Coaching Research

BPS Textbooks in Psychology

BPS Wiley presents a comprehensive and authoritative series covering everything a student needs in order to complete an undergraduate degree in psychology. Refreshingly written to consider more than North American research, this series is the first to give a truly international perspective. Written by the very best names in the field, the series offers an extensive range of titles from introductory level through to final year optional modules, and every text fully complies with the BPS syllabus in the topic. No other series bears the BPS seal of approval!

Many of the books are supported by a companion website, featuring additional resource materials for both instructors and students, designed to encourage critical thinking, and providing for all your course lecturing and testing needs.

For other titles in this series, please go to **http://psychsource.bps.org.uk**

Coaching Researched

A Coaching Psychology Reader

EDITED BY

JONATHAN PASSMORE

&

DAVID TEE

The British
Psychological Society

WILEY

Registered Office(s)
John Wiley & Sons, Inc., 111 River Street, Hoboken, NJ 07030, USA

Editorial Office
111 River Street, Hoboken, NJ 07030, USA

For details of our global editorial offices, customer services, and more information about Wiley products visit us at www.wiley.com.

Wiley also publishes its books in a variety of electronic formats and by print-on-demand. Some content that appears in standard print versions of this book may not be available in other formats.

Library of Congress Cataloging-in-Publication Data
Names: Passmore, Jonathan, editor. | Tee, David, editor.
Title: Coaching researched : a coaching psychology reader / edited by
   Jonathan Passmore & David Tee.
Description: Hoboken, NJ : Wiley, [2019] | Series: 2380 BPS textbooks in
   psychology | Includes index.
Identifiers: LCCN 2020007535 (print) | LCCN 2020007536 (ebook) | ISBN
   9781119656883 (paperback) | ISBN 9781119656906 (adobe pdf) | ISBN
   9781119656890 (epub)
Subjects: LCSH: Personal coaching. | Positive psychology. | Executive coaching.
Classification: LCC BF637.P36 C6355 2019 (print) | LCC BF637.P36 (ebook) |
   DDC 158.3–dc23
LC record available at https://lccn.loc.gov/2020007535
LC ebook record available at https://lccn.loc.gov/2020007536

Cover Design: Wiley
Cover Image: © James Lee/Unsplash

Set in 10/12pt Dante by SPi Global, Pondicherry, India
Printed and bound by CPI Group (UK) Ltd, Croydon, CR0 4YY

10 9 8 7 6 5 4 3 2 1

All of the royalty proceeds from this title have been gifted to the British Psychological Society by the contributors, authors, and editors.

"Bernard of Chartres used to compare us to dwarfs perched on the shoulders of giants. He pointed out that we see more and farther than our predecessors, not because we have keener vision or greater height, but because we are lifted up and borne aloft on their gigantic stature"

John of Salisbury, Metalogicon, 1159

This book is dedicated to Prof Anthony M Grant, whose work inspired many and set the foundations for an evidenced-based approach to coaching through the development of coaching psychology.

Contents

Foreword

We live in a world of change and transition. We cannot always control our environment or indeed what happens in our lives, but we can choose how we respond to it. We need to adapt to new ways of working and enhance how we interact with our world and those around us. At times, it can be challenging to see the way ahead or to explore different options. This is true for world and business leaders as it is for the rest of us in our daily lives. As Galileo said, 'we cannot teach people anything; we can only help them to discover it within themselves'. Coaching has increased in popularity over the last 30 years and is now applied in a wide range of contexts – from boardrooms to students, to educational and medical contexts. There is a fine line between coaching, mentoring and indeed counselling; and, as with coaches, practitioners too operate from different models and different perspectives.

We want to create momentum for change – for each person, their teams and the environments in which they live and work. I readily observe this in practice. Take Jenna, the high-flying executive, delivering and exceeding expectations. How can coaching support her? By using evidence-based practice, we can appreciate her experience more clearly. We can enable her to see different opportunities as well as ways to make the most of her social and emotional capital and to leverage resources more effectively. This is simply one example but now multiple the use of research and practice across the thousands of coaching situations and there is power and impact from coaching psychology.

But are we making the most of the research and evidence in the way we apply coaching? What does research tell us about the impact of our interventions, and what data and evidence do we need for future work? This book provides us with insights into these areas and more. As the president of the British Psychological Society, I am delighted that this BPS-sponsored book is being published. My interest in this book is twofold. First, my experience over the last two decades as a practitioner psychologist and executive coach highlights the need for scientific evidence and well-researched frameworks. Second, as a sponsor of the application of science and evidence-based practice in coaching, I want to see the perforation of research evidence and psychological base in coaching interventions.

The BPS Special Group in Coaching Psychology (SGCP) was formed in 2004 in response to the Coaching Psychology Forum (CPF) and the desire to share research as well as practical experiences. As the group evolved, the core focus has been on the scientific study and application of behaviour, cognition and emotion to deepen our understanding of individuals' and groups' performance, achievement and well-being, and to enhance practice within coaching. What has this meant in terms of research and practice?

This book, titled *Coaching Researched: A Coaching Psychology Reader*, is a milestone in our understanding of the psychological research in coaching psychology. Our esteemed colleagues, Jonathan Passmore and David Tee, as editors have brought together a strong mix of researchers and research outcomes to explore the core themes for coaching research as we move into the next phase of coaching development.

In the 20 chapters, they address the core research themes and the evidence behind it, from a qualitative, quantitative and mixed research perspective. They discuss the value of coaching as a behavioural change tool, enabling us to appreciate the core threads and themes for development and coaching, and the value of different frameworks and approaches. They enable us to understand why the investment in coaching psychology adds significant value to clients, practitioners and organisations.

This book enables us to appreciate the value of rigorous research methods and insights. It encourages us to reflect on the coaching practice story and highlights the importance of research for practice, insightful coaching psychology theory and the value of the evidence base. It enables us to think seriously about how we can combine theory and practice. It emphasises the importance of coaching supervision and continuous professional development, and why coaching is an important part of psychology.

Most of all, it is a book that brings in the human perspective and challenges us all to think more broadly about coaching research and practice. Like me, I am sure that you will find this to be a thought-provoking and genuinely interesting insight into coaching psychology. Enjoy!

– Dr Hazel McLaughlin:
President, British Psychological Society and Founder,
MorphSmart Ltd
hazel.mclaughlin@morphsmart.com

About the Editors

Jonathan Passmore

Jonathan is the editor of the British Psychological Society's (BPS) *International Coaching Psychology Review*, the premier peer review coaching psychology journal, distributed across BPS members and psychologists in other English-speaking countries. He is a chartered psychologist, practicing coach, and author. He has published widely with over 100 scientific papers and book chapters, and edited and written 30 books (including *Excellence in Coaching, Appreciative Inquiry for Change Management and Top Business Psychology Models*). Jonathan holds two professorships—one at University of Évora, Portugal and a second at Henley Business School.

David Tee

David is the editor of *The Coaching Psychologist*, published by the BPS. He is a chartered psychologist, practicing coach, who couples work for University of Worcester and University of South Wales alongside independent consultancy. He has published widely including papers in *The Coaching Psychologist, International Coaching Psychology Review* and *Danish Journal of Coaching Psychology*.

List of Figures and Tables

Section I
Insights from the Nature of Coaching Psychology and Coaching Supervision

Jonathan Passmore and David Tee

Coaching psychology has emerged from the wider tradition of coaching and has frequently struggled to provide a clear identity for itself as something distinct or separate from coaching. In the same way, coaching supervision has struggled to shake off its roots as a therapeutic process used by therapists to provide a space for reflection and guidance about their highly emotionally charged work.

In this first section of the book, we offer two papers from the *International Coaching Psychology Review*. The first explores the nature of coaching and coaching psychology, offering the reader multiple definitions to consider. Maybe one of coaching psychology and coaching's strengths is the diversity of its application and thus multiplicity of its definitions. One key aspect for psychologists is the central nature of evidence. If coaching psychology is anything it is evidenced-based practice, which explores the behavior, cognition, and emotion of coaching.

The 2010–2020 period has seen a growth in coaching research, promoted not only by coaching journals such as the *International Coaching Psychology Review* and *The Coaching Psychologist*, but also through meta-analysis papers (Grover & Furnham, 2016) which have brought together the research data to provide fresh insights and through systematic reviews, have sought to synthesize coaching research to provide an integrated understanding of published research (Athanasopoulou & Dopson, 2017). Through these meta-studies, we hope coaching psychology, in its many forms, can lead to the refinement of practice.

In the second paper, the topic of supervision is explored; its role and the growing evidence for its contribution as a tool to aid reflective practice. While the jury may still be out in terms of the specific contribution which coaching supervision plays, there is mounting evidence that supervision is a useful resource worthy of further research (Hawkins, Turner, & Passmore, 2019).

REFERENCES

Athanasopoulou, A., & Dopson, S. (2017). A systematic review of executive coaching outcomes: Is it the journey or the destination that matters the most? *Leadership Quarterly, 29*(1), 70–88. doi:10.1016/j.leaqua.2017.11.004

Grover, S., & Furnham, A. (2016). Coaching as a developmental intervention in organisations. *PLoS One, 11*(7), e0159137. doi:10.1371/journal.pone.0159137

Hawkins, P., Turner, E., & Passmore, J. (2019). *The supervision manifesto.* Henley-on-Thames: Henley Business School.

1 Coaching Psychology: Exploring Definitions and Research Contribution to Practice

Jonathan Passmore and Yi-Ling Lai[1]

INTRODUCTION

Since coaching started its journey of development as a separate discipline in the early 1980s (Brock, 2012; Passmore & Theeboom, 2016), definitions of coaching have been part of the debate within coaching practice and research across the literature, from practitioners' guides to academic texts. While there has been broad agreement over these years, the focus and emphasis have varied, reflecting the orientation and focus of different writers (e.g., Grant & Palmer, 2002; Passmore & Fillery-Travis, 2011; Whitmore, 1992).

The search for a formal definition of coaching may be considered to be an academic pursuit. However, Grant (2011) argues that a clear definition is needed for the purpose of the development of evidence-based practice, such as coach training and education. Summarizing from previous discussions on the need for a standardized coaching definition, we conclude that marking the boundaries of a domain is vital for three reasons. First, it is essential for practice; a standardized definition of an intervention makes it clear to clients what they can expect from a service provider (their coach), namely a regulated professional service. This view is shared by the International Coach Federation (ICF), which encourages coaches to include an exploration of the nature

[1] First published as Lai, Y-L. & Passmore, J. (2019). Coaching psychology: Exploring definitions and research contribution to practice? *International Coaching Psychology Review, 14*(2), 69–83.

of coaching during the contracting phase with clients, ensuring both have a shared understanding of the process and what the client can expect (International Coach Federation, 2017). Second, it's vital for research. We need to clearly delineate the domain to understand the phenomena being studied. As coaching is still an emerging research domain, it is crucial to define the key components to differentiate coaching from other similar helping interventions (e.g., counseling) and provide a platform from which theoretical contributions can develop. Third, a consistent definition is vital for coaching education and qualification, with a scientific-based framework to support its pedagogy. Meanwhile, we consider a distinct description and characterization of coaching helps us to have a better understanding of whether coaching psychology is a unique discipline, and what the essential body of knowledge is to support its theoretical domain.

This paper starts with reviewing the definitions of coaching, following with the distinctions between subspecialized practices under coaching, such as executive, health, and life coaching. In addition, we also provide a comparative analysis to differentiate coaching from other similar professional helping interventions (e.g., counseling). Moreover, we summarize the interpretations of psychology-based coaching approaches considering that the term, coaching psychology, has been used and perceived as a developed (or developing) discipline in some regions (e.g., Australia and the UK). Nevertheless, it is still not widely accepted or used in other parts of the world. Therefore, we attempt to clarify whether the theoretical foundation of what so-called "coaching psychology" is different from coaching and what the body of knowledge is under its domain from existing research evidence through reviewing the most used definitions. The term "coaching psychology" is used hereafter to maintain consistency in this paper. Finally, we integrate key perspectives and findings from recent systematic reviews and meta-analyses on coaching to consider the psychological contribution to coaching practice.

DEFINING COACHING

Grant (2001) indicated the first reference to coaching in the workplace dates back to 1937. This has subsequently been cited by multiple research papers over the past two decades. The paper, a journalist's report by C.B. Gordy, the Detroit editor of *Factory Management and Maintenance*, examined the role of worker development (through training and coaching) to improve factory processes. The journalist offered little in the way of a formal definition of coaching. In fact, the only reference to coaching by Gordy comes at the very end of the paper: "whereas supervisors found it advisable in the early years to coach employees in the importance of spoiled work and cost reduction, it is now found the older men voluntarily assume this task in training the younger employees" (Gordy, 1937, p. 83). Gordy appeared to suggest that coaching and training are almost synonymous, with progress from what might be a short and informal approach to training (coaching) to a more formal training intervention.

Our own literature search, using the term "coaching" through the Henley One database, which searches multiple business databases, has revealed earlier references to the term. As early as 1911, the term was being used in journals to reflect its use as an educational tool within university and school debating societies, helping members improve their debating skills (Huston, 1924; Trueblood, 1911). As with Gordy, there is little description in these papers of the process, and no explicit definition of the term. Also, as with Gordy, the term appears to be used interchangeably with training. More workplace coaching papers were written during the 1930s (Bigelow, 1938). At the same time, sports coaching was developing too, where the first connections were made between coaching and psychology (Griffith, 1926). But these works were relatively few and far between, until the eruption of coaching in the 1980s.

As the literature evolved from a sporadic collection of papers, often with little if any definition of terms, Whitmore's seminal book placed a marker in the sand, and provides a clear definition of coaching. For Whitmore, coaching was about "unlocking a person's potential to maximise their own performance. It is helping them to learn rather than teaching them—a facilitation approach" (Whitmore, 1992, p. 8). Whitmore drew heavily on Timothy Gallwey's inner game model. Gallwey had noted in sports performance that the internal state of a player was a significant factor. He went further to argue that it was more significant even than the opponent in individual sports like tennis and golf. If the individual could control their self-talk, sizable performance gains could be made (Gallwey, 1986) At the core of coaching for John Whitmore was a belief that the purpose of coaching was helping individuals develop greater self-awareness and personal responsibility: "Performance coaching is based on awareness and responsibility" (Whitmore, 1992, p. 173).

Other founding writers offered alternative definitions. Laura Whitworth, one of the pioneers in the United States, along with Thomas Leonard (Brock, 2009), developed co-active coaching, which defined coaching as "a relationship of possibilities ... based on trust, confidentiality" (Whitworth, Kinsey-House, & Sandahl, 1998).

These perspectives highlighted the nature of the coaching process and its dependency on people, interpersonal interactions, and collaboration. This relational aspect distinguishes coaching from other tutoring or training interventions, where arguably knowledge exchange is at the heart of the process and has led to one stream of coaching research focusing on interpersonal and relational aspects, in the belief that if the relationship is sound, effective outcomes will result.

Passmore and Fillery-Travis (2011) offered a more process-based definition in an attempt to differentiate coaching from mentoring, counseling, and other conversation-based approaches to change. They suggested coaching involved "a Socratic based dialogue between a facilitator (coach) and a participant (client) where the majority of interventions used by the facilitator are open questions which are aimed at stimulating the self awareness and personal responsibility of the participant."

Bachkirova, Cox, and Clutterbuck (2010) have suggested that coaching is "a human development process that involves structured, focused interaction and the use of appropriate strategies, tools and techniques to promote desirable and sustainable change for the benefit of the coachee" (Bachkirova et al., 2010, p. 1), while Lai (2014) suggested coaching is defined as a "reflective process between coaches and coachees which helps or facilitates coachees to experience positive behavioural changes through continuous dialogue and negotiations with coaches to meet coachees' personal or work goals." Again, positive behavioral changes are pointed out as the main purpose of coaching, with a recognition that a structured process is involved. Moreover, "negotiation" is put forward in Lai's reinterpretation of coaching that reflects back the previous definitions; coaching is a relationship-based learning and development process.

SUBSPECIALIZED PRACTICES UNDER COACHING

As the coaching industry has grown, definitions have split into a series of subsets of coaching. These have included executive coaching, health coaching, and life coaching. The following sections summarize the definitions and characteristics of these most prevalent subspecialized areas of coaching.

EXECUTIVE COACHING

The application of coaching in the workplace, and specifically with senior managers, has led to the development of what has been labeled executive coaching. At its simplest, executive coaching could be defined as coaching for senior, or c-suite, managers. Kilburg suggested executive coaching was distinctive in being

> a helping relationship formed between a client who has managerial authority and responsibility in an organization and a consultant who uses a wide variety of behavioural techniques and methods to help the client achieve a mutually identified set of goals to improve his or her professional performance and personal satisfaction and, consequently, to improve the effectiveness of the client's organization within a formally defined coaching agreement. (Kilburg, 1996, p. 142)

Similarly, de Haan, Duckworth, Birch, and Jones (2013), echoing earlier relational definitions, indicated executive coaching is a relationship-focused development intervention. Their research and practice perceive executive coaching as a form of leadership development that takes place through a series of contracted, one-to-one conversations, with a qualified "coach." The process itself is tailored to individuals, so that they learn and develop through the reflective conversation, but that such learning occurred because of the unique relationship based on trust, safety, and support.

Both definitions highlight the professional working relationship in the coaching process and the importance of "contracting" beforehand. However, the definition by de Haan et al. (2013) specifies the term "qualified coach," which raises the awareness of a "standard" coaching qualification. Given de Haan's own background as facilitator and coach trainer, this is not surprising, but his definition opens up the discussion, what does "qualified coach" mean and who decides.

HEALTH COACHING

A further strand that has emerged and is continuing to grow in popularity is health coaching. The approach has grown in both the UK, within the National Health Service (NHS) (Evidence Centre, 2014), in the United States through private providers and globally. A literature review identified 275 published studies, with the approach now widely used by nurses, doctors, and allied health professionals such as physiotherapists and health advisors (Evidence Centre, 2014).

The study defined health coaching as:

> a patient-centred process that is based upon behaviour change theory and is delivered by health professionals with diverse backgrounds. The actual health coaching process entails goal setting determined by the patient, encourages self-discovery in addition to content education, and incorporates mechanisms for developing accountability in health behaviours. (Evidence Centre, 2014, p. 3)

A similar definition was offered by Palmer, Stubbs, and Whybrow (2003), who defined health coaching as "the practice of health education and health promotion within a coaching context, to enhance the wellbeing of individuals and to facilitate the achievement of their health-related goals" (Palmer et al., 2003, p. 91). The distinction is the focus on self-discovery, which echoes Whitmore's primary aims of coaching: self-awareness and personal responsibility.

However, what is less clear from these definitions is where health coaching starts and finishes. If coaching is employed to help individuals with chronic conditions and to improve health outcomes, does this include approaches such as motivational interviewing, which are widely used for drug and alcohol treatment, or brief solution focus therapy and cognitive-behavioral therapy (CBT), which might be considered to be included within the definitions above, but which the practitioner delivering it might consider to be counseling or therapy. This lack of a more clearly defined boundary has made it difficult to study and compare coaching interventions within health coaching (Boehmer et al., 2016).

One useful, although controversial, distinction we have offered is to use the time focus of the conversation, with coaching focused on future behavioral change for health improvement, while counseling or therapy focused on coping with managing or making sense of the past.

LIFE COACHING

Like health coaching, life coaching has become a popular means of helping nonclinical populations in setting and reaching goals and enhancing their well-being (Green, Oades, & Grant, 2006).

Life coaching can be broadly defined as a collaborative solution-focused, result-orientated, and systematic process in which the coach facilitates the enhancement of life experience and goal attainment in the personal and/or professional life of normal, nonclinical clients (Grant, 2014). In other words, life coaching has often been considered to be coaching outside of the work arena, for example in education (Green, Grant, & Rynsaardt, 2007) or coaching for well-being (Green et al., 2006).

One possible distinction between life coaching and health coaching is that health coaching is often defined in terms of the qualification of those providing it, as the coaching is delivered by health professionals, while life coaching is delivered by those outside of the health sector. In the UK and Australia, the term itself has slipped in popularity, being replaced by the term well-being coaching. Although the term life coaching remains popular in North America, coaching continues to grow and spread to new areas beyond business and sports to areas including driving development (Passmore & Rehman, 2012; Wilmott & Wilmott, 2018), safety coaching (Passmore, Krauesslar, & Avery, 2015), maternity and childcare (Golawski, Bamford, & Gersch, 2013), and marital relationships (Ives & Cox, 2015; Williams & Williams, 2011).

REFLECTIONS OF THE DEVELOPING NATURE OF COACHING DEFINITIONS

Reflecting back on the wide-ranging definitions, a common theme is the facilitative nature of coaching. First, the role of the agent (the coach) is not to guide, direct, or instruct, but to "facilitate." The process is to support the client (coachee) in making new discoveries and insights, and moving closer to their goals. A second observation from reviewing these multiple definitions is that coaching has been refined and redefined continually over this period as it has changed, developed, and spread into new areas. This brings not only challenges, but could also be considered to be coaching's strength, reflecting a vibrant, dynamic, and developing area of practice. As Palmer and Whybrow note "definitions seldom stay static, unless the area has stagnated" (2007, p. 3).

The situation has been less fluid in coaching psychology. While there have been various definitions of coaching psychology offered since the turn of the millennium, the variety and volume of change have been markedly different, with only two or three alternative definitions offered in publications (Passmore, Peterson, & Freire, 2013).

THE DIFFERENCES BETWEEN COACHING AND OTHER HELPING INTERVENTIONS

One way of understanding the essential defining elements of coaching is a comparison with other relevant facilitation activities. Traditionally, coaching has been compared with therapy/counseling and mentoring (Bachkirova, 2008) because they share very similar features and processes. In this discussion, we also include a discussion about organizational change. Various writers have discussed the key similarities and differences among coaching, therapy/counseling, mentoring, and change agent (e.g., Bachkirova, 2008; Leonard, Lewis, Freedman, & Passmore, 2013). Table 1.1 summarizes the key features subsequent to reviewing a number of related papers and book chapters (Bachkirova, 2008; Gray, 2006; Joo, 2005; McDowall & Mabey, 2008; Passmore et al., 2013).

Table 1.1 *Differences and Similarities Between Coaching and Other Similar Professional Helping Interventions*

Aspects	Counseling/ therapy	Coaching	Mentoring	Change agent
Ultimate purpose and benefits	Development and well-being of individual.	Development and well-being of individual (if sponsored, also benefit for the sponsoring organization).	Development and well-being of individual (if sponsored, also benefit for the sponsoring organization).	Development and organizational change.
Initial motivation	Eliminating psychological problem and dysfunctions.	Enhancing life, improving performance.	Enhancing life, improving performance.	Enhancing life, improving performance at the workplace.
Context of interventions	Open to any and potentially to all areas of client's life.	Specified by the contract according to the client's goals, the coach's area of expertise and the assignment of a sponsor if involved.	Specified by the contract according to the client's goals, the coach's area of expertise, and the assignment of a sponsor if involved.	Specified by the contract according to the client's goals, the coach's area of expertise and the assignment of a sponsor if involved.
Client's expectations for change	From high dissatisfaction to reasonable satisfaction.	From relative satisfaction to much higher satisfaction.	From relative satisfaction to much higher satisfaction.	From relative satisfaction to much higher satisfaction.

(Continued)

Table 1.1 *(Continued)*

Aspects	Counseling/ therapy	Coaching	Mentoring	Change agent
Possible outcome	Increased well-being, unexpected positive changes in various areas of life.	Goal attainment, increased well-being, and productivity.	Goal attainment, increased well-being, and productivity.	Goal attainment, increased well-being, and productivity.
Theoretical foundation	Psychology and philosophy.	May include psychology, education, sociology, philosophy, management, health, and social care, etc.	May include psychology, education, sociology, philosophy, management, health, and social care, etc.	May include psychology, education, sociology, philosophy, management, and organizational change theories, etc.
Main professional skills	Listening, questioning, feedback, use of tools, and methods specific to particular approaches.	Listening, questioning, feedback, use of tools, and methods specific to particular approaches.	Listening, questioning, feedback, use of tools, and methods specific to particular approaches.	Listening, questioning, feedback, use of tools, and methods specific to particular approaches.
Importance of relationship in the process	High	High	High	High
Importance of the client's commitment	High	High	High	High
Role of the practitioner's self in the process	Very important	Very important	Important	Less important
Degree of formality	High	High	Less formal	High
Frequency	Variable, but usually several sessions needed based on client's individual situations.	Variable, but usually several sessions needed based on client's individual situations.	Variable, but usually several sessions needed based on client's individual situations.	Variable, usually based on the original contract with the organization.
Ownership of data/ feedback	It is confidential data. Only shared between therapist and client.	Coach and individual, some data often shared with line manager. It depends on the agreed contract.	Mentor and the mentee. Some data and information are shared with the organization based on the initial agreement.	Most of the data and information are shared with the organization.

Note. Revised from Joo (2005); Gray (2006); Bachkirova (2008); McDowall and Mabey (2008); and Passmore et al. (2013).

COACHING COMPARED WITH COUNSELING/THERAPY

The need for a clearer differentiation between counseling/therapy and coaching is emerging as the use of psychological models and tools in coaching interventions has increased considerably (Bachkirova, 2008). Such differentiation is essential to ensure a quality coaching engagement if the clearer orientation and required knowledge are defined in the coaching evaluation and training agenda. The similarities between the counseling/therapy and coaching domains are that both are concerned with the "relationship," there is a need for engagement or "client's/coachee's commitment," and both rely on the "practitioner's (coach's) self-awareness" to both facilitate the relationship and keep the conversation moving forward. In both cases, the aim is to facilitate a person's change through an interpersonal interactive process, the relationship between practitioner and client, and how the practitioner facilitates an effective relationship is essential for a positive outcome. In addition, the counseling/therapy and coaching principle share a number of basic required professional skills such as listening, questioning, summarizing, reflection, and affirmations.

We suggest that there are at least three differentiating aspects. First, the initial motivation of clients to undertake counseling/therapy is different from coaching. For example, the individual usually expects to eliminate psychological problems and dysfunctions through counseling/therapy sessions. In this sense, it may be considered to be primarily problem-focused. In contrast, coaching clients are seeking more.

The coachee arrives in anticipation of an improvement in personal and professional development. In this sense, it may be considered to be solution-focused. Second, the focus of counseling/therapy may involve any matters relevant to the client's personal well-being, while the coaching process is usually restricted to the agreed and contracted goals. The expected outcomes and evaluation methods are usually defined prior to the first session with the involved parties (e.g., coachee, supervisors, and other stakeholders). Third, the time horizon for the work is longer. While the coach may contract for 4, 6, or possibly 12 sessions, the therapist contracts week by week, with a view that it takes as long as it takes.

COACHING COMPARED WITH MENTORING

The similarity between coaching and mentoring is that they both provide a one-to-one relationship that is designed to enhance a person's career development (Feldman & Lankau, 2005). However, there are notable differences between these two activities.

First, mentoring is a form of tutelage, which means a more senior or experienced mentor conveys knowledge and insight to a junior mentee about how to improve in a specific job, role, vocation, or organization. Passmore et al. (2013) referred to the definition of mentoring from Eby, Rhodes, & Allen (2007, p. 16): workplace mentoring involves a relationship between a less experienced individual (protégé) and a more experienced person (the mentor), where the purpose is the personal and professional growth of the protégé. The mentor may be a peer at work, a supervisor, or someone else within the organization but outside the protégé's chain of command. Both coaching and mentoring disciplines highlight the importance of "relationship." However, coaching is typically conducted without the expectation of an equal relationship between the two parties, with less focus on technical knowledge (Joo, 2005). Besides, the main purpose of coaching is considered to be improving performance or workplace well-being through self-awareness and learning, whereas the purpose of mentoring varies widely from socialization of newcomers to management development (Joo, 2005). Some have also argued that coaching also differers from mentoring in its use of a structured process, involving specific tools and assessments, to provide both awareness in the client and the development of specific plans for improvement (Joo, 2005), which is in turn reflected in the timelines, with mentoring often running over several years and coaching over several months.

COACHING COMPARED TO CHANGE AGENT

A change agent is defined as being an individual who initiates and manages change in the organization (Lunenburg, 2010). Similar to the coaching intervention, the change agent can be assigned from internal staff (e.g., managers or in-house HR professionals) or hired from external specialists (Tschirky, 2011). Integrating contemporary theoretical interpretations between the coach and change agent, these two roles share several common features and historical development processes. First, coaches and change agents are commissioned to transform individuals to fit into the norms (e.g., behaviors, attitudes, performance, thinking styles) of societies or organizations at the early stage of both practices (Bennis, Benne, & Chin, 1969; Kilburg, 1996; Parsloe, 1999). A "planned" change in the organizational setting has usually been expected by the change agency (i.e., the sponsored organization) since the late 1950s (Lippitt, Watson, & Westley, 1958). The primal definitions of coaching, as well as an emphasis on the purposes of coaching, are related to "corporate vision and goals," "team performance," "organisational productivity," and "professional development" (Parsloe, 1999; Sperry, 2008). These descriptions of being a coach and change agent focus on the task, instead of people; and the process is viewed as an instrumental tool generating conformity in the organization. Nevertheless, a broader view of both practices is established alongside the development of relevant theories, such as motivation to change. For instance,

Zaltman and Duncan (1977) indicated the change agent is an individual who transforms the status quo even though the operation is not sanctioned. In addition, Caldwell (2003) indicates the role of change agents has been shifted away from a planned approach to change, with a bottom-up approach advocated. Meanwhile, the objective of coaching is expanded from specific corporate-related goals to stimulation of personal potential and responsibility (Passmore & Fillery-Travis, 2011).

The evolution of both practices is grounded on the idea that people's behavioral change is highly associated with their intention (i.e., motivation) to change (Webb & Sheeran, 2006). Accordingly, the focus of changing process research transfers to change recipients' needs and intrinsic motivation in this changing and learning process. Second, facilitating a collaborative and equal working relationship is encouraged in both practices. Zaltman and Duncan's study (1977) indicates change agents are more likely to be effective if they keep a flexible working relationship with the change recipient; for instance, acknowledging their needs, maintaining a collaborative process, and being receptive to new ideas. In the meantime, the quality of the professional helping relationship is recognized as an essential antecedent for positive coaching outcomes (Bozer & Jones, 2018; de Haan et al., 2013) through numerous primary studies. Third, psychology plays an essential part in both practices. The involvement of psychology in the change process can be traced back to the 1970s. Several papers indicate change agents as "consultants in behavioural clothing" or "psychological consultants".

The explicit inclusion of a psychological perspective within coaching can be attributed to Grant (2001). Following Grant's Ph.D. (2001), the consideration of the psychological effects of coaching—both processes and outcomes—has been a popular area of research (Bono, Purvanova, Towler, & Peterson, 2009; Smither, 2011). More recently, several systematic reviews and meta-analyses have established psychologically informed research at the vanguard of coaching research (Athanasoupoulou & Dopson, 2018; Bozer & Jones, 2018; Jones, Woods, & Guillaume, 2016; Theeboom, Beersma, & van Vianen, 2014). Nevertheless, in terms of practice, some papers (e.g., Bono et al., 2009; Passmore, Palmer, & Short, 2010) have argued that there is little evidence of differences in practice between coaching psychologists and nonpsychologically trained coaches. Despite these debates as to whether psychological training informs coaching practice, we would argue there is little doubt that psychology theory, be it behavioral change theory or psychological theories of human relationships, have informed all coach training. The understanding of human behavior, emotions, cognition, and motivation are key skills for all coaches, not just psychologists. Fourth, both practices involve managing a complex social context. According to O'Neill (2000), the change agent often has no direct authority over the implementer; therefore, it is a natural triangular working relationship between the sponsor, implementer, and agent. A similar relationship exists in the coaching context. More and more coaching studies (Ianiro, Lehmann-Willenbrock, & Kauffeld, 2015; Louis & Fatien Diochon, 2014; Shoukry & Cox, 2018) have acknowledged the significance of the social dynamic in the coaching process. For example, Ianiro et al.'s study (2015) highlighted the importance of interpersonal interactions between the coach and coachee and how these are altered by different social circumstances.

DEFINING COACHING PSYCHOLOGY

Given this debate, the question remains, what, if anything, is the difference between coaching and coaching psychology? At its birth, coaching psychology's Godfather, Anthony Grant, offered a definition of coaching psychology that subsequently established the foundation of a coaching psychology definition within the British Psychological Society. According to Grant (2001, p. 10):

> Coaching psychology can provide a useful platform from which to investigate the psychological factors involved in purposeful, directed behavioural change in normal populations, and in this way further the contribution of psychology to the enhancement of performance, productivity and quality of life of individuals, organizations and the broader social community.

In Grant's (2001) definition, coaching psychology is:

1. An empirically-validated framework of change that facilitates the coaching process.
2. A model of self-regulation that allows delineation of the processes inherent in self-regulation, goal setting, and goal attainment.
3. A methodology of how behavior, thoughts, and feelings interact, and how behavior, thoughts, and feelings can be altered to facilitate goal attainment.

Drawing on Grant's Ph.D. thesis, Palmer and Whybrow reformulated the definition for the British Psychological Society's Special Group in Coaching Psychology (SGCP). Coaching psychology is for: "enhancing well-being and performance in personal life and work domains, underpinned by models of coaching grounded in established adult learning or psychological approaches" (Palmer & Whybrow, 2006).

Passmore et al. (2010), as noted above, argued such definitions draw a false distinction between nonpsychologist coaches and coaching psychologists. Passmore argued that many coaches draw upon psychological models in their practice and that coach training had over the past two decades adopted more evidence-based approaches, thanks in part to the work of Grant, Cavanagh, Green, Bachkirova, and Palmer, who had published widely and argued the case for evidence-based coaching. Passmore's position appears to be supported by research evidence, which suggests in terms of behaviors (Jenkins, Passmore, Palmer, & Short, 2012), and in wider practice (Passmore, Brown, & Csigas, 2017), there is little difference between coaches and coaching psychologists and coaches.

In contrast to focusing on psychological approaches, Passmore sought to recast coaching psychology as a separate domain of study, parallel to occupational, health, or forensic psychology. He defined coaching psychology as "the scientific study of behaviour, cognitive and emotion within coaching practice to deepen our understanding and enhance our practice within coaching" (Passmore, 2010, p. 4).

Passmore suggested that while there are few observable differences between coaches and coaching psychologies in their practice, the study of psychology can enhance practice, and may lead to materially different outcomes. However, this view remains the subject of debate. In this paper, we might go further to suggest that coaching psychologists may be able to more clearly articulate what they do and the underpinning theory supporting their approach. Further, as a result of the robust ethical standards set by national psychological societies such as the British Psychological Society (BPS), Australian Psychological Society (APS), New Zealand Psychological Society (NZPS). Psychological Society of South Africa (PsySSA), Canada Psychology Association (CPA), and American Psychological Association (APA), psychologists may act to raise ethical standards when working with coaching clients. Of course, this last point is highly contentious, given the complex and diverse nature of ethics, what is ethical, and the diversity of ethical standards between different coaching body members and different national cultures (Passmore et al., 2017).

In response to an invitation (Passmore, Stopforth, & Lai, 2018), researchers and practitioners have come forward with their own definitions of coaching psychology. Our role here is not to suggest that one is right or wrong, but recognize that different traditions, cultural perspectives, and working environments shape and influence these different perspectives. Our purpose is to simply bring these perspectives together as part of the debate.

Grant offers a fresh take from the vantage point of Australia.

> Coaching psychology is a branch of psychology that involves the systematic application of behavioural science to the attainment of professional or personal outcomes that are valued by the coachee. Such outcomes or goal typically focus on the enhancement of personal or professional life experience, work performance and/or well-being, and can be used for individuals, groups and/or organisations. Coaching does not aim to treat issues related to mental illness. (Grant, Personal Communication 2018)

Michel Moral, a leading name in French coaching, research, and practice, has suggested that

> coaching psychology is a way of doing coaching which uses and combines all the theatrical and technical resources of psychology in intrapersonal, interpersonal and systemic areas of knowledge. It allows the coach to be fully aware of what they are doing in service of the coaching mission. (Moral, Personal Communication 2018)

The South African Psychologists Coaching Group draw on the work of Odendaal and Le Roux (2016, p. 3) in the following definition of coaching psychology:

> Coaching Psychology, as practiced by a registered practitioner, is a conversational process of facilitating positive development and change towards optimal functioning, well-being

and increased performance in the work and personal life domains, in the absence of clinically significant mental health issues, through the application of a wide range of psychological theories and principles. The intervention is action-orientated with measureable outcomes, and is also reflective towards creating greater self-awareness and meaning, and is directed at individuals, groups, teams, organisations and communities within a culturally-specific context. (Gail C. Wrogemann, Chair Group Sub-Committee, PsySSA, Personal Communication, 2019)

The NZPS Special Group use the following definition: Coaching psychology

draws on and develops established psychological approaches, and [is] the systematic application of behavioural science to the enhancement of life experience, work performance and well-being for individuals, groups and organisations who do not have clinically significant mental health issues or abnormal levels of distress. (Jonathan Black, Co-Chair of Coaching Psychology Special Interest Group [CPSIG], Personal Communication, 2019)

While different psychological groups and practitioners hold differing perspectives, a common feature is the link to psychological theory and a common purpose to promote evidence-based practice through a psychological understanding of what it is to be human, within a "normal" (nonclinical) range of functioning. Coaching psychology is "the well" that refreshes the wider coaching profession. It is the heart of scientific inquiry about coaching practice for work with nonclinical populations, and while practices may not diverge, understanding of psychological theory, ethical standards, and contribution to research mark coaching psychologists and coaching psychology apart.

KEY FINDINGS FROM RECENT SYSTEMATIC REVIEWS ON COACHING PSYCHOLOGY

While the ongoing debates between psychologists and nonpsychologists have continued, several systematic reviews on coaching psychology have identified key factors for a positive coaching outcome (Athanasoupoulou & Dopson, 2018; Bozer & Jones, 2018). First, the working alliance that refers to the quality and strength of the collaborative relationship between the client and therapist (Hatcher & Barends, 2006) has been recognized as a key indicator of coaching outcomes (Grover & Furnham, 2016; Lai & McDowall, 2014). Second, self-efficacy, which focuses on how individuals perceive their acquisition of a skill or knowledge (Gist & Mitchell, 1992), has been found to be an important antecedent of affective coaching outcomes as reflected in perceived coaching effectiveness (Bozer & Jones, 2018; de Haan et al., 2013; de Haan, Grant, Burger, & Eriksson, 2016). Third, the coachee's readiness to change (i.e., motivation to change) is a critical variable to outcomes (Bozer & Jones, 2018). Moreover, the leader-member exchange (LMX) theory (Aryee, Budhwar, & Chen, 2002), which explains the support from the coachee's leader and organization to their coachee, has a key role to play in outcomes (Bozer & Jones, 2018). Summarizing from these critical reviews on existing coaching evidence, we can conclude psychology continues to play a significant part in shaping contemporary coaching research, specifically, frameworks from psychotherapy (e.g., the working alliance framework) and organizational psychology (e.g., motivational theory and LMX). As coaching research continues, we suspect that the contribution of both psychological theory and psychological research methods will inform and shape the development of evidence-based coaching practice. We can also conclude that evidence-based practice will increasingly become the core modality for qualified coaching practitioners, as the draw from the well of coaching psychology research.

DISCUSSION

This review paper answers several questions on contemporary coaching study, practice, and the need for a coach's training and development. We can initially conclude that coaching intervention cannot be detached from psychological perspectives in considering that the main activity embedded in the coaching process relies on "interpersonal interactions," such as dialogs and conversations. In addition, some research (Ianiro et al., 2015) indicated "body languages" and "unspoken manners" between the coaching dyad act a key role for a successful coaching outcome. Therefore, the psychological professional relationship is embedded in all coaching settings, regardless of the technique or framework.

Further, most of the current research evidence indicated theories in psychotherapy, such as therapeutic working alliance, provide a theoretical foundation in coaching alliance study. Nevertheless, social-psychological perspectives are highlighted in recent coaching research domains due to the power dynamics and cultural differences in most of the coaching contexts (e.g., hierarchy in the social settings of coaches and expectations in different cultural backgrounds). Moreover, motivational theories that are usually studied in organizational psychology and adult learning areas are identified as the fundamental factor for an effective coaching alliance. Therefore, building trust and rapport at the beginning of the coaching relationship is the key to opening up the coachee's mind and enhancing their motivation to change. Consequently, we argue that while psychology is not the only theoretical discipline to facilitate an effective coaching process and outcome, it plays an essential part in this human-relationship-focused intervention.

CONCLUSIONS

The evidence for investment in coaching intervention will continue to be a major concern for scholars in relevant domains, as well as for organizational stakeholders. While the development of coaching has been transformed from a "business model or service"

(Briner, 2012) toward a more scientific rooted profession, more rigorous research is still required to inform practice.

Coaching research has evolved from the "infant" stage and has moved toward its teenage years. It has established that coaching works and produces moderate effect sizes (Theeboom et al., 2014). Further, it has a role beyond the coaching dyad, such as sponsoring organizations, cultural influences, and coachees' social environments (Passmore & Theeboom, 2016). Its next stage of development must be to identify the active ingredients in coaching and measure what effect each has. It must also start to differentiate between individuals and presenting problems. What type of coaching fits what type of person, and what type of issue? To suggest that all are equal (Kilburg, 2005) is not supported by the growing evidence from other behavioral change domains, such as motivational interviewing (MI) and CBT. These have shown that different approaches can be better suited to specific types of presenting problem. We hypothesize that coaching will find that personality factors of the coach and coachee, as well as presenting problems and levels of readiness to change, all influence outcomes: My coaching need is not your coaching need. To move closer to this understanding, a renewed energy is needed, with closer collaboration between coaching psychologists with the research skills and coaching practitioners to deliver the hundreds of data points needed for this type of research to bear fruit. If the past 15 years of coaching psychology have been growing and learning, the coming decade of coaching psychology will be a coming of age.

REFERENCES

Aryee, S., Budhwar, P. S., & Chen, Z. X. (2002). Trust as a mediator of the relationship between organizational justice and work outcomes: Test of a social exchange model. *Journal of Organizational Behaviour: The International Journal of Industrial, Occupational and Organizational Psychology and Behaviour, 23*(3), 267–285.

Athanasoupoulou, A., & Dopson, S. (2018). A systematic review of executive coaching outcomes: Is it the journey or the destination that matters the most? *Leadership Quarterly, 29*(1), 70–88.

Bachkirova, T. (2008). Role of coaching psychology in defining boundaries between counselling and coaching. In S. Palmer & A. Whybrow (Eds.), *Handbook of coaching psychology: A guide for practitioners* (2nd ed., pp. 351–366). Hove: Routledge.

Bachkirova, T., Cox, E., & Clutterbuck, D. (2010). *The complete handbook of coaching.* London: Sage.

Bennis, W. G., Benne, K. D., & Chin, R. (1969). *The planning of change.* New York, NY: Holt, Rinehart and Winston.

Bigelow, B. (1938). Building an effective training program for field salesmen. *Personnel, 14,* 142–150.

Boehmer, K. R., Barakat, S., Ahn, S., Prokop, L. J., Erwin, P. J., & Murad, M. H. (2016). Health coaching interventions for persons with chronic conditions: A systematic review and meta-analysis protocol. *Systematic Reviews, 5*(1), 146.

Bono, J., Purvanova, R., Towler, A., & Peterson, D. (2009). A survey of executive coaching practices. *Personnel Psychology, 62*(2), 361–404.

Bozer, G., & Jones, R. J. (2018). Understanding the factors that determine workplace coaching effectiveness: A systematic literature review. *European Journal of Work and Organizational Psychology*, *27*(3), 342–361.

Briner, R. (2012). Does coaching work and does anyone really care? *OP Matters*, *17*, 4–12.

Brock, V. (2009). Coaching pioneers: Laura Whitworth and Thomas Leonard. *International Journal of Coaching in Organisations*, *1*(1), 54–64.

Brock, V. (2012). *The sourcebook of coaching history* (2nd ed.). Self-published.

Caldwell, R. (2003). Models of change agency: A fourfold classification. *British Journal of Management*, *14*(2), 131–142.

de Haan, E., Duckworth, A., Birch, D., & Jones, C. (2013). Executive coaching outcome research: The contribution of common factors such as relationship, personality match, and self-efficacy. *Consulting Psychology Journal: Practice and Research*, *65*(1), 40.

de Haan, E., Grant, A. M., Burger, Y., & Eriksson, P.-O. (2016). A large-scale study of executive and workplace coaching: The relative contributions of relationship, personality match, and self-efficacy. *Consulting Psychology Journal: Practice and Research*, *68*, 189–207.

Eby, L. T., Rhodes, J. E., & Allen, T. D. (2007). Definition and evolution of mentoring. In L. T. Eby & T. D. Allen (Eds.), *The Blackwell handbook of mentoring: A multiple perspectives approach* (pp. 7–20). Oxford: Blackwell.

Evidence Centre. (2014). *Does health coaching work?* Retrieved 10 January, 2019, from http://eoeleadership.hee.nhs.uk/sites/default/files Does%20health%20coaching%20work%20-%20 summary.pdf

Feldman, D. C., & Lankau, M. J. (2005). Executive coaching: A review and agenda for future research. *Journal of Management*, *31*(6), 829–848.

Gallwey, T. (1986). *The inner game of tennis*. London: Pan.

Gist, M. E., & Mitchell, T. R. (1992). Self-efficacy: A theoretical analysis of its determinants and malleability. *Academy of Management review*, *17*(2), 183–211.

Golawski, A., Bamford, A., & Gersch, I. (2013). *Swings and roundabouts: A self-coaching workbooks for parents and those considering becoming parents*. Abingdon: Karnac.

Gordy, C. (1937). Everyone gets a share of the profits. *Factory Management and Maintenance*, *95*, 82–83.

Grant, A. (2011). Developing an agenda for teaching coaching psychology. *International Coaching Psychology Review*, *6*(1), 84–99.

Grant, A. M. (2001). *Toward a psychology of coaching: The impact of coaching on metacognition, mental health and goal attainment*. Sydney: Coaching Psychology Unit, University of Sydney.

Grant, A. M. (2014). Autonomy support, relationship satisfaction and goal focus in the coach–coachee relationship: Which best predicts coaching success? *Coaching: An International Journal of Theory, Research and Practice*, *7*(1), 18–38.

Grant, A. M. & Palmer, S. (2002). Coaching Psychology. Meeting held at the Annual Conference of Division of Counselling Psychology, British Psychological Society, Torquay, May 18.

Gray, D. E. (2006). Executive coaching: Towards a dynamic alliance of psychotherapy and transformative learning processes. *Management Learning*, *37*(4), 475–497.

Green, L. S., Oades, L. G., & Grant, A. M. (2006). Cognitive-behavioural, solution-focused life coaching: Enhancing goal striving, well-being, and hope. *The Journal of Positive Psychology*, *1*(3), 142–149.

Green, S., Grant, A. M., & Rynsaardt, J. (2007). Evidence-based life coaching for senior high school students: Building hardiness and hope. *International Coaching Psychology Review*, *2*(1), 24–32.

Griffith, C. R. (1926). *Psychology of coaching: A study of coaching methods from the point of view of psychology*. New York, NY: Scribner.

Grover, S., & Furnham, A. (2016). Coaching as a developmental intervention in organisations: A systematic review of its effectiveness and the mechanisms underlying it. *PLoS One, 11*(7), e0159137.

Hatcher, R. L., & Barends, A. W. (2006). How a return to theory could help alliance research. *Psychotherapy: Theory, Research, Practice, Training, 43*(3), 292–299.

Huston, R. E. (1924). Debate coaching in high school. *The Quarterly Journal of Speech Education, 10*, 127–143.

Ianiro, P. M., Lehmann-Willenbrock, N., & Kauffeld, S. (2015). Coaches and clients in action: A sequential analysis of interpersonal coach and client behaviour. *Journal of Business and Psychology, 30*(3), 435–456.

International Coach Federation. (2017). *ICF Core Competencies*. Retrieved on February 5, 2019, from https://coachfederation.org/core-competencies

Ives, Y., & Cox, E. (2015). *Relationship coaching: The theory and practice of coaching with singles, couples, and parents*. Hove: Routledge.

Jenkins, L., Passmore, J., Palmer, S., & Short, E. (2012). The nature and focus of coaching in the UK today: A UK survey report. *Coaching: An International Journal of Theory, Research and Practice, 5*(2), 132–150.

Jones, R., Woods, S., & Guillaume, Y. (2016). The effectiveness of workplace coaching: A meta-analysis of learning and performance outcomes from coaching. *Journal of Occupational and Organizational Psychology, 89*(2), 249–277.

Joo, B. K. B. (2005). Executive coaching: A conceptual framework from an integrative review of practice and research. *Human Resource Development Review, 4*(4), 462–488.

Kilburg, R. R. (1996). Toward a conceptual understanding and definition of executive coaching. *Consulting Psychology Journal: Practice and Research, 48*(2), 134–144.

Kilburg, R. R. (2005). Executive coaching: The road to dodoville needs paving with more than good assumptions. *Consulting Psychology Journal: Practice and Research, 57*(1), 90–96. doi:10.1037/1065-9293.57.1.90

Lai, Y.-L. (2014). *Enhancing evidence-based coaching through the development of a coaching psychology competency framework: Focus on the coaching relationship*. Guildford, UK: School of Psychology, University of Surrey.

Lai, Y.-L., & McDowall, A. (2014). A systematic review (SR) of coaching psychology: Focusing on the attributes of effective coaching psychologists. *International Coaching Psychology Review, 9*(2), 120–136.

Leonard, H. S., Lewis, R., Freedman, A. M., & Passmore, J. (Eds.). (2013). *The Wiley-Blackwell handbook of the psychology of leadership, change and organizational development*. Chichester: Wiley Blackwell.

Lippitt, R., Watson, J., & Westley, B. (1958). *The dynamics of planned change: A comparative study of principles and techniques*. New York, NY: Harcourt, Brace.

Louis, D., & Fatien Diochon, P. (2014). Educating coaches to power dynamics: Managing multiple agendas within the triangular relationship. *Journal of Psychological Issues in Organizational Culture, 5*(2), 31–47.

Lunenburg, F. C. (2010). Managing change: The role of the change agent. *International Journal of Management, Business, and Administration, 13*(1), 1–6.

McDowall, A., & Mabey, C. (2008). Developing a framework for assessing effective development activities. *Personnel Review, 37*(6), 629–646.

Odendaal, A., & Le Roux, A. (2016). Contextualising coaching psychology within multicultural context. In L. E. van Zyl, M. W. Stander, & A. Odendaal (Eds.), *Coaching psychology:*

Meta-theoretical perspectives and applications in multicultural context (pp. 2–25). New York, NY: Springer International Publishing.

O'Neill, M. B. (2000). *Executive coaching with backbone and heart.* San Francisco, CA: Jossey-Bass.

Palmer, S., Stubbs, I., & Whybrow, A. (2003). Health coaching to facilitate the promotion of healthy behaviour and achievement of health-related goals. *International Journal of Health Promotion and Education, 14*(3), 91–93.

Palmer, S., & Whybrow, A. (2006). The coaching psychology movement and its development within the British Psychological Society. *International Coaching Psychology Review, 1*(1), 5–11.

Palmer, S., & Whybrow, A. (2007). *Handbook of coaching psychology: A guide for practitioners.* London: Routledge.

Parsloe, E. (1999). The Manager as Coach and Mentor, (2nd Ed) London: Chartered Institute of Personnel.

Passmore, J. (2010). A grounded theory study of the coachee experience: The implications for training and practice in coaching psychology. *International Coaching Psychology Review, 5*(1), 48–62.

Passmore, J., Brown, H., & Csigas, Z. (2017). *The state of play in European coaching and mentoring.* Henley-on-Thames: Henley Business School & EMCC.

Passmore, J., & Fillery-Travis, A. (2011). A critical review of executive coaching research: A decade of progress and what's to come. *Coaching: An International Journal of Theory, Research and Practice, 4*(2), 70–88.

Passmore, J., Krauesslar, V., & Avery, R. (2015). Safety coaching: A critical literature review of coaching in high hazard industries. *Industrial and Commercial Training, 47*(4), 195–200. doi:10.1108/ICT-12-2014-0080

Passmore, J., Palmer, S., & Short, E. (2010) *Results of an online UK survey of coaching and coaching psychology practitioners.* Unpublished survey.

Passmore, J., Peterson, D., & Freire, T. (2013). The psychology of coaching and mentoring. In J. Passmore, D. Peterson, & T. Freire (Eds.), *The Wiley-Blackwell handbook of the psychology of coaching and mentoring* (pp. 1–13). Chichester: Wiley Blackwell.

Passmore, J., & Rehman, H. (2012). Coaching as a learning methodology—A mixed methods study in driver development using a randomized controlled trial and thematic analysis. *International Coaching Psychology Review, 7*(2), 166–184.

Passmore, J., Stopforth, M., & Lai, Y.-L. (2018). Defining coaching psychology: Debating coaching and coaching psychology definitions. *The Coaching Psychologist, 14*(2), 120–124.

Passmore, J., & Theeboom, T. (2016). Coaching psychology research: A journey of development in research. In L. E. van Zyl, M. W. Stander, & A. Odendaal (Eds.), *Coaching Psychology: Meta-theoretical perspectives and applications in multicultural contexts* (pp. 27–46). New York, NY: Springer International Publishing.

Pearl, A. (1974). The psychological consultant as change agent. *Professional Psychology, 5*(3), 292.

Reddin, W. J. (1971). Effective management by objectives, New York: McGraw-Hill.

Shoukry, H., & Cox, E. (2018). Coaching as a social process. *Management Learning, 49*(4), 413–428.

Smither, J. (2011). Can psychotherapy research serve as a guide for research about executive coaching? An agenda for the next decade. *Journal of Business and Psychology, 26*(2), 135–145.

Sperry, L. (2008). Executive coaching: An intervention, role function, or profession? *Consulting Psychology Journal: Practice and Research, 60*(1), 33–37.

Theeboom, T., Beersma, B., & van Vianen, A. E. M. (2014). Does coaching work? A meta-analysis on the effects of coaching on individual level outcomes in an organizational context. *Journal of Positive Psychology, 9*(1), 1–18.

Trueblood, T. C. (1911). Coaching a debating team. *Public Speaking Review, 1*, 84–85.

Tschirky, H. (2011). *Managing innovation-driven companies: Approaches in practice.* New York, NY: Palgrave Macmillan.

Webb, T. L., & Sheeran, P. (2006). Does changing behavioural intentions engender behaviour change? A meta-analysis of the experimental evidence. *Psychological Bulletin, 132*(2), 249–268.

Whitmore, J. (1992). *Coaching for performance.* London: Nicholas Brealey.

Whitworth, L., Kinsey-House, H., & Sandahl, P. (1998). *Co-active coaching: New skills for coaching people towards success in work and life.* Mountain View, CA: Davies Black.

Williams, J., & Williams, J. (2011). *Marriage coaching.* Springfield, MA: GTRC.

Wilmott, G., & Wilmott, C. (2018). *Who's in the driving seat.* Oldham: Active Driving Solutions.

Zaltman, G., & Duncan, R. (1977). *Strategies for planned change.* Wiley.

2 The State and Future of Coaching Supervision

J. Thomas Tkach and Joel A. DiGirolamo[1]

Coaching can trace its roots back to many different fields and ideological movements, including philosophy, psychology, and the business world (see Figure 2.1). One of the biggest influences on coaching comes from the human potential movement in the 1960s, which sought to help individuals to reach their full potential (Brock, 2008; DeCarvalho, 1991). The human potential movement was influenced in part by humanistic psychologists Abraham Maslow and Carl Rogers, who emphasized the concepts of unconditional positive regard, self-awareness, personal growth, and self-actualization (DeCarvalho, 1991; Maslow, 1943; Rogers, 1957).

While it is hard to determine where specific practices in coaching originated, similarities between coaching and clinical or counseling psychology suggest influences from these domains as well as social work. For example, all of these modalities frequently involve one-to-one helping relationships, which require confidentiality (Hart, Blattner, & Leipsic, 2001). Supervision is another area where psychology may be influencing coaching (Carroll, 2007).

Supervision in counseling and other forms of psychological therapy can trace its roots all the way back to Freud (Carroll, 2007; Watkins, 2013). The first known requisite for supervision came in the 1920s when it became a formal requirement for psychoanalytic training at the Berlin Poliklinik, which was largely funded and influenced by Max Eitingon (Carroll, 2007; Watkins, 2013). From these roots in Europe, supervision eventually made its way to the North American continent. Other helping professions such as social work, counseling, probation, and teaching began incorporating supervision into their practices, although we are unable to

[1]First published as Tkach, J. & DiGirolamo, J. (2017). The state and future of coaching supervision. *International Coaching Psychology Review, 12*(1), 49–63.

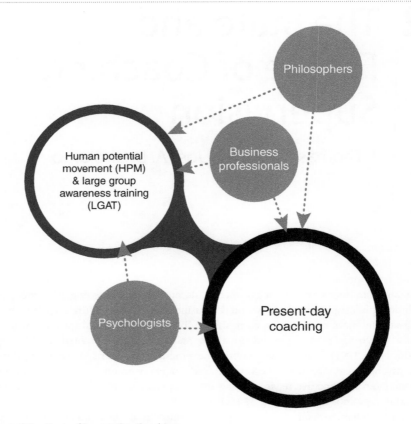

Figure 2.1   *Roots of Present-Day Coaching*

discern if a connection exists between the use of supervision in psychoanalysis and a migration to other professions or vice versa (Carroll, 2007).

In the United States, supervision evolved from a counseling process to a more educational process. In the 1970s, U.S. universities conducted abundant research to create supervision models and theories, and it soon became a requirement for training in counseling. During the late 1970s and early 1980s, these models and theories had a significant influence in Britain. There, the British Association for Counseling and Psychotherapy not only made it a requirement for training but also required all members to receive ongoing supervision—a requirement that remains to this day (Carroll, 2007).

PREVALENCE OF COACHING SUPERVISION

Supervision has since spread to the coaching field. Although it is impossible to know for sure, the regional differences in counseling supervision between the United States and the UK may have influenced how coaching supervision is regarded today. Reports indicate that coaching supervision is gaining popularity in the UK (Hawkins & Schwenk, 2006a, 2006b; Hawkins & Turner, 2016, 2017).

Research on how widely coaching supervision is practiced has been limited in quantity and scope. Only a handful of coaching supervision research studies have been conducted, and most are confined to a specific geographic region. This has made it difficult to compare supervision trends over time and across regions. Differing methodology has also made it challenging to compare these studies.

A 2006 study conducted by the Chartered Institute of Personnel and Development found a large discrepancy between coaches' beliefs about the importance of supervision and the actual practice of supervision in the UK. The study reported that 86% of coaches believed that coaches should have regular, ongoing supervision, while only 44% reported receiving supervision (Hawkins & Schwenk, 2006a, 2006b). However, follow-up research conducted in 2014 by Hawkins and Turner (2016, 2017) indicated that over 92% of coaches in the UK reported having some form of coaching supervision.

Coaching supervision appears to be popular in other regions. A study by Grant (2012) reported that 83% of Australian coaches were receiving supervision, although only 26% was formal supervision. Hawkins and Turner (2017) also reported that a high percentage (81%) of European coaches outside of the UK receive supervision.

Although supervision is prevalent in Australia, the UK, and other parts of Europe, little is known about the prevalence of coaching supervision in other parts of the world. Findings by Hawkins and Turner (2017) suggest that supervision is much less popular in North America. Although this is likely true, one must be cautious with the data since the sample size is quite low (42 participants). Data from Australia and New Zealand, Asia, Africa, and Latin America were also included in this study but had even smaller sample sizes.

The rise in coaching supervision in the UK and other parts of Europe over the last ten years could be attributed to a number of factors, including cultural influences and accrediting body requirements. For example, when stating the top two reasons coaches participated in supervision, 36% of UK coaches listed "professional body requirement." Confounding matters further, 87% of UK coaches reported "personal commitment to good practice" as one of their top two reasons (Hawkins & Turner, 2017). This data suggests a complicated relationship between external pressures and intrinsic motivation. Future robust studies are needed to understand coaching supervision prevalence and regional differences in attitudes, motivation, and growth trends.

STATE OF COACHING SUPERVISION

Functions and definitions of coaching supervision

Coaches, clients, accrediting bodies, and organizations that procure coaching services all have a stake in coaching supervision, and each has a somewhat unique perspective. Consequently, supervision may serve different functions for different stakeholders.

For example, research conducted in 2006 in the UK found that most coaches (88%) sought supervision for developmental reasons while the majority of organizations (70%) were most interested in the quality assurance function of supervision (Hawkins & Schwenk, 2006a, 2006b). This disparity makes it difficult to identify a universal purpose of supervision. It also highlights a difference between supervision in the therapeutic fields versus coaching, namely that coaching frequently involves a third party, the employer of the client (Bachkirova, 2008), and further, that the employer of the client may view supervision solely as a quality control function (Hawkins & Schwenk, 2006a, 2006b).

Some researchers and organizations have attempted to outline the primary functions of supervision. A popular framework of the purpose of supervision is outlined by Hawkins and Smith (2006), which offers three functions of coaching supervision: developmental, resourcing, and qualitative. These functions were adapted from similar functions developed for social work by Kadushin (1976). The developmental function serves to develop "the skills, understanding and capacities of the supervisees" (Hawkins & Smith, 2013, p. 173). This is an exploration of the dynamic between the supervisee and their clients through reflection. The resourcing function is about supporting supervisees emotionally (Hawkins & Smith, 2013). Finally, the qualitative function provides "quality control." This ensures not only the quality of the supervisee's work but also that they are following ethical guidelines (Hawkins & Smith, 2013, p. 173).

Research seems to support the existence of these three functions, especially the developmental and qualitative functions (Champion, 2011; Hawkins & Schwenk, 2006a, 2006b; Lawrence & Whyte, 2014; Passmore & McGoldrick, 2009). Some have argued that the resourcing function may be more applicable to the fields of social work or therapy (Lawrence & Whyte, 2014; Moyes, 2009). Others have found, however, that supervision can help supervisees feel less isolated (Champion, 2011; McGivern, 2009; Passmore & McGoldrick, 2009). It has been suggested that group supervision in particular "provides a supportive atmosphere of peers in which practitioners can share anxieties and realize that others are facing similar issues" (Hawkins & Smith, 2013, p. 209).

Due to the varying functions of supervision, defining supervision has been challenging. No universally accepted definition for coaching supervision exists (Moyes, 2009). Table 2.1 compares several popular coaching supervision definitions, and each of these is provided in the Appendix 2.A.

Within these definitions, the most common themes were: learning or development, reflection, and support, which echo the developmental and resourcing functions described above. Monitor or evaluate and client protection, which most closely resembles the qualitative function, was represented in almost half of the definitions examined. Although understanding client-systems or organizations is only mentioned in 2 of the 10 definitions, some have argued for the importance of a systemic approach to coaching supervision (Bachkirova, Jackson, & Clutterbuck, 2011; Hawkins & Smith, 2013). The popularity of Hawkin's "seven-eyed model" (Bachkirova et al., 2011; DeFilippo, 2013) seems to reflect this trend.

Table 2.1 Themes in Definitions of Coaching Supervision[a]

	Formal process	Learning or development	Monitor or evaluate	Reflection (on work and self)	Support	Understanding client-system or organization	Client protection (ethics)
Association for Coaching (2015)	✓			✓			
Bachkirova (2008)	✓	✓	✓	✓	✓		
Bluckert[b]		✓		✓	✓		✓
Carroll (2007)		✓		✓			
de Haan and Birch (2010)		✓					
European Mentoring and Coaching Council (2016)		✓	✓		✓		✓
Hawkins and Schwenk (2006b)	✓	✓			✓	✓	
Hawkins and Shohet (2012)		✓		✓	✓	✓	
International Coach Federation (2016)		✓		✓	✓	✓	
Stevens (2004)	✓	✓	✓	✓	✓		

[a] Definitions were compared as they were explicitly stated.
[b] Bluckert (2004), as quoted in Hawkins and Schwenk (2006b).

Differences among accrediting bodies

When examining the different definitions and functions supervision can play, it is important to understand how different accrediting bodies approach the issue. Each organization has its own definitions, policies, and positions regarding supervision, and therefore comparing their positions is difficult.

The International Coach Federation (ICF), for example, makes a distinction between mentoring and supervision. According to the ICF, mentoring is defined as "coaching for the development of one's coaching" (International Coach Federation, 2014) whereas supervision is defined as "a collaborative learning practice to continually build the capacity of the coach through reflective dialogue and to benefit his or her clients and the overall system" (International Coach Federation, 2016). This distinction is not made with the European Mentoring and Coaching Council (EMCC) and the Association for Coaching (AC). Interestingly, Gray (2010) describes a model that utilizes a mentor more for career and business development.

These differences are most apparent when comparing the accreditation requirements of these organizations. For instance, the EMCC and AC require supervision for accreditation, whereas the ICF does not (Association for Coaching, 2016; European Mentoring and Coaching Council, 2012; International Coach Federation, 2015). However, the ICF does require mentoring in lieu of supervision. It is hard to determine if this translates to measurably different practices and outcomes or whether these differences are simply a matter of semantics.

These organizations also differ when it comes to ongoing supervision. The *Global Code of Ethics*, which both the AC and EMCC endorse, states:

> To support their learning and ongoing professional development, members will engage in regular reflective practice. Members will engage in supervision with a suitably qualified supervisor or peer supervision group with a level of frequency that is appropriate to their coaching or mentoring practice. (Association for Coaching & European Mentoring and Coaching Council, 2016, p. 5)

Contrasting this, the ICF does not require ongoing supervision (International Coach Federation, 2015). According to the EMCC *Guidelines on Supervision*:

> Coaches/mentors should undertake no less than one hour of supervision per 35 hours of practice, ensuring a minimum of four hours per year, evenly distributed if possible. (European Mentoring and Coaching Council, 2016, p. 3)

The AC does not outline the amount of time or the type of supervision (one-to-one, group, formal, informal, peer, etc.). The only publicly available information comes from an AC newsletter, which states:

> Best practice would be no less than quarterly and ideally monthly. If you have a lower caseload you may consider attending group rather than one-to-one supervision. (Lucas, 2015, p. 2)

Coaching supervision models

As mentioned previously, one of the earliest models for supervision in general was proposed by Kadushin (1976) and subsequently adapted or developed independently by others (e.g., Proctor, 1987). This model has considerable utility. Kadushin proposed three components: administrative, educational, and supportive. The administrative component centers on client case management, rights, and ethics. Monitoring and self-care fall into the supportive component in order to maintain job satisfaction and prevent burnout. Lastly, the educational component entails personal and skill development. This fundamental model continues to provide utility in supervision research to date (e.g., Bambling, 2014; Hodge, 2016). It also plays into the concept that "supervision should be a mix of simultaneous challenge and support" (Cavanagh, Stern, & Lane, 2016, p. 178).

As demonstrated earlier, the history of coaching supervision has been heavily influenced by psychotherapy and social work (Carroll, 2007). Similarities between the fields and an increasing number of therapists training as coaches may also have an influence (Bluckert, 2005; Butwell, 2006; Moyes, 2009). Thus, the most popular models and functions in the literature can trace their roots back to these fields. Some have argued that these models, functions, and definitions are incompatible with coaching:

> Coaching is not counselling or psychotherapy and one could argue that we should not assume that we can blithely transpose one set of standards across to another arena. (Butwell, 2006, p. 49)

Consequently, practitioners and researchers have expressed the need to develop coaching models, definitions, and functions that are unique to coaching (Hawkins & Schwenk, 2006b):

> One of the dangers of a coach going for supervision to a counsellor, or counselling psychologist, is that the supervisor's professional focus will tend towards understanding the psychology of the client. (Carroll, 2006a, p. 3)

The most widely used model of coaching supervision is the seven-eyed model created by Peter Hawkins. Originally developed for use in counseling and psychotherapy, the seven-eyed model was adapted for use in coaching beginning in the mid-1990s (Hawkins & Schwenk, 2011). This model uses a systemic approach to supervision. Figure 2.2 illustrates the model and explains the seven "eyes," or modes, contained within. Several other coaching supervision models based on Hawkins' seven-eyed model also exist, including Megginson and Clutterbuck's seven conversations model (Clutterbuck, 2011) and the three worlds four territories model (Turner, 2011). The seven-eyed model is comprehensive since it includes all parties in the conversation—the client, coach, supervisor, and organization or other external context. It is also valuable since it includes elements internal to each of the parties as well as their relationships with each other.

Coaching supervision models are not limited to the seven-eyed model and its variants, however. Other models and techniques include the reflective coaching practitioner

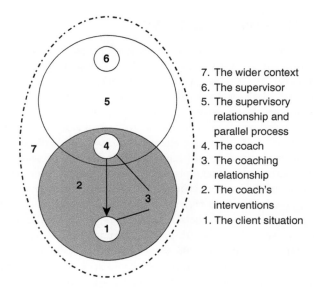

7. The wider context
6. The supervisor
5. The supervisory
   relationship and
   parallel process
4. The coach
3. The coaching
   relationship
2. The coach's
   interventions
1. The client situation

Figure 2.2 *Hawkin's Seven-Eyed Model of Supervision*
Note. Reproduced from Hawkins, 2014, with permission from Sage Publishing

model developed from Schon's work in social work and psychotherapy in the 1980s (Campone, 2011), the full spectrum model (Murdoch & Arnold, 2013), action learning supervision (Childs, Woods, Willcock, & Man, 2011), the gestalt supervision model (Gillie, 2011), nondirective supervision (Thomson, 2011), and narrative supervision (Congram, 2011), although the use, development, and establishment of these models vary greatly. For a more in-depth review of these models and techniques, refer to Bachkirova et al. (2011), Hawkins and Shohet (2012), Murdoch and Arnold (2013), and Passmore (2011).

A case for a systemic approach to supervision

Supervision was originally focused solely on the therapist's client (Carroll, 2006a). However, with the growth of counseling in organizations, supervision began to take a more systemic approach (Carroll, 2006a). Guidelines from the American Psychological Association now mention the importance of understanding the contexts and systems involved in clinical supervision (American Psychological Association, 2014). Several proponents have argued that coaching supervision should also have a systemic focus (Carroll, 2006a; Gray, 2007; Hawkins, 2011; Hay, 2007). Carroll (2006a, p. 2) explains:

> Unlike workplace counselling where what happened in the counselling room was dictated by the client and the organisation had little say in that agenda, suddenly with executive coaching it is the organisation that often sets the agenda.

Self-deception is another concern for coaches. Bachkirova (2015) interviewed six coaching supervisors about self-deception in their supervisees and found examples, including:

> Overstepping the boundaries of coaching when clients wished to work on issues more appropriate for therapy; pushing the client too much for their own reasons; ignoring ethical dilemmas; and colluding with powerful clients. (Bachkirova, 2015, p. 11)

One influence of self-deception reported was wider influences such as "power balance, organizational culture [and the] current state of society" (Bachkirova, 2015, p. 13), further adding to the case for a more systemic approach to supervision.

In addition to supervision models for the supervisor/supervisee relationship, several meta-models describe the interactions between the different elements within a supervisory relationship (Carroll, 2006a, 2006b; Gray, 2007). Carroll (2006a) presents a model (see Figure 2.3) that expands upon other models by highlighting the connections between different "subsystems" in a coaching supervision relationship:

> While the visible focus of executive coaching supervision is usually two people or a small group of people (peer, team, group supervision), to ignore the systemic side of supervision is to miss the unseen but very active participants in the wider field who impact dramatically on the executive coaching, the coachee and their work together. Supervision inevitably involves a number of subsystems, even if they are invisible participants in the process. (Carroll, 2006a, p. 48)

Gray (2007) also presents a meta-model of supervision (see Figure 2.4), which provides context for the supervisory relationship.

In addition to these models, Hawkins has developed the "four pillars of systemic supervision." These pillars emphasize the importance of a systemic perspective in coaching supervision, which focuses on the organizations, relationships, and processes that surround and interact with the coach, client, and supervisor. Within the four pillars is the CLEAR process model, which outlines the five stages that take place during supervision: contract, listen, explore, action, and review (Hawkins, 2011).

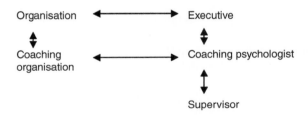

Figure 2.3 *Systemic Overview of Coaching Psychology Supervision*
Note. Reproduced from Carroll (2006a, 2006b), with permission from the British Psychological Society

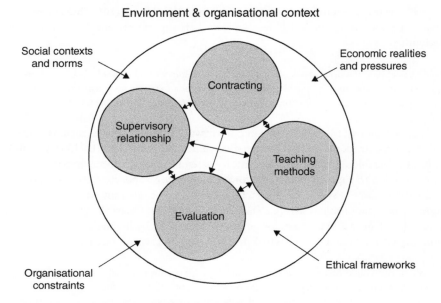

Figure 2.4 *Systemic Meta-Model of Coaching Supervision*
Note. Reproduced from Gray (2007), with permission from the Australian Psychological Society

Best practices

Currently, there are no universally accepted guidelines or best practices for coaching supervision. However, Hawkins and Schwenk (2006a, 2006b) have outlined eight "good practices" based on their research. Although these practices have not been validated, findings from a study by Passmore and McGoldrick (2009) support these guidelines. They include:

- takes place regularly
- has balance of individual, group, and peer supervision
- manages ethical and confidentiality boundaries
- generates organizational learning
- provides support for the coach
- quality assures coaching provision (provides quality assurance in regards to ethics and competence)
- provides continuing professional development to the coach
- focuses on client, organization, and coach needs (Hawkins & Schwenk, 2006b, p. 8)

The Special Group in Coaching Psychology (2007) published guidelines for coaching psychology supervision, which included a discussion of the appropriate formats for supervision (one-to-one, peer, and group), agreements, confidentiality, climate, frequency, roles and responsibilities, and competencies.

In the domain of clinical supervision, a distinction has been made between supervision competencies and best practices. Borders (2014) defines competencies as knowledge and best practices as the procedures used in carrying out the supervision.

The Association for Counselor Education and Supervision commissioned a task force to "formulate a relevant and useful set of best practice guidelines for clinical supervisors, regardless of work setting" (ACES Task Force, 2011, p. 1). The resulting document is a comprehensive guideline, which includes elements of process, inclusion of diversity considerations, relationship, ethics, supervision format, and supervisor responsibilities. These guidelines were created through a consensus process among task force members after a review of the supervision and ethics literature, as well as gathering data from task force members.

A developmental approach is considered important by many (e.g., Bambling, 2014; Cavanagh et al., 2016; Hodge, 2014). This orientation considers the need for early practitioners to work on skill acquisition, skill development, and maintaining consistent quality in their work. Mid-level practitioners may wish to hone their skills and integrate techniques sufficiently that their approach feels fluid and seamless to clients. Coaches at the master level may choose to co-create their supervision plan and remain more open to what arises during the supervision process. This approach brings to mind the shift away from a hierarchical model that Watkins and Milne (2014) have observed:

> First, if there is one feature that now seems to characterise the tenor of all supervision models, it might best be stated as follows: Across the decades, supervision conceptualisation and conduct have come to increasingly reflect a more egalitarian, collaborative, co-partici-pative, and co-constructed vision of process and outcome, where supervisor and supervisee actively and fully work together to create a supervision experience that is jointly optimal and productive. At its core, that evolving shift is ultimately about power, influence, and agency——the move toward recognising that: (a) both supervisor and supervisee have power and influence in the supervisory endeavour, and (b) supervision works best when that power and influence are mutually used and shared for its enhancement. (p. 676)

Supervision outcomes and experiences

Studying and measuring coaching supervision efficacy would be an extremely diffi-cult, expensive, and time-consuming process due to the number of supervisors, coaches, and clients that would need to be involved, the length of time needed for the study, and the number of assessments needed to be given to each of the three parties. Consequently, no study to date has attempted to do so. However, anecdotal findings from several studies suggest that coaches who undergo supervision generally report having positive outcomes and experiences. The most common themes were develop-mental in nature and included increased self-awareness, confidence, objectivity, resourcefulness, and capability (Champion, 2011; DeFilippo, 2013; Lawrence & Whyte, 2014; Lucas, 2012; McGivern, 2009; Passmore & McGoldrick, 2009). A sense of belonging and reduced feelings of isolation were also described, especially in group supervision settings (Butwell, 2006; Passmore & McGoldrick, 2009).

Barriers to supervision

Despite mostly positive perceptions about coaching supervision, some have described negative experiences. For example, Grant found that 30% of participants had poor experiences. However, despite these negative experiences, 91% of these same participants also agreed or strongly agreed that "it is very important that all professional coaches should have regular on-going supervision on coaching" (Grant, 2012, p. 27). When asked about these negative experiences, 26% expressed dissatisfaction with the supervisor's skill level. Not surprisingly, 35% of participants reported the lack of good supervisors as a barrier to receiving coaching supervision. Of all the participants in this study, 39% used peer supervision and 18% had informal supervision, which may have contributed to the reported poor experiences (Grant, 2012). Cost was also cited as a barrier (Salter, 2008). Grant (2012) reported that 32% of participants listed cost as an obstacle to receiving supervision. In 2006, 17% of UK coaches listed cost as a reason for not receiving supervision (Hawkins & Schwenk, 2006a, 2006b). Recent research has suggested that the cost and negative experience barriers may be falling away (Hawkins & Turner, 2017). However, the participants in this study were mostly pulled from the UK, so this finding may not apply to other regions of the world.

FUTURE OF COACHING SUPERVISION

Should supervision be mandatory?

Although most research indicates that coaches are in favor of coaching supervision, there has been some debate about whether or not it should be mandatory. Some coaches argue that supervision directly affects coaching quality and could help strengthen the profession. Others have reasoned that supervision stifles creativity, breeds conformity, and violates confidentiality (Salter, 2008). A survey of 218 coaches across the United States, Canada, and Europe found that 63% of coaches do not believe supervision should be mandatory, although overarching generalities and conclusions cannot be made from a single study (Salter, 2008).

Bachkirova (2008, p. 16) argues that supervision is actually more important for coaches than therapists:

> Coaches have more than one client in each coaching engagement and so have a greater need to see the complexity of the relationship and the many perspectives of the various stakeholders in their work. Furthermore, coaches are less equipped than counsellors to identify mental health issues impinging on the boundaries of coaching, so they would benefit from another pair of eyes to check their concerns.

However, even with this strong endorsement of supervision, Bachkirova et al. (2011, p. 4) state, "we hope and believe that discretionary supervision is likely to work better than if it were mandatory." More recently, Hodge (2016) states:

> When the coach takes personal responsibility for their supervision (including preparation and subsequent reflections) this gives them a wider purpose than just meeting imposed accreditation requirements … This voluntary approach may potentially conflict with the coaching associations' mandated approach in their wish to establish standards of professional practice. (p. 101)

Hodge (2016) also concludes "one-to-one supervision alone is not enough to support coaches in this work" (p. 98).

Based upon the fact that no robust studies exist identifying the efficacy of coaching supervision, one would be hard-pressed to defend a position mandating coaching supervision on an ongoing basis.

Future research

Despite a growing number of books and academic articles, the scope of research on coaching supervision is still rather limited. This is most likely due to the fact that "supervision is a complex intervention" (Watkins & Milne, 2014, p. 683) and lacks generally accepted models and standardized instruments. For example, the recent dissertations of DeFilippo (2013) and Hodge (2014) do not develop or employ similar coaching supervision models.

Wheeler and Barkham (2014) discuss the deficiencies in clinical supervision research, such as weak procedures and methodologies. Additionally, their research showed very little overlap in the instruments used from study to study. To overcome the instrumentation deficiency, Wheeler and Barkham (2014) have proposed a fixed battery of five assessments to begin gathering consistent data. While this will move the industry forward, it still lacks client measurement—a critical measure of supervision efficacy.

Based on the exposition herein, coaching supervision research that incorporates the following elements is recommended:

- randomized control and experimental groups
- client, coach, and supervisor outcome measures
- client, coach, and supervisor characteristics
- measures of coach–supervisor bond
- measures of coach–supervisor tasks
- assessment of supervisor flexibility to adapt to coach developmental level

Conducting a robust study with sufficient statistical power will require a large number of clients, coaches, and supervisors over an extended period of time, even if the effect size turned out to be large. Obviously, such a study will be considerably expensive.

Until such a study is undertaken, however, an approach similar to Wheeler and Barkham (2014) would provide small steps toward that goal. Development, validation, and agreement among researchers on tools needed to conduct such a robust study will pave the way for that ultimate journey.

CONCLUSION

This review of the coaching supervision literature highlights the steady progress made toward a better understanding of what takes place in coaching supervision. The latest studies have shone light on the coaching supervision process and effects on coaches as well as supervisors. These studies also highlight the need for standardized elements such as models and instruments. While the seven-eyed model is sufficient to illustrate the players, relationships, and context, it does not speak to the activities and processes taking place within supervision. Development and agreement among researchers of standardized measures will prove very helpful in moving the industry forward.

We have seen that with the apparent consensus among clinical supervision researchers on measures, they will be able to gather large quantities of data, albeit with somewhat limited usefulness, since client outcomes will not be measured. However, the coaching industry can continue to observe the clinical field for additional clues into coaching supervision.

REFERENCES

ACES Task Force. (2011). *Best practices in clinical supervision*. Retrieved March 28, 2016, from http://www.saces.org/resources/documents/aces_best_practices.doc

American Psychological Association. (2014). *Guidelines for clinical supervision in health service psychology*. Retrieved March 22, 2016, from http://www.apa.org/about/policy/guidelines-supervision.pdf

Association for Coaching. (2015). *Coaching supervision guide*. Retrieved March 24, 2016, from http://www.associationforcoaching.com/media/uploads/ac_coaching_supervision_guide.doc

Association for Coaching. (2016). *AC coach and executive coach accreditation scheme overview: Choosing your application level*. Retrieved March 22, 2016, from http://www.associationforcoaching.com/media/uploads/ac_coach_accreditation_overview_final.pdf

Association for Coaching & European Mentoring and Coaching Council. (2016). *Global code of ethics for coaches and mentors*. Retrieved March 22, 2016, from http://www.associationforcoaching.com/media/uploads/global_code_of_ethics_-_version_1.0_dated_february_2016.pdf

Bachkirova, T. (2008). Coaching supervision: Reflections on changes and challenges. *People and Organisations at Work, Spring*, 16–17.

Bachkirova, T. (2015). Self-deception in coaches: An issue in principle and a challenge for supervision. *Coaching: An International Journal of Theory, Research and Practice, 8*(1), 4–19.

Bachkirova, T., Jackson, P., & Clutterbuck, D. (2011). Introduction. In T. Bachkirova, P. Jackson, & D. Clutterbuck (Eds.), *Coaching and mentoring supervision: Theory and practice* (pp. 1–14). New York, NY: Open University Press.

Bambling, M. (2014). Creating positive outcomes in clinical supervision. In C. E. J. Watkins & D. L. Milne (Eds.), *The Wiley international handbook of clinical supervision* (pp. 445–457). Chichester: Wiley.

Bluckert, P. (2005). The similarities and differences between coaching and therapy. *Industrial and Commercial Training, 37*(2), 91–96.

Borders, L. D. (2014). Best practices in clinical supervision: Another step in delineating effective supervision practice. *American Journal of Psychotherapy, 68*(2), 151–162.

Brock, V. G. (2008). *Grounded theory of the roots and emergence of coaching.* Unpublished doctoral dissertation, International University of Professional Studies, Maui, HI.

Butwell, J. (2006). Group supervision for coaches: Is it worthwhile? *International Journal of Evidence Based Coaching and Mentoring, 4*(2), 1–11.

Campone, F. (2011). The reflective coaching practitioner model. In J. Passmore (Ed.), *Supervision in coaching: Supervision, ethics and continuous professional development* (pp. 11–29). Philadelphia, PA: Kogan Page.

Carroll, M. (2006a). Supervising executive coaches. *Therapy Today, 17*(5), 47–49.

Carroll, M. (2006b). Key issues in coaching psychology supervision. *The Coaching Psychologist, 2*(1), 4–8.

Carroll, M. (2007). One more time: What is supervision? *Psychotherapy in Australia, 13*(3), 34–40.

Cavanagh, M. J., Stern, L., & Lane, D. A. (2016). Supervision in coaching psychology: A systemic developmental psychological perspective. In D. A. Lane, M. Watts, & S. Corrie (Eds.), *Supervision in the psychological professions: Building your own personalized model* (pp. 173–194). Maidenhead: Open University Press.

Champion, C. K. (2011). Beyond quality assurance: The Deloitte story. In T. Bachkirova, P. Jackson, & D. Clutterbuck (Eds.), *Coaching and mentoring supervision: Theory and practice* (pp. 281–290). Maidenhead: Open University Press.

Childs, R., Woods, M., Willcock, D., & Man, A. (2011). Action learning supervision for coaches. In J. Passmore (Ed.), *Supervision in coaching: Supervision, ethics, and continuous professional development* (pp. 31–44). Philadelphia, PA: Kogan Page.

Clutterbuck, D. (2011). Using the seven conversations in supervision. In T. Bachkirova, P. Jackson, & D. Clutterbuck (Eds.), *Coaching and mentoring supervision: Theory and practice* (pp. 55–66). New York, NY: Open University Press.

Congram, S. (2011). Narrative supervision: The experiential field and the 'imaginal'. In J. Passmore (Ed.), *Supervision in coaching: Supervision, ethics, and continuous professional development* (pp. 81–98). Philadelphia, PA: Kogan Page.

de Haan, E., & Birch, D. (2010). Quality control for coaching. *Training Journal,* August, 71–74.

DeCarvalho, R. J. (1991). *The founders of humanistic psychology.* New York, NY: Praeger.

DeFilippo, D. J. (2013). *Executive coach supervision: The dynamics and effects.* Unpublished doctoral dissertation, University of Pennsylvania.

European Mentoring and Coaching Council. (2012). *European individual accreditation v2 EIA v2 guide to applying for non-EQA certificate holding applicants.* Retrieved March 22, 2016, from http://www.emccouncil.org/webimages/EU/EIA/ON-EQA_certificate_holding_applicants.pdf

European Mentoring and Coaching Council. (2016). *EMCC guidelines on supervision.* Retrieved November 18, 2016, from http://www.emccouncil.org/src/ultimo/models/Download/7.pdf

Gillie, M. (2011). The Gestalt supervision model. In J. Passmore (Ed.), *Supervision in coaching: Supervision, ethics, and continuous professional development* (pp. 45–64). Philadelphia, PA: Kogan Page.

Grant, A. (2012). Australian coaches views on coaching supervision: A study with implications for Australian coach education, training and practice. *International Journal of Evidenced Based Coaching and Mentoring, 10*(2), 17–33.

Gray, D. E. (2007). Towards a systemic model of coaching supervision: Some lessons from psychotherapeutic and counselling models. *Australian Psychologist, 42*(4), 300–309.

Gray, D. E. (2010). Towards the lifelong skills and business development of coaches: An integrated model of supervision and mentoring. *Coaching: An International Journal of Theory, Research and Practice, 3*(1), 60–72.

Hart, V., Blattner, J., & Leipsic, S. (2001). Coaching versus therapy: A perspective. *Consulting Psychology Journal: Practice and Research, 53*(4), 229.

Hawkins, P. (2011). Systemic approaches to supervision. In T. Bachkirova, P. Jackson, & D. Clutterbuck (Eds.), *Coaching and mentoring supervision: Theory and practice* (pp. 167–179). New York, NY: Open University Press.

Hawkins, P. (2014). Coaching supervision. In E. Cox, T. Bachkirova, & D. Clutterbuck (Eds.), *The complete handbook of coaching* (2nd ed., pp. 391–404). London: Sage.

Hawkins, P., & Schwenk, G. (2006a). *Coaching supervision: Paper prepared for the CIPD coaching conference.* London: Chartered Institute of Personnel and Development.

Hawkins, P., & Schwenk, G. (2006b). *Coaching supervision: Maximising the potential of coaching.* London: Chartered Institute of Personnel and Development.

Hawkins, P., & Schwenk, G. (2011). The seven-eyed model of coaching supervision. In T. Bachkirova, P. Jackson, & D. Clutterbuck (Eds.), *Coaching and mentoring supervision: Theory and practice* (pp. 28–40). New York, NY: Open University Press.

Hawkins, P., & Shohet, R. (2012). *Supervision in the helping professions* (4th ed.). Maidenhead: Open University Press.

Hawkins, P., & Smith, N. (2006). *Coaching, mentoring and organizational consultancy: Supervision, skills, and development.* Maidenhead: Open University Press.

Hawkins, P., & Smith, N. (2013). *Coaching, mentoring and organizational consultancy: Supervision, skills, and development* (2nd ed.). Maidenhead: Open University Press.

Hawkins, P., & Turner, E. (2016). Coming of age: The development of coaching supervision 2006–2014. *Coaching at Work, 11*(2), 30–35.

Hawkins, P., & Turner, E. (2017). The rise of coaching supervision 2006–2014. *Coaching: An International Journal of Theory, Research and Practice, 10*(2), 102–114.

Hay, J. (2007). *Reflective practice and supervision for coaches.* New York, NY: Open University Press.

Hodge, A. (2014). An action research inquiry into what goes on in coaching supervision to the end of enhancing the coaching profession. Unpublished manuscript, Middlesex University. Retrieved from http://eprints.mdx.ac.uk/13707

Hodge, A. (2016). The value of coaching supervision as a development process: Contribution to continued professional and personal wellbeing for executive coaches. *International Journal of Evidence Based Coaching and Mentoring, 14*, 87–106.

International Coach Federation. (2014). *Mentor coaching duties and competencies.* Retrieved March 22, 2016 from http://www.coachfederation.org/credential/landing.cfm?ItemNumber=2210&navItemNumber=3364

International Coach Federation. (2015). *Associate Certified Coach (ACC) application requirements.* Retrieved March 22, 2016, from http://www.coachfederation.org/credential/landing.cfm?ItemNumber=2199&navItemNumber=744

International Coach Federation. (2016). *Coaching supervision*. Retrieved December 7, 2016, from http://www.coachfederation.org/credential/landing.cfm?ItemNumber=4259

Kadushin, A. (1976). *Supervision in social work*. New York, NY: Columbia University Press.

Lawrence, P., & Whyte, A. (2014). What is coaching supervision and is it important? *Coaching: An International Journal of Theory, Research and Practice, 7*(1), 39–55.

Lucas, M. (2012). Exploring the double-value of supervision: A developmental perspective for internal coaches. *International Journal of Mentoring and Coaching, 10*(2), 21–38.

Lucas, M. (2015). *What's so 'Super' about supervision?* London: Association for Coaching. Retrieved March 22, 2016, from http://www.associationforcoaching.com/media/uploads/mber_-_coaching_supervision_1%5B4%5D.pdf

Maslow, A. H. (1943). A theory of human motivation. *Psychological Review, 50*(4), 370–396.

McGivern, L. (2009). Continuous professional development and avoiding the vanity trap: An exploration of coaches' lived experiences of supervision [Special Issue 3]. *International Journal of Evidence Based Coaching and Mentoring*, 22–37.

Moyes, B. (2009). Literature review of coaching supervision. *International Coaching Psychology Review, 4*(2), 162–173.

Murdoch, E., & Arnold, J. (2013). *Full spectrum supervision: Who you are is how you supervise*. St. Albans, Herts: Panoma Press.

Passmore, J. (2011). *Supervision in coaching: Supervision, ethics, and continuous professional development*. Philadelphia, PA: Kogan Page.

Passmore, J., & McGoldrick, S. (2009). Super-vision, extra-vision or blind faith? A grounded theory study of the efficacy of coaching supervision. *International Coaching Psychology Review, 4*(2), 145–161.

Proctor, B. (1987). Supervision: A co-operative exercise in accountability. In A. Marken & M. Payne (Eds.), *Enabling and ensuring: Supervision in practice* (pp. 21–23). Leicester: Leicester National Youth Bureau & Council for Education and Training in Youth and Community Work.

Rogers, C. R. (1957). The necessary and sufficient conditions of therapeutic personality change. *Journal of Consulting Psychology, 21*(2), 95–103.

Salter, T. (2008). Exploring current thinking within the field of coaching on the role of supervision [Special Issue 2]. *International Journal of Evidence Based Coaching & Mentoring*, 27–39.

Special Group in Coaching Psychology. (2007). Guidelines on supervision for coaching psychology. *The Coaching Psychologist, 3*(2), 95–102.

Stevens, P. (2004). Coaching supervision. *Training Journal, 1*, 18–19.

Thomson, B. (2011). Non-directive supervision of coaching. In J. Passmore (Ed.), *Supervision in coaching: Supervision, ethics, and continuous professional development* (pp. 99–116). Philadelphia, PA: Kogan Page.

Turner, M. M. (2011). The three worlds four territories model of supervision. In T. Bachkirova, P. Jackson, & D. Clutterbuck (Eds.), *Coaching and mentoring supervision: Theory and practice* (pp. 41–54). New York, NY: Open University Press.

Watkins, C. E. (2013). The beginnings of psychoanalytic supervision: The crucial role of Max Eitingon. *American Journal of Psychoanalysis, 73*(3), 254–270.

Watkins, C. E. J., & Milne, D. L. (2014). Clinical supervision at the international crossroads: Current status and future directions. In C. E. J. Watkins & D. L. Milne (Eds.), *Wiley international handbook of clinical supervision* (pp. 673–696). Chichester: Wiley.

Wheeler, S., & Barkham, M. (2014). A core evaluation battery for supervision. In C. E. Watkins & D. L. Milne (Eds.), *The Wiley international handbook of clinical supervision* (pp. 367–385). Chichester: Wiley.

APPENDIX: DEFINITIONS OF COACHING SUPERVISION

Association for Coaching (2015): A formal and protected time for facilitating a coach's in-depth reflection on their practice with an experienced coaching supervisor. Supervision offers a confidential framework within a collaborative working relationship in which the practice, tasks, process, and challenges of the coaching work can be explored. The primary aim of supervision is to enable the coach to gain ethical competence, confidence, and creativity to ensure the best possible service to the coaching client, both coachees and coaching sponsors. Supervision is not a "policing" role, but rather a trusting and collegial professional relationship.

Bachkirova (2008): Coaching supervision is a formal process of professional support, which ensures continuing development of the coach and effectiveness of their coaching practice through interactive reflection, interpretative evaluation, and the sharing of expertise.

Bluckert (2004) (as quoted in Hawkins and Schwenk, 2006b): Supervision sessions are a place for the coach to reflect on the work they are undertaking, with another more experienced coach. It has the dual purpose of supporting the continued learning and development of the coach, as well as giving a degree of protection to the person being coached.

Carroll (2007): Supervision is a forum where supervisees review and reflect on their work in order to do it better.

De Haan and Birch (2010): Coaching supervision takes place either in groups or on a one-to-one basis. Its purpose is to help the coach bring the best of themselves to their work with clients; in practical terms, this means ensuring that they are sufficiently well-resourced to help their clients take responsibility for their behavior and their choices at work.

European Mentoring and Coaching Council (2016): The interaction that occurs when a mentor or coach brings their coaching or mentoring work experiences to a supervisor in order to be supported and to engage in reflective dialog and collaborative learning for the development and benefit of the mentor or coach, their clients, and their organizations.

Hawkins and Schwenk (2006b): A structured formal process for coaches, with the help of a coaching supervisor, to attend to improving the quality of their coaching, grow their coaching capacity, and support themselves and their practice. Supervision should be a source of organizational learning.

Hawkins and Shohet (2012): Supervision is a joint endeavor in which a practitioner, with the help of a supervisor, attends to their clients, themselves as part of their client practitioner relationships and the wider systemic context, and by so doing improves the quality of their work, transforms their client relationships, and continuously develops themselves, their practice, and the wider profession.

International Coach Federation (2016): Coaching supervision is a collaborative learning practice to continually build the capacity of the coach through reflective dialog and benefit their clients and the overall system.

Stevens (2004): Coaching supervision is a formal learning process in which a coach engages with a more experienced coaching practitioner in order to articulate, reflect on, evaluate, and receive support to monitor their coaching practice.

Section II
Insights from Coaching Psychology Theory

Jonathan Passmore and David Tee

This book is intended to be a "coaching psychology reader," yet this section is labeled as "coaching" (as opposed to coaching psychology) theory. We think this distinction matters. While there is broad consensus concerning the conceptualization and definition of coaching psychology (see the introduction to Section I), Passmore, Stopforth, & Lai (2018) make clear that the nature of what is coaching remains a contested space.

Although activities that have been labeled as "coaching" have been conducted in a range of settings, from sports to university debating societies, for many years, formal coaching is argued to have emerged during the 1980s (Grant & Cavanagh, 2007) and to have experienced a rapid growth since that time (Briner, 2012).

Ives (2008) emphasizes both practical and conceptual issues that separate the conflicting coaching practitioner paradigms. These include humanist, behaviorist, systemic, cognitive, and positive psychology coaching. To take one example, some coaching researchers (see Bachkirova, 2012; Cavanagh, 2006) dispute the tenet that coaches, acting only as facilitative guides, must always refrain from giving advice to clients. In this respect, coaching contrasts with mentoring, where the mentor shares their wisdom, experience, and insights for the benefit of the mentee. Parsloe and Wray (2000), as well as Connor and Pakora (2012), argue that this distinction between coaching and mentoring is false. Passmore too has argued that in practice coaching and mentoring sit on a continuum that the experienced executive coach navigates in the best interests of, and reflecting the developmental stage and experience of, their client (Passmore, 2007).

Given the diversity and debate that (arguably) may simultaneously plague and enrich coaching, it is therefore unsurprising that there is no one clear body of theory or a theoretical framework that can easily be identified as the foundation on which the recent growth in coaching has been built: to point to a "theory of coaching" would be problematic indeed.

To return to the distinction between coaching and coaching psychology: the latter is regarded as diverse and interdisciplinary (Cowan, 2013; McDowall & Short, 2012), drawing on theories from counseling, sports and exercise, occupational, and other domains of psychology. The former is stated by Bachkirova, Cox, and Clutterbuck (2018) to indeed draw from psychology, but also draw from management, philosophy, education, and the social sciences, each of which are rich in their own bodies of theory. Taken collectively, these diverse roots are based upon varying etic, emic, axiological, and other philosophical assumptions. Western (2012) therefore states that coaching has lots of theories: what it is actually in need of is a metatheory. Without this, coaching may well continue to merely appropriate from elsewhere: to be "dressed in borrowed clothes" (Hawkins & Schwenk, 2006).

If the function of theory is considered, then the effect of the absence of a coaching-specific theory and the reliance on acquired theories from multiple related disciplines can be understood. Theory allows the creation of a conceptual scheme to describe and understand a phenomenon; it creates a set of variables that generate a systematic view of the phenomenon of interest; that specifies and articulates the hypothesized relationships between those variables.

Clothes borrowed from multiple wardrobes may struggle to achieve a coordinated fashion statement. Coaching as a practice may celebrate the breadth and variety of sources it draws upon, but this very variety, this range of variables that were never intended to be related or interconnected, this series of "conflicting paradigms" (Ives, 2008) that has typified the formative years of coaching and coaching psychology, point to a plausible explanation as to why Western's (2012) plea for a metatheory as yet goes unanswered.

As editors of this book, and of the British Psychological Society's two coaching peer review publications (*International Coaching Psychology Review* and *The Coaching Psychologist*), we believe a unifying theory of coaching is needed. If we look at other domains such as medicine, chemistry, or most other scientific disciplines, there is one theory, one model of evidence-based practice. As psychologists, we believe coaching is not an art but a science. While humans are highly variable, as with medicine or psychiatry, evidence-based practice dominates, informed by rigorous and robust research. Over the coming decade, we hope to see (and encourage through our coaching journals) the development of a single unifying theory of evidence-based coaching which supports and sustains evidence-based practice.

REFERENCES

Bachkirova, T. (2012). Nature of evidence, quality of research and self-deception in coaching and coaching psychology. *Annual Conference of the Special Group in Coaching Psychology*, British Psychological Society, Aston, UK, 7 December.

Bachkirova, T., Cox, E., & Clutterbuck, D. (2018). Introduction. In E. Cox, T. Bachkirova, & D. Clutterbuck (Eds.), *The complete handbook of coaching* (3rd ed., pp. xxix, xlviii). Sage.

Briner, R. B. (2012). Does coaching work and does anyone really care? *OP Matters, 16,* 4–11.

Cavanagh, M. (2006). Coaching from a systemic perspective: A complex adaptive approach. In D. R. Stober & A. M. Grant (Eds.), *Evidence-based coaching handbook* (pp. 313–354). Hoboken, NJ: Wiley.

Connor, M., & Pokora, J. (2012). *Coaching and mentoring at work* (2nd ed.). Maidenhead, UK: Open University Press.

Cowan, K. (2013). Ready, set, goal. *Coaching at Work, 8*(4), 33–35.

Grant, A. M., & Cavanagh, M. J. (2007). Evidence-based coaching: Flourishing or languishing? *Australian Psychologist, 42,* 239–254.

Hawkins, P., & Schwenk, G. (2006). *Coaching supervision: Maximizing the potential of coaching.* London, UK: Chartered Institute of Personnel and Development.

Ives, Y. (2008). What is 'coaching'? An exploration of conflicting paradigms. *International Journal of Evidence Based Coaching and Mentoring, 6*(2), 100–113.

McDowall, A., & Short, E. (2012). Editorial. *Coaching: An International Journal of Theory, Research and Practice, 4*(2), 67–69.

Parsloe, E., & Wray, M. (2000). *Coaching and mentoring.* London, UK: Kogan Page.

Passmore, J. (2007). Coaching & mentoring: The role of experience and sector knowledge. *International Journal of Evidence based Coaching and Mentoring,* (S1), 10–16.

Passmore, J., Stopforth, M., & Lai, Y.-L. (2018). Defining coaching psychology: Debating coaching and coaching psychology definitions. *The Coaching Psychologist, 14*(2), 120–123.

Western, S. (2012). *Coaching and mentoring: A critical text.* London, UK: Sage.

3 Does Coaching Work or Are We Asking the Wrong Question?

Annette Fillery-Travis and David A. Lane[1]

Successful organizations in the emerging knowledge economy innovate continually to maintain their place in such a dynamic marketplace. But it is the individual employee who must develop the flexibility and creativity needed to effectively drive growth and deliver appropriate results. They expect (and are expected) to constantly upgrade their technical and leadership skills. While individuals view this professional development as predominantly their own responsibility, they look to their organization to partner them in accessing and resourcing it (Lane, Puri, Cleverly, Wylie, & Rajan, 2000). The challenge for the employer is how to achieve this within the constraints of efficient time and financial resource management.

In facing this challenge, organizations are turning away from the traditional training initiatives with the implied ethos of one size fits all. Flexibility and speed of response are imperative, and thus development has become more person-centered and tailored to the individual. In this environment it is, therefore, unsurprising that coaching has grown in popularity as an option to meet the emerging needs of organizations and, as such, has become widespread and well accepted.

As identified by Dr. Michael Cavanagh in his keynote address at the 2nd Annual Conference of the Special Group in Coaching Psychology at the British Psychological Society (BPS), "coaching has been around too long to be a management fad." It is an established part of the development portfolio available to the executive.

The market is still growing, and recent estimates put its size as $2 billion per year. In this context, it is not surprising that the question being raised by buyers of coaching is "Does it work?"

---

[1] First published as Fillery-Travis, A. & Lane, D. (2006). Does coaching work or are we asking the wrong question? *International Coaching Psychology Review*, 1(1) 23–36.

In other words, does coaching provide a return on its investment in driving performance up and impacting the bottom-line? We argue here that this is the wrong question.

Before we can ask whether coaching works, we must ask what it is being used for. Is all coaching addressing similar aims that can be quantified by a standard method, or is there a number of purposes to the coaching? If the latter, then we need to consider if these purposes are coherent and form part of a framework of practice for the profession or whether the aims are too disparate to formalize.

We have looked to the academic and practitioner literature to address this issue as well as our own research. It is clear that coaching practice has evolved almost as quickly as it has grown, and there is now a range of roles, coaching models, and frameworks of practice. At first sight, there seems to be a diversity of practice where few established norms can be assumed.

It can be argued that such diversity is to be welcomed, and indeed expected, as coaches respond to the individual needs of the client. We would agree if we were considering the *process* of coaching only, that is, the nature and description of the coaching relationship. But within this paper, we are looking at how coaching is being used, its *purpose*, and if it is considered effective by its clients and their sponsoring organizations. Therefore, as a review document, this work does not fully expand upon underpinning issues such as the emergence and development of learning organizations, nor does it explicitly cite the psychology literature that underpins the process of coaching.

Instead, we have reviewed the academic literature on the efficacy of coaching published between 1990 and 2004, although where there is insufficient work, some references are cited from the 1930s. Similarly, we have identified the general trend of the practitioner publications (both articles and books) to identify the focus of practice. We will also draw upon our own research into the experience of over 30 HR directors or buyers of coaching (Jarvis, Lane, & Fillery-Travis, 2006). The first point of note is that in common with previous reviewers (Kampa & White, 2002) we have found that the evidence base for coaching has not increased at the same rate as practice. Research into the efficacy of coaching has lagged behind, and it has only started to develop seriously over the last 5 years. As identified by Grant (2003) the literature is at the point of expansion in response to the practice development.

We have focused our interest on the following questions:

1. How is coaching being used within organizations, and who is doing it?
2. Is there a coherent framework of practice across the identified modes of coaching?
3. Is it perceived or quantified as being effective?

The consideration of these questions structures the rest of this paper. Within it, we identify the coaching agenda or purpose to be an underpinning concept that allows us to develop a framework of practice that encompasses both coaching mode and role. It is against this framework that the question can then be asked: "Does it work?"

HOW IS COACHING BEING USED WITHIN AN ORGANIZATION?

The School of Coaching survey (Kubicek, 2002) last year provided data on which coaching modes are being used within organizations:

- 51% used external coaches;
- 41% trained internal coaches; and
- 79% manager coaches.

We will consider each of these in turn and also briefly mention team coaches.

External coaches

Various surveys have been undertaken in recent years to investigate the use of this type of coaching within the UK; the Coaching Study published by the University of Central England (a survey of 1,153 organizations across the UK) and The Institute of Employment Studies (IES) report (Carter, 2001) are but two of them. Each sought to identify what coaches were being commissioned to do within organizations. Considering this information together with the journal and research literature, we can group the potential functions for an external coach under two main headings:

1. The coaching of a senior executive to their own agenda.
2. The coaching of managers after training to consolidate knowledge acquisition and work with the individual to support and facilitate resulting behavior change in relation to a specific organizational agenda.

The tasks associated with the first function included: supporting the induction of a senior manager, supporting particular individuals identified as high potential or as targets for extra support, and acting as a critical friend or sounding board for a senior manager where mentors are not appropriate or practical. It is also clear that coaching is being seen as a reward for senior managers and part of a retention package. Indeed it has been noted within the IES (Carter, 2001) study that the phenomenon of "coaching envy" is a reality for the members of its research forum. As cited by Hall, Otazo, and Hollenbeck (1999), "Executives like the confidentiality and personal attention: they also like what coaching does for their careers."

So once coaching is introduced to a company, other executives within the company want a coach.

Traditionally within this first option, the coaching agenda is totally free and defined only by the coachee. It is not even constrained to the work role but allows exploration of any issues that the coachee identifies as interesting. In our previous study on the efficacy of coaching (Jarvis et al., 2006) we found that organizations were increasingly aware of the potential difficulties for an organization of "free agenda" coaching. These include a perceived "lack of control" with the potential for distraction of the coachee from the primary task and also the lack of a defined return on investment (ROI). In addition, there is the real possibility that the coachee may be "coached out of a job."

Organizations react to this latter issue in one of two ways: either by acknowledging that the coaching is revealing a hidden problem thereby creating an opportunity to manage it effectively or by reducing the potential for this type of crisis to occur by restricting the agenda of the coaching at the start of the contract.

In the latter strategy, the sponsoring organization will seek to have more direct involvement in the contracting phase, usually through involvement with the line manager or the HR department. Within our own research, HR directors were increasingly requiring their external coaches to undergo a familiarization process covering the company's culture and ethos and to undertake to keep within a proscribed agenda.

The issues identified within the coaching agenda will, in general, be diverse and the external coach can be working at a variety of levels of engagement. Categorization of these levels of engagement has been developing within the literature for some time. Grant and Cavanagh (2004) identify three generic levels:

1. skills coaching, which can be of short duration and which requires the coach to focus on specific behaviors;
2. performance coaching, which will focus on the process by which the coachee can set goals, overcome obstacles, and evaluate and monitor their performance; and finally,
3. developmental coaching, which takes a broader, more holistic view, often dealing with more intimate, personal and professional questions. This can involve the creation of personal reflective space, often referred to as "therapy for the people who don't need therapy."

Other categorizations have been also been developed, for example, Witherspoon and White (1996) identify four distinct roles for the coach: coaching for skills, for performance, for development, and for the executive's agenda. For Peterson (1996) there are three different types: targeted, intensive, and executive. At the present time, there are no universally identified definitions of these roles. But it is clear that the level of competence and skill required of the coach increases with the level of engagement, and at the highest level it is generally acknowledged that a mastery of practice is needed. Defining what "mastery" of practice means in this context has been the work of professional bodies in recent years, and the interested reader is referred to their websites and publications for further information.

It is while considering these levels that the concepts of professional practice—that is, specified body of knowledge, accreditation, and ethical basis of practice—are brought into focus (Garman, Whiston, & Zlatoper, 2000). As Lane (Jarvis, Lane, & Fillery-Travis, 2006) points out,

> This is not proposed as an argument that only psychologists should coach but rather that those who work as coaches to address complex personal and professional development should adopt the hallmarks of a profession and work to an evidence based agenda rather than promote untested propriety models built on ideas drawn from sources both spurious and credible.

Primary to this goal is the supervision of the coach. The various coaching professional bodies are currently developing frameworks of professionalism and accreditation of coaching and coaches. Central to the majority of these is the supervision of the coach. For example, the European Mentoring and Coaching Council (EMCC) states in its code of ethics, "A coach/mentor must maintain a relationship with a suitably qualified supervisor, who will regularly assess their competence and support their development." The external coach will be expected to be under supervision but may also provide supervision for others. We will deal with this in more detail later.

This free agenda coaching engagement is in stark contrast to the second option for the executive coach: training consolidation (Smither, London, Flautt, Vargas, & Kucine, 2003). It is now widely accepted that sustained behavior change after training can only be achieved through monitoring and consolidation activities that continue after the training itself. In the past, this has been in the form of "follow on workshops," and so on, but external coaches are now taking a role in providing one-to-one assessment and feedback on the learning undertaken. This is obviously limited in duration, typically one or two sessions, and there is a highly constrained agenda defined by the training event or focus, with an outcome of facilitating behavior change to affect the required response. One area where it is highly used is in the training of manager coaches and the supervision of internal coaches. We will deal with those in due course.

Manager coaches

Although current research has focused on the coach as an external consultant, there is a literature dating back to the 1930s on manager coaches (Grant, 2003). Graham, Wedman, and Garvin-Kester (1993) reported an evaluation of a coaching skills program for 13 sales managers with a total of 87 account representatives reporting to them. Although this focus for research has declined in the last couple of decades, it is still an active and distinct modality of coaching, particularly given the recent emphasis on the learning organization. Quoting again from the recent survey by the School of Coaching—"Is coaching being abused?" (Kubicek, 2002)—"Most organisations will say 'yes our managers are coaching' and 'yes we support it. '"

This survey of 179 senior HR managers in the UK during February 2002: found that most organizations in the sample (79%) were providing coaching by line managers to their direct reports. Middle managers were the most likely group of employees to be receiving coaching (74%). It was interesting that only 38% of organizations had an initiative in place to develop their managers' coaching skills and these were primarily for middle managers. Most of the respondents (70%) had coaching as part of their development strategy, with 40% mentioning performance measures and 37% a competency framework.

An in-depth example of the use of mentoring and coaching within a human resource strategy is provided by Coca-Cola Foods (Veale, 1996). Here coaching is viewed in its widest description, which includes instruction and problem solving, but the cohesiveness of the approach is worth investigation.

A study by Ellinger and Bostrum (1998) has attempted to define, through a qualitative critical incident study, the ways exemplary managers facilitate their employee learning. They describe a range of behaviors and the interested reader is referred to this paper as well as the range of literature on learning organizations that can inform our training and development of the manager coach.

The coaching agenda for managers is usually solely concerned with the requirements of the organization and is focused explicitly on the achievement of work goals. It does not have the open agenda commonly used by external coaches and it is set for the mutual benefit of manager and coachee. The manager needs the output from the employee and seeks to develop it. The employee needs to satisfy the requirements of the post and needs the help and advice of the manager in achieving this. This mutuality sets the focus for the engagement and has an impact both on the learning needs the coaching can address and on the training and supervision required for the coach.

The benefits of this coaching are clear—the coach is on-the-spot with a clear identification of organizational culture and an assessment of the coaching needs of the individual. There is minimal time delay between identification of need and coaching intervention. As one of our case studies identified, "the business environment is changing too fast so we cannot continually retrain everyone—we need to use coaching to constantly update and upgrade."

It is unlikely and probably unethical for the coaching to be at the developmental level where disclosure of personal and intimate information is required. But it will certainly address skills and probably performance levels. Thus the level of skill and competence required of the manager coach is significantly lower than that of the external coach. However, some level of competence is still necessary. In the School of Coaching Study (Kubicek, 2002) concern was raised that on average the manager coaches received only 3 days of training to develop their coaching skills and that 67% of companies had no policy/strategy/vision with regard to the use of coaching (a strategy was more likely the bigger the organization). As identified by Geber (1992), the task of coaching for the manager is, "the most difficult one to perform and requires the biggest paradigm shift of any new system."

We should expect managers to need support to attain competence in this role. It is, therefore, not surprising that, as we indicated previously, external coaches are contracted to provide some of this support and help consolidate behavior change. Alternatively, this support can also be supplied by internal coaches, who we will consider next.

Internal coaches

The coach manager is not the only form of internal coach. As discussed in "The emerging role of the Internal Coach" (Frisch, 2001), "Coaching is now seen as an investment in the organisation's future. Perhaps concurrent with this has been the emergence of the internal coach."

When used in the remedial role, it can be argued that the external coach's separateness is essential to reduce defensiveness on the coachee's part and allow focus on their development. However, in the senior development role, the trained colleague or internal coach's knowledge of the organization and immediate availability can be beneficial.

It can be argued that HR professionals have always undertaken some coaching within their job descriptions, but it was "informal and normally transactional." Internal coaches are now identified and acknowledged by their organizations and coaching professional bodies. Frisch defines internal coaching as: "a one-to-one developmental intervention supported by the organisation and provided by a colleague of those coached who is trusted to shape and deliver a program yielding individual professional growth."

There are several points arising from this definition:

1. The internal coach is outside line management, that is, distinct from the manager coach.
2. They will not always use standard assessment as external coaches as they will already know significant background information and have access to the results of organizational assessment.
3. Multiply interventions are assumed—it is not a single informal discussion but an ongoing program.

This interaction was identified as different from the many other training and advice-type engagements, such as discussion with HR and training, as these are organizationally focused as opposed to the individual focus of the internal coaching relationship. The advantages were seen to be the ability to see the coachee within their role and knowledge of the environment within which the coachee is working. The emergence of the internal coach can be seen as "a tangible manifestation of the learning organisation."

We have shown previously (Jarvis et al., 2006) that the tasks associated with this role are:

- coaching individuals where manager coaches are not fully used;
- providers of coach training to managers;
- supervision of manager coaches providing support and further skills as and when required; and
- specialist coaches for senior managers.

The coaching agenda within this mode is still well focused upon organizational objectives but it has a broader vision to that observed with the manager coach. There will be an element of mutual benefit although it can be considered "indirect" as with external coaching. The coaching agenda can explore the underpinning aspects of the behavior or change required, although it will still be restricted to some extent by the organizational framework. As indicated previously, supervision of internal coaches is necessary and is often subcontracted to external coaches.

A FRAMEWORK OF PRACTICE?

In summary, current practice, as identified within our review, can be characterized by the agreed coaching agenda and the role level employed. Coaching is practiced within three modes; external, internal, and manager. The breadth and freedom of the coaching agenda will increase as indicated in Figure 3.1 and the coach will employ a level of intervention appropriate to the agenda.

These, in turn, will impact upon the outputs that are expected. For instance, a restricted coaching agenda is unlikely to impact upon the development of the coachee at the personal level. It may, however, address very specific skill enhancements that can be quantified by, for example, comparing sales figures before and after coaching in relationship building. Similarly, external coaching with a broad agenda in which the coach is acting within a development role will address issues such as purpose and self for the coachee. Measurement of the impact of the coachee's development may be difficult to quantify.

Before we consider the efficacy of coaching, there are several points upon which we would like to comment. From the "Is coaching being abused?" survey, there is also a perception that manager coaching is good for middle managers but not for those at the top. This has led to a lack of integration within the corporate strategies. Within this survey, 63% used coaching at senior manager level, and 74% and 69% at junior and middle managers level. Blackman-Sheppard (2004) argues convincingly that "executive" coaching should be a resource available to all employees. There is an interesting question that has not been addressed within the literature as yet: Does the mode of coaching on offer depend upon your seniority within the organization?

Another critical point is that coaching is not being confined to individuals—team coaching has started to be the subject of both discussion and research publications. Diedrich (2001) discusses the lessons learned from practice and identifies a number of principles of practice. Within his practice he does *not* identify team coaching with team building or team development.

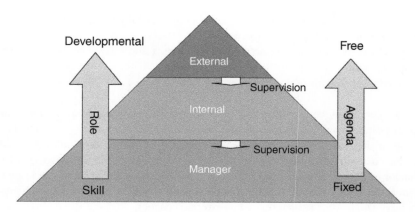

Figure 3.1   *Coaching Role, Agenda, and Supervision*

The coaching of a team is a process where the consulting psychologist has an ongoing, helping relationship with both the team and the individual executives; that is he or she has time for the team as well as one-to-one coaching contacts with the team members over time. Coaching a team is an iterative process for both the team and the individual that is developmentally orientated as opposed to being a problem-centred quick fix for the team.

Within the literature, there is not complete agreement with this view, and some team coaches positively rule out coaching of individual members except for specific tasks. "Coaching at the Top" (Kralj, 2001) is a case study of an intervention to enable a company to redesign their organization. All the interventions were kept to a systems or team level. The authors make a case that coaching should be expanded to include such team engagements.

DOES IT WORK?

As with all human interactions, there is a multiplicity of factors that will impact on whether the interaction has the desired effect. Indeed, when considering coaching there will even be a variety of criteria for what constitutes an "effect"? For instance, is it sufficient that the coachee perceives coaching to have enabled them to achieve an identified goal? Or does the output have to percolate down to the bottom-line in terms of a quantifiable performance measure for the organization?

To date, there are only two studies prepared to quote an ROI, that is, identify an impact upon the bottom-line. Both of these are concerned with external coaching. The most frequently cited was carried out by Right Management Consultants and published in the *Manchester Review* (McGovern et al., 2001). The quoted figure for ROI was 5.7 in terms of "tangible" or quantifiable outputs such as increased productivity. There is a difficulty with this study in terms of reliability as it surveyed the clients of the consultancy where the author was based, and the results were based upon the coachee's own estimates. However, it does identify how the clients perceived coaching had impacted their behavior and hence the perceived ROI. In particular, it is of note that the frequency of impact was higher for the intangible impacts, such as improving relationships (77%) and teamwork (73%), then for the tangible impacts such as productivity (53%) and quality (48%). The other study is provided by the Phillips ROI institute (Phillips, 2008), quoting a figure of 2.21. However, to date, this study has not been published and is only available from their website.

Generally, published investigations have concentrated on the self-reporting of improvement by the coachee but some studies have looked at assessment (of improvement) by colleagues and reports. Several seek to quantify improvement of performance of the coachee's department or team, but as we shall see, these have so far delivered only tentative results. All studies identified the satisfaction of the coachee was good or high and where self-reporting was used, then the coaching was identified as having impact on the development of the individual. Where the studies use quantifiable performance measures, other than multisource feedback, the effectiveness is less well evidenced.

For ease of reading, we have classified the studies into those addressing external coaching, internal coaching, manager coaching, and team coaching.

External coaching

The most researched task of the external coach has been supporting the impact of multisource feedback and promoting improvement in performance. We will consider three such studies.

The first study, and the only study to date that compares the performance of coached and noncoached individuals, is that by Smither et al. (2003). They also go beyond self-reporting of improvement and compare 360 degree feedback pre- and post-intervention. The advantages of 360 degree feedback are well established in that it provides information on how the coachee is perceived by others; on what should be improved and obtains these ratings from a variety of groups. However, as Smither et al. (2003) identify, there can be major problems in working with this information; there can be an overwhelming amount of information, the difference between self and others' ratings can be difficult to reconcile and there is often a need for guidance and help to figure out the next step. Locke and Latham (1990) have shown that feedback alone is not the cause of behavior change, it is the goals that people set in response to feedback that promote change. The question asked by this study was: Could coaching facilitate this goal setting with appropriate follow-through and hence enhanced performance? The subjects of the study were 1,361 senior managers in a global corporation who received multisource feedback in autumn 1999. After feedback, 404 of the managers received coaching (5 to 7 hr covering review of feedback within two to three individual sessions) and then responded to a brief online questionnaire. In the autumn of 2000, another multisource feedback program was carried out in which 88.3% of managers from the initial survey received feedback. In July 2002, a brief survey was carried out in which raters evaluated the progress of the manager toward the goals set by the manager themselves, based on the initial feedback.

Managers who worked with a coach were more likely to set specific (rather than vague) goals (d = 0.16) and to solicit ideas for improvement from their supervisors (d = 0.36). They had a higher performance improvement in terms of direct report and supervisor ratings. However, the effect size (d = 0.17) was small.

It should be noted that the multisource feedback was being used within the appraisal system in a high accountability culture; for example, salary and resources were both linked to the results so the effect of the coach might be masked by this driver for change. Also, this was a very short intervention with 55% of the managers having three or more conversations, 29.4% having two, and 15.6% having just one.

In a similar vein, the second study, by Thach (2002), also investigated the quantitative impact of coaching and 360 degree feedback on the leadership effectiveness of 281 executives within a single company. Within the first phase of the research, a pilot program with

57 executives was run in which the coaching concentrated on one to three development actions arising from a 360 degree assessment. After feedback from participants of Phase 1, the program was launched in Phase 2 with 168 executives over one year. The participants received four coaching sessions in all before a mini 360 degree and participant survey. This was run the next year in Phase 3 for a further 113 participants. There was no choice of coach and the duration of coaching was short, although it was noted many paid for further sessions from their own funds. However, the 360 degree was not linked to appraisal and hence the impact of the coaching intervention should have been more clearly defined. Unfortunately, no comparison was made with noncoached executives.

The overall percentage increase in leadership effectiveness was 55% in Phase two and 60% in Phase 3. The coaching impact was also assessed through the average number of times met with coach (3.6) and it was noted that there was a trend toward higher contacts giving higher scores. From the qualitative feedback from the participants, the factor of greatest impact was the relationships with the coach themselves, with the 360 degree feedback as the factor of second importance. The third study, by Luthans and Peterson (2003), was on a smaller scale but with a similar remit, and again used multisource assessment in conjunction with coaching. They identified that there is usually a discrepancy between the self-rating and that of others. This is lessened by increasing the self-awareness of the coachee. Their proposition was that 360 degree program should not seek to deal with this by lowering self-rating but by raising performance to the level of the initial self-rating.

The authors conducted a study involving all 20 managers in a small firm to determine how effective coaching was at facilitating this improvement. At the start of the study, and again 3 months later, 360 degree ratings were collected. After the initial assessment the managers were met for a coaching session to analyze the results. All managers met the same coach and followed the same process. The feedback was confidential to the client and the coaching was developmental not assessment orientated. The process was structured around: what are the discrepancies; why they were present; what can be done; with the final part of the session concentrating on the responsibility of the individual to make the changes. Follow-up checks were then carried out randomly and qualitative data collected on whether the coachees had made the changes discussed.

Given the short timescale of the study and the short duration of the coaching, it is perhaps surprising that the initial discrepancy between self- and others' rating was eliminated in all three factors tested—behavioral competence, interpersonal competence, and personal responsibility. The reduction in discrepancy was brought about through the elevation of the others' rating, not the reduction in the coachee's ratings. There was an improvement in both the managers' and their employees' work attitudes with a significant increase in job satisfaction with the work itself, supervision, and co-workers. Organizational commitment also increased.

Thus, it is suggested that coaching has a part to play in getting the most from feedback to obtain benefits such as positive attitude to work and reduced turnover. The authors also found evidence of an improvement in organizational performance, for example in sales figures (seasonally adjusted) following coaching and feedback. However, as they are systems-level indicators they were not deemed sufficiently controlled to link directly with the individual coaching intervention.

Other studies have concentrated upon the perception of impact by clients after a coaching program. Usually, groups of clients are surveyed after completion of the coaching program. In general, these have provided a universally positive response from the clients, and researchers have sought to dissect the positive impact into its constituent parts by asking "what worked?" These have been less successful and indicate alternative research designs will be necessary to go beyond the first-order question.

A study that didn't include multisource feedback, was conducted by Harder+Company Community Research in the United States (2003). In this design, 24 executives from various organizations were coached for 40 hr over 13 months, and three peer round-table events were also included for the sharing of experience and support. The executive were given a choice of coach from a pool of 12 coaches recruited for their diversity of background and interest. The coachees had less than 4 years' experience at the executive level but no prior experience of coaching.

A learning contract was drawn up for all coachees and the research design was a survey (before, middle, and end), semi-structured interviews (over phone for 20), and case studies of five. At the end of the study the overall satisfaction of the coachees was 4.6 on a scale of 5. One point of note was that significant change was apparent at 6 months but this rate of improvement was not sustained at 12 months.

A doctoral thesis from the United States (Dawdy, 2004) provides a comparative design exploring the perceived effectiveness of coaching and methods. The design of the study was to identify whether "one size fits all." Does executive coaching suit everyone? The criterion used to group the executives was personality type.

Sixty-two participants took part in the study, all from a large engineering firm. They were all white males between 40 and 50 years of age. They had participated in a coaching program for at least 6 months and completed it. The coaching was provided by a single firm using the in-house framework although little detail is given. A survey of the participants was conducted and 90% of them considered coaching to be effective, 91% thought it was valuable to their relationships outside work, and 75% thought it was valuable to their relationships within work. On the question of whether it had facilitated behavior change on a scale of 1 (*not met*) to 7 (*met far beyond expectations*), the mean was 4.34 SE0.15. There was no effect of personality type.

There was no significant difference in perception of the success of various coaching tools, such as interviews and feedback, although 88% of those who had experienced 360 degree feedback rated it as positive or neutral. A similar result was found for communication with the coach (82% agreed), acquiring new skills (74%) and coach's encouragement (87%). Thus, this study agrees with the norm—people like to be coached and people perceive that they have changed behaviors as a result. But it goes not further.

Another thesis from the United States (Dingman, 2004) asked the question "How does the extent and quality of participation in an executive coaching experience affect levels of self-efficacy and job-related attitudes in job satisfaction, organisational commitment and the conflict between work and family?"

The design used sought to identify the quality of the coaching experienced for each individual, that is, whether generic elements of the coaching process had been implemented and the perception of the coaching relationship. These were then related to the change in self-efficacy and job-related attitudes of the coachee. The assumption implicit in the work is that positive job-related attitudes correlate with high job performance and thus job-related attitudes indicative of more quantifiable outputs, such as specific measures of tasks completed.

The author had chosen to take investigation of the relationship between coach and coachee a stage further and ask the executive to rate their coach in terms of three specific behaviors that illustrate their relation: interpersonal skills, communication style, and instrumental support.

All coachees were coached using the same program to control some variables but this does restrict the generality of the results. The author looked at the evidence for executive coaching efficacy at each point using Kirkpatrick's (1983) training evaluation criteria.

The research instrument was an online survey distributed to the clients of one coaching center. The response rate was 52%, and 82% of clients were male with an average age of 42. A number of coaches were used with 53% of them having a post-graduate degree.

The hypotheses tested were that there was a significant relationship between the coaching process/quality and job satisfaction and self-efficacy. The quality of the relationship was positive for self-efficacy but negative for job satisfaction. This may have been because the executives were being coached out of their jobs or alternatively there may be some aspect of relationship that was not tested and hence skewed results.

The author goes further in the analysis and identifies that the process and quality of coaching impact on self-efficacy of the coachee and mediate job-related attitudes.

There was no support for the relationship between coaching and life/work conflict or organizational commitment, but we are not given any information as to whether these are considered within the particular coaching model used.

A very extensively cited study concerns the use of a specific tool within a coaching context (Foster & Lendl, 1996). Eye movement desensitization and reprocessing (EMDR) was integrated into an executive coaching program and four case studies are reported. Participants received 1–10 hr of coaching in which EMDR was used to desensitize an upsetting event that was standing in the way of the coachee's performance. The intervention was successful in all cases and each coachee progressed well toward their identified goals. However, the study tests the use of EMDR within a coaching context and not the coaching interaction itself.

Internal coaching

The first reported attempt at examining effects of coaching in a public sector municipal agency was undertaken by Olivero, Bane, and Kopelman (1997). Although they describe the mode of coaching used as executive coaching, within the definitions we are using here their study investigated the effectiveness of internal coaching.

Their interest was in the effectiveness of using coaching as a means to translate training into behavior change. It is known that two of the most dominant factors that influenced this process are the opportunity for practice and constructive feedback (Anderson & Wexley, 1983). They used an action research methodology to determine if coaching could provide this support. Thirty-one managers underwent a conventional managerial training program. Then eight of the managers underwent a coach training program and coached their peers, every week for 2 months, as they undertook a real-life project. A knowledge inventory was completed before and after the workshop.

The productivity of each of the managers was measured after training and after coaching. The measures chosen were appropriate to the specific work of the manager, were quantifiable, and of benefit to the organization. The result was a 22.4% increase in productivity after the management training but an 88% increase after coaching.

Although these figures seem clear-cut, there are a number of issues that have to be borne in mind. By their very nature the projects undertaken while the managers were being coached would also have contributed to enhanced productivity. It is also unclear whether the intervention was coaching or action research facilitation. The authors themselves are clear that this study design cannot address all the issues, but the output does provide scarce information on how coaching can affect the bottom-line.

Manager coach

A rare study looking at effectiveness of leaders as coaches and the performance of teams was conducted in 2001 (Wageman, 2001). The basis of the study was the generation of self-managing teams. It is suggested that the principal reason for their failure is a lack of motivation and the inability of the manager to create the right conditions for them to thrive.

In this field study of the company Xerox, two factors are investigated: the design of the team and the coaching by the manager. Thirty-four teams of between three to nine members were used, split between consistently high performers and consistently poor performers (18 superb teams and 15 poor teams). Multiple measures of team design and manager coaching were identified through structured interviews and a survey of the participants. These were then used to assess the teams. Quantitative measures of performance were obtained from the organization and these related to bottom-line quantities such as response rate, parts expenses, and machine reliability. The data analysis was rigorous and large effects were seen.

The hypothesis that well-designed teams exhibit more self-management and are more effective then teams with design flaws was supported as expected. The hypothesis that well coached teams exhibit more self-management but *not* higher task performance was also supported.

There was a negative coaching aspect and a positive coaching aspect. Negative aspects were for behaviors such as identifying team problems and task intervention while positive was providing cues, informal rewards, and problem-solving consultancy. There was no support for the hypothesis that coaching alone influenced the bottom-line factors. The hypothesis that coaching and design interacted positively was supported for self-management but not for performance or satisfaction. Overall, positive coaching worked best for well-designed teams and negative coaching impacted more on poorly designed teams.

Graham, Wedman, and Garvin-Kester (1993) identified that training could develop manager coaching skills, at least within a sales environment, through a study of 87 account representatives who worked for 13 sales managers. Seventy per cent of account representatives indicated that they had observed a positive change in their managers. This was most shown by those who had worked for their managers for 2 years, whereas for lesser or more time with the same boss the percentage decreased.

DOES COACHING WORK?

In all the studies undertaken, investigating whatever mode of coaching, the conclusion was the same—everyone likes to be coached and perceives that it impacts positively upon their effectiveness. Thus, to the first order, the answer is "Yes it does."

But, if we consider the question within the context of our suggested framework of practice, we can start to develop a more structured and useful answer, particularly in terms of ROI.

For external or executive coaching where the coaching agenda is broad and, by definition, unconstrained then the identified outputs will be of both direct and indirect impact to the bottom-line. This is well illustrated within the two studies specifically aimed at producing an ROI. Both of these studies identified that the outputs of the coaching would have "tangible" and "intangible" elements. Tangible elements such as productivity and sales figures are relatively easy to measure and correct for external factors. The "intangible" elements such as leadership or relationship handling can be identified and even quantified but their relative impact upon the bottom-line must, by definition, be considered on an individual basis. Any study seeking to address this must specifically design in this issue at the start of the investigation.

To date studies of external coaching have concentrated on quantifying the "intangibles" and assuming these will impact favorably upon the bottom-line. The improvement in coachee behaviors, and so on, post-coaching was consistent across all studies, whether the coachees self-reported or the quantification was through 360 degree feedback.

If we now consider the more restricted and organizationally focused coaching agenda found with internal and manager coaching then the research studies are, by definition, more closely focused on "tangible," bottom-line outputs. The study by Olivero et al. (1997) is of particular note. The design used productivity as the factor to be measured before and after coaching and this was also the case with the study at Xerox. Both of these studies show significant improvement in bottom-line measures after the coaching intervention.

It is clear from this analysis that when we ask "Does coaching work?" we must first identify where within the framework of practice the coaching is actually placed, how constrained is the coaching agenda and whether a tangible or intangible output is being sought. Only then can we identify if the evidence is available to answer the question as posed.

REFERENCES

Anderson, J. P., & Wexley, A. (1983). Application-based management development: A method to promote practical application of managerial and supervisory training. *Personnel Administrator, 28,* 39–43.

Blackman-Sheppard, G. (2004). Executive coaching. *Industrial and Commercial Training, 36,* 5–8(4).

Carter, A. (2001). *Executive coaching: Inspiring performance at work* (Vol. Report 379). London: The Institute for Employment Studies.

Dawdy, G. N. (2004). *Executive coaching: A comparative design exploring the perceived effectiveness of coaching and methods.* Unpublished Doctorate, School of Education, Capella University.

Diedrich, R. C. (2001). Lessons learned in – and guidelines for – coaching executive teams. *Consulting Psychology Journal: Practice and Research, 53,* 238–239.

Dingman, M. E. (2004). *The effects of executive coaching on job-related attitudes.* School of Leadership Development, Regent University.

Ellinger, A., & Bostrom, R. (1998). Managerial coaching behaviours in learning organisations. *Journal of Management Development, 18.*

Foster, S., & Lendl, J. (1996). Eye movement desensitisation and reprocessing: Four case studies of a new tool for executive coaching and restoring employee performance after setbacks. *Consulting Psychology Journal: Practice and Research, 48,* 155–161.

Frisch, M. H. (2001). The emerging role of the internal coach. *Consulting Psychology Journal: Practice and Research, 53,* 240–250.

Garman, A. N., Whiston, D. L., & Zlatoper, K. W. (2000). Media perceptions of executive coaching and the formal preparation of coaches. *Consulting Psychology Journal: Practice and Research, 52,* 201–205.

Geber, B. (1992). From manager into coach. *Training, 29,* 25–31.

Graham, S., Wedman, J. F., & Garvin-Kester, B. (1993). Manager coaching skills: Development and application. *Performance Improvement Quarterly, 6,* 2–13.

Grant, A.M. (2003). Keeping up with the cheese again! Research as a foundation for professional coaching of the future. *International Coach Federation Conference Symposium on Research and Coaching,* 1–26.

Grant, A. M., & Cavanagh, M. (2004). Toward a profession of coaching: Sixty-five years of progress and challenges for the future. *International Journal of Evidence Based Coaching and Mentoring, 2,* 7–21.

Hall, D. T., Otazo, K. L., & Hollenbeck, G. P. (1999). Behind closed doors: What really happens in executive coaching. *Organizational Dynamics, 27,* 39–53.

Jarvis, J. Lane, D. & Fillery-Travis, A. (2006). The Case for coaching; Making evidenced based decisions. London: CIPD Publications.

Kampa, S., & White, R. P. (2002). The effectiveness of executive coaching: What we know and what we still need to know. In R. L. Lowman (Ed.), *The California School of Organisational Studies: Handbook of organisational consulting psychology: A comprehensive guide to theory, skills, and techniques* (pp. 139–158). San Francisco, CA: Jossey Bass.

Kirkpatrick, D. L. (1983). Four steps to measuring training effectiveness. *Personnel Administrator, 28*(11), 19–25.

Kralj, M. M. (2001). Coaching at the top: Assisting a chief executive and his team. *Consulting Psychology Journal: Practice and Research, 53,* 108–116.

Kubicek, M. (2002). Is coaching being abused? *Training,* May, 12–14.

Lane, D., Puri, A., Cleverly, P., Wylie, R., & Rajan, A. (2000). *Employability: Bridging the gap between rhetoric and reality*. London: Professional Development Foundation.

Locke, E. A., & Latham, G. P. (1990). *A theory of goal setting and task performance*. Englewood Cliffs, NJ: Prentice-Hall.

Luthans, F., & Peterson, S. J. (2003). 360 degree feedback with systematic coaching: Empirical analysis suggests a winning combination. *Human Resource Management, 42*, 243–256.

McGovern, J., Lindemann, M., Vergara, M., Murphy, S., Barker, L., & Warrenfeltz, R. (2001). Maximising the impact of executive coaching. *Manchester Review, 6*, 1–9.

Olivero, G., Bane, K., & Kopelman, R. E. (1997). Executive coaching as a transfer of training tool: Effects on productivity in a public agency. *Public Personnel Management, 26*, 461–469.

Peterson, D. B. (1996). Executive coaching at work: The art of one-on-one change. *Consulting Psychology Journal: Practice and Research, 48*, 78–86.

Phillips, P. & Phillips, J. (2008). Roi Fundamentals: Why and when to measure Return on Investment. New York: Pfeiffer.

Research, H. C. C. (2003). *Executive Coaching Project: Evaluation of findings*.

Smither, J. W., London, M., Flautt, R., Vargas, Y., & Kucine, I. (2003). Can working with an executive coach improve multi-source feedback ratings over time? A quasi-experimental field study. *Personnel Psychology, 56*, 23.

Thach, E. C. (2002). The impact of executive coaching and 360 degree feedback on leadership effectiveness. *Leadership and Organization Development Journal, 23*, 205–214.

Veale, D. (1996). Mentoring and coaching as part of a human resource development strategy: An example at Coca-Cola foods. *Leadership & Organization Development Journal, 17*(3), 16–20.

Wageman, R. (2001). How leaders foster self-managing team effectiveness: Design choices versus hands-on coaching. *Organisation Science, 12*, 559–577.

Witherspoon, R., & White, R. P. (1996). Executive coaching: A continuum of roles. *Consulting Psychology Journal: Practice and Research, 48*, 124–133.

4 A Languishing–Flourishing Model of Goal Striving and Mental Health for Coaching Populations

Anthony M. Grant[1]

It is often said that coaching is not therapy and that coaching does not aim to treat psychological problems, mental illness, or other issues of pathology. Rather, coaching clients are looking for ways to better attain their goals, improve their performance, and enhance their quality of life (see, for example, Whitworth, Kimsey-House, & Sandahl, 1998). Are these mantras in fact true? If not, how can we integrate issues related to mental health and goal striving within a coaching-related model?

As the practice of coaching develops and as research into coaching advances, our understanding of the parameters of the coaching industry and demographics of coaching clients has become more sophisticated. As this knowledge has developed, it has become increasingly clear that there is a discrepancy between espoused ideas about what coaching "should" be and the reality of what happens in real-life coaching practice. In reality, the boundaries between coaching practice and therapeutic practice are somewhat blurred.

[1] First published as Grant, A. M. (2007). A languishing-flourishing model of goal striving and mental health for coaching populations. *International Coaching Psychology Review*, 2(3), 250–264.

Coaching Researched: A Coaching Psychology Reader, First Edition. Edited by Jonathan Passmore and David Tee.

That there has been little theoretical or empirical research exploring the boundaries between coaching and therapy is a serious shortcoming in the coaching literature. Clearly, the coaching industry and coaching psychology would benefit from coaching-related models that delineate issues of goal striving, mental health/mental illness, and psychopathology.

In this paper, past approaches to distinguishing coaching from therapy are discussed. The key foci of coaching—goal striving, well-being enhancement, and goal attainment—are distinguished from the foci of therapeutic interventions that are identified as the treatment of psychopathology. Drawing on recent languishing–flourishing work in the area of positive psychology (Keyes, 2003), this paper then presents a new provisional model of goal striving and mental health/mental illness for use in coaching research and practice. Recent comparative research, presented in this paper, suggests that coaching clients who voluntarily seek life coaching have higher levels of psychopathology than individuals who undertake coaching as part of a workplace coaching program. These findings underscore the importance of coaches having a sophisticated understanding of the issues related to coaching and mental health.

COACH OR COUCH?

A wide range of factors has been used to differentiate coaching from therapy. Coaching is said to have a greater emphasis on structured conversations and goal attainment (Hart, Blattner, & Leipsic, 2001), and greater variation in modes of delivery, with coaching being conducted in short sessions, face-to-face, by phone or email (Richard, 1999). Coaching is also said to be more focused on solution construction rather than problem analysis, and focuses on the present rather than on the past (Berg & Szabo, 2005) or unconscious facets of behavior (Levinson, 1996).

However, for each distinction offered, alternative viewpoints have been presented. For example, it has been proposed that coaching is developmental rather than goal focused (Kilburg, 2000), should incorporate the past as well as the present (Kemp, 2005), should focus on emotions rather than actions (Schlegelmich & Fresco, 2005), and should prioritize the delivery of expert skills-based knowledge rather than focusing on self-directed learning (Fox, 1983).

Such distinctions center on how coaching is conducted, rather than who the coaching client is, or the specific focus or goals of the coaching intervention. While distinctions based on how coaching is conducted give a useful overview of what coaches do with their clients, they give an incomplete picture of the differences between coaching and therapeutic modalities, and they give little guidance to coaches about how to deal with psychopathology within a coaching engagement (for further discussion, see Bluckert, 2005).

THE NORMAL CURVE: DISTINGUISHING THE ABNORMAL POLLUTION?

Another way that coaching has been differentiated from therapy considers the different levels of degree of psychopathology seen in coaching, counseling, and clinical populations. This somewhat simplistic approach is based on the distribution of psychopathology in the general population, which is represented as lying on the normal distribution (Krabbendam et al., 2004). In such approaches, the extreme end of the normal distribution of psychopathology (say, approximately three to four standard deviations below the mean) can be deemed to be a psychiatric population, with less extreme sections of the distribution being deemed clinical, counseling, and coaching populations respectively (see Figure 4.1; see Cavanagh (2005) and Sperry (2004) for detailed discussions of this issue).

This approach to delineating coaching from therapeutic modalities is based on two fundamental assumptions. First, that coaching clients do not present clinically significant problems for treatment or are from a "nonclinical" section of the population. Second, that coaching is primarily about enhancing goal striving and well-being rather than treating mental illness or distress. This is an important and central philosophical assumption about coaching and coaching psychology and reflects the espoused viewpoint of a large number of organizations, including the Association of Coaching (AC), the European Mentoring and Coaching Council (EMCC), the International Coach Federation (ICF), the Worldwide Association of Business Coaches (WABC), and a wide range of individual commentators such as Parkes (1955), Whitmore (1992), and Williams and Thomas (2004).

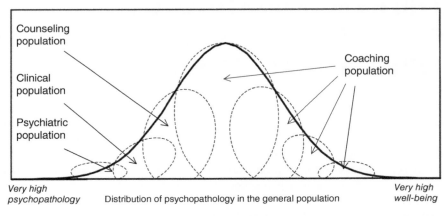

Figure 4.1 *Theoretical Distribution of Psychopathology in the Psychiatric, Clinical, Counseling, and Coaching Populations*

The notion that a range of client groups per se can be distinguished by reference to varying degrees of psychopathology is central to the Australian Psychological Society (APS) distinctions between coaching, counseling, and clinical psychology. The APS Interest Group in Coaching Psychology (IGCP) defines coaching psychology as "the systematic application of behavioral science, which is focused on the enhancement of life experience, work performance and well-being for individuals, groups and organizations with *no clinically significant mental health issues or abnormal levels of distress*" (italics added; Australian Psychological Society IGCP, 2003).

The APS distinguishes counseling psychology as being predominantly focused on the use of "therapeutic techniques" in the amelioration of distress. Thus "individuals may seek assistance from a counselling psychologist to help them to … 'manage stress and conflict at home and work, deal with grief, loss and trauma, [and] overcome feelings of anxiety and fear'" (Australian Psychological Society, 2007a).

In contrast, "clinical psychologists are specialists in the assessment, diagnosis and treatment of psychological problems and *mental illness*" (italics added; Australian Psychological Society, 2007b), with the majority of the training of clinical psychologists primarily focusing on the identification and treatment of psychopathological states.

The focus of coaching psychology then is subtly different to that of clinical and counseling practice. As can be seen from the above APS definitions, the primary focus of clinical and counseling practitioners is the alleviation of psychopathology or distress and addresses such issues directly. In contrast, the primary focus of coaching is not explicitly on alleviating psychopathology or primarily dealing with distress, rather it is about assisting clients in articulating goals and helping them systematically strive toward goal attainment. These goals may be developmental or focused on enhancing performance or acquiring a specific skill set.

THE PSYCHOPATHOLOGY OF COACHING CLIENTS: THREE RECENT STUDIES

There has been very little empirical research into the levels of psychopathology found in coaching clients. Although there have been concerns that coaching is being used as a de facto form of therapy (Berglas, 2002), and various authors have reported anecdotal concerns about the overlap between coaching and therapy (Naughton, 2002), to the present author's best knowledge only three studies have quantitatively collected data on the extent to coaching populations manifest psychopathology.

As part of a study of the effectiveness of life coaching, Green, Oades, and Grant (2005) surveyed a total of 107 potential life coaching clients from a community sample and found 52% had clinically elevated scores (a score of two standard deviations above the mean) on the Brief Symptom Inventory (BSI: Derogatis & Melisaratos, 1983). The BSI is a well-validated self-report health screening instrument designed to be used with both clinical and nonclinical populations (Preston & Harrison, 2003).

Reflecting Green et al.'s (2005) finding, and using another community sample and the same BSI screening criteria, Spence and Grant (2007) found that 25% of 84 participants in a life coaching program had clinically elevated BSI scores. It worth noting that while Green et al. (2005) drew their sample from a regional center with a relatively low socioeconomic status, Spence and Grant (2007) drew their sample from a capital city with a relatively higher socioeconomic status. The comparative results of these two studies suggest that individuals who seek life coaching may have higher than average levels of psychopathology, and such levels may be reflective of the specific population from which the sample is drawn.

A third study examined the extent of psychopathology in 43 participants who took part in a workplace coaching program in an Australian high school. Using the Depression, Anxiety, and Stress Scales (DASS; Lovibond & Lovibond, 1995), Grant, Green, and Rynsaardt (2007) found that 4.6% of participants had levels of depression at the 90th percentile or above, 21.9% had levels of anxiety at the 90th percentile or above, and 18.6% had stress levels at the 90th percentile or above (note: percentiles used follow recommendations of Crawford & Henry, 2003). These levels of depression, anxiety, and stress appear to be in accord with the general levels found in the teaching profession (see van Dick & Wanger, 2001).

The DASS is a well-validated self-report measure of depression, anxiety, and stress suitable for use in both clinical and nonclinical populations (Clara, Cox, & Enns, 2001; Henry & Crawford, 2005).

The sample sizes in these three studies are not large enough to draw definitive conclusions. However, they provide useful preliminary empirical evidence about psychopathology in coaching populations, and indicate that these levels can vary considerably depending on the specific population. This point is further reinforced by recent Australian research examining the mental health of 7,500 individuals from a number of professions, which found that 15% of lawyers, 10% of accountants, and 9% of information technology professionals had symptoms indicative of moderate or severe depression (*Australian Financial Review*, 2007). Together these findings illustrate the inadequacy of differentiating coaching from counseling or clinical populations merely by means of levels of population psychopathology and emphasize that coaches need more sophisticated theoretical frameworks.

PSYCHOPATHOLOGY: A LANGUISHING–FLOURISHING DISTINCTION

Given that a proportion of clients presenting for coaching will have mental health problems, do such issues exclude them from coaching? Can a professional coach ethically coach someone with an anxiety disorder, when the goals of the coaching engagement are about a work or leadership development-related issue, or if the client

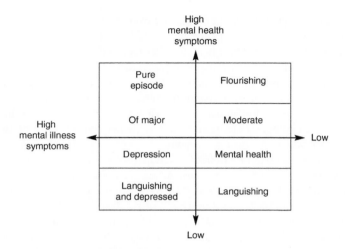

Figure 4.2 *Keyes's Model of Mental Health and Diagnostic Categories*
Note. Reproduced with permission from Keyes (2003)

becomes depressed during the coaching engagement? How are we to understand such mental health issues in relation to goal attainment within a coaching context?

Recent theorizing from within the positive psychology area may be useful here. Keyes (2003) has proposed a model for use in the study of mental health and mental illness within the positive psychology framework. Keyes conceptualizes mental health and mental illness as being separate constructs with two orthogonal dimensions: the mental health continuum and the mental illness continuum (see Figure 4.2). In brief, within Keyes's model the mental health dimension is represented by high or low levels of psychological well-being, for example, self-acceptance, positive relations with others, personal growth, purpose in life, environmental mastery, and autonomy (Ryff & Keyes, 1996). The mental illness dimension is represented by a presence or absence of symptoms indicative of depression; for example, anhedonia, insomnia, or hypersomnia.

For Keyes, mental health is far more than the mere absence of mental illness symptoms. Individuals high in mental health and low in mental illness are designated as *flourishing* in life, whereas those low in mental health and low in mental illness symptoms are designated as *languishing*. Those with low mental health and high mental illness are designated as both languishing and depressed (for details, see Keyes, 2003). Keyes estimates that only approximately 25% of the population can be considered to be flourishing.

Languishing has been defined as "a state in which an individual is devoid of positive emotions toward life, is not functioning well psychologically or socially, and has not been depressed within the past year," whereas flourishing can be understood as "a state in which an individual feels positive emotions toward life and is functioning well psychologically and socially" (Keyes, 2003, p. 294).

The languishing–flourishing delineation may have considerable utility for coaching. However, Keyes's approach as it stands does not explicitly incorporate the elements of goal striving and goal attainment so central to coaching practice. Coaching is after all primarily focused on facilitating intentional goal striving and goal attainment (Whitmore,

1992). Thus, a useful adaptation of Keyes's approach for use in coaching would need to explicitly incorporate both a mental health/illness dimension and a goal-striving dimension.

GOAL STRIVING AND COACHING

Goal striving sits at the very heart of coaching. Implicit in the notion of goal striving is the concept of intentionality; the purposeful pursuit of the goal. It is thus important to distinguish between "strivings" and "aspirational goals." The concept of striving implies that the individual has somehow invested in the intentional pursuit of a goal, and is actually engaged in its pursuit. This can be contrasted with the notion of aspirational goals.

The notion of aspirational goals has traditionally referred to higher-order, values-based goals that an individual hopes to achieve (see, for example, Zimmerman & Bandura, 1994). However, the contemporary meaning of the term "aspirational goal" has taken a new direction and reflects recent political rhetoric (Milbank, 2007). In line with recent usage "aspirational goals" can be understood as goals that an individual expresses interest in achieving, but in reality is unwilling or unable to work toward or make a commitment to. For example, political leaders may have an aspirational goal of reducing global greenhouse gas emissions and global warming, but not have actually begun the striving process by setting specific pollution reduction benchmarks or enacting legislation.

Of course, not all goals are created equal. Different types of goals differently impact on individuals' performance and their subjective experience of the goal-striving process. For example, Coats, Janoff-Bulman, and Alpert (1996) found that people who tended to set avoidance goals had higher levels of depression and lower levels of well-being. Other studies have found that approach goals are associated with both higher levels of academic performance and increased well-being (Elliot & McGregor, 2001). Performance goals tend to focus individual's attention on issues of personal ability (Gresham, Evans, & Elliott, 1988), and such attentional focus can actually impede performance when the task is complex or the goal is perceived as highly challenging, and the individual is not skilled or is low in self-efficacy. In such cases, learning (or mastery) goals may better facilitate task performance (Seijts & Latham, 2001).

SELF-CONCORDANCE, GOAL STRIVING, AND MENTAL HEALTH

Sheldon and Elliot (1998) noted that not all personal goals are personal. Individuals can pursue specific goals for a wide range of reasons, and the specific motivations underpinning goal striving can have an important impact on well-being. For example, the degree to which a specific goal is self-concordant has an important impact on the emotions associated with the goal (Koestner, Lekes, Powers, & Chicoine, 2002). Self-concordance refers to the degree to which a goal is perceived by the individual as being autonomous, that is, emanating from the self (an internal perceived locus of causality indicating greater self-concordance), as compared with a goal that is perceived by the individual as being controlled by factors outside of the self or by the introjected ideas of others (external perceived locus of control indicating less self-concordance) (Sheldon & Elliot, 1998). It is important to remember that goals are nearly always motivated by a complex combination of internal and external factors (Spence, Oades, & Caputi, 2004). Thus a dimensional rather than categorical approach is appropriate here.

Goals that are self-concordant and in alignment with the coachee's core personal values or developing interests are more likely to be engaging, and self-concordant goals are associated with higher levels of goal attainment, greater goal satisfaction, and well-being (Sheldon & Elliot, 1999; Sheldon & Kasser, 1995). Further, both goal content (intrinsic or external) and goal motivation (autonomous or controlled) make significant contributions to psychological well-being or lack of well-being (Sheldon, Ryan, Deci, & Kasser, 2004).

As can be seen from the above discussion, goal striving and goal attainment may not necessarily be associated with mental health or well-being. Indeed, individuals may have high levels of goal striving and goal attainment, yet have low levels of well-being and mental health. These observations have important implications for a coaching-related model of mental health and goal striving.

A LANGUISHING–FLOURISHING MODEL OF GOAL STRIVING AND MENTAL HEALTH

The proposed model of goal striving and mental health presented in Figure 4.3 has two key dimensions: (a) the mental health-illness spectrum; and (b) intentional goal striving (high or low).

There has been considerable discussion attempting to define the differences between mental health and mental illness. One approach argues that mental health is more than the mere absence of mental illness (e.g., Keyes & Lopez, 2002; Seligman & Csikszentmihalyi, 2000). This view posits that the presence of mental health is best indicated by high levels of psychological and subjective well-being, rather than the mere absence of depression, anxiety, or stress, whereas mental illness is indicated by the presence of high levels of depression, anxiety, or stress.

Measures of well-being and life satisfaction tend to correlate between −.40 and −.55 with measures of psychopathology such as depression, indicating a shared variance of about 25% (Keyes, 2003). Given the degree of shared variance, one useful way of visually representing the relationship between mental health and mental illness is

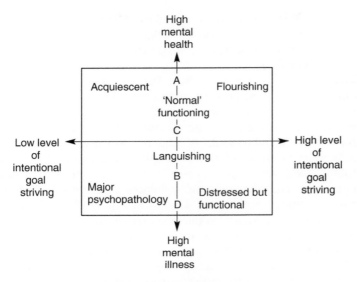

Figure 4.3 *Proposed Model of Goal Striving and Mental Health*

in a Venn diagram with separate but overlapping dimensions representing mental health and mental illness (following the work of Grünbaum (2003) this is represented as a quadratic polygon in Figure 4.3).

It should be noted that the areas within this diagram are representative only, and are not meant to imply any specific distribution pattern in terms of numbers or percentages of coaching clients in each specific area, and of course, individuals will move from one area to another over time.

The mental health area is represented in the figure as falling between point *A* and point *B* (where *A* represents high mental health, and *B* represents low mental health) with the mental illness area is represented as falling between point *C* and point *D* (where *C* represents low mental illness and *D* represents high mental illness). Snyder et al. (2003) advocate the use of a dimensioning approach to the process of labeling and measuring mental health and illness, and argue that "all dimensions would have the inherent capability of yielding information that varies in content from maladaptive to adaptive" (p. 29).

Flourishing

The concept of flourishing used in this model extends Keyes's construct. Where Keyes defines flourishing by primary reference to the presence of mental health and the absence of mental illness, flourishing in the present proposed model is defined also by explicit reference to the intentional pursuit of goals. The far top right-hand area of this figure is where individuals have high levels of mental health and are engaging in high levels of intentional goal striving. This is the area of flourishing. Many would consider this area to be the ultimate goal of the coaching process. Goals in this area can be expected to be highly self-concordant because the long-term pursuit of self-concordant goals is associated with higher levels of well-being (Sheldon et al., 2004). The relationship of levels of self-concordance to this area is of course an empirical issue, and further research is needed here.

In relation to workplace coaching, clients in this area can be expected to be fully engaged in their work, find meaning and purpose in their work lives, and have positive relations with others in the workplace. However, it is important to note that high levels of intentional goal striving are not necessarily equivalent to "getting things done," "upward and onward," or "high performance." An individual may be intentionally striving to achieve less, for example, increasing the quality rather than quantity of their work performance, or redefining their career path based on personal values, rather than corporate or social definitions of success. Indeed, increasing numbers of executives are engaging in such career plateauing (The Families and Work Institute, 2004). Individuals in this area may also be engaging in practices of intentional nonstriving, as in Buddhist and some meditative traditions. Paradoxically, such mindful or meditative activities can be also understood as being strivings in the pursuit of acceptance goals. Such acceptance goals may be articulated as "My goal is to unconditionally accept whatever I experience, by bringing my attention back to my breathing whenever my attention wanders." Although the concept of strivings in the pursuit of acceptance goals may appear contradictory, such attitudes of purposeful awareness and intentional acceptance are central to mindfulness meditation (Kabat-Zinn, 1995).

Acquiescence

The top left-hand section of Figure 4.3 is where individuals have good mental health but have low levels of intentional goal striving, although they may well hold aspirational goals. This is the area of acquiescence. Here individuals enjoy psychological and subjective well-being but are not actively engaged in an intentional goal-striving process characteristic of the flourishing domain. To be acquiescent is to assent tacitly, to consent, to agree with others' wishes, and is the act or process of accepting. In this quadrant, goals are likely to be only moderately self-concordant, as individuals may well show a greater tendency to accept decisions made for them by others or by setting aside the pursuit of their own goals in preference for the goals of others.

The notion that individuals can have good levels of mental health, and yet not be intentionally pursuing goals of their choice may at first glance appear to be incongruent. However, many parents will be familiar with the experience of having to set aside their own personal career goals so that their partner or children have the opportunity of pursuing their goals. Paradoxically, setting aside their own goals may still result in parents experiencing psychological well-being, on dimensions such as positive relations with others and purpose in life (Ryff, 1989).

In the workplace, individuals in this area are the "happy but disengaged." It can be expected that individuals in this quadrant would be physically and emotionally present, but not actively engaged with the goals of the organization. Although some individuals may well purposefully choose the kind of work that does not demand engagement, it may be that individuals in this area over time will become increasingly bored with the daily work routine, and may well drift into the area of languishing.

Languishing

The overlapping area between points *B* and *C* represents individuals who have low levels of psychological or subjective well-being without elevated levels of depression, anxiety, or stress. This is the area of languishing. While individuals who are languishing may be intentionally striving toward goals (possibly with the assistance of a coach), in general their lives are likely to be devoid of the pleasure often associated with intentional goal striving (Street, 2002). Such individuals may well be engaged in the pursuit of conditional goals.

Conditional goals are goals that are pursued because the individual believes that its attainment will bring happiness and well-being (Street, 2002). For example, an individual may be striving to acquire a specific sum of money in the belief that "everything will be fine" once that sum is in the bank. Such goals are likely to have a relatively low level of self-concordance. The languishing state at the higher end of the goal-striving dimension thus encompasses the notion of "deferred happiness syndrome" in which individuals persist in the long term with life situations that are difficult, stressful, and exhausting in the belief that this sacrifice will pay off in the long term (Breakspear & Hamilton, 2004).

Distressed but functional

The bottom right-hand area of Figure 4.3 is the area of distressed but functional clients. Here we find individuals presenting for coaching who have high levels of intentional goal striving. They may be highly functional, in terms of work performance, social status, and earning capacity, yet still be dysthymic or even clinically depressed, anxious, or stressed. Issues of mental health or mental illness here can range from moderately dysthymic or distressed (as represented by the areas aligned with point *C*) to more serious levels of mental illness (as represented by the areas aligned with point *D*).

This is an area of significant challenge for coaches who do not have clinical or counseling training (Cavanagh, 2005). This is because contrary to popular belief, it is not always easy to recognize depression or anxiety, particularly for those who are untrained in such diagnostics (Leimkuhler, Heller, & Paulus, 2007; Preville, M., Cote, G., Boyer, R., & Hebert, R., 2004). Indeed, coachees in this area are unlikely to present for treatment for mental illness, and may not even be aware that they have such problems. The coachee is far more likely to present with issues related to time management, interpersonal communication difficulties, or workplace disengagement.

Major psychopathology

The bottom far left-hand area in the model is the area of major psychopathology. Here we find clients with high levels of mental illness, which might include illness such as major depression, major anxiety disorders, serious chemical dependencies, self-defeating behavior patterns, or major personality disorders. In addition, clients in this area have low to very low levels of intentional goal striving and low to very low levels of functionality.

The term functionality in this context refers to the degree to which an individual is capable of carrying out the activities of daily living in occupational, social, or personal domains (see Roper, Logan, & Tierney, 1980). According to the Global Assessment of Functioning Scale as presented in the Diagnostic and Statistical Manual of Mental Disorders (American Psychiatric Association, 2000) very low functioning might be characterized by a danger of harm to self or others, a failure to maintain personal hygiene, serious impairment in judgment, serious impairment in either occupational or school functioning, interpersonal relationships, judgment, thinking, and/or mood.

Although it may appear self-evident that individuals in the bottom far left-hand area of Figure 4.3 are not suitable candidates for coaching, some commentators have suggested that coaching might be a more acceptable alternative to therapy, especially for those who are resistant to therapy (Filippi, 1968; McKelley & Rochlen, 2007). Coaching methodologies have been found to be effective in enhancing skills generalization in social skills training programs for schizophrenia (Gottlieb, Pryzgoda, Neal, & Schuldberg, 2005) and for improving adherence to antidepressant treatment among primary care patients (Brook et al., 2005). Further, some have suggested that life coaching might be a suitable therapeutic intervention for disorders such as Adult Attention Deficit Disorder (Ratey, 2002).

It is in this quadrant that the boundaries between coaching and therapy become dangerously blurred. While a solid argument can be made in favor of trained mental health professionals using coaching methods to treat some forms of psychological disorder (e.g., schizophrenia, depression), this would be ethically unacceptable for coaches who are not trained mental health professionals (Spence, Cavanagh, & Grant, 2006). This is because overconfident, poorly trained coaches may not recognize the limits of their competency and inadvertently do harm to their clients (for further discussion on these issues, see Buckley & Buckley, 2006; Cavanagh, 2005; Sperry, 2004).

CAN INAPPROPRIATE COACHING INTERVENTIONS DO HARM?

There has been very little discussion within the coaching literature as to whether coaching interventions can be harmful (Berglas, 2002). This is an important question particularly for coaching clients in the lower section of the model between points *C* and *D*, where individuals have increased vulnerabilities. The somewhat limited coaching outcome literature to date suggests that coaching interventions per se tend to be effective (for a recent review, see Grant & Cavanagh, 2007), but to date there has been little or no work examining the possible negative effects of coaching in vulnerable populations.

Support for the notion that, under certain conditions, coaching may be harmful to vulnerable populations comes from the clinical literature. First, it has been shown that not all interventions are equally effective. For example, cognitive-behavioral interventions tend to be more effective than noncognitive-behavioral therapies for generalized anxiety, social phobia, and obsessive-compulsive disorders (Chambless & Ollendick, 2001), and this suggests that some coaching interventions will be more effective than others.

Second, and more worryingly, the inappropriate use of psychological treatments can result in enduring psychological or physical damage. Lilienfeld (2007) lists a number of therapies that can be explicitly harmful through inappropriate usage. For example, expressive-experiential therapies can be harmful to some clients, as can be confrontational "boot-camp" style interventions for conduct disorder, recovered memory therapy, and critical stress debriefing.

Additionally, while some interventions might be ineffective and not directly harmful, they may carry *indirect* harm (such as elongated periods of suffering) and various "opportunity costs" (such as lost time). Lilienfeld (2007) cautions that the costs of indirect harm should not be underestimated. This warning may be particularly salient for organizational and executive coaching clients, where both personal and business costs should be taken into account. For example, failure to address clinical levels of stress or depression in a senior executive who is receiving coaching could result in an escalation of mental health problems, burnout, and eventual executive derailment, and this could have serious consequences for the coachee, their family, and for organizational stakeholders as a whole. Coaches who are highly skilled and well-informed about mental health issues are ideally placed to help prevent such unfortunate occurrences.

ETHICAL ISSUES

If a coach is not qualified as a mental health professional they still have a legal and ethical duty of care to address the issue by making a preliminary assessment and considering referral options (Spence et al., 2006). Even in the face of obvious symptomology, many clients are reluctant to accept a mental illness diagnosis or preliminary assessment and are often reluctant to accept a referral to a qualified mental health professional (Bluckert, 2005).

Thus a key challenge for the coach is to determine if and how to work with the coachee. If the coachee is not prepared to accept a referral to a qualified mental health practitioner for treatment, the coach needs to make a decision about whether or not to continue coaching. Ethically, this is problematic because the focus of therapy is the explicit treatment of psychopathology. Coaches offer coaching services, not therapy. Thus, most coaches would be acting unethically if they engaged in therapy with clients, as they would be acting beyond the boundaries of their competence (Association of Coaching, 2006; International Coach Federation, 2005; Worldwide Association of Business Coaches, 2003). In line with the understandings of coaching outlined above, a coach who is not a trained mental health professional may ethically work with a coachee from the distressed but functional population as long as the goal of coaching is not *intended* to primarily address psychopathology or serious intrapersonal or interpersonal distress, and as long as the coaching does not impede recovery from such distress.

However, for coachees in the far lower right-hand area, their distress may be of such a magnitude that it significantly impedes their progress toward their coaching goals. Such clients are the ones where, despite robust goal setting at the beginning of each session the coaching conversation keeps returning to therapeutic issues, and the coach finds themselves repeatedly acting as a supportive counselor. At some point, the coach may have to take a firm stand and insist that the coachee seeks treatment. One way to deal with this is for the coach to highlight how the presenting symptoms are preventing goal attainment, and how appropriate treatment will help the attainment of the goals of coaching. Supervision for the coach is essential here and ideally from a supervisor or mentor with extensive experience in such issues.

If, on the other hand, the coachee is willing and prepared to accept a referral to a qualified mental health practitioner, the challenge for the coach then becomes one of how to establish a working relationship with a suitability trained therapist. This is about managing the possible three-, four-, or even five-way relationship between (for example) the therapist, the coachee, the sponsoring organization, family members, and the coach themselves. This is not an endeavor for the unskilled or fainthearted. Managing the boundaries and interests of multiple stakeholders takes tact and a considerable investment in time and effort. Done poorly it can have a considerable negative influence on outcomes. Conversely, done well, there may be considerable potential to foster growth and recovery.

FUTURE DIRECTIONS IN RESEARCH AND PRACTICE

This paper has presented an initial theoretical model that integrates goal striving and mental health illness and has discussed ethical issues related to coaching and mental illness. This has begun the process of developing a framework that situates the concepts of languishing, acquiescence, and flourishing within the coaching and goal-striving process. The model presented in this paper has utility for individual coaching and in organizational contexts. Future research should seek to empirically validate this model, for example, by developing screening tools that map on to this model and that cover the full mental health and mental illness spectrum. We also need to discover the relative percentages of coaching clients in each area. This model also has potential in organizational context in terms of mapping well-being and workplace engagement, and when coupled with validated assessments may prove to be a useful framework for coaching for well-being in the workplace.

The main focus of coaching is on helping clients move from languishing or acquiescence to flourishing. It is the energizing sense of fulfillment inherent in helping clients move from "good to great" that attracts many individuals to work in the coaching industry. But just because we are solution-focused and positively-orientated does not mean we should be problem-phobic. It is all too easy to avoid the difficult issues of mental health and mental illness in coaching clients. In the past, the coaching industry has side-stepped this issue with the mantra of "it's coaching, not therapy." This is no longer good enough.

Given that a significant number of coaching clients will have problems related to mental illness, it may be high time for the major coaching bodies to make basic training in mental health issues, understanding of mood disorders, and referral procedures a compulsory part of any coach certification process. In addressing this issue with coaches who are not psychologists, organizations such as the AC, ECMC, ICF, and WABC should take a proactive position on this issue. Indeed, not to take such action is to fail to meet the basic ethical duty of care requirements for our coaching clients, the coaching industry, and society at large.

The proposed model presented in this paper is meant to be a starting point for future discussion and research about the integration of mental health, mental illness, and goal striving within a coaching context. A sophisticated understanding of the issues related to coaching, goal striving, and mental health can only help the coaching industry further flourish.

REFERENCES

American Psychiatric Association. (2000). *Diagnostic and statistical manual of mental disorders: DSM-IV-TR* (4th ed.). Washington, DC: American Psychiatric Association.

Association of Coaching. (2006). *Association of Coaching Code of Ethics*. Retrieved September 15, 2007, from http://www.associationforcoaching.com/about/about02.htm

Australian Financial Review. (2007). Pressure cooker lives push lawyers into depression. *Australian Financial Review*, 22, Monday, April 23.

Australian Psychological Society. (2007a). *Counselling Psychologists*. Retrieved August 15, 2007, from www.psychology.org.au/community/specialist/counselling/

Australian Psychological Society. (2007b). *Clinical Psychologists*. Retrieved August 15, 2007, from http://www.groups.psychology.org.au/cclin

Australian Psychological Society Interest Group in Coaching Psychology (APS IGCP). (2003). *About Us*. Retrieved August 15, 2007, from http://www.groups.psychology.org.au/igcp/about_us/.

Berg, I. K., & Szabo, P. (2005). *Brief coaching for lasting solutions*. New York, NY: Norton.

Berglas, S. (2002). The very real dangers of executive coaching. *Harvard Business Review*, 80(6), 87–92.

Bluckert, P. (2005). The similarities and differences between coaching and therapy. *Industrial and Commercial Training*, 37(2), 91–96.

Breakspear, C. & Hamilton, C. (2004). *Getting a life: Understanding the downshifting phenomenon in Australia: Discussion Paper No. 62*. Canberra: The Australian Institute.

Brook, O. H., van Hout, H., Stalman, W., Nieuwenhuyse, H., Bakker, B., Heerdink, E., et al. (2005). A pharmacy-based coaching programme to improve adherence to anti-depressant treatment among primary care patients. *Psychiatric Services, 56*(4), 487–489.

Buckley, A., & Buckley, C. (2006). *A guide for coaching and mental health: The recognition and management of psychological issues*. Hove, UK: Routledge.

Cavanagh, M. (2005). Mental-health issues and challenging clients in executive coaching. In M. Cavanagh, A. M. Grant, & T. Kemp (Eds.), *Contributions from the behavioural sciences: Vol. 1. Evidence-based coaching*. (pp. 21–36). Bowen Hills, QLD: Australian Academic Press.

Chambless, D. L., & Ollendick, T. H. (2001). Empirically support psychological interventions: Controversies and evidence. *Annual Review of Psychology, 52*, 685–716.

Clara, I. P., Cox, B. J., & Enns, M. W. (2001). Confirmatory factor analysis of the depression, anxiety and stress scales in depressed and anxious patients. *Journal of Psychopathology and Behavioral Assessment, 23*(1), 61–67.

Coats, E. J., Janoff-Bulman, R., & Alpert, N. (1996). Approach versus avoidance goals: Differences in self-evaluation and well-being. *Personality and Social Psychology Bulletin, 22*(10), 1057–1067.

Crawford, J. R., & Henry, J. D. (2003). The Depression, Anxiety and Stress Scales (DASS); normative data and latent structure in a large non-clinical sample. *British Journal of Clinical Psychology, 42*, 111–131.

Derogatis, L. R., & Melisaratos, N. (1983). The Brief Symptom Inventory: An introductory report. *Psychological Medicine, 13*, 595–605.

Elliot, A. J., & McGregor, H. A. (2001). A 2 × 2 achievement goal framework. *Journal of Personality and Social Psychology, 80*(3), 501–519.

Families and Work Institute. (2004). *Generation and gender*. New York, NY: Families and Work Institute.

Filippi, R. (1968). Coaching: A therapy for people who do not seek help. *Zeitschrift Für Psychotherapie und Medizinische Psychologie, 18*(6), 225–229.

Fox, D. (1983). Coaching: The way to protect your sales training investment. *Training & Development Journal, 37*(11), 37.

Gottlieb, J. D., Pryzgoda, J., Neal, A., & Schuldberg, D. (2005). Generalisation of skills through the addition of individualised coaching: Development and evaluation of a social skills training programme in a rural setting. *Cognitive and Behavioral Practice, 12*(3), 324–338.

Grant, A. M., & Cavanagh, M. (2007). Evidence-based coaching: Flourishing or languishing? *Australian Psychologist, 42*(4), 239–254.

Grant, A. M., Green, L. S. & Rynsaardt, J. (2007). *A randomised controlled study of 360 degree feedback-based workplace coaching with high school teachers*. Paper presented at the third Australian evidence-based coaching conference, University of Sydney, Australia.

Green, S., Oades, L. G., & Grant, A. M. (2005). An evaluation of a life-coaching group programme: Initial findings from a waitlist control study. In M. Cavanagh, A. M. Grant, & T. Kemp (Eds.), Theory, research and practice from the behavioural sciences: *Vol. 1. Evidence-based coaching* (pp. 127–142). Bowen Hills, QLD: Australian Academic Press.

Gresham, F. M., Evans, S., & Elliott, S. N. (1988). Academic and social self-efficacy scale: Development and initial validation. *Journal of Psychoeducational Assessment, 6*(2), 125–138.

Grünbaum, B. (2003). *Convex polytopes*. New York, NY/London, UK: Springer.

Hart, V., Blattner, J., & Leipsic, S. (2001). Coaching versus therapy: A perspective. *Consulting Psychology Journal: Practice and Research, 53*(4), 229–237.

Henry, J. D., & Crawford, J. R. (2005). The short-form version of the Depression Anxiety Stress Scales (DASS-21): Construct validity and normative data in a large non-clinical sample. *British Journal of Clinical Psychology, 44*(2), 227–239.

International Coach Federation. (2005). *International Coach Federation Code of Ethics*. Retrieved September 15, 2007, from http://www.coachfederation.org/ICF/For+Current+Members/Ethical+Guidelines/Code+of+Ethics/

Kabat-Zinn, J. (1995). *Wherever you go, there you are: Mindfulness meditation in everyday life.* New York, NY: Hyperion.

Kemp, T. J. (2005). Psychology's unique contribution to solution-focused coaching: Exploring client's past to inform their present and design this future. In M. Cavanagh, A. M. Grant, & T. Kemp (Eds.), *Theory, Research and Practice from the Behavioural Sciences: Vol. 1. Evidence-based coaching* (pp. 37–48). Bowen Hills, QLD: Australian Academic Press.

Keyes, C. L. M. (2003). Complete mental health: An agenda for the 21st century. In C. L. M. Keyes & J. Haidt (Eds.), *Flourishing: Positive psychology and the life well-lived* (pp. 293–290). Washington, DC: American Psychological Association.

Keyes, C. L. M., & Lopez, F. G. (2002). Towards a science of mental health: Positive directions in diagnosis and interventions. In C. R. Snyder & F. G. Lopez (Eds.), *The handbook of positive psychology* (pp. 45–62). New York, NY: Oxford University Press.

Kilburg, R. R. (2000). Coaching and the psychodynamics of executive character and organisations. In R. R. Kilburg (Ed.), *Executive coaching: Developing managerial wisdom in a world of chaos* (pp. 97–120). Washington DC: American Psychological Association, xiv, 253

Koestner, R., Lekes, N., Powers, T. A., & Chicoine, E. (2002). Attaining personal goals: Self-concordance plus implementation intentions equals success. *Journal of Personality and Social Psychology, 83*(1), 231–244.

Krabbendam, L., Myin-Germeys, I., de Graaf, R., Vollerbergh, W., Nolen, W. A., Iedema, J., et al. (2004). Dimensions of depression, mania and psychosis in the general population. *Psychological Medicine, 34*, 1177–1186.

Leimkuhler, A., Heller, J., & Paulus, N. (2007). Subjective well-being and 'male depression' in male adolescents. *Journal of Affective Disorders, 98*(1–2), 65–72.

Levinson, H. (1996). Executive coaching. *Consulting Psychology Journal: Practice and Research, 48*(2), 115–123.

Lilienfeld, S. O. (2007). Psychological treatments that cause harm. *Perspectives on Psychological Science, 2*(1), 53–70.

Lovibond, S. H., & Lovibond, P. F. (1995). *Manual for the depression anxiety stress scales.* Sydney: Psychology Foundation of Australia.

McKelley, R. A., & Rochlen, A. B. (2007). The practice of coaching: Exploring alternatives to therapy for counseling-resistant men. *Psychology of Men & Masculinity, 8*(1), 53–65.

Milbank, D. (2007, June 1). As the world warms, the White House aspires. The Washington Post, A02.

Naughton, J. (2002). The coaching boom: Is it the long-awaited alternative to the medical model? *Psychotherapy Networker, 42*, 1–10.

Parkes, R. C. (1955). We use seven guides to help executives develop. *Personnel Journal, 33*, 326–328.

Preston, N. J., & Harrison, T. J. (2003). The Brief Symptom Inventory and the positive and negative syndrome scale: Discriminate validity between a self-reported and observational measure of psychopathology. *Comprehensive Psychiatry, 44*(3), 220–226.

Preville, M., Cote, G., Boyer, R., & Hebert, R. (2004). Detection of depression and anxiety disorders by home care nurses. *Aging & Mental Health, 8*(5), 400–409.

Ratey, N. (2002). Life coaching for adult ADHD. In S. Goldstein & A. T. Ellison (Eds.), *Clinicians' guide to adult ADHD: Assessment and intervention* (pp. 261–277). San Diego, CA: Academic Press.

Richard, J. T. (1999). Multimodal therapy: A useful model for the executive coach. *Consulting Psychology Journal: Practice and Research, 51*(1), 24–30.

Roper, N., Logan, W. W., & Tierney, A. J. (1980). *The elements of nursing.* Livingstone: Churchill.

Ryff, C. D. (1989). Happiness is everything, or is it? Explorations on the meaning of psychological well-being. *Journal of Personality and Social Psychology, 57*, 1069–1081.

Ryff, C. D., & Keyes, C. L. M. (1996). The structure of psychological well-being revisited. *Journal of Personality and Social Psychology, 96*(4), 719–727.

Schlegelmich, A., & Fresco, D. (2005). Emotion- focused therapy: Coaching clients to work through their feelings. *Counselling Psychology Quarterly, 18*(3), 225–226.

Seijts, G. H., & Latham, G. P. (2001). The effect of distal learning, outcome, and proximal goals on a moderately complex task. *Journal of Organizational Behavior, 22*(3), 291–307.

Seligman, M. E., & Csikszentmihalyi, M. (2000). Positive psychology: An introduction. *American Psychologist, 55*(1), 5–14.

Sheldon, K. M., & Elliot, A. J. (1998). Not all personal goals are personal: Comparing autonomous and controlled reasons for goals as predictors of effort and attainment. *Personality and Social Psychology Bulletin, 24*(5), 546–557.

Sheldon, K. M., & Elliot, A. J. (1999). Goal striving, need satisfaction, and longitudinal well-being: The self-concordance model. *Journal of Personality and Social Psychology, 76*(3), 482–497.

Sheldon, K. M., & Kasser, T. (1995). Coherence and congruence: Two aspects of personality integration. *Journal of Personality and Social Psychology, 68*(3), 531–543.

Sheldon, K. M., Ryan, R. M., Deci, E. L., & Kasser, T. (2004). The independent effects of goal contents and motives on well-being: It's both what you pursue and why you pursue it. *Personality and Social Psychology Bulletin, 30*(4), 475–486.

Snyder, C. R., Lopez, S. J., Edwards, L. M., Pedrotti, J. T., Prosser, E. C., Walton, S. L., et al. (2003). Measuring and labelling the positive and negative. In S. J. Lopez & C. R. Snyder (Eds.), *Positive psychological assessment: A handbook of models and measures* (pp. 21–39). Washington, DC: APA.

Spence, G., Cavanagh, M., & Grant, A. M. (2006). Duty of care in an unregulated industry: Initial findings on the diversity and practice of Australian coaches. *International Coaching Psychology Review, 1*(1), 71–85.

Spence, G., & Grant, A. M. (2007). Professional and peer life coaching and the enhancement of goal striving and well-being: An exploratory study. *Journal of Positive Psychology, 2*(3), 185–194.

Spence, G., Oades, L., & Caputi, P. (2004). Emotional intelligence and goal self-integration: Important predictors of emotional well-being? *Personality and Individual Differences, 37*(3), 449–461.

Sperry, L. (2004). *Executive Coaching: The essential guide for mental health professionals.* New York: Brunner-Routledge.

Street, H. (2002). Exploring relationships between goal setting, goal pursuit and depression: A review. *Australian Psychologist, 37*(2), 95–103.

van Dick, R., & Wanger, U. (2001). Stress and strain in teaching: A structural equation approach. *British Journal of Educational Psychology, 71*, 243–259.

Whitmore, J. (1992). *Coaching for performance.* London: Nicholas Brealey.

Whitworth, L., Kimsey-House, H., & Sandahl, P. (1998). *Co-active coaching: New skills for coaching people towards success in work and life.* Palo Alto, CA: Davies-Black.

Williams, P., & Thomas, L. J. (2004). *Total life coaching.* New York, NY: Norton.

Worldwide Association of Business Coaches. (2003). Worldwide Association of Business Coaches code of ethics and integrity. Retrieved September 15, 2007, from http://www.wabccoaches.com/regulation/code_of_ethics.htm

Zimmerman, B. J., & Bandura, A. (1994). Impact of self-regulatory influences on writing course attainment. *American Educational Research Journal, 31*(4), 845–862.

5 Addressing Deficit Performance Through Coaching: Using Motivational Interviewing for Performance Improvement at Work

Jonathan Passmore[1]

Coachee ambivalence about change is a reality for coaching psychologists working with executives in the workplace. Yet coaching models are limited in their value in addressing coachee ambivalence. So far, there has been little discussion of the readiness of the coachee for change and few of the current coaching models consider the "stage" of change a coachee may be at, before commencing with the coaching process. Motivational interviewing (MI) may be a useful contribution to the skill set of executive coaches when used alongside behavioral and cognitive-behavioral models (Passmore, 2007a).

This paper first discusses the development of MI and the theoretical bases in which it is grounded. The practice of MI is described with reference to the research literature. The paper then considers evidence from the application of MI in coaching, where MI

[1] First published as Passmore, J. (2007). Addressing deficit performance through coaching: Using motivational interviewing for performance improvement at work. *International Coaching Psychology Review*, 2(3), 265–275.

has been applied in an organizational setting to resolve ambivalence about change. Finally, the paper offers suggestions as to when the coaching psychologist could most effectively use MI alongside more traditional coaching interventions.

DEVELOPMENT OF MI

MI was largely developed in clinical environments by therapists working with drug and alcohol dependency. Therapists working with clients from these groups found that change processes in therapy mirrored natural change outside therapy. Firstly, a key predictive factor whether people would change or not was the way they spoke about change during their sessions with the therapist. Clients who made statements that signaled a high level of motivation and a strong commitment to change were more likely to make change than those demonstrating resistance. Secondly, there was a recognition that the language used by the client could be influenced by interpersonal interactions with the therapist (Miller & Rollnick, 2002). Thirdly, changes in the words and language used by the client were a strong predictor of future behavior change. It was observed that the style of interaction affected the change talk of the client, with empathic styles facilitating stronger change talk, and more confrontational methods generating less strong change talk or resistance talk (Miller & Rollnick, 2002).

The strong facilitative nature of MI has links to the humanistic counseling tradition, with its person-centered method of communication (Joseph, 2001). In the case of MI, these person-centered discussions are goal-related, which contrasts with person-centered therapy. MI aims to enhance intrinsic or internal motivation toward behavioral change, by helping the resolution of ambivalence to change that is felt by the client (Miller & Rollnick, 2002; Resnicow et al., 2002).

The approach also contrasts with traditional behavioral coaching approaches that are grounded in extrinsic motivators such as praise (Passmore, 2007b). In these cases, the coach may seek to encourage a behavior change through recognizing and praising the efforts of the coachee, and encouraging actions that move the coachee toward the organization's expressed goals. MI takes the view that such approaches can have an adverse effect, and strengthen resistance to change. In MI, the coach explores the values and goals of the coachee, and how their current behavior may be discrepant with their ideal behaviors. The aim of the coach in this approach is to help the coachee clarify their ambivalence toward change.

THEORY BASE OF MI: TRANSTHEORETICAL MODEL

A key concept of MI is to assess the coachee's state of readiness to change. The transtheoretical model (Diclemente & Prochaska, 1998) is a well-researched and influential model, describing how people prepare to change, and how successful change is maintained. The model argues that individuals progress through certain stages, as part of a change cycle.

The transtheoretical model argues that people experience different thought patterns at different stages of change. These include consciousness raising, where a person learns new facts or ideas that support making change, occurring at the contemplation stage, and self-liberation, such as making a commitment to change, occurring at the action or maintenance stages (Perz, Diclemente, & Carbonari, 1996). Likewise, the balance between the pros and cons of a specific behavior varies with an individual's stage of change. The coachee in the preparation stage experiences more negative cognitions and emotions toward their current behavior than a person in the contemplative stage of change.

Miller notes that movement through the stages is not always a straight path from pre-contemplation to maintenance, with relapse to an earlier stage, and spiraling through the stages, typically occurring before long-term maintenance is achieved.

A key concept of MI is the importance of tailoring interventions to meet an individual's stage of change; it has been discovered that the style of helping must match the motivation of the person (Project MATCH Research Group, 1997) (Table 5.1).

At the pre-contemplative, contemplative, or sometimes preparation stages ambivalence is experienced by the client. This may be summarized by the statement; what's the point of changing? Ambivalence can often keep the client grounded, and not able

Table 5.1 *Using MI and Other Interventions Within a Model of Change*

Change stage	Intervention model	Focus for work
Pre-contemplation	Motivational interviewing	Encourage the coachee to reflect on their current behavior.
Contemplation	Motivational interviewing and cognitive-behavioral	Encourage the coachee to explore their current behavior, its wider affect on their network (colleagues, friends, and family).
Planning	Motivational interviewing and behavioral	Encourage Coachee to establish a plan of action; long-term and intermediate goals.
Action	Behavioral	Encourage coachee to reflect on barriers and stakeholders. Who is going to be on their side and who is against them? Who will encourage and who will block their moves for change?
Maintenance	Behavioral	Hold the coachee to account, reflecting back previous goals and discussing barriers and stakeholders and referring back to values (motivators).

Note. Passmore adaption from Diclemente and Prochaska (1998), *Five-Stage Model of Change.*

to make the required change. It often explains why the person has not responded to demands from their partner and others to attend the training course or to correct the deficit behavior, such as drug taking or abuse.

A therapist's response to such ambivalence may be to offer unwelcome advice, education, or options of action. Such interventions from the therapist are likely to result in resistance from the client, and frustration for both therapist and client. Resistance behaviors are often responses to the style of interaction, that is, a mismatch between the client's stage of change, and the therapist's approach. In organizational settings, this may result in a coachee showing reluctance to attend the coaching sessions, complaints about the organization being unfair in mandating attendance, or complaints about the coach.

When applied to coaching, the MI approach requires the coaching psychologist to recognize and understand ambivalence as a natural part of the change process (Miller & Rollnick, 2002) and to work with it. In line with MI, it is essential for the coach to know which stage of change the coachee is at. One way of doing this is to ask the coachee to rate their perceived readiness to change on a scale of 0–10, with 10 being that they have already made change, and 0 being not at all interested in changing.

This can be rephrased, depending on the nature of the relationship to "If 10 was you would bust down the door to make this happen and 1 is you can't be bothered to get up from the chair, how motivated are you to …" An alternative way of doing this is to draw the dimensions and ask the coach to mark where they are with a cross on the scale between 1 and 10 (Figure 5.1).

A second key concept of MI is that there is a discrepancy between the coachee's values and goals, and their current behaviors. For successful change to occur, the individual first needs to be willing to believe that the target behavior is personally important to them. This often means that the goal is aligned to their personal values. Second, they must be ready to make the change a priority in their life.

The third element of MI involves the concept of self-efficacy (Bandura, 1977). In the "ready, willing, and able" triumvirate, no amount of readiness will compensate for perceived inability (Rollnick, 1998). In the case of a skills deficit, the coach can step back into the role of trainer, mentor, and facilitator to support the coachee in learning the new behaviors or skills required. This may involve drawing on behavioral-based models (Alexander, 2006; Skiffington & Zeus, 2003), or a facilitative model for supporting the development of the required skills.

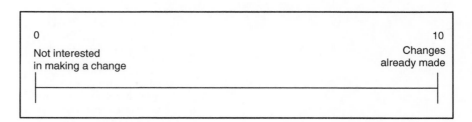

Figure 5.1 *Change Continuum*

One source of hope for coachees from the MI approach is that there is no "right way" to change, and if one given plan for change does not work, a coachee is only limited by their creativity as to the number of other approaches that may be tried.

These three concepts of MI are related; for example, readiness relies on a perception of intrinsic importance and confidence to change (Miller & Rollnick, 2002). A coachee who does not see change as important is unlikely to be ready to change. Furthermore, a coachee who perceives change to be impossible is unlikely to rate their readiness to change as very high. Exploring coachee ambivalence through the practice of MI helps to clarify which of these three concepts is keeping a client stuck in ambivalence, in turn identifying to the coach which aspect of motivation needs to be the focus of change talk.

CLINICAL RESEARCH

Most of the evidence base for MI comes from the clinical psychology environment where MI has been extensively used in drug and alcohol counseling, with strong evidence of effect (Burke, Arkowitz, & Menchola, 2003; Miller & Moyers, 2002; Solomon & Fioritti, 2002). It has also been applied to the field of chronic illness management; for example, helping people with diabetes to achieve better control of blood glucose (Channon, Smith, & Gregory, 2003; Prochaska & Zinman, 2003), in teenagers' contraception interventions (Cowley, Farley, & Beamis, 2002), and in cardiac management (Kazel, 1998). However, to date, MI has remained within the health and clinical psychology environment, yet it has potential for wider application such as in coaching psychology, when combined with individual models for change such as the transtheoretical model described above and when used as part of a wider repertoire of skills such as behavioral and cognitive-behavioral coaching interventions.

APPLYING MI IN COACHING PSYCHOLOGY

This approach has been developed based on MI as a coaching tool to help address deficit performance. It aims to retain the core spirit of the counseling-based approach, but focus its application within a workplace context.

The basis behind MI interactions is that the relationship between coach and coachee is collaborative. The coach provides empathy and support, never criticizing the coachee's efforts. The relationship is like a partnership, with the coachee being responsible for their progress, which fits with the application of behavioral and cognitive-behavioral interventions, as these too can be highly collaborative.

In applying the techniques from MI a number of key lessons can help increase the likelihood of success. The coach should avoid suggesting options until the coachee has resolved ambivalence and is getting ready to take action. Coachees are free to choose their own method of change, in turn increasing the likelihood of long-term success. Coaches may try to persuade the coachee about the urgency and the potential benefits of change. However, such tactics generally increase resistance and diminish the probability of change (Miller & Rollnick, 1991). Overall, the coach should aim to make the coaching session between the coach and coachee feel more like a dance than a wrestling match.

In this approach, MI has been applied in three separate phases. The first phase involves exploring the ambivalence of the coachee. The second phase involves building the intrinsic motivation and self-efficacy of the coachee. The third phase involves strengthening the coachee's commitment to change.

In the first phase, the coach uses open questions to encourage the coachee to talk about their situation at work, what has happened, what they feel and why they feel as they do. In this approach, the aim would be to come alongside them. Initially this is difficult as, unlike most coaching assignments where the coachee is either self-referred or is a keen participant, for these assignments the coachee has often been a less willing or a suspicious participant. As a result, the starting point is to make clear during the contracting stage that the coach's role is as servant to the coachee, but also that the coach is not there to provide advice or to tell them what they should do; their actions are their choice and each carries associated consequences. The aim during the early phase is to get the coachee to do most of the talking, with the coach listening and promoting the coachee to reflect on their values and goals, in contrast to their actions. A second core skill at this first stage is reflective statements demonstrate active listening and empathy to the coachee. This requires the coach to hold back from moving rapidly toward more directive and action-orientated questions that are more typical of behavioral and cognitive-behavioral interventions (Alexander, 2006; Neenan, 2006). Reflection is not a passive process. It is the coach who decides what to reflect on and what aspects to ignore. In this way, the coach can direct the attention of the coachee and encourage them to focus on aspects that may help them to reframe the situation or move forward (Figure 5.2).

Ambivalence to change may be apparent because importance is high but confidence is low. To assess confidence to change, a confidence ruler can be employed, followed by: "Why are you an X on the scale and not a zero?" and "What would it take for you to go from X to a higher number?" (Figure 5.3)

> Coachee: *"I have been referred by my manager for this meeting."*
> Coach: *"You've been asked by your manager to attend some coaching."*
> Coachee: *"I don't really feel that it's fair. In fact most of what she does is not fair. I don't need coaching. It's not me who needs to change it's her."*
>
> Coach: *"So, it seems to you that your manager has been unfair in referring you for coaching and that she has to look at her own behaviour as well."*

Figure 5.2 *Reflective Listening*

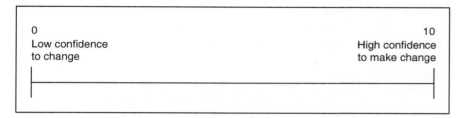

Figure 5.3   *Ambivalence Continuum*

Offering affirmations also has an important place in MI. Affirmations facilitate an atmosphere of acceptance, helping to build confidence to change in the coachee and demonstrating the coach is working as an ally of the coachee.

During phase one, the processes highlighted above help to clarify and explore ambivalence. However, there is a danger of the coach becoming stuck in ambivalence with the coachee. In order to maintain momentum, the coach can utilize directive processes, for eliciting and reflecting on change talk.

In order to elicit change talk, the ruler method described previously may be utilized. For example, it may be appropriate to clarify the coachee's rating of importance to address change and then to ask:

"Why are you at an X (x being a number) and not a zero?"

"What would it take for you to go from X to a higher number?"

It may be useful for a coachee to fill in a decisional balance sheet (see Figure 5.4), to reflect and reinforce ambivalence previously explored and discussed with the coachee. However, from personal experience coachees can be reluctant to complete the sheet for themselves. As a result, the coach can help in this process and capture responses from the coachee, verbally summarizing these and noting them down on the sheet. In this way, the coachee has a record of their thinking at the end of the discussion.

Whether a person will continue to explore change talk or veer away depends on how the coach responds. When resistance occurs, it is a sign that the coachee is not keeping up.

Benefits of activity	Costs of activity	Benefits of change	Costs of change

Figure 5.4   *Coaching for Change Balance Sheet*

Two summarizing techniques can be useful to the coach to amplify the reaction or to reframe it. Amplified reflections with an exaggerated emphasis encourage the coachee to elicit the opposite argument of their ambivalence:

Amplified reaction

Coachee: "I couldn't accept a transfer to a new role in the organization, my colleagues will think that I have failed in my current job and delays are my fault?"

Coach: "You couldn't handle your colleagues' reaction?"

Reframing is a technique that acknowledges the validity of the coachee's claim, but the information is reflected back in a new light, more supportive of change:

Reframing

Coachee: "I have applied for promotion so many times, they don't want me to have it and that's it. I am stuck in this role until I retire."

Coach: "It sounds as though you have been amazingly determined. In spite of the disappointments you have received when you have applied in the past, you are still determined to progress your career here and fulfill your potential."

Emphasizing personal choice and control or shifting the focus away from the resistance may be other useful strategies to help roll with rather than confront resistance.

The third phase of the MI process involves strengthening commitment. The coach needs to look for signs of decreased resistance and decreased discussion about the problem from the coachee's perspective. Continuing the example from Figure 5.2, the coachee may say, "Well I guess I also need to do something too, to help my manager recognize the skills I have."

A discrepancy between a person's goals and their current behaviors should now be clear. The next step is to help the coachee consider methods to achieve their goals. One route would be to brainstorm options; the coachee's task is then to select a preferred option. A plan for change can then be devised, including summarizing issues such as: why change is important, how specific goals can be reached, predicting obstacles, and evaluating how change will be measured. The more the coachee verbalizes the plan, the more commitment is strengthened. All of this has strong similarities with action planning within the behavioral and cognitive-behavioral approaches.

The key elements of MI practice may be summarized as:

- seeking to understand and affirm the coachee's perspective via summaries and reflective listening;
- keeping the coachee focused on change talk, through selectively reinforcing the coachee's own motivational statements;
- monitoring degree of readiness to change, and rolling with resistance; and
- accepting and affirming the coachee's choice of change and self-direction.

THE EVIDENCE FOR MI IN COACHING PSYCHOLOGY

MI is a new approach within coaching. As an advanced technique it requires a high level of skills in framing questions, active listening, and accurately summarizing. It also requires an appreciation of human behavior and motivation. Coaching psychologists are rightly keen to review the efficacy of each intervention. As yet, the evidence for the efficacy of coaching in the workplace is still in its infancy (Passmore & Gibbes, 2007) and MI is no exception to this. The evidence for MI to date shows it to be a valuable approach in counseling addictive and habitual behaviors, but as yet no studies have been undertaken in respect of its efficacy in the workplace. Initial evaluation evidence from coachees who have experienced MI coaching suggests that MI may be worthy of more detailed research investigation. This evidence is drawn from reviews from coachees of their experience on the completion of the coaching intervention.

Three short cases are presented here with quotes from the coachee as an illustration of the range of opinions expressed. While the reaction level evaluation shows coachees appreciate the coaching interaction and there appears to be some impact on motivation, such evaluation is inadequate for us to conclude that MI coaching is effective as a tool for addressing deficit performance and low motivation. A further rider to the studies is that all of them were drawn from coaching in the UK with middle managers. However, based on this sample evidence MI is worthy of further investigation as coaching psychologists plan and prepare the randomized controlled trial (RCT) studies that counseling has employed to demonstrate its value as a one-to-one intervention.

The first case is Susan, a middle manager in a public sector organization. The coaching relationship involved four coaching sessions. The initial referral was from the organization's human resources team who had been asked by Susan's line manager to "sort her out." Susan revealed during her coaching session that she had worked for the organization for 30 years, she had less than 5 years to go until retirement, and that the place had changed under the new senior appointments. The session spent a significant proportion of the time exploring values and life goals, which contrasts with a more behavioral or cognitive approach. At the conclusion of the relationship, Susan fed back that she was now reflecting on her motivation levels and how she might address her low motivation so she could feel better about going to work each day: "You have made me think about why I keep coming to work, and what I have to give to colleagues who are just starting out on their careers."

In Susan's case, the reaction feedback suggested that she had moved through the contemplation stage of the transtheoretical model, but had not completed the planning stage. As a result, there was no action at a behavioral level that was planned or being tested out. Unfortunately, given the nature of coaching in real organizations, there was no evidence of Susan's plan or her subsequent actions.

Jack is a middle manager who lost out on internal promotion. He felt bitter about the appointment process, and while able to welcome his new boss and get on with his old job, he was going through the motions. The reaction feedback at the end of the coaching relationship identified his need to act. Jack identified action plan choices as making the decision to move by starting to look for a new job, or finding tasks in his current role that he did enjoy and focusing his energies on these to make a difference. Jack too was able to identify that a failure to change could result in him becoming a victim of the organization. His language changed during the coaching and as it progressed he was quoting stories of other managers from earlier in his career who had become characters of derision as they were "old buffers" stuck in the past. Jack was determined not to become a source of ridicule from younger colleagues. By the end of the coaching, Jack had identified a plan to take control of the situation. This involved planning his own departure and finding a new role that he found more rewarding, with a fresh challenge in a different organization. He had allocated himself 12 months to find the role, and set other criteria that were essential and others that were desirable, to evaluate potential opportunities against.

The third case is Phil, a manager of a large team of building staff that had a strong masculine culture. The behavior and language used were inappropriate for the environment, and the appointment of a female director responsible for the business had brought Phil into conflict with the director and subsequently the human resources director. Phil was referred on the basis of "coaching, but if he can't change it will be disciplinary action." The MI interventions offered an opportunity to explore how his elder mother, aunt, and his daughter, would react to the work styles in the team. The reframing conversations moved Phil's view toward one where he was able to express that such language in what had been an all-male environment may have been acceptable, but in a mixed work environment, the style of working could result in people being offended and upset. Further that, as with his daughter, women had skills and the right to work in an environment where they were free from inappropriate remarks. In reviewing his approach, Phil described how he viewed the situation differently, and while it was harmless fun, it could upset people. His change of heart in what was appropriate and inappropriate enabled a fresh approach in tackling such behaviors across the whole team, which he led, challenging his colleagues in their behavior, and having a plan to help him change his behavior, so leading by example. In Phil's case he was able to make the move over 6 months from a fixed position to a new perspective, moving through pre-contemplation:

> This is not a problem, we have done this for years and no one has ever complained. It's all to do with my new boss, who is a woman.

Through the contemplation stage:

> Well, I would not like my daughter to be called that word.

Into the planning stage:

> I have heard that at XYZ they took down the calendars and there is a swear box, we could try ideas like that too I guess.

The final step was a plan of action that Phil implemented, helping him address his and his team's behaviors.

A word of caution from the transtheoretical model, and from what we know of human behavior—human behavior is difficult to change. The desire to change our behavior and an actual change are two different things. We may have the desire to change (willing), plan of action (ready), and the skills (able), but to succeed, we need to be persistent. This maintenance aspect requires the individual to continually catch themselves slipping back into old behavior patterns and reenergize themselves to return to the plan. Support during this phase should not be underestimated, so the use of rewards and allies can help the coachee to continue after the coaching assignment has ended.

In selecting MI as an approach, initial reaction evidence suggests that it is best suited where the coachee is not the client, but instead has been referred by others within the organization. In cases of working with deficit performance, we have found that more traditional approaches such as behavioral and cognitive-behavioral interventions were not helping the coachee to move forward. In these situations, the coachee seemed highly resistant to change, yet they continued to attend coaching, as the organization had mandated their attendance. This can occur in mergers and planned change, where new roles have been identified and people allocated to new roles, or where they have been asked to change and adopt the new ways of working of the lead partner in the merger.

A second circumstance is where the coachee is referred for coaching as a final step prior to the commencement of capability or disciplinary action. In this situation the threat of consequences is clear, but from my experience, the coachee either rejects their manager's view that they need to change or believes that their manager is being unfair. The coachee is thus "stuck" and is heading for a direct collision with the organization (Passmore & Whybrow, 2007).

PROPOSED MODEL

In these cases outlined above, the organizational client is often seeking explicit behavioral change. However, before behavioral-based coaching can commence, the coach needs to explore and resolve the ambivalence to the situation, or threat faced by the coachee. Behavioral and cognitive-behavioral interventions can then be used to develop new skills or beliefs for success.

Research by Passmore (2007c) suggests coaching psychologists already use a wide range of interventions, effectively using an integrated approach through combining humanistic, behavioral, and cognitive-behavioral elements. Motivaitional interviewing is a complementary set of techniques that can be added to their repertoire with the appropriate training, although the nature of the intervention may make it less suitable for nonpsychologists. The integrative coaching model (Passmore, 2007a) offers one way that the approach can be combined with other widely used coaching approaches such as behavioral, cognitive-behavioral, and facilitative (Palmer & Whybrow, 2006).

While not explored in this paper, MI also has strong potential for application by coaching psychologists in other areas of work such as health coaching and could complement current cognitive-behavioral practice, which has already been shown to be widely effective in health coaching intervention (Palmer, Tubbs, & Whybrow, 2003). Examples could include the application of MI to support smoking cessation, either working with organizations encouraging their employees to adopt more healthy lifestyles or working with local health trusts (primary care trusts in the UK) to promote behavioral changes where motivation is a factor.

CONCLUSION

The development of MI as a tool within coaching offers a new departure. Its integration as an element within a wider model could help coach psychologists to broaden their repertoire and offer a distinct approach that is grounded in psychological practice and is complementary to already popular approaches.

REFERENCES

Alexander, G. (2006). Behavioural coaching: The Grow coaching model. In J. Passmore (Ed.), *Excellence in coaching: The industry guide* (pp. 83–93). London: Kogan Page.

Bandura, A. (1977). Self-efficacy: Towards a unifying theory of behaviour change. *Psychological Review, 84*, 191–215.

Burke, B. L., Arkowitz, I. I., & Menchola, M. (2003). The efficacy of motivational interviewing: A meta-analysis of controlled clinical trials. *Journal of Consulting and Clinical Psychology, 71*, 843–861.

Channon, S., Smith, V. J., & Gregory, J. W. (2003). A pilot study of motivational interviewing in adolescents with diabetes. *Archives of Disease in Childhood, 88*(8), 680–683.

Cowley, C. B., Farley, T., & Beamis, K. (2002). 'Well, maybe I'll try the pill for just a few months.' Brief motivational and narrative-based interventions to encourage contraceptive use among adolescents at high risk for early childbearing. *Families, Systems, & Health, 20*, 183.

Diclemente, C. C., & Prochaska, J. O. (1998). Toward a comprehensive, transtheoretical model of change: Stages of change and addictive behaviours. In W. R. Miller & N. Heather (Eds.), *Treating addictive behaviours* (2nd ed., pp. 3–24). New York, NY: Plenum Press.

Joseph, S. (2001). *Psychopathology and therapeutic approaches: An introduction.* Basingstoke: Palgrave.

Kazel, R. (1998). Cardiac coaching produces better health savings. Business Insurance, October 19.

Miller, J. H., & Moyers, T. (2002). Motivational interviewing in substance abuse: Applications for occupational medicine. *Occupational Medicine, 17*(1), 51–65.

Miller, W. R., & Rollnick, S. (1991). *Motivational interviewing: Preparing people to change addictive behaviour*. New York, NY: Guilford Press.

Miller, W. R., & Rollnick, S. (2002). *Motivational interviewing: Preparing people for change* (2nd ed.). New York, NY: Guilford Press.

Neenan, M. (2006). Cognitive behavioural coaching. In J. Passmore (Ed.), *Excellence in coaching: The industry guide* (pp. 110–122). London: Kogan Page.

Palmer, S., Tubbs, I., & Whybrow, A. (2003). Health coaching to facilitate the promotion of health behaviours and achievement of health-related goals. *International Journal of Health Promotion and Education, 41*(3), 91–93.

Palmer, S., & Whybrow, A. (2006). Shifting perspectives: One year into the development of the BPS Special Group in the UK. *International Coaching Psychology Review, 1*(2), 75–85.

Passmore, J. (2007a). An integrative model for executive coaching. *Consulting Psychology Journal: Practice and Research, 59*(1), 68–78.

Passmore, J. (2007b). Behavioural coaching. In S. Palmer & A. Whybrow (Eds.), *The handbook of coaching psychology: A guide for practitioners* (pp. 73–85). London: Routledge.

Passmore, J. (2007c). *Coaching behaviours: What's effective?* Paper to the 2nd International Coaching Conference, London, December, 2006.

Passmore, J., & Gibbes, C. (2007). The state of executive coaching research: What does the current literature tell us and what's next for coaching research? *International Coaching Psychology Review, 2*(2), 116–128.

Passmore, J. & Whybrow, A. (2007). Motivational interviewing: A specific approach for coaching psychologists. In S. Palmer & A. Whybrow (Eds.), *The handbook of coaching psychology: A guide for practitioners* (pp. 160–173). London: Routledge.

Perz, C. A., Diclemente, C. C., & Carbonari, J. P. (1996). Doing the right thing at the right time? The interaction of stages and processes of change in successful smoking cessation. *Health Psychology, 15*, 462–468.

Prochaska, J. O., & Zinman, B. (2003). Changes in diabetes self-care behaviours make a difference in glycemic control: The Diabetes Stages of Change (DISC) study. *Diabetes Care, 26*, 732–737.

Project MATCH Research Group. (1997). Matching alcoholism treatments to client heterogeneity: Project MATCH post-treatment drinking outcomes. *Journal of Studies on Alcohol, 58*, 7–29.

Resnicow, K., DiIorio, C., Soet, J. E., Borrelli, B., Hecht, J., & Ernst, D. (2002). Motivational interviewing in health promotion: It sounds like something is changing. *Health Psychology, 21*(5), 444–451.

Rollnick, S. (1998). Readiness and confidence: Critical conditions of change in treatment. In W. R. Miller & N. Heather (Eds.), *Treating addictive behaviours* (2nd ed., pp. 49–60). New York, NY: Plenum.

Skiffington, S., & Zeus, P. (2003). *Behavioural coaching: How to build sustainable organisational and personal strength*. North Ryde, NSW: McGraw-Hill.

Solomon, J., & Fioritti, A. (2002). Motivational intervention as applied to systems change: The case of dual diagnosis. *Substance Use and Misuse, 37*(14), 1833–1851.

6 Does Coaching Psychology Need the Concept of Formulation?

David A. Lane and Sarah Corrie[1]

Since its introduction to clinical psychology regulation in 1969, formulation has become a defining skill of applied psychology. Different forms of professional psychology define the term in different ways, and the extent to which formulation has a scientific basis and is drawn directly from psychological theory varies between disciplines (see Lane & Corrie, 2006). Nonetheless, there is fairly broad agreement that the ability to construct formulations is central to applied psychology practice (British Psychological Society, 2005; Corrie & Lane, 2006; Johnstone & Dallos, 2006) and much time, during initial training and subsequent professional development, will be spent in the service of acquiring and refining this complex skill.

However, the role that formulation should play in the emerging discipline and profession of coaching psychology is yet to be adequately considered. In this paper, we argue for the centrality of formulation in coaching psychology and propose that the quality of coaching practice can be significantly enhanced by elevating formulation to the heart of the coach–client partnership.

In order to contextualize our argument, we begin with an overview of the way in which formulation has been conceptualized in the literature more broadly, and consider some of the debates concerning its role in practice. We then examine some of the factors that may have led to this being a relatively neglected topic in coaching psychology, and consider ways in which elevating formulation to the heart of coaching

[1] First published as Lane, D.A. & Corrie, S. (2009). Does coaching psychology need the concept of formulation? *International Coaching Psychology Review*, 4(2), 195–208.

psychology might contribute to the development of high-quality practice. Finally, we propose an approach to formulation that can help coaches achieve a more rigorous and systematic approach, regardless of their theoretical preferences. This approach is, we believe, relevant regardless of whether the coaching journey is undertaken with an individual seeking personal guidance, a team seeking higher levels of performance, or an organization seeking a strategic change of direction. Coaching is very broadly based and the formulation process happens at different scales (dyad, triad, group, organization, etc.). Consequently, there are multiple stakeholders. We argue that formulation must encompass or reflect these nested contexts. Hence, formulation is not a single moment in time but an iterative process. Formulations are co-created sometimes in the coaching dyad, but at other times may represent in an organizational context both coach and coachee's evolving apprehension of the stakeholder situation.

FORMULATION AND ITS ROLE IN PSYCHOLOGICAL PRACTICE: A BRIEF REVIEW OF THE LITERATURE

When the coaching psychologist sits alongside a client, what is their first duty as a professional? Arguably, it is one of ensuring that the client feels heard and that their story is understood and accepted. However, the client is also seeking assistance from the psychologist to identify a way forward. The client is, therefore, assuming that a psychological perspective is potentially relevant and helpful. The coach becomes a partner in the client's story, contributing ideas derived from theory, research, and prior professional experience to help formulate a coherent explanation of the puzzle, problem, or concern that the client is facing.

In general terms, formulation can be understood as an explanatory account of the issues with which a client is presenting (including predisposing, precipitating, and maintaining factors) that can form the basis of a shared framework of understanding and which has implications for change. It is reasonable to assume that this explanatory account will draw upon a wide range of data, including psychological theory, general scientific principles, research from the wider literature, and professional experience, in addition to being informed by the nuances of the client's self-told story. The stories that clients tell in coaching are often the way into a rich narrative (Drake, 2009).

Formulation is believed to serve a variety of functions. These include (although are by no means limited to) facilitating an informed understanding of the client's needs, prioritizing client concerns for the purposes of goal setting, identifying hypotheses worthy of further investigation, selecting intervention strategies, and guiding systematic thinking about lack of progress (see Bieling & Kuyken, 2003; Butler, 1998; Corrie & Lane, 2010).

Formulation has also been described as an aid to engagement, particularly in those instances where a client's actions may challenge the practitioner's empathic ability (as, for example, in the case of sexual offending; see Haarbosch & Newey, 2006; Sheath, 2010).

However, the empirical literature on formulation would appear to challenge its status as a cornerstone of effective practice. Most notably, there is a lack of consensual definition (Corrie & Lane, 2010); poor inter-rater reliability, particularly in relation to the explanatory components of cases where greater inference is required (Bieling & Kuyken, 2003); and an equivocal relationship to outcome (Schulte, Kunzel, Pepping, & Shulte-Bahrenberg, 1992). Moreover, a number of clients appear to find formulations of their needs unhelpful (Chadwick, Williams, & Mackenzie, 2003; Evans & Parry, 1996).

One question arising from these ambiguous findings is that of who should "own" the formulation and thus, who is entitled to devise, change, or discard it. Crellin (1998), for example, has noted how formulation tends to take the form of translating clients' experiences into testable hypotheses. However, she argues that while this may render complex client experiences more manageable for practitioners, such reductionism prevents us from grasping the very experiences we seek to understand. A similar concern has been expressed by Duncan and Miller (2000) and Worrell (2010), who warn that our theoretically- and empirically-derived formulations all too easily become professional expositions imposed on clients, rather than useful ideas that might form the basis of new possibilities.

The evidence base for formulation raises a question about whether our faith in formulation as the route to effective practice is misplaced. Moreover, we must consider the implications of these debates for coaching psychology itself. In light of this literature, to what extent should coaching psychology adhere to the established view that formulation is a central component of effective practice? Is a formulation always essential for effective, ethical coaching, or are there times when it is unnecessary? What questions might an understanding of the role of formulation generate that assists coaching psychology in its task of helping clients re-author their stories? These questions are considered next.

DOES COACHING PSYCHOLOGY NEED THE CONCEPT OF FORMULATION?

In recent texts reviewing the field (for example, Palmer & Whybrow, 2007), it is apparent that the concept of formulation is largely absent (see Palmer & Szymanska, 2007; Szymanska, 2009, for an exception). This is despite the fact that many coaching models "borrow" constructs and approaches from clinical psychology, counseling psychology, and psychotherapy.

There are a number of reasons why formulation may be a neglected topic. First, it may relate to the purpose of coaching. Formulation may not be necessary for all forms of coaching, particularly where there is a clear goal and action plan and where a new understanding of causal or maintenance factors does not appear to be required. Grant and Cavanagh (2004) identify three generic levels of engagement within the coaching agenda: skills coaching (typically of short duration where the focus is on specific behaviors); performance coaching (where the focus is on the process by which the coachee can set goals, manage obstacles, and monitor their performance); and developmental coaching (which takes a more holistic view and addresses personal and professional questions in the context of a "reflective space"). Formulation is unlikely to be required to the same degree across all three levels. Thus, where horizontal change is involved (for example, where the client aims to extend what they already know and can do and where the focus is essentially one of skills coaching), formulation may be less relevant. However, where vertical change is involved (for example, where the client will need to fundamentally alter the way they perceive a situation and acquire new ways of thinking and doing), the need to challenge how they see and apply new learning becomes more critical. As Olson (2008) points out, although we arrive at our perspectives on our worlds in different ways, if we want to understand we have to make our assumptions explicit. Formulation, we would contend, is a useful part of such a process of explication.

A second reason for the relative absence of formulation in the coaching literature may lie in the roles played in coaching by client and coach and the existence of three- or four- (or more) cornered contracts, which imply that multiple stories have to be addressed or integrated. For example, in a study of transfer of gains, Stewart, Palmer, Wilkin, and Kerrin (2008) found that the multiple interactions typical of coaching contracts in organizations required an understanding of a complex interplay of factors beyond the idea of the coach–coachee relationship. They suggested that organizations must adopt a holistic guardianship of their coaching provision.

A third reason for the relative neglect of formulation in the coaching psychology literature may relate to the domain in which client concerns have traditionally been located. In her review of the literature, Butler (1998) highlights how approaches to formulation have tended to focus on predisposing, precipitating, and maintaining factors that are concerned primarily with individual, internal, or intrapsychic factors. At the same time, social, cultural, and historical factors have suffered relative neglect. A similar argument has been made by Lazarus (1973), whose multimodal model has come to be known through the acronym BASIC ID, where each letter stands for a particular sensory modality (biology, affect, sensation, imagery, cognition, interpersonal factors and the need for drugs or pharmacological intervention). Palmer (2008) has explored these arguments in coaching.

Although the neglect of the social, cultural, economic, and political domains is a criticism that has been levied against applied psychology (see Masson, 1990; Smail, 1993, 1996), there may have been compelling reasons for practitioners' pursuit of internal factors. In their analysis of what they term "the zeitgeist of internal causation," Martell, Addis, and Jacobson (2001) highlight how Western culture tends to blame individuals for difficulties that society attributes to "deviant behavior." (They illustrate this culture of blame through reference to the social discourse surrounding HIV and AIDS, where those affected have been labeled either as "innocent victims" or "those who got what they deserved.") In contrast, by attributing difficulties to internal factors over which the individual has no direct control (e.g., an imbalance in brain chemistry or genetic features), the difficulty is redefined as one of illness, with the burden of stigma concurrently reduced. The focus on internal factors has, therefore, served the function of legitimizing distress in a culture that is highly judgmental of human dilemmas.

However, as a direct consequence, coaching psychologists may now find themselves faced with an array of theories and models that are inadequate for the contexts in which they work. In coaching psychology practice, multiple stories are involved. The traditional overreliance on internal factors while engaged in a process that is essentially, because of the multiple relationships involved, interrelational has been raised by Spinelli (2008). He argues the need for a broader exploration and quality of relationship. We are in what Spinelli (quoting Jopling, 2007) calls "fuzzy space," where multiple relationships and perspectives need to be addressed.

This may also generate the fourth possible reason. Many coaches have become concerned about boundary issues between coaching and therapy. As it is often associated with *clinical* case conceptualization, it may be that formulation seems too close to the boundary of therapy to feel safe. Thus, while some concepts from therapy are embraced others are not, and there are issues over the uses of such theory (Lane, 2006) and the range to which it is applied. The issue of boundaries has greatly exercised many in the field. (See, for example, debates in Bachkirova, 2007; Lane, Stelter, & Stout Rostron, 2009; Spinelli, 2008.)

A fifth potential reason for the relative neglect of formulation in the coaching psychology literature is its equivocal relationship to outcome. The empirical status of the construct of formulation, as well as some of the well-documented biases in decision making that underpin it, has led some (e.g., Meehl, 1954, 1986; Wilson, 1996, 1997) to argue that individual formulations should be bypassed in favor of manual-based, empirically-validated interventions wherever possible. There is certainly a pressure toward manual-based coaching interventions, where a simple process can be taught in a short training program and will supposedly deliver consistent results (Lane, 2009).

However, despite some of the challenges, abandoning formulation in coaching psychology may be premature. As noted previously, formulation has continued to be regarded as a central skill of applied psychologists, despite a growth in manualized interventions (British Psychological Society, 2005). Moreover, the many functions that formulation serves relate to the content, process, planning, and evaluation of psychological interventions. This implies a highly sophisticated skill that relies on a range of higher-order skills in both problem solving and design—some of which may be more amenable to empirical examination than others. For example, practitioners bring to their inquiries theoretical knowledge and prior professional experience that shape how they listen, respond to, and understand their clients' concerns from the earliest stages of engaging with them. Hence, they operate using covert formulations that direct the process of the inquiry from the outset (Butler, 1998).

Additionally, as noted by Dowie and Elstein (1988), professional judgments are not isolated cognitive events and can be understood only in relation to a particular task in a specific context. They are judgments about situations and experiences that are constantly evolving, rather than static events that lend themselves well to statistical analyses of accuracy (Hogarth, 1981). Is coaching psychology fundamentally different in this respect? We believe not. As Butler (1998) proposes, the aim of a formulation is not to provide answers but rather to generate a rich source of questions and ideas that add value to the work. Interpreted in this light, investigating the effectiveness of formulation should perhaps focus on the properties of powerful questions and how those questions can be used to create leverage for change (Adams, 2004).

Kuyken, Padesky, and Dudley (2009) have also proposed that the reason formulations are not always positively received by clients is that they tend to focus on unilaterally derived, practitioner-determined accounts presented to clients rather than being constructed in partnership. This emphasis on partnership is critical to devising explanations that are both acceptable to all those involved and useful in their implications. The issue of partnership and the forms it takes has featured centrally in much of the coaching literature (Bachkirova, 2007; Spinelli, 2008). Hence, if formulation is to take its place within coaching psychology, building appropriate relationships in which the multiple purposes served and stories heard, constructed, deconstructed and reconstructed will be necessary.

In consequence, we argue that:

1. Formulation has a potentially crucial role to play in the development of coaching psychology, despite the ambiguities in the literature. It may not be necessary for all levels of engagement (particularly where the focus is on skills coaching) but will be crucial in working with clients at the levels of performance and developmental coaching, as well as work involving any degree of complexity.
2. Formulation can serve many functions ranging from the identification of relevant issues and goals to enhancing coach empathy and collaboration.
3. There is currently insufficient knowledge of the factors that make our formulations optimally useful for coaches and their clients.

We might also conclude that if formulation is to prove "fit for purpose" for coaching psychologists and their clients, it will be necessary to:

1. Develop a model or framework that is consistent with a client partnership framework in which it is possible to incorporate a variety of stakeholder positions.
2. Develop a model or framework that can take account of a broader range of factors than the individual and internal (that is, an approach that is not restricted by the "zeitgeist of internal causation").
3. Develop a model or framework of formulation that has relevance to all contexts, regardless of the goals chosen, theoretical position adopted, or techniques for change used (that is, the framework or approach to formulation must be replicable across time, place, and contract).

In the next section we consider how, in the light of the criteria identified, it might be possible to develop a systematic approach to formulation, regardless of the theoretical perspective taken.

TOWARD A MODEL OF FORMULATION FOR COACHING PSYCHOLOGY: INTRODUCING THE PURPOSE, PERSPECTIVE, PROCESS MODEL AS A FRAMEWORK FOR FORMULATION

In previous work (Corrie & Lane, 2006; Lane & Corrie, 2006) as well as current work (Corrie & Lane, 2010), and drawing on empirical findings establishing the effectiveness of this approach (Lane, 1990), we have defined formulation as the co-construction of a narrative that provides a specific focus for a learning journey. This learning journey takes the client from where they are now to where they want to be, based on a process of negotiating appropriate goals. The task of formulating centers on the creation of a shared framework of understanding that has implications for change. This shared framework centers on the three core themes of purpose, perspective, and process as follows:

1. What purpose is the formulation designed to serve? For example, is the purpose to help the client construct a meaningful narrative that enables them to make sense of their situation? Or is it to ease communication with professional colleagues? Unless we understand that purpose, it is difficult to make any decision to apply a psychological approach to its resolution. Making a decision with the client about whether coaching is appropriate is part of our responsibility in the initial encounter. It may, for example, be the case that a management consultancy or organizational design approach has more to offer.
2. What *perspective* informs the development of the formulation? The purpose of any inquiry will influence its direction. The intentions of the different stakeholders, their beliefs and views on human experience, and the nature of the evidence that needs to underpin any psychological intervention will all inform the journey taken. In working psychologically there are many perspectives upon which we might draw. Some of these are the client's, some our own, some belong to other authors,

and some are prescribed or proscribed by the context in which the work takes place. Those perspectives help us to make sense of the purpose we have agreed as the "shared concern."

3. Given the purpose and perspective, what process is needed? Based on your understanding and the context in which you have defined your purpose and identified your perspective, what intervention strategies, approaches, methods, or tools do you select? In undertaking that work, we follow a process determined partly by how we have defined the purpose of the inquiry and partly by the perspectives that underpin our approach.

We argue that as a generic framework, the purpose, perspective, process model meets the criteria outlined in the previous section and can usefully guide practitioners in understanding the issues relevant to each stage of a client inquiry. We now consider each of the components of the purpose, perspective, process model in turn.

Purpose (where we are going and why?)

In undertaking any inquiry within coaching psychology, it is vital to be clear about its fundamental purpose. The shape that your inquiry takes and the stories you tell about that inquiry will follow logically from there. Thus, the shared journey begins as you define the purpose of your work together. Critical questions in this regard include: What is the purpose of working with the client? Where are you going with this client? What do they want to achieve? Where do they want to go in their overall journey with you as their guide? Who are the stakeholders and what do they want? This is more than defining a contract for work, it is defining the purpose of the enterprise.

Defining the purpose of the work comprises four essential elements:

1. understanding the question you wish to explore
2. understanding the expectations of key stakeholders
3. clarifying the role that each party wishes to play
4. appreciating the wider context that gives meaning to the purpose and the way in which it has come to be defined

1. *Understanding the question to which you seek an answer or wish to explore*
   Establishing the core question that you and the client will explore provides the basis for deciding where the work is headed. This may start with the client's sense of dissatisfaction with the current situation and a desire to move to a new preferred state, but it must also include an agreement that the journey itself is worthwhile. Questioning why it is important to undertake the work is critical in this regard, the reasons for which may include arriving at a new understanding of something that has hitherto seemed incomprehensible, anticipated improvements in current circumstances, or the pursuit of a new vision (Lane, 1973). In developing this understanding we recommend considering the following questions:

- Is a generic intent to explore an area sufficient to justify the journey—that is, an open inquiry that may lead to an unknown destination?
- Does the question need a fixed-point resolution—is there a problem to be solved, an issue to be unraveled, or a solution to be found that is recognized as appropriate by key stakeholders?
- Is it possible in advance to know what an appropriate resolution will look like—that is, might performance criteria be devised?
- Is it impossible (or at least unlikely) to know in advance what an appropriate resolution might look like? For example, something entirely unexpected might emerge as a resolution. Are the principal stakeholders prepared to allow for such a disruptive learning experience?
- Is the question to be explored agreed between stakeholders? Alternatively, do you need to work to obtain such an agreement, or at least partial agreement, sufficient to begin the journey?

2. *Understanding the expectations of key stakeholders*

This entails achieving a sense of clarity about what you, the client and others involved expect to achieve from having undertaken the journey. The objectives of relatives, other professionals, managers, or sponsors who have an investment in the outcome must be considered, as must the extent to which those objectives are congruent with what the client wishes to achieve. Anticipated outputs or results in terms of what the client will experience as different, and any behavioral change the client and others will recognize (e.g., an increased sales turnover following the more effective use of delegation) are critical to establish, as are the anticipated learnings from engaging in the process of change. Thus, in understanding the expectations of key stakeholders, we would recommend the need to identify the following:

- the intention behind this inquiry (i.e., what the practitioner, client, and others involved intend as the aim of the engagement)
- the key stakeholders and the objectives of each party
- the anticipated outputs or results and how these relate to the objectives of each party
- what will be different as a consequence of achieving these outputs or results
- the new learning that it is hoped will occur as a result of undertaking the journey
- the areas in which the stakeholders share the concern or take divergent positions

3. *Clarifying the role that each party wishes to play*

Given the main objectives and anticipated results, it is important to establish the role that each invested party will play. Will the purpose be defined in such a way that the journey occurs solely between practitioner and client? Or will multiple stakeholders contribute to the way in which the journey unfolds? In some examples of psychological practice, it will be sufficient to focus the inquiry on the practitioner–client dyad (as is often the case in executive coaching). In other forms of practice, several parties will wish to contribute or be required to contribute (e.g., when working with a team). In clarifying the role of each stakeholder, it is important to identify:

- those who should play a role in identifying key hypotheses and data gathering
- the role that each party will play
- the investment that each party will be expected to make in terms of time, energy, and resources, and their willingness and ability to do so
- the way in which each party will be initiated into the inquiry to ensure that a sense of ownership is achieved

4. *Appreciating the wider context that gives meaning to the purpose and the way in which it has come to be defined*

Once the practitioner has clarified the question to be explored, the expectations of key stakeholders and the role that each party wishes to play, they are able to make an initial decision to engage on the journey with the client. However, deciding if they are the right person to undertake that journey raises a further set of considerations. In essence, these focus on the context in which the journey will happen and the practitioner's competencies to facilitate that journey. Critical questions here include:

- What does the client need to make it possible for them to tell their story and feel heard? Can you meet that need?
- What type of client purpose is best served by your service context? Do you have a match or mismatch in this particular case?
- What boundaries do you place on the purpose of the work that would require you to refer the client elsewhere? Should the client be referred?
- With whom would you not work and where is the margin of that boundary?
- Have you been able to define a shared concern that fits within the identified boundaries and is best served by working with you rather than another professional or profession?
- Have you identified and understood the position of other key stakeholders who might be beneficiaries (or victims, Checkland, 1989) of the intervention?

Once you have defined the purpose of your service you are in a position to explore the perspective that will inform the journey.

Perspective (what will inform our journey?)

As part of an agreed purpose, it is important to be able to define what you bring to the encounter. The perspective component of the purpose, perspective, process model is concerned with trying to understand those factors that influence the expectations of, and inform the journey for, both practitioner and client. This includes the range of explanations with which your professional knowledge equips you (e.g., explanations grounded within diagnostic and theoretical perspectives), as well as your beliefs about that knowledge, your sense of what you do well in relation to that knowledge and the limits of your competence. However, clients bring perspectives of their own that will inform the work and that must, therefore, be given equal consideration in the enquiry that follows. Engaging with these perspectives gives rise to questions such as:

- What perspectives are informing your approach to the inquiry?
- What perspectives are informing the client's approach to the inquiry?
- What are the beliefs (and prejudices) that you each bring to the encounter?
- Some journeys prescribe and proscribe certain routes of investigation and intervention. How do you ensure coherence between your journey and the journey of the client?
- What do you do to ensure that the client is able to explore their beliefs, knowledge, and competencies within the encounter? Clarity about the perspectives that underpin our work and the ways in which we attempt to engage our clients is vital. It enables us to scrutinize those ideologies, assumptions about human nature, and beliefs relating to the nature of the evidence that is dominant in the current climate and which also infiltrates our work (with or without our knowledge).

From our reading of the literature, contemporary approaches to formulation within the psychological professions are typically informed by at least one of five key perspectives. These are as follows:

1. *Formulation derived from diagnostic classification*
   Formulation derived from, and built around, a particular diagnosis is an approach that has a long history in psychology. The most obvious current influence lies with the *Diagnostic and Statistical Manual of Mental Disorders* (DSM) and the *International Classification of Diseases* (ICD), from which particular formulations of distinct diagnostic profiles can then be constructed. The challenge facing those who use these "medical models" to classify disorders and formulate intervention is to identify how the client's idiosyncratic story can be incorporated. However, in coaching psychology we are frequently faced with diagnosis of client issues based on psychometrics not of their choosing, in which managers or sponsors determine what is wrong or needs to be fixed (what Jarvis, Lane, & Fillery-Travis, 2006, call fixed agenda coaching).

2. *The formulation of the scientist-practitioner*
   The formulation is viewed as an essentially "scientific" or empirical enterprise and works from the assumption that we can identify, define, and test hypotheses to arrive at an accurate and useful explanation of the factors that are influencing the client's behavior. The practitioner using this approach must consider how it is possible to use data from multiple sources to co-construct formulations, and avoid the temptation to determine in advance what frame will fit the client (see Cavanagh & Grant, 2006).

3. *Formulation as a theoretically-driven story*
   Practitioners approaching formulation from a distinct theoretical perspective, whichever theory they prefer, need to identify how their prior assumptions inform the task of formulation. A significant challenge concerns how our professionally sanctioned theories determine where the focus of change is located. The issue of how our theories cause us to notice and overlook particular aspects of the client's story has to be addressed. We can see the benefits that the coherent

use of a particular theory may bring (see, for example, Cavanagh & Palmer, 2007), but need to be aware of the narrowing impact of any one stance (e.g., House & Loewenthal, 2008).

4. *Strategic formulation*

A number of psychologists have adopted "forward-looking" approaches, such as design, systemic, and solution-focused models that challenge traditional models oriented toward problems and analyzing the influencing process. While this is often seen as a departure point between coaching and therapy, the distinction is far from clear (Spinelli, 2008). The strategic approach looks at the future and the strengths people bring to achieve desired states. Here, questions arise about the justifications for, and implications of, using this framework for formulation. What, for example, is left out of the client's account, and what knowledge of potential value held by the client and practitioner is unavailable to use?

5. *Formulation and its role as a means of social control*

Critiques of psychological approaches have pointed to their role as a means of social control in educational, clinical, forensic, and occupational settings. This debate, which ranges from the control of ethnic minorities to the control of dangerous people, presents a critical challenge to the impact of our work on the individual and society. To what extent are we taking into account how our approach to formulation reflects more subtle belief systems and prejudices that penetrate the professions in which we operate, and to what extent as coaches do we operate for the benefit of the powerful (see, for example, Guilfoyle, 2008)?

Each of the five perspectives listed above favors an approach that provides a rationale for choosing between interventions and through which practitioners are able (at least in principle) to demonstrate that strategies based upon their formulations bring about change. To give just one example, the diagnostic perspective assumes that diagnosis (or some forms of psychometrics or 360° evaluations) is a representation of some "real" quality that can be measured.

We believe it is reasonable to assert that regardless of the approach taken, it is important to avoid squeezing the client into the perspective you prefer. The risk is that you lose the essence of the person or context within which your work together is happening. All practitioners, even where specializing in a single model (perspective) applied to a specific goal, must have a means for deciding whether their offer of service makes sense for a particular client. Of course, there can on occasion be good reason for specializing in offering a service from the perspective of one particular theory. As research evidence highlights the contribution of specific ways of working to particular kinds of difficulties, it makes sense that certain models will be used in preference to others and that the process of exploration may be shortened for very good reasons. However, the critical issue is do we know when and why we are foreshortening exploration? Are we aware of what we are not attending to as a result of framing an inquiry in one way rather than another and the implications of this for our clients?

Process (how will we get there?)

Once you have been able to define the purpose of your work and the perspectives that underpin it, then it is possible to structure a process for the work that you and your client intend to undertake. Without the purpose and perspective defined, the process becomes a technical application uninformed by psychology. Manualized interventions can be effective and have provided substantial benefits to many clients. However, we would argue that they are based less on the client's own story, told in their own words, than they are on one view of evidence and one view of science that may lack the means to grasp the innovative. Indeed, the context in which practitioners work is often one that favors improvement over innovation. For example, many current initiatives in public health, education, and social service sectors quite specifically seek to reduce complexity in pursuit of conformance with a protocol in the belief that this is an indication of quality. Is the same pressure appearing in coaching? Quality systems in industry appeal to those who want a reliable product or service rather than an outstanding one (Lane, 2002).

Recent years have witnessed a considerable increase in this type of intervention in both clinical and occupational work where a product, skills training or 360° feedback is offered without understanding the features of the learning journey of the client (Lane, 1993). In such cases, a given procedure is applied to a client based on a minimal definition of some aspect of their behavior (e.g., the linking of a 360° feedback result to a specific intervention). Arguably, the client as a person is absent, as is the psychological investigation necessary to determine what is happening in the client's life that leads them to the point of change. In this context, the key question becomes: What process (including any method or tool) is necessary to ensure that the purpose is met within the constraints of the perspectives available to us?

Process is what happens as you work. It refers to what an outsider, the client, or the sponsor could observe. Process is not of itself a model, although often wrongly described as such, and thus a process for working is confused with the perspectives that underpin it. There are many step-based frameworks available in the literature that provide a structure to work with clients and a series of questions to take clients through the steps. In the clinical arena, these have appeared in numerous treatment protocols as well as the notion of "stepped care" (see Bower & Gilbody, 2005, for a review). In the coaching arena, Stout Rostron (2009) has identified a series of generic question frameworks ranging from 2 to 10 steps. The same abundance can be found in step frameworks for medical, clinical, forensic, and occupational arenas, among others. Stout Rostron, whose own research distinguishes frameworks (architecture for the process) and models (analogies about the world), has identified a range of what she terms "stage frameworks" that can be useful for considering the architectural design of our own approach to process.

These frameworks represent a mere portion of the stage and question frameworks available in one small area of practice. However, although each framework (including those based on protocols) has the potential to add value, significant limitations to thinking and action occur when they are used as a short cut to formulation without reference to the perspective that sits behind it and the purpose for which it has been developed. If we substitute the idea of coaching as a stepwise process for one involving individual formulation we gain a great deal.

THE PURPOSE, PERSPECTIVE, PROCESS MODEL: IMPLICATIONS FOR THE FUTURE

It has been noted elsewhere that coaching research, although increasing, does not yet match the growth in coaching practice (Linley, 2006). There remains a lack of well-defined theory on which coaches base their work (Global Convention on Coaching, 2008) and also a lack of consensus on the distinct skill set of coaching psychologists (Bennett, 2006). Although its role in coaching psychology is yet to be fully determined, we would argue that greater attention to formulation will be a vital contributor to developing systematic approaches to practice in a field that is highly diverse.

In the absence of a full discussion of the benefits and limitations of a formulation-driven approach, the aims of this paper have been to raise awareness of some of the debates and controversies surrounding formulation, and to highlight ways of navigating these debates more successfully for the benefits of ourselves, our clients, and the future development of our profession. It is our view that however we approach the task of making sense of psychological puzzles, we should be able to articulate the choices we are making and to recognize the advantages and disadvantages of choosing one approach over another. Equally, the processes we use at each stage of a psychological inquiry need to be defined or at least be capable of definition. Formulation helps us achieve this particular brand of rigor and should, therefore, feature more clearly in the teaching and practice of coaching psychology, as part of our professional duty of care. We argue that it is important to understand the perspective and purpose that underpin a powerful change process if you are offering yourself as a facilitator of change.

However, in order to add something of substantive value, formulation can and must be consistent with a client partnership framework into which it is possible to incorporate a variety of theoretical positions and the different scales within which the coaching relationship happens. The purpose (where are we going and why?), perspective (what will inform our journey?), process (how will we get there?) model (Corrie & Lane, 2010) is presented as one of a number of possible approaches that might enable us to co-construct more elegant, thought-provoking, and empowering psychological explanations that can accommodate both the available evidence base and the client's personal story.

However, it is only one of a number of possible approaches, so this leaves us with a number of questions:

- If formulation is to feature more widely in the teaching and practice of coaching psychology (which we suggest it should), what other frameworks can be used to enhance the distinct role that coaching psychology might bring?
- In the coaching context, what questions that remain unanswered from the broader literature (such as utility as opposed to accuracy) are important for coaching psychology—are they the same questions or will quite different issues emerge?
- Where might we look for alternative frameworks, especially as coaching psychologists often grow their practice from other disciplines? Should those disciplines provide starting points for the debate? For example, occupational psychologists often use the consultancy cycle (identification of client's needs, analysis, formulation of solution, implementation, and evaluation) and educational psychologists an assessment cycle (see Lane & Corrie, 2006).

We invite readers to contribute to the debate any other outstanding questions that the wider use of the concept of formulation in coaching psychology might generate.

REFERENCES

Adams, M. G. (2004). *Change your questions, change your life.* San Francisco, CA: Berrett-Koehler Publishers.

Bachkirova, T. (2007). Role of coaching psychology in defining boundaries between counselling and coaching. In S. Palmer & A. Whybrow (Eds.), *Handbook of coaching psychology* (pp. 351–366). London: Routledge.

Bennett, J. L. (2006). An agenda for coaching-related research: A challenge for researchers. *Consulting Psychology Journal: Practice and Research, 58*(4), 240–249.

Bieling, P., & Kuyken, W. (2003). Is cognitive case formulation science or science fiction? *Clinical Psychology: Science and Practice, 10*(1), 52–69.

Bower, P., & Gilbody, S. (2005). Stepped care in psychological therapies: Access, effectiveness and efficiency. *British Journal of Psychiatry, 186*, 11–17.

British Psychological Society. (2005). *Subject benchmarks for applied psychology.* Leicester: British Psychological Society.

Butler, G. (1998). Clinical formulation. In A. S. Bellack & M. Hersen (Eds.), *Comprehensive clinical psychology* (Vol. 6, pp. 1–24). Oxford: Pergamon.

Cavanagh, M., & Grant, A. (2006). Coaching psychology and the scientist-practitioner model. In D. A. Lane & S. Corrie (Eds.), *The modern scientist-practitioner. A guide to practice in psychology* (pp. 130–145). Hove, East Sussex: Routledge.

Cavanagh, M., & Palmer, S. (Eds.). (2007). *International Coaching Psychology Review*, [Special issue], (1), 2.

Chadwick, P., Williams, C., & Mackenzie, J. (2003). Impact of case formulation in cognitive behaviour therapy for psychosis. *Behaviour Research and Therapy, 41*, 671–680.

Checkland, P. (1989). An application of soft systems methodology. In S. Rosenhead (Ed.), *Rational analysis for a problematic world* (pp. 101–119). Chichester, West Sussex: Wiley.

Corrie, S., & Lane, D. A. (2006). Constructing stories about clients' needs: Developing skills in formulation. In R. Bor & M. Watts (Eds.), *The trainee handbook. A guide for counselling and psychotherapy trainees* (2nd ed., pp. 68–90). London: Sage.

Corrie, S., & Lane, D. A. (2010). *Constructing stories telling tales: A guide to formulation in applied psychology*. London: Karnac.

Crellin, C. (1998). Origins and social contexts of the term 'formulation' in psychological case-reports. *Clinical Psychology Forum, 112*, 18–28.

Dowie, J. A., & Elstein, A. S. (1988). *Professional judgement. A reader in clinical decision-making*. Newcastle-upon-Tyne: Cambridge University Press.

Drake, D. B. (2009). Using attachment theory in coaching leaders: The search for a coherent narrative. *International Coaching Psychology Review, 4*(1), 49–58.

Duncan, B. L., & Miller, S. D. (2000). *The heroic client: Doing client-directed, outcome-informed therapy*. San Francisco, CA: Jossey-Bass.

Evans, J., & Parry, G. (1996). The impact of reformulation in cognitive-analytic therapy with difficult-to-help clients. *Clinical Psychology and Psychotherapy, 3*, 109–117.

Global Convention on Coaching. (2008). *White paper of the working group on a research agenda for development of the field*. Dublin: GCC.

Grant, A. M., & Cavanagh, M. (2004). Toward a profession of coaching; sixty-five years of progress and challenges for the future. *International Journal of Evidence Based Coaching and Mentoring, 2*, 7–21.

Guilfoyle, M. (2008). CBT's integration into societal networks of power. In R. House & D. Loewenthal (Eds.), *Against and for CBT: Towards a constructive dialogue?* (pp. 233–240). Ross-on-Wye: PCCS Books.

Haarbosch, V., & Newey, I. (2006). Feeling one's way in the dark: Applying the scientist-practitioner model with young people who sexually offend. In D. A. Lane & S. Corrie (Eds.), *The modern scientist-practitioner. A guide to practice in psychology* (pp. 130–145). Hove, East Sussex: Routledge.

Hogarth, R. (1981). Beyond discrete biases: Functional and dysfunctional aspect of judgmental heuristics. *Psychological Bulletin, 90*, 197–217.

House, R., & Loewenthal, D. (2008). *Against and for CBT: Towards a constructive dialogue?* Ross-on-Wye: PCCS Books.

Jarvis, J., Lane, D. A., & Fillery-Travis, A. (2006). *The case for coaching: Making evidence-based decisions on coaching*. Wimbledon, UK: Chartered Institute of Personnel and Development.

Johnstone, L., & Dallos, R. (Eds.). (2006). *Formulation in psychology and psychotherapy: Making sense of people's problems*. Hove, East Sussex: Routledge.

Jopling, A. (2007). The fuzzy space: Exploring the experience of space between psychotherapy and executive coaching. London: Unpublished MSc dissertation, New School of Psychotherapy and Counselling.

Kuyken, W., Padesky, C. A., & Dudley, R. (2009). *Collaborative case conceptualisation: Working effectively with clients in cognitive-behavioural therapy*. New York, NY: Guilford Press.

Lane, D. (2009). Coaching in the UK: An introduction to some key debates. *Coaching: An International Journal of Theory, Research and Practice, 2*(2), 155–166.

Lane, D. A. (1973). Pathology of communication: A pitfall in community health. *Community Health, 5*(3), 157–162.

Lane, D. A. (1990). *The impossible child*. Stoke-on-Trent: Trentham Books.

Lane, D. A. (1993). Counselling psychology in organisations. *Revue Européenne de Psychologie Appliquée, 43*, 41–46.

Lane, D. A. (2002). *The emergent models in coaching*. Cambridge, UK: European Mentoring and Coaching Council.

Lane, D. A. (2006). Brave new world. *Coaching at Work, 1*(7), 17.

Lane, D. A., & Corrie, S. (2006). *The modern scientist-practitioner. A guide to practice in psychology*. Hove, East Sussex: Routledge.

Lane, D. A., Stelter, R., & Stout Rostron, S. (2009). The future of coaching as a profession. In E. Cox, T. Bachkirova, & D. Clutterbuck (Eds.), *The Sage handbook of coaching*. London: Sage.

Lazarus, A. A. (1973). Multimodal behaviour therapy: Treating the 'BASIC-ID'. *The Journal of Nervous and Mental Disease, 156*, 404–411.

Linley, P. A. (2006). Coaching research: Who? What? Where? When? Why? *International Journal of Evidence Based Coaching and Mentoring, 4*(2), 107.

Martell, C. R., Addis, M. E., & Jacobson, N. S. (2001). *Depression in context: Strategies for guided action*. W. W. Norton.

Masson, J. (1990). *Against therapy*. London: Fontana.

Meehl, P. (1954). *Clinical versus statistical prediction: A theoretical analysis and a review of the evidence*. Minneapolis, MN: University of Minnesota Press.

Meehl, P. (1986). Causes and effects of my disturbing little book. *Journal of Personality Assessment, 50*, 370–375.

Olson, P. O. (2008). A review of assumptions in executive coaching. *The Coaching Psychologist, 4*(3), 151–159.

Palmer, S. (2008). Multimodal coaching and its application to the workplace, life and health coaching. *The Coaching Psychologist, 4*(1), 21–29.

Palmer, S., & Szymanska, K. (2007). Cognitive behavioural coaching: An integrative approach. In S. Palmer & A. Whybrow (Eds.), *Handbook of coaching psychology: A guide for practitioners* (pp. 86–117). Hove, East Sussex: Routledge.

Palmer, S., & Whybrow, A. (2007). *Handbook of coaching psychology: A guide for practitioners*. Hove, East Sussex: Routledge.

Schulte, D., Kunzel, R., Pepping, G., & Shulte-Bahrenberg, T. (1992). Tailor-made versus standardised therapy of phobic patients. *Advances in Behaviour Research and Therapy, 14*, 67–92.

Sheath, M. (2010). Case formulation: The dilemmas posed by child sex offenders. In S. Corrie & D. A. Lane (Eds.), *Constructing stories telling tales: A guide to formulation in applied psychology*. London: Karnac.

Smail, D. (1993). *The origins of unhappiness: A new understanding of personal distress*. London: Secker and Warburg.

Smail, D. (1996). *How to survive without psychotherapy*. London: Constable.

Spinelli, E. (2008). Coaching and therapy: Similarities and divergences. *International Coaching Psychology Review, 3*(3), 241–249.

Stewart, L. J., Palmer, S., Wilkin, H., & Kerrin, M. (2008). Towards a model of coaching transfer: Operationalising coaching success and the facilitators and barriers to transfer. *International Coaching Psychology Review, 3*(2), 87–109.

Stout Rostron, S. (2009). *Business coaching international: Transforming individuals and oganisations*. London: Karnac.

Szymanska, K. (2009). The case for assessment and case conceptualisation in coaching. *Coaching Psychology International, 2*(1), 6–9.

Wilson, G. T. (1996). Manual-based treatments: The clinical application of research findings. *Behaviour Research and Therapy, 34*(4), 295–314.

Wilson, G. T. (1997). Treatment manuals in clinical practice. *Behaviour Research and Therapy, 35*(3), 205–210.

Worrell, M. (2010). Existential formulations of therapeutic practice. In S. Corrie & D. A. Lane (Eds.), *Constructing stories telling tales: A guide to formulation in applied psychology*. London: Karnac.

7 An Integrated Model of Goal-Focused Coaching: An Evidence-Based Framework for Teaching and Practice

Anthony M. Grant[1]

Although Coaching is typically thought of as being a goal-focused activity, the use of goals in coaching is somewhat controversial. Common arguments against the use of goal setting in coaching include the propositions that goal setting is an overly-linear process that constricts the coaching conversation and acts as a barrier to working with emergent issues within the complex dynamic system that is the coaching conversation; or that goal setting is associated with coaches cajoling coachees in the blind pursuit of a previously-set but inappropriate goal, leading to "lazy" join-the-dots mechanistic coaching; or even that goals typically focus on issues that may be easy to measure but are of little real importance (see Clutterbuck, 2008, 2010).

Some coaches say that they never use goals in coaching, rather they assert that as coaches their role is to help clients explore their values, clarify their intentions, and then to help them achieve their personal aspirations. Yet others seem to steadfastly avoid

[1] First published as Grant, A. M. (2012). An integrated model of goal-focused coaching: An evidence-based framework for teaching and practice. *International Coaching Psychology Review*, 7(2), 146–165.

using the word "goal," but talk about helping clients chart a course, navigate the waters of life, foster transformational change, or re-author personal narratives. Goal setting has even gained a bad reputation in some sections of the academic psychology press, with some authors asking if goal setting has gone wild, and decrying the supposed overprescription of goal setting (Ordóñez, Schweitzer, Galinsky, & Bazerman, 2009).

While some of these points have merit, goal theory per se has much to offer coaching research and practice. There is a considerable body of literature on goals and goal setting (Locke & Latham, 2002). A search of the database PsycINFO in May 2012 accessing the broader psychological literature base and using the keyword "goals" found over 59,530 citations. Yet the academic literature on the use of goals within the area of executive coaching is far smaller, with the keywords "goals" and "executive coaching" producing only 30 citations. Most of these report on the various uses of goal setting in executive coaching practice (e.g., Bono, Purvanova, Towler, & Peterson, 2009; Lewis-Duarte, 2010; McKenna & Davis, 2009b; Stern, 2009; Sue-Chan, Wood, & Latham, 2012), with a few empirical studies examining how executive coaching facilitates goal attainment (e.g., Benavides, 2009; Burke & Linley, 2007; Freedman & Perry, 2010; Grant, Curtayne, & Burton, 2009; Milare & Yoshida, 2009; Schnell, 2005; Smither, London, Flautt, Vargas, & Kucine, 2003; Turner, 2004).

To date, there have been surprisingly few articles detailing theoretical frameworks that explicitly link goal theory to executive or organizational coaching. Three key examples are Sue-Chan et al.'s (2012) work, which explored the differences between promotion and prevention goals as a foci for coaching, and the role of implicit fixed beliefs about ability and implicit incremental beliefs on coaching outcomes; Gregory, Beck, and Carr's (2011) work, which argues that control theory (in which goals and feedback are two crucial elements) can provide an important framework for coaching; and Grant's (2006) initial work on developing an integrative goal-focused approach to executive coaching.

This chapter draws on and extends previous work (e.g., Grant, 2002, 2006, 2012; Gregory et al., 2011; Locke & Latham, 2002) and, utilizing the goal-setting literature from the behavioral sciences, discusses the concept of goal, presents a definition of goals that can be helpful in coaching practice, and describes a new model of goal-focused coaching and new preliminary research that highlights the vital role that coaches' goal-focused skills play in determining successful coaching outcomes.

SMART GOALS CAN DUMB-DOWN COACHING

Goals and goal constructs have been extensively researched within academic psychology (Moskowitz & Grant, 2009), and sophisticated understandings of goals are evident within the broader psychological literature. This is not the case within the coaching-related literature. From an overview of the coaching literature it appears that many coaches' understanding of goals is limited to acronyms such as SMART (specific, measurable, attractive, realistic, and timeframed), originally delineated by Raia (1965) and that typically goals are equated with being specific, measurable, attainable, relevant, and timeframed action plans (note: the exact delineation of the SMART acronym varies between commentators).

While the ideas represented by the acronym SMART are indeed broadly supported by goal theory (e.g., Locke, 1996), and the acronym SMART may well be useful in some instances in coaching practice, I think that the widespread belief that goals are synony-mous with SMART action plans has done much to stifle the development of a more sophisticated understanding and use of goal theory within the coaching community, and this point has important implications for coaching research, teaching, and practice.

It is worth reflecting that acronyms such as SMART may provide useful mnemonics— mnemonics being memorable surface markers of deeper knowledge structures. However, the use of such mnemonics without a clear understanding of the deeper underpinning knowledge may well result in ill-informed decision making, and the cultivation of inaccu-rate practice doctrines and mythologies about goals and goal theory. Unfortunately, such misconceptions may make it even more difficult for practitioners to engage with the broader knowledge -base. Clearly, there is a case here for coach educators and trainers to draw more extensively on the broader goal theory literature. My hope is that this chapter will make a contribution in encouraging this course of action.

WHAT ARE GOALS?

If this article is to make a meaningful contribution in terms of the more sophisticated use of goals and goal theory in coaching, it is important to develop a clear understanding of the goal construct. The term "goal" is generally understood as being "the purpose toward which an endeavour is directed; an objective or outcome" (see, for example, www.thefreedictionary.com). Although such understandings are adequate for everyday use, a far more nuanced understanding of the goal construct is needed in coaching.

In attempting to develop more sophisticated understandings of the goal construct, a wide range of other terms have been used over the years, including the terms "reference values" (Carver & Scheier, 1998), "self-guides" (Higgins, 1987), "personal strivings" (Emmons, 1992), or "personal projects" (Little, 1993). However, although such broad linguistic repertoires can be useful, the lack of precision in such definitions makes it hard to distinguish between var-ious aspects of the goal construct such as "aims," "objectives," "desires," or "outcomes," and they also fail to capture the true essence of the goal construct.

Goals are defined as playing a key role in transitions from an existing state to a desired state or outcome (e.g., Klinger, 1975; Spence, 2007). As the goal construct has been variously defined in terms of cognitions (Locke, 2000), behavior (Bargh, Gollwitzer, Lee-Chai, Barndollar, & Trötschel, 2001; Warshaw & Davis, 1985), and affect (Pervin, 1982) (for further discussion on these points, see Street, 2002). These three domains are of great relevance for coaching, and an understanding of goals for use in coaching should encompass all three domains.

Cochran and Tesser (1996) present a comprehensive description of a goal as "a cognitive image of an ideal stored in memory for comparison to an actual state; a representation of the future that influences the present; a desire (pleasure and satisfaction are expected from goal success); a source of motivation, an incentive to action" (as cited in Street, 2002, p. 100). This understanding of goals is particularly useful for coaching because, as Street (2002) points out, it emphasizes the role of cognition (in terms of cognitive imagery), as well as affect and behavior, in addition to the notion that the purpose of a goal as "a source of motivation and an incentive." However, while this definition is more sophisticated than notions that situate goals as being synonymous with SMART action plans, it is still somewhat unwieldy as a working definition.

One definition that is succinct, captures the essence of the above issues, and is clearly applicable to coaching is Austin and Vancouver's (1996) notion of goals as being "internal representations of desired states or outcomes" (p. 388).

GOALS AS "INTERNAL REPRESENTATIONS OF DESIRED STATES OR OUTCOMES" ARE CENTRAL TO COACHING

Although there are many definitions of coaching, all capture common themes. The Association for Coaching defines coaching as "A collaborative solution-focused, results-orientated and systematic process in which the coach facilitates the enhancement of work performance, life experience, self-directed learning and personal growth of the coachee" (Association for Coaching, 2012). The International Coach Federation defines coaching as "partnering with clients in a thought-provoking and creative process that inspires them to maximize their personal and professional potential" (International Coach Federation, 2012). The World Association of Business Coaches defines business coaching as a structured conversation designed to "enhance the client's awareness and behaviour so as to achieve business objectives for both the client and their organisation" (World Association of Business Coaches, 2012). The European Mentoring and Coaching Council defines coaching (and mentoring) as "activities within the area of professional and personal development ... to help clients ... see and test alternative ways for improvement of competence, decision making and enhancement of quality of life ... with the purpose of serving the clients to improve their performance or enhance their personal development or both" (European Mentoring and Coaching Council, 2011).

It is clear that there is considerable agreement within professional coaching bodies about the nature of coaching. All of these definitions indicate that the process of coaching is essentially about helping individuals regulate and direct their interpersonal and intrapersonal resources in order to create purposeful and positive change in their personal or business lives. In short, all coaching conversations are either explicitly or implicitly goal-focused and are about helping clients enhance their self-regulatory skills so as to better create purposeful positive change.

GOAL-FOCUSED SELF-REGULATION SITS AT THE CORE OF THE COACHING PROCESS

The core constructs of self-regulation are a series of processes in which the individual sets a goal, develops a plan of action, begins action, monitors their performance, evaluates their performance by comparison to a standard, and based on this evaluation changes their actions to further enhance their performance and better reach their goals (Carver & Scheier, 1998). The coach's role is to facilitate the coachee's movement through the self-regulatory cycle and onward toward goal attainment. Figure 7.1 depicts a generic model of self-regulation (Grant, 2003).

In practice, the steps in the self-regulatory cycle are not clearly separate stages. Each stage overlaps with the next, and the coaching in each stage should aim to facilitate the

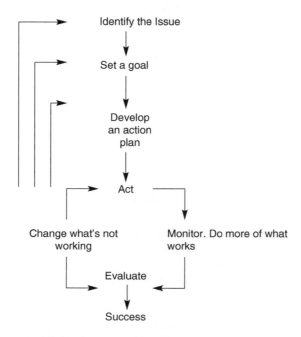

Figure 7.1   *Generic Model of Goal-Directed Self-Regulation*

process of the next. For example, goal setting should be done in such a way as to facilitate the development and implementation of an action plan. The action plan should be designed to motivate the individual into action, and should also incorporate means of monitoring and evaluating performance, thus providing information on which to base follow-up coaching sessions (Grant, 2006). This self-regulatory cycle sits at the core of the coaching process.

Knowing how and when to set goals in coaching, knowing how to gage the client's readiness to engage in a robust and explicitly goal-focused conversation or when to work with more vaguely defined or more abstract goals, are skill sets that distinguish the novice or beginner coach from more advanced or expert practitioners (Grant, 2011; Peterson, 2011). Having a solid understanding of the multifaceted nature of goals is thus important in making the novice–expert shift, and are thus of relevance for both the teaching and practice of coaching. It is to this issue that we now turn.

GOALS ARE NOT MONOLITHIC ENTITIES

If we are to understand coaching through the lens of goal theory, it is important to distinguish between different types of goals. Goals are not monolithic. Indeed, there are over 20 types of goals that can be used in coaching. These include outcome goals, distal and proximal goals, approach and avoidance goals, performance and learning goals, and higher- and lower-order goals, as well as the actual results that the coachee aims to achieve. These distinctions are important because different types of goals impact differently on coachees' performance and their experience of the goal-striving process.

TIMEFRAMING: DISTAL AND PROXIMAL GOALS

The timeframing of goals is an important part of the goal-setting process, and timeframes can influence the coachee's perception of the attainability of the goal (Karniol & Ross, 1996). Distal goals are longer-term goals, and are similar to the vision statements often referred to in business or management literature or the "broad fuzzy vision" referred to in the life-coaching literature (Grant & Greene, 2004). Proximal goals are shorter-term and tend to stimulate more detailed planning than distal goals (Manderlink & Harackiewicz, 1984), and hence are important goals when used in action planning. In essence, the action steps typically derived in coaching sessions are a series of short-term proximal goals. Combining both distal with proximal goals in the coaching and action planning process can lead to enhanced strategy development and better long-term performance (Weldon & Yun, 2000).

OUTCOME GOALS

Many coaching programs focus entirely on setting outcome goals. Such goals tend to be a straightforward statement of some desired outcome (Hudson, 1999); for example, "to increase sales of widgets by 15% in the next three months." This is a useful approach to goal setting, because for individuals who are committed and have the necessary ability and knowledge, outcome goals that are difficult and are specifically and explicitly defined, allow performance to be precisely regulated, and thus often lead to high performance (Locke, 1996). Indeed, many coaching programs focus purely on the setting of specific SMART goals and this approach is supported by some of the goal-setting literature (Locke & Latham, 2002).

However, there are times when overly-specific outcome goals will alienate the coachee, and may actually result in a decline in performance (Winters & Latham, 1996). For individuals who are in a highly deliberative mindset, it may be more useful to purposefully set more abstract or quite vague goals and focus on developing a broad "fuzzy vision" (Grant & Greene, 2004), rather than drilling down into specific details and setting more concrete goals. For individuals at this point in the change process, vague or abstract goals are often perceived as being less threatening and less demanding (Dewck, 1986).

AVOIDANCE AND APPROACH GOALS

Avoidance goals are expressed as a movement away from an undesirable state, for example, "to be less stressed about work." Although this presents a desired outcome, as an avoidance goal it does not provide a specific outcome target or provide enough details from which to define those behaviors that might be most useful during the goal-striving process; there are almost an infinite number of ways one could become "less stressed." In contrast, an approach goal is expressed as a movement toward a specific state or outcome, for example, "to enjoy a fulfilling balance between work demands and personal relaxation," and these can indeed help define appropriate goal-striving behaviors.

Not surprisingly, there are differential effects associated with avoidance or approach goals. Coats, Janoff-Bulman, and Alpert (1996) found that people who tended to set avoidance goals had higher levels of depression and lower levels of well-being. Other studies have found that the long-term pursuit of avoidance goals is associated with decreases in well-being (Elliot, Sheldon, & Church, 1997), and that approach goals are associated with both higher levels of academic performance and increased well-being (Elliot & McGregor, 2001).

PERFORMANCE AND LEARNING GOALS

Performance goals focus on task execution and are typically expressed as being competitive in terms of performing very well on a specific task, receiving positive evaluations from others about one's performance, or outperforming others. Performance goals tend to focus the coachee's attention on issues of personal ability and competence (Gresham, Evans, & Elliott, 1988). An example of a performance goal in executive or workplace coaching might be "to be the very best lawyer in my area of practice." Performance goals can be very powerful motivators, especially where the individual experiences success early in the goal-attainment process.

However, it is not so well known that performance goals can in fact impede performance. This is particularly the case when the task is highly complex or the goal is perceived as very challenging, and where the individual is not skilled or is low in self-efficacy, or where resources are scarce.

Furthermore, in highly competitive situations or when there are very high stakes, performance goals can foster cheating and a reluctance to cooperate with peers, and the corporate and business world is replete with such examples (Midgley, Kaplan, & Middleton, 2001).

In many cases learning goals may better facilitate task performance (Seijts & Latham, 2001). Learning goals (sometimes referred to as mastery goals) focus the coachee's attention on the learning associated with task mastery, rather than on the performance of the task itself. An example of a learning goal in executive or workplace coaching might be "learn how to be the best lawyer in my area of practice." Learning goals tend to be associated with a range of positive cognitive and emotional processes, including perception of a complex task as a positive challenge rather than a threat, greater absorption in the actual task performance (Deci & Ryan, 2002), and enhanced memory and well-being (Linnenbrink, Ryan, & Pintrich, 1999). Furthermore, individual performance can be enhanced in highly complex or challenging situations when team goals are primarily framed as being learning goals, and the use of team-level learning goals can foster enhanced cooperation among team members (Kristof-Brown & Stevens, 2001). One benefit of setting learning goals is that they tend to be associated with higher levels of intrinsic motivation, which in turn is associated with performance (Sarrazin, Vallerand, Guillet, Pelletier, & Cury, 2002).

The differences in the articulation of these different types of goals is more than a matter of mere semantics because the way a goal is expressed has important implications for coachee engagement (Rawsthorne & Elliott, 1999), and coaches need to be attuned to such nuances if they are to work effectively within a goal-focused coaching paradigm.

COMPLEMENTARY AND COMPETING GOALS

Coaches also need to be attuned to the existence of competing or conflicting goals. These occur when the pursuit of one goal interferes with the pursuit of another goal. Some goal conflict is easy to identify, for example in the case of the two goals "to spend more time with my family" and "to put more time into work in order to get a promotion." However, goal conflict may not always be immediately evident. For example, the goal "to get my sales force to sell more products" may be in perceived conflict with the goal "to have a more hands-off leadership style" if the coachee (a sale manager) finds delegation difficult and is used to a more controlling management style in dealing with their sales force (Grant, 2006).

The skill of the coach here is to help the coachee find ways to align seemingly conflicting goals and develop complementary goals, and Sheldon and Kasser (1995) have argued that such congruence is important in facilitating goal attainment and well-being.

UNCONSCIOUS GOALS?

Human beings are goal-orientated organisms. Without goals we could not exist as conscious sentient beings. Indeed, Carver and Scheier (1998) argue that all human behavior is a continual process of moving toward or away from mental goal representations. This is not to say that all goals are consciously held. Under many conditions, we enact complex outcome-directed behaviors even though we may not have consciously set specific goals.

For example, I might be sitting at home writing an article on coaching, and decide to walk to the corner store to buy some biscuits so I can enjoy afternoon tea and biscuits at home. I am aware that I have been sitting at the desk writing for some hours, and that taking a walk will help maintain flexibility in my back, and I am keen to try to prevent the development of back problems as I get older. However, my overarching and consciously set goals are to get biscuits and then make and enjoy some afternoon tea. With this goal in mind, I put on my shoes, take my keys from the shelf, check my wallet, open the door, close and lock the door (to maintain home security and avoid loss of personal property). I then walk to the store, taking care to look both ways as I cross the road (so as to avoid being knocked over by a car or other vehicle), find my way to the biscuit shelf, select my biscuits from a wide range of biscuit products (some of which I don't like), chat with the storekeeper about Saturday's football match, purchase my biscuits, return home safely (opening and then closing the front door behind me), and put the kettle on.

All of these individual actions themselves involve a goal of some kind and all influenced my behavior at any point in time, yet hardly any of these goals were consciously set.

Because goal-states influence our behavior even though we may not have consciously set specific goals, goal theory is particularly helpful in coaching contexts and as a means of understanding human behavior. Goal theory can provide a framework from which to help clients explore, identify, and then change unhelpful implicit goals in order to better facilitate purposeful positive change (for an informed discussion on how actions are initiated even though we are unconscious of the goals to be attained or their motivating effect on our behavior, see Custers & Aarts, 2010).

SELF-CONCORDANT GOALS

Self-concordance is important in goal setting because goals that are self-concordant and in alignment with the coachee's core personal values or developing interests are more likely to be engaging and elicit greater effort. Self-concordance theory (Sheldon & Elliot, 1998) is a useful framework from which to understand and work with the reasons and motivations associated with goal selection and goal strivings.

Self-concordance refers to the degree to which a goal is aligned with an individual's intrinsic interests, motivations, and values. Derived from self-determination theory (Deci & Ryan, 1980) this can be a simple and powerful framework for understanding the link between values and goals. The self-concordance model emphasizes the extent to which an individual perceives their goals as being determined by their authentic self, rather than compelled by external forces.

The self-concordance approach delineates the perceived locus of causality as varying on a continuum from controlled (external) factors to internal (autonomous) facets. A key point here is that it is the individual's perception of the locus of causality that is the key in determining the extent to which the goals are deemed to be self-integrated and where they sit on the external–internal continuum. To maximize the probability of genuinely engaged and motivated action, and to increase the chances of goal satisfaction upon goal attainment, it is important that a coachee's goals are as self-congruent as possible, and coaches may need to play quite an active role in helping their coaches align goals in order to make them personal and congruent. There are at least four factors from this perspective that may influence successful goal alignment (Sheldon & Elliot, 1999).

First, the coachee needs to be able to identify the enduring and authentic from transitory or superficial whims or desires. Second, the coachee needs the personal insight and self-awareness to be able to distinguish between goals that represent their own interests and goals that represent the interests of others (Sheldon, 2002). Given that there are significant individual variations in levels of self-awareness (Church, 1997), some coachees may find this quite challenging. Third, the goal content needs to be expressed in a way that aligns the goals with the coachee's internal needs and values. Fourth, the coach needs to have the ability to recognize when a goal is not self-concordant, and then be able to re-language and reframe the goal so that it does align with the coachee's needs and values.

GOAL HIERARCHIES: LINKING VALUES, GOALS, AND ACTIONS STEPS

The relationships between values, goals, and action steps are generally not well understood in coaching, yet these are central to coaching practice. Goal hierarchy frameworks are one way of making explicit the links between values, goals, and specific action steps, and are also a useful way of operationalizing the notion of goal self-concordance (see Figure 7.2).

Goals can be considered as being ordered hierarchically, with concrete specific goals being subsumed under higher-order and broader, more abstract goals (Chulef, Read, & Walsh, 2001) in a fashion similar to the "Big Five" personality traits (Costa & McCrae, 1992). Hence, higher-order abstract goals such as "to be a great business leader" can be understood as being situated vertically higher than the lower-order and more specific goal "to increase business profits by 25% in the next quarter" and there is some empirical support for this notion (Chulef et al., 2001; Oishi, Schimmack, Diener, & Suh, 1998).

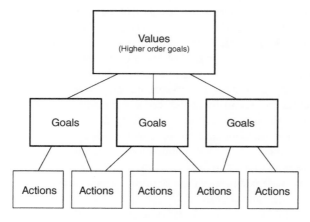

Figure 7.2 *Goal Hierarchy Framework*

Higher-order goals from this perspective equate to values. A valuable model for using goal theory in coaching involves thinking of values as higher-order abstract goals that are superordinate to lower order, more specific goals, which in turn are superordinate to specific action steps. Indeed, visualizing values, goals, and actions as being part of a hierarchy in this way provides coaches with an extremely useful case conceptualization framework for coaching practice, teaching, and supervision, and also makes the notion of values more tangible to many coaching clients.

In using this model in coaching practice, it is important to try to ensure both vertical and horizontal congruency. That is, to ensure that goals are aligned with the client's higher-order values and that any actions designed to operationalize the goals are themselves similarly aligned (vertical alignment). It is also important to try to ensure horizontal alignment so that goals complement, support, and energize each other rather than being, as previously mentioned, being competing or conflicting goals resulting in the pursuit of one goal interfering with the pursuit of another.

Of course, such alignment may not always be possible. Nevertheless, simply drawing the coachee's attention to the existence of any competing or conflicting goals, and highlighting any disconnect between goals and values can provide the coachee with important insights and alternative perspectives, which may in turn facilitate more useful ways of facilitating change.

In addition, in terms of teaching coaching and coaching psychology, this model can be used as a practical template to help student coaches develop a more sophisticated understanding of the goal alignment process.

GOAL NEGLECT

The hierarchical model is also very useful to coaches as it can be used to illustrate the effect of goal neglect. The notion of goal neglect is not well known in the coaching literature but has very useful implications for coaching practice.

The term goal neglect refers to the disregard of a goal or a task requirement despite the fact that it has been understood or is recognized as being important (Duncan, Emslie, Williams, Johnson, & Freer, 1996). In essence, goal neglect occurs when we fail to pay attention to a specific goal of importance, but instead focus our attention on some other goal or task, resulting in a mismatch between the actions required to attain the original goal, and the actions that are actually performed.

Human beings are essentially goal-directed organisms. All our behavior (behavior here is broadly defined to include thoughts, feelings, and physical actions) is shaped and given direction, purpose, and meaning by the goals that we hold, and of course much of our behavior is shaped and directed by goals and values that are outside of our immediate conscious awareness. In relation to the goal hierarchy model, it is the higher-order (or superordinate) values that give direction, meaning, and purpose to the lower-order goals and actions.

When self-regulation at upper levels of a goal hierarchy has been suspended (for example, by not enough attention being paid to those values), the goals at a lower level

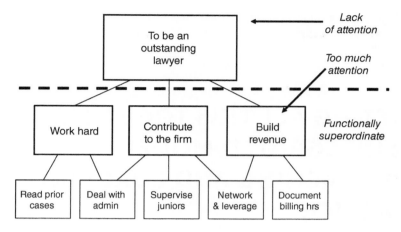

Figure 7.3   *Goal Hierarchy Framework Illustrating the Outcomes of Goal Neglect*

become functionally superordinate in guiding overt behavior and actions (Carver & Scheier, 1998). That is to say that the guidance of the human system defaults (regresses) to lower levels (see Figure 7.3).

This seemingly technical psychological point has important implications for coaching practice. This is because, typically, lower-order goals in the hierarchy are not in themselves relatively meaningful in comparison to the higher-order values. In fact, in many cases the lower-order goals and actions may not be pleasant activities at all. They are often only made palatable by the notion that reaching those lower-order goals activates the higher-order value.

When we fail to consistently pay attention to the higher-order values in the goal hierarchy system, and overly focus on attaining lower-order goals, the lower-order goals become the superordinate or dominant values in the cognitive system, and these lower-order goals are often inherently dissatisfying in themselves.

In the example above, the higher-order value is "to be an outstanding lawyer," and many individuals may enter the law profession with the intention of becoming an outstanding lawyer and ensuring that their clients receive justice. In order to become an outstanding lawyer, they would need to work hard, make explicit contributions to their firm or practice, and build a revenue stream. The attainment of these mid-level goals is in turn made possible by the enactment of lower-order goals and actions such as dealing with administration, documenting billing hours, and so on. However, frequently individuals place their attention on the lower-order goals (e.g., revenue building or documenting billing hours), over time neglecting their higher-order values, and this can easily result in goal dissatisfaction and disengagement.

The hierarchical framework can give coaches and their coachees very useful insights into the psychological mechanics underlying goal dissatisfaction and can be used to develop practical tools and techniques to help clients in the coaching processes. For example, by helping clients purposefully refocus their attention on their higher-order values, we help them reconnect with the meaning inherent in their higher-order values, redefining their goals if necessary, with the result that they may well feel revitalized and reengaged in the enactment of purposeful positive change.

PUTTING ALL THIS TOGETHER: AN INTEGRATED MODEL FOR TEACHING AND COACHING PRACTICE

As can be seen from this brief overview, goal theory has much to offer coaching practice. The question is, how can we organize this information in a way that makes this useful in coaching practice? It may be that goal theory has not been widely taught in coaching programs because there is a vast amount of material on goal and the goal-attainment process, and making explicit links between these bodies of knowledge and then relating this material to coaching practice is not easy.

One way of integrating this diverse body of knowledge is to develop a visual representation or model of the various factors related to goal-focused coaching, and such a model is presented in Figure 7.4. This model may be useful for teaching coaching and the psychology of coaching because it attempts to capture the key aspects involved in the goal-focused approach to coaching and highlights some of the factors that a coach may consider during the coaching engagement.

A word of caution: as with all models this is only a broad representation of some of the possible ways that these factors relate in the coaching process. This model represents my own personal experience and understanding, and I would encourage readers to explore the limitations of this model by reference to their own understanding and coaching experience, and then adapt and extend this model in order to create their own frameworks. Indeed the development of such personalized models can be useful teaching aids.

Examining this model, it can be seen that the coaching process is driven by needs (represented on the left-hand side of the model). Both individual and contextual / organizational factors play important roles in determining the perceived need for coaching, which gives rise to the individual's intentions to participate in the goal selection process. Individual factors at play here include perceived deficits and opportunities, psychological needs, personality characteristics, and available resources (or lack thereof). Contextual or organizational factors include system complexity, social and psychological contracts, rewards and punishments, and available resources (or lack thereof).

The goal selection process is often not straightforward. Even where coaching has been mandated by an organization with specific outcomes in mind, the goal-setting process can be convoluted and complex. The rush to seize and set a specific goal too early in the coaching process is a key derailer—a common trap for the novice. Certainly,

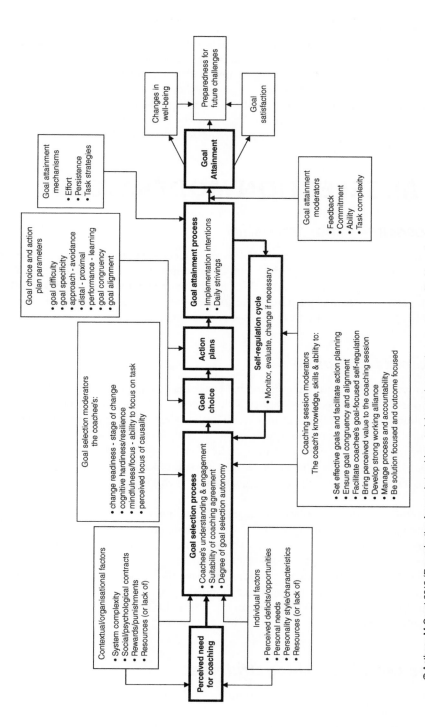

Figure 7.4 *Integrative Model of Coach-Facilitated Goal Attainment*

© Anthony M Grant 2012 (Reproduction for use in teaching, training and research purposes permitted by author)

key issues and broad initial goals should be discussed quite early in the coaching process in order to give the conversation direction and purpose, but the coach should also be paying attention to a number of factors during the goal selection process. These include the coachee's understanding of, and engagement with, the coaching process.

Some coachees arrive for their first coaching session with little idea of the nature of coaching. The suitability and clarity of the coaching agreement (be that formal or informal) will play an important role in engaging the coachee in the goal selection process, as will the degree of autonomy the coachee has in goal selection.

GOAL SELECTION MODERATORS

The coachee's characteristics

There are a number of moderator variables that influence the strength of a relationship between coaching goals and the eventual outcomes of coaching. These include the coachee's ability to focus on the tasks at hand, their ability to adapt in the face of adversity, and the perceived purpose of the goal and the extent to which they feel that they have agency and autonomy in the goal selection process.

Readiness to change

The coachee's readiness to change is another factor that will impact on the goal selection process. Coaches need to consider if the coachee is in the pre-contemplation, preparation, or action stage of change (for a useful reference on applying the transtheoretical model of change to a wide range of goals, see Prochaska, Norcross, & DiClemente, 1994). The transtheoretical model of change posits that change involves transition through a series of identifiable, although somewhat overlapping stages. Five of these stages have direct relevance for goal setting in coaching. These stages are:

1. Pre-contemplation: No intention to change in the foreseeable future.
2. Contemplation: Considering making stages, but have not yet made any changes.
3. Preparation: Increased commitment to change, intend to make changes in the near future and often have started to make small changes.
4. Action: Engaging in the new behaviors, but have made such changes for only a short period of time (usually less than 6 months).
5. Maintenance: Consistently engaging in the new behavior over a period of time (usually 6 months).

Stage-specific coaching strategies

For individuals in the pre-contemplation stage, the general principle is to raise awareness, increasing the amount of information available to the coachee so that they can move forward into action. There are many ways of raising awareness, including multi-rater feedback sales, qualitative feedback, sales or performance data, or other relevant information.

The key characteristic of the contemplation stage is ambivalence; the conjoint holding of two or more conflicting desires, emotions, beliefs, or opinions. The general principle for individuals in the contemplation stage is to help the coachee explore their ambivalence, rather than pushing them into setting a specific goal before they are ready. Setting specific or stretching goals too soon in this stage often results in the coachee disengaging from the goal selection process. In the preparation stage, the coachee is getting ready to make the change. Here the aim is to build a commitment to change. In terms of goals, the coach should be helping the coachee focus on developing a clear vision of the future (abstract goals) and using goals that involve small, easily attainable but consistent action steps. Progress throughout this stage should be monitored closely and new desired behaviors positively reinforced by acknowledging and celebrating the attainment of small subgoals. Clearly, there is a considerable art to the effective use of goals in coaching.

In the action and maintenance stages, the key is to build on past successes and maximize self-directed change, working on using more stretching goals and developing strategies to sustain the change over time.

Coaching session moderators: the coach's skill set

There are a number of other factors related to the coaching session itself that impact on the goal selection process and act as moderator variables. These include the coach's ability to set effective goals and facilitate action planning, and the coach's ability to maximize goal congruency and goal alignment while also facilitating the coachee's goal-focused self-regulation.

The success of the above is also dependent on the coach's ability to bring perceived value to the coaching session and develop a strong working alliance with the coachee (Gray, 2007). All the theoretical knowledge in the world about goal theory is of no importance unless the coach can put this theory into practice, managing the goal-striving process while holding the coachee accountable and being solution-focused and outcome-focused.

GOAL CHOICE AND ACTION PLANNING

Goal choice and action planning are outcomes of the goal selection process. It is important to note that although the model represents these as linear processes, in reality these are iterative, with an amount of back and forth movement between stages. The goal choice and action planning parameters include goal difficulty and goal specificity, whether the goals are approach or avoidance goals, timeframing (distal or proximal), or a performance or learning orientation.

Goal choice is a necessary but not sufficient part of the coaching process—action plans must be developed and enacted. Action planning is the process of developing a systemic means of attaining goals and is particularly important for individuals who have low self-regulatory skills (Kirschenbaum, Humphrey, & Malett, 1981). The coach's role here is to develop the coachee's ability to create a realistic and workable plan of action and to help them define task strategies that will facilitate the goal-striving process while promoting persistence in the face of adversity—in this way clients can enhance their self-regulation abilities and build resilience (Grant et al., 2009).

One key outcome of successful action planning is the coachee's transition from a deliberative mindset to an implementational mindset (Gollwitzer, 1996; Heckhausen & Gollwitzer, 1987). The deliberative mindset is characterized by a weighing of the pros and cons of action and examination of competing goals or courses of action (Carver & Scheier, 1998). The implementational mindset is engaged once the decision to act has been made. This mindset has a determined, focused quality, and is biased in favor of thinking about success rather than failure—factors that are typically associated with higher levels of self-efficacy, self-regulation, and goal attainment (Bandura, 1982).

THE SELF-REGULATION CYCLE, FEEDBACK, AND GOAL SATISFACTION

The monitoring and evaluation of actions and the generation of feedback as the coachee moves through the self-regulation cycle is a vital part of the coaching process. However, self-reflection does not come naturally to many people (Jordan & Troth, 2002), and so the coach may need to find ways to develop action plans that focus on observable, easily monitored behaviors.

What is monitored will, of course, vary according to the coachee's goals and context. Some behaviors will be easier to monitor than others. Exercise or physical activity-based actions can be relatively straightforward to monitor. Intrapersonal issues, interpersonal skills, or communication patterns in the workplace may be more difficult to monitor, and the coach and coachee may have to be quite creative in devising means of monitoring and evaluating these.

Care should be taken to set the kinds of goals that will generate useful feedback, because the right feedback is vital in providing information about how (or if) subsequent goals and associated actions should be modified, and this process, if done well, will eventuate in successful goal attainment (Locke & Latham, 2002). Goals that have been aligned with the coachee's intrinsic interests or personal values are more likely to be personally satisfying when achieved, and the positive emotions associated with such goal satisfaction may well play an important part in priming the coachee for engagement in future challenges (Sheldon, 2002).

SO WHAT? DOES GOAL THEORY MATTER IN PRACTICE?

Although it is clear from the above discussion that goal theory can inform what happens within coaching sessions and also has great relevance for the broader coaching process, the question arises: does goal theory really matter in actual practice? Is the coach's ability to be goal-focused related to coaching outcomes? This is a key question for the further development of evidence-based coaching practice.

A significant body of research within the psychotherapeutic literature holds that the most important factors in determining therapeutic outcomes are the so-called "common factors"—the ability of the therapist to develop a working alliance with the client that embodies trust, warmth, and respect for the client's autonomy (Lampropoulos, 2000). Not surprisingly, it is often assumed in the coaching literature that this is also the case for coaching (McKenna & Davis, 2009a). However, coaching is not therapy. The aims and process of coaching and therapy are different.

To date, there have been few studies that have sought to explore the importance of goals in the coaching relationship, so I was interested to see which aspect of the coaching relationship was more positively related to coaching outcomes—a goal-focused approach to coaching, or the so-called "common factors" associated with the person-centered approach (Grant, 2012). To explore this issue I designed a within-subjects (pre-post) coaching study, in which 49 mature age coachees (males = 12; females = 37; mean age 37.5 years) set personal goals and completed a 10- to 12-week, five-session, solution-focused cognitive-behavioral personal coaching program using the GROW model (goal, reality, options, will)[2] (Whitmore, 1992).

Participants were asked to identify their desired outcome for the coaching relationship (i.e., their goal) and then rated the extent to which they had achieved this outcome on a scale from 0% (*no attainment*) to 100% (*complete attainment*). Psychological health was also assessed using the Depression Anxiety and Stress Scale (DASS-21: Lovibond & Lovibond, 1995) and an 18-item version of Ryff's Psychological Well-being Scales (Ryff & Keyes, 1995). In addition, self-insight was assessed using the Insight subscale of the Self-Reflection and Insight Scale (SRIS; Grant, Franklin, & Langford, 2002).

In order to see which aspect of the coaching relationship was the better predictor of coaching success, two key measures of the coaching relationship were used. The goal-focused aspect of the coaching relationship was measured using an adaptation of the Goal-focused Coaching Skills Questionnaire (GCSQ; Grant & Cavanagh, 2007). Items on this scale include: "The coach was very good at helping me develop clear,

---

[2] The GROW model is a commonly-used way of structuring the coaching conversation by setting a goal for the coaching session, then discussing the reality of the situation, exploring options and finally wrapping up the session by delineating some action steps. Although this may appear to be a simplistic linear process, in fact the GROW model can be used in a sophisticated and iterative fashion, with the conversation cycling back and forth between steps. For an extended discussion on the use of the GROW model, see Grant (2011).

simple and achievable action plans"; "We discussed any failures on my part to complete agreed actions steps"; "The goals we set during coaching were very important to me"; "My coach asked me about progress towards my goals"; "The goals we set were stretching but attainable."

The "common factors" aspect was assessed using an adaptation of Deci and Ryan's (2005) Perceived Autonomy Support Scale (PASS). Items on this scale included: "My coach listened to how I would like to do things"; "I feel that my coach cares about me as a person"; "My coach encouraged me to ask questions"; "I feel that my coach accepts me"; "I felt understood by my coach"; "I feel a lot of trust in my coach."

The coaching program appeared to be effective and successful in helping the clients reach their desired outcomes for the coaching relationship: there was a significant increase in goal attainment following the coaching program (t 1,48 (11.43); $p < .001$), as well as insight (t 1,48 (2.61); $p < .05$), and significant decreases in anxiety (t 1,48 (2.89); $p < .01$) and stress (t1,48 (2.13); $p < .05$). No changes in levels of depression or psychological well-being were observed.

The main area of interest was the relationship between coaching success and the various aspects of the coaching styles used by the coaches. There was a significant correlation between coaching success as defined by the extent to which the client had achieved their desired outcome (i.e., goal attainment) and the GCSQ ($r = .43$; $p < .01$), and there was also a significant correlation between coaching success (as defined by the extent to which the client had achieved their desired outcome) and the PASS ($r = .29$; $p < .05$). Not surprisingly, there was also a significant correlation between the GCSQ and the PASS ($r = .61$; $p < .001$). This suggests that both a goal-focused coaching style and a "common factors" person-centered coaching style contribute to coaching success.

However, and this is a key point, the correlation between coaching success (goal attainment) and the goal-focused coaching style measured by the GCSQ remained significant even when statistically controlling for a "common factors" person-centered coaching style as measured by the PASS ($r = .31$; $p < .05$). It should also be noted that, when controlling for the goal-focused coaching style as measured by the GCSQ, the relationship between the PASS and coaching success (goal attainment) was not significant ($r = .03$; $p = .81$).

These findings strongly suggest that the use of goals in coaching is indeed of practical importance in that the use of a goal-focused coaching style is more effective than a "common factors" person-centered coaching style in the coaching context. This is not to say that a person-centered relationship is not important. Rather, this reminds us that the coaching relationship differs from the counseling or therapeutic relationship, and that coaches need to be mindful of the fact that they are employed by their clients to help make a purposeful and positive change in their personal and professional lives.

CONCLUSION

Coaches may use metaphors such as helping clients chart a course, navigate the waters of life, or re-author their lived narratives, and such metaphors may well be powerful vehicles for facilitating change. Some coaches may prefer to talk about their role in terms of helping clients explore their values, clarify their intentions, or working to help them to achieve their personal aspirations, rather than using the perceived jargon of goal theory. Clearly, coaches should feel entirely free to express themselves and describe their work as they choose. However, at its core coaching is necessarily a goal-directed activity, regardless of linguistic gymnastics or variations in meaning-making perspectives, and goal theory can indeed provide a useful lens through which to understand coaching. The integrative goal-focused model presented here is a multifaceted evidence-based methodology for helping individuals and organizations create and sustain purposeful positive change. Because the coaching conversation is inherently iterative and frequently unpredictable and nonlinear, the key issue for coaches is one of informed flexibility in using goal theory. Goal use in coaching is far more than the simplistic SMART acronym implies.

By understanding the different types of goals and their relationship to the process of change, and through facilitating the goal alignment and goal-pursuit processes, skillful professional coaches can work more efficiently with their clients, helping them to achieve insight and behavioral change that enhances their workplace performance, their professional working lives and, most importantly, their personal well-being and sense of self. After all, that is surely the overarching goal of the coaching enterprise itself.

REFERENCES

Association for Coaching. (2012). Association of Coaching definition of coaching. Retrieved April 19, 2012, from http://www.associationforcoaching.com/about about03.htm

Austin, J. T., & Vancouver, J. B. (1996). Goal constructs in psychology: Structure, process, and content. *Psychological Bulletin, 120*(3), 338–375.

Bandura, A. (1982). Self-efficacy mechanism in human agency. *American Psychologist, 37*(2), 122–147.

Bargh, J. A., Gollwitzer, P. M., Lee-Chai, A., Barndollar, K., & Trötschel, R. (2001). The automated will: Non-conscious activation and pursuit of behavioural goals. *Journal of Personality and Social Psychology, 81*(6), 1014.

Benavides, L. (2009). *The relationship between executive coaching and organisational performance of female executives as a predictor for organisational success.* San Francisco: University of San Francisco.

Bono, J. E., Purvanova, R. K., Towler, A. J., & Peterson, D. B. (2009). A survey of executive coaching practices. *Personnel Psychology, 62*(2), 361–404.

Burke, D., & Linley, P. (2007). Enhancing goal self-concordance through coaching. *International Coaching Psychology Review, 2*(1), 62–69.

Carver, C. S., & Scheier, M. F. (1998). *On the self-regulation of behaviour.* Cambridge, UK: Cambridge University Press.

Chulef, A. S., Read, S. J., & Walsh, D. A. (2001). A hierarchical taxonomy of human goals. *Motivation and Emotion, 25*(3), 191–232.

Church, A. H. (1997). Managerial self-awareness in high-performing individuals in organisations. *Journal of Applied Psychology, 82*(2), 281–292.

Clutterbuck, D. (2008). What's happening in coaching and mentoring? And what is the difference between them? *Development and Learning in Organisations, 22*(4), 8–10.

Clutterbuck, D. (2010). Coaching reflection: The liberated coach. *Coaching: An International Journal of Theory, Research and Practice, 3*(1), 73–81.

Coats, E. J., Janoff-Bulman, R., & Alpert, N. (1996). Approach versus avoidance goals: Differences in self-evaluation and well-being. *Personality and Social Psychology Bulletin, 22*(10), 1057–1067.

Cochran, W., & Tesser, A. (1996). The "What the hell" effect: Some effects of goal proximity and goal framing on performance. In L. Martin & A. Tesser (Eds.), *Striving and feeling* (pp. 99–123). New Jersey: LEA.

Costa, P. T., & McCrae, R. R. (1992). *Revised neo personality inventory and neo five-factor inventory: Professional manual.* Florida: Psychological Assessment Resources.

Custers, R., & Aarts, H. (2010). The unconscious will: How the pursuit of goals operates outside of conscious awareness. *Science, 329*(5987), 47.

Deci, E. L., & Ryan, R. M. (1980). Self-determination theory: When mind mediates behaviour. *Journal of Mind & Behaviour, 1*(1), 33–43.

Deci, E. L., & Ryan, R. M. (Eds.). (2002). *Handbook of self-determination research.* Rochester, NY: University of Rochester Press.

Deci, E.L. & Ryan, R. M. (2005). Perceived Autonomy Support Scale. Retrieved August 5, 2006, from http://www.psych.rochester.edu/SDT/measures needs_scl.html

Dewck, C. S. (1986). Motivational processes affecting learning. *American Psychologist, 41*(10), 1040–1048.

Duncan, J., Emslie, H., Williams, P., Johnson, R., & Freer, C. (1996). Intelligence and the frontal lobe: The organisation of goal-directed behaviour. *Cognitive Psychology, 30*(3), 257–303.

Elliot, A. J., & McGregor, H. A. (2001). A 2 × 2 achievement goal framework. *Journal of Personality and Social Psychology, 80*(3), 501–519.

Elliot, A. J., Sheldon, K. M., & Church, M. A. (1997). Avoidance personal goals and subjective well-being. *Personality and Social Psychology Bulletin, 23*(9), 915–927.

Emmons, R. A. (1992). Abstract versus concrete goals: Personal striving level, physical illness and psychological well-being. *Journal of Personality and Social Psychology, 62*, 292–300.

European Mentoring and Coaching Council. (2011). European Mentoring and Coaching Council code of conduct for coaching and mentoring. Retrieved April 19, 2012, from http://www.emccouncil.org/src/ultimo/models Download/4.pdf

Freedman, A. M., & Perry, J. A. (2010). Executive consulting under pressure: A case study. *Consulting Psychology Journal: Practice and Research, 62*(3), 189–202.

Gollwitzer, P. M. (1996). The volitional benefits of planning. In P. M. Gollwitzer & J. A. Bargh (Eds.), *The Psychology of Action* (pp. 287–312). New York, NY: Guilford Press.

Grant, A. M. (2002). Towards a psychology of coaching: The impact of coaching on metacognition, mental health and goal attainment. Dissertation Abstracts International Section A: Humanities and Social Sciences, 63/12, p.6094 (June).

Grant, A. M. (2003). The impact of life coaching on goal attainment, metacognition and mental health. *Social Behaviour and Personality: An International Journal, 31*(3), 253–264.

Grant, A. M. (2006). An integrative goal-focused approach to executive coaching. In D. Stober & A. M. Grant (Eds.), *Evidence based coaching handbook* (pp. 153–192). New York: Wiley.

Grant, A. M. (2011). Is it time to regrow the GROW model? Issues related to teaching coaching session structures. *The Coaching Psychologist, 7*(2), 118–126.

Grant, A. M. (2012). Making a real difference: Insights and applications from evidence-based coaching research in the lab, workplace and reality TV. Paper presented at the 2nd International Congress of Coaching Psychology, Sydney, Australia.

Grant, A. M., & Cavanagh, M. (2007). The goal-focused coaching skill questionnaire: Preliminarily findings. *Social Behaviour and Personality: An International Journal, 35*(6), 751–760.

Grant, A. M., Curtayne, L., & Burton, G. (2009). Executive coaching enhances goal attainment, resilience and workplace well-being: A randomised controlled study. *The Journal of Positive Psychology, 4*(5), 396–407.

Grant, A. M., Franklin, J., & Langford, P. (2002). The self-reflection and insight scale: A new measure of private self-consciousness. *Social Behaviour and Personality, 30*(8), 821–836.

Grant, A. M., & Greene, J. (2004). *Coach yourself: Make real changes in your life* (2nd ed.). Harlow, UK: Pearson Education.

Gray, D. E. (2007). Towards a systemic model of coaching supervision: Some lessons from psychotherapeutic and counselling models. *Australian Psychologist, 42*(4), 300–309.

Gregory, J. B., Beck, J. W., & Carr, A. E. (2011). Goals, feedback, and self-regulation: Control theory as a natural framework for executive coaching. *Consulting Psychology Journal: Practice and Research, 63*(1), 26.

Gresham, F. M., Evans, S., & Elliott, S. N. (1988). Academic and social self-efficacy scale: Development and initial validation. *Journal of Psychoeducational Assessment, 6*(2), 125–138.

Heckhausen, H., & Gollwitzer, P. M. (1987). Thought contents and cognitive functioning in motivational versus volitional states of mind. *Motivation and Emotion, 11*(2), 101–120.

Higgins, E. (1987). Self-discrepancy: A theory relating self and affect. *Psychological Review, 94,* 319–340.

Hudson, F. M. (1999). *The handbook of coaching.* San Francisco: Jossey-Bass.

International Coach Federation. (2012). International Coach Federation code of ethics. Retrieved April 19, 2012, from http://www.coachfederation.org/ethics

Jordan, P. J., & Troth, A. C. (2002). Emotional intelligence and conflict resolution: Implications for human resource development. *Advances in Developing Human Resources, 4*(1), 62–79.

Karniol, R., & Ross, M. (1996). The motivational impact of temporal focus: Thinking about the future and the past. *Annual Review of Psychology, 47,* 593–620.

Kirschenbaum, D. S., Humphrey, L. L., & Malett, S. D. (1981). Specificity of planning in adult self-control: An applied investigation. *Journal of Personality and Social Psychology, 40*(5), 941–950.

Klinger, E. (1975). Consequences of commitment to and disengagement from incentives. *Psychological Review, 82,* 1–25.

Kristof-Brown, A. L., & Stevens, C. K. (2001). Goal congruence in project teams: Does the fit between members' personal mastery and performance goals matter? *Journal of Applied Psychology, 86*(6), 1083–1095.

Lampropoulos, G. K. (2000). Definitional and research issues in the common factors approach to psychotherapy integration: Misconceptions, clarifications, and proposals. *Journal of Psychotherapy Integration, 10*(4), 415–438.

Lewis-Duarte, M. (2010). *Executive coaching: A study of coaches' use of influence tactics.* Claremont, CA: Claremont Graduate University.

Linnenbrink, E. A., Ryan, A. M., & Pintrich, P. R. (1999). The role of goals and affect in working memory functioning. *Learning and Individual Differences, 11*(2), 213–230.

Little, B. R. (1993). Personal projects: A rationale and method for investigation. *Environment and Behaviour, 15,* 273–309.

Locke, E. (2000). Motivation, cognition, and action: An analysis of studies of task goals and knowledge. *Applied Psychology, 49*(3), 408–429.

Locke, E. A. (1996). Motivation through conscious goal setting. *Applied and Preventive Psychology, 5*(2), 117–124.

Locke, E. A., & Latham, G. P. (2002). Building a practically useful theory of goal setting and task motivation. *American Psychologist, 57*(9), 705–717.

Lovibond, P. F., & Lovibond, S. H. (1995). The structure of negative emotional states: Comparison of the Depression Anxiety Stress Scales (DASS) with the Beck Depression and Anxiety Inventories. *Behaviour research and therapy, 33*(3), 335–343.

Manderlink, G., & Harackiewicz, J. M. (1984). Proximal versus distal goal setting and intrinsic motivation. *Journal of Personality and Social Psychology, 47*(4), 918–928.

McKenna, D., & Davis, S. L. (2009a). Hidden in plain sight: The active ingredients of executive coaching. *Industrial and Organisational Psychology: Perspectives on Science and Practice, 2*(3), 244–260.

McKenna, D., & Davis, S. L. (2009b). What is the active ingredients equation for success in executive coaching? *Industrial and Organisational Psychology: Perspectives on Science and Practice, 2*(3), 297–304.

Midgley, C., Kaplan, A., & Middleton, M. (2001). Performance-approach goals: Good for what, for whom, under what circumstances, and at what cost? *Journal of Educational Psychology, 93*(1), 77–86.

Milare, S. A., & Yoshida, E. M. P. (2009). Brief intervention in organisations: Change in executive coaching. *Psicologia em Estudo, 14*(4), 717–727.

Moskowitz, G. B., & Grant, H. (Eds.). (2009). *The psychology of goals.* New York: The Guilford Press.

Oishi, S., Schimmack, U., Diener, E., & Suh, E. M. (1998). The measurement of values and individualism-collectivism. *Personality and Social Psychology Bulletin, 24*(11), 1177–1189.

Ordóñez, L. D., Schweitzer, M. E., Galinsky, A. D. & Bazerman, M. H. (2009). Goals gone wild: The systematic side effects of over-prescribing goal setting. Academy of Management Perspectives, February, 6–16.

Pervin, L. A. (1982). The stasis and flow of behaviour: Toward a theory of goals. In M. M. Page (Ed.), *Nebraska symposium on motivation* (pp. 1–53). Nebraska: Lincoln.

Peterson, D. B. (2011). Good to great coaching. In G. Hernez-Broome & L. A. Boyce (Eds.), *Advancing executive coaching: Setting the course of successful leadership coaching* (pp. 83–102). San Francisco: Jossey-Bass.

Prochaska, J. O., Norcross, J. C., & DiClemente, C. C. (1994). *Changing for good.* New York: Avon Books.

Raia, A. P. (1965). Goal setting and self-control: An empirical study. *Journal of Management Studies, 2*(1), 34–53.

Rawsthorne, L. J., & Elliott, A. J. (1999). Achievement goals and intrinsic motivation: A meta-analytic review. *Personality and Social Psychology Review, 3*(4), 326–344.

Ryff, C. D., & Keyes, C. L. M. (1995). The structure of psychological well-being revisited. *Journal of Personality and Social Psychology, 69*(4), 719–727.

Sarrazin, P., Vallerand, R., Guillet, E., Pelletier, L., & Cury, F. (2002). Motivation and dropout in female handballers: A 21-month prospective study. *European Journal of Social Psychology, 32*(3), 395–418.

Schnell, E. R. (2005). A case study of executive coaching as a support mechanism during organisational growth and evolution. *Consulting Psychology Journal: Practice and Research, 57*(1), 41–56.

Seijts, G. H., & Latham, G. P. (2001). The effect of distal learning, outcome, and proximal goals on a moderately complex task. *Journal of Organisational Behaviour, 22*(3), 291–307.

Sheldon, K. M. (2002). The self-concordance model of healthy goal striving: When personal goals correctly represent the person. In E. L. Deci & R. M. Ryan (Eds.), *Handbook of self-determination research* (pp. 65–86). Rochester, NY: University of Rochester Press.

Sheldon, K. M., & Elliot, A. J. (1998). Not all personal goals are personal: Comparing autonomous and controlled reasons for goals as predictors of effort and attainment. *Personality and Social Psychology Bulletin, 24*(5), 546–557.

Sheldon, K. M., & Elliot, A. J. (1999). Goal striving, need satisfaction and longitudinal well-being: The self-concordance model. *Journal of Personality and Social Psychology, 76*(3), 482–497.

Sheldon, K. M., & Kasser, T. (1995). Coherence and congruence: Two aspects of personality integration. *Journal of Personality and Social Psychology, 68*(3), 531–543.

Smither, J. W., London, M., Flautt, R., Vargas, Y., & Kucine, I. (2003). Can working with an executive coach improve multisource feedback ratings over time? A quasi-experimental field study. *Personnel Psychology, 56*(1), 23–44.

Spence, G. B. (2007). Gas-powered coaching: Goal attainment scaling and its use in coaching research and practice. *International Coaching Psychology Review, 2*(2), 155–167.

Stern, L. R. (2009). Challenging some basic assumptions about psychology and executive coaching: Who knows best, who is the client, and what are the goals of executive coaching? *Industrial and Organisational Psychology: Perspectives on Science and Practice, 2*(3), 268–271.

Street, H. (2002). Exploring relationships between goal setting, goal pursuit and depression: A review. *Australian Psychologist, 37*(2), 95–103.

Sue-Chan, C., Wood, R. E., & Latham, G. P. (2012). Effect of a coach's regulatory focus and an individual's implicit person theory on individual performance. *Journal of Management, 38*(3), 809–835.

Turner, C. A. (2004). *Executive coaching: The perception of executive coaching from the executive's perspective.* Malibu, CA: Pepperdine University.

Warshaw, P. R., & Davis, F. D. (1985). The accuracy of behavioural intention versus behavioural expectation for predicting behavioural goals. *The Journal of Psychology, 119*(6), 599–602.

Weldon, E., & Yun, S. (2000). The effects of proximal and distal goals on goal level, strategy development, and group performance. *The Journal of Applied Behavioral Science, 36*(3), 336–344.

Whitmore, J. (1992). *Coaching for performance.* London: Nicholas Brealey.

Winters, D., & Latham, G. P. (1996). The effect of learning versus outcome goals on a simple versus a complex task. *Group & Organisation Management, 21*(2), 236–250.

Worldwide Association of Business Coaches. (2012). Worldwide Association of Business Coaches definition of business coaching. Retrieved April 19, 2012, from http://www.wabccoaches.com/includes/popups definition.html

Section III

Insights from Qualitative Coaching Psychology Research

Jonathan Passmore and David Tee

Coaching research review papers at the start of the twenty-first century typically contrast the growth in coaching as an organizational developmental practice with the relatively low level of research and evidence accompanying that growth (see Feldman & Lankau, 2005; Kampa-Kokesch & Anderson, 2001). Researchers called for an increase in the amount of empirical research, without which they claimed coaching psychology would remain a "protoscience" (Grant & Cavanagh, 2007; Passmore & Fillery-Travis, 2011). Adjectives such as "solid" or "highest quality" were used to differentiate quantitative research from any other design, with Furnham (personal correspondence, cited in Grant & Cavanagh, 2007) likening coaching to "alternative medicine," until it was able to demonstrate through empirical evidence its value.

Yet, there may have been an understandable reason for the absence of large numbers of empirical studies in the early years of coaching psychology. Passmore and Fillery-Travis (2011) detailed a three-phase model for new domains of inquiry, stating the maturation process that coaching psychology was undergoing typified that experienced in other research areas. The initial phase, where the phenomenon is explored and practitioner experiences shared, is followed by a second phase. Here, Passmore and Fillery-Travis stated:

> The initial part of this phase is often marked with case studies and small qualitative research. This gradually shifts towards theory building and randomised controlled trial studies with large sample sizes, and finally to meta-analysis. (p. 71)

In this narrative, the prevalence of qualitative research in the early years of coaching psychology was associated with, and arguably a necessary part of, the emergence of this field of knowledge, rather than an inferior research approach that needed to be replaced if coaching psychology were to be taken seriously.

The intervening years have seen Passmore and Fillery-Travis's predicted increase in the number of empirical studies within the field take place, to the point where systematic reviews and meta-analyses are now being produced (see the introduction to Section IV). In this same time period, voices within the coaching psychology research community have argued for the distinct contribution that qualitative studies can make to advancing our understanding: it is now recast as "other" rather than "lesser."

For instance, Grant (2016a), in considering what should constitute evidence, suggests that qualitative designs, such as case studies, have unique and valuable characteristics that meta-analyses and randomized controlled trials may not provide. One justification for this viewpoint may be that some legitimate areas of inquiry related to the coaching experience are not appropriate for reductivist approaches: examples include the phenomenon of peak experiences during coaching (Honsová & Jarošová, 2018) or any critical moments experienced by clients during coaching sessions (de Haan & Nieß, 2015—included in this section). Axiological assumptions of coaching as a value-laden endeavor can also be seen in Stelter's (2007) argument that social meaning-making is a central concept within coaching, and one that should therefore be studied from a phenomenological paradigm.

With the very early years of coaching psychology as a discipline now behind us, qualitative research is accepted as both inherently worthwhile and also complementary to positivist studies. Tooth et al. (2013), in determining the effectiveness of a coaching survey instrument, conclude that certain outcomes of coaching (they cite increases in client self-efficacy as an example), can indeed be quantified. However, their conclusion about how the impact of coaching should be determined is more nuanced:

> Coaching survey data can provide valuable insights into patterns and themes in coaching and can inform coaching practice, but there are many other aspects of the coaching experience that do not lend themselves to measurement. (p. 149)

Kilburg (2016) goes further in asserting the relevance of quantitative research to coaching. Arguing against Furnham's call for more empirical data, Kilburg states that the biomedical approach, likening executive clients to patients with common symptoms and diagnoses, is not appropriate and that coaching operates in a much more complex and dynamic setting that does not lend itself to such research designs.

Therefore, qualitative studies have a distinct contribution to make in advancing coaching research, theory, and practice. This section features papers with a variety of qualitative research methods, from interpretative phenomenological analysis to grounded theory, and a range of topics, from coaching supervision to how coaches work with emotion. The papers also demonstrate the role that qualitative studies play, such as generating theories and conceptual frameworks, highlighting future research avenues, shedding light on processes and perceptions rather than just outcomes and informing real-world decisions (examples in this section include scoping coaching supervisor-specific training and indicating where university-situated coaching might create value for students).

Hopefully, with coaching psychology's growing pains as a field of scholarly research in the past, and with the variety of benefits that qualitative studies can generate, Grant (2016b, p. 318) states the time has come to push aside "nefarious dichotomies that posit one [approach] as better than the other." To have a full understanding of coaching as a phenomenon, and to steal from Grant's article title, "counting numbers is not enough."

REFERENCES

Feldman, D. C., & Lankau, M. J. (2005). Executive coaching: A review and agenda for future research. *Journal of Management, 31*(6), 829–848.

Grant, A. M. (2016a). What constitutes evidence-based coaching? A two-by-two framework for distinguishing strong from weak evidence for coaching. *International Journal of Evidence-Based Coaching and Mentoring, 14*(1), 74–85.

Grant, A. M. (2016b). The contribution of qualitative research to coaching psychology: Counting numbers is not enough, qualitative counts too. *Journal of Positive Psychology, 12*(3), 317–318.

Grant, A. M., & Cavanagh, M. J. (2007). Evidence-based coaching: Flourishing or languishing? *Australian Psychologist, 42*(4), 239–254.

de Haan, E., & Nieß, C. (2015). Differences between critical moments for clients, coaches and sponsors of coaching. *International Coaching Psychology Review, 10*(1), 38–57.

Honsová, P., & Jarošová, E. (2018). Peak coaching experiences. *Coaching: An International Journal of Theory, Research and Practice, 12*(1), 3–14.

Kampa-Kokesch, S., & Anderson, M. Z. (2001). Executive coaching: A comprehensive review of the literature. *Consulting Psychology Journal: Practice & Research, 53*(4), 205–228.

Kilburg, R. R. (2016). The development of human expertise: Toward a model for the 21st century practice of coaching, consulting, and general applied psychology. *Consulting Psychology Journal: Practice and Research, 68*(2), 177–187.

Passmore, J., & Fillery-Travis, A. (2011). A critical review of executive coaching research: A decade of progress and what's to come. *Coaching: An International Journal of Theory, Research and Practice, 4*(2), 70–88.

Stelter, R. (2007). Coaching: A process of personal and social meaning making. *International Coaching Psychology Review, 2*(2), 191–201.

Tooth, J., Nielsen, S., & Armstrong, H. (2013). Coaching effectiveness survey instruments: Taking stock of measuring the immeasurable. *Coaching: An International Journal of Theory, Research and Practice, 6*(2), 137–151.

8 Super-vision, Extra-vision, or Blind Faith?: A Grounded Theory Study of the Efficacy of Coaching Supervision

Jonathan Passmore and Susan McGoldrick[1]

Coaching is fast gaining popularity and credibility and the coaching sector as a whole continues to experience significant growth. A recent estimate put this at $2 billion worldwide (Fillery-Travis & Lane, 2006). Given this figure, the UK coaching market may be estimated to be worth approximately £150 million per annum, although such estimates are extremely difficult to substantiate given the diversity of coaching practice, and with the growth of in-house coaching. The reality is that coaching has moved from a niche to a core personal development activity within the UK and the United States. This growth has been supported by a growth in the number of coaching professional bodies, such as the British Psychological Society's Special Group in Coaching Psychology (SGCP), which have acted as catalysts, stimulating research and bringing together professionals to share knowledge. This has been matched by a growth in coach training provision, from short courses over a few days or a week to the more recent development of longer accredited courses, and full-time Masters programs. Alongside this growth in coaching practice, there has been a growth in the advocacy for coaching supervision (Hawkins & Schwenk, 2006; Hawkins & Smith, 2006). This has been largely supported by the emerging professional bodies, such as Association for Coaching (AC), European Coaching & Mentoring Council (EMCC), and Association for Professional Executive Coaches & Supervisors (APECS). It has been argued

---

[1] First published as Passmore, J. & McGoldrick, S. (2009). Super-vision, extra-vision or blind faith? A grounded theory study of the efficacy of coaching supervision. *International Coaching Psychology Review*, 4, 143–159.

that supervision is an important part of maintaining professional standards. Such calls have, however, been made largely without reference to any clear evidence that supervision contributes to enhanced coaching practice.

Coaching has turned to counseling practice for ideas. The models that have been discussed (Carroll, 2006; Hawkins, 2006; Hawkins & Smith, 2006) have their roots in the counseling and social work professional practice (Hawkins & Shohet, 1989; Inskipp & Proctor, 1995). Are these models appropriate to the work of business coaches? More importantly, is supervision the most effective model to manage the challenges and continuous professional development of the coaching practitioner? In light of this, there is a need to review the efficacy of coaching supervision.

WHAT IS SUPERVISION?

The word "supervision" has many meanings. In common terms, it means "to oversee and direct" (Oxford Dictionary, 2008). However, there is more to supervision than merely overseeing another's work. Some writers talk about "Super-vision" (Houston, 1995), while others refer to the term "Extra-vision" (Inskipp & Proctor, 1995) in the context of nursing, social work, and therapy, implying that such support and guidance is outside of the line management relationship. Carroll notes that while the term "super" in the word "supervision" can imply that supervisors monitor supervisees from a superior position, in practice this should not be the case (Carroll, 1996).

SUPERVISION IN COACHING

In therapy and the helping professions, supervision is the dominant model for reflective practice. This contrasts with much of management practice where a hierarchical model of management has been dominant; supplemented, more recently, with 360° appraisal and competency frameworks.

Practitioners, while arguing in favor of supervision, have also tried to define the concept within coaching. Bluckert (2005) argues:

> Supervision sessions are a place for the coach to reflect on the work they are undertaking, with another more experienced coach. It has the dual purpose of supporting the continued learning and development of the coach, as well as giving a degree of protection to the person being coached.

Other writers, such as Bachkirova, Stevens and Willis (2005) suggest:

> Coaching Supervision is a formal process of professional support, which ensures continuing development of the coach and effectiveness of his/her coaching practice through interactive reflection, interpretative evaluation and the sharing of expertise. (Bachkirova et al., 2005)

THE GROWTH OF COACHING SUPERVISION IN PRACTICE

The volume of coaching practice, and by implication the number of coaching practitioners, has grown rapidly over the past decade. Following this, there has been a growth in the advocacy for coaching supervision within the UK.

Downey (2003) noted that very few coaches had any supervision but it is a "vital ingredient" in effective coaching. More recently Hawkins and Schwenk (2006) noted, from their research of UK practice, that 88% of organizers of coaching and 86% of coaches believe that coaches should have continuous and regular supervision. However, in comparison only 44% of coaches receive continuous and regular supervision. Drawing on our own personal experience, we would question the representative nature of the sample used in the study. Our own experience in the UK coaching sector, based on coach training, coaching networks in the SGCP and Association for Coaching, suggests the figure may actually be below 25%. Such figures, however, are difficult to establish and vary depending on the sample. What is clear is that a wide range exists with lower participation found among sole practitioners and those undertaking coaching work as a supplementary activity and higher participation among coaches within organizations and those seeing coaching as a professional activity in their work portfolio.

Coaches' reasons for not seeking supervision include that it is not required by organizations, it is too expensive (17%), or they can't find a supervisor (17%) (Hawkins & Smith, 2006). For organizations, the reasons for not providing supervision include that it is too expensive (19%) and they can't find supervisors (13%). While not acknowledged, we believe one explanation for this gap between expressed desire and actual practice is the lack of evidence as to whether supervision is an effective tool for enhancing coaching practice. A second reason may be the lack of understanding of how supervision can enhance practice. However, further research, with a wider sample, is needed to explore these issues, possibly through collaboration with one or more of the coaching membership bodies.

In the absence of a body of good coaching supervision research or theories, a limited amount of coaching specific training available, and inadequate numbers of trained coaching supervisors, many coaches have turned to counselors, psychologists, and psychotherapists for supervision (Hawkins & Smith, 2006). Given the differences between coaching and therapy, which have been widely discussed elsewhere (Palmer & Whybrow, 2007; Passmore, 2006), are these individuals the most appropriate to deliver coaching supervision? These differences include the more future-focused nature of coaching, the management of different boundaries when working in organizational settings, and in organizational setting understanding the dynamics and complexity of organizational life.

Given the lack of research on coaching supervision, this paper explores the perceived benefits of the supervision process and builds a conceptual framework for coaching supervision that could be subjected to further testing. In this respect, a grounded theory methodology was selected (Glaser & Strauss, 1967; Strauss & Corbin, 1990).

METHOD

Participants

This study involved a total of six participants in a two-part process. The first stage involved an observational study of a coaching supervision session. The second stage involved recorded interviews with six participants including the two participants from the observed session.

In the observed supervision session the two participants were white British, aged 40–55, one was female, the other male. The first participant (S1) (supervisor) had more than 20 years' experience of working in supervision, initially in therapy and more recently in coaching. The second participant (C1) (coach) was a trained coach, with approximately 18 months' post-qualification experience. She also worked as a senior HR manager and had more than 20 years' experience in HR and people management.

The second part of the study involved semi-structured interviews with six participants. Five of the participants were white British and one was black British/Caribbean. The ages of the participants ranged from 30 to 65. The two coaches (C2 and C3) were both female and were full-time self-employed coaches who had been coaching for more than 3 years and were receiving formal coaching supervision. One coach did most of her coaching in the corporate environment (mainly private sector), while the other coach was mostly involved with coaching leaders and managers in the further education sector. The supervisors (S2 and S3) were both male, experienced executive coaches and trained coaching supervisors who offered regular coaching supervision. Both supervisors had been practicing for more than 10 years.

Data collection

The study was designed as a two-phase data collection process. The first phase involved the observation and aimed to offer an understanding of the supervision process. This was then used to develop and refine the interview questions. The second phase, involving semi-structured interviews with six participants, was the data collection phase.

The observation session of a coaching supervision meeting was recorded. This took place in a private interview room equipped with two-way mirrors and audio and video recording equipment.

In the second phase of data collection, semi-structured interviews were undertaken with the six coaches and coaching supervisors. The interviews were focused on participants' experiences of the coaching supervision process. The interviews were recorded and transcribed using a revised version of the Jefferson framework (Jefferson, 1985; O'Connell & Knowal, 1996). Both phases were conducted prior to detailed engagement in the literature, as consistent with the grounded theory method (Glaser & Strauss, 1967), as adapted by Strauss and Corbin (Strauss & Corbin, 1990).

Each participant provided informed consent for their session to be recorded. As part of the process, the opportunity was offered at the end for the data to be destroyed. In all cases, participants agreed that the data could be used for the research study.

Data analysis

Following the transcription of the first two interviews, margin memos and noting was used to identify themes. An initial set of themes was identified. This was used to further explore issues during the second set of four interviews. An iterative process was employed during the analysis as the researchers sought saturation of the data in the development of the descriptive codes. Following this process, the material was set to one side and after a period further work was undertaken to develop the conceptual categories that were used for the framework. The conceptual codes were critically reviewed by the researchers in the production of the final version.

RESULTS

The results of the analysis are reported using the main descriptive categories as headings and the subcategories that make them up as subheadings. For ease of reference, the main categories and subcategories are listed in Table 8.1. In this paper, we have selected quotes that illustrate a theme or topic, but other statements were also made in relation to these codes.

Influencing factors

The data suggested a number of factors influenced the supervision process. These include expectations, attitudes (of the coach), and the preceding "need" for supervision.

The first influencing factor was the expectations of the coach. These played an important role in the personal experience of supervision, and its ultimate success or failure. It is interesting to note that none of the coaches had any understanding or expectations of coaching supervision before they started it.

> when I started supervision I didn't really understand what it was all about … I s'pose I just thought it was just like having a different level of coaching experience, but of course I discovered it is a whole lot more than that. (C2: 7–10)

Once the coaches were receiving regular supervision, their expectations were varied and included expectations of the supervisor and of the environment/relationship.

Table 8.1 *Table of Categories, Subcategories, and Themes*

Main categories	Subcategories	Themes
1. Influencing factors	Expectations (coach/supervisor)	Of supervisor Of relationship/environment Of coach
	Coach attitudes to supervision	Proactive and positive Seeking out issues Opportunity to reflect Faith in supervision
	Need for supervision	Coach aware of issue The hidden need
2. Process of supervision	Coach's role	Active and primary role Open and present Critical appreciation
	Supervisor's role	Facilitator Support and challenge Quality feedback Knowledge over time Awareness of coach body language
	Properties of supervision	Frequency Type Consistency of supervisor
	Relationship and environment	Safe Role clarity and equality Develops over time Working together Coach–supervisor "fit"
	Group supervision	Learning from others Experimentation Objectivity
3. Necessary conditions	Supervisor	Trained coaching supervisors
	Knowledge, skills, and experience	Contextual knowledge Supervision informs practice
	Ethical practice	Ethical function of supervision Ethics training for supervisors
4. Limiting factors	Limited understanding of supervision	
	Bringing issues to supervision	
	Coach–supervisor relationship	
	Supervisor behavior	Too directive
	Coach behavior	Reliant on supervisor's opinion Impression management
5. Supervision potential	Individual	Enhanced capacity to challenge Qualitative function of supervision CPD
	Organizational	Opportunity for organizational learning and change
6. Outcomes	Individual	Difficult to quantify Raised awareness Confidence in coaching Perseverance in coaching Sense of belonging Professionalism "Internal supervisor"

Having engaged in supervision for a period of time, the coaches' expectations of the process increased. They expected their supervisor to be trained and have a specific set of skills and experience.

> I guess, having somebody who's been trained in supervision and is following a process and model … not just a coach who's decided to call it supervision and raise their game sort of thing, but a different skill set or set of processes. (C2:136–138)

The coaches indicated a desire for supervisors to stimulate their thinking and offer them a different perspective on their practice. Coaches expected to feel safe and comfortable in their supervision environment, and able to discuss their issues freely and openly without being judged. Particularly important was the guarantee of confidentiality in supervision and freedom to discuss important issues.

Supervisors also held expectations of their coaches. There was an expectation that coaches should be open to constructive challenge and open to supervision in general and be "present" in the supervisory relationship. One supervisor said that the coach plays an active and primary role in supervision and that "it is the coach that makes it work" (S2: 13). The coach has a responsibility in the supervisor's eyes to be willing to stand back and reflect on their practice, reflect on themselves in the context of the coaching conversation. In essence, the coach needed to be able to "sit in a different seat in the room … and look at their work from a different angle" (S2: 16–17).

A second theme was the coach's attitude toward supervision. Having a positive attitude toward supervision was viewed as important if the coach was to engage in an open and constructive way. The coaches reported adopting a proactive attitude toward their supervision by actively looking for issues in their coaching.

> I don't always bring something—sometimes there's nothing that's cropped up in the month, but I'm looking for things to bring if you see what I'm saying. (C2: 39–41)

In addition, the coaches saw supervision as an opportunity to reflect on their practice, and as a resource with potential benefit for their practice.

> If I've got a new client, I'll be thinking about using it as an opportunity, so where do I feel least comfortable with this client, what can I ask. So I think of supervision as a resource that I can kind of latch onto and get what I can out of it. (C2: 24–26)

A third influencing factor was the need for supervision. The coaches in the study highlighted how the need for supervision at specific instances contributed to their practice.

Such incidents were often about difficult or challenging themes within their coaching work that they were unsure of how to manage.

> I went to the person that ran the program I was on and asked for a one-to-one supervision session, because I just felt that this was really important and I needed to do something now. (C3: 41–42)

The supervisors also highlighted the need for supervision, but held the view supervision should be regular rather than only at times of need. They highlighted that on occasions there was value in discussing issues that were outside of the immediate awareness of the coach. Two of the supervisors expressed concern for coaches who only sought supervision when they had a particular issue to discuss. One supervisor made the interesting point that coaches can learn from their good practice (to find out what they are doing well) and not only from the issues and problems they seek help with. Both supervisors recommended that supervision be attended on a regular, consistent basis, and that coaches should be able to request further supervision at times when there is a particular issue they wish to address.

The process of coaching supervision

Coaching supervision is a dynamic process between two people or more (for group supervision), which takes place in a wider coaching and organizational context. The themes that emerged through the data regarding the process of coaching supervision were: the coach's role, the supervisor's role, properties of coaching supervision, the supervisory relationship and environment and, finally, a rather separate theme: the process of group supervision.

As previously indicated, coaches tended to take a proactive role in their supervision. It became clear from the participants that the coach's role was not limited to the actual supervision session. It involves a considerable amount of preparation in the form of active and ongoing reflection on their coaching practice. In the actual supervision session, the coaches also described taking a lead role. They described how they took responsibility for providing the supervisor with accurate and sufficient information regarding the coaching relationship. They noted that the quality of the supervision relied on the quality of information the coach brought to the supervision session, as well as their ability to reflect on their practice openly in the session with help from the supervisor.

In order that the coach is able to bring enough information to supervision, it emerged from both coach and supervisor participants that the coach should be able to be open and fully present during the session. This commitment to supervision and the ability to be open are also some of the behaviors supervisors expected from the coach. Without openness or commitment, the real work of supervision could not be successfully undertaken.

Further, coaches highlighted the importance of adopting a critical stance for new insights to emerge. However, such insights were for reflection, not wholesale adoption. In this sense, the coach was operating as a separate autonomous individual, influenced but not directed by the supervisor.

> To be a good supervisee I think is to take on board any insights, comments, and suggestions but to still have the confidence not to throw your own ideas out the window, because somebody else has suggested something different. (C2: 161–164)

It was noted by participants that the supervisor also had an important role to play in coaching supervision. It emerged that the supervisor took a facilitative role in the process of coaching supervision by opening up the "critical reflective space" (S2: 92) for the coach. It was suggested that the supervisor should encourage the coach to step back and reflect on their practice and hold this reflective space without supplying solutions. To achieve this the supervisor drew on multiple methods; employing open questioning, stimulating the coach's thinking and exploring together the issue, including the emotions of the coach and coachee in the coaching relationship.

> So having a supervisor who's shining a light on the part of the process you haven't been aware of. (C2: 126–128)

Data from the first part of the study (the videotaped supervision session) illustrated this. In the session, the supervisor used a wide range of interventions to help the coach explore the issue from an alternative perspective. Examples of interventions from this observed coaching supervision session are summarized in Table 8.2.

The supervisor, in this facilitative role, was supportive of the coach, yet maintained a strong element of challenge in order to assist the coach in their reflective process. Feedback was a further aspect identified by both coaches and supervisors as an important role of the supervisor.

Coaches also highlighted the value of an ongoing relationship with their supervisor. This allowed the supervisor to become more knowledgeable of the coach's approach, tendencies, and behavioral patterns. This knowledge informed the practice of supervision in a way that helped the coach to raise their awareness of behaviors that may be affecting their coaching practice. As a result, it was perceived that the quality of supervision deepened over time:

> Having the same supervisor every month, so they get to know your patterns, means that you'll get more insightful feedback from them. (C2: 131–133)

Table 8.2   *Sample Questions Used in the Observed Coaching Supervision Session*

Supervisor questions
- How do you see that?
- And where would you sense that?
- … the statement behind those questions would be?
- What do you think he might say?
- Who would be saying this?
- And what's happening between you and your coachee?
- So how did you get that feedback then?
- What were you wanting to say to your boss?
- So what would be your challenge to him?
- How do you think he would describe you differently when you get into the six-month review than how he described you at the beginning?
- So, what would the confident, assertive you be saying to me?
- How does that feel?

Supervisors noted the importance of being aware of nonverbal cues, alongside the spoken words of the coach. It was assumed that this awareness also developed over time, and what was important was not the behavior itself but how the behavior contrasted with the "typical" behavior of the coach while engaging with the supervisor. One of the supervisors noted:

> People's verbal version of it isn't that accurate ... because how we remember ... but what we do know is what a person shows you physically, in the room, what they replicate is much more accurate. If you film a coaching session and then film the supervision on it, you'd be able to pick out elements that are transferred, in terms of uh, paralleling from that one into this one. (S1: 40–44)

This reference to a parallel process was also found within the first part of the study. In the filmed supervision session, the supervisor picked up on the coach's closed body language. This provided a clue as to the underlying feelings of the coach and by pointing it out the supervisor opened up an avenue for exploration in the observed supervision session.

Supervisor:

> So, how are you doing with your assertiveness and confidence in here? ... I'm just noticing that the times when we go into here, um it's like (demonstrates closed body language), is that OK, or ...? If you were being confident and assertive with me, here, what would you be saying, right now? (Extract from the observed supervision session)

A third theme was the properties of the session that were judged to be important. The data suggest a few common elements in terms of the frequency, type of supervision, and consistency of supervisor.

The strongest message related to the frequency of coaching supervision with both supervisors and coaches recommending regular, scheduled supervision sessions. It is interesting to note that from the interviews, although one coach received monthly supervision and the other two coaches received quarterly supervision, all considered their supervision to be regular, so there is a certain relativity regarding the regularity of supervision in the eyes of the coach.

> Very regular, yeah, so it's quarterly, but I will ask for supervision if I need something. (C3: 39)

One of the supervisors pointed out that the regularity of supervision was dependent on the amount of coaching done. Perhaps the most important point raised about the frequency or regularity of supervision is that it should be formal and scheduled, rather than a voluntary and ad hoc arrangement for the coach. However, coaches valued the flexibility of being able to seek extra coaching supervision in addition to their scheduled sessions if there was an issue they needed to address urgently. This could be through phone contact with their supervisor or through arranging an extra session

> Because, you know, the thing with supervision is that you've got an issue now, you can't wait three months to sort it out! (C3: 42–43)

In terms of the type of supervision, there was strong support by both coaches and supervisors for a mixed approach, rather than purely one-to-one sessions. Both coaches and supervisors valued the dynamics and learning opportunities provided by group supervision, which will be discussed below.

> I have found it valuable to not just have one-to-ones. (C2:138–139)

There was also support, from both sides, for having the same supervisor over time. The reason provided for this was to build up a supervisory relationship and benefit from the development of enhanced knowledge and rapport of one another over time.

> Having the same supervisor every month, so they get to know your patterns, means that you'll get more insightful feedback from them. (C2: 131–133)

Both coaches and supervisors drew attention to the relationship as a dynamic process, with roles and responsibilities on both sides and a reported sense of equality in terms of power, while retaining clarity of roles in the relationship. The issue of contracting was also noted and comparisons made to the equal importance to this within the coach–coachee relationship.

The last subtheme mentioned in this cluster was the fit between the coach and the supervisor. It was seen as favorable by the coach to have a supervisor who stimulated their thinking and whose approach to supervision complemented their approach to coaching.

While much of the debate was about the benefits of one-to-one supervision, coaches pointed out that they enjoyed and benefited from attending group supervision in addition to their regular one-to-one sessions. One of the main reasons provided by both coaches and supervisors was the opportunity for coaches to gain a wider perspective and to learn from other coaches. One of the supervisors said that while he had "immense time for one-to-ones" (S3: 68), he believed that the dynamics of group supervision added value to coaching supervision. Coaches shared this view of the dual benefits from both one-to-one and group supervision:

> I actually like having a small group environment as well … you've got more dynamics going … it's quite interesting to hear other people's case studies … the process on somebody else, being able to relate it to yourself. (C2: 142–144)

It was noted that in a group the coach was able to learn from the experiences of other coaches and relate to these common issues. The result of this was a sense of belonging to the "coaching community" and a feeling that the coach was not alone in the issues they were facing in their coaching practice.

Group supervision provided the coach with an opportunity to receive insights and opinions from other group members in an environment where experimentation was encouraged.

> I thought it was quite experimental. I could say "Well, I tried this and, or this happened" and I didn't feel like there was going to be any comeback really. (C3: 23–24)

Necessary conditions for coaching supervision

Participants suggested there were a number of necessary conditions that had to be in place for coaching supervision to be deemed most effective. Some of these have already been brought to light in this study, such as the creation of an open, safe, confidential, and nonjudgmental environment within which coaching supervision can take place. Other important factors included the supervisor's training, experience, and ethical maturity.

Both coaches and supervisors expected coaching supervisors to have specialist training and to use a specific model that added value to the process. The supervisors pointed out the need for coaching supervisors to have knowledge of the context in which they were supervising. For executive coaches, this would be knowledge and/or experience of the dynamics present in the top tier of organizations and the pressures senior executives experience in their roles. Simply drawing on counseling experiences and transferring these to the coaching space was seen as inadequate.

> There are many counselling supervisors who have never worked in organizations … they don't have the contextual frame or professional frame I think to do good coaching supervision. (S2: 236–239)

Another feature raised was that supervision should inform one's practice. The supervision session should translate into a concrete course of action to which the coach commits. The environment of coaching supervision should thus be one of constant learning and change.

A further point that came over very strongly from all participants was the focus on the ethical function of coaching supervision. Although the issues that coaches face may be of a lower "grade" than those faced in other helping professions, the ethical element in coaching supervision is one that should not be ignored. Supervisors highlighted the ethical responsibility they held to challenge the coach when ethical issues arose. If the coach was not behaving in an ethical manner, the supervisor would intervene, challenging where appropriate. In all cases, the supervisor should act to protect the best interests of the coachee.

It was noted that this competency of ethical maturity required training and personal development on behalf of the supervisor and that the supervision process provided continuous development and learning for the supervisor as well as the coach.

Limiting factors

The participants of the study raised a number of factors that proved limiting to the effectiveness of coaching supervision, both in terms of the supervisory relationship and the process or issues related to one or both of the involved parties. These included: the limited understanding of supervision; the issues or lack of them brought to supervision; the coach–supervisor relationship, the supervisor's behavior; and the behavior of the coach.

As noted above, expectations can play an important part in the process and can both enhance and derail the supervision relationship. It was noted by coaches that they were aware of individuals who attended supervision with counseling supervisors due to the wider availability of such individuals and the lower cost. According to one supervisor in particular, this was not advisable, as they argued that the context in which coaching takes place is fundamentally different from counseling, and the failure to understand these differences can be dangerous for both the coachee and their employing organization.

> I think a lot of coaches have gone to counselling and psychotherapy supervisors ...
> I think on the whole counselling and psychotherapy practice differs 'cause they are there to serve the client in front of them, while the coach has always got at least the client and the organization and the performance. (S1: 156–158)

There was also a sense that the term "supervision" has been used too loosely when applied in the coaching community to a wide range of activities including peer support and peer coaching.

Coaches highlighted that the sometimes rigid nature of supervision meetings could make it difficult to bring a particular issue to the scheduled supervision sessions. As a result, the coach may need to have a supervisor available to deal with a crisis situation rather than wait for two months until the next formal supervision meeting. Supervision contracts should provide for this flexibility to call upon the supervisor between formal meetings. Coaches must be prepared to seek out additional supervision if and when required. It was noted that such a flexible arrangement should be in addition to, rather than a replacement for, formal and regular supervision meetings.

There are dangers in the supervisory relationship that if the necessary conditions and expectations discussed above are not fulfilled, coaching supervision will not be effective. The coach needs to be comfortable to discuss their issues freely and openly. The features of challenge and support come into play to keep the relationship on its "learning edge", to use the words of one of the supervisors.

Supervisor behavior was also highlighted as an important aspect and a potential limiting factor, if the supervisor behaved in ways that undermined the relationship, such as being over-directive. Both supervisors warned against the potential of being too directive, which they considered detracted from the learning potential of supervision. It was indicated that the supervisor should not be offering direct advice or solutions, but should allow the coach to reach these on their own, without being judged by the supervisor.

Coach behaviors also could have a negative effect. Coaches suggested that to gain the most from the process they needed to be open to the alternative perspectives in supervision, while also retaining their individuality and confidence in their ideas. It was acknowledged that the supervisor's assessment of an issue was based on the information the coach discloses and, as a result, the coach should not be too drawn to the supervisor's perspective if they do not feel it is accurate.

Um, if you're too drawn to their assessment of the situation—because … the supervisor's assessment is still going to be based on the limited information that you've brought to the table. (C3: 156–159)

A further danger was the failure by coaches to be truly open and the danger of seeking to present a particular perspective of events. It was felt that this danger increased in a group supervision session, where impression management, due to peer pressure, was more present.

The potential of coaching supervision

Participants suggested that supervision offered a number of potential gains. The perceived potential benefits of coaching supervision range from enhancing the coach's capacity to challenge to enhancing the quality of coaching practice. The third theme in this cluster was the contribution that coaching supervision could make in continuing professional development (CPD). The process of coaching supervision within a group as an action learning set encourages the linkage between theory and practice. One of the supervisors stated that supervision should inform a coach's practice; another mentioned that one's mental models should grow and change over time and this should inform practice. A fourth theme was the potential organizational benefits. For coaches based within organizations, or working with a number of coachees from the same organization, it was suggested that by increasing the coach's capacity, the coach could be more effective with individual coachees and thus contribute to wider organizational change.

Another potential organizational benefit from supervision, based on the participant responses, is the potential ability to assess systemic patterns, through the outcomes of the multiple supervisory conversations (within clear confidentiality boundaries). By drawing on such information, and sharing the high-level themes with the organization, the supervisor can contribute toward wider organizational cultural change.

What are the systemic patterns, what does that tell us about the current state of the culture, and how that matches the vision and strategy, and work out what the organization can do to shift these patterns? (S3: 78–80)

Outcomes of coaching supervision

While coaches and supervisors highlighted the potential benefits, participants in both groups found it more difficult to identify explicit benefits from coaching supervision. Coaches remarked that it was difficult to quantify how their coaching practice had changed or benefited as a direct result of coaching supervision, especially at the time, but looking back they believed they were more effective coaches as a result of supervision.

I'm sure it does, um, it's very difficult to quantify, but I'm sure it makes me more effective. (C3: 92–93)

Coaches valued receiving a wider perspective on their coaching issues and practice. Participants claimed this reflection resulted in a raised awareness and new insights for the coach that had the potential to enhance their coaching practice. The element of surprise at the discovery of a "blindspot" (below) indicates the transformational power of supervision that is alluded to by both Hawkins (2006) and Carroll (2006).

What I find really useful about supervision is noticing my blind spots. I like to think I've looked at every possible angle, and then somebody from the outside spots something and you think "Oh my goodness! How could I have missed that! (laughs)." (C3: 82–87)

However, the coaches in the study were unable to identify specific instances of changes in the practice resulting from insights gained in supervision. Instead, the largest gains were less tangible. Coaches stated having increased confidence in their coaching practice. Along with the confidence to pursue issues came a reported increased ability for coaches to persevere when things become difficult in the coaching relationship.

Both coaches and supervisors indicated support for group supervision. One of the reasons for this, from the coach's point of view, was that group supervision provided coaches with a sense of belonging to the coaching community. In a group supervision, coaches were able to listen to the issues of other coaches, relate them to themselves, and receive input on their own issues. One coach noted:

Coaching is quite a lonely profession in a way, you know, going out, meeting someone, getting back, reflecting on your own. So it brings that sort of community together. (C3: 112–113)

Group supervision helped in the formation of what coaches described as a community. Related to the sense of community, was a raised sense of professionalism and ethical awareness in their coaching practice. The in-depth exploration and reflection on their practice raised questions of how they might conduct themselves in a professional manner. Supervision reminded coaches of their ethical duty and held their focus on professional practice.

I think it helps me be professional, it keeps my professionalism up and reminds me of the ethos behind what I'm trying to do. (C3: 111)

A further theme was what may be termed the "internal supervisor". This related to a coach's growing ability to self-supervise as a result of coaching supervision, as the coach reflected on what the supervisor might say. The supervision process thus offered a form of holding to account, not in any hierarchical sense but in the sense the coach sought to maintain the standards of practice expected of them by their supervisor.

DISCUSSION

Reflecting on the data

The series of interviews, six in all, alongside the video session, provided a wealth of data on coaching supervision.

There was an indication from the data that coaches looked to supervision as a means of dealing with the challenges they experienced in their coaching and that both one-to-one and group supervision models offered potential benefits. However, the actual benefits were harder to quantify. Coaches held a belief that their practice was enhanced, but they were unsure about the specific benefits. There may be an echo of the process identified in coaching (De Meuse & Dai, 2009). De Meuse and Dai demonstrated through a meta-analysis that ratings of coaching's positive impact given by the coachee are significantly higher than ratings given by peers of coaching's impact. This aside, it is of interest in this study that, despite being unable to measure the impact of supervision on coaching practice, coaches displayed faith in the value of supervision in terms of confidence and being able to listen and share their experiences with others.

Both coaches and supervisors shared a common view about what factors contributed and limited the supervision relationship, and on the value of maintaining an ongoing relationship with the same supervisor, who was both trained and had relevant experience.

Reflecting on the literature

The results of this study provide a detailed picture of how coaches and supervisors experience coaching supervision as this field is developing within the UK. The body of literature on coaching supervision is at this stage limited and has been outpaced by the development of coaching supervision practice and the race to claim that supervision is the most effective model for continuous professional development.

Carroll (2006) has identified a series of central principles that underpin coaching supervision:

- coaching supervision is for the learning of the supervisees
- supervisors facilitate supervisee learning
- learning in supervision is transformational (not just transmissional)
- supervision moves from "I-learning" to "We-learning"

The results of this study echo Carroll's first point that coaching supervision is about the learning of the coach. Coaching supervision, as described by the participants, centers on the coach's individual practice with the aim of learning from this experience. The supervisor was expected to be committed to helping the coach with their issue, creating an environment in which the coach was able to be open and honest and learn through a process of critical reflection. The results of the study strongly supported the view that a coaching supervisor takes the role of a facilitator. Supervisors in this study cautioned against overinvolvement and coaches indicated that supervision was not as effective as it might be when supervisors offered too much advice or directive solutions. Coaches noted that, in order for the supervisor to be able to effectively facilitate the session, the coach had a responsibility to be open and honest and to provide sufficient information in the session to explore the issue being presented. Coaches also noted that it was important that they retain their confidence, trust their judgment, and were not too influenced by an overly directive supervisor. For them, supervision was a joint and equal process rather than a hierarchical one of being held to account.

Transformational learning as a theme came across clearly in the study, from both coaches and supervisors. For the supervisors, transformational learning was an aim, while for coaches the learning was experienced, and this experience sometimes resulted in surprise and an openness to change in their coaching approach as a result.

In both the one-to-one and group supervision, participants raised the point that supervision created a two-way learning process. This occurred through the dialog and feedback between supervisor and coach. In a group supervision, coaches were able to learn from the experiences of other coaches. As raised by one of the participants, group coaching supervision should be seen as an action learning set, where learning is necessarily experiential, and reflection informs one's practice. Supervisors also highlighted that learning occurred for them in the process.

This learning, however, only took place when a good relationship existed and this depended on the supervisor being able to adapt their style to suit the needs of the coach. One participant coach, who had had a number of different supervisors over time, indicated the perceived value of coach–supervisor "fit". It was indicated that her learning experience was enhanced by having a supervisor whose approach suited hers, and a mismatch in approaches was a "turn-off". Carroll (2006) also discusses this, saying that supervisors should have an understanding that one size does not fit all in learning terms. He indicates that supervisors should know the learning style and intelligence of their coach/supervisees in order to facilitate their learning. The overriding theme here is that the supervision should be a self-directed learning experience, and supervisors should be able to accommodate the style and learning needs of any supervisee.

The results also appear to support Hawkins and Smith's (2006) three functions of coaching supervision: developmental, resourcing, and qualitative. In terms of the developmental function, the participants indicated that supervision provided them with a regular opportunity to reflect on their practice, gain an alternative perspective, and receive feedback. In terms of the resourcing function, the participants noted that the opinions and feedback of others were valuable resources in gaining a wider perspective. The support and challenge offered by the supervisor helped the coach address the issues openly and without fear. The qualitative function was experienced by the participants as increased ethical capacity and confidence to persevere, allowing them to deliver coaching of superior quality.

The results of the study provide support for Hawkins and Schwenk's (2006) guidelines for best practice. These guidelines include:

- takes place regularly
- balance of individual, group and peer supervision
- manages ethical and confidentiality boundaries
- generates organizational learning
- provides support for the coach
- quality assures coaching provision
- provides continuing professional development of the coach
- focuses on the client, organization, and coach needs

This rosy glow of support for the work of writers in the field should not, however, mask some interesting challenges that the research has brought to light. A significant theme that emerged from the study was that the coaches had no prior understanding or expectations of supervision. Although they both reported positive experiences of supervision and there was an underlying sense that they valued supervision, they might not have sought it out on their own. This echoes our view that coaching supervision is more spoken of than practiced within the wider coaching community in the UK. This may also explain the higher profile of coaching supervision as the model of choice for CPD in the UK and its relative obscurity in other English-speaking countries such as the United States and Australia. Hawkins and Smith (2006) ask the question of why coaching supervision is well-promoted but not so well-practiced.

Another dimension to the lack of clarity of benefits was a lack of understanding of the different forms of CPD, including one-to-one supervision, group supervision, a reflective log or journal, and formal and informal peer mentoring. The research appears to offer some insight into the different benefits of one-to-one and group supervision. However, as was anticipated, there was little understanding among coaches of the potential benefits of other forms of CPD. It may be that different forms may suit different coaches and may be of particular value at different stages of a coach's development. For example, we would argue that new coaches benefit greatly from group supervision, developing a sense of community and shared ethical standards and learning from each other. However, later in their coaching careers, a learning log and peer mentoring may offer a more appropriate model. Further, it may be argued that most benefit can be obtained from using more than one reflective practice approach; combining for example group supervision with a reflective log.

A further issue was the assumption that supervision was a problem-solving forum. However, we would argue supervision is part of a learning forum for new coaches and part of continuous professional development for experienced coaches.

A final theme that is worthy of mention is that of supervision training. While in Australia and the United States coaching supervision training is either nonexistent or virtually nonexistent, there has been a slow growth in the UK. The study highlighted the value of having a trained supervisor who holds to a model of practice and is also experienced in the domain of practice of the coach. The coaches in the study indicated that this was important to them. They wanted to know that the supervisor had a specific set of skills and was following a process, rather than just another coach who wanted to "raise their game". There is currently a shortage of trained coaching supervisors. We would argue that the development of additional coaching supervision training will help to address this issue, as will the recognition of accredited supervisor status by coaching bodies.

Practical implications

Firstly, the study suggests a need for formal coach supervision training within the UK if the supervision model is to be more widely adopted. Such training needs to reflect coaching rather than therapy needs.

Secondly, in selecting supervisors, we would advocate that the coach considers the match between themselves and the supervisor, as well as the supervisor's experience and qualifications. Once a selection is made clear, contracting to set expectations will help in making sessions more productive for both parties.

Thirdly, we would argue that a more flexible approach should be considered before the coaching profession adopts supervision as the gold standard for coaching CPD. There is a danger that supervision is made compulsory in ethical or professional codes. Such a move will reduce the flexibility to meet CPD needs through a variety of routes.

Other CPD models are available and we would argue that these may be more appropriate at different stages of a coach's development. These may include peer mentoring, reflective logs, or diaries.

Finally, this research, while one of the few supervision-based studies published to date, is limited in its scope. The study drew on a limited pool of participants as a qualitative study, and a deeper understanding of the processes and efficacy of coaching supervision is required. This could be achieved by further research in this area of coaching practice.

Developing a conceptual framework

As a grounded theory study, the ultimate aim of the study was to reflect on the factors that emerged from the research and construct a framework that both reflects the state of coaching supervision as a process in the UK and offers a framework that can be the subject of further testing through more focused research into supervision and super-vision practices. Such a model is summarized in Figure 8.1. Here, the supervision process is organized into three core stages: (a) context, such as which aspirations, expectations, and needs inform the process; (b) supervision process, which consists of the behaviors of the coach and supervisor, along with the experience of the supervisor and the fit between the two participants in the relationship; and (c) the outcomes stage. The complexity and intangible nature are represented by the focus on perceived benefits. However, within these may be buried specific and tangible outcomes, which may include enhanced confidence and a holding to account. These may also include aspects such as growth in ethical maturity. It is these factors which, when adopted and used by the coach may, in turn, shape their practice and thus the wider efficacy of coaching, offering gains to the coachee and to the coachee's organization.

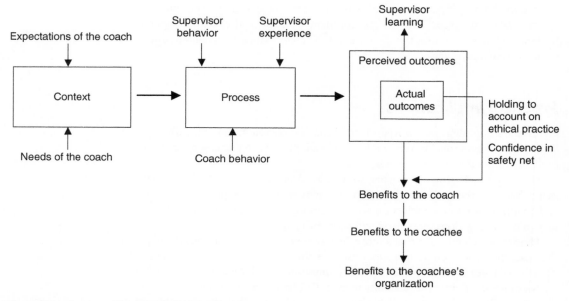

Figure 8.1   *Conceptual Framework: Coaching Supervision*

CONCLUSIONS

This study set out to develop a theoretical model of the process of coaching supervision based on the experiences of coaches and supervisors. A grounded theory methodology was employed. The results of the study gave rise to a theoretical framework of coaching supervision, covering aspects such as influencing factors, the process of supervision, necessary conditions, limiting factors, supervision potential, and experienced outcomes. The results echoed the existing literature on coaching supervision, with coachees expressing a belief that supervision offered benefits to them in their coaching practice, including raising awareness about their practice, increasing confidence, encouraging perseverance, and providing a sense of belonging. The study also highlighted the challenges that coaching supervision faces as a result of the growing coaching industry, and coaches in this study expressed a desire for trained supervisors with relevant contextual knowledge. This places a demand for trained coaching supervisors. Further, the study highlighted the importance of clearly setting expectations in the supervision process.

The study, while unique in exploring a new area of practice through a grounded theory approach, should be viewed as a starting point for wider research into the efficacy of coaching supervision. In this study, participants were quick to describe the perceived benefits. However, they were less able to substantiate the benefits in tangible terms. As a result, further research needs to explore these aspects, comparing supervision with other forms of CPD such as peer coaching and reflective logs, as well as comparing the benefits of one-to-one supervision with group supervision.

REFERENCES

Bachkirova, T. Stevens, P. & Willis, P. (2005). *Coaching supervision*. Oxford Brookes Coaching and Mentoring Society. Retrieved October 1, 2008, from www.brookes.ac.uk

Bluckert, P. (2005). *Coaching supervision*. Retrieved October 1, 2008, from http://www.pbcoaching.com/what-we-do/coaching-supervision

Carroll, M. (1996). *Counselling supervision. Theory, skills and practice*. London, UK: Cassell.

Carroll, M. (2006). Key issues in coaching psychology supervision. *The Coaching Psychologist, 2*(1), 4–8.

De Meuse, K., & Dai, G. (2009). Does executive coaching work: A research analysis. *Coaching: An International Journal of Theory, Research. Practice, 2*(2), 117–134, https://doi.org/10.1080/17521880902882413.

Downey, M. (2003). *Effective coaching. Lessons from the coaches' couch*. New York, NY: Texere/Thomson.

Fillery-Travis, A., & Lane, D. (2006). Does coaching work or are we asking the wrong questions. *International Coaching Psychology Review, 1*(1), 23–36.

Glaser, B., & Strauss, A. (1967). *The discovery of grounded theory: Strategies for qualitative research*. New York, NY: Aldine.

Hawkins, P. (2006). Coaching supervision. In J. Passmore (Ed.), *Excellence in coaching: The industry guide* (pp. 257–272). London, UK: Kogan Page.

Hawkins, P., & Schwenk, G. (2006). *Coaching supervision: Maximising the potential of coaching*. London, UK: CIPD.

Hawkins, P., & Shohet, R. (1989). *Supervision in the helping professions* (2nd ed.). Milton Keynes, UK: Open University Press.

Hawkins, P., & Smith, N. (2006). *Coaching, mentoring and organisational consultancy. Supervision and development*. Maidenhead, UK: Open University Press.

Houston, G. (1995). *Supervision and counselling* (2nd ed.). London, UK: Rochester Foundation.

Inskipp, F., & Proctor, B. (1995). *Art, craft and tasks of counselling supervision*. St Leonards-on-Sea, UK: Cascade Publications.

Jefferson, G. (1985). An exercise in the transcription and analysis of laughter. In T. van Dijk (Ed.), *Handbook of discourse analysis*. London, UK: Academic Press.

O'Connell, D., & Knowal, S. (1996). Basic principles of transcription. In J. Smith, R. Harre, & L. van Langehoven (Eds.), *Rethinking methods in psychology* (pp. 93–105). London, UK: Sage.

Oxford English Dictionary. (2008). Retrieved November 7, 2008, from www.askoxford.com

Palmer, S., & Whybrow, A. (2007). *Handbook of coaching psychology: A guide for practitioners*. London, UK: Routledge.

Passmore, J. (2006). *Excellence in coaching: The industry guide*. London, UK: Kogan Page.

Strauss, A., & Corbin, J. (1990). Grounded theory methodology: An overview. In N. Denzin & Y. S. Lincoln (Eds.), *Strategies of qualitative inquiry* (pp. 158–183). London, UK: Sage.

9 Coaching with Emotion: How Coaches Deal with Difficult Emotional Situations

Elaine Cox and Tatiana Bachkirova[1]

Over the last decade or so there has been a considerable increase in research into the impact and management of emotions in organizations and questions have been raised about the invisibility or marginalization of emotionality in organizational life (Gherardi, 1995). This growing emphasis on the use and management of emotion in the workplace implies that coaches need to be aware of both their own and their clients' emotional reactions, and the contexts in which they occur, in order to be in a position to help their clients. Indeed, Whitmore (1996) has urged coaches to "tap" the emotions.

However, there may be significant apprehension felt by coaches in relation to overt displays of emotions by clients. There may yet be the thought among coaches that emotions should only be explored within a counseling setting and, as in many organizations, the traditional view that emotion interferes with rationality may still influence thinking. Both of these notions may lead to overmanagement of what are considered to be difficult emotions.

Following a review of how emotions have been perceived in organizations, difficult emotions are defined. Then the methodology is explained and the three themes that emerged are explored in turn, using examples from the data. In the conclusion, the implications for coaching practice and further research are considered.

---

[1] First published as Cox, E. & Bachkirova, T. (2007). Coaching with emotion: How coaches deal with difficult emotional situations. *International Coaching Psychology Review*, 2, 178–189.

THE PLACE OF EMOTION
IN THE WORKPLACE

The work of Fineman (2000) has been important in securing the place of emotion in organizational contexts, countering arguments from early philosophers such as Plato and Kant. Fineman highlights the main tension between rationality and emotion, and describes three possible positions that could be held:

- emotions interfere with rationality
- emotions serve rationality
- emotions and rationality entwine

The prevailing view has been that emotions interfere with rationality: Pizarro (2000, p. 356) confirms that Kant, influentially, believed emotional forces to be "sources that tainted the process of moral thinking, primarily because they were antagonistic to the reasoning process" and goes on to summarize the three main reasons for the perpetuation of this view:

1. Emotions can be seen to be partial in that they are aroused in relation to things and people we care about.
2. Emotions arise due to the presence of arbitrary factors.
3. Emotions are beyond our voluntary control and are passively experienced.

Thus emotions, particularly so-called "difficult" emotions, have been seen as interfering with rationality, harmful to decision making, and as unruly, undesirable, and needing to be managed in the workplace in order to reduce unpredictability (Speedy, 2005). Indeed, Smith and Sharma (2002, p. 197) confirm that within organizations emotional reactions are seen as disruptive, illogical, biased, and weak, and consequently as "antithetical to performance".

However, Pizarro refutes this traditional judgment on emotion, arguing that we have the capacity to regulate our emotions; that emotions reflect our pre-existing concerns (our values and our principles). The suggestion here is that emotions help reasoning by focusing our attention on the problem, "allowing us to pay attention to features of the situation that may escape us otherwise" (Pizarro, 2000, p. 358). Gross, Richards, and John (2006, p. 2) also focus on acknowledging and managing emotion, suggesting that strong emotions need to be managed "if we are to keep our appointments, careers and friendships." They claim that "successful emotion regulation is a pre-requisite for adaptive functioning. To get along with others, we must be able to regulate which emotions we have and how we experience and express these emotions."

Simpson and Smith (2005, p. 1) confirm that the "entrance of emotion into considerations of work and organisation has occurred alongside other significant developments concerning the growth in the service economy." This has led to a great need to focus on the eliciting of desired emotions. Emotional labor, sometimes known as "emotion work," has become a feature of the work of many employees, especially in service sectors such as the health service and education. Such public services require employees to be even-tempered and agreeable in the workplace: "the major object of emotional labour is to provide predictability and maintain harmony in the workplace, while enhancing competitive productivity" (Speedy, 2005, p. 4).

The most substantial incursion of emotion into organizational consciousness has, arguably, come through the concept of emotional intelligence (EI). One of the most frequently used definitions of EI is given by Salovey and Meyer (1990, p. 189) as "the ability to monitor one's own and other's feelings and emotions, to discriminate among them, and to use this information to guide one's thinking and action." However, a review of both emotion work and EI carried out by Opengart (2005) concludes that the application of EI is incomplete without an understanding of emotion work as, she claims, the two function together. She highlights how the emotional display rules that guide emotional expression are "learned within an employee's particular work context," (p. 57) and so the management of emotions requires not only EI, but the ability to perceive, learn, and adjust behavior as necessary. Opengart also argues that it is difficult to assess and interpret emotional expression without contextual knowledge since there would be "no basis from which to understand why someone chooses to express a particular emotion" (2005, p. 57).

It can be seen from the brief survey of literature above that there has been renewed interest in the role of emotion in organizational contexts, resulting in a burgeoning literature on the topic (ten Bos & Willmott, 2001; Mark, 2005; Smith & Sharma, 2002). Gender stereotypes in relation to emotion are also being questioned and Brody (1997, p. 369) has argued that "stereotypes about gender and emotional expression tend to be imprecise and misleading. They fail to acknowledge situational, individual, and cultural variations in males' and females' emotional expressiveness." In addition, reservations are now being expressed in relation to the extreme rationality that has tended to govern bureaucratic organizational structures in the past and a more receptive view of emotion as a resource is emerging. A range of factors are seen as influencing this situation; for example, the growth of emotion work, the impact of globalization, and the influx of more women and people from different cultures into organizations.

DEFINING DIFFICULT EMOTIONS

Against the backdrop of conflicting views in relation to the role of emotions in the workplace, coaches have to consider their own position. This study highlights how coaches currently deal with the difficult emotions they encounter in their practice.

Some specific emotions have been described as "difficult" or "negative." Tiedens (2001), for example, has suggested that inwardly directed "negative" emotions, such as depression or fear, have fewer short-term positive functions and tend to elicit negative emotions in others. More recently, Fineman (2005, p. 12) has questioned whether it makes sense to "bracket off" positive emotions, in the way proposed in positive psychology, since this would assume that they are separate states with their own profile and structure, and not intrinsically linked to negative emotions. However, Greenberg (2003) explains how primary emotions, such as fear, are essentially positive. He suggests that primary emotions are either adaptive (healthy feelings) or maladaptive (bad feelings) and suggests that emotions can be divided into four categories:

1. a healthy core feeling (an adaptive primary emotion)
2. a chronic bad feeling (a maladaptive primary emotion)
3. a reactive or defensive emotion that can obscure a primary feeling (a secondary emotion)
4. an influencing or manipulative emotion used by people to get what they want (an instrumental emotion)

In this model, all emotions are seen as normal and "positive" and become maladaptive, secondary, or instrumental as a result of an intervention, such as thinking, or of circumstance. Fineman (2005, p. 13) confirms this view, arguing that "the valuation of an emotion by self or others has no necessary universality." He cites Bagozzi (2003), stressing that the "same" emotion can be felt differently and responded to differently depending on extant cultural and social factors.

For the purposes of this article we want to define difficult emotional situations as those that give the coach a "bad feeling," that is, those that tend to make the coach feel uncomfortable in some way, and to acknowledge that what is termed a difficult emotion may vary from coach to coach and be dependent upon a number of internal and external factors.

METHODOLOGY

This article reports on findings from a wider research study aimed at exploring the personal theories of a sample of organizational and life coaches in order to understand how they deal with difficult emotional situations. The study was aimed at finding out:

- what role emotions play in coaching according to coaches;
- what it is like for them to deal with the emotional side of the process;
- what personal theories coaches have about dealing with emotions; and
- how these theories affect their practice.

This article explores three important themes that emerged from the study, which focus specifically on how coaches deal with difficult emotional situations:

1. difficult situations in terms of dealing with clients' emotions
2. difficult situations in terms of coaches' emotions
3. differentiated and potentially problematic views on male / female client emotions

The study was intended to uncover the range of possible positions held by coaches in relation to emotion in coaching. In order to do this, an interpretative phenomenological study (Smith & Osborn, 2003) was designed that would allow data to be gathered on coaches' personal theories and strategies in relation to emotions in coaching.

We used a questionnaire method built around a set of stem sentences that would engender open, spontaneous, and possibly emotional responses. The questions were educed from a detailed reading of the literature combined with the researchers' own experiences of emotional triggers. Sixty questionnaires were distributed among practicing executive and life coaches in the UK, and 39 were completed—a nearly 70% return rate. The coaches were presented with a series of unfinished sentences, which they then had to complete in a quick and spontaneous manner. Crotty (1996, p. 278) uses stem sentences to encourage the development of metaphors and similes, such as "Learning to start my new small business is like ... walking through a hall of mirrors." This spontaneity and freedom of response is something that we wanted to encourage in our study. Crotty also suggests that the stem-sentence method is an invitation to "open ourselves to the phenomenon as the object of our immediate experience" (1996, p. 278). This appeared to fit well with the research questions and with our proposed grounded theory approach to the data analysis. As a form of phenomenological inquiry, grounded theory focuses on the question: "what is the structure and essence of experience of this phenomenon for these people?" (Merleau-Ponty, 1992, p. 5). This analysis method thus ensured that the knowledge of the respondents was given precedence over that of the researchers.

The stem-sentence questionnaire included 21 stems for completion such as:

When/If my client presents an intense emotion, I ...

- Painful emotions during the coaching process are ...
- Control of emotions during coaching is ...
- Those who freely express their emotion at work ...
- Emotions that are more difficult for me to deal with in coaching are ...
- Consequences of suppressed emotions in coaching ...

Because of the highly interpretative nature of this study, and the lack of existing research in this area, the grounded theory method of analysis was designed to take account of the differing perspectives of the three researchers involved in the data collection. Analysis of this stage of the research was, therefore, a co-ordinated interpretation of data and themes. The answers for each stem sentence were analyzed and categorized by each of the three researchers separately, and the categories compared, discussed, and agreement reached for each stem sentence. The agreed categories were then analyzed in relation to all stem sentences, the overarching categories were identified, and the emerging themes discussed and agreed. This "triangulation" involved significant discussion of the findings as they emerged and ensured that interpretation was as true to respondents' meanings as possible.

FINDINGS

Six initial themes emerged from the data that reflect the personal theories of the sample of coaches. Three of these themes were related to dealing with difficult emotions and are examined here:

1. difficult situations in terms of dealing with clients' emotions
2. difficult situations in terms of coaches' emotions
3. differentiated views on clients' emotions

Each of these three themes is explored in depth below, using extracts from the data. Respondents' identities are protected using an alphanumeric code.

Difficult situations in terms of dealing with clients' emotions

Our analysis of stem responses indicates that there are a number of difficult situations in the coaching process that coaches perceived as relating to the emotional state of the client. They identified examples of where a client may not be aware of the emotions they are presenting, or emotions are not congruent to the coaching process, or they are emotionally detached or anxious. The coaches' responses to these situations appear to take five directions:

i. Coaches analyze their own discomfort in the situation and consider it as a response to an underlying client issue. In this example the coach infers that the client is not expressing emotion adequately:

> He/she will often displace their feelings and/or negate others. (R8)
> In a similar response, the coach confirmed that it would be necessary to:
> Probe to find out what he/she (the client) is covering up. (R16)

ii. Coaches deem the difficult situation to be an outcome of their own actions or the failing dynamics of the relationship:

> I ask myself what's going on here … am I missing something.
> Am I misaligned with where the client is at? (R4)
> I wonder to what extent they are engaged with the coaching relationship. (R7)

iii. The coach tries to actively influence the client's emotion:

> I have a lot of different options and have to act fast. (R2)
> I look for ways of engaging their physicality. (R39)
> It is important to take time to discuss and work on making them congruent. (R37)

I will try to help them to discuss their anxiety perhaps using metaphors or cue cards to help express the nature of this anxiety. (R22)

iv. The coach considers referral (without mention of supervision):

I would suggest they may need a different kind of intervention, e.g. counselling or therapy. (R7)
I may call a halt or suggest a referral. (R16)

v. The coach sees emotions as normal reactions:

I try to remain calm, recognise the emotion and talk about it, ask them what is helpful. (R32)
Blocks and defences occur. (R11)
It opens up possibilities. (R29)

Many of these responses appear to reflect what Fineman (2000) calls the quarrel between rationality and emotion. Coaches that considered a referral, as in (iv) above, may hold to the notion that emotions interfere with rationality and so need to be explored outside of the coaching relationship, maybe in a counseling or psychotherapy setting. Responses in (i) and (ii) also imply that there is something wrong with emotions and the coaches seem to attribute the problem either to the client (covering up or displacing) or they attribute it to themselves and the relationship they have created (missing something, misalignment, are they engaged?).

Where the coach decides to actively influence the emotion, as in (iii) above, it could also be seen as a distrustful reaction to emotion, albeit covert. Although they do not give up on the client immediately and, at first glance, it seems that the coach is working positively with the client, they could, in fact, be seen as trying to change or control the emotion, which subtly implies that there is no room for difficult emotions in the coaching process.

These results, on the whole, imply that the first reaction to emotions by many coaches is to associate them with problems. Emotions are frequently viewed as needing to be managed somehow and some might even argue that control of emotions is a function of coaching. However, research by Richards and Gross (2005) suggests that control of emotions can come at a "cognitive price" in that it may impair the memory of emotional events. Similarly, Bono, Foldes, Vinson, & Muros (2007) report that employees required to manage their emotions at work experience more stress and lower job satisfaction. However, they also point out that if managers use transformational and empowering leadership behaviors then the negative effects of emotional regulation are reduced. Since "transformational" and "empowering" are terms that epitomize the coaching relationship, it would appear that there is a role for coaching here in helping clients to reduce problems such as stress at work—not through control and regulation of their emotions, but by acknowledging and understanding them as normal. A number of coaches did describe how they would work with an emotion, helping the client to express it more fully, name it, and use it productively. It could be assumed from their answers that these coaches, at the very least, are not suspicious of any type of emotion and they would explore them and work with them. Examples from the data are given in (v) above and could be seen to support the aims of coaching. This concurs with Patrick's (2004) research with coaching clients, which suggests that those who work to understand, rather than control their emotions, are more likely to experience significant growth.

Our first finding has confirmed that a proportion of coaches in the current study actively try to influence client emotions. However, some would refer a client, suggesting that emotions are considered as unhelpful to the coaching process, or that they need to be managed in some way. Others described a more client-centered approach that would allow exploration: the role for coaches being to acknowledge and understand emotion as normal.

Difficult situations in terms of coaches' emotions

This theme is divided into two parts: A and B. Part A identifies the emotions and emotional situations that coaches report impact most on their own emotions and test the boundaries of their work as coaches. Part B then moves on to explore the ways in which coaches deal with these emotional responses.

Part A

In addition to perceived difficult situations in relation to client emotions, there seems to be a range of emotions presented by the client that can affect a coach's own emotions and so also create difficult situations in the coaching process. Our study suggests that coaches see difficult emotional situations as testing their understanding of the boundaries of the profession.

> A coach needs to understand the fine line between coaching and counselling. (R22)

> I would suggest they may need a different kind of intervention—e.g., counselling or therapy. (R7)

This is not surprising in the light of the messages given to coaches in statements, such as that provided by the International Coaching Federation (ICF), that clearly suggest that working with emotions belongs to domains other than coaching: "Coaching assumes the presence of emotional reactions to life events and that clients are capable of expressing and handling their emotions. Coaching is not psychotherapy" (International Coach Foundation, 2002). Some emotions could indeed indicate underlying issues that may not be appropriate to work with in coaching and it has been argued elsewhere (Bachkirova & Cox, 2004) for the importance of psychological literacy of coaches in order to define if and when a referral is necessary. However, statements such as the ICF's may lead to coaches being wary of all emotions.

Occasionally, client emotions were identified by coaches as impacting on their own emotions. When this occurs, the client's strong or seemingly inappropriate emotions trigger emotions in the coach, making it hard for the coach to maintain control of their own emotions. Control of these is seen as good and necessary. When asked what kinds of emotions were more difficult to deal with, and why, coaches replied:

> Ones that I can relate to personally might make me feel emotional too. (R38)
> They irritate me, and force me to spend some of my energies concentrating on dealing with my own emotions. (R16)

> I get wrapped up in myself and my own internal dialogue and reasons etc. Self-justification, etc. (R10)

These examples indicate that some coaches are identifying with the client's emotion in some way. Such identification could be interpreted as suggesting a lack of understanding by the coach of the role of empathy. In person-centered therapy and counseling, empathy is an expression of values and understanding that results in a "principled non-directivity" (Schmid, 2001, p. 1). Schmid goes on to remind us that in therapy the attempt to understand is not used "in order to." When coaches work to understand an emotion in order to do something with it or try to use client emotions in order to help them achieve goals or help them to manage their emotions in order to placate work colleagues, this could be seen as a lack of understanding and, it could be argued, is a move away from client-centeredness. Similarly, if coaches avoid particular emotions because they find them uncomfortable to work with, as in the examples above, then this could be seen as a lack of empathy. Empathy involves being in the client's place moment by moment and "feeling as if" (Schmid, 2001, pp. 2–3). Schmid confirms that it is this "as if" that is important since it distinguishes empathy from identification: "identification does not pay attention to, and even ignores, the otherness of the Other. Interpretation closes the eyes to his or her uniqueness." Although closely related, empathy and identification are also different in the affects they produce. Empathy produces acceptance, while identification may result in transference/countertransference. For some of our coaches the dangers of identification, or of ignoring the boundaries between coach and client, are very real and could be seen as unhelpful. There are implications here for coach training and supervision.

In addition, a spectrum of specific client emotions was perceived by coaches as being more difficult to deal with professionally. These included:

> Anger (R8, R12, R13 …)
> Apathy and resignation (R3) Lack of drive, detachment (R33) My own fears (R6)
> Despair, futility (R22) Hopelessness (R25)

Le Bon (2001, p. 86) argues that a central element in emotions is our beliefs, evaluation, and judgments. The feeling of anger, he confirms, includes a judgment that someone has committed a wrong. This implied judgment could account for the fact that, in this study, anger appears most often as a "difficult" emotion. Our findings also support Tiedens's (2001) contention that depression or fear tend to elicit negative emotions in others by evoking uncertainty, pessimism, and risk-averse choices. Similarly, Fischer et al. (2004) report that emotions such as sadness or despair produce reactions of powerlessness and helplessness in others. There was, however, some useful evidence of self-awareness in relation to these specific emotions and the effect they were having, plus recognition of coaches' own vulnerability in terms of human relationships. This level of self-awareness is essential for the further personal and professional development of coaches. In the responses below, the indication is that a rational judgment is being made by coaches regarding their abilities to deal with certain emotions. In particular, coaches expressed uncertainty in how to handle emotions they perceived as difficult, and some indicated a need for ongoing development or training.

> I am not sure how to handle them and I get a sense of panic. (R28)
> I am not sure I have the right tools/training or experience to deal with them effectively. (R36)

Part B

We now consider how coaches reported that they deal with perceived difficulties associated with their own emotions. When they feel a strong emotion, coaches tended to respond in one of four ways:

i. Through reflection and self-examination, either internally, or externally through supervision, seeing it in one of two ways:
   a. their own issue:

   > I will reflect on why this is. (R28)
   > I would need to be aware of the impact on my coaching—stand back and reassess the situation. (R38)

   b. or as their client's issue:

   > I try to get over it but am always aware they might also provoke this in other people so I would consider whether this was my stuff or part of the client issue. (R10)
   > I look for what they are doing to trigger it. (R39)

ii. Through actively exploring the issue with a client
   Flag it up or bring it into the room. (R11) Will if appropriate discuss this with them. (R34)

iii. By termination of the coaching process

   > I question whether I should have that relationship with that individual. (R24)
   > I wouldn't continue the relationship. (R35)

iv. By taking the issue to supervision (although very few respondents mentioned this)

   > I need at least to discuss this with a supervisor. (R9)
   > I call my supervisor/mentor for guidance. (R25)

Only one response was to continue the process on the professional level (this is not unusual for similar professions, e.g., counseling)

> I will discuss with a supervisor to understand why. Professionally, I should not need to feel enthusiastic about all my clients to be effective. (R9)

The strategy in terms of responsible coaching, so as not to recycle problems, is to use some form of supervision. The responses in (i) (b), above, might well indicate unresolved personal issues that may interfere with the coach's ability to work with clients. For example, there could be irrational fears that these coaches have in relation to their experience, and an outcome would be possible termination and giving up on their own and their client's development, as in (iii). Coaches are not required to work with their personal issues in the way counselors are, and as a consequence may be unaware of their limitations in relation to their personal "stuff". This appears to reinforce a need for supervision.

By contrast, in (ii) above there is an indication of a high level of awareness of the coach, one who is prepared to work in-depth. But even actively exploring emotions in this way needs to be reflected on carefully because it could still mask issues such as transference or countertransference. Thus all responses should be explored in supervision.

The second theme has identified responses to difficult emotional situations caused by the range of emotions presented by the client. Two categories of client emotion have been identified as having the most impact: strong emotions and inappropriate emotions, and some of these appeared to affect a coach's own emotions, in some cases revealing a strong identification with the emotion. It was evident that most coaches in this study, however, were aware of the boundaries between themselves and their client. The results suggest that coaches deal with emotional situations in one of three ways:

1. They take time out to analyze and reflect on the emotion, either viewing the issue as their own and self-reflecting or taking it to supervision, or they see it as belonging to their client.
2. They actively explore the emotion with the client in the coaching session and try to use the energy they perceive as captured within it.
3. They refer the client or terminate the process.

Coaches perceived a range of emotions as difficult but saw control of their own emotions during the coaching process as vitally important.

Differentiated views on clients' emotions

Court (1995) considers that beliefs about emotions are still highly gendered. This differentiated aspect of emotion could also have the potential to lead to complex emotional situations for the coach. In the workplace, for example, it has been reported that female executives are expected to control their emotions, as any display of feelings can be perceived as weak or irrational (Sachs & Blackmore, 1998). Lupton (1998) also confirms that femininity has been associated with the emotional and the private, while masculinity has been associated with a more rational and public persona.

Gender issues in relation to emotion were evident in a variety of responses from coaches:

a. Some coaches reported no gender differences in dealing with emotions. When prompted with the stem "When a female/male client presents an emotional reaction, I …" responses included:

> Behave exactly as I would with a male. (R23)
> Respond the same way I would if a female client did so. (R7)
> Treat it on the emotion—not their gender. (R21)
> Respond appropriately irrespective of gender. (R37)

b. Others had somewhat gender-biased responses indicating more tolerance to female emotions and more discomfort in working with male emotions:

> I can probably empathise better. (R2)
> I would probably feel less comfortable than I would if it were a female client. (R5)
> Can probably empathise, being a female myself. (R39)
> Try to deal with it in a professional, sympathetic, but detached way (I am male). (R9)

The recognition by coaches that gender differences exist and that they might approach them differently reflects the situation in the workplace. The conventionally male attributes of rationality, control, and logic are still positively imbued and in opposition to the traditional female qualities of emotionality and irrationality.

The heightened awareness necessary within coaching suggests that coaches need to recognize that they may hold to certain stereotypes and that there is a need to reflect on this. In (b) above it was evident that even in an overtly nonjudgmental occupation such as coaching, some coaches were aware that they are conditioned by stereotypical, gender-biased cultures. Some coaches considered that they would have more empathy with someone of the same sex and may feel less comfortable with male expressions of emotion.

CONCLUSION AND FURTHER RESEARCH

In this paper, we have presented an investigation of how coaches deal with difficult emotional situations in their coaching relationships. The study suggests that coaches have very different viewpoints in relation to dealing with challenging emotional situations and that an enhanced awareness of this is essential.

In the workplace, especially with the current stress on being "emotionally intelligent", or with emphasis on controlling and using the emotions purposefully, as in the case of emotional labor, it is important for coaches to be aware of how emotions can help or hinder the client's progress. It is important too, that they are aware of their own responses, biases, and limitations. Although there was evidence in this study of considerable reflective practice and a focus on development as a coach, the results suggest that there is a significant role for supervision. However, very few immediate responses of coaches to difficult emotional situations included reference to supervision, illustrating probably a stage in the development of the profession when supervision is only gradually starting to playing an important role.

In relation to gender stereotyping, some coaches saw no gender difference in relation to how they would deal with emotions, but others admitted they may be more tolerant with females and experience more discomfort when males displayed their feelings. This is an illustration of how unexamined assumptions about emotions, absorbed from a dominant culture, might hamper the coaching process, and points again to the value of supervision.

This paper has also shown that coaches are significantly affected by their clients' emotions: none of the coaches appears to have been involved in a practice where they could avoid emotion, as the ICF statement above seemed to imply. In fact, the responses of this sample of coaches show that full involvement in the coaching process implies involvement of the total person, including their emotional characteristics. This may well lead to situations that the coach may identify as difficult.

A further observation relates to the individual responses to our stem-sentence questionnaire, which reveal a large variety of intentions and strategies in terms of dealing with emotional situations. We believe that this variety is partly an outcome of the very mixed attitudes to emotions evident in organizations (Fineman, 2000). These attitudes range from suppression and rationalization to acceptance and high expectations, especially in relation to the ability of EI to deliver performance-related outcomes. We have described elsewhere how this ambiguity contributes to the spectrum of personal theories of emotions that coaches hold (Bachkirova & Cox, 2007).

In addition, the stem-sentence method mirrors the spontaneity and immediacy of the coaching conversation and so we would suggest reveals individual tendencies, which, in turn, are colored by elements of professional background and experience. Thus we would argue that the coaches' responses to difficult emotional situations and their personal theories (articulated or unconscious) might be influenced by current attitudes toward emotions, particularly in organizations, but also by their individual differences. Such individual differences include their tolerance of the affective states of others, their own "emotionality", their gender, and their professional training. This is an area for further research.

The implications of these findings for the coaching and mentoring profession are twofold:

1. Education and training would need to include the nature of emotions and their function in individual change; the issue of EI with sufficient criticality applied to the concept, its measurement, and commercial use; the role of individual differences in dealing with emotions; the difference between empathy and identification.
2. The study shows that coaches need appropriate support in order to advance their awareness and understanding of specific emotions in the coaching process and their individual capacity and style of working with these. However, in this study,

very few coaches identified this support with supervision and are, therefore, missing the opportunity to enhance the quality of their coaching work through individually tailored professional support.

This paper has highlighted some of the ways in which coaches currently deal with difficult emotional situations and has reinforced the call for supervision for coaches. However, more research is needed. The next stage of our own project is to examine some of the strategies coaches have for helping clients become aware of their emotions and to see how they perceive the role of emotion in aiding performance and well-being.

REFERENCES

Bachkirova, T., & Cox, E. (2005). A bridge over troubled water: Bringing together coaching and counselling. Counselling at Work.

Bachkirova, T., & Cox, E. (2007). Coaching with emotion in organisations: Investigation of personal theories. *Leadership & Organization Development Journal, 28*(7), 600–612. doi.org/10.1108/01437730710823860

Bagozzi, R. P. (2003). Positive and negative emotions in organisations. In K. S. Cameron, J. E. Dutton, & R. E. Quinn (Eds.), *Positive organisational scholarship* (pp. 176–193). San Francisco, CA: Berrett-Koehler.

Bono, J. E., Foldes, H. J., Vinson G., & Muros, J. P. (2007). Workplace emotions: The role of supervision and leadership. *Journal of Applied Psychology, 92*(5), 1357–1367. https://doi.org/10.1037/0021-9010.92.5.1357

ten Bos, R., & Willmott, H. (2001). Towards a post-dualistic business ethics: Interweaving reason and emotion in working life. *Journal of Management Studies, 38*(6), 769–793. https://doi.org/10.1111/1467-6486.00258

Brody, L. (1997). Gender and emotion: Beyond stereotypes. *Journal of Social Issues, 53*(2), 369–393. https://doi.org/10.1111/j.1540-4560.1997.tb02448.x

Court, M. (1995). Good girls and naughty girls. In B. Limerick & R. Lingard (Eds.), *Gender and changing emotional management* (pp. 150–161). Sydney, Australia: Hodder & Stoughton.

Crotty, M. (1996). Doing phenomenology. In P. Willis & B. Neville (Eds.), *Qualitative research practice in adult education*. Melbourne, Australia: David Lovell Publishing.

Fineman, S. (Ed.). (2000). *Emotions in organisations* (2nd ed.). London, UK: Sage Publications.

Fineman, S. (2005). Appreciating emotion at work: Paradigm tensions. *International Journal of Work Organisation and Emotion, 1*(1), 4–19. https://doi.org/10.1504/IJWOE.2005.007323

Fischer, A., Rotteveel, M., Evers, C., & Manstead, A. (2004). Emotional assimilation: How we are influenced by others' emotions. *Cahier de Psychologie Cognitive, 22*, 223–245.

Gherardi, S. (1995). *Gender, symbolism, and organizational cultures*. Newbury Park, CA: Sage Publications.

Greenberg, L. (2003). *Emotion focused therapy*. Washington, DC: American Psychological Association.

Gross, J., Richards, J., & John, O. (2006). Emotion regulation in everyday life. In D. Snyder, J. Simpson, & J. Hughes (Eds.), *Emotion regulation in couples and families: Pathways to dysfunction and health* (pp. 13–35). Washington DC: American Psychological Association. https://doi.org/10.1504/IJWOE.2005.007323

International Coach Foundation. (2002). The Nature and Scope of Coaching, International Coaching Federation. Accessed April 3, 2006, from http://www.coachfederation.org/ICF/For+Coaching+Clients/Selecting+a+Coach Nature+and+Scope+of+Coaching

Le Bon, T. (2001). *Wise therapy*. London, UK: Continuum.

Lupton, D. (1998). *The emotional self*. London, UK: Sage Publications.

Mark, A. (2005). Organising emotions in health care. *Journal of Health Organization and Management, 19*(4/5), 277–289.

Merleau-Ponty, M. (1992). *Phenomenology of perception*. London, UK: Routledge.

Opengart, R. (2005). Emotional intelligence and emotion work: Examining constructs from an interdisciplinary framework. *Human Resource Development Review, 4*(1), 49–62. https://doi.org/10.1177/1534484304273817

Patrick, C. (2004). Coaching: Should we enquire into emotional aspects of the client's experience? Oxford Brookes University: MA Thesis.

Pizarro, D. (2000). Nothing more than feelings? The role of emotions in moral judgement. *Journal for the Theory of Social Behaviour, 30*(4), 355–374. https://doi.org/10.1111/1468-5914.00135

Richards, J., & Gross, J. (2005). Personality and emotional memory: How regulating emotion impairs memory for emotional events. *Journal of Research in Personality, 40*(5), 631–651. https://doi.org/10.1016/j.jrp.2005.07.002

Sachs, J., & Blackmore, J. (1998). You never show you can't cope: Women in school leadership roles managing their emotions. *Gender and Education, 10*(3), 265–279. https://doi.org/10.1080/09540259820899

Salovey, P., & Mayer, J. (1990). Emotional intelligence. *Imagination, Cognition, and Personality, 9*, 185–211.

Schmid, P. (2001). Comprehension: The art of not knowing. Dialogical and ethical perspectives on empathy as dialogue in personal and person-centred relationships. In S. Haugh & T. Merry (Eds.), *Empathy*. Llongarron, UK: PCCS Books.

Simpson, R. & Smith, S. (2005). Emotional labour and organisations: A developing field. *Highlights*, Autumn. Accessed October 31, 2006, from http://www.inderscience.com/www/newsletter article_winter2006.pdf

Smith, J., & Osborn, M. (2003). Interpretative phenomenological analysis. In J. Smith (Ed.), *Qualitative psychology*. London, UK: Sage.

Smith, P., & Sharma, M. (2002). Rationalising the promotion of non-rational behaviours in organisations. *The Learning Organization, 5*(2), 197–201.

Speedy, S. (2005). Emotions and emotionality in organisations. *Australian Journal of Business and Social Inquiry, 3*. Accessed April 18, 2006, from www.scu.edu.au/schools/socialsciences/ajbsi papers/Vol3/speedy.pdf

Tiedens, L. Z. (2001). Anger and advancement versus sadness and subjugation: The effect of negative emotion on social status conferral. *Journal of Personality and Social Psychology, 80*, 86–94. https://doi.org/10.1037/0022-3514.80.1.86

Whitmore, J. (1996). *Coaching for performance*. London, UK: Nicholas Brealy.

10 Critical Moments of Clients and Coaches: A Direct-Comparison Study

Erik de Haan, Colin Bertie, Andrew Day, and Charlotte Sills[1]

"I don't understand. I just don't understand … I don't understand it at all. I just don't understand." "What's wrong? What don't you understand?" "I've never heard such a strange story." "Why don't you tell me about it?" Opening lines of *Rashomon* (1950), Akira Kurosawa.

Executive coaching—the professional development of executives through one-to-one conversations with a qualified coach—is a discipline within the broader field of organization development (OD), which is comparatively amenable to research. Executive coaching conversations are usually explicitly contracted and bounded in both time and space (fixed duration, similar intervals, quiet and dependable space, away from the client's organization, etc.). Most coaching manuals suggest keeping the space for conversation as much as possible neutral, uncluttered, and comfortable, without interference or distraction (Hawkins & Smith, 2006; Starr, 2003). Coach and client may spend some 10–20 hours in this same environment, in addition to sporadic email and telephone exchanges. The executive coach does not normally have a lot of contact with others in the client's organization unless there are additional coaching clients in that organization or the coaching is part of a larger-scale consulting intervention. This relative simplicity and the underlying unities of space, time, action, and actors, create a relatively bounded *laboratory* in which

---

[1] First published as de Haan, E., Bertie, C., Day, A., & Sills, C. (2010). Critical moments of clients and coaches: A direct-comparison study. *International Coaching Psychology Review*, 5(2), 109–128.

consulting interventions can be studied. This is what makes executive coaching particularly exciting to investigate. In order to understand the impact and contribution of executive coaching and other organizational consulting interventions, it is not enough to just understand general effectiveness or outcome. One also has to inquire into and create an understanding of the underlying coaching processes themselves, from the perspectives of both clients and coaches. The executive coaching profession is still young and although there are several studies on coaching outcome (e.g., Evers, Brouwers, & Tomic, 2006; Ragins, Cotton, & Miller, 2000; Smither, London, Flautt, Vargas, & Kucine, 2003), all rigorous quantitative research papers can probably be counted on the fingers of one hand. For recent overview studies that together cover some 20 serious coaching outcome research papers, see Kampa-Kokesch and Anderson (2001), Feldman and Lankau (2005), and Greif (2007). However much pioneering work has been done in recent years, there is really no comparison with the related but much more established field of psychotherapy, which boasts many hundreds of solid research papers (for an overview of outcome research in psychotherapy, see Wampold (2001)).

Outcome or effectiveness research reduces the whole of the coaching intervention to only one number, or perhaps a set of numbers; for example, averages of psychometric instruments or client ratings. Outcome research has to be silent on what happens within a coaching relationship: the many gestures, speech acts, and attempts at sense-making that make up the whole of the intervention. At best, it can tell us in a statistical manner how the full sum of all those conversations taken together may contribute to a digit on a Likert scale, at worst it may not even tell us that. What interests us in this study is how outcomes are achieved within the coaching intervention, that is, within and between individual coaching conversations. This is the realm of so-called sub-outcome (Rice & Greenberg, 1984): outcome achieved in moments or sessions of coaching.

Research into coaching *process* is not as straightforward as research into coaching *outcome*. While reducing the whole of a coaching relationship to one or a few quantifiable "outcomes" (e.g., a rating by the coach, the client, the client's boss, an independent observer) allows a clear-cut and specific definition of that variable when it comes to process, one has to deal with manifold "sub-outcomes" (Rice & Greenberg, 1984). Moreover, studying an ongoing process will influence that process, which makes it harder to study.

Not withstanding the difficulties with process research, it is of vital importance for coaching practitioners to understand better what happens in their conversations, what both partners in the conversations pay attention to and what they think is achieved through engaging in conversation. This article sets out to find some preliminary answers to the following main research questions:

1. What is the nature of "key moments" that clients and coaches report immediately after their session together?
2. In what ways and to what degree are the reports by coaches and their clients different?
3. How do the results obtained with this new sample of real-time "key moments" compare with findings from earlier studies?

Although, to the best of our knowledge of executive coaching literature, comparison studies into coaches' and clients' experiences of coaching have not been undertaken before, they are not without important precursors in psychotherapy. Admittedly, psychotherapy has distinctive professional qualifications, different ways of working, and a different knowledge base (Spinelli, 2008). However, there is enough similarity in terms of one-to-one conversations with a professional helper to be interested in similar research findings from that field. Yalom and Elkin (1974) famously wrote up their two-year therapy journey, so that for some 75 sessions we have a first-person account from both therapist and client written up independently and shortly after each session. For an overview of more quantitative studies, it seems appropriate to start with Feifel and Eells' (1964) account of therapy outcomes as reported by both patients and therapists. They report "a thought-provoking contrast in the patients' accent on insight changes compared with those of symptom relief and behaviours by therapists" (Feifel & Eells, 1964, p.317). In a more extensive study, where patient and therapist reports after single sessions were compared (Orlinsky & Howard, 1975), "patients and therapists agreed in rating insight and problem-resolution as the dominant goal of the patients, with relief as a prominent although secondary, goal" (p.66). Stiles (1980) did a direct-comparison study of sessions, by comparing clients' and therapists' ratings of sessions that they had together. By correlating ratings, he was able to show that clients' positive feelings after sessions were strongly associated with perceived "smoothness/ease" of the sessions, while therapists' positive feelings were associated with "depth/value" of the sessions. Broadly, clients and therapists tended to agree in their characterizations of sessions. Caskey, Barker, and Elliott (1984) have compared patients' and therapists' perceptions of preselected individual therapist responses and they found reasonable agreement between patients and therapists on therapists' impact and intentions, as well.

Particularly relevant from the perspective of this inquiry is the direct-comparison study of key moments of therapy by Llewelyn (1988). She interviewed 40 patient–therapist pairs and collected 1,076 "critical events" (both helpful and unhelpful) from 399 sessions (an average of 2.7 per session). She found highly significant differences between the selection and description of the events by therapists and by patients. These differences turned out to be greater when the outcome of the psychotherapy was relatively less helpful. Llewelyn used Elliott's (1985) taxonomy to classify the events and found that, while patients valued "reassurance/relief" and "problem solutions" more highly, therapists valued "gaining of cognitive/affective insight" highest, and both patients and therapists valued "personal contact" highly.

Llewelyn (1988) concludes that patients seem to be more concerned with solutions to their problems and that they place a higher value on advice and solutions, provided they feel free to reject them. Therapists, on the other hand, seem more concerned with the etiology of the problems and potential transformation through the patient's insight. Earlier research of critical moments of coaching conversations followed a narrative and retrospective approach. De Haan (2008a, 2008b), de Haan, Bertie, Day, and Sills (2010), and Day, de Haan, Blass, Sills, and Bertie (2008) asked three groups of coaches and one group of clients of executive coaches to describe briefly one critical moment (an exciting, tense, or significant moment) from their coaching journeys. See Table 10.1 for a brief overview of all five inquiries into critical moments of executive coaching from 2002.

Table 10.1 *Five Data Sets of Critical-Moment Descriptions, 2002–2009*

Data set	Who has provided the descriptions?	No. of critical-moment descriptions	Main conclusions	Publication
1	Inexperienced executive coaches: approximately 75% were (internal and external) consultants who had recently completed a full-year program in management consulting and about 25% independent coaches.	80	All critical moments could be expressed as *doubts* of coaches. Critical moments were seen as important sources of information and potential breakthrough moments.	De Haan (2008a)
2	Experienced executive coaches: at least 8 years' experience.	78	All critical moments could be expressed as *anxieties* of coaches. Experienced coaches grapple with recurring struggles in their client work.	De Haan (2008b)
3	New sample of very experienced executive coaches (on average 11.3 years' experience) who were interviewed in-depth.	49	An experienced *rupture* in the relationship (e.g., misunderstanding, anger, re-contracting and referral, withdrawal and termination) was found around every critical moment. Critical to the outcome of that process was whether continued and shared reflection was possible after the critical moment.	Day et al. (2008)
4	Clients of executive coaching.	59	What clients report as most helpful from their experience of coaching are new realizations and insights.	De Haan et al. (2010)
5	Direct comparison of experienced coaches with their clients.	86	Both coaches and clients report new realizations and insights as most critical in their direct experience of coaching, and they are also in substantial agreement about the specific moments that were critical in the sessions and why.	This study

Note. The number of critical moments in the first study (de Haan, 2008a) is lower (56). This is because we have extended this data set beyond the work for that publication.

The studies to date have found quite divergent material, with coaches and clients clearly submitting different descriptions and also placing a different emphasis within the descriptions (see de Haan et al., 2010). The results of previous investigations prompted the present direct-comparison study as a way to explore and clarify some of the differences and also to test the conclusions from earlier papers with the help of a new data set. Direct-comparison in real time is of course not possible without seriously interfering with the executive-coaching sessions themselves. In order to minimize interference, coach and client were interviewed only once and directly after a session. Other than logistical issues, potential relational difficulties were anticipated as the research would impinge on very sensitive, private, and confidential relationships. To quote Elton Wilson and Syme's (2006) pertinent book, *Objectives and Outcomes* (p.82):

> Asking clients for their opinion is a process fraught with controversy, with many thera-
> pists asserting the possibility of harm to the therapeutic alliance or, conversely, affecting
> the transference. In addition, clients may wish to please or praise their therapists or even
> to covertly attack their therapist. Unfortunately, a practitioner's own observations may
> be laden with assumption and a defensive need to prove their own worth or the effective-
> ness of their own theoretical and methodological approach.

The same can very well be true for asking coaches and their clients about their find-ings while they are still engaged in a long-term coaching intervention. One would expect the reports of key moments from their recent conversation to be influenced by what they think of the overall quality of the work and the relationship, by what they expect us as researchers to be looking for, or even by their relationships with us and our institution.

Following de Haan et al. (2010), the main hypothesis for this study was that the perspectives of clients and coaches will be significantly different, as is also the case for critical-event studies in psychotherapy (see, for example, Caskey et al., 1984; Llewelyn, 1988). We were expecting not only substantial differences in the moments that were selected for recall but also in terms of the emphasis within the moment descriptions. To our surprise, we actually found that clients' and coaches' data in this study were very similar; that in more than 50% of cases the same moment, event, or topic was described, and that there were substantial similarities in emphases between the coaches and their clients.

METHOD

Since 2002, we have opted for the study of so-called "critical-moment descriptions" as a way of understanding the impact of executive coaching engagements, following similar methods as pioneered by Flanagan (1954), Elliott, James, Reimschuessel, Cislo, & Sack (1985), and Llewelyn (1988). Critical moments are remembered as exciting, tense, and/or significant moments after coaching conversations. They can be assumed to be a reflection of change through executive coaching as it happens in conversation. Descriptions allow pattern analysis, both qualitatively and quantitatively, and they afford comparison procedures between different data sets. As a comparison with the previous research on critical moments in executive coaching conversations, a setting was devised that allows as much as possible to directly compare clients' and coaches' perceptions of key moments in their sessions, in such a way that the distortions of memory (Goodman, Magnussen, Andersson, Endestad, Løkke, & Mostue, 2006) would be minimized by gathering the critical-moment descriptions as quickly after the session as possible. We contacted directly and personally about 20 executive coaches of our acquaintance and agreed with 14 to work with us on this research programme. Each of these coaches agreed to be interviewed and selected a client who would also be interviewed straight after the coaching session they had together, for a maximum of 30 min. Two of the 14 coaches contributed two client sessions, and one contributed seven client sessions (all different clients). The coach who contributed seven sessions with seven clients did not preselect and just offered us data from all her clients within one particular organization. All interviews were recorded, and in one case the recording equipment did not work so that this data had to be discarded. All in all, the sample size was 21 coaching conversations, yielding 42 recorded interviews.

Of the 14 coaches participating in this inquiry, two were Ashridge, Hult Business School staff, five Ashridge associated coaches who do a lot of executive coaching work for Ashridge, three belonged to a wider network, and four were in the second year of their MSc in Executive Coaching at Ashridge. Nine of the coaches had been accredited by Ashridge, and all had over two years' experience as an executive coach, with an average experience level of more than ten years. The coaches selected the client, coaching conversation, and interview day—the researchers worked as much as possible around their requirements and preferences. Three of the participating coaches were male and 11 were female. Of the 21 participating clients, six were female and 15 were male. Most clients and coaches were white and British/Irish; there was one Israeli and one Australian coach and one South African client. The average number of sessions that coach and client had already had with each other was 5.4—with a minimum of two and a maximum of 15. On average, coach and client had worked with each other for almost 10 months.

As the authors have developed their thinking about critical moments in executive coaching over the years, they decided not to participate in the study as coaches, as clients, or even as interviewers. Two MSc students in Organizational Behavior at Birkbeck College, University of London, Heather Reekie and Monica Stroink, were willing to run all the interviews, as they collected material for their own Masters dissertations. All interviews were conducted in private rooms, mostly close to the location where the coaching had taken place. Some interviews were over the telephone. The interviews with client and coach were done as much as possible by both students to avoid potential biases. Logistically, this was not possible in three cases as the client and coach were promised an interview straight after the coaching session so there would be least memory loss. Also, in four (~10%) of the client interviews, a member of the author group stepped in and conducted the interview.

Unexpected logistical challenges occurred because, for every pair of interviews, two different researchers had to travel to the right location or telephone in at the right time. This sometimes meant hiring a second consulting room. Even with the logistics under control, the interviewees were subjected to detailed questioning, having just come out of presumably intensive and exhausting coaching encounters. Nevertheless, 42 interviews with clients and coaches took place shortly after their sessions, which generated 86 descriptions of key moments of interest.

All interviews had the same structure and they were all transcribed (except one). The core questions about the critical moments were as follows:

1. Looking back on the session, what seems to be the important or key or critical moment(s) of your time together? What happened? Please can you provide a brief description of the moment(s).
2. What tells you that this was a critical moment?
3. What was your role in that moment?
4. What was your partner's role in that moment?
5. How do you think this moment will impact on the future (i.e., the future of these conversations or what you take from the coaching)?

In this way the interviewers were able to obtain 86 critical moments from 21 sessions, that is, an average of just over two per interview and 4.1 per coaching session. Exactly 43 of these moments were obtained from clients and another 43 were obtained from coaches. This article reports on the descriptions of key moments as they are found in the transcripts, that is, mainly answers to questions 1 and 2 above, and occasionally more data were taken from answers to the other questions when this yielded additional clarity.

From this data set the inquiry proceeded as follows:

1. Using grounded theory (Corbin & Strauss, 1990) we came up with 30 shortcodes describing critical aspects in the critical-moment descriptions.
2. Five in the research team (the four authors and one MSc student) coded the data set using as many of these codes as they wanted per critical moment. The four codings were correlated for inter-rater consistency and first conclusions were drawn from the frequencies of codes.
3. The same method of grounded theory was again followed to come up with a much smaller code set, containing only 12 more disparate and mutually exclusive codes, which could be used for this data set but also for all four previous data sets (Day et al., 2008; de Haan, 2008a, 2008b; de Haan et al., 2010).
4. All five sets of critical moments, totaling 352 critical moments, were coded on the new codes using a sort method (exclusive coding of only one code per critical moment), by two of the authors (CB and EH) and by one outsider, a colleague not previously introduced to this research (AC).

RESULTS

First impressions on reading through the data set. The following features of this new data set, some of which clearly different from earlier research data, stand out:

- Both clients and coaches found it easy to come up with critical or key moments. Contrary to earlier research into the experiences of clients of coaching (de Haan et al., 2010), there were no 'no' responses. In fact, there was at least one critical-moment description from every interview and the total amount of key moment descriptions volunteered by clients exactly equals the number of those volunteered by coaches (43, i.e., on average 2.05 key moment descriptions per interview). There is, however, one client who says "There's nothing really that sticks out, obviously it's always a very casual conversation—I think that the biggest thing is that it's always very thought-provoking, it makes you look at yourself quite a lot," but he then continues to volunteer one key moment.

- There was a clear and sustained focus on the client throughout the descriptions: only one of the 43 coach descriptions referred exclusively to the coach's internal process (this one description still referred three times briefly to the client, by name) and only one of the clients described exclusively what the coach was doing. Fifty-three percent of coaches' descriptions referred to themselves and their interventions, and 44% of clients' descriptions referred explicitly to the coach and to what the coach had done.

- The coding of the content of the critical moments with 30 codes similar to those in de Haan et al. (2010) showed that the most prevalent codes were again those about personal realizations (both about issues and about self) and those that are about specific behaviors of the coach (both directive and facilitative interventions). Together these four of the 30 codes make up almost 50% of the coded content. When client and coach descriptions are compared, there are two clusters of codes that are strongly skewed toward the coach critical-moment descriptions: (a) the coach's emotional reactions, which made up five codes but only 6% of the content; and (b) physiological reactions of the client (such as skin tone, agitation, and breathing), a single code that covered 2% of the content.

- A lot of clients and coaches comment on the same moment or situation, and they talk about those moments and situations in similar terms. In fact 46 of the 86 key moment descriptions (53%) were clearly about the same moment or event (examples below are the pairs 3co9 and 3cl10 and 14co51 and 14cl52).

- The descriptions are narrative in nature and seemed to all four authors less exciting or engaging compared with the previous research. They seem to be lower risk and of less immediate impact. At the same time, they can be seen as an illustration of the straightforward, helpful, and practice-based character of our own experience of "everyday coaching."

- The nature of the descriptions is broadly positive and constructive; there was only one moment approximating a rupture in the relationship (see key moment 4co13, below, and compare with Day et al. (2008), which found evidence of ruptures in the relationship in most critical-moment descriptions). So, in summary with the previous conclusion, there seems to be an absence of tension, struggle, and strong emotion. There are three occasions where clients express interest in their coaches, for example, critical moment 8cl30 below. We assumed this was partly because of an implicit psychological contract between the participants, and between the participants and us, to be appreciative and gentle toward one another, which in turn may be due to the pre-selection and the ongoing nature of all relationships.

- The only differences initially found between clients' and coaches' accounts were that coaches place more emphasis on their own actions and they use more jargon and psychological terms to describe what went on compared with their clients. This reminded us of Yalom's (Yalom & Elkin, 1974, p.79) statement that his own observations seemed more sophomoric than his client's writing.

- There was a high number of references by coaches (17 out of 43 moments) to clients' physiological responses (frowning, posture, note-taking, agitation, breathing, etc., for example, vignettes 3co9 and 5co17, below), while clients never referred to these matters.

Vignettes of the 86 real-life critical moments

To help the reader gain a better connection with the full data set we have chosen 17 vignettes from the 86 key moment descriptions. We have chosen this data set purposefully, to give an indication of the range of data and also to show two occasions where coach and client comment on the same moment in the session (the pairs 3co9 and 3cl10 and 4co51 and 4cl52). Rather than showing a random selection here, we have deliberately chosen a more meaningful and engaging range of vignettes. The numbering of these vignettes follows the chronological order of the interviews, that is, conversation number, "co" for "coach moment" and "cl" for "client moment," and then key moment number. We have not edited these fragments. These are just 1,285 words. The full data set is over 27,000 words long.

[1cl2] "I suppose really for me it's through the process of discussion it's the realization on my part that there's something that I have to do. So it's the sort of the processes of opening my eyes to you know, ooh hang on there's something I need to do here that you know wouldn't otherwise. So the, you know, it's the what helps me realize is the point that I get the light bulbs going off to like, hey hang on why haven't I thought about this?"

[1cl4] "So the feeling for me is really say it's sort of a … it's a point that I recognize that there's something that's needed. It's sort of highlighting it. So it's almost a feeling of surprise and realization around there's something there that I'm able to see it's just that I haven't previously been able to."

[3co9] "And that was the tipping point I think, when he recognized that he could use one thing to do the other, he thinks in a very linear way. And he was thinking about I've got to do the projects, I've got to be more approachable but really by linking the two together he was able to see that … I think he recognized that actually I can do both of these together and one will help the other. And that was the … that was the … the key I think. It was partly his erm … he was clearly doing some visualizing sitting there in thought, looking up at the ceiling. So erm … And a period of silence after when he said 'erm yeah I hadn't thought of looking at it like that.' Erm what else did he say? 'I think I've crossed a bridge,' that's what he said."

[3cl10] "I'd written it down as an action to do, which is kind of respective of my style. It's because it's … I describe it as opening my eyes to a blind spot really it's easy with hindsight to say that's a good way of approaching it but prior to the conversation or prior to today I would not have thought of trying to do the project in that particular direction. So it's a change in direction to what I would have done otherwise."

[4co13] "He was asking me to raise an issue outside of the coaching relationship. Erm you know to show I was sort of agreeing with him a form of words that he was … that he would be happy with, for me to sort of try and get something fed back into

the organization that he thought was important. So that was quite an important … err an interesting part of the conversation. Erm well this was an issue about the person's boss … erm and the person's boss is being coached by erm one of my colleagues … so is it was a sort of a 'can you use your influence with the other coach?'"

[5co17] "Er, he started to make notes … actually he started to make notes and started to get more animated in how he was talking about it."

[5co19] "That he began drawing on my pad. And the adult to adult was his meeting. The meetings that he controlled. That was his meeting. The big circle was his meeting."

[6co23] "He sat back and thought about it rather than being accused by it."

[8cl30] "I think the key moment might have been that I asked him what he felt about the work we'd been doing and he said that he was pleased that the report he'd done had led to substantial change and efficiencies and he seemed to take some pleasure in it … I think it was good to hear that he'd taken some pleasure from it himself and felt that … taken some pleasure out of the fact that he'd been effective."

[9cl32] "It's basically stating the obvious, but I didn't see it, it was staring me right in the face."

[11cl40] "Not a lot of other people know about it—I have a limited amount of contact with people to let them know about it and not feel bad and embarrassed about it. It felt like the right thing to do rather than waffle around the edges."

[13cl50] "Organizing our future sessions that definitely was and also you know another bit was maybe time to talk about some other issues you know that are going around you know what we do and I had an opportunity to talk to someone who's not involved as well. So that was probably the important part of it."

[14co51] "It was a bit odd the way that we started off because he thought that he'd sent me some information and I … I'm perfect you see … I knew that I was thinking, I did check all of my emails but I don't recollect what you've sent me you know and I looked through I'm sure I printed everything off that folk had sent me. So we had a kind of a 20-minute forage around whether we could find this information. So it's kind of like erm, it felt like a weird start to the session and I did say to him given that we haven't got the information can you talk to me about what was important to you and what you'd written through and we can cover it here and now. (…) So it's really important to him about appearances and again being professional, doing the right thing, you know doing what he says he's going to do. So it was a real … I was really noticing how I was getting hooked into, well I haven't got the information you know we're looking on computers, I was searching my Blackberry thinking this is bizarre really because we don't need it. So it was this bizarre start to him (…) It really linked into how he wants to get things done and wants to get things right and look good to other people. That's really, really important to him. Erm, so links from that."

[14cl52] "It's important that we got sorted today, the mix up we had at the beginning so we knew where we were going. That was important and I must say within two or three minutes we had it sorted. We realized there'd been a mistake and agreed appropriate action and it got resolved very easily. It wasn't confrontational in any way, don't think that, just a mix up but a few negotiation skills on both our parts

we could resolve it, so we didn't lose anything out of those five minutes of the hour-and-a-half session, so it was very important that we could speak our way round it to recover the situation."

[21cl83] "It was really the characterization. It was just kind of that makes perfect sense to me. I've been thinking, reflecting about this at various levels for a long time. Occasionally you have those moments of realization, you forget them and then when you're reminded it not only provides clarity it provides comfort to the person who's being coached."

[21co84] "My hunch is it's probably more important to my client than it was to me. He can tell you for himself but my hunch was that was new and interesting information that he was quite intrigued by."

[21co86] "I was surprised. So I suppose I was monitoring my own reactions and my own reactions were well that feels like something important and new so I guess it felt like it meant something. Whether it's just because I was worried I missed it I don't know but it was something about this is new and feels significant. My client was very animated in talking about it."

Content analysis of the critical moments

All critical-moment descriptions were coded to identify recurrent themes, with similar codes as in our previous research (see, for example, de Haan et al., 2010). The coding did not show a large or consistent difference between coach and client moment descriptions, and it showed less consistency among markers than before (Cohen's kappa was only 0.34 on average; kappa being the standard measure for correlations between independent coding processes), which can be explained by the fact that the fragments are longer (on average 316 words per description), so there is more information conveyed in every key moment description. Because of the failure of the existing set of codes to divulge distinctive patterns in the data set, and because of the striking differences with earlier data sets, a new more succinct set of codes was drawn up and tested, which would capture all critical aspects across all five data sets. There were four broad categories in these 12 codes: a moment of learning (codes 1 and 2), a moment of relational change (codes 3 and 4), a moment of significant action (codes 5 and 6), and a moment of significant emotional experience (codes 7–12). To provide help with the emotional codes (7–12) a table with the full range of emotions, based on a tree structure built on six primary emotions (three positive and three negative) by Parrott (2001), was provided to the coders. For brief descriptions of the 12 codes, see Table 10.2.

Two of the authors (EH and CB) and one colleague who was not an executive coach (AC) coded the full data set of 352 critical moments with these codes. All codes were at least used three times by every coder, though there were four codes that were used for less than 3% of the data set: 6, 7, 8, and 11. We had anticipated this when drawing up the set of 12 codes, but we kept these codes in to keep a balanced and structurally complete set. Figure 10.1 shows the frequency of use of the codes, for all three observers and the full data set of 352 moments.

Table 10.2 *The 12 Codes Used to Analyze All Five Data Sets*

Code number	Short description of the code
1	A moment of learning: a moment in which new insight was created for coach and—particularly—client.
2	A moment of learning: a moment of working through, reflecting, gaining new perspectives and/or making sense of existing material.
3	A change in the relationship in the moment (positive).
4	A change in the relationship in the moment (negative).
5	Significant action in the moment (coach-led): applying oneself to a unique scripted process such as drawing, visualization, role-play, GROW ...
6	Significant action in the moment (client-led): organizing future sessions, negotiating the session, taking away action points, making notes ...
7	Significant emotional experience in the moment: joy (client); heightened positive emotion.
8	Significant emotional experience in the moment: joy (coach); heightened positive emotion.
9	Significant emotional experience in the moment: anxiety (client); heightened negative emotion.
10	Significant emotional experience in the moment: anxiety (coach); heightened negative emotion.
11	Significant emotional experience in the moment: doubt (client); fundamental not-knowing, often a starting point for reflection.
12	Significant emotional experience in the moment: doubt (coach); fundamental not-knowing, often a starting point for reflection.

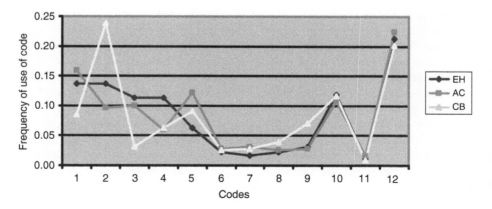

Figure 10.1 *Usage of All Codes (EH, AC, CB)*

To determine inter-rater reliability, Cohen's kappa (Cohen, 1960) was computed between all coders and found an average kappa of 0.44, which seems a reasonable figure given the number of codes: it is more than 30 times chance level. In any case, the coding of individual moment descriptions will not be reported: all conclusions will be based only on the totals of codes used for each of five data sets—see Table 10.1. These sets of totals correlate 0.77 on average between the three coders. High reliability between raters of "helpful events" was also reported in psychotherapy research (Elliott et al., 1985; Llewelyn, 1988).

Biases between the three coders were small (see Figure 10.1). EH codes more negative changes in the relationship (code 4; 40 in total against 21/22 for the other coders) and AC codes more coach-led significance in doing (code 5; 43 in total against 22 for EH), while CB codes more anxieties of clients (code 9; 25 in total against 10/11 for the other coders). The only boundary between codes that seems to have been interpreted differently is the one between codes 1 and 2, which are both "moments of learning"—code 1 describes a sudden realization and code 2 a more reflective working through. In truth, these forms of learning probably do not have a sharp boundary anyway. All coders use codes 1 and 2 in just over a quarter of their coding (mainly in data sets 4 and 5), but AC uses code 1 in 62% of those and CB uses code 1 in only 26% of those, with EH in the middle: 50%.

Figure 10.2 shows an overview of the coding of all data sets, by one of the coders (CB). From the figure, the following conclusions are immediately apparent:

- Data set 1 (critical moments of less experienced coaches) contains a disproportionate amount of "doubts of coaches" (code 12) and "negative changes in the relationship" (code 4). This supports the main conclusions of de Haan (2008a).
- Data sets 2 and 3 (critical moments of experienced coaches) share with data set 1 a high proportion of "anxieties of coaches" (code 10) while they contain significantly less "doubts of coaches." This supports the main conclusions of de Haan (2008b) and Day et al. (2008).

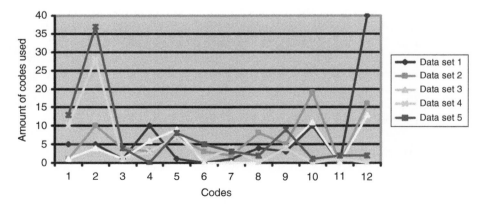

Figure 10.2   *Overview of Coding for All Five Data Sets (CB)*

Note. 1: Less experienced coaches; 2: Experienced coaches; 3: Very experienced coaches (phone interviews); 4: Clients of coaching; 5: Coaches and clients direct comparison (interviews)

- Data set 4 (critical moments of clients of coaching) shows an altogether different profile, with a much higher proportion of "moments of learning" (codes 1 and 2). This supports the main conclusions of de Haan et al. (2010).
- Data set 5 (critical moments of coaches and clients, directly compared) is overall much more similar to data set 4 than to any of the three data sets of executive coaches.
- From data sets 1–4 one can observe that both clients and coaches report more on their own emotions and sensations than on their counterparts' emotions and sensations, that is, descriptions from coaches (data sets 1, 2, and 3) lead to more perceived codes 8, 10, and 12 (coaches' emotions and doubts) than the equivalent 7, 9, and 11 (clients' emotions and doubts) and this is reversed in the clients' descriptions (data set 4). This was also reported in de Haan et al. (2010).

A more in-depth comparison between the five data sets, distinguishing between the 43 "client moments" and the 43 "coach moments" in data set 5, yields the following:

- The clients' critical-moment data set 4 and the new clients' critical-moment descriptions in data set 5 follow a very similar pattern (see Figure 10.3 in the case of coder AC), both having a very high proportion of "moments of learning" (codes 1 and 2). On average, the correlation between the coding of data set 4 and of the client moments in data set 5 of AC, CB, and EH was 0.92, which is remarkably high and gives strong confirmation of the conclusions from a rather disparate set of client moment descriptions in de Haan et al. (2010).
- Surprisingly, there is also a high correlation between data set 4 and the coach moments in data set 5 (see again Figure 10.3, for coder AC). On average, this correlation is 0.58 among the three coders, whereas the correlations between data sets 1, 2, and 3 and the coach moments in data set 5 is 0.003: negligible. We will come back to this surprising finding in the Discussion section.
- The coders found an absence of negative changes in the relationship (code 4) in data set 5, confirming what was concluded more informally at the beginning of the Results section, above, namely that descriptions in the new data set seem positive and constructive as if celebrating or protecting the ongoing relationships.
- Remarkably in data set 5 we have for the first time a higher occurrence of one's partner's emotions than one's own: coaches in data set 5 come up with more anxieties of the client (code 9; see Figure 10.3 for coder AC) than of themselves.
- Coaches still report a significant number of doubts (code 12), consistent with earlier research (Day et al., 2008; De Haan, 2008a, 2008b).

These conclusions are true for all three coders.

Finally, having this rather unique data set 5, which allows a direct comparison of the views of coaches and their clients on the same coaching conversation, also affords the analysis of those descriptions where coach and client seem to be speaking about the very same moment or event within the coaching conversation. Surprisingly, there are 46 key moment descriptions, more than half of the data set, which are obviously relating to the same event or moment within the conversations. Bear in mind that the duration of these conversations was, on average, about 2 hr.

The usage of codes on these particular descriptions were analyzed by computing Cohen's kappa (Cohen, 1960) for this new data set. Cohen's kappas were computed for the coder's choice of code for the "coach moment" compared with the coder's choice of code for the corresponding "client moment." It is a relatively small data set of only 23 measurements, but kappas can be reliably computed. Cohen's kappas were: 0.29 (AC), 0.38 (CB), and 0.47 (EH), each much higher than chance levels, which are around 0.02. With the caveat that this conclusion is based only on a small data set of 46 codes, we can provisionally conclude that these coaches and clients did not only agree in more than 50% of key moments on the particular event or subject matter they described, but they also seem to agree on the nature of those events, which seems a strong agreement between the two partners, particularly if one takes into account the low agreement sometimes reported in psychotherapy (e.g., Tallman & Bohart, 1999; however, Weiss, Rabinowitz, & Spiro, 1996, report variability in the agreement between clients' and therapists' qualitative reports).

DISCUSSION

In summary, the direct comparison data contributed by coaches and clients of coaching (data set 5) suggests the following:

- Clients' and coaches' experiences of coaching conversations are not as different as would have been thought, based on the earlier studies, neither in the nature of selected events (coaches' and clients' descriptions are coded in similar distributions across a fixed set of 12 codes), nor in their specific choice of events (46 of 86 descriptions refer to an event also described by the partner in conversation), nor even in the emphases within their event descriptions (those 46 "shared event" descriptions were coded in a manner correlating about 20 times chance level, for all three observers).
- Clients and coaches use similar language and, apart from one reported rupture in the relationship, all 86 descriptions were broadly positive and indicated learning, progress, and accomplishment. Partly, this may be due to the fact that for 14 of the 21 sessions the client and conversation were chosen by the coach and they will have chosen positive client relationships as they had to invite their client to the research.

Comparing this data set explicitly with all of the earlier data sets of clients' and coaches' descriptions of critical moments of executive coaching led to the following results:

- Overall a strong endorsement of the main conclusions in the earlier articles. Although the new data set correlates strongly only with data set 4, the new data set does also replicate some of the trends found in the other previous data sets. Sixty-two percent of clients' moments in data set 5 were coded as 1 or 2 ("moments of learning"), and 40% of coaches' moments; in data sets 1–4 these numbers had been 59% for clients' moments and 9% for coaches' moments. Another interesting example is the occurrence of coaches' doubts: 56% for inexperienced coaches (data set 1), 18%/27% for experienced coaches (data set 2/data set 3 respectively), 0% for clients of coaching (data set 4) and now in data set 5: 0% for clients and 5% for coaches.

- A high correlation between the coding of these direct-comparison client data and the earlier client critical-moments data set (data set 4, correlations consistently over 0.90).
- No correlation at all between the coding of the new data set (data set 5) and the earlier coach data (data sets 1, 2, and 3), to the extent that the average correlation between the coaches' descriptions from data sets 1 to 3 and from data set 5 was exactly zero.

We think that these findings can be understood best from the realization that this direct-comparison study contains a fair representation of straightforward, "run-of-the-mill," successful and everyday executive coaching, with client and coach being in broad agreement, not only about the goals and outcomes of their sessions but also about their coaching process and coaching relationship. We can assume that this type of "run-of-the-mill" coaching is exactly what the clients in data set 4 also reported on, as many studies have shown executive coaching to be satisfactory and successful in most cases (see, for example, McGovern et al., 2001; de Haan, Culpin, & Curd, 2011). On the other hand, data sets 1, 2, and 3 were drawn from a much broader and deeper experience of executive coaching and have probably included rarer and more extreme examples of transformation, resistance, or ruptures in the working alliance. In other words, while data sets 4 and 5 focus on the everyday learning that takes place in generally positive coaching relationships, data sets 1, 2, and 3 take their inspiration from special occurrences in coaching, moments and events that may occur only a few times in the lifetime of an executive coach—and in particular at the beginning of a coach's career when there are still great insecurities and doubts (de Haan, 2008a).

We cannot rule out the possibility that there are other qualitative differences between what coaches and clients associate with the term "critical moment" when it applies to the session they have just had today (data set 5), as compared to when "critical moment" applies to a whole coaching relationship (data set 4) or to a career of coaching experience, however short in some cases (data sets 1, 2, and 3). It may well be that the term "critical moment" does not apply in the same way to the past hour as to a lifetime of work.

Both run-of-the-mill and exceptional circumstances are part of coaching practice, so all various data sets have something to teach executive coaching practitioners. Studies like these can provide crucial information for the training and development of executive coaches, while they may also help to inform and manage the expectations of clients of executive coaching. Here is a short summary of what we believe these data can teach us:

- Data sets 1, 2, and 3 give an indication that in the careers of most executive coaches there are such things as exceptional moments where the relationship is tested or ruptured and where coaches experience strong doubts and anxieties. Generally, the levels of anxiety of coaches in such events remain high, while the degree of doubting abates over time (de Haan, 2008b).
- Data sets 4 and 5 give an indication that what clients are most looking for in coaching conversations are moments of realization and emerging insight; that is, learning of some form that they can bring to use in their own practice. Coaches can and do

work in such a way that they seem in agreement with their clients about which are the events that matter and the nature of those events. Under exceptional circumstances, a different picture may emerge, where disruptions to the relationship between coach and client become more figural, and then we are back in the realm of data sets 1, 2, and 3.

In summary, more agreement than disagreement was found between clients and coaches:

- Forty-six of 86 moments or events were selected by both clients and coaches (53%);
- The critical-moment descriptions from clients and coaches were similar (see Figure 10.3) and they use similar language apart from a few occurrences of jargon in the language of the executive coaches.
- Clients and coaches place similar emphases within their description of those events, witnessed by the substantial correlations between the coding of these pairs of moments.
- For the first time, one can even notice that the anxieties that both partners in the conversation attend to are in a way similar: they are predominantly the anxieties of the client (see Figure 10.3), as one would hope in executive coaching.

In psychotherapy research there are some indications that clients and therapists are looking for quite different events and moments, and that they have incommensurate memories of the sessions themselves (Elliott, 1983, 1989; Elliott & Shapiro, 1992; Llewelyn, 1988; Rennie, 1990; Tallman & Bohart, 1999); however, one review study investigating all publications to date on agreement between clients and therapists found a high variability (Weiss et al., 1996). One interpretation worth noting is that therapists will address perceived weaknesses more than coaches, and will, therefore, have more emphasis on challenging, disruptive, and even corrective interventions, which may result in less agreement between therapist and client than between coach and client.

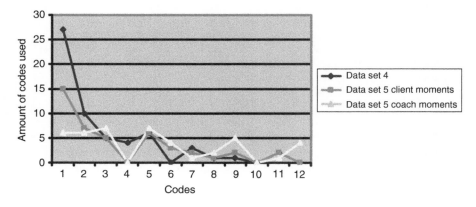

Figure 10.3   *Distribution of Codes Selected by Coder AC*

CONCLUSION

This direct-comparison study of coaches' and clients' critical-moment descriptions that were gathered straight after mutual executive-coaching conversations has produced both a confirmation of earlier conclusions when studying critical moments in executive coaching and a linkage between the various disparate studies hitherto undertaken. We think we now understand better why clients' and coaches' descriptions in earlier studies were so different, and we are beginning to understand how descriptions from clients and coaches coming out of coaching sessions can also be extremely similar, as was the case here.

Interestingly, the results of this direct-comparison study connect with an old debate in psychotherapy process research (Mintz, Auerbach, Luborsky, & Johnson, 1973), which seeks to clarify to what degree the experiences and accounts of both parties in helping conversations are similar versus different. On the one hand, coach and client are essentially similar, being both twenty-first-century professionals with an interest in leadership and development. Moreover, during the conversation, they attend to the same "reality" of the conversation as it emerges between them. On the other hand, one can argue they take up entirely different and complementary roles in the same conversation, with one focusing on own issues and the other focusing on the progress and development of the partner in conversation. So clearly, in the accounts of coaching one would expect *both* a reasonable consensus *and* the "Rashomon experience," named after Akira Kurosawa's classic 1950 Japanese movie *Rashomon*, where four participants retell a single event and come up with equally plausible but totally different and incompatible accounts. Most process research in psychotherapy has confirmed the "Rashomon-side" of the debate, showing that clients and therapists do indeed place an entirely different emphasis in recall, selection, and interpretation of significant events of therapy (Mintz et al., 1973; Weiss et al., 1996). Here is how Yalom (Yalom & Elkin, 1974; p.222) formulates that side of the argument:

> I am struck by … the obvious discrepancies in perspective between Ginny and me. Often she values one part of the hour, I another. I press home an interpretation with much determination and pride. To humour me and to hasten our move to more important areas she "accepts" the interpretation. To permit us to move to "work areas," I on the other hand humour her by granting her silent requests for advice, suggestions, exhortations, or admonitions. I value my thoughtful clarifications; with one masterful stroke I make sense out of a number of disparate, seemingly unrelated facts. She rarely ever acknowledges, much less values my labours, and instead seems to profit from my simple human acts: I chuckle at her satire, I notice her clothes, I call her buxom, I tease her when we role play.

These present results seem to favor the other side of the debate, with a surprising degree of overlap between coach and client accounts, both in their recall/selection and in their emphasis/interpretation. However, given the originality of the design and the limited scope of the data set, it may be too early to argue that coach–client pairs have more in common than therapist–patient pairs.

From the point of view of education and professional development for coaches, the following recommendations can be drawn from this research:

1. Coaches need to be prepared for quite different circumstances in run-of-the-mill coaching and in the presence of real dramatic moments and ruptures. In ordinary coaching, they need to keep the focus with what clients are interested in most: realizations, emerging insight, and reflection. In extraordinary conversations, they need to be able to deal with their own substantive doubt and anxiety, and also with strong emotions in their clients.
2. More effort can be put into preparing coaches for what they can expect in ordinary, successful conversations. The results of this inquiry have shown that coaches need to help clients to look beyond their current solutions and mindset, to achieve new realizations and insight. They need to remain focused on new learning and how they can support their clients to achieve that. Epiphanies are not necessarily what is needed. Sometimes creating a sense of support and reflection is adequate. As concluded before (de Haan et al., 2010), coaches need awareness of the fact that clients seem to be focused on changing their thoughts and reflections—rather than on pure space for reflection, reassurance, or new actions. Coaches should ensure they have the skills to facilitate the emergence of new learning, reflection, realization, and insight.
3. When teaching the important findings of outcome research, for example, the so-called common factors that in psychotherapy have so often been shown to be significantly related to outcome and that teach us the importance of the relationship, expectancy, and personality when it comes to effectiveness (Wampold, 2001), it is important to consider also what sub-outcome research (Rice & Greenberg, 1984) may teach in terms of, for example, what a practicing coach can expect in terms of their own doubts and anxieties, or clients' expectations of session-by-session learning outcomes (realizations, changing perspectives, etc.). When aspects such as the above find their way into coach training and development programs, this would help in making a more clear-cut case for executive coaching for the benefit of purchasers of coaching, including more information on expected benefits and limitations of working with an executive coach.

We would suggest there is a great need for further investigation in this area, particularly in the following domains:

1. Critical moments research, if only to assemble larger data sets upon which firmer conclusions can be based. A larger data set can also be used to (dis)confirm the more tentative conclusions in both this and other articles.
2. Direct-comparison studies such as the present one should be extended into longitudinal studies of coach–client relationships, which could study the progress of the intervention through the evolving reported critical moments. In such research, more care should be taken to minimize interference with the coaching intervention as a whole.

3. We would be most interested in finding out about critical moments and the coaching process from the perspective of the oft-neglected (indirect) clients of coaching, which are the direct colleagues, managers, and reports of the coaching client within the organization of the client. It would be fascinating to investigate what they believe were the critical moments of their colleague's coaching journey.

ACKNOWLEDGMENTS

We would like to thank all the coaches and their clients who generously gave accounts of their experiences. We are also grateful to Monica Stroink and Heather Reekie for doing most of the interviews, to Andy Copeland for helping us with the coding of the moments, and to Shirine Voller who has coordinated this research program from the Ashridge Centre for Coaching.

REFERENCES

Caskey, N., Barker, C., & Elliott, R. (1984). Dual perspectives: Clients' and therapists' perceptions of therapist responses. *British Journal of Clinical Psychology, 23,* 281–290. https://doi.org/10.1111/j.2044-8260.1984.tb01302.x

Cohen, J. (1960). A coefficient of agreement for nominal scales. *Educational and Psychological Measurement, 70,* 213–220. https://doi.org/10.1177/001316446002000104

Corbin, J., & Strauss, A. J. (1990). Grounded theory research: Procedures, canons and evaluative criteria. *Zeitschrift für Soziologie, 19,* 418–427. https://doi.org/10.1007/BF00988593

Day, A., de Haan, E., Blass, E., Sills, C., & Bertie, C. (2008). Coaches' experience of critical moments in the coaching. *International Coaching Psychology Review, 3*(3), 207–218.

de Haan, E. (2008a). "I doubt therefore I coach"—Critical moments in coaching practice. *Consulting Psychology Journal: Practice and Research, 60*(1), 91–105. https://doi.org/10.1037/1065-9293.60.1.91

de Haan, E. (2008b). "I struggle and emerge"—Critical moments of experienced coaches. *Consulting Psychology Journal: Practice and Research, 60*(1), 106–131. https://doi.org/10.1037/1065-9293.60.1.106

de Haan, E., Bertie, C., Day, A., & Sills, C. (2010). Critical moments of clients of coaching: Towards a "client model" of executive coaching. *Academy of Management Learning & Education, 9*(4), 1–31. https://doi.org/10.5465/amle.9.4.zqr607

de Haan, E., Culpin, V., & Curd, J. (2011). Executive coaching in practice: What determines helpfulness for coachees? *Personnel Review, 40*(1), 24–44. https://doi.org/10.1108/00483481111095500

Elliott, R. (1983). "That is in your hands"—A comprehensive process analysis of a significant event in psychotherapy. *Psychiatry, 46,* 113–129. https://doi.org/10.1080/00332747.1983.11024185

Elliott, R. (1985). Helpful and nonhelpful events in brief counseling interviews: An empirical taxonomy. *Journal of Counselling Psychology, 32,* 307–322. https://doi.org/10.1037/0022-0167.32.3.307

Elliott, R. (1989). Comprehensive Process Analysis: Understanding the change process in significant therapy events. In M. J. Packer & R. B. Addison (Eds.), *Entering the circle: Hermeneutic investigations in psychology* (pp. 165–184). Albany, NY: State University of New York Press.

Elliott, R., James, E., Reimschuessel, C., Cislo, D., & Sack, N. (1985). Significant events and the analysis of immediate therapeutic impacts. *Psychotherapy: Theory, Research, Practice, Training, 22*(3), 620–630.

Elliott, R. K., & Shapiro, D. A. (1992). Client and therapist as analysts of significant events. In S. G. Toukmanian & D. L. Rennie (Eds.), *Psychotherapeutic change: Theory-guided and descriptive research strategies* (pp. 163–186). Newbury Park, CA: Sage.

Elton Wilson, J., & Syme, G. (2006). *Objectives and outcomes: Questioning the practice of therapy.* Maidenhead, UK:: The Open University Press.

Evers, W. J. G., Brouwers, A., & Tomic, W. (2006). A quasi-experimental study on management coaching effectiveness. *Consulting Psychology Journal: Practice and Research, 58*(3), 174–182. https://doi.org/10.1037/1065-9293.58.3.174

Feifel, H., & Eells, J. (1964). Patients and therapists assess the same psychotherapy. *Journal of Consulting Psychology, 27*, 310–318. https://doi.org/10.1037/h0046645

Feldman, D. C., & Lankau, M. J. (2005). Executive coaching: A review and agenda for future research. *Journal of Management, 31*, 829–848. https://doi.org/10.1177/0149206305279599

Flanagan, J. C. (1954). The critical incidents technique. *Psychological Bulletin, 51*(4), 327–358.

Goodman, G. S., Magnussen, S., Andersson, J., Endestad, T., Løkke, C. & Mostue, C. (2006). Memory illusions and false memories in the real world. In S. Magnussen & T. Helstrup (Eds.), *Everyday memory* (pp. 169–194). Hove, UK: Psychology Press.

Greif, S. (2007). Advances in research on coaching outcomes. *International Coaching Psychology Review, 2*(3), 222–249.

Hawkins, P., & Smith, N. (2006). *Coaching, mentoring and organisational consultancy: Supervision and development.* Maidenhead, UK: The Open University Press.

Kampa-Kokesch, S., & Anderson, M. Z. (2001). Executive coaching: A comprehensive review of the literature. *Consulting Psychology Journal: Practice and Research, 53*, 205–228. https://doi.org/10.1037/1061-4087.53.4.205

Llewelyn, S. (1988). Psychological therapy as viewed by clients and therapists. *British Journal of Clinical Psychology, 27*(3), 223–237. https://doi.org/10.1111/j.2044-8260.1988.tb00779.x

McGovern, J., Lindemann, M., Vergara, M., Murphy, S., Barker, L., & Warrenfeltz, R. (2001). Maximising the impact of executive coaching: Behavioural change, organisational outcomes, and return on investment. *The Manchester Review, 6*(1), 1–9.

Mintz, J., Auerbach, A. H., Luborsky, L., & Johnson, M. (1973). Patients', therapists' and observers' views of psychotherapy: A 'Rashomon' experience or a reasonable consensus? *British Journal of Medical Psychology, 47*, 319–334. https://doi.org/10.1111/j.2044-8341.1973.tb02233.x

Orlinsky, D. E., & Howard, K. I. (1975). *Varieties of psychotherapeutic experience.* New York, NY: Teachers College Press.

Parrott, W. (2001). *Emotions in social psychology.* Philadelphia, PA: Psychology Press.

Ragins, B. R., Cotton, J. L., & Miller, J. S. (2000). Marginal mentoring: The effects of type of mentor, quality of relationship, and programme design on work and career attitudes. *Academy of Management Journal, 43*(6), 1177–1194. https://doi.org/10.5465/1556344

Rennie, D. (1990). Towards a representation of the clients' experience of the psychotherapy hour. In G. Lietaer, J. Rombauts & R. Van Balen (Eds.), *Client-centred and experiential psychotherapy in the nineties* (pp. 155–172). Leuven, Belgium: Leuven University Press.

Rice, L. N., & Greenberg, L. S. (Eds.). (1984). *Patterns of change: Intensive analysis of psychotherapeutic process.* New York, NY: Guilford Press.

Smither, J. W., London, M., Flautt, R., Vargas, Y., & Kucine, I. (2003). Can working with an executive coach improve multisource feedback ratings over time? A quasi-experimental field study. *Personnel Psychology, 56,* 23–44. https://doi.org/10.1111/j.1744-6570.2003.tb00142.x

Spinelli, E. (2008). Coaching and therapy: Similarities and divergencies. *International Coaching Psychology Review, 3*(3), 241–249.

Starr, J. (2003). *The coaching manual: A definitive guide to the process, principles and skills of personal coaching.* Harlow, UK: Pearson.

Stiles, W. B. (1980). Measurement of the impact of psychotherapy sessions. *Journal of Consulting and Clinical Psychology, 48,* 176–185. https://doi.org/10.1037/0022-006X.48.2.176

Tallman, K. & Bohart, A. C. (1999). The client as a common factor: Clients as self-healers. In M. A. Hubble, B. L. Duncan & S. D. Miller (Eds.), *The heart and soul of change: What works in therapy* (pp. 91–131). Washington, DC: APA Press.

Wampold, B. E. (2001). *The great psychotherapy debate: Models, methods and findings.* Mahwah, NJ: Lawrence Erlbaum.

Weiss, I., Rabinowitz, J., & Spiro, S. (1996). Agreement between therapists and clients in evaluating therapy and its outcomes: Literature review. *Administration and Policy in Mental Health, 23*(6), 493–511. https://doi.org/10.1007/BF02108686

Yalom, I. D., & Elkin, G. (1974). *Every day gets a little closer: A twice-told therapy.* New York, NY: Basic Books.

11 Differences Between Critical Moments for Clients, Coaches, and Sponsors of Coaching

Erik de Haan and Christiane Nieß[1]

Although the term executive coaching refers to a diverse range of interventions relying on different paradigms and methodologies, most researchers and practitioners would probably agree that clients of coaching enter the process with learning and development goals, to increase their performance within their organization, or to reflect upon their own behavior (de Haan & Burger, 2005; Downey, 1999; Parsloe & Wray, 2000; Zeus & Skiffington, 2002). Most professionals would also agree that coaching is an organizational intervention, designed to benefit an organization through working with an individual (Smither, London, Flaw, Vargas, & Kucine, 2003). When clients are asked to evaluate coaching outcomes, they have been found to report higher goal attainment (Grant, 2003), greater self-efficacy (e.g., Baron & Morin, 2010; Evers, Brouwers, & Tomic, 2006), improved social skills (Spence & Grant, 2005; Wasylyshyn, 2003), and better team performance (Sue-Chan & Latham, 2004) in response to coaching interventions. Although some of the coaching outcome studies have used feedback data from peers and managers (Peterson, 1993; Smither et al., 2003; Thach, 2002), what remains largely unexplored is the question of whether and how those positive outcomes are also visible to others in the organization. With organizations spending billions of dollars on coaching interventions globally (Sherman & Freas, 2004), we need research that establishes whether those investments not just pay off for the client of coaching,

[1] First published as de Haan, E. & Nieß, C. (2015). Differences between critical moments for clients, coaches, and sponsors of coaching. *International Coaching Psychology Review, 10*(1), 56–61.

Coaching Researched: A Coaching Psychology Reader, First Edition. Edited by Jonathan Passmore and David Tee.
© 2021 John Wiley & Sons Ltd. Published 2021 by John Wiley & Sons Ltd.

but particularly for others whom the client interacts with at work. The present study, therefore, aims to extend previous research by examining the coaching process not only from the perspective of clients and coaches, but also from that of their sponsors in the organization, who were the clients' direct line-managers, partners, or HR directors.

Making use of a qualitative methodology, we first aim to replicate existing findings on the critical moments of change that clients and their coaches attribute to their coaching assignments (Day, de Haan, Sills, Bertie, & Blass, 2008; de Haan, 2008a, 2008b). Secondly, we build on those previous studies by including critical moments that organizational sponsors notice in response to those same coaching assignments. For this purpose, we are imagining that in executive coaching there are two processes running concurrently: the coaching process with all its twists and turns, and indeed with critical moments as observed by the two partners; and the organizational processes where coachees collaborate with and work toward requirements of their colleagues, clients, and sponsors. In this research, we are comparing the critical moments in this second process to the critical moments from within the coaching process. Our coding of such qualitative data will allow us to identify and quantify similarities and differences in clients', coaches', and sponsors' perceptions of critical moments both within and as a consequence of executive-coaching conversations.

CLIENTS' AND COACHES' CRITICAL MOMENTS IN COACHING

Despite the popularity of coaching interventions in organizations (Sherman & Freas, 2004), rigorous empirical studies on the outcomes of coaching are rather scarce. The research that has been conducted has generally focused on the clients' and partly on the coaches' perspectives concerning the beneficial outcomes that coaching entails (de Haan & Duckworth, 2013). Although we recognize the value of such quantitative outcome studies, we start with more qualitative data in this study. By analyzing the qualitative data rigorously we aim to shed more light on the question of what happens within the coaching process; in other words, we focus more on sub-outcomes than on overall outcomes. Rice and Greenberg (1984) define sub-outcomes as outcomes achieved within the process, from moment to moment, as distinct from outcomes that are generally the result of the process, that is, which can be measured after completing the full coaching assignment.

Several previous research projects have already investigated critical moments in coaching assignments for clients and coaches. More specifically, they have asked clients and coaches the following question: "Describe briefly one critical moment (an exciting, tense, or significant moment) with your coach/client. Think about what was critical in the coaching journey, or a moment when you did not quite know what to do." Study participants were inexperienced coaches (de Haan, 2008a), experienced coaches (Day et al., 2008; de Haan, 2008b), coaching clients (de Haan, Bertie, Day, & Sills,

2010a), dyads of coaches and clients that were interviewed directly after their sessions together (de Haan, Bertie, Day, & Sills, 2010b), and, in a case study, a single dyad of client and coach (de Haan & Nieß, 2012). Collecting such descriptions of what had been found significant, tense, anxiety-provoking, exciting, or pivotal in some way, confirmed that such descriptions of "critical moments" tend to refer to major events in the coaching relationship and can, therefore, be defined as "sub-outcomes" of that relationship: important outcomes or events on a moment-by-moment or session-by-session basis (Rice & Greenberg, 1984).

The critical-moment descriptions collected in those studies were coded by independent coders using the coding scheme displayed in Table 11.1, which is described in more detail in de Haan et al. (2010b). Broadly, the coding scheme refers to four categories:

Table 11.1   *Critical Moments Coding Scheme*

Code number	Short description of the code
1	A moment of learning: new insight. A moment in which new insight was created for coach and—particularly—client.
2	A moment of learning: new connections or perspectives. A moment of working through, reflecting, changing perspective and/or making sense of existing material.
3	A change in the relationship in the moment (positive).
4	A change in the relationship in the moment (negative).
5	Significance in doing in the moment (coach-led). Applying oneself to a unique scripted process such as drawing, visualization, role-play, GROW, …
6	Significance in doing in the moment (client-led). Doing something relevant: organizing future sessions, negotiating the session, taking away action points, making notes …
7	Significant emotional experience in the moment: joy (client). Heightened positive emotion.
8	Significant emotional experience in the moment: joy (coach). Heightened positive emotion.
9	Significant emotional experience in the moment: anxiety (client). Heightened negative emotion.
10	Significant emotional experience in the moment: anxiety (coach). Heightened negative emotion.
11	Significance in being in the moment: doubt (client). Fundamental not-knowing, often a starting point for reflection.
12	Significance in being in the moment: doubt (coach). Fundamental not-knowing, often a starting point for reflection.

Note. Adapted from de Haan et al. (2010b)

1. Moments of learning (code 1 "New insight" and code 2 "New connection/ perspective");
2. Moments of relational change in the coaching relationship (code 3 "Positive change in the relationship" and code 4 "Negative change in the relationship");
3. Moments of significant action (code 5 "Significance in doing in the moment, coach-led" and code 6 "Significance in doing in the moment, client-led"); and
4. Moments of significant emotional experience (code 7 "Joy, client," code 8 "Joy, coach," code 9 "Anxiety, client," code 10 "Anxiety, coach," code 11 "Doubt, client," and code 12 "Doubt, coach").

The main findings of those previous studies into critical moments of coaching suggest very broadly that, while inexperienced coaches express mainly their own doubts as critical moments (de Haan, 2008a), more experienced coaches tend to refer to critical moments as sources of anxiety (de Haan, 2008b). It is important to note, however, that those coaches were asked for a critical moment with one of their clients, which they could well have interpreted as the most significant moment of their whole portfolio of work. It is, therefore, not surprising that these two groups of participants are biased toward reporting particularly dramatic and emotional moments. When, on the other hand, clients of coaching were asked for their critical moments of coaching (with the help of the same question above), they instead reported moments of new realizations and insights as particularly critical. Similar results are obtained when dyads of coaches and clients were interviewed independently after a joint coaching session: *both* parties had a tendency to report new realizations and insights as most critical to the session, and they were in substantial agreement in terms of which moments they selected as being critical in the session they had just completed.

These are important findings and worth testing with a new and wider dataset. The finding that clients are frequently referring to new realizations and insight in their critical-moment descriptions, in combination with the fact that they are mostly selecting positive experiences of coaching (de Haan et al., 2010a), may indicate that coaching clients are particularly helped by acquiring new insight and learning. In other words, it is possible that on a within-session, moment-by-moment level clients prefer to be served by insight-focused interventions and less by the other three main contributions in executive coaching: problem-focused, person-focused, and solution-focused approaches (de Haan & Burger, 2005). It is important, however, to hold such an interpretation of the earlier findings lightly, because growing client insight will be common to all successful approaches and may, therefore, be one of many "common factors" in professional coaching approaches. Nevertheless, our growing understanding of how clients describe their most critical moments in the coaching relationship may inform extensive debates in the coaching literature around which method or approach to offer to clients. Since the present study looks into critical-moment descriptions, each from a single coaching assignment (rather than taken from a whole portfolio of client work), we would expect to replicate this; more specifically, we suggest:

Hypothesis 1: Clients and coaches mostly refer to moments of insight and learning (Codes 1 and 2 in Table 11.1) in their critical-moment descriptions of coaching.

SPONSORS' CRITICAL MOMENTS IN COACHING

While rigorous studies concerning the outcomes of coaching interventions from the perspective of clients and coaches are limited to less than 20 (de Haan & Duckworth, 2013), even fewer studies have investigated whether sponsors notice any positive outcomes that they attribute to the effectiveness of coaching. Nevertheless, preliminary evidence suggests that the beneficial effects of executive coaching are also visible to others in the organization. Studies that estimate the changes caused by executive coaching in terms of 360° feedback show that managers who worked with an executive coach receive better evaluations on the second 360° feedback instrument compared to those who did not work with an executive coach (Smither et al., 2003). Similarly, Thach (2002) found that leaders who were coached for an average of six months received more favorable evaluations through 360° feedback. Managers and HR partners of coaching clients have been found to report more effective leadership behaviors and better interpersonal skills among participants of a commissioned coaching program (Wasylyshyn, Gronsky, & Haas, 2006). Olivero, Bane, and Kopelman (1997) found that managers who participated in a management development program with additional coaching received higher ratings of productivity (an 88% increase) compared with managers who participated in the management development program alone (only a 22% increase in productivity).

In sum, there are a few empirical studies that suggest coaching interventions provide some benefits that are also visible to others in the organization. The second aim of the present study is to extend this line of research by inquiring more deeply into the experience of line managers and sponsors of coaching clients. More specifically, we aim to identify critical moments for sponsors of coaching and to compare triads of clients, coaches, and sponsors in terms of what critical moments they notice in shared coaching assignments. To the best of our knowledge, only two published studies so far have also included clients', coaches', and sponsors' perceptions of coaching outcomes separately, albeit that in the second study they did not necessarily stem from the same assignments. Peterson (1993) studied $N = 370$ leaders from various organizations at three points in time (pre-coaching, post-coaching, and follow-up) with outcome defined by their own coaching objectives and five standard "control" items, rated by at least themselves, their manager, and their coach (multisource ratings). The coaching program was intensive and long-term, with typically 50+ hours of individual coaching with a professional coach over at least a year. Peterson found that clients, on average, achieved significant improvement in all measures of outcome related to coaching objectives (effect sizes $d > 1.5$). Schlosser, Steinbrenner, Kumata, and Hunt (2006) invited triads of clients, coaches, and the clients' managers to report outcomes they attributed to coaching engagements. These participants were asked to select from a list of 25 outcomes the ones that they believed had improved as a result of the coaching engagement. While only $N = 14$ managers responded to the authors' request, results indicated that all three groups (clients, coaches, and managers) regarded employee "engagement" and "promotability" as the main outcomes of coaching. Managers, however, rated the effectiveness of coaching significantly lower than clients and coaches did.

The present study extends these quantitative approaches by looking at the "sub-outcome" level (Rice & Greenberg, 1984) for the first time, on the basis of critical-moment descriptions of triads of clients, coaches, and sponsors working together on the *same* coaching assignment. While we hypothesized that clients and coaches would refer primarily to moments of new insight and learning (codes 1 and 2; see Hypothesis 1), we would argue that such moments of new insight or realization will be less relevant for the sponsors of those assignments who are only indirectly involved (or only involved directly at the contracting and review stages). For this reason, we suggest that sponsors mainly report critical moments that refer to more readily observable moments of *change* (codes 3 and 4) and to *new actions* taken by clients (code 6). If this is confirmed we would have some preliminary evidence for sponsors operating more from a "problem-focused" understanding of executive coaching (de Haan & Burger, 2005).

> *Hypothesis 2:* Sponsors mostly refer to moments of change in the relationship and significant action taken by the client (codes 3, 4, and 6) as critical ones.

The coding scheme that Hypotheses 1 and 2 refer to (see Table 11.1) was originally developed inductively for classifying many hundreds of clients' and coaches' critical moments of executive coaching. Several codes, therefore, refer to critical moments that are likely to arise within coaching sessions that may be less observable for sponsors of coaching, such as the codes referring to emotional states of coaches and clients (codes 7 through 12). Although we expect these codes of the earlier scheme to be less relevant here, we have chosen to retain the scheme as a whole as a first coding system, to allow a direct comparison with the earlier studies.

However, we also felt the need for a second, more tailor-made coding scheme that could test this particular hypothesis.

For this reason, we adopted a grounded theory approach (Glaser, 1992; Strauss & Corbin, 1990) to develop a second coding scheme. The grounded theory approach made use of 41 sponsors' critical-moment descriptions collected at an earlier date (de Haan & Nieß, 2011). In this inductive way, we arrived at another scheme for classifying critical moments of change, particularly from the sponsor perspective but usable for all three parties (clients, coaches, and sponsors). We noticed that our scheme turned out similar to Schein's (1985) conceptualization of the "onion" of organizational culture. This coding scheme, which is depicted in Figure 11.1, suggests that while "outer layers" such as changes in behavior and communication of coaching are visible to outsiders, "inner layers" refer to invisible learning or personal change in, for example, attitudes and knowledge. While clients and coaches directly involved in the coaching assignment may thus notice more of the inner levels of the "onion" model, those inner layers may be less visible to sponsors of coaching. If coding would confirm that sponsors are more occupied with the "outer layers" of the model, this would give support to the idea that sponsors describe their critical moments more from a "problem-focused" perspective and less from an "insight-focused" perspective (see de Haan & Burger, 2005), which we know has been more the perspective of clients and coaches in regular coaching sessions (de Haan et al., 2010b). We therefore propose:

> *Hypothesis 3:* Sponsors refer significantly more than others to moments of communication or change that are visible on the outer layers of the "onion" model (codes 1, 2, 3, 4, and 5), as critical ones.

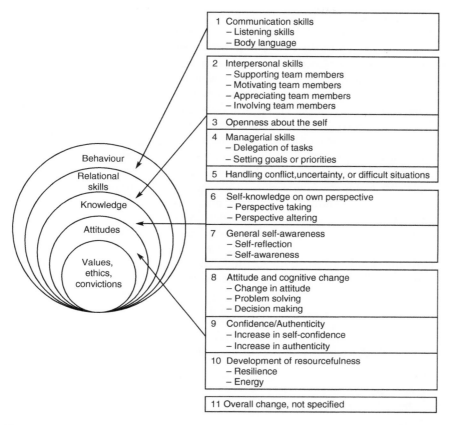

1 Communication skills
   – Listening skills
   – Body language

2 Interpersonal skills
   – Supporting team members
   – Motivating team members
   – Appreciating team members
   – Involving team members

3 Openness about the self

4 Managerial skills
   – Delegation of tasks
   – Setting goals or priorities

5 Handling conflict,uncertainty, or difficult situations

6 Self-knowledge on own perspective
   – Perspective taking
   – Perspective altering

7 General self-awareness
   – Self-reflection
   – Self-awareness

8 Attitude and cognitive change
   – Change in attitude
   – Problem solving
   – Decision making

9 Confidence/Authenticity
   – Increase in self-confidence
   – Increase in authenticity

10 Development of resourcefulness
    – Resilience
    – Energy

11 Overall change, not specified

Behaviour / Relational skills / Knowledge / Attitudes / Values, ethics, convictions

Figure 11.1   *Second Critical-Moments Coding Scheme Based on Schein's (1985) "Onion" Model*

CONGRUENCE BETWEEN CLIENTS, COACHES, AND SPONSORS

Hypotheses 1, 2, and 3 are concerned with the nature of the moments that clients, coaches, and sponsors refer to as critical with regard to the shared endeavor of the executive-coaching work. What, however, remains unexplored so far is the extent to which those three parties actually refer to the *same* moments as being critical to them. More particularly, we were interested in finding out how often triplets of clients, coaches, and sponsors refer to the same moment of change that they notice during or as a result of coaching. This would be important as another way to understand the level of agreement between various participants in the coaching assignment, and also as a way to study the "Rashomon conjecture" proposed and much debated by psychotherapists (Mintz, Auerbach, Luborsky, & Johnson, 1973; Weiss, Rabinowitz, & Spiro, 1996).

Previous research has consistently shown that clients and coaches refer to the same moments as critical significantly above chance level, and thus that there is not much of a "Rashomon effect" in executive coaching, which would be the case when participants in a coaching conversation leave the session with different, incommensurable accounts of their experience together (based on Kurosawa's movie *Rashomon* where a single event is recounted very differently from four different perspectives). De Haan et al. (2010b) showed that in a client–coach direct comparison study, clients and coaches referred to the same moment in 53% of the descriptions, while in a longitudinal investigation where client and coach wrote down their critical moments after each coaching session they referred to the same moment in 47% of the descriptions (de Haan & Nieß, 2012). Not only did clients and coaches refer to the same incidents at a frequency much higher than chance, but they also tended to agree in their descriptions of their critical moments (de Haan et al., 2010b), thereby disconfirming the Rashomon conjecture.

In those two studies, clients and coaches were asked for their critical moments straight after shared coaching sessions, while participants in the present study referred to one coaching assignment consisting of many sessions and they did not normally answer straight after mutual sessions. For this reason, we expect numbers of congruence between clients and coaches to be smaller than in those two previous studies, yet we suggest that they are still above chance. Since sponsors are not directly involved in the coaching assignments, we expect congruence between clients/coaches and sponsors to be smaller than between clients and coaches.

> *Hypothesis 4a:* The incidence of shared critical moments between clients and coaches, that is, the percentage of cases in which they both refer to the same shared incident, will again be well above chance level (chance level is below 1 %) but also significantly below the level found in earlier studies into a single coaching session (47–53%).

> *Hypothesis 4b:* The number of times that sponsors and clients (and also sponsors and coaches) refer to the same moments as being critical is significantly smaller than the number of times that coaches and clients refer to the same critical moments.

METHOD

Sample

Participants of the present study ($N = 177$) were recruited through two different sources. First, potential sponsors of coaching were approached at a Business School in Great Britain and as part of another study (de Haan & Wels, 2011), resulting in an initial sample from sponsors of $N = 30$. Second, we made use of a large-scale online survey where clients, coaches, and sponsors of coaching who were involved in the same coaching assignment were recruited (de Haan & Page, 2013), adding $N = 49$ clients, $N = 49$ coaches, and $N = 49$ sponsors of coaching from matching assignments. Sponsors were nominated by the clients as those work colleagues who sponsored their assignment, so they were mainly their line managers, though in some cases they were HR directors or more senior partners in professional services firms. The overall research questionnaire was completed by 130 sponsors (a response rate of around 20%) and 49 of their answers to the open question could be matched with answers by coaches and clients (38%). Participants were drawn from 22 different countries with the help of a wide network of 366 executive coaches who participated in this worldwide large coaching outcome study. Clients and sponsors had an almost equal gender split, while coaches had an average experience of 13.31 years $(SD = 7.19)$, 67% were female and 86% were external coaches (with the remainder internal mainly in large public organizations), mostly conducting stand-alone executive-coaching assignments.

Materials

Data for this study were obtained by asking participants whether they had "experienced something that felt like a 'critical' moment (an exciting, tense, or significant moment) where they noticed a difference and to describe briefly one (or more) such critical moments"; in the case of clients we added "during coaching"; in the case of coaches we added "in your work with this client," and in the case of sponsors of coaching we added: "with your colleague, where you were directly aware of the impact of executive coaching." We highlighted direct awareness of executive coaching because we were looking for experiences that they somehow related to the coaching work. We chose the word "impact" here because it was the most general term we could think of: it could be interpreted as the sponsor wished without limiting the range of their answers. Clients, coaches, and sponsors were thus asked essentially the same question with small modifications, which was also the same as that in all earlier research programs.

Procedure

After the 49 clients', 49 coaches', and 79 sponsors' critical-moment descriptions had been collected, they were coded three times blindly and independently by four independent coders out of a group of eight coders, one of whom was the first author (in the first two of these coding procedures, critical-moment descriptions were drawn randomly and blindly from all three sources: clients, coaches, and sponsors; in the third of the coding procedures, the source of the critical-moment description had to be revealed to the coder, by definition):

1. The coding was based on the original coding scheme that had already been used in previous studies (see Table 11.1). For this first coding, a forced-choice design was employed, forcing the coders to only attach one code to each critical-moment description. We knew from the earlier studies that coders had never asked for more categories. This was replicated in this study, so forced choice with these 12 codes was straightforward.
2. The second way of coding was developed inductively from moments collected from sponsors of coaching, by using a grounded theory approach, which on the second iteration could be linked with Schein's (1985) "onion" model (see Figure 11.1). According to this model, organizational culture can be regarded as a

metaphorical onion, where visible organizational behaviors are located on the outer layers of the onion, while organizational knowledge refers to less visible, middle layers, and underlying assumptions of the organization are found in the inner layers. More specifically, 11 codes (see Figure 11.1) evolved from the sponsors' critical-moment descriptions collected prior to the present study, which naturally fitted into an "onion" model similar to the one proposed by Schein (1985). The first code, namely changes in communication, such as listening skills or body language, refers to changes in behavior (first layer of the "onion" model). Codes 2 through 5 refer to changes in relational skills (second layer of the "onion" model). They include interpersonal skills (code 2), such as supporting, motivating, appreciating, and involving members of the team, openness about self (code 3), managerial skills (code 4) such as delegating tasks and setting goals and priorities, and handling conflict, uncertainty, or difficult situations (code 5). Codes 6 (self-knowledge, such as perspective-taking and perspective-altering) and 7 (general self-awareness, and self-reflection) represent the middle layer of the "onion" model, namely knowledge. Changes in attitude (fourth layer of the "onion" model) are described by codes 8 through 10. Code 8 implies changes in attitude and cognitive change, such as problem solving and decision making, while code 9 describes changes in self-confidence and authenticity. Code 10 refers to a development of resourcefulness, such as energy or resilience. Code 11 (overall change, not specified) was developed to fit the descriptions that did not mention a specific change. No code was developed to refer to the core of the "onion" model (basic assumptions, ethics, and convictions), as none of the critical-moment descriptions referred to changes on that level. For the coding based on this second coding scheme, we again employed a forced-choice design, in which coders were asked to only administer one code per critical-moment description—however, in this case, the final code is a "remainder" category (see Figure 11.1).

3. For the third way of coding, we asked the coders to indicate whether the critical-moment descriptions from the same assignment (i.e., triplets of client, coach, and sponsor; $N = 49$) were congruent in that they were referring to the *same* moment or incident as being critical. More specifically, we asked them to indicate whether they thought there was a correspondence with regards to content between the client and the coach, between the client and the sponsor, between the coach and the sponsor, and between all three critical-moment descriptions that came from the same coaching assignment.

To estimate the degree of agreement between coders, Cohen's kappa was calculated for each of the three ways of coding. For the first coding scheme, which includes 12 codes, we found a Cohen's kappa of | = .240. For the second coding scheme, using 11 codes, Cohen's kappa was slightly higher at | = .318. Finally, the third way of coding (congruence), which has 5 codes, Cohen's kappa was | = .282. All codings thus indicate fair agreement between coders (Landis & Koch, 1977). We averaged the codings by adding up the times each code was assigned to the critical-moment descriptions by each coder and dividing through the number of coders and critical moments. This procedure ensured that none of the coders' assessments were lost.

Vignettes of raw data

In order to help the reader gain a basic understanding of the critical-moment descriptions collected from clients, coaches, and sponsors of coaching, we have chosen a number of short but representative vignettes, which can be found in Table 11.2. Those data show the range of critical moments that were mentioned by the participants of this study as well as the range of congruence (which is increasing toward the bottom of Table 11.2) between the three different parties.

Table 11.2   *Vignettes of the Critical-Moment Descriptions Within Each Row Data From the Same Coaching Assignment*

	Clients' critical moments	Coaches' critical moments	Sponsors' critical moments
1	Significant moment when I realized, through input from my coach, how a helping conviction can improve your confidence and behavior.	Challenging was the fact that I didn't know if I was the right coach for her. I didn't feel comfortable [...]	In general during interaction with other team members and the client, where my counselee was much more open and engaged in the discussions.
2	The moment I recognized, through my coaching, that I was the one of all my brothers and sisters who organized [...]	I experienced a significant moment when this client realized that his behavior as adult was still influenced by limiting believes from his youth [...]	[...] Before the coaching my colleague usually had a big problem in dealing with difficult situations and put all his energy in defending the approach of his people. It was remarkable that he took his time to listen, ask, and analyze [...]
3	Realizing that my anxiety in groups was created by me most of the time by negative thought patterns and hence I also had the capacity to change that thinking (and hence the feelings).	When she tackled a long-standing area of concern with her partner and had a positive outcome [...]	Increased confidence in conversing at multi-professional meetings where there are strong dominating personalities.
4	There was a session when the coach let me talk to myself in a role playing game.	My client told me about a clash between her and a colleague of hers about her sub-assertive behavior. She got emotional about being unable to gather the courage to stand up to her [...]	She has made advantages especially in situations with a colleague that can be quite snappy. Before coaching, she was swiped off her feet or intimidated, after coaching she stands by her opinion [...]
5	In one of the sessions I realized that I had the know-how in dealing with a confrontational situation, I just had to remain calm and deal with it in a calm manner [...]	At the end of the second session I felt a marked shift in her attitude and confidence in moving forward effectively. She suddenly appeared in control and not just reacting emotionally.	My colleague appears to be more patient with those she manages and appears to be more approachable. There appears to be less conflict situations in the office [...]

Note. Toward the bottom of this table one can observe the degree of "congruence" between the three parties increasing.

RESULTS

Clients' and coaches' critical moments in coaching

Hypothesis 1 suggests that clients and coaches mostly refer to moments of insight or learning (codes 1 and 2) as critical ones. It was tested based on the first coding scheme that was also used in previous studies. Figure 11.2 displays the proportion of codes assigned to clients', coaches', and sponsors' critical-moment descriptions based on this coding scheme. This graphical representation of the data shows that codes 1 and 2 were indeed used most frequently for coding both clients' and coaches' critical-moment descriptions. Paired samples t-tests were conducted to investigate whether this difference was statistically significant (see Appendix 11.A). Results indicated that codes 1 and 2 were indeed used significantly more often than all the other codes at $p < .001$, except for code 5 where the difference was not significant. The results were thus mainly supportive of Hypothesis 1.

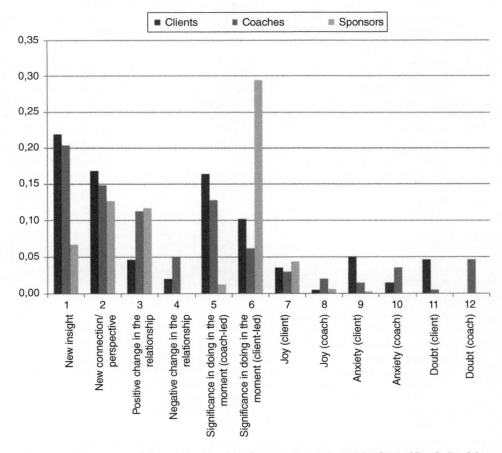

Figure 11.2   *Proportions of Codes Assigned to Critical-Moment Descriptions Within Original First Coding Scheme*

Results for sponsors' critical moments in coaching

Hypothesis 2 states that with respect to the same, original coding scheme, sponsors refer to moments of change and client-led action (codes 3, 4, and 6) as critical ones. Again, Figure 11.2 includes the graphical representation of the data based on this coding scheme. It shows that sponsors of coaching differ substantially from clients and coaches with respect to their critical-moment descriptions: Clients and coaches seem to be more aligned in their critical-moment descriptions when compared to sponsors (a similar alignment between clients and coaches straight after shared coaching conversations was also found in de Haan et al. (2010b) and de Haan and Nieß (2012)).

In order to statistically test Hypothesis 2, we again made use of paired sample t-tests, comparing the frequencies of codes 3, 4, and 6 to the frequencies of the other codes. Results indicated that codes 3 and 6 were indeed used significantly more often at a $p < .01$ level than any of the other codes (except for code 2, where the difference to code 3 was not significant; see Appendix 11.B). Code 4 was, however, not used at all for coding of sponsors' critical moments, possibly because sponsors only reported positive changes as a result of coaching. The results offer strong but partial support for Hypothesis 2: while code 3 (positive change in the relationship) and code 6 (significance in doing in the moment, client-led) were indeed used significantly more to describe sponsors' critical moments, this was not the case for code 4 (negative change in the relationship).

Based on the second coding scheme grounded in the "onion" model of organizational change, Hypothesis 3 states that sponsors mainly refer to moments of change that are visible as they are on the outer layers of the client-as-onion model (codes 1, 2, 3, 4, and 5) as critical ones. Figure 11.3 displays the proportions of codes from the second coding scheme assigned by coders to the critical-moment descriptions for clients, coaches, and sponsors of coaching. The graphical representation of the results suggests that codes 1 (communication skills) and 2 (interpersonal skills) were used very frequently for coding sponsors' critical-moment descriptions, especially when compared to the ratings for clients' and coaches' critical-moment descriptions. Codes 8 (attitude and cognitive change) and 9 (confidence / authenticity) were, however, also used frequently for coding sponsors' critical-moment descriptions. Paired sample t-tests were again conducted to test whether the differences in the frequencies of codes 1, 2, 3, 4, and 5 in comparison to the other codes were statistically significant. Results (see Appendix 11.C) indicated that code 1 was only used significantly more frequently for coding sponsors' critical moments than code 6, but not more frequently than any of the other codes. Code 2 was used more frequently than codes 6, 10, and 11, but there was no difference to the other codes. Codes 3 and 4 were not used significantly more frequently than any of the other codes. Code 5 was used significantly more often than code 6 only. In sum, the results suggest that codes 1 (communication skills) and 2 (interpersonal skills) were indeed used more frequently than some of the other codes, offering only limited support for Hypothesis 3. However, some of the codes on the inner layers of the "onion" model, such as codes 7 (general self-awareness), 8 (attitude or cognitive change), and 9 (confidence / authenticity) were not used significantly less frequently for coding sponsors' critical-moment descriptions.

The results of both coding schemes thus suggest that clients and coaches are more aligned in what they regard as critical moments in their coaching assignments than

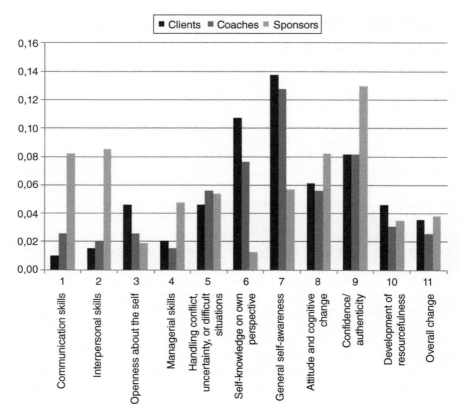

Figure 11.3   *Proportions of Codes Assigned to Critical-Moment Descriptions Within Second Coding Scheme Based on Schein's (1985) "Onion" Model*

sponsors are. With respect to the first, original coding scheme, we tested that finding with paired sample *t*-tests and our results indicate that sponsors of coaching reported fewer moments of new insights (code 1) and coach-led significance in doing in the moment (code 5) than clients and coaches did. Instead, they reported more critical moments that were coded as client-led significance in doing in the moment (code 6) when compared to both clients and coaches. With respect to the second, newly-developed coding scheme, we found that sponsors of coaching referred to significantly more critical moments of communication skills (code 1) than clients, but the difference to coaches was only marginally significant. Sponsors furthermore referred significantly more often to critical moments that were coded as interpersonal skills (code 2) than clients and coaches. Sponsors, however, referred to significantly fewer critical moments that were coded as self-knowledge on own perspective (code 6) or general self-awareness (code 7). Sponsors thus refer to more changes in the outer layers of the "onion" model (codes 1 and 2), while clients and coaches refer more frequently to changes on the inner layers of the onion (codes 6 and 7).

Results for congruence between clients, coaches, and sponsors

We were also interested in the degree of congruence between triplets of clients', coaches', and sponsors' critical-moment descriptions, as they were referring to the same coaching assignments. More specifically, we suggest that the degree to which both clients and coaches refer to the same moments as critical is above chance (Hypothesis 4a) and that the degree to which both sponsors and clients refer to the same moments as critical is smaller than the degree to which both coaches and clients refer to the same moments as critical (Hypothesis 4b). A graphical representation of the results pertaining to those two hypotheses can be found in Figure 11.4. It shows that in almost 40% of the cases there is no congruence between any of the three parties in what moments they refer to as critical ones. Put differently, in almost 40% of the critical-moment descriptions, none of the coders recognized a congruence. In almost half of the cases (46%), clients and coaches, however, refer to the same critical moments of their coaching assignments. Given that these coaching assignments had lasted for an average of near eight sessions (a median of seven sessions), which would be more than 10 hr of coaching on average, this amounts to a correspondence that was well above chance and offers strong support for Hypothesis 4a. Figure 11.4 also shows that correspondence between clients and sponsors (26%) as well as between coaches and sponsors (24%) was considerably smaller, thus offering support for Hypothesis 4b.

However, as this is narrative research we need to be careful with our interpretations: here, we seem to have found congruence between all three parties, and particularly between coaches and clients, a degree of congruence that is clearly above chance. On the other hand, any congruence we found is not—and can never be—full congruence,

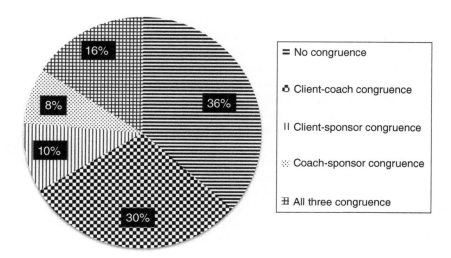

Figure 11.4 *Congruence Between Clients, Coaches, and Sponsors Referring to the Same Coaching Assignments*

because the critical-moment descriptions are by design independent and therefore different. They have only been recognized by coders as belonging to similar instances of the coaching work. Moreover, there is a sample of almost 40% of all critical-moment descriptions remaining where the coders report no congruence across client, coach, or sponsor perspectives. We do not know if in those descriptions completely incommensurable narratives were told, or rather narratives that other parties would easily recognize as well, simply because we have no means to test this retrospectively. So despite the surprisingly high agreement in both selection and nature of description of critical moments (compare Figure 11.2) between clients and coaches, we cannot rule out significant remaining "Rashomon" phenomena where both parties tell very different stories indeed.

DISCUSSION

The aim of the present study was to investigate critical moments of coaching for clients, coaches, and sponsors referring to the same coaching assignments. Our results suggest that overall clients and coaches are considerably more aligned in what they regard as critical moments than sponsors are, even when all three parties are referring to the same coaching assignment. More particularly, we find that clients and coaches mostly refer to moments of new realizations and insights as well as coach-led significance in doing in the moment as critical. They also frequently noticed changes in the inner layers of a metaphorical onion (i.e., understanding and self-awareness) and refer to the same moments as critical ones in almost half of their descriptions. Sponsors, on the other hand, mainly notice positive changes in the relationship with the client as well as client-led significance in doing in the moment as critical moments. Overall, sponsors were very positive in their descriptions, which explains why there were no codes in "negative changes in the relationship" (code 4; see Figure 11.2). This could be due to self-selection because a significant proportion of sponsors in the large-scale research project chose not to answer this question. Also, the changes in terms of the "onion" model are noticed more frequently on the outer layers, such as in clients' communication and interpersonal skills. Finally, coaches and clients seem to be much more congruent (a correspondence of 46%) in terms of which moments they selected as being critical, than either sponsors and clients or sponsors and coaches (correspondences of 26% and 24%, respectively).

These findings become more convincing if they are compared directly with the original datasets of earlier studies, as we have done in Figure 11.5. We can then appreciate that blind coding of all seven datasets of critical-moment descriptions (a total of 555 critical-moment descriptions each coded by at least three coders of which one, AC, coded every dataset) collected from inexperienced coaches, experienced coaches (two datasets), clients of coaching, clients and coaches together after a shared session (two datasets), and sponsors of coaching assignments, are actually very distinct:

1. Critical moments from inexperienced coaches over their whole coaching experience are classified as "doubts of the coach" (code 12) in more than half of cases. The coach's anxieties (code 10) are also prominent.

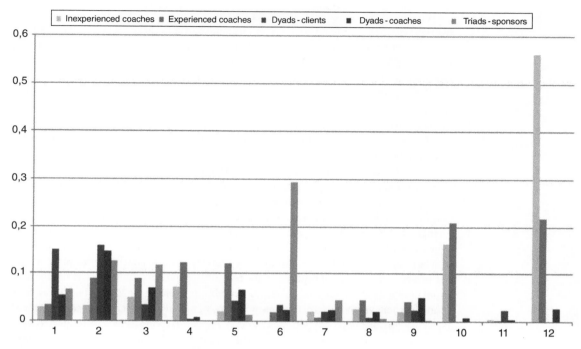

Figure 11.5   *Comparison of Sponsors' Critical Moments With Earlier Research Findings*

2. Critical moments from experienced coaches over their whole coaching experience peak at both "doubts" and "anxieties" of the coach (codes 10 and 12 in equal measure).
3. Critical moments from coaches and clients straight after sessions contain mainly new insights (code 1) and new perspectives (code 2).
4. Critical moments from sponsors of coaching (this research) are coded as "significant action led by the client" (code 6) in almost a third of cases.

Compared with those earlier findings the data from the coaches as collected this time (which are visible in Figure 11.2 and not in Figure 11.5), are a mixture of the earlier patterns as one would expect. This dataset contains mostly experienced coaches but we have not excluded inexperienced coaches and is based on assignments that have just started as well as assignments that have gone on for many hours (in fact we could reliably estimate that on average client and coach had already spent more than seven sessions together). In Figure 11.2 we can see that the coach data in fact contain a significant amount of anxiety and doubt, features we would only expect if either coaches were very inexperienced or if they are reporting the most significant moments of their careers (which was the case in Day et al., 2008 and de Haan, 2008a, 2008b). This may also contribute to the fact that the overlap between client moments and coach moments (46% in this study) is marginally smaller than in the earlier studies (de Haan et al., 2010b, and de Haan & Nieß, 2012, where this degree of overlap was 53% and 47%, respectively).

We would still consider that the fact that almost half of critical-moment selections overlap between client and coach is remarkable, particularly as we know that they had an average of some eight sessions together before answering the questionnaire. Taken together, these findings mean that all earlier conclusions from critical moments in coaching studies that we could test are supported in this study.

The present study extends previous research by also including sponsors' critical-moment descriptions. Figure 11.5 embeds the sponsors' critical-moment descriptions obtained in the present study into previous research conducted with clients, coaches, and coach-client dyads. The figure shows that more than a quarter of the critical-moment descriptions from sponsors have been categorized as containing changes in clients' behaviors (code 6), which is some first evidence that organizational sponsors and managers do attribute behavioral changes in their employees to coaching assignments undertaken.

Together with the earlier qualitative research into critical moments in real, contracted, executive-coaching assignments, this study offers support for the presence of tangible change within and as a result of coaching conversations (e.g., we could confirm Hypothesis 3). We believe that we now have ample evidence that clients and coaches by and large agree on the kind of momentary changes through coaching, except in or near the presence of significant ruptures in the relationship, where coaches report significantly more emotions in the form of anxiety and doubt (de Haan et al., 2010b). Finally, we have found further evidence that also sponsors can recognize significant change coming out of coaching conversations (Hypotheses 2 and 3). However, sponsors draw attention to a different aspect of these changes, namely the actions that the clients initiate as a result of coaching conversations. At this stage of research, we are beginning to see evidence of the organizational experience of coaching conversations, and we are beginning to see the consequences of those conversations through analyzing critical moments experienced by third parties. This kind of scrutiny of critical moments in coaching conversations is giving us some idea of the differences in mindsets engendered by the three roles taken in and around coaching sessions, those of client, coach, and sponsor. These differences in mindsets are well described by the "window on coaching" model put forward by Clutterbuck (1985) and de Haan and Burger (2005):

1. Clients and coaches conducting normal coaching conversations seem to have an "insight-focused" ideology where significant moments are those of new learning: new perspectives and new insights related to self and coaching objectives and themes;
2. Coaches when in the presence of rare ruptures or dramatic events in coaching conversations seem to have a "person-focused" ideology where the orientation is much more toward highly personal anxieties, emotions, and doubts;
3. Organizational sponsors of coaching seem to have more of a "problem-focused" or "solution-focused" mindset that is more action-, behavior-, and future-oriented.

It is interesting that within these overall differences sponsors do mention deeper layers of personality, such as self-awareness, attitude, confidence, and authenticity (see Figure 11.3), even as much as the coaches and clients are doing. The sponsors may be more interested in changes in their relationship with their colleagues (Figure 11.2), but they still define those relationships as multilayered and not just superficially in terms of communication and behavior (Figure 11.3).

Knowing more about the ideology of the various partners that come to build the coaching relationship can be extremely helpful. Coaches can adapt their contracting to what the other parties find most critical in this helping relationship—and they can also adapt their style in the presence of misunderstandings and ruptures. All in all, communication between the various parties working together in this essentially triangular endeavor can be improved by a deeper knowledge of likely default ideologies, such as their orientations toward emotions, problems, solutions, and insights. Finally, we may be discovering how change from executive coaching is being retranslated and refined through the various stakeholders involved: coaches may be focusing a lot on their own anxieties and doubts, yet at the same time translating this sensitivity into new insight for clients (by, for example, free association and making use of countertransference, as in insight-focused approaches; see de Haan & Burger, 2005). Clients may then be able to translate new insight into new behavior and a changed outlook within their organizations, translating their new learning into observable relational change with their sponsors and other counterparts (adapting to work environments that may be more action- and problem-oriented than coaching conversations), as well as, conversely, retranslating new organizational experiences into requests for new insight from coaching, etc. The substantive and measurable emerging changes from executive-coaching conversations that are beginning to come to light in coaching outcome studies (de Haan & Duckworth, 2013) are well captured by the following words from a Chinese proverb: "Carefully watch your thoughts, for they become your words. Manage and watch your words, for they will become your actions. Consider and judge your actions, for they have become your habits. Acknowledge and watch your habits, for they shall become your values. Understand and embrace your values, for they become your destiny." It is as if a coaching conversation creates a "ripple" in the mind, which propagates, first between client and coach, and then in the form of new action into and within the organizational context of the coaching client.

LIMITATIONS

Limitations of the present study were, firstly, that the sponsor dataset is still quite limited (only 79 sponsor critical-moment descriptions of which 49 could be matched to both clients' and coaches' descriptions), despite our having access to a very large-scale research program that has yielded more than 4,000 questionnaires. We think that, because of their more detached and supervisory role, it is harder to collect usable data from organizational sponsors (compare de Haan & Nieß, 2011). A larger dataset would allow us to dig more deeply into the perceptions that organizational colleagues tend to develop toward coaching clients, in their roles of sponsors of executive coaching.

Secondly, that the degrees of agreement between coders are still relatively small (Cohen's kappa around $|$ $=.3$). Kappas are similar to those in previous studies and they are probably small because coders are collapsing whole narratives into single code descriptors. In our view, both larger datasets and finer coding systems will need to be developed if we really want to understand what makes a difference in coaching conversations, and for each party to those conversations.

Thirdly, and following from the previous point, coding in narrative research and the social sciences is bound to suffer from considerable overlap between coding categories and from differences in interpretation of the meaning of both the narratives (the critical-moment descriptions) and the coding categories. Such fuzziness around meaning is hard to avoid without losing the richness of the original experiences, but will further degrade agreement between coders.

FURTHER RESEARCH

Critical-moment descriptions have convincingly been shown to be a promising area of coaching process research, and we can only hope that more studies will appear in the future so that our understanding of "critical incidents," "sub-outcomes," or "momentary changes" in coaching assignments deepens and expands further. In particular, it seems important to explore more deeply the area of (non)congruence of critical-moment descriptions, by not just collecting descriptions of critical moments of coaching but also asking clients, coaches, and perhaps even sponsors, to which degree they can recognize the narratives of the other parties in the common endeavor. Such research should be able to shine more light on the Rashomon conjecture, the question of whether participants in shared sessions develop similar or essentially different narratives of their time spent together.

ACKNOWLEDGMENTS

We would like to thank our Ashridge colleagues Andy Copeland, Stefan Cousquer, Myrna Jelman, Tsheli Lujabe, Niraj Saraf, Charlotte Sills, and Dorothee Stoffels for their careful coding of the critical-moment descriptions.

REFERENCES

Baron, L., & Morin, L. (2010). The impact of executive coaching on self-efficacy related to management soft-skills. *Leadership & Organization Development Journal, 31*(1), 18–38. https://doi.org/10.1108/01437731011010362

Clutterbuck, D. (1985). *Everyone needs a mentor: Fostering talent in your organisation.* London, UK: IPM.

Day, A., De Haan, E., Sills, C., Bertie, C., & Blass, E. (2008). Coaches' experience of critical moments in the coaching relationship. *International Coaching Psychology Review, 3*(3), 207–218.

de Haan, E. (2008a). I doubt therefore I coach: Critical moments in coaching practice. *Consulting Psychology Journal: Practice and Research, 60*(1), 91–105. https://doi.org/10.1037/1065-9293.60.1.91

de Haan, E. (2008b). I struggle and emerge: Critical moments of experienced coaches. *Consulting Psychology Journal: Practice and Research, 60*(1), 106–131. https://doi.org/10.1037/1065-9293.60.1.106

de Haan, E., Bertie, C., Day, A., & Sills, C. (2010a). Critical moments of clients of coaching: Towards a 'client model' of executive coaching. *Academy of Management Learning and Education, 5*(2), 109–128. https://doi.org/10.5465/amle.9.4.zqr607

de Haan, E., Bertie, C., Day, A., & Sills, C. (2010b). Critical moments of clients and coaches: A direct-comparison study. *International Coaching Psychology Review, 5*(2), 109–128.

de Haan, E., & Burger, Y. (2005). *Coaching with colleagues. An action guide for one-to-one learning.* Hampshire, UK; New York, NY: Palgrave Macmillan.

de Haan, E., & Duckworth, A. (2013). Signalling a new trend in coaching outcome research. *International Coaching Psychology Review, 8*(1), 6–20.

de Haan, E., & Nieß, C. (2011). Change through executive coaching. *Training Journal, 7*, 66–70.

de Haan, E., & Nieß, C. (2012). Critical moments in a coaching case study: Illustration of a process research model. *Consulting Psychology Journal: Practice and Research, 64*(3), 198–224. https://doi.org/10.1037/a0029546

de Haan, E., & Page, N. (2013). Outcome report: Conversations are key to results. *Coaching at Work, 8*(4), 10–14.

de Haan, E., & Wels, I. (2011). De link tussen top, topteams en high performance [Development at the top: An inquiry into personal development at executive-board level]. *Management & Consulting, 4*, 44–46. urn:nbn:nl:ui:31-e7646e78-ac65-4c79-bebe-4e5d12904adf

Downey, M. (1999). *Effective coaching.* London, UK: Orion.

Evers, W. J., Brouwers, A., & Tomic, W. (2006). A quasi-experimental study on management coaching effectiveness. *Consulting Psychology Journal: Practice and Research, 58*(3), 174–182. https://doi.org/10.1037/1065-9293.58.3.174

Glaser, B. G. (1992). *Basics of grounded theory analysis.* Mill Valley, CA: Sociological Press.

Grant, A. (2003). The impact of life coaching on goal attainment, metacognition and mental health. *Social Behaviour and Personality, 31*(3), 253–264. https://doi.org/10.2224/sbp.2003.31.3.253

Landis, J. R. & Koch, G. G. (1977). The measurement of observer agreement for categorical data. *Biometrics, 33*(1), 159–174. DOI: 10.2307/2529310

Mintz, J., Auerbach, A. H., Luborsky, L., & Johnson, M. (1973). Patient's, therapist's and observers' views of psychotherapy: A 'Rashomon' experience or a reasonable consensus? *British Journal of Medical Psychology, 46*(1), 83–89. https://doi.org/10.1111/j.2044-8341.1973.tb02233.x

Olivero, G., Bane, K. D., & Kopelman, R. E. (1997). Executive coaching as a transfer of training tool: Effects on productivity in a public agency. *Public Personnel Management, 26*, 461–469. https://doi.org/10.1177/009102609702600403

Parsloe, E., & Wray, M. (2000). *Coaching and mentoring.* London, UK: Kogan Page.

Peterson, D. B. (1993). Skill learning and behavior change in an individually tailored management coaching and training programme (Doctoral Dissertation, University of Minnesota). *Dissertation Abstracts International, 54*(3), 1707–1708.

Rice, L. N., & Greenberg, L. S. (Eds.). (1984). *Patterns of change: Intensive analysis of psychotherapeutic process.* New York, NY: Guilford Press.

Schein, E. H. (1985). *Organisational culture and leadership.* San Francisco, CA: Jossey-Bass.

Schlosser, B., Steinbrenner, D., Kumata, E., & Hunt, J. (2006). The coaching impact study: Measuring the value of executive coaching. *The International Journal of Coaching in Organizations, 4*(3), 8–26.

Sherman, S., & Freas, A. (2004). *The wild west of executive coaching. Harvard Business Review, 82*(11), 82–93.

Smither, J. W., London, M., Flaw, R., Vargas, Y., & Kucine, I. (2003). Can working with an executive coach improve multisource feedback ratings over time? A quasi-experimental field study. *Personnel Psychology, 56*, 23–44. https://doi.org/10.1111/j.1744-6570.2003.tb00142.x

Spence, G. B., & Grant, A. M. (2005). Individual and group life-coaching: Initial findings from a randomised, controlled trial. In M. Cavanagh, A. M. Grant, & T. Kemp (Eds.), *Theory, Research and Practice from the Behavioural Sciences: Vol. 1. Evidence-based coaching* (pp. 143–158). Bowen Hills, Queensland, Australia: Australian Academic Press.

Strauss, A., & Corbin, J. (1990). *Basics of qualitative research: Grounded theory procedures and techniques*. Newbury Park, CA: Sage.

Sue-Chan, S., & Latham, G. P. (2004). The relative effectiveness of external, peer, and self-coaches. *Applied Psychology: An International Review*, *53*(2), 260–278. https://doi.org/10.1111/j.1464-0597.2004.00171.x

Thach, E. C. (2002). The impact of executive coaching and 360° feedback on leadership effectiveness. *Leadership & Organization Development Journal*, *23*(4), 205–214. https://doi.org/10.1108/01437730210429070

Wasylyshyn, K. M. (2003). Executive coaching: An outcome study. *Consulting Psychology Journal: Practice and Research*, *55*, 94–106.

Wasylyshyn, K. M., Gronsky, B., & Haas, J. W. (2006). Tigers, stripes, and behavior change: Survey results of a commissioned coaching program. *Consulting Psychology Journal: Practice and Research*, *58*(2), 65–81. https://doi.org/10.1037/1065-9293.58.2.65

Weiss, I., Rabinowitz, J., & Spiro, S. (1996). Agreement between therapists and clients in evaluating therapy and its outcomes: Literature review. *Administration and Policy in Mental Health and Mental Health Services Research*, *23*(6), 493–511. https://doi.org/10.1007/BF02108686

Zeus, P., & Skiffington, S. (2002). *The complete guide to coaching at work*. New York, NY: McGraw-Hill.

APPENDIX A

Paired Sample t-Tests Comparing Code 1 With Other Codes in Coding Scheme 1; Hypothesis 1

Pair	mean	t	df	p
Code 1	.40	2.52	97	.014
Code 3	.21			
Code 1	.40	4.79	97	.000
Code 4	.09			
Code 1	.40	1.13	97	.260
Code 5	.32			
Code 1	.40	2.02	97	.046
Code 6	.24			
Code 1	.40	5.06	97	.000
Code 7	.09			
Code 1	.40	6.31	97	.000
Code 8	.04			
Code 1	.40	5.01	97	.000
Code 9	.09			
Code 1	.40	5.20	97	.000
Code 10	.08			

Pair	mean	t	df	p
Code 1	.40	4.78	97	.000
Code 1	.10			
Code 1	.40	6.92	97	.000
Code 12	.03			

Paired Sample t-Tests Comparing Code 2 With Other Codes in Coding Scheme 1; Hypothesis 1

Pair	mean	t	df	p
Code 2	.41	2.69	97	.008
Code 3	.21			
Code 2	.41	5.06	97	.000
Code 4	.09			
Code 2	.41	1.24	97	.218
Code 5	.32			
Code 2	.41	2.36	97	.020
Code 6	.24			
Code 2	.41	5.20	97	.000
Code 7	.09			
Code 2	.41	6.46	97	.000
Code 8	.04			
Code 2	.41	5.20	97	.000
Code 9	.09			
Code 2	.41	5.20	97	.000
Code 10	.08			
Code 2	.41	5.01	97	.000
Code 1	.10			
Code 2	.41	6.83	97	.000
Code 12	.03			

APPENDIX B

Paired Sample t-Tests Comparing Code 3 With Other Codes in Coding Scheme 1; Hypothesis 2

Pair	mean	t	df	p
Code 3	.44	3.13	78	.002
Code 1	.20			
Code 3	.44	.74	78	.460
Code 2	.38			
Code 3	.44	4.30	78	.000
Code 7	.14			

(Continued)

Pair	mean	t	df	p
Code 3 Code 8	.44 .03	7.12	78	.000
Code 3 Code 9	.44 .01	7.67	78	.000
Code 3 Code 10	.44 .00	7.88	78	.000
Code 3 Code 1	.44 .00	7.88	78	.000
Code 3 Code 12	.44 .00	7.88	78	.000

Paired Sample t-Tests Comparing Code 6 to Other Codes in Coding Scheme 1; Hypothesis 2

Pair	mean	t	df	p
Code 6 Code 1	.75 .20	7.37	79	.000
Code 6 Code 2	.75 .38	4.54	79	.000
Code 6 Code 7	.75 .14	8.59	79	.000
Code 6 Code 8	.75 .03	14.22	79	.000
Code 6 Code 9	.75 .01	13.81	79	.000
Code 6 Code 10	.75 .00	15.17	79	.000
Code 6 Code 1	.75 .00	15.17	79	.000
Code 6 Code 12	.75 .00	15.17	79	.000

APPENDIX C

Paired Sample t-Tests Comparing Code 1 With Other Codes in Coding Scheme 2; Hypothesis 3

Pair	mean	t	df	p
Code 1 Code 6	.18 .05	2.43	78	.017
Code 1 Code 7	.18 .15	.39	78	.698

Pair	mean	t	df	p
Code 1 Code 8	.18 .23	−.75	78	.453
Code 1 Code 9	.18 .30	−1.79	78	.077
Code 1 Code 10	.18 .1	1.04	78	.300
Code 1 Code 1	.18 .1	1.04	78	.300

Paired Sample t-Tests Comparing Code 2 With Other Codes in Coding Scheme 2; Hypothesis 3

Pair	mean	t	df	p
Code 2 Code 6	.24 .05	3.32	78	.001
Code 2 Code 7	.24 .15	1.35	78	.180
Code 2 Code 8	.24 .23	.17	78	.863
Code 2 Code 9	.24 .30	−.84	78	.401
Code 2 Code 10	.24 .1	2.00	78	.049
Code 2 Code 1	.24 .1	2.00	78	.049

Paired Sample t-Tests Comparing Code 3 With Other Codes in Coding Scheme 2; Hypothesis 3

Pair	mean	t	df	p
Code 3 Code 6	.06 .05	.38	78	.71
Code 3 Code 7	.06 .15	−1.83	78	.070
Code 3 Code 8	.06 .23	−2.97	78	.004
Code 3 Code 9	.06 .30	−3.99	78	.000
Code 3 Code 10	.06 .1	−1.07	78	.288
Code 3 Code 1	.06 .1	−1.16	78	.251

Paired Sample t-Tests Comparing Code 4 With Other Codes in Coding Scheme 2; Hypothesis 3

Pair	mean	t	df	p
Code 4 Code 6	.14 .05	1.98	78	.052
Code 4 Code 7	.14 .15	−.24	78	.810
Code 4 Code 8	.14 .23	−1.54	78	.127
Code 4 Code 9	.14 .30	−2.40	78	.019
Code 4 Code 10	.14 .1	.50	78	.620
Code 4 Code 1	.14 .1	.45	78	.658

Paired Sample t-Tests Comparing Code 5 With Other Codes in Coding Scheme 2; Hypothesis 3

Pair	mean	t	df	p
Code 5 Code 6	.15 .05	2.19	78	.032
Code 5 Code 7	.15 .15	.00	78	1.00
Code 5 Code 8	.15 .23	−1.28	78	.203
Code 5 Code 9	.15 .30	−2.24	78	.028
Code 5 Code 10	.15 .1	.65	78	.516
Code 5 Code 1	.15 .1	.69	78	.495

12 One-to-One Coaching as a Catalyst for Personal Development: An Interpretative Phenomenological Analysis of Coaching Undergraduates at a UK University

Natalie Lancer and Virginia Eatough[1]

The benefits of both one-to-one and group coaching for students have been demonstrated in numerous studies. However, most of these have used quantitative designs and measures such as the General Health Questionnaire (Short, Kinman, & Baker, 2010). These studies are useful as they make clear how coaching affects students in particular domains. For example, in an early study, Grant (2003) found that group coaching for postgraduate mature students was associated with significantly higher levels of goal attainment, along with improvements in metacognitive processing (self-reflection and insight) and mental health (lower depression, stress, and anxiety). Sue-Chan and Latham (2004) compared grades attained and satisfaction for MBA

[1] First published as Lancer, N. & Eatough, V. (2018). One-to-one coaching as a catalyst for personal development: An interpretative phenomenological analysis of coaching undergraduates at a UK university. *International Coaching Psychology Review*, *13*(1) 72–88.

students coached by an external coach with those coached by peers and found that both measures were greater when coached by external coaches. Thus, it seems there are specific benefits to using external or professional coaches.

Coaching studies on undergraduate students have tended to focus on deprived or "special case" populations. For example, Greene (2004) found that one-to-one coaching helped economically and socially disadvantaged undergraduates gain confidence and reduce anxiety. Swartz, Prevatt, and Proctor (2005) found that coaching helped undergraduates with ADHD organize themselves and make positive changes, and Van Zandvoort, Irwin, and Morrow (2009) found that obese female university students attributed their adoption of healthier lifestyles and enhanced self-acceptance to coaching. Robinson and Gahagan (2010) found that coaching resulted in 40% fewer suspended students from a group of academically underperforming students.

There have been a limited number of coaching studies on non-special-case and nonclinical students, which is surprising given that coaching aims to help all types of nonclinical people attain goals and achieve enhancement of their life experience in personal and/or professional spheres (Grant, 2003). The few studies undertaken include Franklin and Doran's (2009) work, which found that two different coaching programs increased academic performance; Short et al. (2010) found that peer coaching significantly reduced the psychological distress of a group of psychology undergraduate students, compared with a control group, while Fried and Irwin (2016) found that stress management and academic performance improved as a result of coaching sessions compared with a control group.

We suggest that the breadth and depth of the existing literature is limited, both due to the nature of the measures used (such as academic performance) in the quantitative studies and to the small number of qualitative studies undertaken. These studies give an overview of coaching, but due to their design cannot explain how coaching is experienced and what it is "like."

There are, however, plenty of qualitative studies that focus on the experience of education (unrelated to coaching) and coaching in contexts other than education. For example, the focus of specific studies using Interpretative Phenomenological Analysis (IPA) includes the personal growth of mature university students (Stevens, 2003) and the experiences of coaching in a business setting (Gyllensten, Palmer, Nilsson, Regnér, & Frodi, 2010). However, there is a dearth of studies that use qualitative approaches to explore coaching in university settings. We posit that IPA's focus on the experience of the participant's world, as lived through their eyes, is important when considering how coaching affects students as it provides insight into their perspective as told through their words. The IPA method of elucidating shared themes is helpful when considering how the group as a whole benefited from coaching. This analysis can be used to tentatively consider how other similar groups of people in a similar context may benefit from coaching.

Arnett (2000) identifies the ages from 18 to 22, the age range of all the undergraduates in this current study, as a distinct life stage of "emerging adulthood," complete with its own dilemmas to explore. Thus, we argue that the reasons to offer coaching to undergraduates are compelling, as not only might it affect academic scores and confidence, but also most undergraduates are making the transition into emerging adulthood, replete with its own distinct issues.

The fact that students are at a time in their lives where support could be beneficial is not the only reason why universities might offer coaching to their undergraduates. In an age of market forces within the university context, students are "consumers" (Naidoo, Shankar, & Veer, 2011) and universities are having to work hard to attract the best. Jackson (2003) estimates that one in four students in the UK drops out. In a separate study, Yorke and Longden (2004) found that students' experience of the course and institution was one of four main reasons for student withdrawal. This, coupled with the fact that tuition fees are increasing in the UK, means that universities are going to have to work hard to make sure all students have a positive experience to both attract and retain them. There is evidence to suggest that coaching can increase student retention. A U.S. government study found that undergraduates who received individual coaching for two semesters were significantly more likely to remain at college up to 18 months after the intervention, compared with those who had not received coaching (U.S. Department of Education, 2012). Furthermore, positive student perceptions of their learning environment had a stronger positive correlation with academic outcomes than previous school achievement (Lizzio, Wilson, & Simons, 2002). Therefore, universities keen to maximize university students' academic outcomes would be wise to consider how to increase these positive student perceptions.

The growing number of student users accessing counseling services (Turner, Hammond, Gilchrist, & Barlow, 2007) may reflect a gap in student support systems. Coaching in the university context may, therefore, "nip in the bud" issues that could otherwise develop into problems requiring counseling services and can thus be viewed as a preventative tool that addresses student health and well-being.

The current research is the first study from a series exploring the personal growth of undergraduates who volunteered to participate in one-to-one coaching sessions over one year. The second study explores the experience of undergraduates who had two years of coaching.

METHODS

Design

A qualitative, longitudinal design was employed and data was gathered using semi-structured interviews at four time-points over 12 months. The transcribed interviews were analyzed using IPA, looking first ideographically, case-by-case, and then moving across the data set to make comparisons in what is shared and what is variable. IPA is an interpretative, experiential approach that focuses on how individuals make sense of a particular experience in a specific context; analysis is a co-construction of knowledge between participant and researcher.

Recruitment strategy and participants

Nine full-time undergraduates responded to a call to participate, which was made in two ways: via the first author's presentation about the study at the beginning of an undergraduate lecture and via an email sent by the subject administrator. Six of the participants were female and three were male; seven were first-year students and two were second-year students. The students were highly articulate and academically able. See Table 12.1 for further participant details.

Procedure

Nine students from a Russell Group university, across various arts and social science subjects, were recruited to receive six one-to-one professional coaching sessions in person and/or by Skype at the beginning of the 2014/2015 academic year. Ten coaches volunteered to give pro bono coaching in response to our notice posted on the European Mentoring and Coaching Council website and through the first author's professional network. The coaches could use whatever coaching approach they preferred. In coaching generally, many coaches use the "systemic eclectic" approach (i.e., they develop their own philosophy and techniques as their knowledge and experience develop) to fit the context and the client (Lancer, Clutterbuck, & Megginson, 2016).

After the researchers led a group briefing with coaches and students, each student was given an information sheet and signed a consent form. The first author paired the students with the coaches randomly. Each student had three 1-hr coaching sessions between October and December 2014 and a further three 1-hr coaching sessions between January and March 2015, in which they were free to discuss whatever issues they wanted. They were also free to change coaches if the pairings did

Table 12.1 *Participant Descriptors*

Pseudonym	Year at university	Subject	Age	Gender
Zara	1st	Humanities	19	Female
Claire	1st	Humanities	20	Female
Natasha	1st	Humanities	20	Female
Lynn	1st	Arts	19	Female
Holly	1st	Arts	19	Female
Martin	2nd	Arts	20	Male
Colin	2nd	Humanities	25	Male
Hermione	2nd	Arts	21	Female
Neil	1st	Humanities	19	Male

not "work," or if there was some other issue. The coaches attended a debrief led by the first author in March 2015. Pseudonyms have been used throughout to protect anonymity (see Table 12.1). The study was approved by the Ethics Committee at Birkbeck, University of London and adhered to British Psychological Society (BPS) ethical guidelines.

IPA requires the participants to have a degree of homogeneity in order for the essence of an experience to be distilled (Smith, Flowers, & Larkin, 2009). Students were recruited from the same university and studying similar subjects. Additional homogeneity arose from the fact that they all had an interest in personal development and were invested in their coaching sessions, as manifested both in terms of attending them all and being keen to discuss them in their interviews.

Data collection

Each student was interviewed, in a comfortable university office, using one-to-one, semi-structured, open-ended interviews by the first author at four time-points: before their first coaching session, after their third, after their sixth, and six months after their last coaching session. Thus, although the data reflects the participants' retrospective sense-making of their coaching experience, for the middle two interviews, the participants' accounts were close in time to the coaching sessions they were describing. Using semi-structured interviews enabled rich data to be collected as although there was an interview schedule, it was used flexibly and we were open to the students speaking about what was important to them within the broad subject matter (Smith et al., 2009). The interview questions were designed to elicit concrete details of the lived experience of coaching and to enable the participants to reflect on how coaching had affected them. The questions were similar at each time-point and are listed below:

- Tell me about the coaching sessions in as much detail as possible.
- What does being coached feel like? What happens in a session or between sessions?
- Would you have learnt what you have learnt on your own eventually or has the coaching added something new?
- What were your expectations of the sessions? Are they what you expected?
- What general themes/topics have you covered?
- Last time, you described a typical day at university. Has the experience of coaching affected how you approach your day or made you think about your day differently?
- How do you think coaching is affecting you, if at all? What about in terms of: contributing to your developing personal growth, life plans, relationships, ambitions, confidence, outlook, academic performance, motivation, and sense of self?
- Overall how would you describe the coaching experience?
- When was the coaching conversation most and least productive?
- What do you think you have achieved through the coaching sessions?
- Do you think you would have achieved those things without the sessions?
- Would you have coaching again? If yes, why? If no, are you pleased you signed up to have coaching? Why wouldn't you have further coaching?

- Would you recommend coaching to your university friends?
- What will take the place of the coaching relationship for you?
- What do you think the future holds for you? Have your coaching sessions influenced your thinking on this?
- Did you think about your coaching sessions at all over the summer?
- Do you think you are still feeling the effects of the coaching sessions from last year?

The interviews were recorded on a digital recorder and transcribed.

Analysis

The four interview scripts for each participant were considered as a joined-up longitudinal account. They were analyzed using IPA. This involves capturing the detailed lived experience of participants on an idiographic level and then looking for patterning across cases. The first author immersed herself in the data, reading all four transcripts for one participant in one sitting while listening to the audio recording. Each transcript was then reread and annotated line by line with keywords, phrases, themes, and ideas. The data was then transferred to a spreadsheet and each answer or question was allocated a cell. Thus, when quoting below we give cell numbers. Each interview was put on a different tab of the same document and each participant was allocated a new spreadsheet. Descriptive comments were noted in the cell to the right of the transcript, key phrases were highlighted in red, and linguistic observations that gave insight into the participant's experience were noted (Smith et al., 2009). Emergent themes that were at a higher conceptual and psychological level than the descriptive themes were noted to the left. All the emergent themes were copied and pasted into one document, duplicates were removed, and themes were grouped into clusters. Some of the themes were used as labels for emergent themes, or a new label was found to capture the ideas of several emergent themes. Careful consideration was given to the superordinate themes. A table of superordinate themes and emergent themes was created, complete with a sample quotation for each one and finally, the table was turned into a thematic diagrammatic structure. This was repeated for each participant. Each diagrammatic structure was then compared for each participant and similarities and differences were analyzed, resulting in an overall thematic structure for the experience of coaching as an undergraduate for the whole group (see Table 12.2).

The first author was consciously reflexive about her experience as a student, university adviser, and professional coach and was open to what the data said on its own terms (Smith et al., 2009). The second author acted as an independent verifier and both authors reflectively discussed the emergent and superordinate themes until consensus was reached. The findings were evaluated using Yardley's (2000) criteria for qualitative methodologies. Firstly, the analysts were sensitive to context, immersing themselves in the relevant philosophical, empirical, and methodological literature. Secondly, they were sensitive to the data itself as analytical claims were grounded in the data with extracts used as evidence to aid transparency, allowing the reader to assess our interpretations. The effect of the researchers' characteristics on the

Table 12.2 *Superordinate and Emergent Themes*

"It was a catalyst for development": Coaching as catalyst	
Superordinate theme one: "It's like more of like a conversation with a friend"—reflections on the experience of coaching	Superordinate theme two: "I'm 100 percent sure I would not have done things that I've done this past six months without the coaching": coaching "wins"
Emergent themes	Emergent themes
Coaching accelerating development	Control: Making tasks and problems more manageable
The nature of the coaching relationship	Balance and focus
Coaching compared with other support mechanisms	Confidence: self-belief, assertiveness, and reassurance
Perceptions of which types of people would benefit from coaching and at what times in their lives	New perspectives

participants both in the interview and in terms of what was subjectively brought to the analysis was reflexively considered. Both analysts are committed researchers and interact with university students in their jobs, and, coupled with the fact that the first author is a professional coach, this meant that rapport could be established quickly and pertinent supplementary questions could be asked, giving rise to high-quality data elicited at interview. The second author is an IPA expert and was a sounding board for the first author to check her analyses were rigorous. A mark of quality of analysis is that the reader gains an understanding of the phenomenon at hand and an appreciation of what it must be like to experience that phenomenon. Finally, the research should bring a new understanding to the topic and this study has added to the literature by focusing on a first-person perspective, illuminating what the experience of coaching is like in a university context. Furthermore, if the findings resonate with the reader then this is an indication of the quality of research (Finlay, 2011).

FINDINGS

The coaching experience was broadly similar for eight of the nine students. One student, Zara, had a very different experience, which acted as a counterpoint, serving as a contrast to emphasize the salient features of the other participants' accounts. Therefore, although she appears less often in the following extracts, her data has an important role to play analytically. The phrase that captures the whole shared experience is "It was a catalyst for development": Coaching as catalyst. This experience was made up of two superordinate themes: "It's like more of like a conversation with a friend"—reflections on the experience of coaching and "I'm 100 percent sure I would not have done things that I've done this past six months without the coaching"—coaching "wins."

The first superordinate theme is about the students' thoughts on the coaching experience, including their relationship with their coach and for whom they felt coaching would be useful in the future. This provides the context for the second superordinate theme, which includes the content of the sessions and how this content was put to use in the students' lives. It was found that coaching helped the students gain control of their lives, achieve greater balance and focus, increase their confidence, and see situations from new perspectives.

Superordinate theme one: "It's like more of like a conversation with a friend": Reflections on the experience of coaching

This superordinate theme comprises the almost unanimous characterization by the participants of coaching accelerating development. It also includes the nature of the coaching relationship, coaching compared with other support mechanisms, perceptions of which types of people would benefit from coaching and at what times in their lives.

Coaching accelerating development

There was a great deal of convergence in the idea that coaching sped up the participants' development like a "catalyst." This word was used spontaneously by one student and the sentiment was echoed by the others:

> I would say that it [coaching] was very helpful in that it was a catalyst for development. (Holly, 3D88)

The word "catalyst" is inextricably linked with temporality—that is, it makes a change or a realization happen faster than it would have done otherwise. The language the students used to describe their coaching experience was very positive. As well as the word "helpful" above, other words included "enjoyable," "active," and "engaging." Claire exemplifies this position:

> I think without coaching you will take longer time to be confident. Coaching just shortened that time period. (Claire, 4D299)

Neil explains that it would have taken longer for him to feel psychologically secure at university if he had not had coaching sessions, and he would have got worse grades:

> Yeah, I still think that without the first one [session] and the others, I suppose, I would have still been insecure about being at [at this university] or it would have taken me longer to get over and I might have got worse grades. (Neil, 4D102)

Several students allude to the fact that coaching decreased the amount of time it would have taken for them to reach the same level of academic performance. Colin wished he could have been as motivated and organized in his first year when he did not have coaching:

Even though the workload was easier and stuff like that, I think if I had been able to approach my work like I did this year, last year, it means I could have come into this year and started straight away. I could have got better results in my first coursework. (Colin, 3D179)

As well as speeding up growth, coaching added new ideas into the mix. The time management techniques that Colin's coach introduced were new to him:

It sounds so simple now that I'm thinking about it but at the time it was like a revelation. It really was. (Colin, 3D141)

The word "revelation" emphasizes the fact that a new way of doing things was revealed to him. He felt that this new way directly improved his academic performance. Martin and Natasha both commented that coaching had stimulated their thinking and that new personal ground had been broken:

It's quite challenging but then it's quite interesting as well because it's making me think of things which I wouldn't think of by myself. (Martin, 2D168)

It's actually new stuff that I've, I've never thought about doing. (Natasha, 2D192)

So we can see that some students believed that coaching accelerated their development and others felt it had introduced new elements of development.

The nature of the coaching relationship

The nature of the coaching relationship influenced how the students responded to the coaching and the benefit they derived from the sessions.

Neil felt that because the coach was a professional (a professional listener and motivator, in a sense) he could open up about himself more:

Yes, I feel like, you know, because he's outside but it's like when you go to a doctor about a physical problem you know they see it all the time, you know I mean I presume, like I mean yes I'm probably younger than a lot of the people that he sees professionally but, no, I just think I'm sure he can deal with this. (Neil, 2D231)

Holly found she had an informal, friendly relationship with her coach:

I found it to be a lot more informal and a lot more casual than I expected in a very good way. (Holly, 3D88)

Claire valued the fact that she did not have any ties to the coach so she could really speak freely:

I think I can feel release because I can talk with someone, yes. I don't know her, she doesn't know me. That we can discuss on one part of my life just only this part and yes. (Claire, 2D216)

Many students experienced these feelings of "relief" and "release" in the process of unburdening themselves in the coaching sessions. Many students were surprised at how the coach was totally focused on them. Neil was touched by how deeply his coach was listening to him:

> Yes within the first, within the first one because it was at the point where he, where he suddenly, he would say something and it showed that he's listened so much you know like a really sort of in-depth comment so at that point you think you know he's not just, he's not just looking at his watch. (Neil, 2D179)

For many students, opening up to their coach was a new experience. Hermione found the opening up that she was able to do, refreshing:

> Yes, I am actually yes, they go pretty quickly and I guess I'm just not that used to talking about my feelings, not used to discussing that sort of thing so it's very refreshing to be able to open up and analyze things like that yes. (Hermione, 2D66)

The word "refreshing" alludes to reinvigorating the self and a restoring of energy. Many students felt that the sessions gave them a boost of energy. Other students also characterized coaching as a boost of motivation:

> It's kind of like a little cheerleader in a way, I think. So, having that as advice and then motivation … it's hard to explain. (Lynn, 3D128)

The coach was a "cheerleader," encouraging Lynn and motivating her.
The very act of having to report back in the next coaching session was inherently motivating:

> I think I had the potential to get there but I almost needed the external push, knowing that I would then have someone to tell that to, to relate that back, it's more motivation to actually do it. (Hermione, 2D116)

The students developed a relationship with the coach such that they did not want to fall short of their expectations:

> I think, I wouldn't like to, I wouldn't like to disappoint him, not that he'll be that bothered but, yes disappoint him in a very vague sense I mean I'm hardly that much of a part of his life. (Neil, 2D209)

Zara was also motivated by coaching but found that the effect dissipated:

> Maybe it had short-term impacts like straight after you'd be like, "Oh I should do this or get going with this." Then it kind of fades after a bit until your next session. (Zara 4D78)

Zara's image of the motivation fading contrasts with Natasha's belief that the coaching's impact would last forever:

> I, I don't think I will freak out because like the stuff I will carry with me for like the rest of my life, like these little tips. (Natasha 2D166)

Thus, it can be seen the students perceived that coaching, in terms of having someone nonpartisan with whom to discuss issues, enabled them to open up and unburden themselves, which gave them the feeling of release and relief. Furthermore, having to report back to their coach in the following session gave the students an extra source of motivation to work on their goals.

Coaching compared with other support mechanisms

Many students made comparisons between coaching and other forms of support including therapy and friendships. Several students expressed the view that the coaching relationship could be achieved within friendships:

> Mike was a lot like a friend in the way that he listened and was compassionate but yeah I think you can get that from actual unpaid friendships as well. (Neil, 3D317)

However, Holly expressed the view that she was pleased that she was able to talk about friends to someone who was not her friend, precluding the need to "bitch" about them:

> It's not the same as counseling but it was very cathartic to be able to talk about things that I didn't feel I had anybody else to talk to about them, so specifically, I could always talk about friends that I didn't want, that I didn't want to have to bitch about a friend to somebody else, so that sort of thing was good. (Holly, 3D88)

She compares coaching to counseling and draws out the cathartic nature of the sessions as a similarity. Martin draws a similar parallel:

> One of my friends is seeing a therapist now, which isn't exactly the same but it's essentially the same sort of thing where you're talking. (Martin, 3D161–162)

However, Natasha found the power relations within coaching to be quite different from those found in counseling. She found that coaching gave rise to a more equal relationship between professional and client, in contrast to her previous experience of therapy where she felt the therapist was writing notes about her as if she were an object who was having therapy done to her, rather than with her:

> So different, I've, I don't feel like someone is domineering the conversation. It's like "and how does this make you feel?" I hate questions like that, it's just. If if I don't say how it makes me feel, I don't want to talk about how it makes me feel. It's completely different and people think therapy is like coaching, completely wrong. It's like more of like a conversation with a friend, just having like a one-on-one conversation. It doesn't feel like someone's writing notes about you like, oh this is your reaction to this equals something. (Natasha, 2D400)

Thus in the participants' eyes, the experience of coaching shared commonalities and differences to therapy and friendships.

Perceptions of which types of people would benefit from coaching and at what times in their lives

The students discussed whom coaching could benefit and when would be a good time in life to have coaching. Over half felt coaching would be useful for people who lacked confidence:

> I think generally people who are less confident or who have less insight into their own lives would be the kind of people who would benefit. (Lynn, 3D136)

Confidence is a concept that permeated the interviews and is clearly something the students felt was very important to cultivate. It seems to hold the key to what was achieved through coaching and what was missing in a lot of students' lives.

The one student who did not benefit from coaching, Zara, attributed this to her inability to open up to a stranger, even though she wanted to talk about relationship issues:

> Yeah. I think maybe I'm just not comfortable talking about more personal stuff with people I don't know that well. (Zara, 3D52)

Zara did in fact change coaches after two sessions, but she felt unable to disclose her issues to either of them. This suggests that it was not the coaches' skills that prevented her from opening up, but, as she herself identified, she was not comfortable doing so, which has important implications for whom coaching is offered in the future. Indeed, Holly highlighted the ability to open up to be important for the success of coaching:

> I think it does take a certain openness of mind to do it. (Holly, 3D208)

When considering the best time to have coaching, many students explained that due to the strangeness of university when they first arrived, the first year of university would be the most beneficial year, which has direct implications for university policy:

> I think first year is a good time because it's kind of chaotic and a time for adjustment. I think in uni years, the first one is probably the best one and then probably the next best time would be like midlife crisis. (Lynn, 3D130)

Indeed, half the students felt that any dramatic life transition would be a good time to have coaching:

> I can't really think on the top of my head of something more appropriate than, a significant transition like university or trying to find a job after university or, or maybe

even somebody who's about to go into retirement as well, just when your complete lifestyle is going through a change or moving, you know when you do something big like a new town or move to a new country even, I think would be very useful. (Holly, 3D232)

Thus, the students felt that people who lacked confidence, but who had the ability to open up, would benefit the most from coaching, and that coaching would be most useful in the first year of university, and also at other transitional times in life.

This superordinate theme has encompassed the experience of coaching as a catalyst for development; the experience of the coaching relationship; the idea that coaching shared common features with other forms of support and that coaching would most benefit first-year university students who lacked confidence and who could open up.

Superordinate theme 2: "I'm 100 percent sure I would not have done things that I've done this past six months without the coaching"—coaching "wins"

This superordinate theme describes the four broad ways in which coaching benefited the students. Firstly, coaching gave the students a sense of control by imparting specific strategies to address tasks and problems. Secondly, coaching helped them achieve greater balance and focus in the different aspects of their lives. Thirdly, coaching sessions increased the students' confidence, which led to them feeling more motivated. Finally, it helped the students see situations from new perspectives, which empowered them to change behaviors, benefiting the students in different ways, such as enjoying improved relationships.

Control: making tasks and problems more manageable

Much of what was addressed and achieved through the coaching sessions for all participants was gaining a sense of control over their work and how to make tasks and problems more manageable. This in turn led to the avoidance of anxiety and, ultimately, a perceived improvement in academic work. Many students spoke of "stress" and "panic attacks" and welcomed methods to reduce these.

Control was partly achieved by introducing time management techniques, including breaking down tasks into smaller components and also simply realizing that there is enough time in the day to do what is needed. Colin serves as an exemplar:

Just setting small goals basically, setting small goals to do certain stuff by a certain date and just, generally just managing my time better, it's really just about setting small goals and then hitting them like doing the research for a paper and then like noting it out so doing a plan and then going on and actually finishing it and then handing in a first draft and getting it back and you know that sort of stuff helps immensely, immensely. (Colin, 2D40)

The practical strategy of breaking issues down led to the students feeling less stressed about their work or aspects of their life:

I think with outlook as well I'm more, because I can be quite a stressed person, quite an anxious person but I feel more relaxed than I was because I think I know how to address the problems if, Henry's taught me sort of how to break down issues in my life and aspects of my life to address them so it's made my outlook on life a lot more relaxed because I don't find it too hard to handle certain things. (Hermione, 3D156)

Hermione became more relaxed as she had learned how to handle issues that previously would have made her stressed. Natasha's coach worked with her to change her perception of how much time there is in the day, obviating the need to panic about not having enough time:

Well it's just got me better at studying, I'm now not leaving everything till the last minute I'm taking more time, I'm like realizing that I have a lot of time in the day so I can get quite a lot done and I previously thought that I couldn't so I'm better at studying and I can do the readings now, I can understand stuff better in lectures and seminars. (Natasha, 3D124)

Thus, adopting time-management techniques helped her space out her work more and decrease procrastination. Time seemed more stretched out for Natasha as she gained greater control over her work.

Both Natasha and Hermione talked about suffering from panic attacks and insomnia respectively:

It's similar to a panic attack except all these bad scenarios keep going around in your head and you're just like, 'This is going to be the worst thing ever. When I have to go up and talk I'm going to fall, I'm going to forget my words. Everyone is going to laugh.' It's just not fun. One of the tips she gave me was to try and make myself laugh. It's weird because you look insane when you're doing it but that really does help. (Natasha, 4D34)

Things like breathing exercises. He had a whole list. I just remember a hot drink, a bath, and reading. Even though that's so simple, for some reason I just always remember that conversation and the list of things to help sleep. (Hermione, 4D128)

The students were given motivational tips that could be applied throughout their lives. Natasha kept coming back to a phrase that had been introduced in her coaching session "you can have everything, just not right now," which became like a motivational mantra for her:

Like this, this one phrase she said to me, it's like "you can have everything, just not right now," which is, like that's quite important to me now because when I first started uni, okay I need to get this, this, and this done. I need to do all these things, not important in my first year but I need to do them. I need to have everything down and I don't actually, like some things can wait until second year. (Natasha, 2D168)

Natasha realized that, although initially she wanted to be on top of everything straight away, there was no rush. She became empowered to engage in her life and take one step at a time through coaching, which relieved the pressure she put on herself.

Claire learned how to face problems through coaching:

> At first if someone tells you what you can do to deal with one problem, then gradually you will know how to deal with the problem yourself. It's important they teach you the skills to deal with problems. That's more important for me. (Claire, 4D117)

She was able to put these problem-solving skills into practice on her own outside the coaching sessions.

Balance and focus

Coaching also helped the students to focus on what was important to them which, in turn, gave rise to a sense of balance. Martin achieved balance between academic work and other pursuits:

> There's a better balance between doing work and … I've always felt really guilty when I'm not doing work, so I've always been doing work 24/7 but I feel like it's helped me balance that a bit better. So, now when I'm watching TV or something I'm not thinking, 'Oh my God! Maybe I should be …' (Martin, 3D110)

The coaching sessions helped the students achieve focus and direction. Lynn spoke implicitly about feeling focused:

> And like, it is sort of like, being able to sort of reorganize clutter in your head, I think, when you're able to talk about stuff in real life. (Lynn, 2D184)

One interpretation of this is that she was taking stock of herself. The fact she was "reorganizing" the clutter means it was once organized, but now she needs to reevaluate it and reorder it in light of her new way of being. The word "clutter" evokes things taking up unnecessary space and things being higgledy-piggledy. Thus, for Lynn, focus was about taking stock and creating order in her life.

Colin's manifestation of focus was in terms of planning his work and knowing how to proceed:

> I just remember being very focused after our sessions and knowing what to do. It was nice it helped me to plan, definitely. (Colin, 4D94)

Focusing for Colin and others was about zoning in on what next steps to take, that is, forward planning.

Coaching helped Natasha keep herself together and stay on an even keel. She felt she would have been a "wreck" without coaching:

> Yes I'm, I'm really happy because it's helped me quite a lot. It's I think, I don't feel that … if I didn't do the coaching I'd be a bit, not worse off but not doing as well as I am now. Especially with certain areas like the procrastination. I'd be, I'd be a wreck actually. (Natasha, 2D160)

The word "wreck" conjures up images that Natasha would have had no compass, no anchor, and would have lost her way in her first year. Coaching enabled her to feel whole, to navigate university, and to survive any turbulent waters.

Confidence: self-belief, assertiveness, and reassurance

The greatest area of convergence for many students was that coaching gave them confidence. This included a growing confidence in their studies and how university "works" as well as the growing of an internal confidence, that is, self-belief. Holly serves as an exemplar:

> I think I've definitely become, become a lot more confident through the process and a lot more able to talk about problems that maybe I was too shy or I didn't think were important enough to talk about. (Holly, 3D170)

She grew in her convictions about what was important to talk about; in other words, her self-belief grew. Other students' confidence also manifested as an increase in self-belief:

> Yeah, just articulating stuff and I think when you do articulate stuff, it gives you confidence and belief in what you're saying. I think it helped in that sense as well. (Lynn, 4D228)

Lynn felt that the very act of articulating her ideas and goals out loud increased her self-belief. Hermione's increase in confidence manifested as assertiveness, which positively affected her social relationships and her participation in societies:

> H: Things, I'm 100 percent sure I would not have done things that I've done this past six months, over the past six months without the coaching, I think that definitely …
> I: Like, like what?
> H: I've become more assertive, like, applying for this job, I probably wouldn't have done it because it's a lot of one-on-one, like going up to people you don't know, interacting so I wouldn't have applied when I applied in like December/January. Going to certain societies, going to debate … I think eventually I would have got there but it's definitely sped up the process and yeah, just, just other social things, I think it's improved the way I react/relate to other people and actually say how I feel without worrying so much so yeah, it's, it's, I definitely feel like I achieved more with it. (Hermione, 3D74–76)

Neil's coach helped increase his confidence by challenging his belief that he should not contribute ideas to tutorials for fear of getting something wrong:

> One of the major things was more confident in lectures and tutorials at actually speaking because I explained how I won't say ideas in a tutorial in case they're wrong, you know and he'd be like 'why would they be wrong?' you know and 'other people get them wrong' and 'who would judge you like that?' you know, so that was a major thing. (Neil, 2D151)

Thus, Neil attributed his change in his academic interactions to coaching.

The students' perceived confidence also increased by gaining reassurance from their coaches. Martin exemplifies this:

M: That [making a film] was, that was kind of feeding off of coaching because it was making me feel like, like I could do it, so I could have but.

I: And what, do, do you feel like you would have done it anyway? You know like, you needed this external encouragement to get going, is that right or …?

M: I don't know really because … I've written things before but then I've just like, I just deleted them or given them to my brother because he makes films but I've never really. Because I could have done it last year and I never did. (Martin, 2D276–298)

For some students, the reassurance of the coach became internalized such that they could hear the coach's voice as they were going about their activities:

It's just really helpful it's like, it's like you have like a second-guessing voice at the back of your head and it helps just like to not reinstate your ideas but like become more like confident in your ideas and that, okay I can do this. It's like a little pep talk now and then, which is nice. (Natasha, 3D138)

The characterization of coaching as a "pep talk" is similar to Lynn's use of the word "cheerleader" in the previous superordinate theme. Reassurance for Holly was in the form of validation of solutions:

Well you see, I think for a lot of things, it was less finding a solution and more validating a solution that I had already found but didn't really know if it was the right solution. So a lot of the time, even with social problems I would, we would talk about the problems and I would already have a solution in mind and that would most likely be the solution I ended up decided on. So a lot of the time it was validation. (Holly, 3D106)

Thus, in the students' lived experience, the reassurance that coaching offered directly increased their confidence. Confidence, in the form of self-belief, assertiveness, and reassurance, was a near-unanimous achievement of coaching.

New perspectives

The coaching sessions gave the students new insights and perspectives on their worlds and thinking. Both Hermione and Martin had considered university to be a "stepping stone"—a temporary place to stop and a means to an end. Both students found that they could now enjoy university in its own right:

My actual uni experience, I'm thinking more as a thing to really enjoy and just get really involved in 'everything uni' and not worry about the future. My view of uni has changed in terms of I see it to enjoy, rather than a stepping stone to a job. (Hermione, 4D262)

> Well, that's the way I've always seen it, a stepping-stone but I feel like I can enjoy it. Martin, 3D140

Just as Hermione and Martin had a shift in attitude to university, so other students experienced a change in outlook that they attributed to coaching:

> The thing that's really stuck with me is that way of thinking. The sheer breadth of not just jumping to a conclusion with a problem. Really considering every single thing you can do to make it easier on yourself or easier on other people, and figure out why you feel the way you do and not just accept that you do feel a certain way. Particularly helpful when figuring out how to come out to my parents and figuring out which way would be easiest for me and which way would be easiest for them. Things like that. (Holly, 4D148)

Through coaching Holly learned a new way of thinking and working through problems, which involved discussing the issue for longer and coming up with several options (or letting go) before jumping to conclusions or premature action/inaction. It can be seen that Holly used what she had learned from coaching to strategize how to come out to her parents, which is something she had been trying to do for years. Thus coaching had a profound outcome for her.

Zara did derive some benefit from coaching. She discussed losing her phone in one of her coaching sessions, which led to a general discussion about militating against risk. This had two ramifications. Firstly, she backed up her files electronically, which was practically useful as she subsequently lost her laptop too. But more importantly, it led her to a change of outlook:

> Just I would say about the whole reacting to things. Like I was thinking of how, you just react to things that happen to you, that maybe we should prepare for them beforehand. That like gave me a different outlook on things. (Zara, 2D194)

Thus, as a result of coaching, she decided to have systems in place to preempt whatever life threw at her.

Another shift in perspective was how students thought and felt about social relationships. For example, Colin, who was a mature student, already had a network of friends and was quite keen not to mix his social life with his university life. However, his coach suggested that making friends at university may enhance his experience:

> She just made me realize how useful it [speaking to people in his class] would be. Like I was saying, that thing about how you need to melt both lives together, it would help it a little bit. She's actually the one who said it would help a little bit and it has. I think it has and I think the more I do it, it will help more. (Colin, 3D109)

Thus, Colin directly attributed having an improved university experience to coaching.

In this superordinate theme, we have seen a great deal of convergence in how coaching benefited the students. Four emergent themes have been discussed: an increased sense of control, the achievement of greater balance and focus, increased confidence, and seeing situations from new perspectives.

DISCUSSION

The phenomenon of the coaching experience was revealed by the lived experience of the students and comprised several features. Firstly, one feature was that coaching was a positive experience that led to perceived accelerated development. Secondly, the relationship with the coach, in most cases, increased the students' ability to open up to them and was itself a source of motivation. Thirdly, the phenomenon disclosed how the students felt about coaching in relation to other sources of support, such as therapy and friendship. Fourthly, it disclosed who they felt would benefit from coaching, that is, first-year university students who lacked confidence and who could open up. Finally, the key feature of the phenomenon of the coaching experience to be revealed by the lived experience of the students was the specific "wins" or outcomes they attributed to coaching. These covered four main areas: an increased sense of control, the achievement of greater balance and focus, increased confidence, and seeing situations from new perspectives. Confidence permeated the experience of coaching: for example, the students identified that people who wanted to work on confidence would benefit from coaching and it was one of the main areas of achievement attributed to coaching.

These findings confirm Gyllensten and Palmer's (2007) study, which found that the coaching relationship was key to reaping the benefits of coaching. Furthermore, this study lends support to Franklin and Doran's (2009) and Fried and Irwin's (2016) findings that coaching positively affected academic performance as several students had the perception that their academic performance had improved as a result of coaching. It would be interesting to explore in a further study whether their academic performance had, in fact, improved in real terms, or whether their perception of improvement was a manifestation of their self-reported improved confidence. Either way, universities would do well to incorporate a coaching component to each undergraduate course. This paper also supports Fried and Irwin's (2016) findings that coaching improved stress management, as many students reported that coaching had helped them in this regard specifically. Greene's (2004) findings that coaching increased confidence are also borne out by this paper, as students reported feeling increased confidence, which they directly attributed to coaching. Greene's research focused on economically and socially disadvantaged undergraduates, whereas this current paper does not focus on a "special case" group. It should be noted that this does not mean that some students in this study were not economically disadvantaged, simply that this was not a criterion for inclusion. Moreover, this paper shows that nonclinical and non-"special case" students reported benefiting from coaching.

Furthermore, this study highlighted the issues with which students need support, namely increasing their sense of control by learning specific techniques, achieving greater balance and focus, increasing their confidence and taking new perspectives. These issues may well be a key component of emerging adulthood (Arnett, 2000), which is a time of life when many people start university.

This paper has focused on the lived experience and active sense-making of the students and fleshes out the previously reported quantitative studies measuring the positive effects of coaching. Therefore, this paper has added to the literature by providing a fine-grained description of what coaching achieved from the students' perspective, which can help inform universities how to support their students in specific ways.

IMPLICATIONS AND CONCLUSIONS

The study has shown that one-to-one coaching can have profound effects on students and can also help them to maximize their time at university, as detailed by their first-person accounts. At most universities, careers services, counseling, and personal tutoring are discrete entities and suffer from a lack of joined-up thinking. In this study, the coach became a tailored one-stop-shop for the students and helped the students make links between different parts of their life, for example, being low in confidence could affect career choices and relationships. If universities are seeking to improve the student experience, prevent student withdrawal, and support their students in general, they would be wise to consider investing in one-to-one coaching for all their students, and not wait until issues become psychological problems. This will also help students to get the most out of their university experience. Universities could provide help in other forms, such as by arranging seminars and workshops on the specific issues detailed in this paper, or by arranging for students to have group-coaching (although the benefits of group coaching in the university context would have to be explored in further research). Furthermore, as an alternative to professional coaches, existing staff members could be trained to take a coaching approach.

LIMITATIONS OF THE STUDY

This study focused on a small group of highly articulate and academically able students at one university and may not be generalizable to other universities or types of students. In addition, this study focused on students studying arts and humanities subjects and these results may not be valid for students on more structured, vocational courses such as medicine or engineering. However, although the findings of this paper only hold true for this particular group in this context, Smith et al. (2009) maintain that "theoretical generalisability" applies "where the reader of the report is able to assess the evidence in relation to their existing professional and experiential knowledge" (p. 4). In other words, to use Finlay's (2011) idea of "resonance," if the study invokes professional or common sense resonance, then it would be reasonable to assume that similar findings may well hold true in similar contexts. Furthermore, the small sample was necessary for an in-depth qualitative study, which is highly appropriate for exploring a novel situation or phenomenon.

Importantly, no account was taken of the coaches' different coaching approaches and techniques and no attempt was made to make this uniform. Therefore, it is unclear if some coaching styles were more beneficial than others in this study but, since this was an exploratory qualitative study, cause and effect of variables were neither sought nor able to be clarified. Moreover, as the coaching sector has burgeoned in recent years, with many different coaching courses on offer, covering a range of approaches, the authors felt it would not be possible to achieve homogeneity in this respect. Since the students presented with different issues, it would also not be possible or wise to use the same techniques on them.

Furthermore, coaches were randomly paired with students without attempting to find a "fit." However, students were given the option to change coaches if they did not get on with their coach. By the very nature of IPA, the data and analysis are subjective at two levels; that is, there is a double sense-making taking place—the participant is making sense of their experience and the researcher is making sense of that (Smith et al., 2009). If an independent assessment of the benefits of coaching students in the university context is required, it would be necessary to introduce some objective measures on a larger sample size to fully understand the benefits of coaching in this context. However, this study has enabled the students' perspectives to come to the fore and has detailed how they experienced and made sense of coaching.

FUTURE RESEARCH

Further research could explore the sustainability of the achievements of coaching by conducting follow-up interviews, for example, a year after coaching had ended. It would be interesting to map the effects of coaching at different stages of the coaching to see, for example, if confidence was built up slowly or whether confidence increased after a certain number of sessions, as this could be an indicator of the optimum number of sessions. It would be highly relevant to explore the benefits of personal tutors (university staff) taking a coaching approach compared with the benefits derived when professional coaches were employed. The effects of coaching on other university cohorts, such as final year undergraduate students, Master's students, students from different subjects and from different universities could be explored in further studies.

REFERENCES

Arnett, J. J. (2000). Emerging adulthood: A theory of development from the late teens through the twenties. *American Psychologist, 55*(5), 469–480. https://doi.org/10.1037/0003-066X.55.5.469

Finlay, L. (2011). *Phenomenology for therapists, researching the lived world.* Oxford, UK: Wiley-Blackwell.

Franklin, J., & Doran, J. (2009). Does all coaching enhance objective performance independently evaluated by blind assessors? The importance of the coaching model and content. *International Coaching Psychology Review, 4*(2), 128–144.

Fried, R., & Irwin, J. (2016). Calmly coping: A motivational interviewing via co-active life coaching (MI-VIA-CALC) pilot intervention for university students with perceived levels of high stress. *International Journal of Evidence Based Coaching and Mentoring, 14*(1), 16–33.

Grant, A. (2003). The impact of life coaching on goal attainment, metacognition and mental health. *Social Behavior and Personality, 31*(3), 253–263. https://doi.org/10.2224/sbp.2003.31.3.253

Greene, T. (2004). Academic coaching: A new approach to supporting student success. *The National Institute for Staff and Organizational Development Innovation Abstracts, 26*(5).

Gyllensten, K., & Palmer, S. (2007). The coaching relationship: An interpretative phenomenological analysis. *International Coaching Psychology Review, 2*, 168–177.

Gyllensten, K., Palmer, S., Nilsson, A.-K., Meland Regnér, A., & Frodi, A. (2010). Experiences of cognitive coaching: A qualitative study. *International Coaching Psychology Review, 5*(2), 98–108.

Jackson, C. (2003). Transitions into higher education; gendered implications for academic self-concept. *Oxford Review of Education, 29*, 321–346. https://doi.org/10.1080/03054980307448

Lancer, N., Clutterbuck, D., & Megginson, D. (2016). *Techniques for coaching and mentoring* (2nd ed.). Oxford, UK: Routledge.

Lizzio, A., Wilson, K., & Simons, R. (2002). University students' perceptions of the learning environment and academic outcomes: Implications for theory and practice. *Studies in Higher Education, 27*(1), 27–52. https://doi.org/10.1080/03075070120099359

Naidoo, R., Shankar, A., & Veer, E. (2011). The consumerist turn in higher education: Policy aspirations and outcomes. *Journal of Marketing Management, 27*(11–12), 1142–1162. https://doi.org/10.1080/0267257X.2011.609135

Robinson, C., & Gahagan, J. (2010). In practice: Coaching students to academic success and engagement on campus. *About Campus, 15*(4), 26–29. https://doi.org/10.1002/abc.20032

Short, E., Kinman, G., & Baker, S. (2010). Evaluating the impact of a peer coaching intervention on well-being amongst psychology undergraduate students. *International Coaching Psychology Review, 5*(2), 27–35.

Smith, J. A., Flowers, P., & Larkin, M. (2009). *Interpretative Phenomenological Analysis*. London, UK: Sage.

Stevens, G. (2003). Late studentship: Academic aspiration, personal growth, and the death of the past. *Journal of Phenomenological Psychology, 34*(2), 235–256. https://doi.org/10.1163/156916203322847155.

Sue-Chan, C., & Latham, G. (2004). The relative effectiveness of external, peer, and self-coaches. *Applied Psychology: An International Review, 53*(2), 260–278. https://doi.org/10.1111/j.1464-0597.2004.00171.x.

Swartz, S., Prevatt, F., & Proctor, B. (2005). A coaching intervention for college students with attention deficit/hyperactivity disorder. *Psychology in the Schools, 42*(6), 647–656. https://doi.org/10.1002/pits.20101.

Turner, A., Hammond, C., Gilchrist, M., & Barlow, J. (2007). Coventry University students' experience of mental health problems. *Counselling Psychology Quarterly, 20*(3), 247–252 https://doi.org/10.1080/09515070701570451.

U. S. Department of Education, Institute of Education Sciences, What Works Clearinghouse. (2012). *WWC review of the report: The effects of student coaching in college: An evaluation of a randomized experiment in student mentoring*. Retrieved February 14, 2017, from https://ies.ed.gov/ncee/wwc Docs/SingleStudyReviews/wwc_studentcoaching_080712.pdf

Van Zandvoort, M., Irwin, J., & Morrow, D. (2009). Co-active coaching as an intervention for obesity among female university students. *International Coaching Psychology Review, 3*(3), 191–206.

Yardley, L. (2000). Dilemmas in qualitative health research. *Psychology and Health, 15*(2), 215–228. https://doi.org/10.1080/08870440008400302

Yorke, M., & Longden, B. (2004). *Retention and success in Higher Education*. Maidenhead, UK: SRHE and Open University Press.

Section IV

Insights from Quantitative Coaching Psychology Research

Jonathan Passmore and David Tee

Coaching psychology has been criticized for lacking methodological rigor—and praised for openly recognizing and acknowledging this fact (Briner, 2012). This criticism is often linked to an assumption that insights and evidence exist in a hierarchy, determined by the research design used to generate them. In this line of argument, randomized controlled trials (RCTs) are situated toward the top of the evidence hierarchy, superseded only by systematic reviews and meta-analyses of those RCTs, with data from case studies and expert opinion situated at the bottom. This assumption about the merit of different designs, found in calls for "evidence-based" management and practice, is acquired from the field of medical research—sometimes openly so (see Rousseau, 2006) and can result in accusations of coaching research relying upon "inferior methodological design" (Grover & Furnham, 2016, p. 5).

While the merit or relevance of applying the rules of rigor from other domains to the field of coaching research can be debated, this position has resulted in calls such as this request from Sheldon (as cited in Grant & Cavanagh, 2007):

> To me, the single most important thing for coaching … to keep in mind is the necessity of collecting rigorous empirical evidence. This may be the only thing that separates the field from earlier humanistic psychology and from current non-validated self-help books. (p. 242)

Returning to the "three-phase" model of research maturation (Passmore & Fillery-Travis, 2011) mentioned in the introduction to Section III, researchers heeding the call of those such as Sheldon have sought to introduce quantitative data collection into the emerging discipline of coaching psychology. Early published empirical research commonly featured subjective, self-reported data for dependent variables and relatively low sample sizes. Examples of these studies can be found in this section, such as Yu, Collins, Cavanagh, White, and Fairbrother (2008) and Madden, Green, and Grant (2011). Nonetheless, these studies marked an important maturation within the field: an effort to move from concentrating solely on establishing effectiveness in the field to determining efficacy within more controlled conditions. So, while these studies were typically conducted in real-world settings, such as workplaces and school classrooms, the random allocation of participants to experimental and control conditions and the attempts to hold other pertinent variables constant allowed these researchers to begin making cautious claims about coaching's impact. With studies such as the featured research from Newnham-Kanas, Irwin, Morrow, and Battram (2011), the move from self-report to the objective measurement of variables continues this effort in coaching psychology research design to adhere to the principles of academic rigor.

Challenges remain. Arguably fundamental to any researcher wishing to isolate and manipulate variables is the fact that the term "coaching" is itself variously defined and operationalized (see Chapter 1). This makes cross-study comparisons, such as systematic reviews and meta-analyses, problematic. Individual studies may appear to be manipulating or measuring the same variable, but the comparisons may not extend beyond surface labels.

The use of placebos is core to the design of RCTs within medical research. If coaching psychology wishes to mature as a field of research and generate a breadth of quantitative research studies as input to future meta-analyses, how can it move beyond wait-list designs, with their associated risks to the internal validity of studies? Such studies require the introduction of the coaching equivalent of a placebo for control condition participants: an intervention that the client and coach both believe to be coaching, or the use of a comparable, parallel intervention.

Finally, coaching psychology is regarded as diverse and interdisciplinary (Cowan, 2013; McDowall & Short, 2012), drawing on theories, models, and techniques from counseling, sports and exercise, occupational and other domains of psychology. This heterogeneity of practice, coupled with wide variance in coaching client goals and a myriad of contextual factors impacting upon any working alliance within coaching, all adds further difficulties in the conduct of quantitative meta-analyses.

Nonetheless, as the selection in this section demonstrates, coaching psychology is now routinely complementing qualitative studies, with all the richness of meaning that their data can provide, with experimental and quasi-experimental research designs. Such studies may well be necessary to satisfy those from wider academia who may be looking in and judging the merits of our field.

REFERENCES

Briner, R. B. (2012). Does coaching work and does anyone really care? *OP Matters, 16,* 4–11.

Cowan, K. (2013). Ready, set, goal. *Coaching at Work, 8*(4), 33–35.

Grant, A. M., & Cavanagh, M. (2007). Evidence-based coaching: Flourishing or languishing? *Australian Psychologist, 42*(4), 239–254.

Grover, S., & Furnham, A. (2016). Coaching as a developmental intervention in organisations: A systematic review of its effectiveness and the mechanisms underlying it. *PLoS One, 11*(7), e0159137.

McDowall, A., & Short, E. (2012). Editorial. *Coaching: An International Journal of Theory, Research and Practice, 4*(2), 67–69.

Passmore, J., & Fillery-Travis, A. (2011). A critical review of executive coaching research: A decade of progress and what's to come. *Coaching: An International Journal of Theory, Research and Practice, 4*(2), 70–88.

Rousseau, D. M. (2006). Is there such a thing as "evidence-based management"? *Academy of Management Review, 31*(2), 256–269.

Madden, W., Green, S., & Grant, A. M. (2011). A pilot study evaluating strengths-based coaching for primary school students: Enhancing engagement and hope. *International Coaching Psychology Review, 6*(1), 71–83.

Newnham-Kanas, C., Irwin, J. D., Morrow, D., & Battram, D. (2011). The quantitative assessment of motivational interviewing using co-active life coaching skills as an intervention for adults struggling with obesity. *International Coaching Psychology Review, 6*(2), 211–228.

Yu, N., Collins, C. G., Cavanagh, M., White, K., & Fairbrother, G. (2008). Positive coaching with frontline managers: enhancing their effectiveness and understanding why. *International Coaching Psychology Review, 3*(2), 110–122.

13 Evidence-Based Life Coaching for Senior High School Students: Building Hardiness and Hope

Suzy Green, Anthony M. Grant, and Jo Rynsaardt[1]

Life (or personal) coaching can be understood as a collaborative, solution-focused, results-orientated systematic process, in which the coach facilitates the enhancement of the coachee's life experience, goal attainment, and well-being, and fosters the self-directed learning and personal growth of the people from normal (i.e., nonclinical) populations.

Recent studies have provided preliminary evidence for the efficacy of evidence-based life coaching. These studies, from the emerging field of coaching psychology, have indicated that an evidence-based life coaching intervention can enhance goal striving, well-being, and hope (Green, Oades, & Grant, 2006), increase goal attainment and satisfaction with life, increase perceived control over environmental factors, and result in greater openness toward new life experiences (Spence & Grant, 2005). In addition, life coaching can increase quality of life and reduce depression, anxiety, and stress (Grant, 2003). To date, such life coaching research has focused on adult community populations.

Within the life-coaching industry, varying niche applications have developed, such as retirement coaching, relationship coaching, and financial coaching. One emerging specialized area lies within the educational setting. Life coaching within educational settings is distinct from educational coaching (or tutoring), which is specifically aimed at improving academic performance. A pilot life-coaching study conducted by Campbell and Gardner (2005) in an educational setting examined the effects of life

[1] First published as Green, S., Grant, A., & Rynsaardt, J. (2007). Evidence-based life coaching for senior high school students: Building hardiness and hope. *International Coaching Psychology Review*, 2(1), 24–32.

coaching on high school students' personal and academic development (Year 12). Their findings indicated that life coaching may have the potential to build resilience and well-being in young people, and help students cope with the stresses of high school. In the Campbell and Gardner (2005) pilot study, only 12 students took part in the life-coaching program, and the coaching was delivered by the school counselor. The present study sought to extend the work of Campbell and Gardner (2005) by training teachers to be the life coaches and by using a larger sample size.

THE CHALLENGE OF SENIOR HIGH SCHOOL

Senior high school (15–18 years) is a difficult time for many students. They frequently feel under considerable pressure to perform well academically, as performance at high school impacts on university entry and future career prospects. A large-scale study in Sydney, Australia, involving over 400 high school students showed that over 50% of respondents had levels of anxiety, depression, and stress that were above the "normal" range (Smith & Sinclair, 2000). High school students typically worry about a range of issues including academic performance, relationships, family, and friends and peers (Amen & Reglin, 1992).

Interventions that have attempted to help students deal with the challenges of high school typically focused on identifying students with problems (Tait & Entwistle, 1996) and delivering study skills training (Zimmerman, Bonner, & Kovach, 1996). However, with the rise of the positive psychology movement, there is interest in developing interventions that build high school students' resilience and well-being, rather than merely treating symptoms of dysfunctionality. Resilience has been described as an individual's capacity for maintenance, recovery, or improvement in mental health following life challenges (Ryff, Singer, Dienberg Love, & Essex, 1998).

COGNITIVE HARDINESS

Cognitive hardiness is an important dimension of resilience (Bonanno, 2004). Hardiness, originally described by Kobasa and Maddi (1977), comprises an individual's commitment to their life goals, a sense of control or belief that they can control life events, and a perception of change as a challenge. Thus hardiness assists individuals to face stressful situations and provides protection from possible damaging effects (Maddi, 2002).

Indeed, it has been shown that hardiness provides a buffering effect on stress and as such protects mental health (Oullete, 1993). College students high in hardiness tend to have more effective coping strategies, lower levels of stress, and better academic grades (McHenry, 1993). Furthermore, they perceive potential future stressors as being more controllable (Gerson, 1998). However, much resilience and hardiness research in student populations has focused on college or university students (e.g., Lindberg, 2002; Mathis & Lecci, 1999) or young elementary students (Borman & Overman, 2004), and such work has tended to focus on dysfunctional or at-risk populations (e.g., Nettles, Mucherah, & Jones, 2000).

There has been little work in looking at the enhancement of hardiness in "normal" high school students, although the hardiness construct seems useful in assisting high school students in dealing with both school-related stressors such as exams and the more personal issues associated with adolescence. The present study sought to address this gap in the literature.

HOPE

Hope is defined as "the process of thinking about one's goals, along with the motivation to move toward those goals (agency) and the ways to achieve those goals (pathways)" (Snyder, 1995, p. 355). Hope as a cross-situational construct has been shown to correlate positively with self-esteem, perceived problem-solving capabilities, perceptions of control, optimism, positive affectivity, and positive outcome expectancies (Snyder et al., 1991).

Hope has predicted problem-focused coping and mental health outcomes (Snyder et al., 1991). Additionally, Hope Scale scores have correlated positively with perceived scholastic competence (Onwuegbuzie & Daley, 1999), greater academic satisfaction (Chang, 1998), and hope has been shown to predict better overall grade point averages (Snyder, Shorey, Cheavens, Pulvens, Adams, & Wiklund, 2002).

It has been found that thinking about goals immediately triggers the agentic and pathways thoughts that are both necessary for goal-directed behavior. Thus, helping individuals to articulate their goals, as is required in an evidence-based, life-coaching intervention, may enhance hope (Snyder, 1999). Snyder (2000) argues that hope enhancement is best achieved by integration of solution-focused, narrative, and cognitive-behavioral interventions, with hope therapy designed to "help clients in conceptualising clearer goals, producing numerous pathways to attainment, summoning the mental energy to maintain the goal pursuit and reframing insurmountable obstacles as challenges to be overcome" (p. 123). These are the key features of the evidence-based approach to life coaching used in the present study.

AIMS OF THE RESEARCH

The present study sought to investigate the impact of an evidence-based, life-coaching program, in an educational setting using a randomized, wait-list control design with a sample of high school students who were not dysfunctional or at-risk. It was anticipated that the life-coaching program would be associated with increases in cognitive hardiness and hope and decreases in depression, anxiety, and stress.

METHOD

Participants

Participants were 56 adolescent females (16–17 years, mean age = 16.09) from a typical (nonclinical) population. Their scores on the Depression, Anxiety and Stress Scale (DASS-21, Lovibond & Lovibond, 1995) all fell within the normal range of psychopathology. Participants were all senior high school students in Year 11 attending a private girls' high school in Sydney, Australia. The 56 participants were randomly assigned to Group 1 (Coaching Group, $N = 28$) or Group 2, a wait-list control group (Control Group, $N = 28$) and completed self-report measures at Time 1 (pre-intervention) and Time 2 (post-intervention). Of the 56 participants assigned to take part in the study, seven participants (four control, three experimental) withdrew from the study prior to completion of the intervention (before Time 2). It should be noted that participants were volunteers and thus self-selected. Sample size was sufficient to detect a medium to large effect size (Cohen, 1977).

Experimental design

A between-subjects design was used. Hope, cognitive hardiness, depression, anxiety, and stress of both groups were assessed at Time 1 and Time 2. Academic performance and goal attainment measures were not taken.

Procedure

The life-coaching program was advertised through an information session held during school hours with all Year 11 girls in attendance. Additionally, the program was advertised in the school newsletter and at an information evening for parents of Year 11 students held at the beginning of the year. Interested students were provided with a participant information sheet and a consent form for both themselves and their parents to sign if they wished to participate in the study.

Participants were assigned to enter the Coaching Group or the Control Group using a wait-list control, randomization procedure with 28 participants in each group. Participants assigned to the Coaching Group completed a 10-session life-coaching program, while those participants randomly assigned to the Control Group completed a 10-week waiting period concurrently.

Participants in Group 1 were randomly assigned to a teacher-coach. Ten teachers were trained as coaches. The teacher-coaches had been trained in the theories of coaching psychology through two half-day workshops conducted by the school counselor who has a Master's in Applied Science (coaching psychology). The workshop was based on a manualized program (available from the authors).

The coaching program

The life-coaching program consisted of ten individual face-to-face coaching sessions with the allocated teacher-coach and was conducted over a period of two school terms (28 weeks including a two-week semester break). The life-coaching program involved participants holistically examining aspects of their lives and identifying two issues that they wished to be coached on; one school-related and one personal. The program was based on a solution-focused cognitive-behavioral framework that has been utilized in two previous randomized, controlled studies on evidence-based life coaching (for details see Green et al., 2006; Spence & Grant, 2005). Each coaching session involved the setting of session goals, followed by a discussion of what was going on in the coachee's life. The aim of the coaching was to raise the coachee's personal awareness of their current situation. Participants were then coached to identify personal resources that could be used in moving toward their goals, and to develop self-generated solutions and specific action steps, systematically working through the self-regulation cycle of setting goals, developing action plans, and monitoring and evaluating progress.

Measures

Participants of both groups completed all of the following questionnaires at Time 1 and Time 2.

The Trait Hope Scale (Snyder et al., 1991) is a 12-item measure of the two dimensions of hope ranging from 1 (*definitely false*) to 4 (*definitely true*). It consists of four agency items (i.e., items that tap the belief in one's ability to initiate and maintain movement toward goals); and four pathways items (i.e., items that tap the ability to conceptualize routes to a goal and four filler items). A total score is used as a measurement of the global concept of hope and is calculated as the sum of the eight agency and pathways items (range = 8 to 32). Test-retest reliabilities for the Hope Scale suggest temporal stability (.83 over a three-week interval, .73 over an eight-week period) (Snyder et al., 1991). Alpha coefficients for the two subscales are acceptable (agency = .71 to .77; pathway = .63 to .80) (Snyder et al., 1991). The alpha coefficients in this study were .79 for agency and .80 for pathways. This instrument demonstrates both internal and temporal reliability, with two separate and yet related factors, as well as an overarching hope factor (Babyak, Snyder, & Yoshinobu, 1993). Several studies have confirmed its convergent and discriminant validity (Snyder, 2000).

The Cognitive Hardiness Scale (Nowack, 1990) was used to measure cognitive hardiness, based on Kobasa's (1979) concept of hardiness comprising the dimension of commitment, control, and challenge. This measure consists of 30 items on a five-point Likert-type scale assessing personal beliefs about life. Nowack (1990) reported an internal consistency of .83. The alpha coefficient in the present study was .78.

The Depression, Anxiety and Stress Scale (DASS-21; Lovibond & Lovibond, 1995) was used as a measure of psychopathology. The DASS-21 is designed to be used with both clinical (Brown, Chorpita, Korotitsch, & Barlow, 1997) and community populations (Antony, Bieling, Cox, Enns, & Swinson, 1998). The scale uses a dimensional rather than a categorical approach to mental health assessment, and views the differences between normal and clinical populations in depression, anxiety, and stress as being essentially differences of degree. As such, it is a useful tool in life-coaching research for screening participants in order to detect mental health issues that require referral, and for monitoring levels of depression, anxiety, and stress that fall within both the normal and clinical ranges. Internal consistency (Lovibond & Lovibond, 1995) and test-retest reliability have been found to be good ($r = .71$ to .81; Brown et al., 1997). The internal reliability in this study was .91.

RESULTS

Before the analyses were conducted, the data were checked for violations of normality. Violations were detected on the variables of depression and anxiety and the appropriate nonparametric tests were used. Means for the Coaching Group and the Control Group on the major variables for Time 1 and Time 2 are shown in Table 13.1.

Hope

A repeated-measures analysis of variance (ANOVA test) revealed a significant treatment by time interaction effect for hope, $F(1,35) = 6.65$, $p < .05$. Follow-up tests revealed significant increases in hope, $t(17) = -4.076$, $p < .001$, for the Coaching Group whereas participants in the Control Group showed no such changes.

A repeated-measures ANOVA test revealed significant treatment by time interaction effect for agency, $F(1,36) = 4.622$, $p < .05$. Follow-up tests revealed significant increases in agency, $t(18) = -4.776$, $p < .001$ for the Coaching Group whereas participants in the Control Group showed no such changes. A repeated-measures ANOVA test revealed a significant treatment by time interaction effect for pathways, $F(1,35) = 4.98$, $p < .05$. Follow-up t-tests revealed significant increases in pathways, $t(17) = -2.601$, $p < .05$ for the Coaching Group whereas participants in the Control Group showed no such changes.

Table 13.1 *Means and Standard Deviations for Major Study Variables for Times 1 and 2*

Variable	Coaching Group		Control Group	
	Time 1	Time 2	Time 1	Time 2
Agency	N = 19		N = 19	
M	21.17	24.84	20.92	18.68
SD	5.43	5.55	5.31	6.86
Pathways	N = 25		N = 24	
M	22.79	24.79	23.03	21.05
SD	4.68	4.28	4.22	7.63
Total hope	N = 25		N = 24	
M	43.86	49.63	43.96	39.74
SD	9.35	9.36	8.70	14.27
Cognitive hardiness	N = 18		N = 17	
M	88.00	108.89	88.00	99.41
SD	7.96	10.79	8.53	10.62
Depression	N = 25		N = 22	
M	14.87	8.63	9.36	8.33
SD	11.33	11.86	6.80	7.77
Anxiety	N = 25		N = 24	
M	11.07	11.00	6.82	6.22
SD	9.11	10.63	6.16	5.82
Stress	N = 16		N = 18	
M	15.25	13.86	13.33	9.22
SD	7.44	10.29	8.00	7.52

Cognitive hardiness

A repeated-measures ANOVA test revealed a significant treatment by time interaction effect for cognitive hardiness, $F(1,33) = 7.631$, $p < .05$. Follow-up tests revealed significant increases in cognitive hardiness, $t(17) = -8.401$, $p < .001$, for the Coaching Group whereas participants in the Control Group showed no such changes.

Depression, anxiety, and stress

The Wilcoxon Signed-Rank Test was performed to examine changes within each group over time for the variables of depression and anxiety. Results revealed significant decreases from Time 1 to Time 2 on the variable of depression ($T = -1.968$, $p < .05$) for the Coaching Group, whereas the Control Group showed no significant change in these scores over the same period. There were no significant changes for either group from Time 1 to Time 2 for anxiety. A repeated-measures ANOVA test on stress revealed no significant treatment by time interaction. It is important to note that all participants fell within the "normal" range of psychopathology, and thus in this respect were not an "at-risk" or dysfunctional population.

DISCUSSION

It has been argued that it is important to investigate holistic salutogenic approaches to health and well-being rather than focusing on issues related to overcoming dysfunction or adverse life events in at-risk populations (Linley & Joseph, 2005). The present study represents a small step in that direction by showing that a holistic life-coaching intervention in a "normal" high school population is associated with increased hope and cognitive hardiness and significant decreases in depression.

Past research has investigated the enhancement of hardiness through training programs specifically designed to target hardiness (e.g., Khoshaba & Maddi, 2001). Maddi, Kahn, and Maddi (1998) describe a four-part training program incorporating: (a) a structured psycho-educational component; (b) cognitive-behavioral techniques such as situational reconstructing (stretching the imagination to develop a broader understanding of the stressor), focusing on bodily sensations in order to develop emotionally based insights; (c) developing of action plans to deal with stressors; and (d) a relapse prevention phase. Such programs are associated with improvement in self-reported hardiness (Maddi et al., 1998), improvements in college grade and retention rates, job satisfaction, and health (Maddi, 2002).

Hardiness training tends to focus specifically on enhancing hardiness and overcoming stressors through a diagnostic psycho-educational process (Maddi, 1987). Although similar to hardiness training in some respects, the life-coaching program used in the present study differed in that it involved participants holistically examining their lives, looking for ways to enhance their life experience, rather than merely addressing issues related to distress. Participants then set goals, identified personal resources and developed goal-focused action steps. Despite the differences in emphasis, the current life-coaching program appeared to be an effective hardiness-enhancing intervention.

In regard to hope, it was found that participants who had completed the life-coaching intervention reported significant increases in agency, pathways, and total hope. These results are consistent with hope theory, which suggests the articulation of goals stimulates hope (Snyder, 1999). In the present study, in addition to talking about their goals and action plans, cognitive-behavioral techniques were used to help participants identify positive self-talk that would help them in the goal-striving process, and in this way were encouraged to increase their agentic thoughts. The use of solution-focused techniques helped participants determine possible routes to their goal, thereby increasing pathways thinking. As such, a cognitive-behavioral, solution-focused coaching intervention, such as the one used in this study becomes a hope-enhancing intervention. These results are consistent with Green et al.'s (2006) study, which also found significant increases in agency, pathways, and total hope as a result of an evidence-based, life-coaching intervention.

Given the correlation between depression, anxiety, and stress (Lovibond & Lovibond, 1995), it is interesting that this study found that only depression (not anxiety or stress) was reduced. The reason for this is not immediately clear. It may be that the items on the DASS that measure depression include questions related to pessimism about the future and being unable to be interested or involved in life, whereas the anxiety and stress scales refer to being panicky, being aware of a dry mouth, breathing difficulties, and pounding of the heart. This study specifically focused on helping participants find ways to enhance their life experience and build hope and resilience, rather than reducing stress or anxiety, thus the primary impact on psychopathology may have been a reduction in depression (which can be viewed as the opposite of hope) rather than a reduction in anxiety or stress.

A limitation in the current study is that participants were self-selected members of a specific community (all females attending a private high school), who may not be representative of the general population. Students volunteered and as such may have been highly motivated. Further, academic performance measures were not taken. This was because the participants were studying a wide range of different subjects, at varying levels of difficulty, and there were no valid or reliable means of making comparisons. In addition, no longitudinal measures were taken, thus it is not known if these results were maintained over time. However, it should be noted that, in a longitudinal study, Green et al. (2006) found that gains from a similar life-coaching program were maintained at a 30-week follow-up.

Whereas many high school-based interventions are aimed at teaching skills targeted at enhancing academic performance, or counseling for bullying or other distressing factors, life coaching programs have the potential to be an effective holistic mental health promotion strategy for high school students. Such positively-framed programs, with a lack of the stigma often associated with remedial counseling, may assist in increasing long-term social and emotional well-being, provide a preventative function, and potentially achieve significant savings in mental health costs. The findings of the present study suggest that meeting life's challenges with a positive and confident attitude regarding one's ability or competence to survive life challenges appears to insulate against depression. This is particularly relevant during major life transitions such as those experienced by senior high school students.

By using a wait-list control and an experimental design, the present study has demonstrated that life coaching can be effective for female high school students. However, it may be that the attention of a caring supportive adult alone would be sufficient to enhance hope and resilience in high school students. It is noteworthy, however, that recent research (Spence & Grant, 2007; Sue-Chan and Latham, 2004) has found that, in an adult sample, peer coaching was not as effective as a professionally-trained coach. Emphasizing the importance of expertise in coaching, Spence and Grant (2007) argued that the presence of a supportive person was a necessary but insufficient condition for enhancing well-being and goal attainment. Future studies using high school students should extend this line of research and compare the effect of a supportive adult with participation in a life-coaching program.

Future research should also use other educational samples (e.g., students in primary and junior high school, and both males and females) and also measure academic performance. Life-coaching interventions that used participants from one specific educational cohort would allow the accurate and meaningful comparison of academic performance. Further, studies that compared life-coaching interventions with educational tutoring or positive parental involvement would provide additional information about the effectiveness of life coaching for students. In addition, it would be useful to conduct longitudinal studies to examine if such life-coaching interventions have a long-term prophylactic effect, and a follow-up study of the present intervention is planned.

SUMMARY

This study is the first controlled study of an evidence-based, life-coaching intervention for senior high school students. It provides preliminary evidence that a cognitive-behavioral, solution-focused life-coaching group program can be effective in increasing hope and cognitive hardiness, and in decreasing self-reported symptoms of depression. This study provides encouraging empirical support for the usefulness of evidence-based life-coaching interventions in an educational setting. An evidence-based life-coaching program implemented in schools may provide a platform for an applied positive psychology, delivering a multitude of benefits that impact positively on students' overall health and well-being.

REFERENCES

Amen, J., & Reglin, G. (1992). High school seniors tell why they are "stressed out.". *The Clearing House, 66*(1), 27–29. https://doi.org/10.1080/00098655.1992.9955920

Antony, M., Bieling, P. J., Cox, B. J., Enns, M. W., & Swinson, R. P. (1998). Psychometric properties of the 42-item and 21-item depression anxiety stress scales in clinical groups and a community sample. *Psychological Assessment, 19*(2), 176–181.

Babyak, M. A., Snyder, C. R., & Yoshinobu, L. (1993). Psychometric properties of the hope scale: A confirmatory factor analysis. *Journal of Research in Personality, 27*, 234–252. https://doi.org/10.1006/jrpe.1993.1011

Bonanno, G. A. (2004). Loss, trauma, and human resilience: Have we underestimated the human capacity to thrive after extremely aversive events? *American Psychologist, 59*(1), 20–28. https://doi.org/10.1037/0003-066X.59.1.20

Borman, G. D., & Overman, L. T. (2004). Academic resilience in mathematics among poor and minority students. *Elementary School Journal, 104*(3), 177–195.

Brown, T. A., Chorpita, D. F., Korotitsch, W., & Barlow, D. H. (1997). Psychometric properties of the depression anxiety stress scales (DASS) in clinical samples. *Behaviour Research and Therapy, 35*(1), 79–89.

Campbell, M. A., & Gardner, S. (2005). A pilot study to assess the effects of life coaching with year 12 students. In M. Cavanagh, A. M. Grant, & T. Kemp (Eds.), *Theory, Research and Practice from the Behavioural Sciences: Vol. 1. Evidence-based coaching.* (pp. 159–169) Bowen Hills, QLD: Australian Academic Press.

Chang, E. C. (1998). Hope, problem-solving ability, and coping in a college student population: Some implications for theory and practice. *Journal of Clinical Psychology, 54*, 953–962. https://doi.org/10.1002/(SICI)1097-4679(199811)54:7<953::AID-JCLP9>3.0.CO;2-F

Cohen, J. (1977). *Statistical power analysis for the behavioral sciences.* New York, NY: Academic Press.

Gerson, M. S. (1998). The relationship between hardiness, coping skills, and stress in graduate students. *Dissertation Abstracts International: Section B: The Sciences and Engineering, 59*(6-B), 3056.

Grant, A. (2003). The impact of life coaching on goal attainment, metacognition and mental health. *Social Behavior and Personality, 31*(3), 253–264. https://doi.org/10.2224/sbp.2003.31.3.253

Green, L. S., Oades, L. G., & Grant, A. M. (2006). Cognitive-behavioural, solution-focused life coaching: Enhancing goal striving, well-being and hope. *Journal of Positive Psychology, 1*(3), 142–149. https://doi.org/10.1080/17439760600619849

Khoshaba, D. M., & Maddi, S. R. (2001). *HardiTraining* (4th ed.). Newport Beach, CA: Hardiness Institute.

Kobasa, S. C. (1979). Stressful life events, personality and health: An inquiry into hardiness. *Journal of Personality and Social Psychology, 79*, 1–11. https://doi.org/10.1037/0022-3514.37.1.1

Kobasa, S. C., & Maddi, S. R. (1977). Existential personality theory. In R. J. Corsini (Ed.), *Current personality theories* (pp. 243–276). Itasca, IL: F. E. Peacock.

Lindberg, M. A. (2002). The role of suggestions and personality characteristics in producing illness reports and desires for suing the responsible party. *Journal of Psychology: Interdisciplinary and Applied, 136*(2), 125–140. https://doi.org/10.1080/00223980209604144

Linley, P. A., & Joseph, S. (2005). The human capacity for growth through adversity. *American Psychologist, 60*(3), 262–264.

Lovibond, S. H., & Lovibond, P. F. (1995). *Manual for the depression anxiety stress scales.* Sydney, Australia: Psychology Foundation of Australia.

Maddi, S. R. (1987). Hardiness training at Illinois Bell Telephone. In J. Opatz (Ed.), *Health promotion evaluation* (pp. 101–115). Stephens Point, WI: National Wellness Institute.

Maddi, S. R. (2002). The story of hardiness: Twenty years of theorizing, research, and practice. *Consulting Psychology Journal: Practice and Research, 54*(3), 175–185. https://doi.org/10.1037/1061-4087.54.3.173

Maddi, S. R., Kahn, S., & Maddi, K. L. (1998). The effectiveness of hardiness training. *Consulting Psychology Journal: Practice & Research, 50*(2), 78–86. http://dx.doi.org/10.1037/1061-4087.50.2.78

Mathis, M., & Lecci, L. (1999). Hardiness and college adjustment: Identifying students in need of services. *Journal of College Student Development, 40*(3), 305–309.

McHenry, S. D. (1993). Hardiness and student status as a noncognitive predictor of academic success and achievement for generic baccalaureate nursing students. Unpublished dissertation, Widener U School of Nursing, PA, United States.

Nettles, S. M., Mucherah, W., & Jones, D. S. (2000). Understanding resilience: The role of social resources. *Journal of Education for Students Placed at Risk, 5*(1–2), 47–60. https://doi.org/10.1080/10824669.2000.9671379

Nowack, K. (1990). Initial development of an inventory to assess stress and health risk. *American Journal of Health Promotion, 4*, 173–180. https://doi.org/10.4278/0890-1171-4.3.173

Onwuegbuzie, A. J., & Daley, C. E. (1999). Relation of hope to self-perception. *Perceptual and Motor Skills, 88*, 535–540. https://doi.org/10.2466/pms.1999.88.2.535

Oullete, S. C. (1993). Inquiries into hardiness. In L. Goldberger & S. Bresnity (Eds.), *Handbook of stress: Theoretical and clinical aspects* (2nd ed., pp. 77–100). New York, NY: Free Press.

Ryff, C. D., Singer, B., Dienberg Love, G., & Essex, M. J. (1998). Resilience in adulthood and later life. In J. Lomaranz (Ed.), *Handbook of aging and mental health: An integrative approach* (pp. 69–96). New York, NY: Plenum Press.

Smith, L., & Sinclair, K. E. (2000). Transforming the HSC: Affective implications. *Change: Transformations in Education, 3*, 67–80.

Snyder, C. R. (1995). Conceptualising, measuring and nurturing hope. *Journal of Counselling and Development, 73*, 355–360. https://doi.org/10.1002/j.1556-6676.1995.tb01764.x

Snyder, C. R. (1999). Hope, goal blocking thoughts, and test-related anxieties. *Psychological Reports, 84*, 206–208. https://doi.org/10.2466/pr0.1999.84.1.206

Snyder, C. R. (Ed.). (2000). *Handbook of hope: Theory, measures and applications.* San Diego, CA: Academic Press.

Snyder, C. R., Harris, C., Anderson, J. R., Holleran, S. A., Irving, L. M., Sigmon, S. T., ... Harney, P. (1991). The will and the ways: Development and validation of an individual differences measure of hope. *Journal of Personality and Social Psychology, 60*, 570–585.

Snyder, C. R., Shorey, H. S., Cheavens, J., Pulvens, K. M., Adams, V. H., & Wiklund, C. (2002). Hope and academic success in college. *Journal of Educational Psychology, 94*(4), 820–826. https://doi.org/10.1037/0022-0663.94.4.820

Spence, G., & Grant, A. M. (2007). Professional and peer life coaching and the enhancement of goal striving and well-being: An exploratory study. *Journal of Positive Psychology, 2*(3), 185–194. https://doi.org/10.1080/17439760701228896

Spence, G. B., & Grant, A. M. (2005). Individual and group life-coaching: Initial findings from a randomised, controlled trial. In M. Cavanagh, A. M. Grant, & T. Kemp (Eds.), *Theory, Research and Practice from the Behavioural Sciences: Vol. 1. Evidence-based coaching* (pp. 143–158). Bowen Hills, QLD: Australian Academic Press.

Sue-Chan, C., & Latham, G. P. (2004). The relative effectiveness of external, peer, and self-coaches. *Applied Psychology: An International Review, 53*(2), 260–278. https://doi.org/10.1111/j.1464-0597.2004.00171.x

Tait, H., & Entwistle, N. (1996). Identifying students at risk through ineffective study strategies. *Higher Education, 31*(1), 97–116 https://doi.org/10.1007/BF00129109.

Zimmerman, B. J., Bonner, S., & Kovach, R. (1996). *Developing self-regulated learners: Beyond achievement to self-efficacy.* Washington, DC: American Psychological Association.

14 Positive Coaching with Frontline Managers: Enhancing Their Effectiveness and Understanding Why

Nickolas Yu, Catherine G. Collins, Michael Cavanagh, Kate White, and Greg Fairbrother[1]

Throughout the past decade, coaching has grown in popularity and is increasingly being used in the health sector, with staff and patients. Coaching is a process that enables people to learn and achieve goals. With staff, coaching is commonly used to enhance work performance, cultivate leadership, and promote positive work cultures. As the academic literature on coaching is relatively young, there are numerous gaps in our understanding of the impact of coaching on work behaviors and well-being, as well as why such changes in behaviors emerge. This paper reports the results of a study undertaken to assess the effectiveness of a workplace coaching program (WCP) aimed at enhancing the work behaviors and well-being of nursing managers in a major Australian hospital. Two types of employee behavior were considered as measures of impact: typical core behaviors (core performance) and proactive behaviors (proactivity). In addition to exploring the impact of the coaching on core performance, proactivity, and well-being, we explored the impact of the intervention on a range of

[1] First published as Yu, N., Collins, C. G., Cavanagh, M., White, K., & Fairbrother, G. (2008). Positive coaching with frontline managers: Enhancing their effectiveness and understanding why. *International Coaching Psychology Review, 3*(2), 110–122.

cognitive and affective mechanisms that are theorized to explain why workplace coaching has a positive impact on employees' behaviors. These mechanisms included: goal attainment, self-insight, and motivation. A hospital setting is a particularly relevant context in which to test the effectiveness of coaching because it is a complex, interdependent workplace where organizational interventions are needed.

COACHING TO ENHANCE CORE PERFORMANCE, PROACTIVITY, AND WELL-BEING

Coaching has been recommended as a strategy to improve performance among professionals in health care (Smeltzer & Truong, 2000). When considering performance, it is also important to take into account well-being, as well-being is likely to optimize (Turner, Barling, & Zacharatos, 2005) and sustain performance.

According to Griffin, Neal, and Parker (2007), employee performance is a multifaceted issue. First, there is a need for core performance, which is the purpose for which individuals are employed. In the hospital setting of the current study, participants' effective core performance included patient care coordination, staffing, bed management, human resources management, financial management, and occupational health and safety. Beyond core performance, organizations also require employees to help build and improve organizational capacity, and create and integrate knowledge, technology, and practice.

Hospitals reflect the complexity that is inherent in the delivery of modern health care. Delivering health care requires the coordination of multiple professionals in order to achieve health or work outcomes. For instance, managing the flow of patients throughout the hospital from point of entry to discharge requires liaison and management from numerous professionals and systems. In such environments, proactive performance behaviors are necessary (Griffin et al., 2007). Proactive behavior refers to "self-initiated, future-oriented action that aims to change and improve the situation or oneself" (Parker, Williams, & Turner, 2006, p. 636)

There are various types of proactivity and the focus of the present study is on proactivity that improves the internal organizational environment, such as work outcomes (e.g., patient safety) and processes (e.g., streamlining systems). This type of proactivity is important because of the organizational need for employees to engage in self-direction, forward-thinking, anticipatory planning, and taking charge behaviors, in order to prevent workplace problems (Parker et al., 2006; Parker & Collins, 2010).

Taking charge and individual innovation are two particularly important proactive behaviors for the hospital context. This is because continuous quality improvement, practice development, clinical leadership, and innovations in models of care are required for health care organizations to be effective. Taking charge refers to "constructive efforts by individual employees, to effect organisationally functional change with respect to how work is executed within the contexts of their jobs, work units, or organisations" (Morrison & Phelps, 1999, p. 403). Individual innovation refers to a process of identifying problems, generating ideas or solutions, building support for and then implementing these (Scott & Bruce, 1994).

Given the importance of core performance and proactivity (e.g., taking charge, individual innovation) in achieving desired organizational outcomes, if coaching is to be a relevant and effective organizational intervention we would expect these factors to be enhanced by a coaching intervention.

Employee well-being is another outcome of substantial interest to organizations. Organizations are particularly interested in maintaining employees' well-being for a variety of reasons. These include the need to attract, engage, and retain good employees; the need to create levels of effective performance that are sustainable in the long term; and the moral and legal responsibility for organizations to provide healthy and safe workplaces. In the literature, well-being has been recognized as a multidimensional construct informed by two major traditions: subjective well-being and psychological well-being (Keyes, Shmotkin, & Ryff, 2002; Ryan & Deci, 2001). Subjective well-being includes positive and negative affect, and life satisfaction (Keyes et al., 2002). In this approach, well-being is defined in terms of pleasure attainment and pain avoidance (Ryan & Deci, 2001). In contrast, psychological well-being focuses on meaning and self-realization. While both types of well-being are of interest in this study, subjective well-being is of particular interest because it is more subject to change in the shorter term.

In summary, we expected an appropriately designed and implemented coaching program to improve employees' core performance, proactivity, and subjective well-being.

WHY WILL COACHING IMPACT THESE EMPLOYEE OUTCOMES?

There are at least three important ways in which coaching might enhance employee behaviors. Firstly, coaching may enhance workplace performance via the development of metacognitive abilities. Metacognition is a process that is central to purposeful, directed change (Carver & Scheier, 2001) and comprises two distinct constructs: self-reflection and self-insight. Self-reflection refers to "the inspection and evaluation of one's thoughts, feelings, and behaviours" (Grant, 2001, p. 179). Self-insight refers to "the clarity of understanding one's thoughts, feelings, and actions" (Grant, 2001, p. 179). Self-insight was expected to be positively impacted by the WCP because coaching is a facilitated conversation in which people are asked questions that often enable new and different perspectives in relation to self, others, and the world (O'Connor & Lages, 2007).

Secondly, goal setting and goal attainment are key features in many of the theories and approaches that commonly inform coaching (e.g., cognitive-behavioral and solution-focused coaching [Grant, 2003], systemic coaching [Cavanagh, 2006], and self-concordance theory [Sheldon et al., 2004]). Goal attainment has also received increased attention in the coaching literature (e.g., Grant, 2003; Green, Oades, & Grant, 2006; Spence, 2007). Goal attainment was expected to be positively impacted by the WCP because coaching is an interaction that explicitly facilitates people through a process of setting goals, developing action plans, monitoring progress, evaluating outcomes, and learning from experience (Grant, 2006). For a fuller discussion of goal setting and its importance in goal attainment, see Latham and Locke (1991).

Thirdly, following Bandura's (1997) social cognitive theory, this paper focuses on self-efficacy as an important motivational factor that has been shown to be a malleable driver of performance. For example, Parker (1998) has shown self-efficacy to improve with positive organizational interventions such as work redesign (Parker, 1998). In particular, we will focus on role-breadth self-efficacy (RBSE), which refers to "employees' perceived capability of carrying out a broader and more proactive set of work tasks that extend beyond prescribed technical requirements" (Parker, 1998, p. 835). Role-breadth self-efficacy was also of interest in this study because it has been found to be an antecedent of proactive behaviors (Crant, 2000). The WCP was expected to positively impact RBSE because coaching is a process that cultivates individual mastery of situations through ongoing, positive feedback (Bandura, 1997). In summary, we expected an appropriately designed and implemented coaching program would improve self-insight, goal attainment, and motivation.

RESEARCH DESIGN

The main objective of this study was to investigate the effectiveness of a coaching program that was aimed at enhancing the work behaviors and well-being of frontline nursing managers in a large Australian teaching hospital. The research used a longitudinal (pre-post test) within sample design.

Description of the workplace coaching program

The WCP was developed with input from 11 experts in the field and three key principles in the literature about processes that contribute to learning, change, and performance (Cunningham & Kitson, 2000; Grant, 2003; Green et al., 2006; Olivero, Bane, & Kopelman, 1997; Spence & Grant, 2007).

Collectively, this information suggested that the WCP be based on three principles. First, a positive approach to change is used (for instance a solution-focused, cognitive-behavioral methodology).

Solution-focused, cognitive-behavioral coaching seeks to identify and describe in detail the coachee's preferred or client's preferred goal state or outcome, identify the resources currently available to the person to achieve that outcome, and build on the progress made toward the goal. This approach also seeks to assist the person to develop performance-enhancing cognitive schemas and behavioral repertoires relevant to goal attainment (Green & Grant, 2003).

The second principle underlying the WCP was that workshop participants need a period of explicit support in order to transfer the learnings and skills acquired in the WCP into the workplace (Olivero et al., 1997). Therefore, individual coaching was used to supplement the coaching skills training delivered in the WCP.

Finally, we believed that for the WCP to be maximally effective it should be personalized to the needs of the individuals and teams participating in the program. Hence a needs-based approach to developing the workshop content was taken. Group coaching was also given to participating teams, and individuals were asked to produce personal development plans. The above principles informed the inclusion of the five major components of the WCP. (See Table 14.1 below for a description of these components.) Coaching was conducted by a tertiary qualified coach with expertise in health care (NY).

Table 14.1 *Various Components of the Workplace Coaching Program*

Component	Description
Coaching seminars	Sixteen coaching seminars were facilitated throughout the WCP.
	Each seminar typically comprised a conceptual overview of the topic, followed by a demonstration or case scenario, role-plays, and a reflective practice activity. These 90-min seminars focused on topics based on requests from participants, and learning needs identified by senior nursing managers and the coach via a pre-intervention educational needs analysis.
Group coaching	Sixteen coaching groups were also facilitated throughout the WCP. These 60-min groups were face-to-face, closed (meaning that no new people entered the group outside of original group participants), and structured according to the GROW coaching model (Whitmore, 1996).
Individual coaching	On average, six individual coaching sessions were provided to participants, throughout the WCP. These 45-min coaching sessions were face-to-face, held away from the participant's office, and structured according to the GROW model (Whitmore, 1996).
	Participants identified a number of important workplace goals that they wanted to achieve early on in the WCP. The goals created the focus for the individual coaching sessions. The content of group and individual coaching was confidential to participants and the coach.
Workplace group projects	Participants worked in four groups to complete a work-based group project. Each group chose a relevant workplace topic, for instance, developing a proposal to initiate a new organizational process such as a nursing council. Each group received coaching in the early part of the WCP, in order to establish clear expectations, timelines, and identify relevant sources of literature. Throughout the WCP, participants received feedback from colleagues in the workplace coaching groups.
Personal development plan (PDP)	The purpose of PDPs was for the participants to set development goals, which were informed by a multisource feedback (MSF) process.
	The coach synthesized MSF for participants and presented these findings to participants in the individual coaching sessions.

Study setting

The setting was a large metropolitan teaching hospital located in Australia. This hospital has a full-time equivalent of approximately 1,000 nurses, 400 beds and 45,000 admissions per year.

Participants

Seventeen frontline nursing managers (15 female, two male; mean age 37 years) took part in the study. Demographic data are presented in Table 14.2. Participants were invited by their line managers to participate in the WCP and, following an information session about the WCP, self-selected to participate. Three participants withdrew from the intervention prior to its conclusion. Fifteen participants completed pre-test surveys and 10 completed post-test surveys. Participants completed questionnaires immediately on enrolment to the WCP and again after the six-month-long coaching intervention.

Measures

Taking charge was measured using the Taking Charge Scale developed by Morrison and Phelps (1999). This ten-item subscale was found to have excellent internal reliability (Cronbach's alpha = .95) in the development studies and good discriminate validity. Examples of items used include "I often try to institute new work methods that are more effective for the company" and "I often try to change organizational rules or policies that are non-productive or counter-productive." The alpha coefficient found in the present study was .71. All items were measured using a five-point scale (1 = *Strongly disagree*, 5 = *Strongly agree*).

Core performance behaviors were assessed with a four-item measure from Morrison and Phelps (1999). The measure was found to have good discriminant validity and the reliability of this scale in development was reported as excellent (Cronbach's alpha = .94). The alpha coefficient found in the present study was .89. Example items from this scale include: "This person meets performance expectations" and "This person adequately completes responsibilities." All items were measured using a five-point scale (1 = *Strongly disagree*, 5 = *Strongly agree*).

Table 14.2 *Demographics of Sample*

Variable	Range
Age range (mean)	26–48 (37)
Years of nursing experience (mean)	6–30 (16)
Years of management experience (mean)	0–10 (2)

A six-item Innovative Behavior Measure (IBM; Scott & Bruce, 1994) was used to measure individual innovation. Example items on this scale include "Promotes and champions ideas to others" and "Investigates and secures funds needed to implement new ideas." All responses were made using a five-point Likert-type scale ranging from 1 = *Not at all* to 5 = *To an exceptional degree*. Cronbach's alpha on this scale at the development scale was reported as .89. The reliability found in the present study was lower (Cronbach's alpha = .660).

The Goal Attainment Scale (GAS) measures participants' perceived difficulty of goals and their expected level of goal attainment by the completion of the WCP. To calculate the goal attainment score we first multiplied the degree of success by the degree of difficulty and, second, divided the number of chosen goals to reach by the mean score (Spence, 2007).

The Self-Reflection Self-Insight Scale (SRIS) was used to assess metacognition. This is a validated and reliable 20-item scale (Grant, Franklin, & Langford, 2002). Good convergent and discriminant validity has been found. The items are divided into two scales. The alpha coefficients for self-reflection (SR, 10 items) and self-insight (SI, 10 items) were both .72 in this study.

Motivation was assessed with the RBSE Scale. This is a valid and reliable ten-item measure (Parker, 1998). In this scale, respondents are asked to rate the level of their confidence in undertaking ten role-relevant tasks. Ratings are made on a five-point Likert scale ranging from 1 = *Not at all confident* to 5 = *Very confident*. Examples of the tasks include: "Representing your work area in meetings with senior management" and "Designing new procedures for your work area." The alpha coefficient found in the present study was .71.

Well-being was assessed in two ways. First, Positive Affect Negative Affect Scale (PANAS), a validated 20-item measure, was used to assess subjective well-being (Watson, Clark, & Tellegen, 1988). The measure has been reported to be internally consistent and with excellent convergent and discriminant properties (Watson et al., 1988). Items are divided into two scales: positive affect (PA) and negative affect (NA), the alphas in this study were .86 and .80 respectively.

Second, Scales of Psychological Well-Being (SPWB) were used. This is a valid and reliable 54-item measure (Ryff, 1989). The items are divided into six scales, each containing nine items: autonomy, environmental mastery, personal growth, positive relations with others, purpose in life, and self-acceptance. Alpha coefficients for the scales ranged from .61 to .81.

RESULTS

Table 14.3 outlines the medians, means, standard deviations, and z scores for each of the measures used at both pre- and post-test times. The Wilcoxon Sign Rank Test was used to assess if there was a statistically significant difference between the measures, pre- and post-coaching intervention. A significance level of $p < .05$ was used. As can be seen in Table 14.3, significant increases between pre- and post-scores were found for

Table 14.3   *Medians (Means), Standard Deviations, z Scores, and Significance Levels (Wilcoxon Sign Rank Test) by Time*

Measure	N	Pre	SD	N	Post	SD	z	p
Goal attainment	17	4 (3.8)	1.9	14	7 (6.7)	1.3	−7.7	<.05
Subjective well-being								
Positive affect	14	4 (3.4)	0.8	10	4 (4.0)	0.4	−2.0	<.05
Negative affect	15	2 (2.2)	0.9	10	1.8 (1.7)	0.7	−1.6	NS
Psychological well-being								
Autonomy	15	3.3 (3.2)	0.7	10	3.5 (3.7)	0.5	−2.0	<.05
Environmental mastery	15	4 (3.7)	0.6	10	4 (4.1)	0.4	−1.9	NS
Personal growth	15	4 (4.0)	0.7	10	4 (4.1)	0.5	−0.7	NS
Purpose in life	15	4 (3.9)	0.6	10	4 (4.0)	0.6	−1.5	NS
Personal relationships	15	4 (4.0)	0.7	10	3.7 (3.8)	0.7	−0.1	NS
Meta-cognition								
Self-reflection	15	3.9 (3.7)	0.5	10	3.9 (3.8)	0.7	−1.1	NS
Self-insight	15	4 (3.8)	0.5	10	4.3 (4.3)	0.6	−2.2	<.05
Proactivity								
Take charge	15	2.7 (2.9)	0.7	10	3.7 (3.6)	0.4	−2.8	<.05
Individual innovation	15	2.7 (2.6)	0.6	10	3.7 (3.6)	0.3	−2.7	<.05
Motivation								
Role-breadth self-efficacy	15	2.8 (2.8)	0.6	10	3.8 (3.8)	0.4	−2.8	<.05
Core performance behavior	15	4 (3.7)	0.8	10	4 (3.9)	0.6	−2.7	<.05

Table 14.4   *Types of Goals Themed Into Major Categories*

Goal type	Description
Goal 1: Well-being	Goals related to positive individual outcomes, e.g., job satisfaction and self-efficacy.
Goal 2: Coaching	Goals related to proactively managing and developing people through change.
Goal 3: Communication	Goals related to effective communication, e.g., managing emotions during difficult conversations.
Goal 4: Strategic thinking	Goals related to higher-level management thinking, e.g., creating job clarity and prioritization of time and tasks.
Goal 5: Technical skills	Goals related to routine management business systems, e.g., rosters, budgets, and staffing.

proactivity (taking charge, individual innovation), core performance, the self-insight subscale of metacognition, motivation (RBSE), well-being (positive affect, autonomy), and goal attainment. A number of the measures did not significantly differ, namely, the self-reflection subscale for metacognition and a number of the well-being subscales (negative affect, environmental mastery, personal growth, purpose in life, and personal relationships).

Further analysis was conducted on the goal-attainment results to explore which of the different types of goals improved. The goals set by participants were therefore clustered into five major goal domains as outlined in Table 14.4.

A by-goal (rather than by-subject) analysis using the Wilcoxon Signed Rank Test was conducted, to explore the relative improvement of the different goal domains. Eighty-two goals arising from the 14 participants were explored in this post-hoc analysis. Significant change was located for each of the five goal domains indicating a uniformity of effect across different types of goals. The technical skills domain attracted somewhat lower ratings than the other goal domains on baseline but improved to reach a similar post-intervention median to the other goal domains.

DISCUSSION

The purpose of this study was to assess the effectiveness of a coaching program aimed at enhancing the work behaviors and well-being of nursing managers.

The results of this study provide some preliminary evidence that coaching enhances workplace behaviors in both core task performance and proactive performance behaviors. Furthermore, a variety of the mechanisms thought to explain why coaching impacts these behaviors were found to be positively impacted by coaching, including goal attainment, the self-insight aspect of metacognition, and motivation (namely RBSE). The impact of coaching on well-being is less conclusive.

This study is unique because it is the first study that has researched the impact of coaching in health care settings using an integrated solution-focused, cognitive-behavioral approach. It is also the first study investigating the impact of coaching on proactivity.

Specifically, the results indicate that, in addition to improving core task performance behaviors, coaching was effective at increasing proactivity focused on control of and bringing about change within the internal organizational environment, such as by improving work methods (i.e., individual innovation and taking charge). These positive findings provide the first empirical support for Kemp's (2005) suggestion that coaching can be used to facilitate proactive behavior. This suggests that coaching is an important way to motivate and support managers in the task of facilitating organizational change.

Social learning theory (Bandura, 1997) and hope theory (Snyder, Rand, & Sigmon, 2005) may help explain these significant increases. The WCP incorporated key social learning theory strategies. Participants were provided with opportunities for repeatedly performing tasks until these tasks were mastered (enactive mastery), observing role models who were effective at performing these tasks (modeling), and receiving realistic encouragement about performance (verbal persuasion) (Bandura, 1997; Parker, 1998; Skiffington & Zeus, 2003). These strategies for behavioral change have previously been demonstrated to enhance RBSE and in turn proactivity (Parker, 1998; Parker et al., 2006). We also found in this study that coaching had a positive impact on RBSE. Future research needs to assess if RBSE mediates the relationship between coaching and performance (core and proactive performance); the sample size in this study was too small to explore this.

Hope theory (Snyder et al., 2005) may provide further explanation for increases in proactivity and core performance. This theory suggests that hope is a function of three types of thinking: (a) goal-directed thinking, which refers to thoughts that set and clarify goals; (b) pathways thinking, which refers to thoughts that develop specific strategies to reach goals; and (c) agency thinking, which refers to thoughts that initiate and sustain the motivation for pathways thinking. The goal-directed, pathways, and agency thinking were all promoted in the WCP.

For example, for the solution-focused approach to coaching facilitated goal-directed and pathways thinking, participants were assisted to develop specific strategies to reach goals in their individual coaching sessions. Specifically, participants were encouraged to: create vivid and attractive images of the future, identify and explore what parts of these future pictures were already present, and harness the strengths and resources people had (or could potentially access) in order to achieve their goals (Green et al., 2006). The cognitive-behavioral coaching approach enabled participants to develop positive and logical thinking patterns about their performance, thus contributing to a greater sense of agency—ways to initiate and sustain motivation (Green et al., 2006).

Coaching was effective in enhancing goal attainment in this study, which reinforces similar findings in previous studies. (Grant, 2003; Green et al., 2006; Spence & Grant, 2007). The present study extends these findings in that it has shown coaching positively affects goal attainment for a range of goal types. Goal attainment was significantly improved for five goal domains: well-being, coaching, communication, strategic thinking, and technical skills. Interestingly, goal attainment remained relatively uniform across these different types of goals. This may suggest that the positive effects of coaching are able to generalize across domains. We suggest that future research explore this issue further. For example, does coaching positively impact on goal attainment outside the focus of the coaching topic? That is, if an individual is being coached at work, does the participant's level of goal attainment improve in their private life?

An aspect of metacognition, self-insight, significantly improved over the time that individuals were coached. This finding is consistent with Grant (2003). The significant increase in self-insight was expected given the solution-focused and cognitive-behavioral approaches taken in the coaching. Within the solution-focused approach, the coach asked questions that enabled participants to take multiple perspectives of human experience and action, while also encouraging experimental and exploratory action that often elicited fresh insights. The cognitive-behavioral approach provided participants with a framework to challenge distorted beliefs and assumptions, and instead engage in positive self-talk that fostered different thoughts, feelings, behaviors, and potential insights. Additionally, self-insight may have been promoted through the coach's purposeful use of skills such as reflecting, clarifying, challenging, and feedback giving.

However, interestingly Grant (2003) found a significant decrease in self-reflection, whereas in this study there was no significant decrease. Rather, our findings are similar to those of Spence and Grant (2007), who found that coaching did not significantly impact self-reflection. Clearly, future research needs to investigate this issue further. For example, does the impact of coaching on self-reflection depend on the content of coaching or sample?

Coaching may have a potentially beneficial impact on well-being. However, the inconsistent findings in this and previous studies (Grant, 2003; Green et al., 2006; Spence & Grant, 2005) point to the need for more research to explore these relationships further.

It appears that coaching was effective in enhancing positive affect and one aspect of psychological well-being—autonomy. An increase in positive affect is an important outcome because positive affect helps build and broaden momentary thought-action repertoires, and enduring social resources (Fredrickson, 2005). The benefits of positive affect over time can also have a positive organizational impact (Losada & Heaphy, 2004). High scores on the psychological well-being autonomy subscale reflect that individuals perhaps became more self-determining and independent, regulating behavior from within, and better able to resist social pressures to think and act in certain ways; rather individuals became better able to evaluate themselves against personal standards (Ryff, 1989).

These findings are consistent with Grant (2003) and Green et al. (2006), who found that coaching had a significant positive impact on well-being. The increase in positive affect could be a function of the positive and expansive principles and questions that were used by the solution-focused coaching approach in the WCP. Also, findings may be partly explained by Hope theory, which posits that positive emotions flow from perceptions of successful goal striving (Snyder et al., 2005).

However, unlike Green et al.'s (2006) study, we did not find a significant decrease in negative affect or a significant increase in other aspects of psychological well-being (i.e., environmental mastery, personal growth, purpose in life, and positive relations with others). Interestingly, these aspects of psychological well-being did not change as a result of coaching in Spence and Grant's (2007) study either. It is also worth noting that the Green et al. (2006) and Spence and Grant (2007) studies were life-coaching studies, whereas our study was set in a workplace context (hospital-based health care) often marked by high demands and strong competition for the allocation of relatively scarce resources. In this context, it is perhaps not surprising that negative affect and other measures of well-being were not significantly improved. Nevertheless, further research needs to explore in detail whether workplace coaching has an impact on global experiences of well-being.

LIMITATIONS

A number of limitations need to be considered when interpreting the above findings. First, due to the absence of a control group, the effects may have occurred as a result of other organizational changes. Although new nursing initiatives are continual features of hospital settings today, to the authors' knowledge there were no systemic large changes occurring for all the nurses involved in the WCP. Second, the sustainability of effects was not measured, as there were only two data collection points. Third, the measures were self-reported and this gives rise to the potential for social desirability and demand effects. This criticism is somewhat countered because we did not find a significant and positive increase for all constructs. Finally, the single-site sample raises questions about the generalizability; future research needs to explore how similar WCPs impact employees working at different organizational levels and within different industries. These limitations are not isolated to this study and are common in young literatures such as coaching when research is exploratory (see Grant, 2003; Green et al., 2006; Spence & Grant, 2007).

These limitations need to be taken into perspective. This pre-post test research design tracked 17 nursing managers over six months. Empirical and longitudinal studies assessing the impact of coaching within organizations are rare. We have provided some initial insights about the positive impact coaching can have for employee behavior and aspects of well-being. This study also provided some evidence why these outcomes may have occurred (i.e., metacognition, motivation, and goal attainment). We encourage future research with larger samples to assess coaching with more rigorous quasi-experimental research designs to tease apart causality. Longitudinal research designs will also be important for understanding the sustainability of effects of the intervention, and thus help understand the frequency with which coaching will be needed.

DIRECTIONS FOR RESEARCH

Future research could also investigate the impact of coaching on other health leaders, rather than just nursing managers as reported in this study. In this study, the intervention was delivered in a graduated format over six months. Future studies could evaluate if similarly positive findings are replicated in a WCP using a different format, for instance, delivering seminars in an intensive format. It would also be valuable to compare the effectiveness of coaching that is underpinned by different theoretical approaches. Research into the differential impact of the various components of WCPs would be useful. Finally, research could investigate the differential impact that coaching has on the well-being of participants who are at various stages of cognitive development (Kegan, 1994).

IMPLICATIONS FOR PRACTICE

At least three implications for practitioners arise from this paper. First, coaching had a positive impact on work performance behaviors—both core behaviors and proactive behaviors. Thus, there is evidence that coaching is an important intervention organizations can use to enhance workplace outcomes. Second, coaching also showed to be important for individual outcomes such as enhancing positive affect, an important well-being outcome. Thus there is evidence that coaching is an important intervention organizations can use to enhance individual outcomes. Finally, some light has been shed on understanding why these changes may have occurred. The change in the mechanisms self-insight, goal attainment, and RBSE implies that WCPs that focus on building these mechanisms are likely to be more effective. We therefore encourage further rigorous empirical testing of this proposition.

SUMMARY

Coaching is a process that can be used by managers, and organizations more broadly, to positively impact workplace outcomes (performance and proactivity) in addition to employee well-being. This study provides support for these coaching outcomes and also supports some of the underlying theories that explain why coaching is an effective organizational intervention. Such interventions are particularly important for health care settings, which are under constant pressure to deal with large workloads, high staff turnover, great complexity, and high stress. This study has the potential to make a valuable contribution to further investigating and understanding coaching as a process that facilitates learning, performance, and human flourishing.

REFERENCES

Bandura, A. (1997). *Self-efficacy: The exercise of control.* New York, NY: Freeman.

Carver, C. S., & Scheier, M. F. (2001). *On the self-regulation of behaviour.* Cambridge, UK: Cambridge University Press.

Cavanagh, M. (2006). Coaching from a systemic perspective: A complex adaptive conversation. In D. Stober & A. M. Grant (Eds.), *Evidence based coaching handbook* (pp. 313–354). New York, NY: Wiley.

Crant, J. (2000). Proactive behaviour in organizations. *Journal of Management, 26*(3), 435–462. https://doi.org/10.1177/014920630002600304

Cunningham, G., & Kitson, A. (2000). An evaluation of the RCN clinical leadership development programme: Part 1. *Nursing Standard, 15*(12), 34–37.

Fredrickson, B. L. (2005). Positive emotions. In C. R. Snyder & S. J. Lopez (Eds.), *Handbook of positive psychology* (pp. 777–796). New York, NY: Oxford University Press.

Grant, A. M. (2001). Towards a psychology of coaching: The impact of coaching on metacognition, mental health, and goal-attainment. Department of Psychology. Sydney, Macquarie University.

Grant, A. M. (2003). The impact of life coaching on goal attainment, metacognition and mental health. *Social Behaviour and Personality, 31*(3), 253–264. https://doi.org/10.2224/sbp.2003.31.3.253

Grant, A. M. (2006). An integrated goal-focused approach to executive coaching. In D. R. Stober & A. M. Grant (Eds.), *Evidence based coaching handbook* (pp. 153–192). Hoboken, NJ: Wiley.

Grant, A. M., Franklin, J., & Langford, P. (2002). The self-reflection and insight scale: A new measure of private self-consciousness. *Social Behaviour and Personality, 30*(8), 821–835. https://doi.org/10.2224/sbp.2002.30.8.821

Green, L. S., Oades, L., & Grant, A. M. (2006). Cognitive-behavioral, solution-focused life coaching: Enhancing goal striving, well-being, and hope. *Journal of Positive Psychology, 1*(3), 142–149. https://doi.org/10.1080/17439760600619849

Griffin, M. A., Neal, A., & Parker, S. K. (2007). A new model of work role performance: Positive behaviour in uncertain and interdependent contexts. *Academy of Management Journal, 50*(2), 327–347. https://doi.org/10.5465/amj.2007.24634438

Kegan, R. (1994). *In over our heads: The mental demands of modern life.* Cambridge, MA: Harvard University Press.

Kemp, T. (2005). The proactive behaviour framework: A reflective process for exploring thinking, behaviour and personal insight. In M. Cavanagh, A. M. Grant, & T. Kemp (Eds.), *Theory, Research and Practice for the Behavioural Sciences: Vol. 1. Evidence-based coaching* (pp. 49–56). Bowen Hills, QLD: Australian Academic Press.

Keyes, C. L. M., Shmotkin, D., & Ryff, C. D. (2002). Optimising well-being: The empirical encounter of two traditions. *Journal of Personality and Social Psychology, 82*, 1007–1022. https://doi.org/10.1037/0022-3514.82.6.1007

Latham, G. P., & Locke, E. A. (1991). Self-regulation through goal setting. *Organizational Behaviour and Human Decision Processes, 50*(2), 212–247.

Losada, M., & Heaphy, E. (2004). The role of positivity and connectivity in the performance of business teams: A non-linear dynamics model. *American Scientist, 47*(6), 740–765. https://doi.org/10.1177/0002764203260208

Morrison, E. W., & Phelps, C. C. (1999). Taking charge at work: Extrarole efforts to initiate workplace change. *Academy of Management Journal, 42*(4), 403–419. https://doi.org/10.5465/257011

O'Connor, J. O., & Lages, A. (2007). *How coaching works.* London, UK: A & C Black.

Olivero, G., Bane, K. D., & Kopelman, R. E. (1997). Executive coaching as a transfer of training tool: Effects on productivity in a public agency. *Public Personnel Management, 26*(4), 461–469. https://doi.org/10.1177/009102609702600403

Parker, S. K. (1998). Enhancing role breadth self-efficacy: The roles of job enrichment and other organisational interventions. *Journal of Applied Psychology, 83*(6), 835–852. https://doi.org/10.1037/0021-9010.83.6.835

Parker, S. K., & Collins, C. G. (2010). Taking stock: Integrating and differentiating multiple proactive behaviors. *Journal of Management, 36*(3), 633–662. https://doi.org/10.1177/0149206308321554

Parker, S. K., Williams, H. M., & Turner, N. (2006). Modeling the antecedents of proactive behavior at work. *Journal of Applied Psychology, 91*(3), 636–652. https://doi.org/10.1037/0021-9010.91.3.636

Ryan, R. M., & Deci, E. L. (2001). On happiness and well-being: A review of research on hedonic and eudaimonic well-being. *Annual Review of Psychology, 52,* 141–166.

Ryff, C. D. (1989). Happiness is everything, or is it? Explorations on the meaning of psychological well-being. *Journal of Personality and Social Psychology, 57*(6), 1069–1081.

Scott, S. G., & Bruce, R. A. (1994). Determinants of innovative behavior: A path model of individual innovation in the workplace. *Academy of Management Journal, 37*(3), 580–607. https://doi.org/10.5465/256701

Sheldon, K. M., Elliot, A. J., Ryan, R. M., Chirkov, V., Kim, Y., Wu, C., … Sun, Z. (2004). Self-concordance and subjective well-being in four cultures. *Journal of Cross-Cultural Psychology, 35*(2), 209–223. https://doi.org/10.1177/0022022103262245

Skiffington, S., & Zeus, P. (2003). *Behavioural coaching: How to build sustainable personal and organisational strength.* Sydney, Australia: McGaw Hill Professional.

Smeltzer, C. H., & Truong, C. P. (2000). Executive coaching- A management tool for achieving success. *Journal of Nursing Administration, 30*(12), 574–576.

Snyder, C. R., Rand, K. L., & Sigmon, D. R. (2005). Hope theory: A member of the positive psychology family. In C. R. Snyder & S. J. Lopez (Eds.), *Handbook of positive psychology* (pp. 257–276). New York, NY: Oxford University Press.

Spence, G. (2007). GAS powered coaching: Goal attainment scaling and its use in coaching research and practice. *International Coaching Psychology Review, 2*(2), 67–79.

Spence, G., & Grant, A. M. (2005). Individual and group life coaching: Initial findings from a randomised, controlled trial. In M. Cavanagh, A. M. Grant, & T. Kemp (Eds.), *Theory, Research and Practice for the Behavioural Sciences: Vol. 1. Evidence-based coaching* (pp. 143–158). Bowen Hills, QLD: Australian Academic Press.

Spence, G., & Grant, A. M. (2007). Professional and peer life coaching and the enhancement of goal striving and well-being: An exploratory study. *Journal of Positive Psychology, 2*(3), 185–194. https://doi.org/10.1080/17439760701228896

Turner, N., Barling, J., & Zacharatos, A. (2005). Positive psychology at work. In C. R. Snyder & S. J. Lopez (Eds.), *Handbook of positive psychology* (pp. 715–728). New York, NY: Oxford University Press.

Watson, D., Clark, L. A., & Tellegen, A. (1988). Development and validation of brief measures of positive and negative affect: The PANAS scales. *Journal of Personality and Social Psychology, 54*(6), 1063–1070.

Whitmore, J. (1996). *Coaching for performance:* London, UK: Nicholas Brealey.

15 Evaluating the Impact of a Peer Coaching Intervention on Well-Being Among Psychology Undergraduate Students

Emma Short, Gail Kinman, and Sarah Baker[1]

The need for research to evaluate the effectiveness of coaching strategies is widely recognized in the emerging field of coaching psychology (Linley, 2006). Indeed, it has been argued that without the systematic empirical evaluation of the success of coaching interventions, coaching practice may be seen as being based on hypothetical theories and conjecture (Biswas-Diener & Dean, 2007). It is, therefore, necessary to develop coaching techniques that are firmly grounded in evidence-based principles (Linley, 2006; Stober & Grant, 2006).

Solution-focused coaching is rapidly gaining popularity in the field. This technique does not seek to alleviate long-term underlying problems but assists people in meeting their goals by helping them develop their skills and resources (Kauffman & Scoular, 2004). By examining the client's core values and life experiences, skills and resources that had

[1] First published as Short, E., Kinman, G., & Baker, S. (2010). Evaluating the impact of a peer coaching intervention on well-being amongst psychology undergraduate students. *International Coaching Psychology Review, 5,* 27–35.

previously been unrecognized may be brought to light. Solutions can subsequently be developed that help achieve the identified goals. Research findings indeed indicate that solution-focused coaching has the potential to enhance goal setting and psychological functioning. Studies have found this technique may improve stress management capabilities and enhance goal striving, emotional well-being, hope, self-confidence, and job satisfaction (Gyllensten & Palmer, 2005; Kauffman & Scoular, 2004; Seligman, 2002). There is some evidence that gains might be maintained over time (Green, Oades, & Grant, 2006).

COACHING IN EDUCATION

Peer-coaching has been described as a relationship between teachers based on sharing experiences, practices, and planning, with learning taking place through observation and skills transfer (Joyce & Showers, 1996; Zwart, Wubbels, Bergen, & Bolhuis, 2007). This technique has been used as a means of facilitating the implementation of new practices and approaches within teaching. The use of peer coaching to enhance the professional development of teachers is strongly endorsed by the UK Department of Education (2001). In the United States, large corporations such as Microsoft sponsor programs to promote the positive benefits of peer-coaching interaction between teachers.

The model of peer coaching used in teaching typically entails groups of two to three teachers coming together to offer support, feedback, and encouragement. Strategies employed include modeling from observed demonstration and skills transfer by assistance. Direct verbal feedback is avoided, however, as it may be perceived by colleagues as evaluative and, therefore, detrimental to the coaching process (Joyce & Showers, 1996). Within these peer-coaching programs, the coach is seen as the person who teaches and the coachee as the person who learns through observation (Joyce & Showers, 1996). It could be argued that this approach has more in common with mentoring than coaching, as the teacher with experience offers guidance to a protégé to help them gain knowledge and skills (Greene & Grant, 2003). Coaching differs from mentoring as it is based on a collaborative relationship that aims to facilitate the development and enhancement of skills and performance through feedback, reflection, and self-directed learning (Greene & Grant, 2003; Green, Grant, & Rynsaardt, 2007).

LIFE COACHING IN EDUCATION

Life coaching is a systematic, structured, and goal-focused approach to helping individuals to construct individual solutions to make positive changes in their lives (Green et al., 2006; Spence & Grant, 2007). In contrast to standard educational tutoring, mentoring, and coaching, which seek to enhance and develop academic performance, the cognitive-behavioral, solution-focused model of life coaching can promote motivation, goal striving and attainment, and enhance personal growth in an educational setting (Grant, 2003, 2008; Green et al., 2007; Green et al., 2006; Spence & Grant, 2007). The coaching process can also exert a strong influence on psychological well-being; studies have found that life coaching can also help students manage anxiety and stress and, accordingly, enhance resilience and perceived quality of life (Campbell & Gardner, 2005; Grant, 2003; Spence & Grant, 2007).

While life coaching is normally conducted in one-to-one sessions by trained professional coaches (Spence & Grant, 2007), it is argued that the use of peer coaching has the potential to enhance the skills and personal development of students. It has also been proposed that there can be benefits for the peer coach as well as the recipient of coaching, in terms of enhanced socioemotional development and improved interpersonal skills such as active listening, questioning, and probing (Ladyshewsky, 2006; Laske, 2006). Although studies have assessed the impact of life coaching in this context, as yet, little systematic research has been conducted that examines the impact of peer coaching techniques in students. The studies that have been conducted tend to yield contradictory findings. Sue-Chan and Latham (2004) and Spence and Grant (2007) reported that an external coach was perceived to be more credible and effective than a peer-coach, whereas other research has yielded more positive findings. Ladyshewsky (2006) observed that student peer coaches have greater credibility than academic or support staff. Peer coaching by and for students has been found to promote self-esteem, motivation, and personal growth and enhance achievement (Hudson, 1999 Ladyshewsky, 2006; Zwart et al., 2007). Despite there being strong evidence that students can experience high levels of stress, especially during assessment periods, the impact of peer coaching on psychological well-being has been little examined in university environments. It is argued that this technique has the potential to enhance well-being in this context.

STUDENT STRESS

There is evidence that university students are subjected to considerable stress and that this has increased in recent years (Benton, Robertson, Wen-Chih, Newton, & Benton, 2003; Gall, Evans, & Bellerose, 2000) The most common stressors reported by students include relationship conflicts, academic pressure, health, financial difficulties, relationships with family, friends, and peers, and life transition problems (Green et al., 2007; Roussis & Wells, 2008). The final year of university study is thought to be particularly stressful owing to anxiety about examinations, dissertation preparation, and plans for the future (Abouserie, 1994; Deary, Watson, & Hogston, 2003; Devonport & Lane, 2006).

It is important for universities to help students manage the stress they experience, as this is likely to lead to impaired academic performance as well as exerting a negative impact on well-being (Akgun & Ciarrochi, 2003; Struthers, Perry, & Menec, 2000). As highlighted above, final-year students may be particularly vulnerable. It is argued that interventions that help students develop their multitasking solutions and enhance their time management skills are likely to provide an additional benefit of providing life-long stress management skills (Hudd et al., 2000).

AIMS OF THE STUDY

Based on the research reviewed above, it is proposed that cognitive-behavioral, solution-focused peer coaching has the potential to help students manage stress and enhance their well-being. This study, therefore, examines the effectiveness of a peer coaching intervention on levels of psychological distress and interpersonal problems in students during the run-up to a final year examination period. As it has been recommended that future research on the effectiveness of peer coaching in university settings should use students from the same cohort (Green et al., 2007), a group of final year psychology students from the University of Bedfordshire was studied.

THE STUDY CONTEXT

Psychology students at the University of Bedfordshire have the option to study coaching psychology during the final year of their undergraduate degree. The module is rigorously evidence-based and incorporates academic and practical components. It aims to provide students with an understanding of the skills of peer coaching, the psychological principles that underlie them, and the opportunity to develop and practice these skills. Students are required to engage in a supervised peer coaching practice with two peers. As the use of a model has been shown to be beneficial to the structure of coaching interventions (Greene & Grant, 2003), the TGROW model is used (Downey, 2003). This is an extension of the GROW (goal, reality, options, will) model proposed by Whitmore (2002). The additional "T" stands for topic or theme, and refers to the broad area on which the coachee wants to work.

Previous research that has evaluated the impact of peer coaching has typically exposed participants to intensive training in coaching techniques through, for example, 1-day workshops (Grant, 2003, 2008; Green et al., 2006). There is evidence that exposing learners to information over an extended period of time and allowing them to gradually accumulate and practice skills is likely to deepen learning and increase insight (Grant, 2007). The present study, therefore, extends previous research by providing coaching training over a 12-week period.

METHOD

Design

This study used a longitudinal design, with two assessment points pre- and post-coaching separated by six weeks.

Participants

Two groups of third-year undergraduate psychology students participated in this study. The coaching group ($N = 32$) comprised 24 females and eight males with a mean age of 25.23 ($SD = 8.07$). This group was registered on a module on coaching psychology and attended a one hour lecture and one hour tutorial each week. There were 33 participants in the control group, which comprised 30 females and three males with a mean age of 24.77 ($SD = 5.57$). As with the study group, the control group were final-year psychology students but were not studying coaching psychology or engaged in peer coaching. The participants for the coaching group and the control group were approached separately during classes. The request to participate was made at the beginning of a lecture by a researcher who was independent of the teaching team.

Measures

Demographic information Age, gender, marital status, dependents, accommodation, education, employment, and ethnicity were assessed.

Psychological distress This was assessed by the 12-item General Health Questionnaire (GHQ-12; Goldberg & Williams, 1988). This questionnaire is widely used as a measure of general distress. Items are rated on a fully anchored four-point scale. An example of an item is "Have you recently felt constantly under strain?," where responses range from "not at all" to "much more than usual." Mean scores were taken across items, with high scores representing poorer well-being.

Interpersonal problems The IIP-32 (Barkham, Hardy, & Startup, 1996) is a reliable and valid short form of the original Inventory of Interpersonal Problems developed by Horowitz, Rosenberg, Baer, Ureno, and Villasenor (1988). The IIP-32 consists of 32 items. Nineteen of the items are based on behavior participants find difficult "It is hard for me to ..." (e.g., "to disagree with other people," "to be supportive of another person's goals in life") and 13 of the items are based on behavior that participants do "too much" (e.g., "I fight with other people," "I open up to people"). Each item is rated on a five-point scale ranging from 0 (*not at all*) to 4 (*extremely*). Mean scores were calculated across items, with high scores indicating general interpersonal problems (Horowitz et al., 1988).

Topics addressed in coaching intervention   A single item investigated the type of problems that students discussed during the coaching intervention. Participants were asked to indicate areas from a specified list (e.g., relationships, health, and career). Participants were also given the option not to disclose this information.

Level of satisfaction with coaching intervention   This was examined by a single item that assessed satisfaction with the peer coaching intervention on a five-point Likert scale ranging from 1 (*not effective*) to 5 (*extremely effective*).

Procedure

Participants in the control group were approached at university and asked to participate as control in a peer-coaching study. The control group comprised final-year undergraduate psychology students who had not taken part in the peer-coaching intervention. Participants in the study group were introduced to the key principles and models of coaching, including the TGROW model (Downey, 2003) used in the study, during lectures on the coaching psychology module. As described earlier, coaching skills were practiced in lectures and seminars.

At Time 1 (pre-coaching intervention), measures of psychological distress and interpersonal problems were taken from both the study group and the control group. The study group subsequently conducted and received five sessions of peer-coaching over six weeks, prior to an examination period.

At Time 2 (post-coaching intervention), measures of psychological distress and interpersonal problems were once again taken from both groups. In addition, measures of perceived effectiveness of the peer-coaching intervention and types of problems addressed in peer coaching were obtained from the study group. Time 2 measures were taken two weeks before the final exam period.

Ethics

The research received full ethical clearance from the departmental ethics committee. Peer coaches were instructed to work within their competencies and to be mindful of the mental health of their coachees. Students were not obliged to participate in the research project. Codes were used to match data from Time 1 and Time 2, meaning that individual respondents were not identifiable to the researchers.

RESULTS

Coaching topics and perceived success of coaching intervention

The most common topics covered in coaching sessions were relationships (36% of participants), health (24%), and career issues (44%). Participants were asked to indicate the extent to which they believed the coaching intervention had been effective. As can be seen from Figure 15.1, 72% found it to be "quite effective" or "moderately effective." No respondents indicated that the intervention had been "very effective" or "not at all effective."

Impact of coaching intervention

The means and standard deviations for the study variables at Time 1 (pre-coaching intervention) are shown in Table 15.1. Independent samples t-tests found no significant differences between the study and control groups on levels of psychological distress ($p = .21$) or interpersonal problems ($p = .32$).

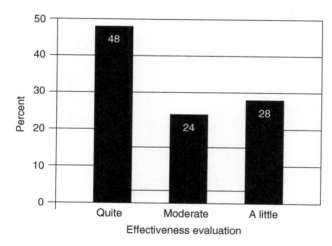

Figure 15.1   *Perceived Effectiveness of Peer Coaching Intervention*

Table 15.1   *Mean Scores for Study Variables at Time 1*

	Study group mean scores (SD)	Control group mean scores (SD)
IIP-32	75.37 (22.85)	68.29 (18.67)
GHQ-12	15.71 (8.01)	14.82 (8.73)

In order to examine whether any significant change in any outcome variable occurred between Times 1 and 2, repeated measures *t*-tests were conducted. Table 15.2 provides details for the study group and the control group. As can be seen, for the study group no statistically significant differences were found between the two time-points. However, the reduction in mean levels of self-reported personal problems at Time 2 approached significance at .06.

For the control group, mean levels of personal problems and psychological distress (indicated by the GHQ-12 scores) were higher at Time 2 than Time 1. The difference in levels of psychological distress was found to be statistically significant ($t = -3.76$, $p = .002$). Figure 15.2 shows the changes in the GHQ-12 scores for the study and control groups at Times 1 and 2.

Table 15.2   *Mean Scores and SD for Study Variables at Times 1 and 2*

	Study group mean scores (SD) T value/significance		*Control group mean scores (SD) T value/significance*	
GHQ-12				
Time 1	15.71 (8.01)		14.82 (8.73)	
Time 2	16.08 (9.06)	−0.59/ns	19. 89 (5.86)	−3.76/p = 0.002
IIP-32				
Time 1	75.37 (22.85)		68.29 (18.67)	
Time 2	68.77 (18.32)	2.00/p = 0.058	71.65 (5.86)	−1.01/ns

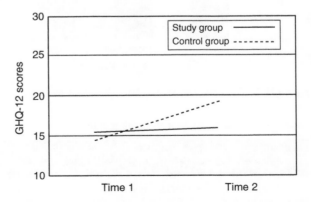

Figure 15.2   *GHQ Scores for Study and Control Groups at Times 1 and 2*

DISCUSSION

The findings of this study provide evidence that a short program of peer coaching may be beneficial for students at a stressful time in their lives. The peer coaching program may have offered some protection from an increase in psychological distress during a stressful period. Some tentative evidence is also provided that peer coaching may protect students from enhanced interpersonal problems during this time. Mean scores for GHQ-12 for both groups were high in comparison with published norms from occupational groups and community samples (Mullarkey et al., 1999). This finding, together with other studies that highlight high levels of stress in final-year students (e.g., Deary et al., 2003), clearly indicates that interventions are required to help them manage their psychological well-being more effectively. Although levels of psychological distress did not reduce after the peer coaching intervention, neither did they increase like those of the control group.

Coaching topics covered during sessions tended to correspond with those highlighted in previous studies as the main sources of stress in students (Roussis & Wells, 2008). Relationships, health, and career issues appear to be the most salient sources of stress for final-year students. Nonetheless, future research might examine the type of problems presented during peer coaching sessions using a freer format, as there may have been topics that were not included in the categories provided.

Previous research findings have suggested that coaching by peers may be seen as less effective than coaching by professionals (Spence & Grant, 2007; Sue-Chan & Latham, 2004). The present study, however, provides strong evidence that peer coaching techniques can be successful in university settings. For the majority of participants (67%), peer coaching was found to be at least moderately effective. This highlights the potential utility of peer coaching interventions for helping students formulate goals and manage stress. Findings have the potential to enhance support structures to foster resilience in student populations. Peer coaching might, therefore, be a practical, fruitful, and low-cost method by which student mental health might be managed during stressful periods.

LIMITATIONS OF THIS STUDY

Although it has added to the evidence base for the effectiveness of solution-focused peer coaching techniques in an educational context, the study had a number of limitations that should be taken into consideration. Firstly, the sample size was relatively small and a cohort from 1 year group. It is possible, therefore, that the results may not be generalized to the larger university population. In addition, self-report data was used, which may be subject to demand characteristics, such as social desirability bias; students may wish to represent their experience as positive, as a way of demonstrating engagement with the coaching process. Moreover, self-report of the benefits attributed to peer coaching may have tempered the validity of the results, as the data reflects a subjective estimate of the competence of the peer coach rather than an objective measure of the benefits provided. It is clear, however, that individual perceptions of the effectiveness of the process and individual well-being are fundamentally important in studies of this type.

CONCLUSION

This exploratory study has presented original data demonstrating some benefits of peer coaching within the higher education context. There are several areas where future research may be fruitful. Although peer coaching has been generally found to be effective, insight into the types of problems that are most receptive to peer coaching techniques is needed. Further work is also required to examine the benefits of peer coaching to student well-being and academic performance, together with the extent to which any benefits are maintained over time. It has been suggested that peer coaching has benefits for the coach as well as the coachee (Ladyshewsky, 2006). The present study did not assess this issue, but the nature of these benefits to well-being and personal development should be further explored in a university environment.

Finally, although this study has examined the coachee's perception of coaching effectiveness, it would be useful to assess the coach's perception of the coachee's readiness and suitability to engage in peer coaching.

ACKNOWLEDGMENTS

We would like to acknowledge the assistance of Guiseppe Turi, Dominika Dainoki, Virag Darida, and Jennifer Vincent in collecting the data for this study.

REFERENCES

Abouserie, R. (1994). Sources and levels of stress in relation to locus of control and self-esteem in university students. *Educational Psychology, 14*(3), 323–331. https://doi.org/10.1080/0144341940140306

Akgun, S., & Ciarrochi, J. (2003). Learned resourcefulness moderates the relationship between academic stress and academic performance. *Educational Psychology, 23*(30), 287–294 https://doi.org/10.1080/0144341032000060129.

Barkham, M., Hardy, G. E., & Startup, M. (1996). The IIP-32: A short version of the inventory of interpersonal problems. *British Journal of Clinical Psychology, 35*, 21–35. https://doi.org/10.1111/j.2044-8260.1996.tb01159.x

Benton, S. A., Robertson, J. M., Wen-Chih, T., Newton, F. B., & Benton, S. L. (2003). Changes in counselling centre client problems across 13 years. *Professional Psychology: Research and Practice, 34*(1), 66–72. https://doi.org/10.1037/0735-7028.34.1.66

Biswas-Diener, R., & Dean, B. (2007). *Positive psychology coaching: Putting the science of happiness to work for your clients.* Hoboken, NJ: Wiley.

Campbell, M. A., & Gardner, S. (2005). A pilot study to assess the effects of life coaching with year 12 students. In M. Cavanagh, A. M. Grant, & T. Kemp (Eds.), *Theory, Research and Practice from the Behavioural Sciences: Vol. 1. Evidence-based coaching* (pp. 159–169). Bowen Hills, QLD: Australian Academic Press.

Deary, I., Watson, R., & Hogston, R. (2003). A longitudinal cohort study of burnout and attrition in nursing students. *Journal of Advanced Nursing, 43*(1), 71–81. https://doi.org/10.1046/j.1365-2648.2003.02674.x

Devonport, T. J., & Lane, A. M. (2006). Cognitive appraisal of dissertation stress among undergraduate students. *The Psychological Record, 56,* 259–266. https://doi.org/10.1007/BF03395549

Department of Education. (2001). *Learning and teaching: A strategy for professional development.* London, UK: Stationery Office.

Downey, M. (2003). *Effective coaching.* London, UK: Texere.

Gall, T. L., Evans, D. R., & Bellerose, S. (2000). Transition to first-year university: Patterns of change in adjustment and across life domains and time. *Journal of Social and Clinical Psychology, 19,* 544–567. https://doi.org/10.1521/jscp.2000.19.4.544

Goldberg, D., & Williams, P. A. (1988). *A user's guide to the general health questionnaire.* Windsor, UK: NFER Nelson Publishing Company Ltd.

Grant, A. M. (2003). The impact of life coaching on goal attainment, metacognition and mental health. *Social Behaviour and Personality, 31*(3), 253–263. https://doi.org/10.2224/sbp.2003.31.3.253

Grant, A. M. (2007). Enhancing coaching skills and emotional intelligence through training. *Industrial and Commercial Training, 39*(5), 257–266. https://doi.org/10.1108/00197850710761945

Grant, A. M. (2008). Personal life coaching for coaches-in-training enhances goal attainment insight and learning. *Coaching: An International Journal of Theory, Research and Practice, 1*(1), 54–70. https://doi.org/10.1080/17521880701878141

Green, L. S., Oades, L. G., & Grant, A. M. (2006). Cognitive-behavioural, solution-focused life coaching: Enhancing goal striving, well-being, and hope. *The Journal of Positive Psychology, 1*(3), 142–149. https://doi.org/10.1080/17439760600619849

Green, S., Grant, A. M., & Rynsaardt, J. (2007). Evidence-based life coaching for senior high school students: Building hardiness and hope. *International Coaching Psychology Review, 2*(1), 24–32.

Greene, J., & Grant, A. M. (2003). *Solution-focused coaching.* Harlow, UK: Pearson Education.

Gyllensten, K., & Palmer, S. (2005). Can coaching reduce workplace stress? *The Coaching Psychologist, 1*(1), 15–17.

Horowitz, L. M., Rosenberg, S. E., Baer, B. A., Ureno, G., & Villasenor, V. S. (1988). Inventory of interpersonal problems: Psychometric properties and clinical applications. *Journal of Consulting and Clinical Psychology, 56,* 885–892.

Hudd, S. S., Dumlao, J., Erdmann-Sager, D., Murray, D., Phan, E., Soukas, N., & Yokozuka, N. (2000). Stress at college: Effects on health habits, health status and self-esteem. *College Student Journal, 34*(2), 217–228.

Hudson, F. (1999). *The handbook of coaching.* Hoboken, NJ: John Wiley & Sons.

Joyce, B., & Showers, B. (1996). The evolution of peer coaching. *Educational Leadership, 53*(6), 12–16.

Kauffman, C., & Scoular, A. (2004). Toward a positive psychology of executive coaching. In P. A. Linley & S. Joseph (Eds.), *Positive psychology in practice* (pp. 287–302). Hoboken, NJ: Wiley.

Ladyshewsky, R. K. (2006). Peer coaching: A constructivist methodology for enhancing critical thinking in postgraduate business education. *Higher Education Research & Development, 25*(1), 67–84. https://doi.org/10.1080/13600800500453196

Laske, O. E. (2006). From coach training to coach education: Teaching coaching within a comprehensively evidence-based framework. *International Journal of Evidence-Based Coaching and Mentoring, 4*(1), 45–57.

Linley, P. A. (2006). Coaching research: Who? What? Where? When? Why? *International Journal of Evidence-Based Coaching and Mentoring, 4*(2), 1–7.

Roussis, P., & Wells, A. (2008). Psychological factors predicting stress symptoms: Metacognition, thought control, and varieties of worry. *Anxiety, Stress and Coping, 21*(3), 213–225. https://doi.org/10.1080/10615800801889600

Seligman, M. E. P. (2002). *Authentic happiness: Using the new positive psychology to realise your potential for lasting fulfilment.* London, UK: Nicholas Brealey.

Spence, G. B., & Grant, A. M. (2007). Professional and peer life coaching and the enhancement of goal striving and well-being: An exploratory study. *Journal of Positive Psychology, 2*(3), 185–194. https://doi.org/10.1080/17439760701228896

Stober, D. R., & Grant, A. M. (2006). *Evidence-based coaching handbook.* Hoboken, NJ: Wiley.

Struthers, C. W., Perry, R. P., & Menec, V. H. (2000). An examination of the relationship among academic stress, copying style, motivation, and performance. *Research in Higher Education, 41*, 581–592. https://doi.org/10.1023/A:1007094931292

Sue-Chan, C., & Latham, G. P. (2004). The relative effectiveness of external, peer, and self-coaches. *Applied Psychology: An International Review, 53*(2), 260–278. https://doi.org/10.1111/j.1464-0597.2004.00171.x

Whitmore, J. (2002). *Coaching for performance* (3rd ed.). London, UK: Nicholas Brealey.

Zwart, R. C., Wubbels, T., Bergen, T. C. M., & Bolhuis, S. (2007). Experienced teacher learning within the context of reciprocal peer coaching. *Teachers and Teaching, 13*(2), 165–187. https://doi.org/10.1080/13540600601152520

16 A Pilot Study Evaluating Strengths-Based Coaching for Primary School Students: Enhancing Engagement and Hope

Wendy Madden, Suzy Green, and Anthony M. Grant[1]

Positive psychology can be understood as being a strengths-based psychology, founded on the humanistic assumption that people want to lead meaningful and fulfilling lives (Seligman, 2002). Positive psychology has also been defined as the study of optimal functioning (Gable & Haidt, 2005). There are an increasing number of positive psychology interventions (PPIs) that are being developed for the purposes of mental health prevention and promotion, with generally promising outcomes (for a recent meta-analysis, see Sin & Lyubormirsky, 2009).

Positive psychology's complementary partner, coaching psychology, can be understood as being "applied positive psychology"—a collaborative, solution-focused, systematic methodology designed to enhance well-being, facilitate goal attainment,

[1] First published as Madden, W., Green, S., & Grant, A. (2010). A pilot study evaluating strengths-based coaching for primary school students: Enhancing engagement and hope. *International Coaching Psychology Review*, 6, 71–83.

and foster purposeful, positive change. There are several research studies that provide support for coaching as a means of increasing aspects of well-being, including hope and hardiness (see, for example, Grant, Green, & Rynsaardt, 2010; Green, Grant, & Rynsaardt, 2007; Green, Oades, & Grant, 2006; Spence & Grant, 2005) and there is a growing evidence base for solution-focused, cognitive-behavioral approaches to coaching in a wide range of settings (Grant, Green, et al., 2010).

Coaching methodologies can provide the opportunity for the application of positive psychology research in areas such as the identification and use of personal character strengths (see, for example, Linley, Nielsen, Gillett, & Biswas-Diener, 2010). While the role of positive psychology in coaching has been discussed previously in the literature, further research in regard to its specific applications is much needed (Biswas-Diener & Dean, 2007; Kauffman, 2006; Linley & Harrington, 2006).

POSITIVE PSYCHOLOGY IN EDUCATION

It might well be said that there have been applications of positive psychology in education for years. This includes programs such as those aimed at enhancing social and emotional learning (SEL), which themselves largely evolved from research on prevention and resilience (see Consortium on the School-Based Promotion of Social Competence, 1994). However, there has been a significant increase in research and interest over the last five years occurring specifically within the field of positive psychology.

In 2009, Professor Martin Seligman formalized the field of "positive education," in part emerging from his own work on depression prevention in schools and the pioneering work at Geelong Grammar in Victoria, Australia. In 2008, Seligman and a team of scholars from the University of Pennsylvania worked with one of Australia's most elite private schools, Geelong Grammar, to implement a program of "teaching positive education," "embedding positive education," and "living positive education." This program sought to infuse positive psychology throughout the entire school, and with encouraging outcomes (Seligman, Ernst, Gillham, & Linkins, 2009). While the program and approach were based on scientifically informed programs and practices, unfortunately it appears that this large-scale program was not itself evaluated using scientifically validated measures; to the best of the present authors' knowledge, no outcome studies of the Geelong Grammar program have been reported in the peer-reviewed press.

There has, however, been significant research conducted on the Penn Resilience Program (PRP), which formed part of the Geelong Positive Education Program. The PRP is a school-based intervention designed to teach students how to think more realistically and flexibly about the problems they encounter (Horowitz & Garber, 2006). Results from studies of over 2,000 individuals in the United States have shown improvements in student well-being from participation in the program (Seligman et al., 2009). The U.S. Department of Education also recently spent $2.8 million to implement a randomized controlled evaluation of the Strath Haven Positive Psychology for Youth (PPY) project. The program, targeting adolescents in high school, was shown to increase students' reports of enjoyment and engagement in school (Seligman et al., 2009).

In the UK, Jenny Fox-Eades is considered to be a pioneer in strengths-based approaches in education and is currently conducting multiple longitudinal research studies, examining the impact of the "Strengths Gym" program on adolescent well-being, including life satisfaction, positive affect, and self-esteem. The "Strengths Gym" program is designed to help individuals identify and use their strengths through a cycle of festivals and storytelling. Positive psychology is woven into the curriculum by using traditional teaching methods of oral storytelling and community celebrations (Eades, 2005).

In Australia, the Coaching Psychology Unit at the University of Sydney hosted the "First Positive Psychology in Education Symposium" in 2009. This provided a forum for a range of applied PPIs being conducted in both private and public schools in Australia. One of the programs presented included "BOUNCE BACK", a resilience program currently taught in several schools across Australia that integrates positive psychology principles within the literacy curriculum (Noble & McGrath, 2008).

Evidence is building for such approaches. For example, a study of solution-focused cognitive-behavioral life coaching for senior high school students conducted by Green et al. (2007) showed significant increases in female senior high school students' levels of cognitive hardiness (a measure of resilience) and hope. This line of research has since been extended to developmental coaching for teachers, again providing evidence for the use of coaching in educational settings to enhance hope, hardiness, and workplace well-being (Grant, Passmore, Cavanagh, & Parker, 2010). The use of solution-focused cognitive-behavioral coaching in educational settings appears to be an area worthy of further study, given preliminary evidence that indicates it may have the potential to build resilience and well-being in young people within educational settings.

APPLIED POSITIVE PSYCHOLOGY IN EDUCATION AS MENTAL HEALTH PROMOTION

Mental health problems are reportedly on the increase among young people, possibly reflecting greater awareness of disorders and also resulting from the frequency and intensity of stressors on young people in the twenty-first century (Broderick & Metz, 2009). Today's youth are exposed to a multitude of threats to their personal well-being (McLoughlin & Kubick, 2004). In a national survey investigating a range of mental health issues, in a stratified, random sample of 4,500 Australian youths (aged 4–17), 14% of those surveyed were found to have mental health problems (Sawyer et al., 2000). Among adolescents, there are also high rates of boredom, alienation, and disconnection from meaningful challenges (Larson, 2000). Efforts to reduce mental health issues and problem behaviors may need to begin in childhood, with special attention to a window of escalating risk in the transition to adolescence (Masten, Herbers, Cutuli, & Lafavor, 2008).

Knowledge and skills that increase resilience, positive emotion, and engagement can be taught. According to Piaget (1977), preadolescent children are entering the formal operations phase of cognitive development and have the cognitive maturity necessary to understand and apply the skills taught. The present study sought to expand on current findings by focusing on primary school students and examining the efficacy of a strengths-based coaching program within this particular age group.

The mission of schools remains one of preparing students academically for the world of higher education, work, and good citizenship. However, increasingly, schools are also responsible for managing students' social and emotional well-being (Broderick & Metz, 2009).

This current study examined a program designed to be easily integrated within the traditional school curriculum, while at the same time addressing a number of the personal development and health outcomes identified on the New South Wales Board of Studies syllabus document (New South Wales Board of Studies, 2007). Embedding the teaching of strengths identification, goal setting, and metacognitive skills within the curriculum provides naturalistic opportunities for students to develop important social-emotional competencies (Noble & McGrath, 2008). Meaningful participation in these kinds of activities also encourages students to take control of and responsibility for their own lives (Oliver, Collins, Burns, & Nicholas, 2006).

AIMS OF THE STUDY

The study sought to investigate the impact of an evidence-based strengths coaching pilot program in a primary educational setting. It was anticipated that participation in the strengths-based coaching program would be associated with increases in male primary school student's levels of engagement and hope.

Engagement

The discipline of positive psychology defines engagement as one of three important realms of happiness; the engaged life, the meaningful life, and the pleasant life (Seligman et al., 2009). The state of "flow," a term coined by Csikszentmihalyi, Rathunde, and Whalen (1993), is a major part of living the "engaged life." It consists of a loss of self-consciousness and deep engagement in the task at hand and can occur when people deploy their highest strengths to meet the challenges that come their way. There is growing evidence to support the concept of engagement as a state that is valuable in its own right, as well as bringing about higher levels of life satisfaction (Seligman et al., 2009).

Strengths

A "strength" can be defined as a natural capacity for behaving, thinking, and feeling in a way that promotes successful goal achievement (Linley & Harrington, 2006). "Signature strengths" refer to the top five character strengths and virtues of a particular individual (Peterson & Seligman, 2004). Signature strengths can convey a sense of ownership and authenticity, and individuals often experience a powerful intrinsic motivation to put them into practice (Linley & Harrington, 2006). Strength-based coaching helps people to identify their strengths and then better direct their talents and abilities into meaningful and engaging behaviors (Peterson & Seligman, 2004). Playing to an individual's strengths has the potential to enhance well-being, because people are then able to do what they naturally do best, thus increasing the chances of meeting their basic psychological needs for autonomy, competence, and confidence (Linley & Harrington, 2006). Finding original ways to use strengths also reflects the importance of ongoing personal effort in producing a flourishing life (Park & Peterson, 2006).

Hope

Hope is defined as "a positive motivational state that is based on an interactively derived sense of successful agency and pathways" (Snyder, 2000; p. 287). The construct of hope is central to successful goal attainment. In order to pursue goals, people need (a) a number of pathways or alternative routes to achieve their goals, because otherwise it is likely that they will give up if the first pathway fails. They also need (b) agency or confidence, in their capacity and ability to reach their goals, so once again if they face setbacks they will persevere in the belief that they can be successful (Snyder, Michael, & Cheavens, 1999).

Hope as a cross-situational construct has been shown to correlate positively with self-efficacy, perceived problem-solving capabilities, perceptions of control, optimism, positive affectivity, and positive outcome expectations (Snyder et al., 1999). In educational settings, higher levels of hope have also correlated positively with perceived scholastic competence (Onwuegbuzie & Daley, 1999) and greater academic satisfaction (Chang, 1998). Higher levels of hope also predict better academic performance while controlling for student intelligence (Snyder, Lopez, Shorey, Rand, & Feldman, 2003).

Consistent with hope theory, an evidence-based approach to coaching can provide the support necessary for individuals to pursue goals, to see themselves as able to generate alternative routes to goals and as having the perceived capacity to use these routes to reach the desired goal(s) (Green et al., 2006). Hope can be engendered in young people by engaging them in solution-focused conversations and activities. For example, children can be asked to set small goals, guided over the hurdles they encounter, and encouraged to persevere until they have succeeded (Snyder, 2000). These are key features of the present study.

METHOD

Participants

Thirty-eight males aged between 10 and 11 years (mean age 10.7 years) from an independent, private primary school in Sydney, New South Wales, Australia.

Procedure

The strengths-coaching program formed part of the school's personal development and health curriculum. Prior to commencing the program, participants were screened by the school psychologist using the Beck Youth Inventory (Beck, Beck, Jolly, & Steer, 2005). As a result of completing this inventory, seven individuals were identified as having higher than expected scores on the inventory (Beck et al., 2005) and were referred to the school psychologist.

Before commencing the program, a note was also sent home to parents giving full details of the program. In line with the International Coach Federation (ICF) Code of Ethics (ICF, 2005), the information clarified that the program did not involve any counseling or therapy for mental illness. Participants completed self-report measures at Time 1 (pre-intervention) and Time 2 (post-intervention) to assess levels of engagement and hope. Participants also completed the Values in Action Strengths Inventory for Youth (Peterson & Seligman, 2004) and were provided with a copy of their results to share with their family. The participants were then randomly assigned to small groups of four or five individuals, with whom they would complete eight group coaching sessions.

The teacher-coach was a qualified primary teacher who, in addition to her teacher training and teaching qualifications, had also completed coach-specific training, held a Master's degree in coaching psychology from Sydney University and had past experience in coaching both child and adult populations.

The coaching program

The coaching program consisted of eight group face-to-face coaching sessions with the teacher-coach. Each coaching session was 45 min in length and was conducted on a fortnightly basis over a period of two school terms (equating to approximately six months). Because this program was run in a school setting in which directive or instructional modalities are commonplace, great care was taken to differentiate this coaching program from general directive or teaching processes by basing this program on a solution-focused cognitive-behavioral framework that had been demonstrated as being effective in two previous randomized, controlled studies on evidence-based life coaching (for details see Green et al., 2006; Spence & Grant, 2005).

There were three key parts to the program. Part 1 focused on raising the participant's self-awareness, including the identification of personal character strengths. Using the Youth Values in Action survey results, the participants were provided with a

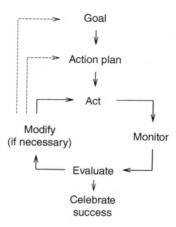

Figure 16.1   *A Generic Cycle of Self-Regulation*

useful vocabulary to both identify and talk about their own character strengths. The participants created "strength shields" representing how they were already using their top five "signature strengths." These shields were openly displayed in the classroom and referred to on a regular basis.

In Part 2 of the program, the participants were coached to identify personal resources and utilize these in working toward individual goals. Using the SMART (specific, measurable, attractive, realistic, and timeframed) goal-setting criteria (for the rationale for SMART, see Locke & Latham, 2002), the participants were coached in identifying personally meaningful goals and to be persistent in their goal striving. The participants applied this knowledge and skills within an ongoing assignment focused on finding novel ways to use one of their signature strengths.

Part 3 of the program was focused on coaching the participants in working through the self-regulation cycle (see Figure 16.1) of setting goals, developing action plans, monitoring, and evaluating progress. Participants were individually coached to identify personal resources that could be utilized in moving toward their goals, and to develop self-generated solutions and specific action steps, and in this way systematically working through the self-regulation cycle.

In addition to the individual coaching process detailed above, group processes were used, in that participants were also given the opportunity to share their results with the group and jointly reflect on what they had learned. Finally, the students completed a "Letter from the future" that involved writing about themselves at their very best, focusing on how their needs and values were being met, and finding solutions to allow for all the things they would like to have happened.

Measures

The Beck Youth Inventory (Beck et al., 2005) was used as a measure of psychopathology. It assesses current levels of anxiety, depression, and anger. It also gives an overall indication of a young person's self-concept. The inventory is designed to assess according to the diagnostic criteria listed in the *DSM-IV-TR* (American Psychiatric Association, 2000). However, it only assesses the current status and does not offer a diagnosis (Beck et al., 2005). It views the differences between normal and clinical populations as differences of degree, hence it is a useful tool for the present study to screen participants for mental health issues that require referral.

To identify character strengths, the participants completed the Values in Action (VIA) Strengths Inventory for Youth Survey (Park & Peterson, 2006). The VIA measure is a self-report survey, allowing the comparison of character strengths across individuals and also identifies an individual's "signature strengths" relative to their other strengths (Park & Peterson, 2008). The VIA youth survey is designed for people aged 10–17 (Park & Peterson, 2006). It reflects each of the character strengths in the VIA classification (Peterson & Seligman, 2004), and is adapted specifically for use with youth, as the items are phrased in simple language and refer to settings and situations familiar to young people (Park & Peterson, 2006). The survey is available online at no cost from www.viacharacter.org (Peterson & Seligman, 2007). It contains 198 multiple-choice items and takes 45 min on average to complete. The survey has good reliability (all item alphas are greater than .70) and good reported construct validity (Park & Peterson, 2008).

To measure the results of the program, participants completed a self-report questionnaire at Time 1 and Time 2. The questionnaire was modified from Snyder's Children's Hope Scale (Snyder, 2000), and the California Healthy Kids Survey (Bernard, 2008). The questionnaire used a seven-point Likert scale ranging from 7 (*strongly agree*) to 1 (*strongly disagree*). The Children's Hope Scale is a self-report measure that is based on the premise that children are goal-directed and that their goal-directed thoughts can be understood according to agency and pathways. The scale is validated for use with children aged 7–16 years and demonstrates both internal and temporal reliability, convergent and discriminant validity (for details, see Snyder, 2000). The California Healthy Kids Survey (CHKS) is sponsored by the California Department of Education as a comprehensive data collection service on youth mental health and resilience (Bernard, 2008). Assisting in its development was an advisory committee consisting of researchers, education practitioners from schools across the state, and representatives from federal and state agencies involved in assessing youth health-related behaviors (Bernard, 2008).

At the completion of the strength coaching program, an informal questionnaire was also used to elicit the student's feedback and opinions about their involvement.

RESULTS

Quantitative findings

It was hypothesized that participation in the coaching program would be associated with increased engagement and hope. The results for all measures are shown in Table 16.1.

Table 16.1   *Results for Measures of Engagement and Hope*

N = 38	Time 1		Time 2				
	M	SD	M	SD	t	p	d
Hope	23.79	3.16	24.87	2.76	3.38	<.001	2.70
Engagement	23.26	4.26	24.98	2.51	3.29	<.01	.98

Note. p values are two-tailed; Cohen's *d* is given as a measure of effect size.

Paired *t*-tests found significant increases in students' self-reported measures of hope, $t(37) = 3.39$, $p = < .01$ and significant increases in students' self-reported measures of engagement, $t(37) = 3.30$, $p = < .001$. Effect sizes were calculated using Cohen's *d*. For hope, an effect size of $d = 2.70$ was observed. This is considered to be a large effect size (Cohen, 1992). For engagement, a medium effect size of $d = .98$ was observed (Cohen, 1992).

Values in action strengths inventory for youth results: class tally

We recorded the top strengths of the class and the number of students who rated each strength as being their highest strength: These strengths, in order of frequency, were; vitality (nine students); creativity (eight students); love (five students); teamwork (three students); love of learning (three students); perseverance (three students); humor (two students); curiosity (one student); leadership (one student); bravery (one student); gratitude (one student); and kindness (one student).

Qualitative findings

To augment the quantitative data reported above, and to further assess the impact of this pilot study, qualitative teacher observations are now reported. These personal observations are made by the teacher-coach who conducted the strengths-based coaching program.

Teacher-coach personal observations

Overall, I felt that the programme was a successful way for a teacher to further develop positive relationships with students. I found that understanding the students' top strengths was very helpful in getting to know the students better, and also in understanding what engages and motivates them. Learning about character strengths also provided students with a useful dialogue to recognise strengths not only in themselves but in others too.

For example, when a new boy joined the school, the students welcomed him into the school community and were quick to point out his strengths, such as bravery and social intelligence, during his first weeks. The students were also very keen to share and discuss their results with their families. The positive feedback from the parents was overwhelming and many of them also did the survey to find out their own character strengths.

Recording the top strengths of the class group provided an interesting insight into the classroom dynamics. Vitality was the top strength of the class. Viewing this as a strength for a class of Year 6 boys, rather than a problem, was both humorous and refreshing.

I found that the students were highly engaged during the goal-setting sessions. They were enthusiastic and excited about their projects and would often stop me in the playground to give updates on their progress. Sharing their successes with their peers was invaluable as they were provided with both positive feedback and recognition. For some students in particular, this was a very special experience, made very clear by their big, beaming grins. The students were also able to transfer their goal-setting skills to their learning in the classroom. Overall, the impact of the program has been profound, with a far more positive, encouraging, and supportive classroom climate.

Examples of student goals

Participants set personal goals as part of the coaching program. These goals were linked with their specific signature strengths. Examples are given below:

Love of learning Signature Strength: Goal was to "read 15 pages of a non-fiction book on cars every night over the next two weeks. Have Mum sign off when I do it. Show (my teacher) Mum's note in our next session and tell her one fact that I learnt about cars."

Leadership Signature Strength: Goal was to "Organise a jelly bean competition with two friends to raise money for the school. Get approval from the principal and my parents. Set up the store outside the canteen every lunch time. Aim to raise at least $100. Bring the money raised to our next session."

Kindness Signature Strength: Goal was to "Help Mum out at home by making both mine and my little brother's beds every morning before school. Ask Dad to sign off that I do it, but don't tell Mum I am doing it for an assignment. Show (my teacher) the note in our next session."

DISCUSSION

The present study was a small-scale pilot study designed to be a preliminary investigation of the effect of a strengths-based coaching program within a school setting. The strengths-based coaching pilot program was associated with significant increases in the students' self-reported levels of engagement and hope. Although the results are promising, it is important not to overgeneralize from these findings. Nevertheless, as we argue below, such strengths-based coaching programs may well have potential as a mental health prevention and promotion intervention in a primary school setting to increase students' well-being and additionally be utilized as an important part of an overall positive education program. Schools already are a major provider of mental health services (Seligman et al., 2009). However, the predominant approach is reactive rather than proactive, in that educational psychology services are available only after students demonstrate difficulties (Noble & McGrath, 2008). A significant proportion of available educational resources is directed toward attempts to remediate young people's problems. This is not surprising, given extra support is provided on the basis of documentation of an individual's assessed problem (Noble & McGrath, 2008). The challenge is to shift the direction and mindset of both educational systems and school personnel from a deficit model to a preventative well-being model (Noble & McGrath, 2008). Problem-focused approaches can be useful in reducing and treating specific targeted problems, but they do not necessarily prepare young people to have healthy, fulfilling, productive lives (Park & Peterson, 2008).

There is growing recognition that effective interventions need to focus on promoting competence and strengths in addition to the prevention and treatment of problems (Masten et al., 2008). We argue that positive psychology offers new directions for working with individual students and for working collaboratively with schools and teachers in designing and implementing school-wide preventative programs (Noble & McGrath, 2008). For example, schools could be adopting more holistic approaches with missions that address the needs of the whole child (McLoughlin & Kubick, 2004). A narrow focus only on cognitive development ignores other critical areas of youth development (Bernard, 2008).

The present pilot study is a very small step in that direction by showing that a strengths-based coaching program can quite easily be integrated within the traditional school curriculum, and can be associated with increased engagement and hope. It should be noted that, even though the present pilot program was part of the school curriculum, and in that sense was compulsory, the student feedback was overwhelmingly positive. Such positively-framed programs, without the stigma often associated with remedial counseling, may provide an effective means of promoting student well-being (Park & Peterson, 2008).

It would appear there are many other potential benefits of strengths-based coaching programs for students, teachers, and schools. For example, when students work with their strengths, they tend to be more motivated and perform at a higher level (Peterson & Seligman, 2004). Similarly, increases in well-being are likely to produce increases in learning, with a positive mood producing broader attention, more creative thinking, and more holistic thinking (Seligman et al., 2009). In addition, students who have positive attitudes toward their teachers and school are more likely to display more appropriate behavior (Huebner, Suldo, Smith, & McKnight, 2004). Indeed, we contend that an evidence-based strengths coaching program, such as the one used in this study, could form an important part of an overall positive education program.

While the importance of happiness and well-being cannot be contested, there is debate about how best to enhance these important aspects of human experience within the traditional educational context (Park & Peterson, 2008). Researchers are concerned by the lack of empirical evidence for most programs (Arthur, 2005, cited in Seligman et al., 2009). Educators and politicians are also concerned such positive educational programs will waste money or even lower achievement by diverting time and money away from academic subjects (Benninga, Berkowitz, Kuehn, & Smith, 2006).

LIMITATIONS

Future research is needed to explore the potential of a range of approaches to positive education. The present study was a small-scale pilot study designed to be a preliminary investigation of the effect of a strengths-based coaching program within a school setting. As such there are a number of limitations that must be taken into account when considering these findings. Firstly, the present study used a within-subject, pre-/post-design. The lack of a control group means that the effects could have occurred naturalistically, rather than being caused by the intervention. Secondly, no longitudinal measures were taken so it is not known if the reported effects would be maintained over time. However, it should be noted a longitudinal study (Green et al., 2006) found that gains in a similar coaching program were maintained at a 30-week follow-up. Thirdly, the present study is also limited by the exclusive use of self-report measures. It would be extremely valuable to move beyond self-report measures and document the effects on observable behaviors from a broader range of outcomes, including students' behavior and academic performance. The findings would also need to be replicated to determine if the program is effective with students from a variety of social-economic and cultural backgrounds. Finally, it should be noted that the teacher-coach was acting in a role as a designated teacher. This could have influenced outcomes by inducing a demand effect, that is, the participants may have felt that they had to report making progress and enhanced well-being in order to please the experimenter.

FUTURE DIRECTIONS

Despite some clear limitations, the results of the present pilot study provide promising initial support for this kind of intervention in a school setting, and future research should be conducted in this area. Further studies that compared interventions with educational tutoring or positive parent involvement would provide additional information about the effectiveness of life coaching for students, and the use of randomized controlled designs would further extend the current research.

Recent research has found that peer coaching was not as effective as a professionally-trained coach (Spence & Grant, 2007) and this finding emphasizes the importance of expertise in facilitating purposeful, positive change in others. Teaching children to employ hopeful thinking requires an interested person who guides the process of goal setting and problem solving with encouragement (Snyder, 2000). For teachers or parents interested in nurturing hope in children, the first step must be to attend to their own hopeful thinking (Snyder, 2000). The "teacher as coach" training program as used in the research of Green et al. (2007) could be used to develop teachers in the evidence-based coaching theories and techniques, which do not currently form part of teacher training. Through such evidence-based coaching programs, teachers may learn to better identify what motivates and inspires each of their students. They could then use this information to design more supportive, positively-orientated teacher-student relationships, which are a defining feature of positive school cultures (Noble & McGrath, 2008).

Of course, there is much more to positive education than a simple stand-alone course (Seligman et al., 2009). There is a need for comprehensive and integrative positive education programs, such as the one recently trialled at Geelong Grammar (Seligman et al., 2009). Rather than running a number of independent initiatives that are not integrated, it may be better to strategically implement an overall positive education policy that is aligned with the overall school climate (Noble & McGrath, 2008).

Clearly, there is a need for further research and for external coaching consultants and educators to work collaboratively with schools in order to create programs with a consistent approach and similar language embedded throughout.

Similarly, there is a need for further research in developing measurement tools to assess the culture and climate of individual schools. With any program or intervention that can be used in schools, a key element is the overall culture and climate that exists within the school environment (Snyder, 2000). Administrators have an important role in educating the school personnel, teachers, and parents about their role in creating a positive school climate. Ultimately, the focus should be on creating a curriculum for students that has genuine relevance, meaning, and connectedness to their lives (Noble & McGrath, 2008). We argue that coaching in school settings has the potential to both shift the culture of the broader educational system and to better enrich the overall individual student experience.

CONCLUSION

This pilot study has examined the impact of an evidence-based strengths coaching program on male primary school students' levels of engagement and hope. It provides preliminary evidence that evidence-based strengths coaching programs may be useful in the primary school setting. The study also illustrates how evidence-based coaching methodologies can be integrated into an educational setting, adding to our collective understanding of what might be included in learning programs designed to enhance well-being. We believe that evidence-based strengths coaching programs can be designed to fit into several existing aspects of the curriculum with relative ease and can address outcomes specified in school syllabus documentation (Noble & McGrath, 2008). This pilot study, while targeting Year Five students, could also be adapted to form part of a school-wide initiative, with a strong practical focus on infusing positive psychology into the whole school curriculum.

With future research in this area, evidence-based coaching may in time become a crucial methodology for the application of positive psychology in educational settings. We look forward to future developments with interest.

REFERENCES

American Psychiatric Association. (2000). *Diagnostic and statistical manual of mental disorders* (4th ed.). Washington, DC.

Beck, J. S., Beck, A. T., Jolly, J., & Steer, R. (2005). *Beck youth inventories of emotional and social impairment* (2nd ed.; BYI–II). Sydney, Australia: Pearson.

Benninga, J. S., Berkowitz, M. W., Kuehn, P., & Smith, K. (2006). Character and academics: What good schools hate. *Phi Delta Kappan, 87,* 448–452.

Bernard, B. (2008). *West Ed Website. California Healthy Kids Survey.* Questionnaires retrieved December 11, 2008, from http://www.wested.org/cs/chks/view/chks_s 17?x–layout=surveys

Biswas-Diener, R., & Dean, B. (2007). *Positive psychology coaching: Putting the science of happiness to work for your clients.* Hoboken, NJ: Wiley.

Broderick, P. C., & Metz, S. (2009). Learning to BREATHE: A pilot trial of a mindfulness curriculum for adolescents. *Advances in School Mental Health Promotion, 2*(1), 35–46. https://doi.org/10.1080/1754730X.2009.9715696

Chang, E. C. (1998). Hope problem-solving ability and coping in a college student population: Some implications for theory and practice. *Journal of Clinical Psychology, 54,* 953–962. https://doi.org/10.1002/(SICI)1097-4679(199811)54:7<953::AID-JCLP9>3.0.CO;2-F

Cohen, J. (1992). A power primer. *Psychological Bulletin, 112*(1), 155–159. https://doi.org/10.1037/0033-2909.112.1.155

Consortium on the School-Based Promotion of Social Competence. (1994). The promotion of social competence: Theory, research, practice, and policy. In R. J. Haggerty, L. Sherrod, N. Garmezy, & M. Rutter (Eds.), *Stress, risk, resilience in children and adolescents: Processes, mechanisms, and interaction* (pp. 268–316). New York, NY: Cambridge University Press.

Csikszentmihalyi, M., Rathunde, K., & Whalen, S. (1993). *Talented teenagers.* Cambridge, UK: Cambridge University Press.

Eades, J. M. F. (2005). *Classroom tales: Using storytelling to build emotional, social and academic skills across the primary curriculum.* London, UK: Jessica Kingsley.

Gable, S. L., & Haidt, J. (2005). What (and why) is positive psychology?. *Review of general psychology, 9*(2), 103–110. https://doi.org/10.1037/1089-2680.9.2.103

Grant, A. M., Green, L. S., & Rynsaardt, J. (2010). Developmental coaching for high school teachers: Executive coaching goes to school. *Consulting Psychology Journal: Practice & Research, 62*(3), 151–168. https://doi.org/10.1037/a0019212

Grant, A. M., Passmore, J., Cavanagh, M. J., & Parker, H. (2010). The state of play in coaching today: A comprehensive review of the field. *International Review of Industrial and Organisational Psychology, 25,* 125–168. https://doi.org/10.1002/9780470661628.ch4

Green, L. S., Grant, A. M., & Rynsaardt, J. (2007). Evidence-based coaching for senior high school students: Building hardiness and hope. *International Coaching Psychology Review, 2*(1), 24–31.

Green, L. S., Oades, L. G., & Grant, A. M. (2006). Cognitive-behavioural, solution-focused life coaching: Enhancing goal-striving, wellbeing and hope. *Journal of Positive Psychology, 1*(3), 142–149. https://doi.org/10.1080/17439760600619849

Horowitz, J. L., & Garber, J. (2006). The prevention of depressive symptoms in children and adolescents: A meta-analytic review. *Journal of Consulting and Clinical Psychology, 74,* 401–415. https://doi.org/10.1037/0022-006X.74.3.401

Huebner, E. S., Suldo, S. M., Smith, L. C., & McKnight, C. G. (2004). Life satisfaction in children and youth: Empirical foundations and implications for school psychologists. *Psychology in the Schools, 41*(1), 81–93. https://doi.org/10.1002/pits.10140

International Coaching Federation. (2005). *Professional coaching core competencies and code of ethics.* Retrieved April 19, 2009, from http://www.coachfederation.org/Downloads/DOCS Ethics/ICF_Code_of_ethics_01_22_05.pdf

Kauffman, C. (2006). Positive psychology: The science at the heart of coaching. In D. Stober & A. M. Grant (Eds.), *Evidence-based coaching handbook* (pp. 219–254). Hoboken, NJ: Wiley.

Larson, R. W. (2000). Towards a psychology of positive youth development. *American Psychologist, 55*(1), 170–183.

Linley, P. A., & Harrington, S. (2006). Strengths coaching: A potential-guided approach to coaching psychology. *International Coaching Psychology Review, 1*(1), 37–46.

Linley, P. A., Nielsen, A. M., Gillett, R., & Biswas-Diener, R. (2010). Using signature strengths in pursuit of goals: Effects on goal progress, need satisfaction, and wellbeing, and implications for coaching psychologists. *International Coaching Psychology Review, 5*(1), 8–17.

Locke, E. A., & Latham, G. P. (2002). Building a practically useful theory of goal setting and task motivation. *American Psychologist, 57*(9), 705–717. https://doi.org/10.1037/0003-066X. 57.9.705

Masten, A., Herbers, J., Cutuli, J., & Lafavor, T. (2008). Promoting competence and resilience in the school context. *Professional School Counselling, 12*(2), 21–34. https://doi.org/10.1177/215 6759X0801200213

Mcloughlin, C. S., & Kubick, R. J. (2004). Wellness promotion as a lifelong endeavour: Promoting and developing life competencies from childhood. *Psychology in the Schools, 41*(1), 131–141. https://doi.org/10.1002/pits.10145

New South Wales Board of Studies. (2007). *Personal Development.* In *Health and physical education K-6 syllabus.* Sydney, Australia: NSW Board of Studies.

Noble, T., & McGrath, H. (2008). The positive educational practices framework: A tool for facilitating the work of educational psychologists in promoting pupil wellbeing. *Educational & Child Psychology, 25*(2), 119–134.

Oliver, K., Collins, P., Burns, J., & Nicholas, J. (2006). Building resilience in young people through meaningful participation. *Australian e-journal for the Advancement of Mental Health, 5*(1), 34–40. https://doi.org/10.5172/jamh.5.1.34.

Onwuegbuzie, A. J., & Daley, C. E. (1999). Perfectionism and statistics anxiety. *Personal and Individual Differences, 26,* 1089–1102. https://doi.org/10.1016/S0191-8869(98)00214-1

Park, N., & Peterson, C. (2006). Moral competence and character strengths among adolescents: The development and validation of the values in action inventory of strengths for youth. *Journal of Adolescence, 29*(6), 891–909. https://doi.org/10.1016/j.adolescence.2006.04.011

Park, N., & Peterson, C. (2008). Positive psychology and character strengths: Application to strengths-based school counselling. *Professional School Counselling, 12*(2), 11–20. https://doi. org/10.1177/2156759X0801200214

Peterson, C., & Seligman, M. E. P. (2004). *Character strengths and virtues: A handbook and classification.* New York, NY: Oxford University Press.

Peterson, C. & Seligman, M. E. P. (2007). Values in Action Institute website. Manuel, D. & Rhoda Mayerson Foundation, OH, Cincinnati. Information retrieved April 22, 2009, from www.viastrengths.org

Piaget, J. (1977). *The grasp of consciousness*. London, UK: Routledge & Kegan Paul.

Sawyer, M. G., Arney, F. M., Baghurst, P. A., Clark, J. J., Graetz, B. W., & Kosky, R. J. (2000). *Mental health of young people in Australia: Child and adolescent component of the National Survey of Mental Health and Wellbeing*. Canberra, Australia: Commonwealth Department of Health and Aged Care.

Seligman, M. E. P. (2002). *Authentic happiness: Using the new positive psychology to realise your potential for lasting fulfilment*. New York, NY: Free Press.

Seligman, M. E. P., Ernst, R., Gillham, K., & Linkins, M. (2009). Positive education: Positive psychology and classroom interventions. *Oxford Review of Education, 35*(3), 293–311. https://doi.org/10.1080/03054980902934563

Sin, N. L., & Lyubormirsky, S. (2009). Enhancing wellbeing and alleviating depressive symptoms with positive psychology interventions: A practice-friendly meta-analysis. *Journal of Clinical Psychology: In Session, 65*(4), 67–487. https://doi.org/10.1002/jclp.20593

Snyder, C. R. (2000). *Handbook of hope: Theory, measures and applications*. San Diego, CA: Academic Press.

Snyder, C. R., Lopez, S. J., Shorey, H. S., Rand, K. L., & Feldman, D. B. (2003). Hope theory, measurements, and applications to school psychology. *School Psychology Quarterly, 18*, 122–139.

Snyder, C. R., Michael, S. T., & Cheavens, J. (1999). Hope as a psychotherapeutic foundation of common factors, placebos and expectancies. In M. A. Hubble, B. Duncan, & S. Miller (Eds.), *Heart and soul of change* (pp. 179–200). Washington, DC: APA.

Spence, G. B., & Grant, A. M. (2005). Individual and group life-coaching: Initial findings from a randomised controlled trial. In M. Cavanagh, A. M. Grant, & T. Kemp (Eds.), *Theory, Research and Practice from the Behavioural Sciences: Vol. 1. Evidence-based coaching* (pp. 143–158). Bowen Hills, QLD: Australian Academic Press.

Spence, G. B., & Grant, A. M. (2007). Professional and peer life coaching and the enhancement of goal striving and wellbeing: An exploratory study. *Journal of Positive Psychology, 2*(3), 185–194. https://doi.org/10.1080/17439760701228896

17 The Quantitative Assessment of Motivational Interviewing Using Co-Active Life Coaching Skills as an Intervention for Adults Struggling with Obesity

Courtney Newnham-Kanas, Jennifer D. Irwin, Don Morrow, and Danielle Battram[1]

The World Health Organization (WHO) reports that globally at least 400 million adults were obese in 2005 (WHO, 2006). Based on these numbers, it is projected that by 2012, obesity levels will rise to 700 million adults worldwide. While obesity was once believed to be a problem in high-income countries, rates are climbing substantially in low- and middle-income countries (WHO, 2006). The recent 2007–2009 Canadian Health Measures Survey (Shields, Tremblay, Laviolette, Craig, & Janssen, 2010) reported that over the past 25–30 years, Canadian adults have become heavier

---

[1] First published as Newnham-Kanas, C., Irwin, J. D., Morrow, D., & Battram, D. (2011). The quantitative assessment of Motivational Interviewing using co-active life coaching skills as an intervention for adults struggling with obesity. *International Coaching Psychology Review*, 6(2), 211–228.

for their heights (Tjepkema, 2006). As a result, 19% of males and 21% of females aged 20–39 were considered obese in 2009 and the percentage increased to one-third for ages 60–69. From 1981 to 2007–2009, the number of obese females aged 40–59 doubled. Based on current waist circumference (WC) measurements, 31% of females and 21% of males aged 20–39 are at high risk for health problems and for ages 60–69, those percentages rose to 65% and 52%, respectively. Body mass index (BMI) has been deemed limited in assessing general health because it does not take the overall distribution of body fat into account. Therefore, WC, which assesses abdominal fat (a predictor of increased risk of disease for both sexes), is used in conjunction with BMI to reflect overall health (Janssen, Heymsfield, & Ross, 2002; Janssen, Katzmarzyk, & Ross, 2002, 2004). If these trends continue, in 25 years, half of all males and females in Canada will be considered obese. These alarming rates of obesity have considerable physical, psychological, and economic consequences for an avoidable noncommunicable disease (Shields et al., 2010).

Because of the drastic rise in obesity in a relatively short period of time (i.e., shorter than needed for genetic changes in a population to be expressed), it is believed that behavioral factors play a more pivotal role rather than biological factors in shaping the development and maintenance of obesity (Stice, Presnell, & Shaw, 2005). While it has been reported widely that inactivity and food consumption are at the root causes of increased rates of obesity, these two behavioral challenges may, in part, be symptoms of other psychosocial challenges (e.g., depression, low self-esteem). Although this problem of underestimating the psychosocial contribution to the obesity epidemic is gaining widespread attention within academic journals and medical sources, new clinical approaches for treating/reducing obesity are lacking (Hardeman, Griffin, Johnston, Kinmonth, & Wareham, 2000; Slevin, 2004). One such treatment is motivational interviewing (MI), which is a directive, client-centered counseling style for eliciting behavior change by helping people explore and resolve their ambivalence for change (Miller & Rollnick, 2002). Motivational interviewing has been well documented as an effective behavior change intervention in the health care field since its inception in 1983, especially in the area of addiction, with particular emphasis on behaviors associated with alcohol use (Brown & Miller, 1993; Miller, 1998; Miller, Yahne, & Tonigan, 2003). Recently, Freedhoff and Sharma (2010) recommended MI as an essential behavioral intervention needed as part of a comprehensive treatment plan for individuals struggling with obesity. A primary concern with using MI as a behavior change intervention has been putting MI principles into action (Mesters, 2009). Previous research and experiences indicate that the tenets and premises of MI are contained entirely within, and brought to fruition via, the skills of CALC (Gorczynski, Morrow, & Irwin, 2008; Irwin & Morrow, 2005; Newnham-Kanas, Gorczynski, Irwin, & Morrow, 2009; Newnham-Kanas, Irwin, & Morrow, 2008; Newnham-Kanas, Morrow, & Irwin, 2010; Whitworth, Kimsey-House, Kimsey-House, & Sandahl, 1998, 2007; van Zandvoort, Irwin, & Morrow, 2008, 2009). Motivational interviewing holds the same principles as CALC and is an accepted methodology that has been utilized in the worlds of medicine and allied health care for some time; CALC builds on these MI roots by providing the tools to effectively put MI principles into action. With MI's potential in aiding individuals struggling with obesity, the recent recommendations by Freedhoff and Sharma, and the application-based tools provided by CALC to properly implement

MI principles into action, MI using CALC skills combine to represent a theoretically sound and evidence-based strategy worth investigating as an intervention for obesity.

When using MI administered via CALC tools as an intervention for obesity, our previous research has demonstrated a statistically significant decrease in WC and increases in self-esteem and functional health status. Qualitatively, participants reported an increase in daily physical activity and healthier dietary choices, feelings of optimism, and greater self-acceptance (Newnham-Kanas et al., 2008). Another study that used CALC as an intervention for obesity found coaching, and particular coaching skills were associated with a trend toward a decrease in WC and clinically significant increases in participants' self-esteem and their mental, physical, and overall health statuses (van Zandvoort et al., 2008). While coaching has been defined historically as a behavior change tool for a nonclinical population, a recent annotated bibliography of 72 critically appraised health-related coaching studies demonstrated that life coaching has been utilized effectively in ameliorating many health issues, including but not limited to diabetes, asthma, poor cardiovascular health, fitness, and depression (Newnham-Kanas et al., 2009). It should be noted that life coaches are not trained as mental health professionals. In fact, Grant and Zackon (2004) reported that only 40% of life coaches received 11 or more hours of training in mental health issues in the form of professional development workshops or programs. In a recent survey of certified professional co-active coaches (CPCC), over 60% of respondents did not have any formal training in recognizing mental health issues (Newnham-Kanas, Irwin, & Morrow, 2011). Therefore, it is crucial that life coaches recognize mental health issues and refer on or work simultaneously with a mental health professional. Participants of the current study were informed that they must continue under a physician's or a trained mental health professional's care for any comorbidities (e.g., depression, diabetes, etc.).

CALC uses MI principles to create a proactive alliance in which coach and client work together as equals to meet the needs of the client. The approach has been evaluated as a theoretically-grounded behavior change method (Irwin & Morrow, 2005) that includes constructs from social cognitive theory (Bandura, 1977), the theory of reasoned action (Fishbein & Ajzen, 1975), and the theory of planned behavior (Ajzen, 1988). Co-active life coaching also shares some of the elements from Egan's skilled helper model (Egan, 1997), self-regulation theory (Kanfer, 1970), and self-determination theory (Ryan & Deci, 2000). From a behavioral perspective, it stands to reason that the MI using the CALC approach may work to produce desirable impacts on obesity because of its impact on self-regulation, and self-regulation in one domain (e.g., life stress) often increases self-regulation in other, unrelated domains (e.g., dietary intake and/or physical activity). Our experience with short-term, MI-obesity research studies suggests that obesity includes modifiable conditions (physical and psychological) that respond to an MI treatment, and a longer-term study is now required (Newnham-Kanas et al., 2008; van Zandvoort et al., 2008, 2009). For a full review of CALC, please refer to Whitworth et al. (1998, 2007). The purpose of this study was to assess the impact of 6 months of MI, administered via CALC skills (hereafter referred to as the coaching intervention), on the body composition, self-esteem, self-efficacy, quality of life, physical activity, dietary intake, and functional health status of eight adults struggling with obesity (aged 35–55; BMI values greater than 30). A secondary purpose was to determine the impact of MI using CALC 6 months after the end of the intervention.

STUDY DESIGN AND METHODS

This study utilized a multiple-baseline, single-subject research design as explained by Kazdin (1982). This quasi-experimental design allows investigators to examine the pattern and stability of two or more behaviors within one participant or of a similar behavior across two or more participants before and during the intervention phase (Kazdin). This design is particularly useful when assessing change in behavior in a small number of participants because this methodology allows for new interventions to be observed on a small number of participants before it is tested on a larger sample size (Hayes, 1981). Eight women participated in this study, which allowed for an attrition rate of two participants, which was a feasible number for the study's single volunteer CPCC. The larger the number of baselines, the clearer the demonstration that the intervention was responsible for the reported change and the smaller the probability that changes between the baseline and intervention phase could be due to chance (Backman & Harris, 1999; Hayes, 1992; Kazdin, 1982). Typically, two baselines are a minimum requirement and for the present study, a minimum of four baselines was conducted to reduce the chance of coincidental extraneous events.

Recruitment

A sample of eight women was recruited via a local London Ontario newspaper. Participants were eligible to participate in the study if they were between the ages of 35 and 55, had a BMI equal to or greater than 30, spoke and read English fluently and continued under a physician's care for any comorbidities (e.g., diabetes). Thirty-five people contacted the researcher and the first eight who met the study's eligibility requirements became the study participants. Ethical approval was received from The University of Western Ontario's Office of Research Ethics.

Participants

All eight participants were White women between the ages of 35 and 55. All participants had a starting BMI greater than or equal to 30. Participants one, two, three, five, seven, and eight had comorbidities that presented after the study began and were under the supervision of a medical professional. The comorbidities included depression, steroid medication, cancer, asthma, and injuries from a car accident. The specific comorbidity is not attached to the corresponding participant to ensure confidentiality. A number of participants also experienced and received physician support for their symptoms related to menopause during the study.

Procedure

During the initial, face-to-face meeting between the lead researcher (CNK) and each participant, the nature of the study and the coaching intervention were explained and each participant received a letter of information for review. Once they agreed to participate (all eight agreed to participate), participants completed a consent form, and their height, weight, and WC (the measuring tape was placed along their belly button to ensure a reliable reading and the same digital scale was used throughout the entire study) were measured and they provided a $10 fee for each coaching session ($180 total). This fee helps to create a sense of personal buy-in from the client, which translates into participants showing up for their appointments on time and doing the work they commit to during their session. Unbeknown to participants, the money would be returned at the end of the intervention. Participants were then asked to complete a series of previously validated tools/questionnaires: specifically, the SF-36 Short Form Functional Health Status Questionnaire (Ware, 1997); the Rosenberg Self-Esteem Scale (Rosenberg, 1989); a self-efficacy questionnaire; the International Physical Activity Questionnaire (IPAQ); a 3-day food record (Chronic Disease and Injury Prevention Team, 2009), and the World Health Organization Quality of Life Scale (WHOQOL-BREF; World Health Organization, 1997). Once the questionnaires were completed, a 10-min semi-structured interview was conducted assessing qualitatively participants' experiences associated with being obese and the effect of these experiences on their lives. The qualitative components of the study are presented in detail elsewhere (Newnham-Kanas et al., 2011). To account for the repeated testing threat to internal validity (i.e., participants remembering correct answers or being conditioned to know the assessments; Cook & Campbell, 1979), baseline assessments (after the initial meeting) and assessments during the intervention consisted of having participants' weight and WC measured only.

Participants one, two, and three had their first coaching session after four baseline assessments, while participants four, five, and six had their first coaching session after five baseline assessments, and participants seven and eight had their first coaching session after six baseline assessments. Baseline assessments were scheduled 1 week apart while assessments during the intervention were spaced at 1-month intervals. To determine whether the intervention might be associated with any changes, participants were asked not to alter their behavior during the pre-intervention phase in order to capture an accurate portrayal of the stability of their weight and WC.

One CPCC known to the researchers donated her time for the study. The coach received her training and certification through the Coaches Training Institute. The CPCC was not involved in the initial meeting with participants and was not privy to any of the information collected during assessments. The only contact that the CPCC and the researchers had about the study was to confirm that participants attended their sessions. After the baseline phases, each participant met with the CPCC at the host university, for her first and only hour-long, face-to-face meeting. The lead researcher (CNK) then scheduled the remaining 35-minute telephone sessions. Each participant received one coaching session per week, after the first session, for 17 weeks. Missed appointments were rescheduled. All participants received all 18 sessions (no attrition occurred throughout the study) over 6 months. For each of these telephone sessions, it was each participant's responsibility to phone the CPCC at the designated appointment time (the CPCC telephoned one participant as a result of a telephone plan arrangement). At the beginning of each telephone coaching session, each participant was free to focus on any issue she wished, whether or not the issue seemed directly related to weight management; previous studies using CALC have demonstrated that obesity issues are connected to a wide variety of apparently unrelated issues extant in each client's life (Newnham-Kanas et al., 2008; van Zandvoort et al., 2008, 2009). The majority of questions and coaching content with a CPCC are unscripted open-ended questions, a primary characteristic of the CALC model (see Whitworth et al., 1998, 2007; van Zandvoort et al., 2008, for additional information about the content of coaching sessions).

At the conclusion of the intervention (i.e., at 6 months post initial coaching session), participants returned to the host university where they completed the same body composition, nutrition, quality-of-life, self-esteem, self-efficacy, physical activity measures, and their checks were returned. Participants returned 1 year post initial coaching session for a final weigh-in and WC measurement.

Data analysis and interpretation

BMI and WC for each participant during the baseline and intervention phase were graphed and analyzed using visual inspection (as described by Kazdin, 1982) to determine the reliability or consistency of the intervention effects. Results from the measures assessing physical activity, self-esteem, self-efficacy, functional health status, quality of life, and nutrition were examined to determine whether a clinically significant difference was attained using effect size. Effect size is a measure of the strength of the relationship between two variables. Cohen's d is defined as the difference between two means divided by a standard deviation for the data (Cohen, 1988).

Values used to determine the effect size for the nutrition data were calculated by inputting the food intake records into a food processor computer program (Food Processor SQL 10.5, ESHA Research Inc., Salem, OR) and an average of the 3 days was calculated. In addition, the number of vegetable and fruit servings according to Eating Well with Canada's Food Guide (EWCFG, 2007) was calculated manually (Health Canada).

RESULTS

Visual inspection

Weight BMI is an appropriate measure when assessing a change across participants because it provides a standard against which to compare (Centres for Disease Control and Prevention, 2011). However, when comparing within a participant, height is already a constant, leaving weight as the only independent variable. As a result, weight was reported in order to highlight the considerable changes these participants experienced. Participant one's weight decreased from a baseline score of 214.2 to 195.8 lbs at the end of the intervention phase. The level decreased 18.4 lbs from the end of baseline to the end of the intervention phase. Weight decreased consistently throughout the study period. However, participant one increased her weight by 14.4 lbs from the end of the intervention to the 6 months follow-up. After using visual inspection, there appeared to be a decrease in participant one's weight across the intervention phase with an increase at the 6 months follow-up, although still 5.4 lbs below her baseline weight. Weight data for participants one to eight are presented in Figure 17.1.

Participant two's weight decreased from a baseline score of 199.2 to 196.0 lbs at the end of the intervention phase. The level decreased 3.2 lbs from the end of baseline to the end of the intervention phase. Weight decreased consistently throughout the study period. However, participant two increased her weight by 11 lbs from the end of the intervention to the 6 months follow-up. Weight decreased slightly at the beginning of the intervention phase and then proceeded to increase half-way through the intervention. After using visual inspection, there appeared to be a very slight decrease in participant two's weight by the end of the intervention with a 6 lbs increase from baseline to the 6 months follow-up.

Participant three's weight decreased from a baseline score of 190.6 to 186.0 lbs at the end of the intervention phase. The level decreased 4.6 lbs from the end of baseline to the end of the intervention phase. Participant three gained 5 lbs from the end of the intervention phase to the 6 months follow-up, although only 0.6 lbs above her baseline weight. Weight decreased slightly throughout the study period. After using visual inspection, there appeared to be a small decrease in participant three's weight across the intervention phase.

Participant four's weight decreased from a baseline score of 172.2 to 143.0 lbs at the end of the intervention phase. The level decreased 29.2 lbs from the end of baseline to the end of the intervention phase. Participant four lost an additional 2 lbs from the end of the intervention phase to the 6 months follow-up. Participant four lost a total of 30 lbs from her baseline weight to the 6 months follow-up. After using visual inspection, there appeared to be a steady and steep decrease in participant four's weight throughout the intervention phase while continuing to maintain her weight from the end of the intervention to the 6 months follow-up.

Participant five's weight decreased from a baseline score of 211.0 to 194.8 lbs at the end of the intervention phase. The level decreased 16.2 lbs from the end of baseline to the end of the intervention phase. Participant five lost an additional 0.6 lbs from the end of the intervention phase to the 6 months follow-up. Participant five lost a total of 19.2 lbs from her baseline weight to the 6 months follow-up. After using visual inspection, there appeared to be a decrease in participant five's weight across the baseline and intervention phases with continued maintenance of her weight from the end of the intervention to the 6 months follow-up.

Participant six's weight decreased from a baseline score of 291.4 to 254.0 lbs at the end of the intervention phase. The level decreased 37.4 lbs from the end of baseline to the end of the intervention phase. Participant six lost an additional 1 lbs from the end of the intervention phase to the 6 months follow-up. Weight decreased consistently throughout the intervention phase. Participant six lost a total of 40 lbs from her baseline weight to the 6 months follow-up. After using visual inspection, there appeared to be a steady decrease in participant six's weight throughout the intervention phase

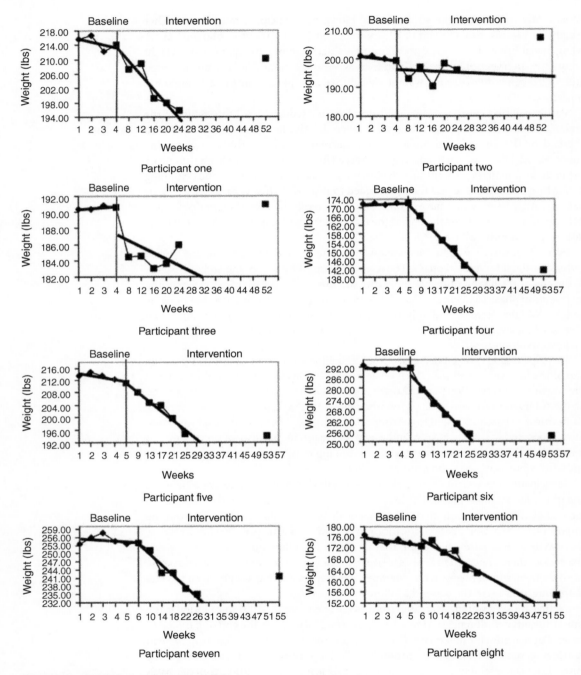

Figure 17.1 *Weight for Participants One to Eight*
Note. The vertical lines indicate the period prior to the intervention's implementation (baseline phase) and when it was implemented (intervention phase).

with a continued maintenance of the weight lost from the end of the intervention phase to the 6 months follow-up.

Participant seven's weight decreased from a baseline score of 254.0 to 235.2 lbs at the end of the intervention phase. The level decreased 18.8 lbs from the end of baseline to the end of the intervention phase. Participant seven gained an additional 6.4 lbs from the end of the intervention phase to the 6 months follow-up. After using visual inspection, there appeared to be a steady decrease in participant seven's weight throughout the intervention phase with an increase in weight from the end of the intervention to the 6 months follow-up, although still 12 lbs below her baseline weight.

Participant eight's weight decreased from a baseline score of 172.8 lbs to a score of 163.0 lbs at the end of the intervention phase. The level decreased 9.8 lbs from the end of baseline to the end of the intervention phase. Participant eight lost an additional 8.2 lbs from the end of the intervention phase to the 6 months follow-up. Participant eight lost a total of 22.2 lbs from her baseline weight to the 6 months follow-up. After using visual inspection, there appeared to be a steady decrease in participant eight's weight throughout the intervention phase with a continued decrease in weight from the end of the intervention to the 6 months follow-up.

To summarize, weight decreased for all participants from baseline to the end of the intervention with a more pronounced decrease for participants one, four, five, six, seven, and eight. Three participants gained part of their weight back that was lost during the 6 months follow-up and five participants maintained and continued to lose additional weight at the 6 months follow-up.

Waist circumference (WC)

Participant one's WC decreased from a baseline score of 43.7 in to a score of 42.0 in at the end of the intervention phase. The level decreased 1.7 in. from the end of baseline to the end of the intervention phase. Participant one maintained her WC from the end of the intervention phase to the 6 months follow-up. After using visual inspection, there appeared to be a decrease in participant one's WC throughout the intervention phase while maintaining her WC from the end of the intervention to the 6 months follow-up. Waist circumference data for participants one, two, three, four, five, six, seven, and eight are presented in Figure 17.2.

Participant two's WC did not change from a baseline score of 39.0 in. to 39.0 in. at the end of the intervention phase. Participant two maintained her WC from the end of the intervention phase to the 6 months follow-up. After applying visual inspection, there appeared to be a slight decrease in participant two's WC throughout the early intervention phase with an increase near the end of the intervention and no change from the end of the intervention to the 6 months follow-up.

Participant three's WC decreased from a baseline score of 42.7 in. to 42.0 in. at the end of the intervention phase. The level decreased by 0.7 in. from the end of baseline to the end of the intervention phase. Participant three maintained her WC from the end of the intervention phase to the 6 months follow-up. After applying visual inspection, there appeared to be a decrease in WC from baseline to the

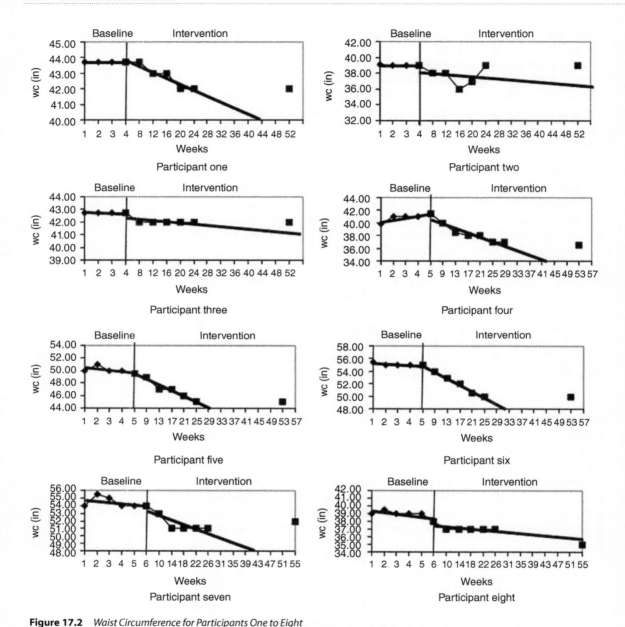

Figure 17.2 *Waist Circumference for Participants One to Eight*
Note. The vertical lines indicate the period prior to the intervention's implementation (baseline phase) and when it was implemented (intervention phase).

beginning of the intervention phase with WC remaining constant throughout the majority of the intervention phase and no change was detected from the end of the intervention to the 6 months follow-up. Participant four's WC decreased from a baseline score of 41.5 in. to 37 in. at the end of the intervention phase. The level decreased by 4.5 in. from the end of baseline to the end of the intervention phase. Participant four decreased her WC by 0.5 in. from the end of the intervention phase to the 6 months follow-up. After applying visual inspection, there appeared to be a decrease in participant four's WC throughout the intervention phase with a slight decrease from the end of the intervention to the 6 months follow-up. Participant five's WC decreased from a baseline score of 49.5 in. to 45 in. at the end of the intervention phase. The level decreased by 4.5 in. from the end of baseline to the end of the intervention phase. Participant five maintained her WC from the end of the intervention phase to the 6 months follow-up. After applying visual inspection, there appeared to be a sharp decrease in participant five's WC throughout the intervention phase and no change was detected from the end of the intervention phase to the 6 months follow-up.

Participant six's WC decreased from a baseline score of 55 in. to 50 in. at the end of the intervention phase. The level decreased by 5.0 in. from the end of baseline to the end of the intervention phase. Participant six maintained her WC from the end of the intervention phase to the 6 months follow-up. After applying visual inspection, there appeared to be a sharp decrease in participant six's WC throughout the intervention phase with no change from the end of the intervention to the 6 months follow-up. It should be noted that participant six could not make time to come in for her final assessment. Her weight and WC were self-reported.

Participant seven's WC decreased from a baseline score of 54 in. to a score of 51 in. at the end of the intervention phase. The level decreased by 3.0 in. from the end of baseline to the end of the intervention phase. Participant seven increased her WC from the end of the intervention to the 6 months follow-up by 1.0 in. After applying visual inspection, there appeared to be a steady decrease in participant seven's WC throughout the intervention phase and a small increase from the end of the intervention to the 6 months follow-up.

Participant eight's WC decreased from a baseline score of 38.0 in. to 37.0 in. at the end of the intervention phase. The level decreased 1.0 in. from the end of baseline to the end of the intervention phase. Participant eight continued to decrease her WC by 2.0 in. from the end of the intervention phase to the 6 months follow-up. After applying visual inspection, there appeared to be a decrease in participant eight's WC when the intervention was applied and remained constant throughout the intervention phase with a continued decrease from the end of the intervention to the 6 months follow-up.

To summarize, WC decreased for participants one, four, five, six, seven, and eight and remained stable for participants two and three. This demonstrates a trend toward a decrease in WC.

CLINICAL SIGNIFICANCE

Pre-post changes in self-esteem, functional health status, quality of life, self-efficacy, physical activity, and nutrition were evaluated for clinical significance by assessing statistical change through an examination of effect size using Cohen's d (Cohen, 1988).

Self-esteem

Participants' scores on the Rosenberg Self-Esteem Scale revealed a large effect (i.e., increase) in self-esteem (Cohen's $d = 1.85$). Collectively, the effect size indicates a clinically significant improvement in participants' self-esteem after completing the coaching intervention.

Functional health status

Participants' scores on the overall health dimension of the SF-36 revealed a considerable increase (i.e., large effect) in overall health status (Cohen's $d = 1.34$). Participants' scores on the physical health dimension of the SF-36 revealed an increase (i.e., large effect) in overall physical health status (Cohen's $d = 0.95$). Participants' scores on the mental health dimension of the SF-36 revealed a considerable increase (i.e., large effect) in overall mental health status (Cohen's $d = 1.89$). Collectively, the effect sizes for physical, mental, and overall health indicate a clinically significant improvement in participants' health status after completion of the coaching intervention.

Quality of life (QOL)

Participants' scores on the overall quality of life (QOL) on the WHOQOL-Bref revealed a moderate to large effect in overall QOL status (Cohen's $d = 0.72$). Participants' scores on the overall health dimension revealed a considerable increase (i.e., large effect) in overall health status (Cohen's $d = 1.21$). Participants' scores on the physical dimension revealed a considerable increase (i.e., large effect) in overall physical health status (Cohen's $d = 1.44$). Participants' scores on the psychological dimension revealed a considerable increase in overall psychological health status (Cohen's $d = 2.36$). Participants' scores on the overall social dimension revealed a moderate increase in overall social status (Cohen's $d = 0.49$). Participants' scores on the environmental dimension revealed a small to moderate effect in overall environmental status (Cohen's $d = 0.38$). Collectively, the effect sizes for QOL dimensions indicate a clinically significant improvement in participants' overall QOL after finishing the coaching intervention.

Self-efficacy

Participants' scores on the self-efficacy barriers to nutrition questionnaire revealed an increase (i.e., large effect) in participants' ability to manage barriers to healthy nutrition (Cohen's $d = 0.77$). Participants' scores on the barriers to physical activity questionnaire revealed a considerable increase in participants' ability to handle barriers to physical activity (Cohen's $d = 1.22$). Participants' scores on the achieving tasks in physical activity questionnaire revealed a moderate increase (i.e., medium effect) in participants' ability to achieve tasks in physical activity (Cohen's $d = 0.51$). Collectively, the effect sizes for self-efficacy indicate a clinically significant improvement in participants' overall self-efficacy after completing the coaching intervention.

Physical activity

Participants' scores on the IPAQ revealed a moderate increase (i.e., medium effect) in participants' level of physical activity (Cohen's $d = 0.6$). The effect size for physical activity does not indicate a clinically significant improvement in participants' overall physical activity level after completing the coaching intervention.

Nutrition

Participants' food records revealed a large increase (i.e., large effect) in vegetables and fruits (Cohen's $d = 1.06$) and protein (Cohen's $d = 1.30$) and a large decrease in sodium (Cohen's $d = -1.53$), total calories (Cohen's $d = -1.50$), and saturated fat (Cohen's $d = -1.08$). There was a moderate decrease (i.e., medium effect) in fiber (Cohen's $d = -0.51$) and total fat (Cohen's $d = -0.52$) and a small to moderate decrease (i.e., small to medium effect) in cholesterol (Cohen's $d = -0.39$). The decrease in carbohydrates was too small to even classify as a small effect (Cohen's $d = -0.04$).

DISCUSSION

The main purpose of this study was to determine the effectiveness of MI using CALC skills as an intervention for decreasing obesity. The secondary purpose was to examine the effect of MI on participants' self-esteem, functional health status, quality of life, self-efficacy, physical activity, and nutrition behaviors.

Weight decreased for all participants directly following the 6 months of coaching. At the 6 months follow-up, participants four, five, six, and eight continued to decrease or maintain their weight. Participants one, two, three, and seven gained weight at the 6 months follow-up but participants one and seven were still below their baseline weight. It should be noted that of the three participants who regained weight, one participant reported an increase in asthma symptoms that reduced her ability to exercise consistently and two participants reported an injury from a car accident as factors that influenced their weight. Based on Shaw, O'Rourke, Del Mar, and Kenardy's (2007) literature review examining psychological interventions for treating obesity, and Douketis, Macie, Thabane, and Williamson's (2005) systematic review that examined methods used for weight loss, these results are not surprising. Both sets of researchers report that longer behavioral interventions result in significantly greater weight loss than shorter behavioral treatments. However, these results are surprising to the researchers of the current study due to the participants' reported comorbidities. One participant was using Prednisone, a steroidal drug used to treat her asthma. Prednisone's side effects include weight gain, fatigue or weakness, joint pain, and severe swelling (Senecal, 1998). In a study conducted by Everdingen, Jacobs, Siewertsz van Reesema, and Bijlsma (2002) that assessed the impact of Prednisone on patients with early active rheumatoid arthritis, the treatment group who received Prednisone had a significant increase ($p = 0.001$) in weight gain with no change in weight in the placebo group. One participant was dealing with depression. According to the Canadian Mental Health Association (2010), depressed individuals have a tendency to eat more, experience a loss of energy, and often feel tired. Three participants were going through menopause and presented symptoms that might have influenced weight, inclusive of aching joints; chronic fatigue; sweet, caffeine, junk food, and carbohydrate cravings; depression and anxiety; dizziness; weight gain; and sleep problems (Greendale & Judd, 1993). One participant received radiation therapy for detected cancerous cells. Radiation side effects include anxiety and depression, changes in appetite, fatigue, and sleep disturbances (Canadian Cancer Society, 2010). Moreover, this same participant quit smoking during the intervention, which can result in an increased appetite, problems sleeping, and slight social withdrawal (American Cancer Society, 2010). Given these comorbidities, it was not expected that participants would decrease their weight. However, participants one, four, five, six, seven, and eight lost as little as 9.8 pounds and as much as 37.4 pounds. In a similar study conducted by Newnham-Kanas et al. (2008), it was suggested that coaching continuing for a longer period of time may garner greater weight loss. Directly following the final coaching session, three participants were no longer obese and two participants moved from Class II obesity to Class I, and Class III obesity to Class II. At the end of the 6 months follow-up, two participants were no longer obese and one participant moved from Class III to Class II. The current study's results highlight the effectiveness of MI using CALC skills for 6 months as a viable intervention for losing weight, even when comorbidities and psychological distress contributing to and/or resulting from obesity are present that may impact the amount of weight lost.

Waist circumference decreased for participants one, three, five, six, seven, and eight directly following the intervention. There was no change in WC for participant two. Waist circumference continued to decrease for participants one and eight at the 6 months follow-up. Participants three, five, and six maintained their WC from the end of the intervention, and participant seven increased her WC but it was lower than her baseline measurement. Waist circumference might have resulted from an increase in physical activity and healthier eating habits as reported in the exit interview. These results are particularly important given that WC is perceived as a more accurate representation of excess body fat which, in turn, is a good predictor of all-cause mortality in middle-aged men and women (Bigaard et al., 2005; Janssen et al., 2004).

Self-esteem increased for participants with a large effect detected. This result is analogous to results reported by a similar study conducted by Newnham-Kanas et al. (2008) and van Zandvoort et al. (2008). Gover (1991) explains that one way to build self-esteem is to become aware of and challenge the individual's inner critic. In coaching, we refer to this inner critic as the saboteur and identifying and confronting the thoughts associated with the saboteur were skills reportedly used by the coach during participants' coaching sessions. Self-concept is integral to increased self-esteem and is determined by the self-talk or internal thoughts the individual has about themselves. By challenging the negative self-talk and thoughts, it is presumed that an individual will be able to set more challenging goals and suggest solutions to their problems (Hall, 2007). In balance coaching, a specific form of CALC, the coach works with clients to envision new perspectives to help them become aware of their current perspective and how to create action plans to generate new perspectives and new ways of looking at life events and challenges (Whitworth et al., 1998, 2007). As reported by the coach of the current study (Newnham-Kanas et al., 2011), balance coaching was one of the styles of coaching used predominately with participants. Increased self-esteem allows individuals to feel worthwhile, capable of helping themselves, and optimistic about the future (Gover, 1991). All of these traits are necessary for weight loss to be possible and may be one reason participants in the current study lost a considerable amount of weight and for some, were able to maintain and even further reduce that weight 6 months later.

Functional health status (FHS) increased for participants with a large effect detected for the overall, physical, and mental dimensions of health. These findings were also reported in studies conducted by Newnham-Kanas et al. (2008) and van Zandvoort et al. (2008). Stress has been reported as an important risk factor for weight loss and maintenance (Elfhag & Rossner, 2005). Additionally, individuals who tend to regain weight have a tendency to increase their eating habits to cope with the stress (Elfhag & Rossner, 2005). All of the participants in the current study struggled with their weight for many years and might fit within that paradigm. These increased FHS results after the coaching sessions suggest that MI applied via CALC aided participants in finding solutions to manage their stress and in turn adopt healthy behaviors that improved their sense of well-being. These results are particularly surprising given the number of comorbidities and resulting stress these participants were dealing with prior to and during the intervention.

Participants' overall QOL increased with a large effect detected for overall, physical, and psychological QOL dimensions. A moderate and small to moderate effect was detected for social and environmental dimensions. Research confirms that increased weight decreases health-related QOL, which would contribute to explaining the mechanism by which participants QOL increased (Jia & Lubetkin, 2005; Pinhas-Hamiel et al., 2005). These results are particularly surprising because it has been reported that as individuals increase in age, their physical QOL scores decrease (Zabelina, Erickson, & Kolotkin, 2009). It is not surprising that psychological dimensions increased as self-esteem and learning to cope with life stressors are key components of the psychological dimension, which increased at the end of the coaching intervention (WHO-QOL-BREF; World Health Organization, 1997). Although social and environment QOL increased moderately, participants reported in their exit interview and focus group (Newnham-Kanas, et al., 2011) that they had been stepping outside of their comfort zone by joining social clubs (e.g., book clubs) and reuniting with old friends.

Participants were viewed by the coach as naturally creative, resourceful, and whole— a cornerstone of the co-active model (Whitworth et al., 2007). In other words, the coach viewed participants as having the capability to find their own solutions to problems and strong enough to work through difficult moments in order to deepen their learning and/or commit to some specific behavioral action to ameliorate their health concern (reflective of another co-active cornerstone). Given the increase in nutrition barriers, physical activity barriers, and physical activity-related task self-efficacy (large and medium effect sizes detected) perceived by participants over the duration of the intervention, it is evident that participants increased their belief and ability to conquer obstacles such as working through issues that were impeding their ability to lose weight, increasing their physical activity (as reported in their post-interviews; Newnham-Kanas et al., 2011), and making healthier nutritional changes. Co-active life coaching tools that support clients in engaging in healthful actions and increasing self-acceptance are some of the reasons MI using CALC skills is believed to be an intervention that can have a more permanent effect on weight loss. These self-efficacy results are different from the study conducted by Newnham-Kanas et al. (2008); our interpretation is that the difference in the present study is due to increasing the number of coaching sessions and the concomitant link to increased self-efficacy scores.

Although a moderate effect size was reported for physical activity, it should be emphasized that even with the comorbidities listed above, participants still found ways to increase their physical activity. As well, six of the eight participants shared in the exit interview that they had to work through "emotional baggage" before they could even contemplate integrating physical activity into their daily lives. Physical activity did increase in this study compared with the results report by Newnham-Kanas et al. (2008); this indicates that increasing the number of coaching sessions might aid in increasing participants' frequency of engaging in healthful behaviors.

Participants reported a large reduction in energy intake of approximately 900 kcal per day, which likely contributed significantly to the observed weight loss. This large reduction in overall energy intake may be attributed to the increase (large effects) in protein and vegetable and fruit intake with a simultaneous reduction in total fat intake—all of which may have enhanced the satiety value of participants' diets. In particular, a diet containing 25% of total energy intake (TEI) from protein, which is similar to that observed in the present study, has demonstrated a spontaneous reduction in energy intake of about 400 kcal per day (Skov, Toubro, Ronn, Holm, & Astrup, 1999). Furthermore, the large increase in vegetable and fruit intake in combination with reductions in total fat, saturated fat, cholesterol, and sodium may reduce participants' risk of developing future chronic diseases, such as Type 2 diabetes and cardiovascular diseases (Institute of Medicine, 2005). With respect to sodium alone, it is estimated that a 1,800 mg/d reduction in sodium intake, which is approximately 50% of what our participants achieved, could reduce systolic and diastolic blood pressure by 5.06 and 27 mmHg respectively and may reduce the overall prevalence of hypertension by 30% (Joffres, Campbell, Manns, & Tu, 2007). It is noteworthy that fiber intake was moderately reduced throughout the study. This is an undesirable finding, as fiber intake is negatively associated with chronic disease development (Institute of Medicine). In future studies, some nutritional education may be warranted to ensure that participants meet their recommended intake of nutrients known to contribute to health and chronic disease prevention.

LIMITATIONS

There are several limitations to the current study. Although recruitment methods were used to attract a variety of individuals, the final group of participants was homogenous in sex and ethnicity. Because the study had only one coach and, due to the multiple-baseline, single-subject design, a small sample size was necessary. As a result of these two factors, these results are not representative of individuals struggling with obesity aged 35–55. Another limitation was the lack of a control group, which could have strengthened internal validity thereby increasing confidence that the measured effects could be attributed to the intervention. However, it should be noted that the current study incorporated suggestions reported by Newnham-Kanas et al. (2008) by standardizing the number of coaching sessions for each participant (all participants completed 18 coaching sessions) and the number of coaching sessions increased from 8 weeks to 6 months, and follow-up continued to 1 year post-baseline.

Even though monthly weigh-in sessions may be viewed as an intervention in and of itself, this is unlikely for the current study. Participants were not shown their weight until the final weigh-in after all coaching sessions were complete. As well, none of the participants in the exit interview reported that the weigh-ins had any effect (positive or negative) on their final weight outcome.

Given the results of the current study, it is apparent that increasing the number of coaching sessions has a beneficial effect on weight loss. Based on suggestions from participants, it is recommended that coaching continues for at least 1 year due to the multiplicity of areas in participants' lives that obesity affects, and that affect obesity. Although a significant amount of weight was lost in only 6 months, it has been reported that dietary/lifestyle therapy can require 2–4 years to maintain weight loss (Douketis et al., 2005). It is also recommended that a larger, more representative sample of participants be used in conjunction with a control group to augment internal validity. Currently, there are two other studies (Newnham-Kanas et al., 2008; van Zandvoort et al., 2008) that have reported MI using CALC skills as an effective intervention for obesity. Thus, MI's effectiveness has been documented and thereby points the way toward integrating formal physical activity and nutritional programs in conjunction with MI to determine what impact these added programs would have on obesity.

CONCLUSIONS

Despite these limitations and suggestions, the following conclusions can be drawn from the reported results:

1. MI applied via CALC was associated with a trend toward a decrease in weight and WC.
2. MI applied via CALC was associated with a trend toward maintaining or continuing to decrease weight and WC 6 months after the last coaching session.

3. MI applied via CALC was associated with clinically significant increases in self-esteem.

4. MI applied via CALC was associated with clinically significant increases in FHS.

5. MI applied via CALC was associated with clinically significant increases in quality of life.

6. MI applied via CALC was associated with clinically significant increases in self-efficacy.

7. MI applied via CALC was associated with a moderately detected increase in physical activity.

As obesity levels continue to rise in Canada and around the world, it is crucial that research continues to test new strategies aimed at helping individuals decrease their weight. As research persists, a common theme of incorporating behavioral treatments with traditional physical activity and nutrition programs is emphasized as vital in aiding obese individuals in decreasing their weight (Foster, Makris, & Bailer, 2005; Kausman & Bruere, 2006). Specifically, treatments that empower individuals to find solutions to their own problems, make healthier choices, and learn to cope with life stressors are deemed effective strategies in losing and maintaining weight (Elfhag & Rossner, 2005; Kausman & Bruere, 2006). Motivational interviewing using CALC skills is one such intervention and it is an effective tool in aiding individuals to conquer their battle with weight.

REFERENCES

Ajzen, I. (1988). *Attitudes, personality, and behaviour*. Chicago: Dorsey Press.

American Cancer Society. (2010). *Guide to quitting smoking*. Retrieved from www.cancer.org/Healthy/StayAwayfromTobacco/GuidetoQuittingSmoking/guide-to-quitting-smoking

Backman, C. L., & Harris, S. R. (1999). Case studies, single-subject research, and N of 1 randomised trials: Comparisons and contrast. *American Journal of Physical Medicine & Rehabilitation, 78*(2), 170–176.

Bandura, A. (1977). Self-efficacy: Toward a unifying theory of behavioural change. *Psychological Review, 84*(2), 191–215.

Bigaard, J., Frederiksen, K., Tjonneland, A., Thomsen, B. L., Overvad, K., Heitmann, B. L., et al. (2005). Waist circumference and body composition in relation to all-cause mortality in middleaged men and women. *International Journal of Obesity, 29*, 778–784.

Brown, J. M., & Miller, W. R. (1993). Impact of motivational interviewing on participation and outcome in residential alcoholism treatment. *Psychology of Addictive Behaviours, 7*(4), 211–218.

Canadian Cancer Society. (February, 2010). *Side effects of radiation therapy*. Retrieved from http://www.cancer.ca/Canada-wide/About percent20cancer/Treatment/Radiation/Side percent20effectspercent20ofpercent20radiation percent20therapy.aspx?sc_lang=en

Canadian Mental Health Association. (2010). *Depression*. Retrieved from http://www.cmha.ca/bins/content_page.asp? cid=3–86–87&lang=1

Centre for Disease Control and Prevention. (2011). *Healthy weight – it's not a diet, it's a lifestyle!* Retrieved from http://www.cdc.gov/healthyweight/assessing bmi/adult_bmi/index.html

Cohen, J. (1988). *Statistical power analysis for the behavioral sciences* (2nd ed.). Hillsdale, NJ: Lawrence Erlbaum.

Cook, T. D., & Campbell, D. T. (1979). *Quasi-experimentation: Design and analysis for field settings*. Chicago: Rand McNally.

Douketis, J. D., Macie, C., Thabane, L., & Williamson, D. F. (2005). Systematic review of long-term weight loss studies in obese adults: Clinical significance and applicability to clinical practice. *International Journal of Obesity, 29*, 1153–1167.

Egan, G. (1997). *The skilled helper: A problem-management approach to helping* (6th ed.). Pacific Grove: Brooks/Cole.

Elfhag, K., & Rossner, S. (2005). Who succeeds in maintaining weight loss? A conceptual review of factors associated with weight loss maintenance and weight regain. *Obesity Reviews, 6*, 68–85.

Everdingen, A. A., Jacobs, J. W. G., Siewertsz van Reesema, D. R., & Bijlsma, J. W. J. (2002). Low-dose prednisone therapy for patients with early active rheumatoid arthritis: Clinical efficacy, disease modifying properties, and side effects: A randomised, double-blind, placebo-controlled clinical trial. *Annals of Internal Medicine, 136*(1), 1–12.

Fishbein, M., & Ajzen, I. (1975). *Belief, attitude, intention and behaviour: An introduction to theory and research*. Reading, MA: Addison-Wesley.

Foster, G. D., Makris, A. P., & Bailer, B. A. (2005). Behavioural treatment of obesity. *The American Journal of Clinical Nutrition, 82*(1), 2305–2355.

Freedhoff, Y., & Sharma, A. M. (2010). *Best weight: a practical guide to office-based obesity management*. Canadian Obesity Network.

Gorczynski, P., Morrow, D., & Irwin, J. D. (2008). The impact of co-active coaching on the physical activity levels of children. *International Journal of Evidence-Based Coaching and Mentoring, 6*(2), 13–26.

Gover, J. (1991). *Building self-efficacy*. Retrieved January 29, 2011, from http://eric.ed.gov/PDFS/ED373298.pdf

Grant, A. M., & Zackon, R. (2004). Executive, workplace and life coaching: Findings from a large-scale survey of International Coach Federation members. *International Journal of Evidence Based Coaching and Mentoring, 2*(2), 1–15.

Greendale, G. A., & Judd, H. L. (1993). The menopause: Health implications and clinical management. *Journal of the American Geriatrics Society, 41*, 426–436.

Hardeman, W., Griffin, S., Johnston, M., Kinmonth, A. L., & Wareham, N. J. (2000). Interventions to prevent weight gain: A systematic review of psychological models and behaviour change methods. *International Journal of Obesity and Related Metabolic Disorders, 24*(2), 131–143.

Hayes, S. C. (1981). Single case experimental design and empirical clinical practice. In A. E. Kazdin (Ed.), *Methodological issues and strategies in clinical research* (2nd ed.). Washington, DC: American Psychological Association.

Health Canada. (2007). *Eating well with Canada's food guide: A resource for educators and communicators*. Ottawa: HC Pub 4667.

Institute of Medicine. (2005). *Dietary reference intakes for energy, carbohydrates, fibre, fat, fatty acids, cholesterol, protein and amino acids*. Washington, DC: National Academy Press.

Irwin, J. D., & Morrow, D. (2005). Health promotion theory in practice: An analysis of co-active coaching. *International Journal of Evidence-Based Coaching and Mentoring, 3*(1), 29–38.

Janssen, I., Heymsfield, S. B., & Ross, R. (2002). Application of simple anthropometry in the assessment of health risk: Implications for the Canadian physical activity, fitness and lifestyle appraisal. *Canadian Journal of Applied Physiology, 27*(4), 396–414.

Janssen, I., Katzmarzyk, P. T., & Ross, R. (2002). Body mass index, waist circumference, and health risk: Evidence in support of current National Institutes of Health guidelines. *Archives of Internal Medicine, 162*(18), 2074–2079.

Janssen, I., Katzmarzyk, P. T., & Ross, R. (2004). Waist circumference and not body mass index explains obesity-related health risk. *American Journal of Clinical Nutrition, 79*(3), 379–384.

Jia, H., & Lubetkin, E. (2005). The impact of obesity on health-related quality-of-life in the general adult US population. *Journal of Public Health, 27*(2), 156–164.

Joffres, M. R., Campbell, N. R. C., Manns, B., & Tu, K. (2007). Estimate of the benefits of a population-based reduction in dietary sodium additives on hypertension and its related health care costs in Canada. *Canadian Journal of Cardiology, 23*, 437–443.

Kanfer, F. H. (1970). Self-regulation: Research, issues, and speculation. In C. Neuringer & J. L. Michael (Eds.), *Behaviour modification in clinical psychology*. New York: Appleton Century-Crofts.

Kausman, R., & Bruere, T. (2006). If not dieting, now what? *Australian Family Physician, 35*(8), 572–575.

Kazdin, A. E. (1982). *Single-case research designs: Methods for clinical and applied settings*. New York: Oxford University Press.

London Health Unit. (2009). *Three-day food record*. Middlesex: Chronic Disease and Injury Prevention Team.

Mesters, I. (2009). Motivational interviewing: Hype or hope? *Chronic Illness, 5*(3), 3–6.

Miller, W. R. (1998). Toward a motivational definition and understanding of addiction. *Motivational Interviewing Newsletter for Trainers, 5*(3), 2–6.

Miller, W. R., & Rollnick, S. (2002). *Motivational interviewing: Preparing people to change addictive behaviour*. New York: The Guilford Press.

Miller, W. R., Yahne, C. E., & Tonigan, S. J. (2003). Motivational interviewing in drug abuse services: A randomised trial. *Journal of Consulting and Clinical Psychology, 71*(4), 754–763.

Newnham-Kanas, C., Irwin, J. D., & Morrow, D. (2008). Life coaching as an intervention for individuals with obesity. *International Journal of Evidence-Based Coaching and Mentoring, 6*(2), 1–12.

Newnham-Kanas, C., Irwin, J. D., & Morrow, D. (2011). Findings from a global sample of certified professional co-active coaches. *International Journal of Evidence-Based Coaching and Mentoring, 9*(2), 23–36.

Newnham-Kanas, C., Morrow, D., & Irwin, J. D. (2010). A functional juxtaposition of three methods for health behaviour change: Motivational interviewing, coaching, and skilled helping. *International Journal of Evidence-Based Coaching and Mentoring, 8*(2), 27–48.

Newnham-Kanas, C. E., Gorczynski, P., Irwin, J. D., & Morrow, D. (2009). Annotated bibliography of life coaching and health research. *International Journal of Evidence-Based Coaching and Mentoring, 6*(2), 1–12.

Pinhas-Hamiel, O., Singer, S., Pilpel, N., Fradkin, A., Modan, D., & Reichman, B. (2005). Health-related quality of life among children and adolescents: Associations with obesity. *International Journal of Obesity*, 1–6.

Rosenberg, M. (1989). *Society and the adolescent self-image* (Rev. ed.). Middletown, CT: Wesleyan University Press.

Ryan, R. M., & Deci, E. L. (2000). Self-determination theory and the facilitation of intrinsic motivation, social development, and well-being. *American Psychologist, 55*(1), 68–78.

Senecal, J-L. (1998). *Lupus: The disease with a thousand faces* (4th ed.). Retrieved January 29, 2011, from http://www.lupuscanada.org/english/living/1000faces_appen2.html

Shaw, K., O'Rourke, P., Del Mar, C., & Kenardy, J. (2007). Psychological interventions for overweight or obesity (review). *Cochrane Database of Systematic Reviews*, (2), CD003818. doi:10.1002/14651858.CD003818.pub2

Shields, M., Tremblay, M. S., Laviolette, M., Craig, C. L., & Janssen, I. (2010). Fitness of Canadian adults: Results from the 2007–2009 Canadian health measures survey. *Health Reports* (Statistics Canada, Catalogue no. 82–003–XPE), *21*(1), 1–15.

Skov, A. R., Toubro, S., Ronn, B., Holm, L., & Astrup, A. (1999). Randomised trial on protein vs. carbohydrate in ad libitum fat reduced diet for the treatment of obesity. *International Journal of Obesity, 23*, 528–536.

Slevin, E. (2004). High intensity counselling or behavioural interventions can result in moderate weight loss. *Evidence-Based Health Care and Public Health, 8*(3), 136–138.

Stice, E., Presnell, K., & Shaw, H. (2005). Psychological and behavioural risk factors of obesity onset in adolescent girls: A prospective study. *Journal of Consulting and Clinical Psychology, 73*(2), 195–202.

Tjepkema, M. (2006). Adult obesity. *Health Reports (Statistics Canada, Catalogue 82–003),, 17*(3), 9–25.

van Zandvoort, M. M., Irwin, J. D., & Morrow, D. (2008). Co-active coaching as an intervention for obesity among female university students. *International Coaching Psychology Review, 3*(3), 191–206.

van Zandvoort, M. M., Irwin, J. D., & Morrow, D. (2009). The impact of co-active life coaching on female university students with obesity. *International Journal of Evidence-Based Coaching and Mentoring, 7*(1), 104–118.

Ware, J. D. (1997). *SF–36 health survey: Manual & interpretation guide*. Boston, MA: The Medical Outcomes Trust.

Whitworth, L., Kimsey-House, K., Kimsey-House, H., & Sandahl, P. (1998). *Co-active coaching: New skills for coaching people toward success in work and life*. California: Davis-Black Publishing.

Whitworth, L., Kimsey-House, K., Kimsey-House, H., & Sandahl, P. (2007). *Co-active coaching: New skills for coaching people toward success in work and life* (2nd ed.). California: Davis-Black Publishing.

World Health Organization. (1997). *WHOQOL Measuring quality of life*. Retrieved September 2009, from http://www.who.int/mental_health/media/68.pdf

World Health Organization. (2006). *Obesity and overweight*. Retrieved from http://www.who.int/mediacentre/factsheets/fs311/en/index.html

Zabelina, D. L., Erickson, A. L., & Kolotkin, R. L. (2009). The effect of age on weight-related quality of life in overweight and obese individuals. *Obesity, 17*(7), 1410–1413.

Section V
Insights from Mixed-Methods Coaching Psychology Research

Jonathan Passmore and David Tee

At present, there is not a sizable literature within coaching psychology focused on the merits of mixed-methods research as a distinct methodology. It is hoped that the gathering of mixed-methods coaching psychology papers in this section may start to redress this imbalance, as equivalent books and papers dedicated to considering mixed methods do exist within coaching-related disciplines (CRDs), such as counseling or organizational research (see Heppner, Kivlighan, & Wampold, 1999; Spencer, 2006).

Mixed methods has been defined as

> the collection or analysis of both quantitative and qualitative data in a single study in which the data are collected concurrently or sequentially, are given a priority, and involve the integration of the data at one or more stages in the process of research (Cresswell, Plano Clark, Gutmann, & Hanson, 2003, p. 212).

Molina-Azorin, Bergh, Corley, and Ketchen (2017) stress the importance of distinguishing between multimethod and mixed methods: whilst multimethod studies may make use of multiple qualitative or multiple quantitative methods within a single study, mixed-methods research will feature studies that include both types of data, "providing opportunities to meaningfully engage with difference" (p. 180). Within mixed methods, Tashakkori and Cresswell (2007) suggest a further distinction: methodology (integrating two approaches to research) and methods (collecting and analyzing two types of data).

Hanson, Cresswell, Plano Clark, Petska, and Cresswell (2005) cite Campbell and Fiske (1959) as the key study in bringing research that uses multiple forms of data into the research community spotlight. As the adoption of mixed-methods research has grown in the decades since 1959, the key argument for this distinct methodology is that the integration or triangulation of different approaches has the potential to enrich our understanding of phenomena in a manner that neither quantitative nor qualitative designs on their own can do (Molina-Azorin et al., 2017). Hanson et al. (2005) suggest, for example, that mixed methods allow study results to be generalized from a sample to a population, whilst simultaneously creating a richer, deeper understanding of the phenomenon under investigation.

The use of both qualitative and quantitative methods within studies in coaching psychology reflects some of the larger debates concerning mixed methods. For instance, Stewart, Palmer, Wilkin, and Kerrin (2008) use the findings of one qualitative "sub-study" to feed into the design of a second quantitative "sub-study." This sequential use of data from different methods acknowledges what Cresswell (2009) describes as the utility of mixed methods and conforms to Cresswell et al.'s (2003) definition. However, sequential use of different data types is not quite the same as the integration of methodologies into one single study, argued by Fetters and Freshwater (2015) to be a key consideration in advancing mixed methods as a distinct approach.

Seven years on from Stewart et al., Bachkirova, Arthur, and Reading (2015) did seek to use a mixed-methods design to allow each form of data to support the other, aiming to address the integration issue and enrich understanding. In addition, they argued that their choice of design was informed by pragmatism, argued by Tashakkori and Teddlie (2003) to be the best paradigm for mixed-methods research. Pragmatism accepts that different methods are informed by different—and perhaps competing—paradigms and that these may well be built upon contradictory philosophical assumptions. Nevertheless, the integrating of different methodologies and methods which "work" in enriching understanding of phenomena, the primacy of addressing the research question over any purist adherence to theory or philosophy, is urged by Tashakkori and Teddlie (2003) to become a hallmark of mixed-methods research.

In the coming years, coaching psychology has the opportunity to learn from other fields of research, not just within CRDs, where mixed methods has a longer tradition as a distinct paradigm. Moreover, just as researchers in coaching psychology have grappled with philosophical and conceptual issues concerning quantitative and qualitative methodologies as tools for advancing understanding of the coaching phenomenon, so they might bring the same consideration to mixed methods as a distinct methodology. Finally, Molina-Azorin et al. (2017) point to barriers in getting mixed-methods research published, with many journals having a bias toward quantitative or qualitative designs, but rarely declaring an active preference and encouragement for mixed-method studies. The following selection of mixed-methods papers from the *International Coaching Psychology Review* (ICPR) hopefully suggests that such a barrier does not exist within our field and that ICPR and similar publications will continue to promote and support mixed-methods studies as a valuable means of advancing coaching psychology.

REFERENCES

Bachkirova, T., Arthur, L., & Reading, E. (2015). Evaluating a coaching and mentoring programme: Challenges and solutions. *International Coaching Psychology Review, 10*(2), 175–189.

Campbell, D. T., & Fiske, D. (1959). Convergent and discriminant validation by the multitrait-multimethod matrix. *Psychological Bulletin, 56,* 81–105.

Cresswell, J. W. (2009). Mapping the field of mixed methods research. *Journal of Mixed Methods Research, 3*(2), 95–108.

Cresswell, J. W., Plano Clark, V. L., Gutmann, M. L., & Hanson, W. E. (2003). Advanced mixed methods research designs. In A. Tashakkori & C. Teddlie (Eds.), *Handbook of mixed methods in social and behavioural research* (pp. 209–240). Thousand Oaks, CA: Sage.

Fetters, M., & Freshwater, D. (2015). The $1 + 1 = 3$ integration challenge. *Journal of Mixed Methods Research, 9,* 115–117.

Hanson, W. E., Cresswell, J. W., Plano Clark, V. L., Petska, K. S., & Cresswell, J. D. (2005). Mixed methods research designs in counseling psychology. *Journal of Counseling Psychology, 52*(2), 224–235.

Heppner, P. P., Kivlighan, D. M., Jr., & Wampold, B. E. (1999). *Research design in counselling* (2nd ed.). Belmont, CA: Wadsworth.

Molina-Azorin, J. F., Bergh, D. D., Corley, K. G., & Ketchen, D. J., Jr. (2017). Mixed methods in the organizational sciences: Taking stock and moving forward. *Organizational Research Methods, 20*(2), 179–192.

Spencer, P. E. (2006). Method variance in organizational research: Truth of urban legend. *Organizational Research Methods, 9,* 221–232.

Stewart, L. J., Palmer, S., Wilkin, H., & Kerrin, M. (2008). Towards a model of coaching transfer: Operationalising coaching success and the facilitators and barriers to transfer. *International Coaching Psychology Review, 3*(2), 87–109.

Tashakkori, A., & Cresswell, J. W. (2007). Editorial: The new era of mixed methods. *Journal of Mixed Methods Research, 1*(1), 3–7.

Tashakkori, A., & Teddlie, C. (Eds.). (2003). *Handbook of mixed methods in social and behavioural research.* Thousand Oaks, CA: Sage.

18 Coaching as a Learning Methodology: A Mixed-Methods Study in Driver Development Using a Randomized Controlled Trial and Thematic Analysis

Jonathan Passmore and Hannah Rehman[1]

The UK government and other governments in the developed world are faced with a challenge of how to improve road safety. Despite persistent attempts at reducing accidents through campaigns, road design, and changes to car design, road traffic accidents remain one of the largest causes of death in the developed world. In 2008, it was reported that around seven fatal incidents occur per day in the UK. Death through a driving-related incident is the single largest cause of death for young people between 17 and 25. Further, around 20% of new drivers are involved

[1] First published as Passmore, J., & Rehman, H. (2012). Coaching as a learning methodology—A mixed methods study in driver development using a randomised controlled trial and thematic analysis. *International Coaching Psychology Review, 7*(2), 166–184.

in an incident within the first six months of acquiring their license (Driving Standards Agency, *Learning to Drive* consultation paper, 2008).

While drivers are often blamed individually for incidents, behind this are issues of national culture, personal attitude, and driver learning. Leading coaching practitioners such as Whitmore (2010) have questioned the current methods for learning to drive and have suggested that coaching may be a more effective method for driver learning, compared with the current instructor-led approach.

The DSA in its consultation paper (2008) discussed ways of revising the current approach by changing the system's focus on merely teaching the skills required to pass the test, with a view toward developing greater use of higher-order skills. As part of this process, the DSA is engaged in a five year project to assess which methods are more effective in enhancing road safety. Serious questions have, however, been raised concerning the methodology of the study, even before initial results have been published (Passmore, 2010; Passmore, 2011). These include questions about cross-contamination between the coaching and control group, where it is reported that members of the control group have previously received training in coaching skills.

In the UK, the key requirements for acquiring a large-goods vehicle (LGV) license are that the individual must have a full category B license (car), meet the eyesight criteria, and be a minimum of 21 years of age. An LGV license is required for all vehicles that weigh over 3.5 t. Similar to driving a car, the LGV learner must complete a theory, hazard perception, and practical test. The British Army have a large need for LGV drivers, which is supplied by the Defence Driving School of Transport (DST), who train British Army learners for cars (category B), lorries (LGVs; category C and C + E) and passenger-carrying vehicles (category D and D + E), in addition to special vehicles such as tanks and specialist off-road vehicles.

The methods for teaching a learner how to drive a lorry and car in the British Army are the same as a commercial driving school, with instructors using instruction-led techniques (Defence Instructional Techniques Manual, 2009). This typically involves the instructor providing explicit instruction on the mechanics and operation of the vehicle, instruction on risks, as well as commands during the drive on what to do (i.e., "use your mirror before you signal") and where to go (i.e., "turn right at the next junction").

Training standards are considered high and the DST "Road Traffic Accident Statistics" in 2008 reveal there was a decrease of 11% in road accidents. However, the total number of "vehicle driver" deaths increased compared to 2007. While instruction has produced positive outcomes, a pressure for change was internal financial challenges and the increasing demand for trained drivers—a direct result of operations in Iraq and Afghanistan.

Coaching was identified as a possible solution to improve driver outcomes and DST was interested in exploring these ideas. In parallel, other work was underway in other areas of driver training, which has provided evidence of coaching's potential contribution to driver development (Passmore & Mortimer, 2011; Passmore & Townsend, 2012). These previous studies in the learner driver and police advanced driver environments have revealed the perceived value by driving instructors of coaching in supporting driving pupil's learning, improving the learning relationship between "instructor" and learner, and the perception that learning was more effective when the instructor used coaching in comparison to instruction. However, not all studies have seen positive results (Passmore & Velez, 2012).

At this stage, the contribution of coaching to adult learning remains theoretical. There are many theories that attempt to explain how adults learn. The most widely used theory is Kolb's (1984) experiential learning theory (ELT). Kolb defines learning as "the process whereby knowledge is created through the transformation of experience. Knowledge results from the combination of grasping and transforming experience" (Kolb, 1984, p. 41). Kolb emphasizes experience as an important aspect of how adults learn (Kolb & Kolb, 2005), within a four-stage cycle of learning (Figure 18.1). While Kolb notes that learning can occur at any point in the cycle, it generally begins with the process of "concrete experience" (Rakoczy & Money, 1995).

According to the ELT, learning involves developing a theory, forming hypotheses, and then testing those hypotheses. On the whole, the four stages of the cycle involve the learner in self-reflect, observation, and testing (Rakoczy & Money, 1995). Kolb highlights that for learning to be a success, the learner needs to actively complete all four stages of the cycle. Argyris (1991) has further developed learning theory through his "double-loop" analogy. Argyris argues that "double-loop learning" consists of asking yourself questions and then testing them. "Double-loop learning" occurs at the third stage of Kolb's cycle, whereby adults learn to apply their hypotheses and theories to new conditions.

It can be hypothesized that coaching further aids the learning process described by Kolb (1984), as coaching creates a sense of personal responsibility of the learning and stimulates the double-loop learning described by Argyris, as the coachee is encouraged

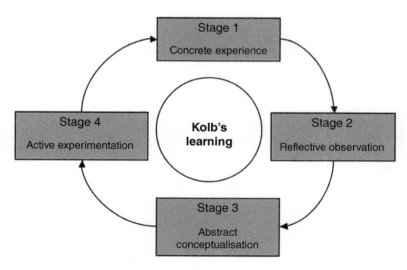

Figure 18.1   *Kolb's (1984) Stages of Learning Cycle.*

Note. Adapted from Kolb & Kolb (2005)

to reflect on their situation and its implications through questions from the coach. These models of learning suggest that an individualized coaching approach might help enhance the efficacy of LGV driver training beyond the traditional directive, instructor-led approach.

A number of previous studies of coaching have indicated the effectiveness of using coaching and training simultaneously to help the learner personalize learning and thus enhance its application to workplace activities (e.g., Olivero, Bane, & Kopelman, 1997). However, to date, no direct comparisons have been made comparing instructional and coaching approaches as learning methodologies. Further, the randomized trials that have been undertaken have tended to focus on the development of psychological characteristics, for example, resilience or behavioral skills (see Grant, Passmore, Cavanagh, & Parker, 2010, for a fuller discussion), rather than a comparison of coaching with other developmental interventions.

Research, however, is still limited even in the area of the development of behavioral skills and even rarer in using coaching with people who may have poor literacy skills. Allison and Ayllon (1980) used a behavioral coaching strategy with 23 participants to aid the learning of specific skills in sports. They found that the behavioral coaching approach enhanced performance and appropriate use of the skills by an average of 50%. The findings of this study suggest that a behavioral coaching approach might be successful in driver training with a diverse population, as driving involves learning a motor skill, which needs to be executed correctly to ensure driver safety beyond the training. However, it also involves higher-order cognitive skills, such as decision making, which themselves are affected by emotional state, personality, and attitudes. As a result, a cognitive-behavioral approach, combining basic behavioral coaching with an exploration of cognition, may enhance driver development outcomes (Figure 18.2).

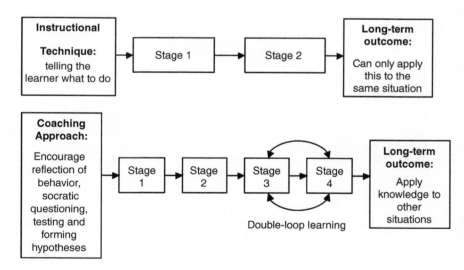

Figure 18.2 *A Model Comparing the Outcomes of the Coaching and Instructional Approaches.*
Note. Adapted from Kolb's (1984) Stages of Learning Cycle

A review of the driver development literature reveals there is currently no empirical research looking at the effects of coaching on driver training, with the exception of the papers noted above conducted as part of this wider review of coaching and driving (Passmore & Mortimer, 2011; Passmore & Townsend, 2012; Passmore & Velez, 2012).

In terms of the wider driver training arena, some work has been conducted. Work by Senserrick and Haworth (2005) has noted the central role of attitudes. Stanton, Walker, Young, Kazi, and Salmon (2007) have suggested hazard perception programs to help improve the effects of training. Senserrick and Swinburne (2001) noted the value of advanced "insight" training courses, which made drivers more aware of the risks involved in driving. Hutton, Sibley, Harper, and Hunt (2002) have highlighted the role of feedback on driver safety behaviors and have found a positive effect of using feedback to change negative behaviors. Boorman (1999) found that an advanced driver training program conducted with the Post Office lorry drivers significantly improved fleet performance and also resulted in a reduction in accidents after the program. These studies lend preliminary support to the notion that driver training can be enhanced with the addition of supplementary approaches.

Given this context, leading driving researchers (Dorn, 2005) have suggested that coaching may be an appropriate methodology for driver training. Rismark and Solvberg (2007) proposed a dialog similar to feedback and coaching to improve the effects of driver training in Norway. The study looked at how to improve driver training in terms of its content through enhancing the communication between the instructor and learner. This approach helped enhance self-awareness and reflection in the driver, which led to better driving behavior beyond training. Similarly, Stanton et al. (2007, p. 1213) evaluated the effectiveness of an advanced coaching driving intervention, training drivers in the "information," "position," "speed," "gear," and "accelerate" system (IPSGA). They conducted the study with 75 participants, who were either put in the coaching group, an observation group with no coaching, or a control group with no observation or coaching being given. The participants were adults between the ages of 23 and 65 with several years of driving experience. The researchers found that the experimental coaching group significantly improved their attitudes, situational awareness, and skills related to driving. They proposed that their findings suggested that a formal one-to-one coaching course would help produce safer drivers, emphasizing that the content and methods of an advanced training program were the key to its success. These findings indicate that coaching will be useful for improving driver development for all vehicles, and in particular for lorry driver training, to help facilitate the acquisition of the specific skills and to enhance road safety beyond the test. Nevertheless, a major weakness identified with their study was the nature of participation in the study. Their sample for the coaching group was self-selected and this group was "motivated to improve their driving" (Stanton et al., 2007, p. 1231). Stanton et al. (2007) and Rismark and Solvberg (2007) provide evidence and support for the use of coaching as an independent and formal program.

These studies were identified by the EU's HERMES Project (2007), which has explored the role of coaching as a learning approach for novice drivers. It has suggested ways that driving instructors can incorporate coaching into driver training (see, for example, HERMES Project, 2010). HERMES also highlighted

Table 18.1   *Goals for Driver Education (GDE) Matrix*

Hierarchical levels of driver behavior	*Competency 1: Knowledge and skill*	*Competency 2: Risk-increasing aspects*	*Competency 3: Self-assessment*
Level 4: Goals for life and skills	Lifestyle, age, group, culture, social position, etc. vs. driving behavior	Sensation seeking Risk acceptance Group norms Peer pressure	Introspective competence Own preconditions Impulse control
Level 3: Goals and context of driving	Modal choice Choice of time Role of motives Route planning	Alcohol, fatigue Low friction Rush hours Young passengers	Own motives influencing choices Self-critical thinking
Level 2: Driving in traffic	Traffic rules Cooperation Hazard perception Automation	Disobeying rules Close-following Low friction Vulnerability	Calibration of driving skills Own driving style
Level 1: Vehicle control	Car functioning Protection systems Vehicle control Physical laws	No seatbelts Breakdown of vehicle systems Worn-out tires	Calibration of car control skills

Note. Adapted from Hatakka, Keskinen, Glad, Gregerson & Hernetkoski (2002, pp. 209–210) and Gregerson (2005, p. 9).

"Goals for Driver Education" (Table 18.1). The matrix defines the goals and competencies required for teaching individuals how to drive, using a "hierarchical approach." Level 1 "vehicle control" is gaining skills in the basic manual handling of the vehicle, such as maneuvring and general car maintenance. Level 2 "driving in traffic" consists of gaining control in traffic situations and different road and weather conditions; it is the mastery of driving in varied conditions. Level 3 "goals and context of driving" and Level 4 "goals for life and skills for living" are the higher-order skills required for driving, such as understanding driver motives and intentions for driving, factors related to driver personality and values, "self-awareness," "emotions," and being able to understand driver personal strengths and weaknesses. They can be seen as the "what, where, when, and how" of a journey and understanding the rationale for making decisions. The matrix can be used to understand what the current traditional approaches to driver training need to revise and reconsider.

While the instructor-led approach focuses on Levels 1 and 2 of the matrix, which are formally assessed on the driving test, it is suggested that the coaching approach helps develop Levels 3 and 4 of the matrix, as coaching helps challenge one's beliefs (HERMES Project, 2010). The evidence suggests that these factors are important and have a large impact on driving behavior (Dorn, 2005; Dorn & Brown, 2003). The HERMES report argues that for driver training to be successful it needs to incorporate all levels on the matrix.

It can be questioned whether a more enhanced coaching approach to driver training will enhance its effectiveness.

Driving involves both cognitive skills, such as calculating other road user speed, intended direction, and associated risks of maneuvers, and behavioral skills, such as vehicle control. For coaching to be successful in driver training, it needs to adopt approaches that enable these aspects of skills development to be addressed. Grant (2001) found that a combined approach of cognitive and behavioral methods was more effective in enhancing learning for adult learners, finding that it led to "deeper" understanding, as well as reducing anxiety, and these effects were also maintained at follow-up.

The current study aimed to explore whether coaching could improve the efficiency and effectiveness of driver training. Unlike the small number of driving studies that focus on young novice drivers, the current study focuses on adult learners who already know how to drive and have passed their test for category B (motor car).

METHOD

This study investigated the impact of coaching on LGV driver training with the DST in the UK. The first part of the study used a randomized controlled trial (RCT), where participants were randomly allocated to the coaching experimental group or the instruction control group. In this study, the independent variable identified was the coaching style of teaching learners how to drive an LGV. The dependent variables were the total number of hours spent in training, the total number of kilometers (km) spent driving in training prior to passing the test, the number of tests taken to pass the driving test, and passing the driving test on the first attempt. The design of the study was a between-subjects design, as there were different participants in each group. The experimental group ("Group 1") received the coaching style of teaching and "Group 2" was the control who received the standard instruction style of teaching. Participants in each group were matched according to their LGV driving test category; whether they were training to acquire their category C license, which is for "vehicles over 3,500 kg, with a trailer up to 750 kg"; or training for their C + E license, which is the same as category C with the exception of a trailer weighing "over 750 kg". The data was collected by members of the DST and subjected to analysis by the researchers. The second part of the study involved a series of short semi-structured interviews, transcription, and thematic analysis to identify common themes.

Participants

The RCT part of the study involved 208 participants, with 104 participants in each group. Participants were serving members of the British Armed forces who were learning to drive a lorry with the DST. The sample included both English as a second language (mainly from Nepal and Kenya) and native English speakers. Participation in the study was voluntary. Participation by learners in each group was randomly assigned, through an ABAB process, following posting to DSA. The driving instructors were all members of unit D, one of seven units involved in driver training. The selection of this group was random. The driving instructors attended five days of coach training. The training covered basic skills in coaching and included a basic coverage of behavioral and cognitive-behavioral coaching models. Participants also completed coaching practice during which they were observed and received feedback, along with a subsequent assessment

The qualitative study involved 11 participants, four instructors, and seven learners, who were interviewed by independent researchers. These were selected at random from each of the groups. Participation was again voluntary.

Materials

1. *Participants:* For each participant (learner driver) a record of the hours spent in training, kilometers driven, number of tests taken, and the date and time of all lessons and tests were recorded using individual learner record sheets. The summary data for each individual was transferred to an Excel spreadsheet for analysis.

    Each participant (learner driver) was given a workbook, worksheets, and an instructor resource to refer to post-training (Performance Learning and Development, 2008a, 2008b).

2. *Trainers:* Twelve DST staff were trained in the coaching approach. The training was designed to develop the driving instructors' knowledge, skills, and attitude to learners and to be able to undertake coaching with confidence and competence. The aim of the training program was to ensure that the trainers (driving instructors) were skilled in the approach so that they could then train other instructors within their organization. The training content is summarized in Table 18.2.

3. *Data collection:* Trainers (driving instructors) were asked to monitor the hours spent in training, kilometers driven, and test details on a record sheet for each student at the end of each session. The collection of such information was part of the instructors' normal role. Data were collected from January to July 2009. During this period, each instructor trained approximately ten students.

Trainers (driving instructors) trained participants (learner drivers) in the experimental group how to drive a lorry, using techniques from both coaching and instruction. Instructors who had not received the additional coaching training taught participants (learner drivers) in the control using the DST's instructional style.

Participants (learner drivers) were randomly allocated to a trainer (driving instructor). Each participant was informed that their details would be monitored during their lessons. In addition, each received an explanation that the army was reviewing its driver learning methods; although precise details were not disclosed as to the types of training methodology or whether the participant was in the experimental or control group.

Eleven semi-structured interviews were also conducted with both trainers and learners to gain further insight into their experiences of the coaching approach. Each

Table 18.2   *Training Objectives*

Day	Objectives
1	• Introduce the coaching process—define coaching and how it compares with other forms of learning • Core coaching skills—listening, questioning, summary, and reflection
2	• Core coaching models, for example, the GROW model, goal setting (SMART goals) • Coaching practice
3	• Models of adult learning—learning cycle, social learning, and double-loop learning • Learning styles • Supplementary models—cognitive-behavioral approach and techniques • Coaching practice
4	• Building learning relationships with learners • Driving lesson planning—combining instruction and coaching • Coaching practice
5	• Integrating the skills • Coaching practice • Personal review and action planning

interview lasted between 10 and 20 minutes. Interviews were conducted with four instructors who had been trained to use coaching to teach learners how to drive. The interviews explored the effects of the coaching course on their role as an instructor, in particular, looking at ways in which it might have changed the way they teach and the effects that this teaching style had on their learners. Seven learners were interviewed. All the learners interviewed were either doing their C or their C + E LGV category license training with the British Army through the DST. All learners had already acquired their category B (car driving) license. The learners were asked if they had noticed any differences in the way they had been taught between their previous instructor and the new coaching instructor and about the learning experience.

RESULTS

Quantitative data

In this section, the findings from the statistical analysis are reviewed for each of the four hypotheses. The level of statistical significance adopted for this study was $p < .01$. An initial review of the data using a One-Sample Kolmogorov test revealed that the data was more or less normally distributed, therefore the Independent Samples t-test was a robust enough test for the data obtained. The t-test also copes better with outliers and is the test of significance for comparing the difference between two groups.

The comparisons made between the experimental group (coaching) and control group (instruction) included:

- total number of hours in training to pass the test
- total number of kilometers driven in training to pass the test
- average number of tests taken to pass the driving test
- whether the learners passed their test on the first attemp

Hypothesis 1: Learners in the coaching group will spend fewer hours in training compared to the instruction control group.

Table 18.3 shows the average number of hours spent driving in training in order to pass the test for the coaching and instruction groups. It can be seen that there is a difference in the number of hours driving between the two groups (control $M = 30.12$, coaching $M = 21.43$).

The coaching group spends fewer hours in training in order to pass their test, indicating a mean difference in hours spent in training of 8.69 (hours). An Independent Samples *t*-test was conducted to determine whether this difference in total hours spent driving was significant. Levene's test for equality of variances was $p < .05$ ($p = .026$). The analysis revealed that the difference between these two groups was significant ($t = 4.014$, $p < .01$, $p = .0005$, one-tailed), indicating that the coaching group on average takes less time in training to pass their test. The null hypothesis can therefore be rejected.

Hypothesis 2: Learners in the coaching group will drive fewer kilometers to pass the test compared to the instruction control group.

Table 18.4 demonstrates the mean for the total number of kilometers driven in training to pass the driving test for both groups. There appears to be a difference between the mean for the instruction control group ($M = 449.99$) and the coaching group ($M = 394.44$).

Table 18.3   *Total Number of Hours Driving to Pass the Test*

Type of training	No. of learners (N)	Min.	Max.	Mean	SD
Instruction group (control)	104	10.15	106.75	30.12	17.78
Coaching group	104	7.00	81.00	21.43	13.06

Table 18.4   *Total Number of Kilometers Driven in Training to Pass the Test*

Type of training	No. of learners (N)	Min.	Max.	Mean	SD
Instruction group (control)	104	90	1,934	449.99	310.76
Coaching group	93	100	2,350	394.44	327.44

The mean difference between the two groups was 55.55 km. The Levene's test for equality of variances was $p > .05$ ($p = .621$), using the top row of values for t, the equal variances assumed row. However, an Independent Samples t-test revealed that this difference in kilometers spent driving in training was not significant ($t = 1.221$, $p > .01$, $p = .112$, one-tailed), thus the null hypothesis failed to be rejected, as coaching showed no improvement in the kilometers driven in training to pass the test.

Hypothesis 3: There will be a decrease in the number of tests taken to pass the test for learners in the coaching group.

Table 18.5 shows the average number of tests taken for the learners to pass in both groups. It can be seen that on average the coaching group takes fewer driving tests to pass ($M = 1.38$).

The difference between the two groups in the number of tests taken to pass their driving test was small (0.33). An Independent Samples t-test analysis revealed that the difference between the number of tests taken for both groups was significant ($t = 2.659$, $p < .01$, $p = .005$ one-tailed). Levene's test for equality of variances was $p < .05$ ($p = .004$) and so the bottom row of values for t were used. As predicted, there was a decrease in the number of tests taken to pass the test for the coaching group and the null hypothesis can therefore be rejected.

Hypothesis 4: Learners in the coaching group are more likely to pass their test on the first attempt.

The data for hypothesis 4 was categorical and thus the chi-square nonparametric test was used for analysis. Table 18.6 shows the average number for whether the learners passed their test on their first attempt for the coaching and control group. It can be seen that there is a difference between the coaching group ($M = 1.00$) and the instruction control group ($M = 1.45$) for whether they pass their test first time.

Table 18.5   *Total Number of Tests Taken to Pass the Driving Test*

Type of training	No. of learners (N)	Min.	Max.	Mean	SD
Instruction group (control)	104	1	6	1.71	1.01
Coaching group	104	1	4	1.38	.74

Table 18.6   *Passing the Driving Test on First Attempt*

Type of training	No. of learners (N)	Mean	SD
Instruction group (control)	77	1.45	.501
Coaching group	77	1.00	.000

Table 18.7 *Cross-Tabulation for Whether Both Groups Pass the Driving Test on the First Attempt*

			Coaching or control group		
			Coaching	Control	Total
Whether they passed their test first time	Yes	Count	77	42	119
		Expected count	59.5	59.5	119.0
	No	Count	0	35	35
		Expected count	17.5	17.5	35.0
Total		Count	77	77	154
		Expected count	77.0	77.0	154.0

Table 18.7 indicates that all learners in the coaching group ($N = 77$) passed their test on the first attempt, indicating that on average a coaching style of teaching will help learners pass their test first time. A chi-square analysis revealed that there is a significant association between the two groups ($x^2 = 45.294$, df $= 1$, $p < .01$, $p = .0005$, one-tailed). The analysis supports the hypothesis that learners who receive a coaching style of teaching are more likely to pass their test on the first attempt and the null hypothesis can, therefore, be rejected.

Qualitative data

Data from the semi-structured interviews were transcribed and analyzed using a thematic analysis approach. This approach can help understand emerging ideas from one's research (Aronson, 1994). "Thematic analysis is a method for identifying, analysing, and reporting patterns (themes) within data" (Braun & Clarke, 2006, p. 6). An advantage of using this approach is that it allows for flexibility (Braun & Clarke, 2006).

The process of analyzing the data firstly entailed becoming familiar with the interview data. The second stage involved identifying the themes and patterns from all the interviews by moving back and forth between the interview data. During this stage, all patterns and trends found in the data were coded. The third stage involved a review of the patterns and trends to form and define the specific themes. The fourth stage combined common or similar themes together in order to create sub-themes. The final stage of analysis was to identify the data that was related to these themes (see Braun & Clarke, 2006).

Trainers

Table 18.8 summarizes the key themes that arose from the interviews with the trainers. The trainers felt that their teaching style had improved from using the new coaching method and could see marked improvements in their learners who had received this style of teaching. Trainers felt that they "reflected back" more when using the coaching style, they gave more feedback, worked in a more collaborative style with their student, set clear goals, helped their students to actively learn through practice rather than instructing and that they asked their students more questions in order to explore whether their student understood the task. The trainers also mentioned that coaching was a useful tool for teaching their learners, commenting that this technique definitely

Table 18.8 *Key Themes From the Interviews With the Trainers*

Themes	Trainers' thoughts/comments
Driving instructor–learner relationship	Trainers felt that coaching helped to build good relationships with their students, creating a good atmosphere to teach in.
Coaching as a complementary methodology	Coaching helped to enhance the skills they were already using.
Enhanced opportunity for learner self-reflection	The approach encouraged more self-reflection and helped learners to become more tolerant of situations that they are faced with. Using reflection also helped to find out if the learner understood the issue and provided the opportunity to then cover again material if the concept was not fully understood.
Flexibility with using the coaching style to teach	Trainers felt that they were able to use a variety of methods to teach, which is tailored to each individual learner's needs.
Feedback and preparation	These were regarded as an important process in their teaching methods.
Involvement	Coaching has made them more aware of ensuring that both learners' needs are met and that they keep them interested through more involvement, for example, by having more conversations with them.
Exploring through questions for deeper understanding	Trainers felt that they now explain more to their learners by asking more questions. They explained that it helps the learner understand and also gives an insight into how much help the learner needed.
Working collaboratively with the learner	They work in partnership with the learners and that working together toward the same goal helped make the experience more enjoyable for everyone.
Setting goals and objectives	They now set more clear goals with their learners, and reassure them that they can do it through using positive reinforcement.
Responsibility of the learner	Trainers now let their learners take control of their learning so that they're not constantly telling them what to do. They found that by giving the learner responsibility of their learning helped them to focus and learn.
Active learning	Actively learning through practice helps the learner to hold onto those skills, making them more able to use those skills outside of training.

worked with their students and would recommend the wider use of the technique in other areas of training. Comments from trainers included:

> I think it's certainly made me a little bit more enthusiastic in getting out there and doing it. No doubt ... well, job satisfaction. (T5-278–282)

> I've got that little bit that's really helping me and I can see the big difference in my students. (T3-140–142)

> You're getting the answer out of them rather than you telling them. You're asking the questions they're giving you the answer then you're waiting for the response of that student. (T3-26–29)

> It's totally different now because now all I'm doing is I'm bringing the best out of the students I'm praising them, everything they do ... the Q & A technique, it's worked so well for me because, now it's making my job easier they're now thinking for themselves a lot earlier. (T3-128–136)

> It's definitely got a place in driver training. (T2–227)

Learners

From interviews with the learners, four of the seven learners interviewed noted no difference in the teaching of the coaching style and felt that their experience was similar to other instructors. Two out of the seven learners interviewed noticed that there was a difference in the teaching style compared to when they did their category B (car driving) course. They commented that the instructors were more careful with them as individuals.

These two learners also noticed the difference in the teaching style compared to their previous instructors and commented that the coaching style of teaching helped them to retain the skills learned after the course and that this would help them when they were out in the field. Learners felt that their new instructors were very good, gave them more one-to-one attention, helped them to increase their confidence in driving, had more conversations with them, and explained what to do more. They commented that they had learned the importance of safety and checking while on the roads. Overall, the learners expressed satisfaction with the course and their trainers and had no negative comments. On average, all the learners interviewed were ready for their test within 5–8 days of training from a coached instructor. Comments from learners included:

> It's more one-to-one as opposed to in a classroom with 20 other students—I think it's a lot better. (L4-42–43)

> I've got the confidence now ... so it's good. (L5-50–51)

> It's helped me to observe more. (L5–85)

> He kinda knows where he needs to explain things to you and he...overemphasizes on a lot of things so he'll help you understand things a lot more. (L4-68–71)

DISCUSSION

The study investigated whether a coaching style of teaching learners to drive a heavy-goods lorry would improve driver training outcomes. In particular, the study aimed to directly compare the differences between a coaching style of learning and the traditional instructional approach used to teach learner drivers.

British Army driver training was selected as there are clearly defined measures of success; namely, a driving test undertaken by an independent examiner. Further, rather than compare coaching with a control group on a waiting list or a group that receives no intervention, driver training offers a commonly used method of learning (Instruction), which coaching could be directly compared with. A third benefit was that both instruction and coaching took place one-to-two, so there was a direct comparison of the learning time. Finally, by using a sample drawn from an organization, such as the British Army, meant that a relatively large sample could be collected, ensuring a reliable and that record-keeping was highly accurate and was completed in full by all trainers.

The results indicated that there was a significant difference between the coaching and instruction (control) group in the number of hours they spent in training to pass their test ($p < .01$). As such, it was found that the coaching group spent fewer hours in training. This finding suggests that the coaching approach of teaching helps learners to grasp the techniques required for lorry driving quicker than the instructional method. A possible explanation for this finding could be that the use of Socratic questions and the self-reflection methods used in coaching aid the learner to make more meaningful links between their existing knowledge and new knowledge, and personalize the learning so the focus of learning is on the learners' needs, rather than a fixed course time and content (Table 18.9).

The expectation that learners in the coaching group would drive fewer kilometers to pass the test compared to the instruction control group, failed to reach significance ($p > .01$). It was assumed that coaches would spend more time at the side of the road discussing the drive, while instruction would take place during driving. This hypothesis reflected earlier research with learner drivers that suggested it may be difficult on occasions to use coaching while the learner was driving, due to the cognitive demands that both learning to drive and reflective questions place on the driver's mental workload (Passmore & Mortimer, 2011). While the coaching group was found to drive fewer kilometers in training in order to pass their driving test, the analysis revealed that the difference between the two groups was in fact small (55.55 km). One of the reasons for such a finding could be that the coaches were in practice coaching while their learner was driving. This view is consistent with the ELT, which highlights that in order for adults to learn effectively, they need to engage in the four stages of learning involving observation, reflection, and testing (Kolb, 1984). However, the finding that the learners in the coaching group spent fewer hours in training supports the theory that coaching was a more time-efficient method, as these learners significantly spent less time to procure the necessary skills for lorry driving.

Table 18.9   *Key Themes From the Interviews With the Learners*

Themes	Learners' thoughts/comments
Course quality and Instructor competence	Learners felt that their instructors and the course were very good and that they helped them to be ready for their test early.
One-to-one learning	Some felt that their instructors had more one-to-one time for them, making their experience more personal.
Flexible learning	Flexible learning Some felt that there was more flexibility in the coaching approach to teaching and were given a choice of techniques.
Increased confidence	All learners commented that their instructors helped them to increase their confidence in their ability to use the skills learned. Their increased confidence helped to deal with difficult situations.
Conversational	Some learners felt that their instructors were very approachable, friendly, informal, and easy to talk to. They talked to them more, explained things and asked more questions to help enhance their understanding.
Deeper understanding	All the learners highlighted that their instructors helped them to understand why they were undertaking activities.
New skills	Some felt they learned many skills through the style of teaching, specifically to think about safety on the road and interaction with other road users.

It was hypothesized that the learners in the coaching group would take fewer tests in order to pass their driving test compared to the instruction control group. A significant difference was found between the two groups in the number of tests taken to pass their test ($p < .01$). On average, the coaching group were found to take less driving tests to pass compared to the instruction control group. The analysis also revealed that the prediction that those in the coaching group were more likely to pass their test on the first attempt was significant ($p < .01$). As highlighted in the Goals for Driver Education Matrix (GDE), safe driving behavior involves not only the manual control of the vehicle, but also requires interpersonal and situational awareness for making safe decisions (Hattaka, Keskinen, Gregerson, Glad, & Hernetkoski, 2002). This study suggests that a coaching style of teaching can be used to optimize driver training outcomes by addressing the higher-level goals for driving as outlined in the GDE.

Although coaching improved the process of the training and was found to be a more time-efficient method as opposed to the instruction approach; the difference between both groups was actually small (0.33), thus these significant findings could have been due to a type 1 error, whereby other confounding variables influenced the results. One of the variables identified is that individual characteristics, such as attributions about the driving lessons and cultural experiences of the learner, could have influenced the way that they responded to the coaching and thus the findings of this study. Other possible explanations were individual differences. Gregory, Levy, and Jeffers (2008) discuss the influence of individual differences, such as gender and age, on the coach's questioning skills. In a future study, it might be beneficial to match the coach and coachee to try and control for this variable. Weather conditions have also been reported as another confounding variable that can impact on driver performance (Gregerson, 1996, 2005). However, it could be argued that these confounding variables were inevitable and difficult to control in this study. Overall, in light of these difficulties, coaching was consistently found to help learners pass their driving test with fewer attempts.

As noted above, there is limited research that evaluates the efficacy of a coaching intervention in learning and specifically within driver development. Nevertheless, the results of the study are consistent with the view that coaching can help to enhance the effectiveness of current driver training approaches by teaching learners the higher-order skills associated with driving (Dorn, 2005; HERMES Project, 2007; Senserrick & Haworth, 2005). The wealth of research on coaching suggests that it helps with knowledge and skill acquisition and enhances performance of individuals in organizational settings (e.g., Feggetter, 2007; Olivero et al., 1997; Tee, Jowett, & Bechelet-Carter, 2009), suggesting that coaching is a highly effective methodology for adult learning. The results of this study further support the fact that coaching can be used successfully to improve outcomes in driver training with a diverse population.

Clark, Ward, Bartle, and Truman (2005) and the National Road Safety Statistics (2008) reveal that lorry drivers are more likely to display unsafe driving behavior compared with? presumably drivers of other vehicles?. Although driver safety was not directly measured in this study, nor was data collected on subsequent accident rates from both groups (the subject of current research), it can be hypothesized that the results from this study suggest that a coaching methodology may help learners to become more aware of the risks associated with unsafe behaviors. Parallels can be drawn between the results from this study and similar findings of research that has evaluated the impact of advanced driver training programs and shown that these additional courses help increase self-awareness, thereby leading to a reduction in accidents (e.g., Gregerson, 1996; Gregerson & Bjurulf, 1996; Lund & Williams, 1985; Rosenbloom, Shahar, Elharar, & Danino, 2008; Senserrick & Haworth, 2005). For instance, Molina, Sanmartin, Keskinen, and Sanders (2007) found that a one-day advanced course helped promote a "safer driving style" up to nine months post-training. However, in contrast to other driving studies, this study, we believe, is the first to look at the impact of a formal coaching program directly on drivers, whereas the majority of the driver training literature assesses the impact of a short advanced course, such as "insight training" or "hazard awareness" training. Evidence for such advanced courses is also mixed, as some studies have revealed that while they are helpful in targeting unsafe behavior, their overall effect is "weak" (Ker et al., 2005; Lonero, 2008). Thus, whether coaching does indeed help learners become safer drivers requires further investigation.

The weaknesses with the traditional instructional approaches of teaching learners to drive have been well documented (e.g., HERMES Project, 2007). As such, the literature documents that the current approach to driver training does not equip learners with the skills required to be safer drivers. This study challenges the current driver training teaching methods by providing an alternative approach that can help overcome the issue of safety and retention of skills beyond the test. It has been highlighted that coaching can help address the higher-cognitive skills required for driving safely (HERMES Project, 2007). Similarly, Stanton et al. (2007) have suggested that an advanced coaching program can help improve driver knowledge, skills, and attitudes.

Grant et al. (2010) have highlighted that many coaching studies lack the use of a control group, making it difficult to firmly assert that the changes produced were due to the coaching itself or some other variable. It is reported that out of the 16 between-subjects studies, there have only been 11 RCT coaching studies to date (e.g., Green, Grant, & Rynsaardt, 2007; Spence & Grant, 2007). However, a number of these have been with relatively small sample sizes. This study was thus untypical in using an RCT method with a relatively large sample and an equal and comparable control, which allows the placebo effect to be removed.

There has been growing UK and EU government interest in the use of coaching in driver training, as highlighted in the HERMES Project (2007) and the Driving Standards Agency consultation paper (2008). This research contributes to this wider agenda and begins to provide support for coaching as a useful learning methodology.

As recommended by Dorn (2005) and Rismark and Solvberg (2007), the current study has attempted to answer the questions raised about the effectiveness of driver training. The results in this study demonstrate that coaching improved learning outcomes, and in this context was more efficient and effective than instructional learning. The results suggest that the coaching approach of teaching learners to drive has the potential to offer significant benefits in the driver training domain.

More generally, the findings from the study provide useful evidence about the value of coaching as a learning methodology when compared to traditional instruction. The paper extends the work of Olivero et al. (1997) through its use of a larger and consistent sample and through using comparable interventions producing statistically significant results on both learning outcomes (percentage of those reaching the required standard/passing the test) and in the time taken to reach the standard (learning hours).

LIMITATIONS OF THE STUDY

Despite these strengths, a number of limitations are acknowledged with the design of the current study. No demographic information about the participants was collected and therefore the sample could not be matched according to their background. This was due to constraints placed on the study by the British Army regarding publishing data on forces personnel. This barrier leads to a question over whether it is reasonable to generalize the results of this study to other groups and to learning environments. Questions could also be raised whether these findings apply to other drivers; for example, non-forces personnel, and driving test categories, such as motor cars. A further limitation of the study was that learner attitudes, driving behavior and safety outcomes were not assessed. The driving literature indicates that one of the problems with the current approaches to driver training is that they do not produce safer drivers, as accident rates are still on the rise (National Road Safety Statistics, 2008; Clark et al., 2005; Senserrick & Haworth, 2005). In order to assess whether coaching helped produce safer drivers it was, therefore, important to have a measure of safety. For example, Boorman (1999) found that an advanced training program improved fleet performance and led to a reduction in accident rates post-training. Similarly, Stanton et al. (2007) measured driving attitudes in the coaching and non-coached group using the "Montag Driving Internality Externality (MDIE) LOC Questionnaire" developed by Montag and Comrey (1987, cited in Stanton et al., 2007, p. 1214). Future coaching and driving studies should, therefore, assess knowledge, skills, attitudes, and behavior by administering a similar questionnaire pre- and post-training or through assessing driver behavior or instructor, as well as assessing accident rates as a measure of safety. Further research is underway on driver accident rates and also of instructor behavior following coaching training using the GDE matrix within a police driving context, and data is currently being analyzed on a study involving "professional drivers" and accident rates (initiated by the same research team).

CONCLUSION

This study aimed to explore the effectiveness and efficiency of coaching as an adult method of learning with a driver learning context. The study provides evidence that coaching is a more effective learning methodology than instruction for driver training. Further research is needed to explore whether coaching may be a more effective methodology than instruction for other aspects of learning, such as leadership development or presentation skills. We believe this study provides is a useful contribution to the debate on both driver development and the wider use of coaching in adult learning.

REFERENCES

Allison, M. G., & Ayllon, T. (1980). Behavioural coaching in the development of skills in football, gymnastics and tennis. *Journal of Applied Behaviour Analysis, 13*(2), 297–314. https://doi.org/10.1901/jaba.1980.13-297

Argyris, C. (1991). Teaching smart people how to learn. *Reflections, 4*(2), 4–15. Retrieved 18 March 2010, from: http://www.velinleadership.com/downloads chris_argyris_learning.pdf

Aronson, J. (1994). A pragmatic view of thematic analysis. *The Qualitative Report, 2*(1), 1–3. Retrieved March 3, 2010, from https://nsuworks.nova.edu/tqr/vol2/iss1/3

Boorman, S. (1999). Reviewing car fleet performance after advanced driver training. *Occupational Medicine, 49*(8), 559–561. https://doi.org/10.1093/occmed/49.8.559

Braun, V., & Clarke, V. (2006). Using thematic analysis in psychology. *Qualitative Research in Psychology, 3*(2), 77–101.

Clark, D. D., Ward, P., Bartle, C. & Truman, W. (2005). An in-depth study of work-related road traffic accidents. Department for Transport. *Road Safety Research Report No. 58.* Retrieved March 18, 2010, from www.orsa.org.uk/guidance/pdfs/indepth_study_work_related_road_accidents.pdf

Defence Instructional Techniques Manual. (2009). Retrieved March 3, 2010, from http://cabmonsta.tripod.com/sitebuilder content/sitebuilderfiles/ditprecisbooklet.doc

Dorn, L. (2005). Driver coaching: Driving standards higher. In L. Dorn (Ed.), *Driver behaviour and training* (Vol. 2) (pp. 471–480). Surrey, UK: Ashgate Publishing.

Dorn, L., & Brown, B. (2003). Making sense of invulnerability at work: A qualitative study of police drivers. *Safety Science, 41*(10), 837–859. https://doi.org/10.1016/S0925-7535(02)00036-X

Driving Standards Agency. (2008). *Learning to Drive: A consultation paper.* Department for Transport. Retrieved November 29, 2009, from http://dsa.gov.uk/Documents/Consultation ltd/FINAL%2020080508.pdf

Feggetter, A. J. W. (2007). A preliminary evaluation of executive coaching: Does executive coaching work for candidates on a high potential development scheme? *International Coaching Psychology Review, 2*(2), 129–136.

Grant, A. M. (2001). *Coaching for enhanced performance: Comparing cognitive and behavioural approaches to coaching.* Paper presented to Spearman Seminar: Extending Intelligence: Enhancement and New Constructs, Sydney. Retrieved January 18, 2010, from www.psych.usyd.edu.au/psychcoach CBT_BT_CT_Spearman_Conf_Paper.pdf.

Grant, A. M., Passmore, J., Cavanagh, M., & Parker, H. (2010). The state of play in coaching today: A comprehensive review of the field. *International Review of Industrial and Organisational Psychology, 25*, 125–168. https://doi.org/10.1002/9780470661628.ch4

Green, S., Grant, A. M., & Rynsaardt, J. (2007). Evidence-based life coaching for senior high school students: Building hardiness and hope. *International Coaching Psychology Review, 2*(1), 24–32.

Gregerson, N. P. (1996). Young drivers' overestimation of their own skill: An experiment on the relation between training strategy and skill. *Accident Analysis and Prevention, 28*(2), 243–250. https://doi.org/10.1016/0001-4575(95)00066-6

Gregerson, N. P. (2005). *EU MERIT Project: Driving instructors' education in Europe: A long-term vision.* Working paper for workshop 1: The content of driving instructor training with regard to driving behaviour and safety, based on the GDE matrix. Brussels, Belgium: EU.

Gregerson, N. P., & Bjurulf, P. (1996). Young novice drivers: Towards a model of their accident involvement. *Accident Analysis and Prevention, 28*(2), 229–241. https://doi.org/10.1016/0001-4575(95)00063-1

Gregory, J. B., Levy, P. E., & Jeffers, M. (2008). Development of a model of the feedback process within executive coaching. *Consulting Psychology Journal: Practice and Research, 60*(1), 42–56. https://doi.org/10.1037/1065-9293.60.1.42

Hattaka, M., Keskinen, E., Gregerson, N. P., Glad, A., & Hernetkoski, K. (2002). From control of the vehicle to personal self-control: Broadening the perspectives to driver education. *Transportation Research Part F, 5*, 201–215. https://doi.org/10.1016/S1369-8478(02)00018-9

HERMES Project. (2007). *State of the art report on Coaching and optimal communication skills for driving instructors.* Retrieved March 3, 2010, from www.alles-fuehrerschein.at/HERMES index.php?page=documentation

HERMES (2010). EU Hermes project final report - High impact approach for enhancing road safety through more effective communication skills in the context of category B driver training. Retrieved 10th March 2010, from http://ec.europa.eu/transport/road_safety/pdf/projects/hermes_final_report_en.pdf

Hutton, K. A., Sibley, C. G., Harper, D. N., & Hunt, M. (2002). Modifying driver behaviour with passenger feedback. *Transportation Research Part F, 4*, 257–269. https://doi.org/10.1016/S1369-8478(01)00027-4

Ker, K., Roberts, I., Collier, T., Beyer, F., Bunn, F., & Frost, C. (2005). Post-licence driver education for the prevention of road traffic crashes: A systematic review of randomised controlled trials. *Accident Analysis and Prevention, 3*(2), 305–313. https://doi.org/10.1002/14651858.CD003734

Kolb, A. Y., & Kolb, D. A. (2005). Learning styles and learning spaces: Enhancing experiential learning in higher education. *Academy of Management Learning and Education, 4*(2), 193–212. https://doi.org/10.5465/amle.2005.17268566

Kolb, D. A. (1984). *Experiential learning: Experience as the source of learning and development.* Upper Saddle River, NJ: Prentice-Hall.

Lonero, L. P. (2008). Trends in driver education and training. *American Journal of Preventative Medicine, 35*(3), 316–323. https://doi.org/10.1016/j.amepre.2008.06.023

Lund, A. K., & Williams, A. F. (1985). A review of the literature evaluating the defensive driving course. *Accident Analysis and Prevention, 17*(6), 449–460. https://doi.org/10.1016/0001-4575(85)90040-5

Molina, J. G., Sanmartin, J., Keskinen, E., & Sanders, N. (2007). Post-licence education for novice drivers: Evaluation of a training programme implemented in Spain. *Journal of Safety Research, 38,* 357–366. https://doi.org/10.1016/j.jsr.2006.10.010

Montag, I., & Comrey, A. L. (1987). Internality and externality as correlates of involvement in fatal driving accidents. *Journal of Applied Psychology, 72*(3), 339–343. https://doi.org/10.1037/0021-9010.72.3.339

National Road Safety Statistics. (2008). Retrieved on 12th April 2020 from https://www.gov.uk/government/collections/road-accidents-and-safety-statistics

Olivero, G., Bane, K. D., & Kopelman, R. E. (1997). Executive coaching as a transfer of training tool: Effects on productivity in a public agency. *Public Personnel Management, 26*(4), 461–469. https://doi.org/10.1177/009102609702600403

Passmore, J. (2010). *Coaching in driver development.* Paper presented to Coaching and Driving Conference, University of East London, UK.

Passmore, J. (2011). A review of coaching skills training for ADIs in the UK. Unpublished study – available from the Coaching Psychology Unit, University of East London, UK.

Passmore, J., & Mortimer, L. (2011). The experience of using coaching as a learning technique in learner driver development: An IPA study of adult learning. *International Coaching Psychology Review, 6*(1), 33–45.

Passmore, J., & Townsend, C. (2012). The role of coaching in police driver training – an IPA study of coaching in a blue light environment. *An International Journal of Police Strategies, 35*(8), 785–800. https://doi.org/10.1108/13639511211275698

Passmore, J., & Velez, M. (2012). Coaching fleet drivers: A randomised controlled trial (RCT) of short coaching interventions to improve driver safety in fleet drivers. *The Coaching Psychologist, 8*(1), 20–26.

Performance Learning & Development. (2008a). *Coaching for performance: Coaching programme.* Wiltshire, UK: PLD.

Performance Learning & Development. (2008b). *Peak performance and coaching: A training development resource for peak performers, performance coaches and attitude change technology practitioners.* Wiltshire, UK: PLD.

Rakoczy, M., & Money, S. (1995). Learning styles of nursing students: A three-year cohort longitudinal study. *Journal of Professional Nursing, 11*(3), 170–174. https://doi.org/10.1016/S8755-7223(95)80116-2

Rismark, M., & Solvberg, A. M. (2007). Effective dialogues in driver education. *Accident Analysis and Prevention, 39,* 600–605. https://doi.org/10.1016/j.aap.2006.10.008

Rosenbloom, T., Shahar, A., Elharar, A., & Danino, O. (2008). Risk perception of driving as a function of advanced training aimed at recognising and handling risks in demanding driving situations. *Accident Analysis and Prevention, 40,* 697–703. https://doi.org/10.1016/j.aap.2007.09.007

Senserrick, T. & Haworth, N. (2005). *Review of literature regarding national and international young driver training, licensing and regulatory systems. Monash University Accident Research Centre. Report No. 239.* Retrieved November 29, 2009, from www.monash.edu.au/muarc/reports muarc239.pdf.

Senserrick, T.M. & Swinburne, G.C. (2001). *Evaluation of an insight driver-training programme for young drivers. Monash University Accident Research Centre. Report No. 186.* Retrieved November 29, 2009, from www.monash.edu.au/muarc/reports muarc186.pdf.

Spence, G. B., & Grant, A. M. (2007). Professional and peer life coaching and the enhancement of goal striving and well-being: An exploratory study. *The Journal of Positive Psychology, 2*(3), 185–194. https://doi.org/10.1080/17439760701228896

Stanton, N. A., Walker, G. H., Young, M. S., Kazi, T., & Salmon, P. M. (2007). Changing drivers' minds: The evaluation of an advanced driver coaching system. *Ergonomics, 50*(8), 1209–1234. https://doi.org/10.1080/00140130701322592

Tee, S. T., Jowett, R. M., & Bechelet-Carter, C. (2009). Evaluation study to ascertain the impact of the clinical academic coaching role for enhancing student learning experience within a clinical masters education programme. *Nurse Education in Practice, 9,* 377–382. https://doi.org/10.1016/j.nepr.2008.11.006

Whitmore, J. (2010). *Coaching and driving.* Paper presented to Coaching and Driving Conference. University of East London, UK.

19 Evaluating a Coaching and Mentoring Program: Challenges and Solutions

Tatiana Bachkirova, Linet Arthur, and Emma Reading[1]

For the last two decades, we have been witnessing unprecedented growth of the coaching industry. Many organizations invest in coaching programs. It seems, however, that the pace of growing evidence of the added value of coaching that should come from research does not yet match the speed of the implementation of coaching programs. Consequently, many organizations aim to gather their own evidence about the effectiveness of these programs to justify the return on investment (ROI). The London Deanery is one such organization.

The London Deanery established a coaching and mentoring service for doctors and dentists in London in 2008. The coaches were trained by an established leadership coaching provider and their performance was assessed at the end of the training. The outcome of the service was measured by individual feedback from the service users. However, it was viewed that although this provided some data on how the service was performing, it was not sufficient to identify any performance changes in the recipients. The service was publicly funded. thus it was important that it should be properly evaluated to ensure value for money. Preliminary work looking at the literature evaluating the benefits of coaching and mentoring did not reveal an established methodology for conducting such a review. The Oxford Brookes team of researchers won a bidding process for the research based on their proposals for developing novel methodologies for the evaluation of the service. The aim of the study was to establish whether the

[1] Bachkirova, T., Arthur, L., & Reading, E. (2015). Evaluating a coaching and mentoring programme: Challenges and solutions. *International Coaching Psychology Review, 10*(2), 175–189.

measures selected could identify changes in the performance and attitudes of doctors undergoing the coaching intervention, since ultimately the purpose of the program is to improve the effectiveness of doctors and dentists for the benefit of the patient.

It appears that the London Deanery task is not dissimilar to questions asked by many HRD practitioners. However, as Lawrence and Whyte (2014) recently argued, these practitioners "have not yet collectively identified a satisfactory approach to evaluating the efficacy of coaching" (p. 6). This is not surprising because the problem of measuring the impact of organizational intervention is not new: it has been actively discussed since Kirkpatrick's (1977) methodology for evaluating training programs (e.g., Ely et al., 2010) but it is still debated, particularly in relation to the evaluation of training (Passmore & Joao Velez, 2014). Kirkpatrick admitted that it is extremely difficult, if not impossible, to evaluate certain programs in terms of the results (Kirkpatrick, 1977) because of the numerous factors influencing the outcomes. Other authors continue to echo this conclusion (de Haan & Duckworth, 2012; Ely et al., 2010). A financial addition to Kirpartick's methodology—ROI has been particularly critiqued in relation to coaching with recent conclusions that are not dissimilar to Kirkpatrick's premise (de Haan & Duckworth, 2012; De Meuse, 2009; Grant, 2012, 2013; Passmore & Fillery-Travis, 2011; Theeboom, Beersma, & van Vianen, 2013).

The evaluation of coaching programs is considered to be even more difficult than the evaluation of training programs (de Haan & Duckworth, 2012; Ely et al., 2010; Grant, 2012). The problems are exacerbated by a number of factors, such as the diversity of outcomes of coaching compared with the relatively fixed expectations of training; the highly individual approach of the coach, which prevents more explicit knowledge of the process; and the confidentiality that surrounds specific details of the goals and consequent outcomes.

On the other hand, as coaching programs tend to be expensive there appears to be a stronger need to justify such expenditure, particularly in the public sector. Therefore, in spite of the additional costs involved in undertaking a full-scale research study on assessing the effectiveness of a coaching program, the London Deanery chose this option. However, such evaluations face similar issues and obstacles as large-scale outcome research projects on organizational interventions (De Meuse, Dai, & Lee, 2009; Passmore & Fillery-Travis, 2011; Theeboom et al., 2013), particularly the use of established paradigms. If traditional positivist methodologies are considered as the gold standard of evaluation, there is a danger that the complexity of coaching interventions may be overlooked (de Haan & Duckworth, 2012; Ely et al., 2010). This paper explores how some specific challenges of the evaluation of a large-scale coaching program were addressed and will suggest a methodology that is more in line with the philosophy of coaching. This will be discussed together with the results of the actual evaluation.

LITERATURE REVIEW

While recognizing that there are wider debates on the evaluation of organizational interventions (for example, Passmore & Joao Velez, 2014), this literature review is only focused on the evaluation of the effectiveness of coaching programs. Typically this literature addresses three main themes: (a) issues of evaluation in principle depending on the main stakeholders; (b) most acceptable methodologies of evaluation; and (c) specific measures of evaluation.

In relation to the general issues of evaluation, Grant (2013) suggests that we need to start with a question: "who is interested in evaluation—and why" (p. 15). The first group concerned with this question is the coaches. On the one hand, they wish coaching to be seen as effective for marketing purposes; on the other hand, they are interested in improving their practice. Purchasers of coaching ask the question of whether coaching works because they want to know if coaching is cost-effective. Both coaches and purchasers seem to have vested interests in the results of evaluation. In comparison, researchers and academics are well placed to explore the effectiveness of coaching using rigorous research methods and are interested in developing evidence-based practice for coaching (Briner, 2012; Fillery-Travis & Lane, 2006; Passmore & Fillery-Travis, 2011). However, they are probably more than others aware of many difficulties in applying scientifically respected methods to researching coaching practice (Drake, 2009; Ellam-Dyson, 2012; Ely et al., 2010; Grant, 2012).

One of the main problems is that many of these research methods require significant oversimplification of the nature of practice. Coaching is a complex intervention influenced by the interplay of different factors such as the client's attitude, coach's skill, and the coach/client relationship, all of which are subject to complex dynamics affected by contextual issues (de Haan & Duckworth, 2012; Ely et al., 2010). In addition, if coaching is sponsored by an organization it is difficult to establish who the main provider of information about the effectiveness of coaching should be: the client, the coach, the purchaser of the service, or those on the receiving end of the changes that are made by the client. In terms of more specific issues, various authors also question a typical assumption that coaches from different backgrounds, training, and styles deliver the same type of coaching and whether it is possible to treat coaching as a homogeneous intervention, allowing general conclusions to be drawn about its effectiveness (Theeboom et al., 2013).

In terms of acceptable methodologies of evaluation, the literature confirms again multiple issues with different methodologies. It is accepted that there are certain advantages and disadvantages in each methodology. Grant (2013) differentiates as rigorous three types of outcome studies with an indication of potential issues associated with them:

1. Case studies that can provide valuable descriptive data but do not allow generalized evaluations or the comparison of results between different coaching interventions.
2. Within-subject outcome research that allows comparison of the impact of coaching on a group of individuals. The group is assessed before and after the coaching interventions. This is the most commonly used study design in the literature and can provide valuable quantitative data of change, but causation cannot be attributed only to coaching.
3. Between-subject and randomized controlled trials (RCTs), which are considered by some to be the "gold standard," particularly in medical research. Although they can measure change and relate it to the intervention, the utility of these designs for studying coaching is contested (de Haan & Duckworth, 2012; Greif, 2009; Passmore

& Fillery-Travis, 2011) due to problems with delineating a control group, maintaining the "blind" condition, and constructing "placebo" interventions. Uses of self-coaching, peer-coaching, or "waiting list" are considered practical issues in terms of implementation in relation to coaching studies (Franklin & Doran, 2009; Greif, 2009; Hicks, 1998; Williams, 2010).

The traditional research literature on evaluations, typically associated with a positivist paradigm, focuses on searching for general relationships between a small number of discrete variables across a wide variety of context. However, these contexts, from a constructionist's point of view, have a large impact on these relationships (Fishman, 1999, p. 235). Without consideration of context, the findings of such studies may lead to conclusions that are so generic that their practical value becomes questionable (de Haan & Duckworth, 2012; Greif, 2007; Orlinsky, Grawe, & Parks, 1994).

It is not surprising that some research communities resist the idea that only one notion of research is recognized as science: the one identified with modernistic positivism. It has been argued that there are other meanings of science, for example, as disciplined, critical, reflective thought that compares and contrasts evidence, arguing for alternative interpretations or explanations of a particular phenomenon (Cronin & Klimoski, 2011; Fishman, 1999). In coaching research, Grant (2013) argues,

> an evidence base per se does not purport to prove that any specific intervention is guaranteed to be effective, nor does it require that a double-blind, randomised, controlled trial is held as being inevitably and objectively better than a qualitative case study approach (2013, p. 3)

This means that the evaluations of coaching could be approached from different research paradigms (pragmatism, contextualism, interpretivism) and may benefit from mixed designs. For example, it can include retrospective questionnaires validated by traditional positivist procedures (Passmore, 2008), but also include new instruments that were developed with considerations of factors such as the type of coaching, the organizational level of the coachee, and the specific objectives and context of each coaching engagement (De Meuse et al., 2009; Ely et al., 2010).

The theme of specific measures that could be used for evaluation of coaching is not an easy one either. According to Fillery-Travis and Lane (2006), before we can ask whether coaching works we must ask why it is being used. A fundamental difficulty of coaching outcome research is the extreme heterogeneity of issues, problems, and goals, which can be picked out as themes in different coaching interventions. This could be compared with therapy, where it is possible to offer general indicators of the quality of service, such as subjective well-being, symptom reduction, and life functioning (e.g., Mental Health Index, Howard, Moras, Brill, Martinovich, & Lutz, 1996). In coaching, however, it is difficult to identify the outcome measures applicable to the whole range of coaching interventions (Greif, 2007, p. 224). Grant (2013), providing many examples from the vast range of issues addressed in coaching, concludes that there is an almost endless list of applications. The majority of these outcomes are difficult to quantify. This is why sometimes the target outcomes are selected because they can be measured, rather than because they are appropriate for individual clients or reflect the nature of coaching (Easton & Van Laar, 2013).

Often practitioners create a battery of measures, which might reflect the context of the study, their priorities, and those of their client or organization commissioning the evaluation. A combination of measures or indicators can sometimes help to avoid oversimplification with an intention to work toward meeting a particular target that is measured (Easton & Van Laar, 2013). Greif (2007), for example, proposes general measures (degree of goal attainment and client satisfaction with coaching) and specific measures such as particular social competences; performance improvement, and self-regulation. The choice of these measures has to be justified by the theories tested in the independent research or by the practical needs of the organization commissioning the evaluation.

Overall, there is recognition in the literature that outcome research and evaluation of the effectiveness of coaching face significant challenges. Therefore, there is a need for pragmatic and creative approaches to this task, which could assure rigor as the result of competent inquiry.

METHODOLOGY OF THE PROJECT

This project was designed as a pragmatic inquiry requiring mixed methods (Tashakkori & Teddli, 2010) with a large proportion of the data, as requested by the client, of a quantitative nature, using qualitative data to construct a questionnaire and further inform the results.

The quantitative element of the study aimed to establish whether the coaching and mentoring provided by London Deanery practitioners had an impact on clients by comparing their scores from Time 1 (pre-coaching) and Time 2 (post-coaching) online measures. In this project, the London Deanery was interested in two variables, which are theoretically related to the individual change process and were considered by them as relevant for the situation: employee engagement and self-esteem. To give a fair representation of the aspect of self-esteem the researchers suggested two measures: self-efficacy and self-compassion.

Selected measures

Schaufeli and Bakker (2003) describe employee engagement as a positive, fulfilling, work-related state of mind that is characterized by vigor, dedication, and absorption. Research over the past 10 years has shown the importance of this concept in relation to understanding key organizational outcomes, such as low turnover (Schaufeli & Bakker, 2004), high organizational commitment (Demerouti, Bakker, Janssen, & Schaufeli, 2001), and customer-rated employee performance (Salanova, Agut, & Peiró, 2005). This has the potential to provide an indirect relationship between the effect of coaching and "customer-rated" employee performance, as well as reduced turnover and increased organizational commitment. Employee engagement is also negatively related to burnout, which was particularly important to the London Deanery.

The Oxford Brookes University team used a typical instrument for measuring employee engagement, the Utrecht Work Engagement Scale (UWES; Schaufeli & Bakker, 2003). This scale consists of 17 items, six of which measure vigor, six measure absorption, and five measure dedication. Vigor is characterized by high levels of energy and mental resilience while working, the willingness to invest efforts in one's work and persistence even in the face of difficulties. Dedication refers to being strongly involved in one's work and experiencing a sense of significance, enthusiasm, inspiration, pride, and challenge. Absorption is characterized by being fully concentrated and happily engrossed in one's work, whereby time passes quickly and one has difficulties with detaching oneself from work (Schaufeli & Bakker, 2003).

The scale consists of seven points: 0 (*never had this feeling*), 1 (*almost never, a few times a year or less*), 2 (*rarely, once a month or less*), 3 (sometimes, a few times a month), 4 (*often, once a week*), 5 (*very often, a few times a week*), and 6 (*always, every day*). The mean scale score of the three subscales is computed by adding the scores on the particular scale and dividing the sum by the number of items of the subscales involved. A similar procedure is followed for the total score.

Perceived self-efficacy refers to beliefs about one's competence to deal with challenging encounters and the "belief in one's capabilities to organise and execute the courses of action required to produce given attainments" (Bandura, 1997, p. 3). It is clear why this concept is related to beneficial coaching and mentoring outcomes. There is now a large body of research that supports a relationship between measures of perceived self-efficacy and performance (Stajkovic & Luthans, 1998).

Self-Efficacy was measured using the Generalized Self-efficacy Scale (GSE: Schwarzer & Jerusalem, 1995). Cross-cultural research has been carried out that confirms the validity of this scale, showing consistent evidence of associations between perceived self-efficacy and other psychological constructs (e.g., health behaviors, well-being, social cognitive variables, and coping strategies; see Luszczynska, Scolz, & Schwarzer, 2005).

The 10 items are scored using a four-point scale: 1 (*not at all true*), 2 (*hardly true*), 3 (*moderately true*), and 4 (*exactly true*). Schwarzer and Jerusalem (1995) found that the internal consistency varied across cultures but ranged from .78 to .91, and concluded that it was very satisfactory, considering that the scale only has 10 items. Scherbaum, Cohen-Charash, and Kern (2006) used Item Response Theory to test the GSE Scale and found that it works best for individuals with average or below-average levels of GSE. The GSE Scale is less precise at above-average levels of GSE. As low self-esteem has been frequently associated with negative social comparisons and internalized self-judgments, self-compassion (Neff, 2009) was introduced as an individual measure that is also a predictor of the ability to cope effectively with adversity and good mental health. Self-compassion comprises being kind and understanding toward oneself when experiencing pain or failure as opposed to being harsh and self-critical. Research studies have consistently linked self-compassion to reduced fear of failure, enhanced perceived competence, and emotionally-focused coping strategies, suggesting that this indicator is a promising one for coaching (Neff, 2009; Neff & Lamb, 2009; Neff & Vonk, 2009).

Self-compassion has three basic components: (a) extending kindness and understanding to oneself; (b) seeing one's experiences as part of the larger human experience rather than as separating and isolating; and (c) holding one's painful thoughts and feelings in balanced awareness and not overidentifying with them (Baumeister, Bushman & Campbell, 2000, as reported by Neff, 2003).

Self-compassion is measured with the Self-Compassion Scale (SCS, Neff, 2003). The 12-item scale was used with items 2 and 6 for self-kindness, items 11 and 12 for self-judgment, items 5 and 10 for common humanity, items 4 and 8 for isolation, items 3 and 7 for mindfulness, and items 1 and 9 for overidentification. Subscale scores are computed by calculating the mean of subscale item responses. To compute a total self-compassion score, reverse score the negative subscale items—self-judgment, isolation, and overidentification (i.e., $1 = 5, 2 = 4, 3 = 4, 4 = 2, 5 = 1$)—then compute a total mean. Neff (2003) found that internal consistency was above the acceptable: .75 level for overall and subscales. Test/re-test reliability of overall scale plus subscales was also found to be acceptable (.93 overall).

A bespoke questionnaire

We made the decision to develop another instrument for this evaluation for two main reasons. The first was responding to the need of the client-organization to address the more specific contextual relationship between the coaching service provided to London Deanery clients and noticeable behavioral and attitudinal changes that might be linked to their work performance and, consequently, patient care. The second was recognizing the importance of being creative when facing various issues associated with measurement. In this case, our intention was to capture not just the static estimation of particular aspects of the clients' working lives but directly addressing the degree of changes that happened in relation to these aspects by the end of the coaching process.

To create this measure we interviewed appropriate stakeholders: three users of service (two consultants and one GP), two coach/mentors and two matchers, those referring clients to this service and identifying a suitable coach. A grounded theory approach (Strauss & Corbin, 1990) was used as the main methodology for analysis. The following themes that emerged as the result of the qualitative analysis were particularly useful in the development of the bespoke questionnaire:

1. Impact on patients
   1. Improved interactions with patients.
   2. Improved feedback from patients.
   3. Use of coaching/mentoring techniques with patients.
   4. Changes in patients' behavior, such as reduced dependency, better use of doctors' time.
2. Impact on colleagues
   1. Improved interactions and communication with colleagues.
   2. Use of coaching/mentoring techniques with colleagues.

3. Impact on self
    1. Improved confidence.
    2. Better time management at work, leading to an improved work-life balance.
    3. Improved capacity to solve problems and make decisions, including career decisions.
    4. Better relationships with family members.
    5. Made them decide to stay within the profession after seriously considering leaving the NHS.

These questions allowed generation of contextually meaningful data for this evaluation. Although this added an important element for measuring the potential impact of coaching we had to acknowledge that in this type of study, without a control group, it was impossible to claim that changes happening to coached clients were the results of coaching rather than any other influences or combination of influences. In order to minimize this limitation, we added another question to our bespoke questionnaire in which clients themselves could indicate to what degree coaching contributed to each identified change. Although this indication is a self-estimation we believe that the well-educated and self-aware clients in this study were conscious agents of their life situation and therefore had sufficient insight into the relationship between various influences in their lives. We believed in their unique position to isolate the role of the service they received from the complex array of other factors in their life and to be completely open about this under the conditions of this particular study when there was no reason for them to misrepresent their responses.

This questionnaire was piloted internally to check the questions and appropriate adjustments were made following feedback. The final questionnaire, the Specific Work-Related Questionnaire (SWRQ), became part of the Time 2 questionnaires.

To summarize, the Time 1 questionnaire consisted of demographic questions and three scales measuring employee engagement, self-efficacy, and self-compassion. The demographic questions were developed to capture the respondents' age group, sex, ethnic origin, whether trained inside or outside the UK, and career level. The Time 2 questionnaire included the above three scales of the Time 1 questionnaire and the SWRQ scale that aimed to identify changes in aspects of working life of the client and degree to which the client attributed each change to coaching. All the questionnaires asked for the unique registration number allocated on application in order to pair the Time 1 and Time 2 responses for each individual, while maintaining anonymity.

Research process

Once the potential participants of the evaluation research applied for the coaching program online they were informed about the evaluation study and were given an option to opt out if they did not wish to take part. Once accepted, clients were sent their registration number (CLT number) and then an online link to the Time 1 Survey on Surveymonkey. The next stage was the normal process of the coaching program as provided by the London Deanery. The participants were rung by one of a small team of matchers, all trained Deanery coaches. A structured conversation was held with the client, checking their reasons for seeking coaching, their understanding of the process, and practical requirements such as venue and time. The participant was then sent an email with the description of three coaches attached for them to identify their preferred coach. Clients were offered coaches outside their specialty and outside their place of work to ensure externality to the coaching process. The coaching intervention consisted of four sessions of 60–90 minutes taken over a period of 6 months. When the coaching was completed, participants were sent a link with an invitation to complete the Time 2 questionnaires. The research was conducted with consideration of good practice and strict ethical guidelines.

RESULTS

Overall, there were 189 Time 1 responses and 137 Time 2 responses. After matching responses and taking out responses where the clients had not completed the minimum number of sessions, there was a total of 120 matched Time 1 and Time 2 responses. Therefore, the final response rate was 78%.

The demographic data show that 48.3% of respondents were aged between 30 and 39, 20.8% were aged between 20 and 29, 23.3% were aged between 40 and 49 and 7.5% were aged between 50 and 59. There were no respondents aged over 60. The majority of respondents were female (66.7%). Nearly all respondents were trained within the UK (92%). The majority of respondents (46.7%) were less than 2 years' post-qualification with a further 25.8% more than 2 years' post-qualification and 18.3% foundation trainees. The majority of respondents were White British, followed by 18.3% who were Asian or Asian British: Indian.

The results of the three selected established measures (Tables 19.1 and 19.2) indicate that clients benefited from the program in relation to each of them.

Table 19.1 shows the descriptive data for both Time 1 and Time 2 for employee engagement, self-efficacy, and self-compassion. The first line of data looks at the means and it is clear that all Time 2 means (average) are higher than the Time 1 means (average).

However, before exploring whether these differences are statistically significant, it is important to consider levels of employee engagement, self-efficacy, and self-compassion before the coaching began. Table 19.2 describes the differences in results of the sample of doctors that was used in the UWES manual. These results suggest that the clients in this study had higher levels of employee engagement before they started the coaching than the sample from the UWES manual. What is also important to point out is the minimum and maximum scores and the resulting range of scores. While the average employee engagement levels are reasonably high there is a wide range of scores, with the lowest being 1.60 (which equates to "at least once a year") and the highest being 5.80 (which equates to "a couple of times a week or daily"). At Time 2, the range of scores is reduced, as is the standard deviation, which measures dispersion around the average value.

Although self-efficacy scores had the largest effect size (Table 19.3) the ranges of scores and standard deviation stayed nearly the same. As with employee engagement, scores for self-compassion showed decreases in range of scores.

Table 19.1 *Descriptive Data From Time 1 and Time 2 Questionnaires*

	Employee Engagement Time 1	Employee Engagement Time 2	Self-Efficacy Time 1	Self-Efficacy Time 2	Self-Compassion Time 1	Self-Compassion Time 2
Mean/Standard Deviation	4.13 (.78)	4.37 (.71)	2.99 (.39)	3.17 (.39)	2.98 (.61)	3.22 (.63)
Median/Range of scores	4.2 (4.20)	4.4 (3.94)	3 (1.9)	3.1 (1.9)	2.92 (3.17)	3.25 (2.84)
Minimum score	1.60	1.93	2	2.1	1.25	1.58
Maximum score	5.80	5.87	3.9	4	4.42	4.42

Table 19.2 *Comparing UWES Sample and London Deanery Sample*

	UWES Manual Sample	London Deanery Sample
Number	655	120
Mean	3.10	4.13
Coding	"At least a couple of times a month"	"At least once a week"
Nationality	Dutch and Finnish	English
Background	Completed career counseling questionnaire	Applied to coaching program

Table 19.3 *Paired Sample t-Tests to Measure Whether Time 2 Means Are Higher Than Time 1 Scores*

Scale	Standard Deviation	t	Df	Sig. (2-tailed)
Employee engagement	.66	3.968	119	.000
Self-efficacy	.36	5.423	119	.000
Self-compassion	.47	5.586	119	.000

The results of the paired sample *t*-tests in Table 19.3 show a positive impact on mean scores of employee engagement, self-efficacy, and self-compassion (at the .01 level) with a highly significant effect for mean scores on all three scales. Effect sizes were calculated based on Cohen's calculations for paired sample *t*-tests. Effect size for employee engagement is .32, for self-efficacy .45, and for self-compassion .38. This shows that the effect sizes vary between small and medium (employee engagement and self-compassion) and medium (self-efficacy). It is also important to highlight that there is evidence that the UWES is better at measuring lower compared to high levels of employee engagement. Therefore, it is possible that the coaching had more of an impact on coaches than these effect sizes suggest. The General Self-Efficacy Scale is also better at measuring lower scores than higher ones.

This means that all three measures selected for their capacity to illustrate meaningful changes in the clients as the result of their coaching confirm that these changes were significant. The clients reported higher levels of employee engagement, self-efficacy, and self-compassion after being coached in comparison to the levels of these aspects in their lives before they engaged with the coaching program. The results were not driven by any particular subgroup and benefit was seen across subgroups in race, gender, stage of career, and age.

Another type of analysis was made available by using the SWRQ developed for this study. This questionnaire was designed to explore the changes that are perceived by the clients in relation to their work.

The results of this analysis are shown in Figures 19.1 and 19.2 and in Table 19.4.

Figure 19.1 represents the results of the analysis of the participants' responses to Question 5: "How the following aspects of your work have changed since starting

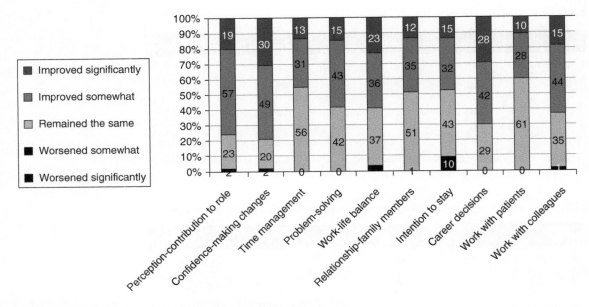

Figure 19.1 *Changes Perceived in Working Life as the Result of Coaching*

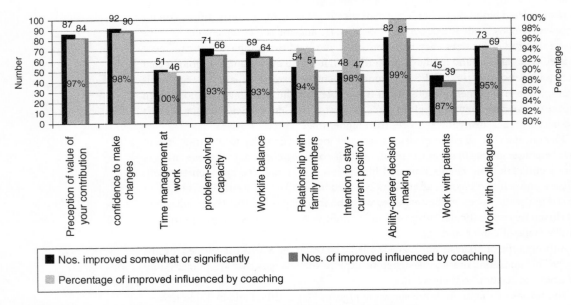

Figure 19.2 *Perception of Participants on How Changes Occurred Are Attributable to Coaching*

Table 19.4 *Summary of Qualitative Analysis*

Theme (no. of comments)	Example of the comments
Confidence (32)	"Substantially increased my confidence in the workplace in the context of being a new consultant joining a well-established senior team."
Change/problem solving (22)	"I can now confidently formulate strategies to help me achieve my goals."
Self-awareness (17)	"gave me insight into the tools I possess myself to change my work and personal life."
Reflection (16)	"taught me how to analyze my experiences objectively—reflecting, thinking about things a lot deeper than I usually would."
Work-life balance (12)	"It has improved my perspective on what I am able to achieve at work and so improved my work-life balance significantly. I feel better able to cope as a result."
Seeing things in perspective (8)	"helped me to see my position, behavior and current options in better perspective."
Career development (7)	"focused my ideas of where I want to be in the future and how to influence and use the resources open to me now to reach these roles."
Being listened to/sharing (6)	"I was able to safely discuss a very difficult situation at work."
General positive (14)	"An immense difference—turned my life around."
General negative (7)	"not all problems have a solution."

coaching." This figure illustrates how, according to clients themselves, certain aspects of their working life were changing or remained the same after the period when they undertook coaching. Different shades of gray represent the degree to which the clients perceived the changes. It is clear that the category "worsened significantly" is not present in the figure. The result suggests that the majority of these aspects improved or improved significantly. Only a very small number of responses (21) indicated that some particular aspects of their working life "worsened somewhat." It is interesting to notice that ten of these responses are related to the "Intention to stay in the current position," which could be interpreted as a positive outcome in some situations when a radical action is beneficial for both the employee and the employer.

Particularly positive perceptions of changes were demonstrated in relation to perception of values of the client contribution to their current role, confidence to make changes in the workplace, and ability to make career decisions. In comparison to other factors, it appears that the coaching program was particularly successful in empowering the clients and improving their perception of themselves at work. This indication of changes corresponds with the data of self-efficacy and self-compassion in the Time 1 and Time 2 questionnaires.

Although the results of changes demonstrated in Table 19.2 and Figure 19.2 show significant changes in clients who undertook the coaching program, it could be argued that these changes might indicate the influence of a combination of factors other than coaching. Because we had no control group we do not know to what degree the changes that we have seen are due to the coaching that they received. In order to compensate for this issue, we included question 6 in our SWRQ, which asked this question directly: "Please indicate the extent to which coaching/mentoring contributed to this change." In relation to each change from Question 5 the clients could indicate if the change could be attributed to coaching and the degree they believed the coaching influenced this change.

The results of the analysis of responses to this question are demonstrated in Figure 19.2.

The black bar in Figure 19.2 highlights the number of respondents who felt that there had been some improvement (either somewhat or significant) in the areas highlighted in the SWRQ. The dark gray bar highlights the numbers of respondents who felt that the coaching had influenced the positive change that is highlighted by the black bar. The light gray bar sitting in front of two other bars highlights what percentage of positive improvement was attributed to the coaching. For example, as was already shown in Figure 19.1, the three areas of work where respondents felt there had been the most improvement were "perception of value of your contribution," "confidence to make changes at work," and "ability to make career decisions." In these areas of work where there had been improvements, respondents felt that a large percentage of the improvement was due to the coaching that they had received—on average 98% for these three most changed areas of life.

The lowest change is indicated in the area of work with patients, which may indicate that although Time 2 responses reflect increased confidence and the way participants felt about themselves, it may take time to recognize such changes in action, particularly with their work with patients. It is also possible that the junior doctors may be fairly remote from patient satisfaction questionnaires (this tends to happen at a departmental level) and, therefore, find it difficult to notice the effect of their internal changes on patients.

Findings from the open question in SWRQ Question 9 in the SWRQ asked participants in a word or phrase to describe what difference the coaching and mentoring program had made to them. All participants responded to this question. Three researchers, first independently and then together, analyzed these responses and identified the following themes (see Table 19.4). These themes are described in the order of the number of comments considered as representing each theme (from highest to lowest).

On the whole the qualitative analysis suggests an overwhelmingly positive impact of coaching on clients and a wide variety of the benefits associated with participation in this program. The overarching patterns of the benefits are:

1. Confidence improvement and increased self-awareness.
2. Specific areas of working life where there was a significant difference as the result of coaching such as career development and work-life balance.
3. Acquiring a range of skills that could make participants more capable of addressing potential issues, such as the skills of problem solving, reflection and seeing things in perspective.

It would be unusual if the effect of coaching were universally positive. A small percentage of general negative comments (4.96%) illustrate that there are circumstances in which this particular type of intervention is not the best solution. There could be, of course, other explanations (e.g., not the best match between coach and client); however without further investigation these are only speculations.

DISCUSSION AND CONCLUSIONS

The evaluation described in the report with the support of both quantitative and qualitative methods indicates that the London Deanery coaching program provides an effective service for their clients. Well-validated measures that were selected for this evaluation project conclusively show that employee engagement, self-efficacy, and self-compassion of the participants significantly improved. It could be argued that the measures selected for this project have been sufficient for the purposes of the evaluation. They appropriately reflect the nature of this program, which is by definition individually focused. However, as the program is delivered and paid for by public funding, the benefits for the individuals have to be meaningful in the context of the added value to the ultimate users: in this context, patients. Therefore, an additional questionnaire, the SWRQ, was developed with a focus on evaluating changes in the context specific to London Deanery coaching clients. The questionnaire allowed unique information to be elicited about the nature of changes that clients identified as the result of the program related to their place of work and consequently showed improvements particularly to the aspect of self (confidence in their ability). We believe that this questionnaire would be useful for future evaluations and the data collected in this project can be used for developing the scale for further investigations.

In terms of the design of the evaluation, needless to say that projects with features of the randomized control study would be easier to defend in the traditional scientific community. However, there are many reasons to expand this position and we propose to consider at least three of them.

The first is simply pragmatic. Considering many issues that constrain the use of RCTs in coaching research (Cavanagh & Grant, 2006; Greif, 2009; Passmore & Fillery-Travis, 2011), not the least the cost-effectiveness of the evaluation itself, we need to develop research designs that are possible to execute. A more positively formulated reason for creating new measures for evaluating coaching programs relates to giving more status to the participants according to the nature of coaching itself. Coaching is about valuing the voice of the individual, empowering the person and trusting in their ability to make a judgment about the issues that reflect their life. Research that actively includes the voice of participants in judging the changes they have experienced is better aligned with coaching than research that treats participants as only capable of answering very simple questions leaving the analysis to an "objective" researcher.

A third and probably the most important reason for being more daring and creative in searching for new approaches to evaluation is based on the acknowledgment that the outcomes we aim to assess result from the complex interaction of multiple elements in systems with emerging properties. Jones and Corner (2012) recently argued that mentoring should be seen as a case of complex adaptive system (CAS) and their arguments are more than relevant also for coaching. Seeing coaching engagement through this lens brings to the fore many issues that were very difficult to account for in this research. For example, the changes that occurred within the clients are directly and complexly related to their context, and it is impossible to isolate all the influences without losing the essence of the process and the layers of meaning for each individual involved. This means that we need to look at research methods that include new ideas different from traditional science, because it implies a different view of the world.

In particular, we suggest wider use of qualitative methods that can enrich understanding of the effect of coaching. Some of these methods can include, for example, vignettes constructed around actual experiences, by using situations provided by participants before and after coaching. These rich descriptions of actual experiences can be seen as snapshots of the complexity reflected in one particular case without losing the link with its context. We can use the SWRQ for evaluation of coaching programs as an addition to other methods and an alternative solution when RCT is not possible / appropriate, as it includes a self-estimation by the respondents about the extent to which they can attribute each change to the received coaching also without losing the view of the systemic nature of their situations.

We also wish to advocate further building of the theoretical base of coaching by extending evaluation research from the question of effectiveness of coaching to exploring further questions such as the following:

1. What elements of coaching in this program have particularly contributed to positive outcomes?
2. Are the changes identified by the clients sustained over a longer period?
3. To what type of clients is this program most suited?
4. What difference does the matching process make?
5. In what way can the changes identified by the client actually affect their work with patients?

Research into the effect of the coaching program on a large scale was on the agenda for the London Deanery at the start of this project. Although this could be an important and ambitious undertaking, we believe that this current project has provided a positive answer to the question about the effectiveness of the coaching program on a reasonable scale. In light of these findings, we would argue that the questions that aim at improvement of the service, which are of a more precise nature, similar to the questions listed above, would be no less important and probably more pertinent for the ultimate stakeholders of the London Deanery's coaching program.

ACKNOWLEDGMENTS

We are deeply grateful to all participants in this study and our advisors from the London Deanery Dr. Rebecca Viney and Dr. Sue Morgan for constructive feedback at all stages of the project.

REFERENCES

Bandura, A. (1997). *Self-efficacy: The exercise of control.* New York: Freeman.

Briner, R. (2012). Does coaching work and does anyone really care? *OP Matters, 16,* 4–12.

Cavanagh, M. J., & Grant, A. M. (2006). Coaching psychology and the scientist-practitioner model. In D. A. Lane & S. C. Corrie (Eds.), *The modern scientist-practitioner* (pp. 146–157). Hove, UK: Routledge.

Cronin, M., & Klimoski, R. (2011). Broadening the view of what constitutes evidence. *Industrial and Organisational Psychology, 4*(1), 57–61.

de Haan, E., & Duckworth, A. (2012). Signalling a new trend in executing coaching outcome research. *International Coaching Psychology Review, 8*(1), 6–19.

De Meuse, K., Dai, G., & Lee, R. (2009). Evaluating the effectiveness of executive coaching: Beyond ROI? *Coaching: An International Journal of Theory, Research and Practice, 2*(2), 117–134.

De Meuse, K. P. (2009). Driving team effectiveness. *A comparative analysis of the Korn/Ferry T7 model with other popular team.* Accessed from https://jocon.com/fileadmin/download/pdf/Teamswhitepaper.pdf

Demerouti, E., Bakker, A. B., Janssen, P. P. M., & Schaufeli, W. B. (2001). Burnout and engagement at work as a function of demands and control. *Scandinavian Journal of Work, Environment & Health, 27,* 279–286.

Drake, D. (2009). Evidence is a verb: A relational view of knowledge and mastery in coaching. *International Journal of Evidence Based Coaching and Mentoring, 7*(1), 1–2.

Easton, S., & Van Laar, D. (2013). Evaluation of outcomes and quality of working life in the coaching setting. *The Coaching Psychologist, 9*(2), 71–77.

Ellam-Dyson, V. (2012). Coaching psychology research: Building the evidence, developing awareness. *OP Matters, 16,* 13–16.

Ely, K., Boyce, L., Nelson, J., Zaccaro, S., Hernez-Broome, G., & Whyman, W. (2010). Evaluating leadership coaching: A review and integrated framework. *The Leadership Quarterly, 21,* 585–599.

Fillery-Travis, A., & Lane, D. (2006). Does coaching work or are we asking the wrong question? *International Coaching Psychology Review, 1*(1), 23–36.

Franklin, J., & Doran, J. (2009). Does all coaching enhance objective performance independently evaluated by blind assessors? The importance of the coaching model and content. *International Coaching Psychology Review, 4,* 128–144.

Grant, A. (2012). ROI is a poor measure of coaching success: Towards a more holistic approach using a well-being and engagement framework. *Coaching: An International Journal of Theory, Research and Practice, 5*(2), 74–85.

Grant, A. (2013). The efficacy of coaching. In J. Passmore, D. Peterson, & T. Freire (Eds.), *The Wiley-Blackwell handbook of the psychology of coaching and mentoring.* Chichester: John Wiley & Sons.

Greif, S. (2007). Advances in research on coaching outcomes. *International Coaching Psychology Review, 2*(3), 222–245.

Hicks, C. (1998). The randomised controlled trial: A critique. *Nurse Researcher, 6*(1), 19–32.

Howard, K. I., Moras, K., Brill, P. L., Martinovich, Z., & Lutz, W. (1996). Evaluation of psychotherapy: Efficacy, effectiveness, and patient progress. *American Psychologist, 51,* 1059–1064.

Jones, R., & Corner, J. (2012). Seeing the forest and the trees: A complex adaptive systems lens for mentoring. *Human Relations, 65*(3), 391–411.

Kirkpatrick, D. (1977). Evaluating training programs: Evidence vs. proof. *Training and Development Journal, 31*(11), 9–12.

Lawrence, P., & Whyte, A. (2014). Return on investment in executive coaching: A practical model for measuring ROI in organisations. *Coaching: An International Journal of Theory, Research and Practice, 7*(1), 4–17.

Luszczynska, A., Scolz, U., & Schwarzer, R. (2005). The general self-efficacy scale: Multicultural validation studies. *The Journal of Psychology: Interdisciplinary and Applied, 139*(5), 439–457.

Neff, K. D. (2003). Development and validation of a scale to measure self-compassion. *Self and Identity, 2,* 223–250.

Neff, K. D. (2009). The role of self-compassion in development: A healthier way to relate to oneself. *Human Development, 52,* 211–214.

Neff, K. D., & Lamb, L. M. (2009). Self-compassion. In S. Lopez (Ed.), *The encyclopedia of positive psychology.* Oxford: Blackwell.

Neff, K. D., & Vonk, R. (2009). Self-compassion versus global self-esteem: Two different ways of relating to oneself. *Journal of Personality, 77,* 23–50.

Orlinsky, D., Grawe, K., & Parks, B. (1994). Process and outcome in psychotherapy. In A. Bergin & S. Garfield (Eds.), *Handbook of psychotherapy and behavior change* (4th ed.). New York: Wiley.

Passmore, J. (Ed.). (2008). *Psychometrics in coaching.* London: Kegan Page.

Passmore, J., & Fillery-Travis, A. (2011). A critical review of executive coaching research: A decade of progress and what's to come. *Coaching: An International Journal of Theory, Research and Practice, 4*(2), 70–88.

Passmore, J., & Joao Velez, M. (2014). Training evaluation. In K. Kraiger, J. Passmore, A. Dos Santos, & S. Malvezzi (Eds.), *The Wiley and Blackwell handbook of the psychology of training, development and performance improvement* (pp. 136–153). Chichester: Wiley Blackwell.

Salanova, M., Agut, S., & Peiró, J. M. (2005). Linking organisational resources and work engagement to employee performance and customer loyalty: The mediation of service climate. *Journal of Applied Psychology, 90,* 1217–1227.

Schaufeli, W. B., & Bakker, A. B. (2003). Utrecht work engagement scale: Preliminary manual. *Occupational Health Psychology Unit, Utrecht University, Utrecht, 26,* 64–000.

Schaufeli, W. B., & Bakker, A. B. (2004). Job demands, job resources and their relationship with burnout and engagement: A multi-sample study. *Journal of Organisational Behavior, 25,* 293–315.

Scherbaum, C., Cohen-Charash, Y., & Kern, M. (2006). Measuring general self-efficacy: A comparison of three measures using item response theory. *Educational and Psychological Measurement, 66*(6), 1047–1061.

Schwarzer, R., & Jerusalem, M. (1995). Generalised self-efficacy scale. In J. Weinman, S. Wright, & M. Johnston (Eds.), *Measures in health psychology: A user's portfolio. Causal and control beliefs.* Windsor, UK: NFER–NELSON.

Stajkovic, A., & Luthans, F. (1998). Self-efficacy and work-related performance: A meta-analysis. *Psychological Bulletin, 124*(2), 240–261.

Strauss, A., & Corbin, J. (1990). *Basics of qualitative research: Grounded theory procedures and techniques.* London: Sage.

Tashakkori, A., & Teddli, C. (Eds.). (2010). *Sage handbook of mixed methods in social and behavioural research.* London: Sage.

Theeboom, T., Beersma, B., & van Vianen, A. (2013). Does coaching work? A meta-analysis on the effects of coaching on individual level outcomes in an organisational context. *The Journal of Positive Psychology, 9*(1), 1–18.

Williams, B. A. (2010). Perils of evidence-based medicine. *Perspectives on Biology and Medicine, 53*(1), 106–120.

20 Toward a Model of Coaching Transfer: Operationalizing Coaching Success and the Facilitators and Barriers to Transfer

Lorna J. Stewart, Stephen Palmer, Helen Wilkin, and Maire Kerrin[1]

Increasingly organizations are employing executive coaching as a means to enhance their human resource assets (Sherman & Freas, 2004). While coaching research is amassing, a lack of an agreed definition or the operationalization of a successful coaching outcome (SCO) means that methods of evaluation are underdeveloped. Furthermore, research has paid little attention to understanding the factors associated with transfer to or maintenance of coaching benefits within the workplace.

Training and coaching are similar insofar as they both involve learning and seek its application beyond the learning environment. These commonalities suggest that poor training transfer estimates (Baldwin & Ford, 1988) may be a caution that the transfer of coaching's benefits to the workplace is not guaranteed. However, while coaching and training both seek to effect positive developmental change, the distinctiveness of coaching objectives (Carter, Wolfe, & Kerrin, 2005), the eclectic nature of the methodologies

---

[1] First published as Stewart, L.J., Palmer, S., Wilkin, H, & Kerrin, M. (2008). Towards a model of coaching transfer: Operationalising coaching success and the facilitators and barriers to transfer. *International Coaching Psychology Review*, 3, 87–109.

employed to achieve them, and the exclusivity of relationships in which they are nurtured, complicate the modeling and measuring of coaching outcomes.

In order to obtain research evidence to inform best practice, and to advise coaching stakeholders on how to facilitate the transfer of coachee-acquired coaching development to the workplace, this study aimed to extend a model of training transfer into the coaching field; thus, providing a basis for coaching evaluation. In addition, it developed frameworks detailing the unique characteristics of coaching success and the factors that impact upon its transfer to the workplace.

EXECUTIVE COACHING

Coaching within organizations falls within two main categories: coaching as a day-to-day management activity predominantly conducted by line managers; and executive coaching (Peltier, 2001). This study was concerned with executive coaching. Executive coaching was recognized as "a form of tailored work-related development for senior and professional managers which spans business, functional, and personal skills" (Carter, 2001, p. x), and as a development activity for less senior high-potential managers (Judge & Cowell, 1997). The term coachee was adopted to represent individuals participating in coaching.

Although coaching strives to be acknowledged as an independent discipline, it incorporates aspects of counseling, mentoring, training, and consulting (Greene & Grant, 2003). Consequently, theoretical knowledge and research methodologies drawn from these disciplines all provide a useful basis for coaching research. The current study drew on training transfer research to provide a framework for coaching evaluation.

Positive training transfer refers to the "implementation of knowledge, skills, attitudes, and other qualities acquired during training into the workplace" (Gumuseli & Ergin, 2002, p. 81). Extrapolating from this concept, the current study proposed a similar construct for positive coaching transfer; specifically, the sustained application of knowledge, skills, attitudes, and other qualities acquired during coaching into the workplace.

MEASURING COACHING TRANSFER

Evaluating coaching relies upon a measure of successful coaching transfer. Such a measure must include: (a) the process under scrutiny; (b) the outcomes it is measured against; and (c) from whose perspective success is being judged (Carter et al., 2005). In terms of outcomes, studies suggest coaching can result in increased: (a) self-awareness (Gegner, 1997); (b) self-esteem (Wales, 2003); (c) emotional intelligence (Kleinberg, 2001); (d) self-efficacy

(Gegner, 1997); and (e) job-satisfaction (Olivero, Bane, & Kopelman, 1997). While this list is not exhaustive, currently no consensus exists regarding what constitutes an SCO.

As the current study sought to understand workplace transfer of coachee-acquired coaching-based development, the primary perspective adopted was that of the coachee. Using the coachee's opinion of an SCO, the study sought to develop a coachee-focused measure of positive transfer. Coaches' and organizational stakeholders' perspectives were also investigated to explore the validity of the coachee-focused measure.

TOWARD A MODEL OF COACHING TRANSFER

Several models of training transfer have been proposed (e.g., Baldwin & Ford, 1988), all of which, fundamentally, seek to integrate the influence of training inputs, training outputs, and conditions of transfer on training transfer. Although Baldwin and Ford's model has been criticized for its simplicity (e.g., Machin, 2002), it provides a straightforward transfer framework. Training inputs are broadly classifiable as trainee characteristics, training design, and work environment factors, and these are suggested to have both direct and indirect effects on transfer (Baldwin & Ford, 1988).

The current study was interested in factors outside of the coachee–coach relationship; in particular, those that can be targeted by transfer enhancing interventions. Hence, only coachee characteristics and work environment factors were explored.

Coachee characteristics

An enduring conceptualization within occupational psychology is that an individual's cognitive ability and motivation are key determinants of learning and work performance (Herold, Davis, Fedor, & Parsons, 2002; Kanfer & Ackerman, 1989). Within the training literature, these factors have been associated with positive transfer and so these factors may also have an impact on coaching transfer. However, the executive coaching population is likely to have a reasonably high, restricted range of cognitive ability (Goleman, 2002). Furthermore, as both cognitive ability and personality are considered relatively stable (Ackerman & Heggestad, 1997) they are not easily manipulated via intervention. Accordingly, while a model of coaching transfer could include cognitive ability, personality, and motivation, only motivation can be actively influenced.

Motivation is recognized as a key determinant of training transfer (Cheng & Ho, 2001), with both motivation to learn and transfer (Noe, 1986) being significant. The current study proposed motivation would be associated with coaching transfer.

Hypothesis 1: Coachee motivation will be positively associated with coaching transfer.

Work environment factors

Work environment factors associated with training transfer include social support, and situational facilitators and constraints (Mathieu & Martineau, 1997). Social support refers to individuals' beliefs about: (a) the opportunities their workplace affords them to use their learning; and (b) the likelihood they will receive support and feedback for their transfer endeavors (Clarke, 2002). Social support sources include subordinates, peers, supervisors, and top management (Facteau, Dobbins, Russell, Ladd, & Kudish, 1995). Within a coaching environment, the final three groups are the most likely to be aware the coachee is attending coaching, provide transfer opportunities, and give feedback on transfer endeavors.

Within the coaching literature, findings related to peer support are limited. Goldsmith and Morgan (2005) found that participants who sought peer input into their development showed marked improvement. Others have found positive links between peer influences on training transfer (e.g., Facteau et al., 1995; Holton, Bates, Seyler, & Carvalho, 1997; Newstrom, 1986). Hence, positive peer support appears likely to be associated with coaching transfer.

Hypothesis 2: Positive peer support will be positively associated with coaching transfer.

The training literature reports ambiguous findings regarding the influence of supervisor support on transfer. Holton et al. (1997) found supervisor support was associated with transfer, whereas Facteau et al. (1995) found it negatively related to transfer. Despite this mixed evidence, McGovern et al. (2001) found the coachee's manager positively influenced coaching success.

Hypothesis 3: Positive supervisor support will be positively associated with coaching transfer.

Little is known about top-management's influence on training transfer. Lim and Johnson (2002) found top-management support was associated with training transfer; whereas Facteau et al. (1995) failed to find a significant relationship. Within coaching, top-management support is discussed indirectly. For example, coaching is described as best when there is collaboration between the coachee, coach, and the organization (Wasylyshyn, 2003). The current study therefore aimed to provide preliminary evidence with regard to the relationship between top-management influences and coaching transfer.

Finally, regarding work environment factors, studies suggest training transfer is affected by facilitators and constraints resident in the workplace. These include the availability of job-related information, equipment, financial support, and time (Huczynski & Lewis, 1980; Mathieu & Martineau, 1997; Porras & Hargis, 1982) and the opportunity to use new skills on the job (Holton et al., 1997). However, other studies have either found no relationship between constraints and performance (Peters, O'Connor, Eulberg, & Watson, 1988), or have found constraints are only significant when they are severe (Facteau et al., 1995). Within the coaching literature, McGovern et al.'s (2001) study cites the coachee's availability and time pressures as affecting coaching effectiveness. The current study proposed the presence of situational facilitators and the absence of severe constraints (collectively referred to as positive situational factors) would be associated with coaching transfer.

Hypothesis 4: Positive situational factors will be positively associated with coaching transfer.

SUMMARY OF COACHING INPUTS

This study proposed three categories of coaching inputs: coachee characteristics, coaching factors, and the work environment. Anticipated coaching outcomes were categorized into coachee development, and the application, generalization, and maintenance of this development within the workplace. Figure 20.1 presents a conceptual model of coaching transfer developed from Baldwin and Ford's (1988) transfer of training model.

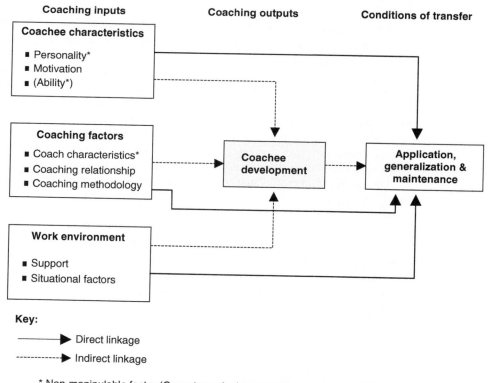

Figure 20.1 *Conceptual Coaching Transfer Model.*

Note. Based on Baldwin and Ford's (1988) transfer of training model.

Verifying this model necessitated a coaching outcome measure. To achieve the study's aims two sub-studies were conducted. Study 1 sought to operationalize an SCO and the facilitators and barriers to coaching transfer. Study 2 sought to verify the proposed coaching transfer model by exploring the aforementioned four hypotheses.

STUDY 1: OPERATIONALIZING A SUCCESSFUL COACHING OUTCOME AND THE FACILITATORS AND BARRIERS TO COACHING TRANSFER

A descriptive qualitative approach was chosen to explore perceptions of an SCO and the facilitators and barriers to transfer. Semi-structured interviews (Kvale, 1996) sought participants' views of what constitutes an SCO and evidence indicative of positive coaching transfer. An adapted critical incident technique (Flanagan, 1954) was used to explore participants' perceptions of the facilitators and barriers of positive transfer. A total of 39 individuals were interviewed: 25 managers and executives, each of whom had completed an average of seven coaching sessions within a variety of coaching programs; nine coaches, each with six or more years' experience; and five senior managers who had recommended staff attend coaching. Interviews lasted approximately one hour. Our findings focus on the coachees as they are critical to transfer.

Themes arising from the interviews were explored via content analysis (Weber, 1990). The sentence was the unit of analysis and complex sentences were broken down into thematic units. Abbreviated text extracts, each containing one theme, were noted in a spreadsheet for each question for every participant. When all extracts were identified, constructs developed to capture meaning and enable comparisons between participants were noted in a separate column alongside each extract. Participants were asked to verify the accuracy of the constructs associated with their comments.

Each construct for each participant was first coded with the participant number and the question number and then transferred onto cards. A card sort was conducted, whereby each card was classified into mutually exclusive groupings (Step 1) (Jankowicz, 2004). A category definition was written for each group (Step 2). The results of the card sort were recorded in a table containing: (a) the coded numbers of the constructs allocated to each category; and (b) the number of constructs in the category, also expressed as a percentage of the total number of constructs (Step 3). To check reliability, the categorization procedure (Steps 1–3) was repeated by an independent researcher. A reliability matrix was constructed and each researcher independently placed the constructs into the matrix cells (Step 4). Inter-rater reliability was calculated using the kappa coefficient of agreement (Cohen, 1960) (Step 5). The initial reliability indices fell below the target of .8 (Stemler, 2001). To improve reliability, the researchers negotiated the category meanings, recalculating the reliability indices after each redefinition. After reaching the .8 agreement threshold, each researcher independently sorted the constructs into the new categories and tabulated their results (Step 3 above). To check reliability, steps four and five were repeated. Separate analyses were conducted for coachees, coaches, and stakeholders.

STUDY 1 RESULTS

Defining an SCO

Analyses identified 738 clusters for coachees, 296 for coaches, and 146 for organizational stakeholders. Within each referent group, two categories emerged: personal outcomes and performance outcomes. Kappa coefficients were: coachees = .86, coaches = .89, and stakeholders = .92. Table 20.1 displays the constructs within each category. For each group personal outcomes had the largest number of constructs.

Personal outcomes

Personal outcomes comprised five clusters: resilience, career management, self-management, social awareness, and self-awareness. Enhanced resilience was the most frequently cited SCO cluster. Coaching was seen as enhancing individuals' capacity to avoid, and/or the ability to recover quickly from, psychological suffering, assaults, and setbacks in a work environment. This manifested as an enhanced attitude toward work, greater psychological and physical resilience, and increased confidence. For example:

> I'm more optimistic in my outlook. Before I felt jaded. I want to come to work now. I feel inspired about what I'm doing, and I'm eager to get on with it. (Coachee 13, lines 34–37)

Interviewees suggested coaching enhanced coachees' personal career management via assisting them to develop the capacity to successfully organize, control, and direct the progress of their working life.

> I'm not settling for a career in which I don't know where I'm going. I'm more focused on achieving in my job, though not necessarily through promotion. (Coachee 11, lines 44–45)

They also indicated that coaching aided coachees to develop their ability to control and direct their behavior (i.e., enhanced self-management) to maximize their work-related performance. This was represented by: (a) enhanced self-monitoring (e.g., monitoring behavior and/or attitudes at work); and (b) using efficiency and effectiveness strategies (e.g., enhanced prioritizing).

> I'm not so random. I have a more focused and less scattered approach to thinking about things. (Coachee 17, lines 19–20)

Table 20.1 *Defining a Successful Coaching Outcome*

	Coachees		Coaches		Stakeholders	
	Freq	*%*	*Freq*	*%*	*Freq*	*%*
Personal outcomes	586	79.40	219	73.99	79	54.11
Enhanced resilience	177	23.98	100	33.78	27	18.49
Enhanced personal career management	140	18.97	44	14.86	18	12.33
Enhanced self-management	124	16.80	50	16.89	26	17.81
Enhanced self-awareness	118	16.00	16	5.40	5	3.42
Enhanced social awareness	27	3.66	9	3.04	3	2.05
Performance outcomes	152	20.60	77	26.01	67	45.89
Enhanced job performance	74	10.03	41	13.85	38	26.03
Enhanced relationship management	54	7.31	27	9.12	20	13.70
Enhanced job-specific knowledge and/or skills	24	3.25	9	3.04	9	6.16
	738	100	296	100	146	100

Although coachees were the most likely to mention enhanced self-awareness, all groups suggested that coaching assisted coachees to acquire a balanced and honest consciousness of their personality, dispositions, and motivators, including the ability to interpret external stimuli in accordance with their view of self.

> Through coaching I connected with my core self. My role had forced me to suppress things about myself. Now I know what I need to be happy in a role, and what motivates me when I am at work, I actually want to go to work. (Coachee 13, lines 29–31)

This manifested as an enhanced understanding of job-related strengths and limitations, motivators and stressors.

> I'm more aware of what triggers me to feel stressed; mostly it's when I have to work outside of my strengths, then I feel less dynamic and out of control. My strategy has become to delegate my weaknesses. (Coachee 6, lines 55–58)

Interviewees suggested coaching enhanced coachees' knowledge and mindfulness of others (i.e., enhanced social awareness). This was characterized by greater appreciation of others' strengths, weaknesses and motivators, and of how to respond to others appropriately.

> It helped me understand other people's perceptions. Knowing more about myself made me more aware that not everyone works the same. We all have different combinations of strengths and weaknesses. I'm better able to recognize these in others. (Coachee 7, lines 71–77)

Performance outcomes

Three clusters fell within this category: job performance, relationship management, and job-specific knowledge and/or skills. Coachees, coaches, and stakeholders all cited enhanced job performance as the key performance outcome. It was signified by tangible outcomes associated with heightened job effectiveness and/or efficiency (e.g., enhanced quality of output). For example:

> My appraisal grades have gone up. I've had better feedback from the people I work with. My manager gave me a pat on the back (laughs). (Coachee 20, lines 30–32)

Enhanced efficiency referred to completing the same amount of work in less time, or more work in the same time. Enhanced work-life balance emerged as a product of enhanced efficiency.

Interviewees suggested coaching assisted coachees in developing the ability to successfully organize, coordinate, and influence their interpersonal and team relationships (i.e., enhanced relationship management).

> I know more about why people behave the way they do, and I'm better at shaping the way I behave to get the reaction I want from them. I'm better at taking people along with me; I'm also more open to what they have to say. It cuts both ways. (Coachee 2, lines 34–38)

Some interviewees' comments suggested coaching resulted in the acquisition of new and/or deeper job-specific knowledge and/or skills, although this tended to be objective specific.

> I'd got by without anyone realizing I lacked certain basics, like budget forecasting. It wasn't the main part of my role, but I felt my weakness was becoming more evident, especially as I was up for promotion. My coach put me in touch with someone who helped me. It only took a couple of hours to get rid of all that stress. (Coachee 20, lines 57–61)

Structure of SCO development

Some coachees' comments suggested that self-awareness formed a foundation for subsequent personal outcomes and performance outcomes (i.e., forward-flow development). Specifically, enhanced awareness led to greater resilience, personal career management, and self-management, which in turn led to enhanced job performance. For example:

> The main difference is I'm more aware of my strengths and limitations. I try to work within my strengths 70% of the time, and push the boundaries to develop myself the rest of the time. As a result both the quality and the quantity of my work have improved. (Coachee 25, lines 20–22)

Developmental influences also appeared to operate between personal outcomes and self-awareness, and between performance outcomes and self-awareness (i.e., feedback-flow development). Feedback influences seemed to produce changes in self-awareness, which subsequently led to further forward-flow development.

> I received negative feedback about the way I was working. I realized a middle ground between what I did before and what I learnt in coaching was more appropriate. (Coachee 24, lines 31–34)

Feedback-flow development appeared to be initiated by: (a) circumstances that caused coachees to reflect on the value and validity of their development; and (b) logistical constraints that prevented the implementation of coaching outcomes. There was also suggestion that development led to enhanced awareness that further development was required.

> I applied what I'd learnt, and this helped me resolve some of the problems; but it also made me more aware of other areas I needed to improve on. (Coachee 5, lines 32–34)

Coachees' comments suggested that an SCO results in the development of a general personal-professional competence that appears to be located in the personal outcomes category. Coachees expressed it as a: (a) toolkit for tackling diverse problems; and (b) new approach that had enhanced their all-round performance.

Defining coaching transfer

Analyses identified 112 constructs for coachees, 54 for coaches, and 38 for stakeholders. Within each group, three clusters emerged: application, maintenance, and generalization. These clusters represented one category: evidence of coaching transfer (EoT). Kappa coefficients were: coachees = .91, coaches = .94, and organizational stakeholders = .90. For each referent group, application was most frequently discussed. For coachees and coaches the second most frequent category was generalization, followed by maintenance. Stakeholders reversed this trend to maintenance and generalization. Table 20.2 displays the category and clusters.

Coaching transfer

Evidence of coaching transfer comprised three clusters: application, maintenance, and generalization. Interviewees suggested that application requires evidence that a significant proportion of the coaching development has been used within the workplace, with a relatively high frequency, and that it has positively impacted on their performance. For example:

Table 20.2   *Defining Coaching Transfer*

	Coachees		Coaches		Stakeholders	
	Freq	%	Freq	%	Freq	%
Coaching transfer	112	100	54	100	38	100
Application	45	40.18	26	48.15	21	55.26
Maintenance	31	27.68	9	16.67	11	28.95
Generalization	36	32.14	19	35.19	6	15.79
	112	100	296	100	146	100

I am achieving so much more. I do more in less time, and it is of a higher quality. My boss has given me much better feedback than this time last year. (Coachee 22, lines 37–40)

All groups expected that the use of coaching development would be sustained or increased within the workplace after the end of the formal coaching period (i.e., maintenance), and that coachees' proficiency and confidence in using their development would be maintained or increase over time.

I persisted in applying what I'd learnt in coaching, and now it seems natural. These days no one would ever know I'd struggled with these things; I forget I did too. (Coachee 25, lines 33–36)

They also suggested that transfer requires evidence that coachees have applied their coaching development to areas beyond those for which it was initially sought and/or applied, including beyond the workplace (i.e., generalization).

Over time I felt more comfortable to bring it into different parts of my job. At first I was worried it wouldn't work beyond what we'd discussed and practiced in coaching—but gradually as I used it I saw the potential for applying it elsewhere, I have and it works. I find some of it useful at home too. (Coachee 16, lines 43–47)

Facilitators and barriers to coaching transfer

Analyses of incidents of facilitation identified 507 clusters for coachees; 383 for coaches, and 164 for stakeholders. Analyses of incidents of barriers to transfer identified 336 clusters for coachees; 289 for coaches, and 63 for stakeholders. Within each group, three categories emerged: positive psychosocial support vs. psychosocial barriers to development, pro-development vs. development-unsupportive organizational culture, and pro-development vs. development-indifferent coachees. The kappa coefficients for the analyses were: (a) facilitator analyses coachees = .82, coaches = .89, stakeholders = .88; and (b) barrier analyses coachees = .89, coaches = .86, stakeholders = .94. Table 20.3 displays the categories and clusters.

Psychosocial support

Psychosocial support emerged as the key category for all groups in both the facilitator and barrier analyses. Positive psychosocial support included the physical and emotional availability of a quality developmental champion: someone senior to the coachee, usually within their organization, who took an interest in the coachee's development by virtue of their role in the organization (e.g., immediate manager) or via a sense of responsibility (e.g., volunteer mentor).

> My manager talked about things in a positive way; he didn't put down what I wanted to do, although in hindsight some of it must have seemed a bit naïve. (Coachee 3, lines 103–105)

The absence of a quality champion posed the chief barrier to transfer.

> My boss could have been more welcoming and interested in me and my coaching. I felt that he didn't want me in his department. I had to seek him out to discuss my coaching and he avoided me. He was arrogant and obnoxious. (Coachee 15, lines 114–118)

Positive psychosocial support also involved the formation of a partnership for developmental action between the coachee and their champion. The champion's role involved assisting the coachee to refine a development plan that integrated the coachee's coaching-generated objectives with their job priorities and overall development plan. Supportive champions were also proactive in helping coachees implement their development. Further, they monitored coachees' progress toward objectives and provided constructive feedback. It was crucial for the champion to fulfill any promised action. For example:

> He gave me feedback about what I'd achieved; and he gave me a few attempts to get it right, he didn't jump down my throat and say "you've got to do it this way." He paid more attention to my successes, which I appreciated. (Coachee 1, lines 80–84)

Poor champions were seen as blocking coachee's development plans, not providing practice opportunities, and not offering or failing to follow through on facilitative action.

> My manager understood that I wanted to make changes but he kept dumping work on me. He could have intervened too when more senior people piled work on me. He cared more about making the department look good than about his staff. (Coachee 23, lines 94–97)

Peer support received less mention than champion support and tended to be viewed as the absence of obstruction. Peers acted as barriers to transfer when they sabotaged coachees' development efforts, including being critical of coaching. Interviewees' comments suggested that the relationship between peer support and coaching transfer may be mediated by: (a) the nature of the development; (b) competition for promotion; (c) whether coachees share with their peers that they are attending coaching; and (d) the organizational culture. For example:

> My peers weren't involved. I didn't tell them. It's very competitive for promotion, and we're rated against our peers. (Coachee 4, lines 111–114)

The findings also suggested that the boundary between supervisors and peers may become contrived at the executive level. For example:

> I see my relationship with them [senior managers] as a friendship. We went to the pub and talked through my [development] options. (Coachee 7, lines 110–111)

Organizational culture

Organizational culture was the second most frequently mentioned facilitator of transfer by all groups. As a barrier it was the coachees' and coaches second most frequently mentioned category; stakeholders, however, mentioned it the least frequently. Of the three culture-related clusters, coachees and stakeholders mentioned workload the most frequently. Coachees' quantity of work, and/or continual tight deadlines, was said to impede transfer by not affording time to implement their development.

> They're too focused on the tangible aspects of success. They forget we're people and not machines. There is no time to think about your coaching. At the worst times, it can be impossible to find the time to go to coaching; sometimes I went before or after work. (Coachee 8, lines 143–148)

A pro-development climate, fostered by a positive attitude toward development, was viewed as assisting transfer. Likewise, organizations that facilitate access to development by offering and financially supporting developmental activities were seen as encouraging transfer.

> Coaching is not frowned upon, and it is available to all. They encourage you to get involved in things that will develop you. They don't view coaching as something for weak people; it's about wanting to make the best of yourself. (Coachee 14, lines 98–103)

Procedural support for development (e.g., having a strategy for post-coaching support) was seen as a transfer facilitator.

> I wanted to change my job as a result of coaching. It was made a lot easier for me that my organization had a procedure for internal job change, and that other people had done it too. (Coachee 25, lines 89–91)

Development-unsupportive cultures were characterized by having an antidevelopment climate (e.g., cultural ethos devalues coaching).

> They paid lip-service to coaching. No-one wanted to go as if you went then you were seen as weak and that was a problem if you wanted to be promoted. (Coachee 6, lines 127–129)

Transfer hampering cultures were also viewed as having structures and processes unsupportive of development (e.g., coaching objectives change with management changes).

Table 20.3 *Coaching Transfer Facilitators and Barriers*

| | Coachees | | | | Coaches | | | | Stakeholders | | | |
| | Facilitators | | Barriers | | Facilitators | | Barriers | | Facilitators | | Barriers | |
	Freq	%	Freq	%	Freq	%	Freq	%	Freq	%	Freq	%
Psychosocial support	269	53.06	165	49.11	172	44.91	147	50.87	64	39.02	28	44.44
Availability of a developmental champion	86	16.96	74	22.02	46	12.01	72	24.91	13	7.93	12	19.05
Champion-coachee partnership for	112	22.09	57	16.96	95	24.80	49	16.96	44	26.83	11	17.46
Peer support	71	14.00	34	10.12	31	8.09	26	9.00	7	4.27	5	7.94
Organizational culture	177	34.91	120	35.71	115	30.03	87	30.10	52	31.71	14	22.22
Organizational climate regarding development	88	17.36	17	5.06	57	14.88	32	11.07	20	12.20	2	3.17
Access to development/workload	69	13.61	80	23.81	31	8.09	23	7.96	25	15.24	9	14.29
Procedural support for development	20	3.94	23	6.95	27	7.05	32	11.07	8	4.88	3	4.76
Coachee's attitude toward development	61	12.03	51	15.18	96	25.07	55	19.03	48	29.27	21	33.33
Approach to development	15	2.96	17	5.06	54	14.10	23	7.96	24	14.63	7	11.11
Goal pursuit	46	9.07	34	10.12	42	10.97	32	11.07	23	14.02	14	22.22
	507	100	336	100	383	100	289	100	164	100	63	100

My manager changed three times during my coaching and my goals kept being changed. It would have been helpful if they could have left them alone and let me get on with it. (Coachee 10, lines 135–138)

Coachee's attitude toward development

The coachee's attitude toward development was the least frequently mentioned transfer facilitator by all groups. It was also the least frequently mentioned transfer barrier by coachees and coaches. Coachees with a pro-development approach (e.g., they assume responsibility for their own development) were viewed as more likely to transfer their development.

I sought out people more senior than me and bounced ideas off them. They gave me the clarity I needed and suggested options for my development. They're in a better position to advise me than my peers. (Coachee 13, line 98)

Proactive goal pursuit, whereby coachees sought to progress their coaching-related development beyond the coaching relationship, was associated with positive transfer.

I realised that the only person who could change this was me, and the only person holding me back was me, so I took responsibility and worked through my beliefs of not being good enough. I stopped waiting for people to help me make things happen and did it on my own. (Coachee 16, lines 152–156)

Conversely, coachees who placed low priority on their own development and coachees who obstructed their own development (e.g., by behaving negatively in coaching) were viewed as less likely to transfer their development.

I could have been more proactive in pursuing the changes earlier. I could have translated my development into action earlier. (Coachee 12, lines 137–140)

DISCUSSION

Defining an SCO

Our findings echo those of other studies exploring coaching outcomes (e.g., Gegner, 1997; McGovern et al., 2001; Olivero et al., 1997; Wasylyshyn, 2003). However, the current study went beyond replicating these independent findings to suggesting a generic SCO framework. It also suggested that coaching-related development could be bidirectional and iterative, and that it may include the development of generalizable competence. Suggestions that require further exploration.

Development of a generic SCO framework The emergence of two SCO categories suggests that coaching results in two definite outcomes: personal outcomes and performance outcomes. While the reported personal outcomes were predominantly job-related they were classified as distinct from performance outcomes, as the benefit of their achievement would only extend beyond the individual coachee when translated into a performance outcome.

Within the personal outcomes category, it appears development can be further classified; specifically, enhanced self-awareness can be considered primary intrapersonal development (IPD) and IPD that occurred as a consequence of self-awareness (e.g., enhanced confidence) can be deemed secondary IPD. These distinctions suggested the conceptual coaching transfer model be revised to incorporate three classes of coaching outputs: (a) primary coaching outputs (self-awareness); (b) secondary coaching outputs (personal outcomes); and (c) tertiary coaching outputs (performance outcomes). Of which only the final two outputs would be measurable in transfer assessments.

Evidence of bidirectional and iterative development The conceptual coaching transfer model proposed that development progressed in a linear forward fashion. This was partially supported by suggestions that self-awareness formed a foundation for subsequent personal and performance outcomes. However, indications that feedback-flow influences operate between personal outcomes and self-awareness, and between performance outcomes and self-awareness, suggested that coaching development is potentially bidirectional and iterative. Hence, the conceptual model requires revision to accommodate both forward-flow and feedback-flow development linkages. Figure 20.2 illustrates the linkages.

Evidence of generalizable competence Coaching methodologies typically stress the importance of goal setting (e.g., GROW model, Whitmore, 2002). The current study's findings suggest that an SCO goes beyond the achievement of discrete goals to the development of a general personal-professional competence. This finding has implications for coaching evaluation: assessing general competence may overcome some of the problems associated with appraising coaching's efficacy against the diverse goals set by coachees. Future research is needed to determine if the content of coaching goals markedly affects the essence of general competence.

Defining coaching transfer

The definition of coaching transfer employed in our conceptual model viewed transfer as the sustained application of the knowledge, skills, attitudes, and other qualities acquired during coaching into the workplace. The finding that coachees', coaches', and stakeholders' expectations of the usage of coaching development fell within the clusters application, maintenance, and generalization supported the proposed definition.

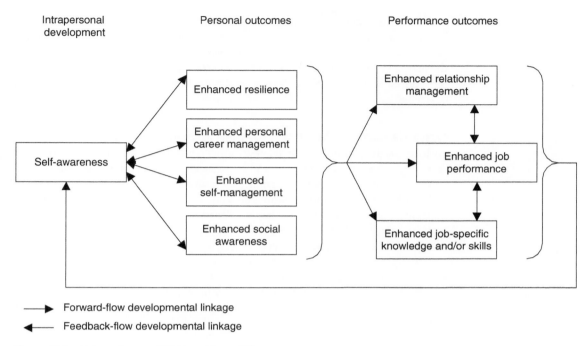

Figure 20.2 *Linkages Between SCO Categories and Clusters*

Coaching facilitators and barriers

The three categories (i.e., psychosocial, organizational culture, and coachee attitude factors) that emerged during the analyses of incidents that facilitated or hampered coaching transfer supported the proposed coaching transfer model (Figure 20.1). Psychosocial factors appeared to correspond to the support subset of the proposed input work environment. Organizational cultural factors appeared to correspond to the situational facilitators and constraints subset of the proposed input work environment. This category also included indicators of organizational precedents and procedures, suggesting that top-management support manifested as organizational norms. This category will be referred to as situational factors. Coachee factors appeared to be a subset of the proposed coaching input coachee characteristics; furthermore, its interview-derived indicators suggested it related to motivation.

Psychosocial factors The training literature suggests that supervisor support is positively linked to transfer (Holton et al., 1997). Also, the coaching literature has alluded to a link between supervisor support and coaching success (McGovern et al., 2001). Similarly, Study 1's results suggested that positive support provided by a developmental champion facilitates coaching transfer. Conversely, the absence of a quality support was viewed as a transfer barrier.

While the training literature offers strong evidence of a positive relationship between peer support and training transfer (Newstrom, 1986), the current findings associated were less clear. The impact of peer support appeared to be influenced by the nature of the development, including whether this aroused peers' competition for promotion, and whether coachees shared with their peers that they are attending coaching.

Organizational factors Coachees, coaches, and stakeholders suggested positive coaching transfer was related to: (a) a pro-development organizational climate; (b) access to development; and (c) procedural support for development. This agrees with findings within the training literature associating transfer with the availability of job-related information and supplies, funding, and time (Mathieu & Martineau, 1997). The finding that workload pressure emerged as a key transfer barrier, agrees with McGovern et al.'s (2001) finding that time pressures on the coachee detract from coaching effectiveness.

Coachees tended to view top-management support as an organizational level factor. Top management was seen as establishing the organizational culture and precedents associated with development and coaching. Hence, preliminary evidence suggests that top management influences coaching transfer, via influencing organizational factors.

Motivation The training literature suggests motivation influences transfer via motivation to learn and motivation to transfer (Noe, 1986). Study 1's facilitators and barriers clusters appear to correspond with these processes. In particular, a coachee with a pro-development approach appeared to possess high levels of motivation to learn, whereas development-indifferent coachees appeared to have low levels of motivation to learn. Coachees with high levels of proactive goal pursuit appeared to possess high levels of motivation to transfer, and coachees who obstructed their own development appeared to have low levels of transfer motivation.

Implications for evaluation due to the differing outcome emphasis across referent groups

While the category structures that emerged for all three referent groups in all three frameworks were structurally similar, the subtle differences in emphasis between the groups have implications for coaching evaluation. There are two noteworthy differences. First, in defining an SCO, stakeholders were more likely than coachees and coaches to emphasize performance outcomes, in particular enhanced job performance. The consequence of this is that stakeholders are more likely to desire and value evaluations that explore coaching efficacy in terms of enhanced job performance. Care must be taken that such evaluations are truly objective and involve multiple measures, as coachees' emphasis on personal outcomes may dispose them to underestimate their performance outcomes. Furthermore, research on gender differences in self-evaluations (e.g., Deaux, 1979; Maccoby & Jackin, 1974) suggests that gender may influence the way coachees respond to self-report evaluations of performance change.

Second, coachees and coaches were more likely than stakeholders to emphasize organizational cultural factors as a barrier to transfer; instead, stakeholders were more likely to attribute transfer problems to the coachee. Prima facie this may represent a form of evading responsibility and blame. Nonetheless, organizations seeking to maximize their coaching investment may benefit from developing the cultural factors conducive to transfer. Selecting coachees for coaching who have a history of being proactive in pursuing their goals and who display a positive approach to development may also be worthwhile.

STUDY 2: VERIFICATION OF THE PROPOSED COACHING TRANSFER MODEL

Method

Participants A convenience sample of 110 participants (60 male and 40 female) was recruited via an email sent to coaches, coaching organizations, and web-based coaching interest groups. Each participant had attended an average of seven coaching sessions from a variety of coaching programs. The average length of coaching engagement was eight months, the minimum of three months, and the maximum of 18 months. The participants included three junior managers, 25 managers, 42 senior managers, 32 partner/directors, and three CEOs. The reasons they had attended coaching were to accelerate their career development (no identified performance concern) (41%), to gain career direction clarity (21.8%), to address personally identified performance concerns (19.1%), on the advice of someone senior (7.3%), and to prepare for an upcoming challenge (5.4%). The majority had volunteered for coaching (63.6%). The modal age category was 36–40 years (30.9%), followed by 46–55 years (28.2%).

Measures The interview-derived indicators from the SCO, EoT, and the coaching transfer facilitator and barrier frameworks developed in Study 1 were used to generate measures of: (a) coaching transfer questionnaire (CTQ); (b) motivation (MVT); (c) manager psychosocial support (MgrPS); (d) peer psychosocial support (PeerPS); and (e) positive situational factors (SitF). The scales were combined into a single 151-item questionnaire.

The questionnaire was piloted and modified before being completed by the 110 participants. The final CTQ comprised 27 items: (a) 21 items related to the application of coaching acquired development (CTApp), of which one item was reverse-coded; and (b) six items related to the generalization and maintenance of coaching acquired development (CTG&M). The final facilitators and barrier scales comprised: (a) MgrPS 15 items, nine reverse-coded; (b) PeerPS five items, four reverse-coded; (c) SitF eight items, two reverse-coded; and (d) MTV eight items, three reverse-coded. Cronbach's alpha ranged from $r = .803$ (MVT) to $r = .929$ (PeerPS). Participants were asked to indicate their agreement against a five-point Likert-type scale, ranging from 1 (*strongly disagree*) to 5 (*strongly agree*).

RESULTS AND DISCUSSION

Analysis of scales

Owing to the unproven nature of the CTQ, its underlying structure was explored using principal component analysis. Six components reached eigenvalue significance of one, explaining 34.07%, 11.86%, 6.75%, 4.76%, 4.39%, and 4.09% of the variance. The scree plot revealed a clear break after the second component, and two components were retained. Varimax rotation revealed a simple two-factor structure. Three of the CTQ items did not load on either component and were removed from subsequent analyses. Varimax rotation was performed on the remaining 24 items. The rotated solution showed all items loaded substantially onto either component. The final two-factor solution explained a total of 51.23% of the variance, with Component1 contributing 32.62% and Component2 18.61%. Component1 comprised items associated with the application of coaching development ($N = 18$), and Component2 comprised items associated with generalization and maintenance ($N = 6$). The means, standards deviations, and alpha coefficients for all scales are presented in Table 20.4.

Table 20.4   *Means, Standard Deviations, and Alpha Coefficients for All Scales*

Scale	No. of items	Min	Max	Mean	SD	Alpha
CTQ						
CTAQ	18	29.00	88.00	66.93	10.03	.924
CTGMQ	6	14.00	30.00	23.07.13	3.58	.856
Facilitator and barrier scales						
MgrPS	15	17.00	75.00	54.96	11.58	.942
PeerPS	5	9.00	25.00	19.53	3.40	.864
SitF	8	13.00	33.00	25.74	4.61	.812
MVT	8	22.00	40.00	33.97	3.70	.737

Note. N = 11.

Pearson product-moment coefficient correlations were used to explore the study's hypotheses. Prior to these calculations preliminarily analyses were performed to ensure no violations of the assumptions of normality, linearity, and homoscedasticity.

Coaching transfer and motivation

Hypothesis 1 proposed that individuals who are more motivated would be more likely to apply, sustain, and generalize their coaching development. Correlation analysis indicated that MVT formed a large positive correlation with CTApp ($r = .588$, $p < .005$) and a moderate positive correlation with CTG&M ($r = .371$, $p < .05$). This suggests that motivation positively impacts both the application, and generalization and maintenance components of coaching transfer. This finding upholds Hypothesis 1; furthermore, it echoes training research that suggests motivated trainees are more likely to transfer their training (Cheng & Ho, 2001).

Coaching transfer and psychosocial factors

Hypotheses 2 and 3 suggested links between manager and peer support with coaching transfer. While a moderate positive correlation was observed between CTApp and MgrPS ($r = .319$, $p < .005$), statistically significant relationships were not found between: (a) CTApp and PeerPS; and (b) CTG&M and either MgrPS or PeerPS. Further analyses were undertaken to determine if the relationship between coaching transfer and psychosocial factors was influenced by the type of development sought via coaching. The data set was categorized on developmental type: (a) permission-dependent (PermisDep—requires approval to implement); (b) non-permission-dependent (NonPermisDep—does not require approval, but requires others' participation); and (c) other-independent (OthrIndep). Pearson product-moment coefficient was then employed to explore the relationships between MgrPS and PeerPS with CTApp and CTG&M within each type of development. The results are presented in Table 20.5.

Table 20.5 *Correlations Between Coaching Transfer Variables and Psychosocial Factors and Split on Development Type*

		PermisDep (N = 37)		NonPermisDep (N = 32)		OthrIndep (N = 41)	
		r	sig (2-tailed)	r	sig (2-tailed)	r	sig (2-tailed)
MgrPS	CTA	.440**	.006	.531**	.002	.104	.518
	CTGM	.033	.847	.244	.179	.068	.672
PeerPS	CTA	.312	.060	.494**	.004	−.236	.138
	CTGM	−.066	.698	.357*	.045	−.105	.512
MVT	CTA	.519**	.001	.656**	.000	.619**	.000
	CTGM	.101	.551	429*	.014	.506**	.001

Note. ** $p < .005$, * $p < .05$ (2-tailed).

Investigating the relationships between permission-dependent development and psychosocial support revealed a moderate positive correlation between MgrPS and PermisDep application ($r = .440$, $p < .005$). A statistically significant relationship was not found with PermisDep generalization and maintenance. The relationship between supervisor support and the application of permission-dependent development may suggest that the application of development that requires manager permission to implement more likely succeeds with manager support. The lack of an observed relationship between MgrPS and CTG&M possibly occurred as permission-dependent development may involve the achievement of a finite goal (e.g., promotion). Thus, once the development has been applied, generalization and maintenance may not occur, be necessary, or require supervisor support.

Statistically significant relationships were not found between PeerPS and either PermisDep application or generalization and maintenance. The nature of permission-dependent development may explain these findings. Permission-dependent development may be associated with development overtly related to coachees' promotion or rewards; and, as suggested by Study 1, such development may: (a) dispose peers to competitiveness; and (b) prevent coachees from sharing with their peers that they are attending coaching, which precludes support. Furthermore, the structural nature of permission-dependent goals may render peer support redundant.

Exploring the relationships between non-permission-dependent development and psychosocial support revealed a large positive correlation between MgrPS and NonPermisDep application ($r = .531$, $p < .005$). A statistically significant relationship was not found with NonPermisDep generalization and maintenance. PeerPS showed: (a) a moderate correlation with NonPermisDep application ($r = .494$, $p < .005$); and (b) a large positive correlation with NonPermisDep generalization and maintenance ($r = .357$, $p < .05$).

These findings suggest that although non-permission-dependent development does not require approval it requires psychosocial support; furthermore, it appears peer and/or supervisor support can create the conditions conducive to its application. The overlap of peer and supervisor support may occur because: (a) as suggested by Study 1, at the executive level the boundaries between peers and supervisors may become contrived; and/or (b) any type of support may suffice.

The finding that peers were associated with creating conditions conducive to the ongoing application of non-permission-dependent development is interesting, since peer support was not associated with either permission-dependent development application or generalization and maintenance. The difference may arise as, compared with permission-dependent development, non-permission-dependent development may be: (a) less overtly related to promotion/reward, and thus may engender peer support; and/or (b) be of a nature where peer support is valid and useful. Furthermore, the finding of a relationship between manager support and application, and not between manager support and generalization and maintenance, of non-permission-dependent development is also interesting. Potentially, once development has been implemented coachees may not require ongoing manager support, and/or managers may not avail ongoing support.

On balance, the influence of peer support in creating the conditions associated with the transfer of non-permission-dependent development appears wider-ranging than that of supervisor support. This agrees with Clarke (2002), who suggested peer support mechanisms may have greater impact than supervisor support for professionals. However, the current study goes beyond Clarke in suggesting that whichever has the stronger influence is determined by the type of development.

Investigating the relationships between other-independent development and psychosocial support did not reveal statistically significant relationships between MgrPS and PeerPS with either OthrIndep application or generalization and maintenance. Since other-independent development doesn't require permission or the involvement of others, its application, and generalization and maintenance, are likely less impacted by others and more likely associated with the coachee. Indeed, motivation was strongly associated with both CTApp ($r = .619$, $p < .005$) and CTG&M: ($r = .506$, $p < .005$). Together these results suggest a coachee with sufficient motivation to apply and sustain their development will likely do so despite a lack of peer and/or supervisor support. Furthermore, extrapolating from Facteau et al.'s (1995) finding that task constraints only have an effect when severe, a sufficiently motivated coachee may succeed in transferring other-independent development despite almost all but the most severe obstruction and sabotage by supervisors and peers.

The above findings offer partial support for Hypotheses 2 and 3. Hypothesis 2 proposed peer support would be positively associated with coaching transfer: Peer support was only found to be associated with the transfer of non-permission-dependent development. Hypothesis 3 proposed positive supervisor support would be associated with coaching transfer: Supervisor support was only found to be associated with the application of permission-dependent and non-permission-dependent development, but not their generalization and maintenance.

Coaching transfer and situational factors

Hypothesis 4 suggested that positive situational factors would be positively associated with coaching transfer. Correlation analysis indicated that SitF formed a large positive correlation with CTApp ($r = .503$, $p < .005$) and a small positive correlation with CTG&M ($r = .281$, $p < .005$). These findings suggest positive situational factors are associated with both the application, and generalization and maintenance components of coaching transfer.

The best predictor of coaching transfer (application)

A standard multiple regression analysis of CTA with MgrPS, PeerPS, SitF, and MVT revealed a final model comprising MgrPS, SitF, and MVT. The model explained 42.7% of the variance in CTA [$R^2 = .427$, $F(3,110) = 26.310$, $p < .005$]. MVT made the largest unique significant contribution [beta $= .459$, $t(110) = 5.601$, $p = .000$]. SitF [beta $= .318$, $t(110) = 3.509$, $p = .001$] also made a statistically significant unique contribution. These results suggest that whether coaching-based development will be applied to the workplace depends heavily on both the coachee (motivation) and conditions created by the organization (situational factors). Nonetheless, 57.3% of the variance in application goes unexplained and is likely to be, at least partly, attributable to factors within the coachee–coach relationship.

Although MgrPS did not significantly contribute to the regression, post hoc evaluation of its correlation with CTApp revealed that it was significantly different to zero ($r = .319$, $p < .001$); hence, it is possible that the relationship between manager support and application is mediated by the relationships between motivation and situational factors with application. Future research could explore this.

The best predictor of coaching transfer (generalization and maintenance) A standard multiple regression analysis of CTG&M with MgrPS, PeerPS, SitF, and MVT revealed a final model, comprising SitF and MVT, and explaining 15.7% of the variance in CTG&M [$R^2 = .157$, F(2,110) = 9.947, $p < .005$].

Of the variables, MVT made the only unique significant contribution [beta = .307, $t(110) = 3.144$, p = .002].

These results suggest that motivation was the single strongest predictor of whether applied development would be sustained and generalized. That 84.3% of the variance in CTG&M goes unexplained is of interest. It may be due to: (a) work environment factors that were included in the facilitators and barriers framework not being incorporated in the SitF scale and thus not being measured; (b) coachee characteristics, such as conscientiousness, recognized as a reliable predictor of job performance (Robertson & Smith, 2001), not being measured; and/or (c) the inability of the CTG&M scale to tap generalization and maintenance once development is integrated into the coachee's behavioral repertoire. Future research could investigate further.

Post hoc evaluation of SitF's correlation with CTG&M revealed that it was significantly different to zero ($r = .371$, $p < .001$); hence it is likely that the relationship between situational factors and generalization and maintenance is mediated by the relationship between motivation and generalization and maintenance. Again, future research could explore this.

GENERAL DISCUSSION

The current study proposed a conceptual model of coaching transfer. To verify the model it investigated the nature of coaching outputs, the nature of the conditions associated with transfer, and hypotheses relating certain manipulable inputs to transfer.

The conceptual coaching transfer model was underpinned by four hypotheses that suggested coachee motivation, peer and manager support, and positive situational factors would be associated with creating conditions conducive to positive coaching transfer. Full support was not found for all hypotheses. The results suggested the model be revised to accommodate the specific transfer conditions required by the interactions of: (a) two types of coaching outputs (i.e., personal and performance outcomes); three types of development (i.e., permission-dependent, non-permission-dependent, and other-independent); and (c) two stages of transfer (i.e., application,

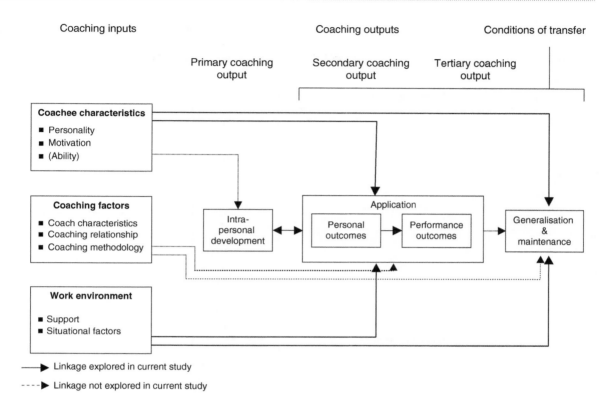

Figure 20.3 *Coaching Transfer Model (Revised)*

and generalization and maintenance). Figure 20.3 displays the revised coaching transfer model.

The first revision arose as the study's results suggested coaching outputs differ from the current conceptualization of training outcomes. Whereas training outcomes tend to be portrayed as one-dimensional performance outcomes (e.g., Baldwin & Ford, 1988), coaching outputs appear to comprise personal outcomes and performance outcomes. Furthermore, while the learning arising from training tends to be separated from its application (e.g., Kirkpatrick's [1983] hierarchy of training outcomes), coaching's secondary and tertiary coaching outputs appear to include the application of development. Moreover, the suggestion that coaching development may be bidirectional and iterative is contrary to Kirkpatrick's (1983) view that training outcomes develop via causal hierarchical linkages—an idea that has dominated training evaluation (Holton, 1996). These findings have implications for coaching evaluation.

The second revision concerns the study's finding that the conditions of transfer appear governed by the stage of transfer and the nature of the development. Evidence was found that suggested the application of coaching development requires different conditions of transfer to its generalization and maintenance. Evidence was also found that suggested conditions of transfer depend on the type of development sought via

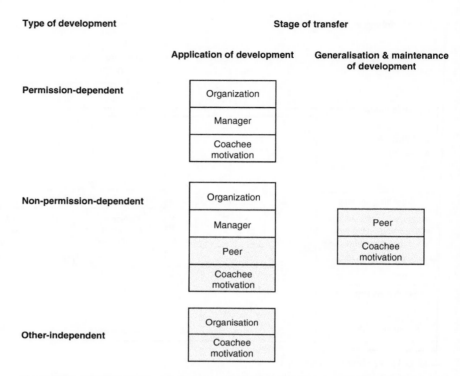

Figure 20.4   *Conditions of Transfer Associated With Types of Development and Stages of Transfer*

coaching. Figure 20.4 illustrates the relationships between types of development, types of transfer, and types of support.

The results of this study have implications for coaching research and organizational interventions. First, while this study sought to develop a coachee-based measure of coaching transfer, analyses of coachees', coaches', and stakeholders' views of an SCO resulted in three frameworks so structurally similar that their overlap formed a common SCO framework. This common SCO framework could inform the development of a generic measure of positive coaching transfer. A generic transfer measure would have four key merits. It would enable organizations to measure specific (i.e., performance outcomes) and general development (i.e., personal outcomes). It would also enable organizations to assess and compare coaching success across the diverse range of coaching goals their staff pursue in coaching. It could provide a means for coachees, coaches, and stakeholders to review development from their perspective and appreciate it from others'. Lastly, it could assist coaching providers in persuading organizations of the value of coaching. Furthermore, while the current study focused on coaching transfer, and hence only sought to measure secondary and tertiary coaching outputs, incorporating a scale relating to primary outputs (IPD) would create a comprehensive measure of an SCO. Such a measure would go some way to providing a generic coaching evaluation tool. Future research could extend the transfer measure to a comprehensive SCO measure by incorporating the IPD category.

The second implication arising from this study concerns its finding that the conditions for positive transfer appear to depend on coachee motivation, manager and to a lesser extent peer psychosocial support, and organizational factors. This suggests that organizations seeking to maximize transfer could assess organizational and coachee readiness for coaching, and manager suitability to act as a developmental champion.

The final implication concerns the finding that coaching transfer appears to be associated with motivation, psychosocial, and situational factors. This suggests organizations could employ transfer enhancing interventions that target these inputs.

The study suffered several methodological limitations. First, it relied exclusively on self-report data. Future research could employ a multiple-methods approach, incorporating more objective sources of evidence (e.g., performance appraisal data). Second, it was based on a convenience sample and may also be in part a snowball sample, both of which are more likely than random samples to suffer sampling bias (Loewenthal, 2001). Third, since motivation was a variable investigated in Study 2, response bias, whereby less motivated individuals did not respond to the survey, may have distorted the results. Fourth, Study 2 analyses were based on relatively small sample sizes, which may have compromised the integrity of the outcomes. Finally, as coaching cannot be isolated from the coachees' professional and personal spheres, any changes coincident with coaching may be attributable to factors unrelated to coaching. Matched coaching and non-coaching comparison group studies would go some way to identifying changes attributable to coaching.

In sum, this study extended coaching research by providing an initial understanding of the influence of the factors that impact on coaching transfer. The findings have implications for coaching research and organizational practice. In particular, they highlight that to maximize their coaching return on investment, organizations must adopt a holistic guardianship of their coaching provision, including coaching readiness assessments and transfer enhancement interventions. They also suggested that if coaching research is to provide comprehensive guidance to underpin practice and develop theory, then the complex interplay of factors beyond the coachee–coach relationship must be explored. Nonetheless, this study was exploratory, and its ultimate value lies in the possibilities for future research that it raised.

REFERENCES

Ackerman, P. L., & Heggestad, E. D. (1997). Intelligence, personality, and interests: Evidence for overlapping traits. *Psychological Bulletin, 121*(2), 219–245. https://doi.org/10.1037/0033-2909.121.2.219

Baldwin, T. T., & Ford, J. K. (1988). Transfer of training: A review and direction for future research. *Personnel Psychology, 41,* 63–105. https://doi.org/10.1111/j.1744-6570.1988.tb00632.x

Carter, A. (2001). *Executive Coaching: Inspiring Performance at Work* (IES Report 379). Brighton, UK: The Institute for Employment Studies.

Carter, A., Wolfe, H., & Kerrin, M. (2005). Employers and coaching evaluation. *International Journal of Coaching in Organizations, 2005*(4), 63–72.

Cheng, E. W. L., & Ho, D. C. K. (2001). A review of transfer of training studies in the past decade. *Personnel Review, 30*(1), 102–118. https://doi.org/10.1108/00483480110380163

Clarke, N. (2002). Job/work environment factors influencing training transfer within a human service agency: Some indicative support for Baldwin and Ford's transfer climate construct. *International Journal of Training and Development, 6*(3), 146–162. https://doi.org/10.1111/1468-2419.00156

Cohen, J. (1960). A Coefficient of Agreement for Nominal Scales. *Educational and Psychological Measurement, 20*, 37–46. https://doi.org/10.1177/001316446002000104

Deaux, K. (1979). Self-evaluation of male and female managers. *Journal of Sex Roles, 5*, 571–580. https://doi.org/10.1007/BF00287661

Facteau, J. D., Dobbins, G. H., Russell, J. E. A., Ladd, R. T., & Kudish, J. D. (1995). The influence of general perceptions of the training environment on pretraining motivation and perceived training transfer. *Journal of Management, 21*(1), 1–25. https://doi.org/10.1016/0149-2063(95)90031-4

Flanagan, J. C. (1954). The critical incident technique. *Psychological Bulletin, 51*(4), 327–358. https://doi.org/10.1037/h0061470

Gegner, C. (1997). *Coaching: Theory and practice. Unpublished master's thesis.* University of San Francisco, California.

Goldsmith, M., & Morgan, H. (2005). Leadership as a contact sport. *Leadership Excellence, 22*(8), 6–7.

Goleman, D. (2002). *The new leaders: Transforming the art of leadership into the science of results.* London, UK: Little, Brown.

Greene, J., & Grant, A. (2003). *Solution-focused coaching: Managing people in a complex world.* Harlow, UK: Pearson Education.

Gumuseli, A. I., & Ergin, B. (2002). The manager's role in enhancing the transfer of training: A Turkish case study. *International Journal of Training and Development, 6*(2), 80–97. https://doi.org/10.1111/1468-2419.00151

Herold, D. M., Davis, W., Fedor, D. B., & Parsons, C. K. (2002). Dispositional influences on transfer of learning in multistage training programmes. *Personnel Psychology, 55*, 851–869. https://doi.org/10.1111/j.1744-6570.2002.tb00132.x

Holton, E. F., III (1996). The flawed four level evaluation model. *Human Resource Development Quarterly, 7*, 5–21. https://doi.org/10.1002/hrdq.3920070103

Holton, E. F., III., Bates, R. A., Seyler, D. L., & Carvalho, M. B. (1997). Toward construct validation of a transfer climate instrument. *Human Resource Development Quarterly, 8*(2), 95–113. https://doi.org/10.1002/hrdq.3920080203

Huczynski, A. A., & Lewis, J. W. (1980). An empirical study into the learning transfer process in management training. *Journal of Management Studies, 17*(2), 227–240. https://doi.org/10.1111/j.1467-6486.1980.tb00086.x

Jankowicz, D. (2004). *The easy guide to repertory grids.* Chichester, UK: Wiley.

Judge, W. Q., & Cowell, J. (1997). The brave new world of executive coaching. *Business Horizons, 40*(4), 71–77.

Kanfer, R., & Ackerman, P. (1989). Motivation and cognitive abilities: An integrative/aptitude-treatment interaction approach to skills acquisition. *Journal of Applied Psychology Monograph, 74*, 657–690. https://doi.org/10.1037/0021-9010.74.4.657

Kirkpatrick, D. L. (1983). Four steps to measuring training effectiveness. *Personnel Administrator, 28*(11), 8–12.

Kleinberg, J. A. (2001). A scholar-practitioner model for executive coaching: Applying theory and application within the emergent field of executive coaching. *Dissertation Abstracts International, 61*(2), 4853. (UMI No. 9999048)

Kvale, S. (1996). *InterViews: An introduction to qualitative research interviewing.* London, UK: Sage.

Lim, D. H., & Johnson, S. D. (2002). Trainee perceptions of factors that influence learning transfer. *International Journal of Training and Development, 6*(1), 36–48. https://doi.org/10.1111/1468-2419.00148

Loewenthal, K. M. (2001). *An introduction to psychological tests and scales* (2nd ed.). New York, NY: Psychology Press.

Maccoby, E. E., & Jackin, C. N. (1974). *The psychology of sex differences.* Stanford, CA: Stanford University Press.

Machin, M. A. (2002). Planning, managing and optimizing transfer of training. In K. Kraiger (Ed.), *Creating, implementing, and managing effective training and development* (pp. 263–301). San Francisco, CA: Jossey-Bass.

Mathieu, J. E., & Martineau, J. W. (1997). Individual and situational influences on training motivation. In J. K. Ford (Ed.), *Improving training effectiveness in work organizations* (pp. 193–221). New York, NY: Lawrence Erlbaum Associates.

McGovern, J., Lindemann, M., Vergara, M., Murphy, S., Barker, L., & Warrenfeltz, R. (2001). Maximizing the impact of executive coaching: Behavioural change, organizational outcomes, and return on investment. *The Manchester Review, 6*(1), 1–9.

Newstrom, J. A. (1986). Leveraging management development through the management of transfer. *Journal of Management Development, 5*(5), 33–45. https://doi.org/10.1108/eb051628

Noe, R. A. (1986). Trainee attributes: Neglected influences on training effectiveness. *Academy of Management Review, 11*(4), 736–749. https://doi.org/10.5465/amr.1986.4283922

Olivero, G., Bane, K. D., & Kopelman, R. E. (1997). Executive coaching as a transfer of training tool; effects on productivity in a public agency. *Public Personnel Management, 26*(4), 461–469. https://doi.org/10.1177/009102609702600403

Peltier, B. (2001). *The psychology of executive coaching.* Abingdon, UK: Routledge.

Peters, L. H., O'Connor, E. J., Eulberg, J. R., & Watson, T. W. (1988). An examination of situational constraints in air force work settings. *Human Performance, 1*(2), 133–144. https://doi.org/10.1207/s15327043hup0102_4

Porras, J. L., & Hargis, K. (1982). Precursors of individual change: Responses to a social learning theory based on organization intervention. *Human Relations, 35,* 973–990. https://doi.org/10.1177/001872678203501103

Robertson, I. T., & Smith, M. (2001). Personnel section. *Journal of Occupational and Organizational Psychology, 74,* 441–472. https://doi.org/10.1348/096317901167479

Sherman, S., & Freas, A. (2004). The wild west of executive coaching. *Harvard Business Review, 82,* 82–90.

Stemler, S. (2001). An overview of content analysis. Practical Assessment, Research & Evaluation, 7(17). Retrieved November 26, 2006, from http://PAREonline.net/getvn.asp?v=7&n=17

Wales, S. (2003). Why coaching? *Journal of Change Management, 3*(3), 275–282. https://doi.org/10.1080/714042542

Wasylyshyn, K. M. (2003). Executive coaching: An outcome study. *Consulting Psychology Journal: Practice and Research, 55*(2), 94–106.

Weber, R. P. (1990). *Basic content analysis* (2nd ed.) (Quantitative Applications in the Social Sciences No. 07-049)). Newbury Park, CA: Sage.

Whitmore, J. (2002). *Coaching for performance: Growing people, performance and purpose* (3rd ed.). London, UK: Nicholas Brealey.

Section VI
The Future of Coaching Research

Jonathan Passmore and David Tee

INTRODUCTION

In this collected volume we have aimed to review, through some 20 papers, the development journey of coaching psychological research. But how can we make sense of the past decades of coaching research and more importantly what are the future trends or themes that are likely to emerge in coaching research over the coming decades?

In previous papers, one of us has offered a conceptual framework of coaching research, developed with Annette Fillery-Travis (Passmore & Fillery-Travis, 2011). This was later developed in a book chapter with Tim Theeboom (Passmore & Theeboom, 2016). In each, we examined coaching papers to provide an insight into the development of coaching research.

We argued that coaching research has progressed from an examination of individual opinions expressed in case reports and case studies, through a number of defined phases of development. We now wish to take the next step in this approach, reviewing our predictions, reformulating the framework, and also considering possible future coaching psychology research themes.

As we already noted in the previous paper and book chapter, our selection reflects how we saw this journey of development. We recognized there were other ways the development of coaching research could be segmented, and that our view was just one perspective. This perspective remains the same. Here, we offer one interpretation. We encourage others to challenge this view and offer alternative perspectives.

Our aspiration is that this section and the others in this book will provide coaching psychology students, and those studying coaching research, with a summarized "history" of the development of coaching psychology. In the past two decades, we have become more serious about the research, but in truth the history of examining coaching dates back at least 100 years. What has changed over this period is the rigor of the research methods used and the insights such methods provide into the nature of coaching as a development and behavioral change tool.

A BRIEF REVIEW OF COACHING PSYCHOLOGY RESEARCH

As coaching practitioners who have both engaged and published coaching psychology research we have both been challenged in the past by coaches: "So why is research important? My clients are happy, I am happy, we all know coaching works." For many practitioners, that is enough. However, when decisions need to be made about whether to invest in coaching, or clients ask "how do you know it works," as psychologists we believe we need to get behind the coaching conversation to explore the science of what is happening and what measuring effects coaching has on people and organizations.

As psychologists, we would also argue that research can provide valuable benefits for us as practitioners. Scientific research aims to identify and define the knowledge base upon which practitioners work. Such research helps us to define the boundaries of our intervention: "when does coaching become counseling." It also provides an evidence base for what we teach: "what works best, when should I do X as opposed to Y, what effect do X and Y have, when Z is present."

The past 25 years have seen an explosion of coaching psychology research from the mid-1990's papers, often published in the American Psychological Association's *Consulting Psychology Journal*, and from 2003 with the emergence of several specialist journals such as the pioneering *International Journal of Evidence Based Coaching and Mentoring*, published by Oxford Brookes University; *International Coaching Psychology Review*, which emerged in 2006, published by the British Psychological Society (BPS); and *Coaching: An International Journal of Theory, Practice and Research*, first published in 2008 by Routledge in partnership with the Association for Coaching (AC). More recently yet, other journals have appeared: *The Coaching Psychologist*, with shorter research papers, published by the BPS; in 2012, the *International Journal of Mentoring and Coaching in Education*, published by Emerald; and in 2016, *The Philosophy of Coaching Journal*.

The developmental journey has witnessed the emergence of new methodologies and approaches that have each sought to answer different questions. In the earlier papers exploring the development of coaching we categorized these as "phases." However, it would be more accurate to describe them as "research themes." The earlier term implies that researchers move from one phase to the next. In reality, a new theme simply joins established themes, as the debate broadens and develops like a growing river. Early themes remain present but are joined by new themes using new and untested methods within the field.

While coaching can be traced back to Gordy's 1937 paper about factory worker performance, earlier papers have revealed it was also a popular tool in the 1910s and

1920s as a word to describe a form of learning within U.S. college debating societies (Huston, 1924; Trueblood, 1911). However, these papers were sporadic and were more reports of events than research studies. The term was also used for sports development in the same period (Griffith, 1926).

These papers and a resurgence of interest in coaching in the 1990s can, taken together, be considered to be the first theme. The papers, or reports, could be considered to be experiential, using case study and survey methods. In this phase, the report, coaches, or consultants shared their experiences of working with students, clients, or fellow coaches. Surveys can be considered to occupy similar ground; while useful in providing a snapshot of practice, they provide no insights on theory development or theory testing.

A second theme emerged with the use of qualitative methods. In this phase, researchers were seeking to build an understanding of the coaching process through semi-structured interviews offering insights of the felt experience of conceptual models, using Interpretative phenomenological analysis (IPA), or providing conceptual models using methodologies such as grounded theory.

In theme three, small-scale quantitative studies were used. These used randomized controlled trials (RCTs) and experimental designs. The aim of the researchers was to provide insights into coaching effectiveness and measure the impact of coaching on stress, or emotional intelligence or leadership development. Generally, these studies had sample sizes of 40 or fewer and often used wait-list designs. While these studies continued, a number of larger sample size studies appeared. These had sample sizes in some cases over 100 participants and compared interventions.

We predicted a fourth theme of meta-analysis studies would emerge as the number of RCT studies grew. This proved to be the case, initially in 2009 a small-scale meta-study reviewing the effect size across four studies (De Meuse, Dai, & Lee, 2009) and later several other meta-studies followed (Grover & Furnham, 2016; Jones, Woods, & Guillaume, 2015; Sonesh et al., 2015; Theeboom, Beersma, & van Vianen, 2014).

Theme five has also started with the emergence of systematic literature review (Athanasopoulou & Dopson, 2018; Bozer & Jones, 2018). These papers aim to synthesize the literature, identifying themes and highlighting insights.

We are suggesting in this paper that there are two further themes that we expect to emerge to join the others. The sixth research theme will be an exploration of the active ingredients. To date, we have only debated and speculated about the active ingredients in coaching, although these are often discussed as facts (McKenna & Davis, 2009). Counseling has done a significantly better job, as has motivational interviewing (MI is a parallel conversational approach to coaching, used to help clients with dependency behaviors) in providing insights into the active ingredients within these approaches.

Within coaching, however, research has been lacking. This is partly the challenge of undertaking coaching research, where funding has been lacking, and where commercial clients are often reluctant to invest the time or financial resources into program evaluations. We hope and expect that research grant funding could trigger a number of studies that would provide insights into active ingredients over the coming decade. These studies will explore which factors are the most important, and what are their antecedents and moderators that influence coaching outcomes.

One example may be the coach–client relationship, often asserted to be central to coaching effectiveness. However, the evidence to support this is anecdotal. Is the relationship universally an important factor? Our hypothesis is that the quality of the relationship is a significant factor in some coaching work, such as middle coaching for leadership development or managing stress, but is of less relevance in other work, such as telephone health coaching, where a more anonymous and distant relationship allows greater disclosure.

The final and seventh theme we predict will be individual exceptions. These studies will seek to answers questions such as: When is coaching likely to cause damage? What models or approaches best suit particular presenting issues? What types of clients benefit from what type of approach? There has been a view that all approaches are of equal value (Kilburg, 2004). This is in our view naïve and is based on data that when different types of presenting issues and different individuals are mixed, the different coaching approaches balance out to be all of equal value. However, research from other domains, not least MI, reveals that some interventions are more effective than others for specific presenting issues (Vasilaki, Hosier, & Cox, 2006).

REFERENCES

Athanasopoulou, A., & Dopson, S. (2018). A systematic review of executive coaching outcomes: Is it the journey or the destination that matters the most? *The Leadership Quarterly, 29*(1), 70–88.

Bozer, G., & Jones, R. J. (2018). Understanding the factors that determine workplace coaching effectiveness: A systematic literature review. *European Journal of Work and Organizational Psychology, 27*(3), 342–361. doi:10.1080/1359432X.2018.1446946

De Meuse, K. P., Dai, G., & Lee, R. J. (2009). Evaluating the effectiveness of executive coaching: Beyond ROI? *Coaching: An International Journal of Theory, Research and Practice, 2*, 117–134.

Gordy, C. (1937). Everyone gets a share of the profits. *Factory Management & Maintenance, 95*, 82–83.

Griffith, C. R. (1926). *Psychology of coaching: A study of coaching methods from the point of view of psychology*. New York: Scribner.

Grover, S., & Furnham, A. (2016). Coaching as a developmental intervention in organisations: A systematic review of its effectiveness and the mechanisms underlying it. *PlosOne.* doi:10.1371/journal.pone.0159137

Huston, R. E. (1924). Debate coaching in high school. *The Quarterly Journal of Speech Education, 10*, 127–143.

Jones, R. J., Woods, S. A., & Guillaume, Y. R. F. (2015). The effectiveness of workplace coaching: A metaanalysis of learning and performance outcomes from coaching. *Journal of Occupational and Organizational Psychology, 89*(2), 249–277.

Kilburg, R. R. (2004). Trudging toward Dodoville: Conceptual approaches and case studies in executive coaching. *Consulting Psychology Journal Practice and Research, 56*(4), 203–213.

McKenna, D. D., & Davis, S. L. (2009). Hidden in plain sight: The active ingredients of executive coaching. *Industrial and Organizational Psychology, 2*(3), 244–260.

Passmore, J., & Fillery-Travis, A. (2011). A critical review of executive coaching research: A decade of progress and what's to come. *Coaching: An International Journal of Theory, Research and Practice, 4*(2), 70–88.

Passmore, J., & Theeboom, T. (2016). Coaching psychology: A journey of development in research. In L. E. Van Zyl, M. W. Stander, & A. Oodendal (Eds.), *Coaching psychology: Meta-theoretical perspectives and applications in multi-cultural contexts* (pp. 27–46). New York, NY: Springer.

Sonesh, S., Coultas, C. W., Lacerenza, C. N., Marlow, S. L., Benishek, L. E., & Salas, E. (2015). The power of coaching: A meta-analytic investigation. *Coaching: An International Journal of Theory, Practice and Research, 8*(2), 73–95.

Theeboom, T., Beersma, B., & van Vianen, A. E. M. (2014). Does coaching work? A meta-analysis on the effects of coaching on individual level outcomes in an organizational context. *Journal of Positive Psychology, 9*(1), 1–18.

Trueblood, T. C. (1911). Coaching a debating team. *Public Speaking Review, 1*, 84–85.

Vasilaki, E., Hosier, S. G., & Cox, W. M. (2006). The efficacy of motivational interviewing as a brief intervention for excessive drinking: A meta-analytic review. *Alcohol and Alcoholism, 41*(3), 328–335.

Index

Coaching Researched: A Coaching Psychology Reader, First Edition. Edited by Jonathan Passmore and David Tee.
© 2021 John Wiley & Sons Ltd. Published 2021 by John Wiley & Sons Ltd.